# Lecture Notes in Computer Science 2769

Edited by G. Goos, J. Hartmanis, and J. van Leeuwen

T0142097

Lecture Notes in Computer Science
Edited by G. Goos, J. Hartmanis, and J. van Leeuwen

Springer
*Berlin*
*Heidelberg*
*New York*
*Hong Kong*
*London*
*Milan*
*Paris*
*Tokyo*

Traugott Koch  Ingeborg Torvik Sølvberg (Eds.)

# Research and Advanced Technology for Digital Libraries

7th European Conference, ECDL 2003
Trondheim, Norway, August 17-22, 2003
Proceedings

 Springer

Series Editors

Gerhard Goos, Karlsruhe University, Germany
Juris Hartmanis, Cornell University, NY, USA
Jan van Leeuwen, Utrecht University, The Netherlands

Volume Editors

Traugott Koch
Lund University Libraries, NetLab, Knowledge Technologies Group
P.O. Box 134, 22100 Lund, Sweden
E-mail: traugott.koch@lub.lu.se

Ingeborg Torvik Sølvberg
Norwegian University of Science and Technology
Dept. of Computer and Information Science
7491 Trondheim, Norway
E-mail: ingeborg.solvberg@idi.ntnu.no

Cataloging-in-Publication Data applied for

A catalog record for this book is available from the Library of Congress

Bibliographic information published by Die Deutsche Bibliothek
Die Deutsche Bibliothek lists this publication in the Deutsche Nationalbibliographie;
detailed bibliographic data is available in the Internet at <http://dnb.ddb.de>.

CR Subject Classification (1998): H.3.7, H.2, H.3, H.4.3, H.5, J.7, J.1, I.7

ISSN 0302-9743
ISBN 3-540-40726-X Springer-Verlag Berlin Heidelberg New York

Springer-Verlag Berlin Heidelberg New York
a member of BertelsmannSpringer Science+Business Media GmbH

http://www.springer.de

© Springer-Verlag Berlin Heidelberg 2003
Printed in Germany

Typesetting: Camera-ready by author, data conversion by PTP-Berlin GmbH
Printed on acid-free paper     SPIN: 10931004      06/3142      5 4 3 2 1 0

# Preface

Welcome to ECDL 2003 and to these conference proceedings, featuring all the papers presented at the 7th European Conference on Research and Advanced Technology for Digital Libraries.

Following Pisa (1997), Heraklion (1998), Paris (1999), Lisbon (2000), Darmstadt (2001) and Rome (2002), ECDL 2003 in Trondheim reaches some of the northernmost shores of the continent.

Being the seventh in an annual series of conferences represents, for better and for worse, a considerable tradition in the fast changing world of digital-library-related research and development. It is still a difficult and slow job to change traditional forms and formats of communication at – and related to – scientific conferences, and also to change participants' expectations. Yet each new conference builds upon the topics and communities involved in previous events and inherits the commitment to quality established by its predecessors.

Each year, ECDL has to live up to its role of being "the major European forum focusing on digital libraries and associated technical, practical, and social issues," bringing diverse disciplines and application communities together. There are still challenges in this respect ahead of us, but the quality and range of papers and other contributions, combined with opportunities for debate, should ensure that ECDL 2003 sets high standards for the future.

ECDL 2003 invited contributions from the broadest spectrum of digital-library-related research, development and practice, an array of 24 topics under the following headings:

- general concepts, methods, standards, economics and strategies
- collection building, management and integration
- architectures and interoperability
- knowledge organization, discovery and retrieval
- mediation, user interaction and collaboration

All 24 conference topics were covered by paper submissions and by expert reviewers. As can be seen from all parts of the conference program, even after highly selective peer review this wide coverage is to a large degree preserved.

The 69 Program Committee members who participated in the review work represent 27 countries from all continents and many digital-library-related disciplines. A further 66 referees shared the peer-review work, assuring three reviews per submission.

The call for papers resulted in 161 paper submissions, 25% of which were declared as short papers. This response is one of the largest number of papers ever submitted to an ECDL conference.

We were able to accept 47 papers, 8 of which are short papers. This is a rather low acceptance rate of 29% compared with the many highly rated submissions we received. So the competition turned out to be fierce and high ratings from the reviewers were required to make the final list of papers for inclusion. The 47 accepted papers are clustered in 13 sessions in two parallel tracks.

The outcome of the lengthy but quality-assuring review process is demonstrated by the high quality of papers included in this volume of proceedings.

The other elements of the conference program were also subject to quality assurance processes. 72 posters and demonstrations were submitted to ECDL 2003, a very high number. "Only" 52 could be selected for presentation, 36 posters and 16 demonstrations. At least 9 are combined formats. A late deadline allowed an invitation to submit demonstrations related to accepted papers, and posters presenting late-breaking results. The posters will be on display throughout the whole conference.

Three excellent and widely known colleagues agreed to be the invited speakers at ECDL 2003: Karen Sparck Jones, Clifford Lynch and John Lervik.

Three exciting panel topics aim at stimulating controversy, lively debate and active participation of the audience.

The number of tutorials and workshops also far exceeded the number that could be accommodated. We feature a very rich tutorial program: nine tutorials are on offer with a good mix of the established and successful with several new topics on both introductory and advanced levels. The five workshops cover a broad spectrum of application areas. Tutorials and workshops turn out to be a good complement to the topics of the paper sessions.

We hope that the interactive potential of these formats will be fully exploited by conference participants. It will be especially interesting to see if the wireless network – providing almost ubiquitous Internet access at the conference venue – can provide new opportunities regarding conference work and communication.

Finally, we want to thank all those who contributed their time and efforts to make this conference possible: the local Organizing Committee, all the conference chairs, the Program Committee and the additional referees, the host institutions and sponsors, the invited speakers, the panellists, tutorial and workshop leaders, all presenters, speakers, session chairs and participants. A conference is a truly collective effort.

You will find references to everything related to the conference and further information at the Web site http://www.ecdl2003.org/.

We are confident that we shall, all together, make ECDL 2003 a well attended, high-quality and successful conference, offering all participants rich and fruitful opportunities to share ideas, results and experiences, to gain insights and make valuable contacts.

June 2003                                                    Traugott Koch
                                                Ingeborg Torvik Sølvberg

# Organization

### General Chair

Ingeborg Torvik Sølvberg, Norwegian University of Science and Technology

### Program Chair

Traugott Koch, NetLab, Lund University, Sweden

### Organizing Chairs

Trond Aalberg, Norwegian University of Science and Technology
Roger Midtstraum, Norwegian University of Science and Technology

### Demonstration Chairs

José Luis Borbinha, National Library of Portugal
Stuart Sutton, University of Washington, USA

### Poster Chairs

Ragnar Nordlie, Oslo College, Norway
Linda Hill, University of California, Santa Barbara, USA

### Panel Chairs

Anders Ardö, Lund University, Sweden
Carol Peters, IEI-CNR, Italy

### Workshop Chairs

Liz Lyon, University of Bath, UK
Christine Borgman, University of California, Los Angeles, USA

### Tutorial Chairs

Andreas Rauber, Vienna University of Technology, Austria
Ronald Larsen, University of Pittsburg, USA

### Publicity Chair

Lesly Huxley, ILRT, University of Bristol, UK

# Program Committee

Maristella Agosti, University of Padua, Italy
Daniel E. Atkins, University of Michigan, USA
Ricardo Baeza-Yates, University of Chile
Thomas Baker, Fraunhofer Gesellschaft, Germany
Nick Belkin, Rutgers University, USA
Alejandro Bia, University of Alicante, Spain
Katy Boerner, Indiana University, USA
Jose Borbinha, National Library of Portugal
Christine Borgman, University of California, Los Angeles, USA
Svein Arne Brygfjeld, National Library of Norway
Gerhard Budin, University of Vienna, Austria
Warwick Cathro, National Library of Australia
Hsinchun Chen, University of Arizona, USA
Key-Sun Choi, KAIST, Korea
Gregory Crane, Tufts University, USA
Ron Daniel, Jr., Taxonomy Strategies, USA
Alberto Del Bimbo, University of Florence, Italy
Lorcan Dempsey, OCLC, USA
Martin Doerr, ICS FORTH, Greece
Matthew Dovey, Oxford University, UK
Jacques Ducloy, CNRS INIST, France
Dieter Fellner, Technical University of Braunschweig, Germany
Ed Fox, Virginia Tech, USA
Michael Freeston, University of California, Santa Barbara, USA
Norbert Fuhr, Duisburg University, Germany
Richard Furuta, Texas A&M University, USA
Carole Goble, University of Manchester, UK
Stefan Gradmann, Hamburg University, Germany
Jane Greenberg, University of North Carolina, Chapel Hill, USA
Juha Hakala, Helsinki University Library, Finland
Sigrun Klara Hannesdottir, National Library of Iceland
Margaret Hedstrom, University of Michigan, USA
Jane Hunter, University of Queensland, Australia
Ole Husby, BIBSYS, Norway
Yannis Ioannidis, University of Athens, Greece
Poul Henrik Joergensen, Portia System, Denmark
Leonid Kalinichenko, Russian Academy of Sciences
Stephen Katz, Food and Agriculture Organization of the UN
Jaana Kekäläinen, University of Tampere, Finland
Juergen Krause, IZ Bonn, and University of Koblenz and Landau, Germany
Carl Lagoze, Cornell University, USA
Ray Larson, University of California, Berkeley, USA
David Levy, University of Washington, USA
Ee-Peng Lim, Nanyang Technical University, Singapore

# Additional Referees

Giuseppe Amato
Anders Ardö
Jurgen Assfalg
David Bainbridge
Maria Bruna Baldacci
Stefano Berretti
Marco Bertini
George Buchanan
Francesco Carreras
Carlos Castillo
Wingyan Chung
Panos Constantopoulos
Daniel Cunliffe
Sally Jo Cunningham
Annakim Eltén
Jörgen Eriksson
Peter Fankhauser
Nicola Ferro
Claudio Gennaro
Torsten Grabs
Kai Grossjohann
Norbert Gövert

Jon Olav Hauglid
Jon Heggland
Otthein Herzog
Linda Hill
Lieming Huang
Zan Huang
Fathi Husein
Kai Jauslin
Matt Jones
Sara Kjellberg
Claus-Peter Klas
Predrag Knezewic
Jessica Lindholm
Sigfrid Lundberg
Gary Marsden
Byron Marshall
Daniel McDonald
Roger Midtstraum
Andrea Miene
Michael Mlivoncic
Gonzalo Navarro
Claudia Niedereé

Henrik Nottelmann
Walter Nunziati
Giorgio Maria Di Nunzio
Nicola Orio
Pasquale Pagano
Pietro Pala
Jeff Pan
Dimitris Plexousakis
Jialun Qin
Heri Ramampiaro
Dietmar Saupe
André Schaefer
Xijun Shi
Martin Steinebach
Manuel Sánchez-Quero
Roman Tzschoppe
Can Türker
Alejandro Vaisman
Gang Wang
Andreas Wombacher
Jennifer Xu
Yiwen Zhang

# Sponsoring Institutions

ABM – Norwegian Archive, Library and Museum Authority
BIBSYS – Norwegian Service Center for Libraries
ERCIM – European Research Consortium for Informatics and Mathematics
Fast Search & Transfer ASA
NFR – Research Council of Norway
NORDINFO – Nordic Council for Scientific Information,
NTNU (Norwegian University of Science and Technology), Department of
Computer and Information Science
NTNU Library
SINTEF Telecom and Informatics
Sun Microsystems

# Table of Contents

## Uses, Users, and User Interaction

## Metadata Applications

## Annotation and Recommendation

## Automatic Classification and Indexing

## Web Technologies

## Topical Crawling, Subject Gateways

## Architectures and Systems

## Knowledge Organization: Concepts

## Collection Building and Management

# Knowledge Organization: Authorities and Works

# Information Retrieval in Different Application Areas

# Digital Preservation

# Indexing and Searching of Special Document and Collection Information

# Users and Uses of Online Digital Libraries in France

Houssem Assadi[1], Thomas Beauvisage[1], Catherine Lupovici[2], and
Thierry Cloarec[2]

[1] France Telecom R&D, 38 rue du Général Leclerc,
92794 Issy Les Moulineaux, France
{houssem.assadi, thomas.beauvisage}@francetelecom.com
http://www.francetelecom.com/rd/

[2] Bibliothèque Nationale de France, Quai François-Mauriac
75706 Paris Cedex 13, France
{catherine.lupovici, thierry.cloarec}@bnf.fr
http://www.bnf.fr

**Abstract.** This article presents a study of online digital library (DL) uses, based
on three data sources (online questionnaire, Internet traffic data and interviews).
We show that DL users differ from average Internet users as well as from classical library users, and that their practices involve particular contexts, among
which personal researches and bibliophilism. These results lead us to reconsider
the status of online documents, as well as the relationship between commercial
and non-commercial Web sites. Digital libraries, far from being simple digital
versions of library holdings, are now attracting a new type of public, bringing
about new, unique and original ways for reading and understanding texts. They
represent a new arena for reading and consultation of works alongside that of
traditional libraries.

## 1   Introduction

This article presents a study of online digital library (DL) uses called the BibUsages
project. This project – a partnership between France Telecom R&D and the French
National Library (Bibliothèque Nationale de France) – took place in 2002.

### 1.1  Objectives

The objective of the BibUsages project was to study online digital library usage. Such
usage, although innovative, is part of well-established practices. Immediate access to
a large body of works enables researchers to imagine unique and original research,
which was not technically possible previously without access to large digital corpora.
In addition, teachers find electronic libraries an inestimable resource to produce
course materials.

T. Koch and I.T. Sølvberg (Eds.): ECDL 2003, LNCS 2769, pp. 1–12, 2003.

The main project objective was to describe online uses of digital libraries, notably that of Gallica, the online digital library of the French National Library (http://gallica.bnf.fr), through a cross-sectional analysis of usage with user-population characteristics. Another objective was to show how emerging patterns of use both affect and modify well-established practices (in the present case, those involving academic research and teaching, but also personal researches).

By use of methods originating from the social sciences, the objective was to explain, on the one hand, well-established usage (several electronic libraries are already available for free consultation on the Web), but of which a more thorough understanding would enable expansion upon the current range of innovative uses, while at the same time better adapting to user needs and characteristics. On the other hand, the study made use of innovative Internet traffic capture and analysis technologies in order to develop a user-centered approach, an approach that is rarely found in large-scale web-usage studies.

In this paper, we present the main results of the BibUsages project. After describing our methodology (§1.2) and giving a quick overview of the state of the art (§1.3), we give detailed results from our study: section 2 shows the specificities of the studied population (visitors of the Gallica Web site); section 3 gives a precise description of the way the studied population uses Internet and particularly DLs and other types of Web sites, data comes both from both Internet traffic analysis and interviews; and finally, section 4 is a discussion of the main qualitative results of this study.

## 1.2  Methodology

In the BibUsages project, we combined qualitative and quantitative methodologies to fully describe the studied population and their uses of online DLs, and more generally of the Internet.

The 12-month-long project, held in 2002, took place in three stages:

1. Online survey on the Gallica web site (March 2002).

   For a three-week period in March 2002, Gallica web-site visitors were asked to respond to a questionnaire, in order to obtain a precise picture of the Gallica web site visitors and to recruit volunteers for a user-panel the Web traffic of which was to be recorded.

   Other than the socio-demographic characteristics of Gallica Users, the questionnaire was tied into two main subject areas: usage of Gallica and general Internet usage. At the end of the questionnaire, respondents were asked to participate in the user panel that was being established.

   At the end of this first stage, 2,340 people had responded to the questionnaire and 589 had accepted to take part in the user-panel.

2. Formation of a user-panel, installation of the system to capture user-panel Web traffic and collection of data.

At the end of the inscription and installation procedure, the panel consisted in 72 volunteers with socio-demographic characteristics which were representative of those of all the respondents to the survey. Panel-member usage data was collected from July to December 2002.

3. Holding interviews with a volunteer user-sample taking part in the panel (October 2002).
   These interviews concerned 16 panel participants out of 72 and revolved, in particular, around three specific areas under investigation: general Internet usage, Gallica and DL usage, and links with "off-line" reading and cultural practices.

The cross-analysis of these three data sources — online questionnaire, traffic data and interviews — enabled the establishment of a highly-informative panorama of usage beyond the scope of online practices per se.

## 1.3  State of the Art

The users of "traditional" libraries are relatively well-known, thanks to the investigations and studies undertaken by the main institutional libraries on their visitors. On the other hand, as far as we know, there is no general study of the uses of a diversified population of remote users of a digital library, population constituted of university researchers and postgraduate students, but also of high school teachers and students or individuals leading personal researches.

The conference *"The economics and usage of digital library collections"* – hosted by the University of Michigan Library in March 2000 – provides information about the behaviour of digital libraries users coming mainly from user surveys by questionnaire. The conclusions of the conference well summarize the situation: electronic access obviously increases the use of the documents but we do not yet completely understand the variety of uses. Who uses the documents? What are the objectives of these uses? Which value does this use represent?

The Association of Research Libraries (ARL) initiated in October 1999 a *New Measures Initiative* program for research projects on statistics of electronic resources usage. The library community has been working for five years on the refinement of the standard services measurement and assessment guidelines to cover the electronic services. The proposed combination of approaches includes:

– Transaction-based measures made by sampling or by transaction logs. They can record interactive sessions, downloads, hits, images or files counting.
– Use-based measures on user activities, user satisfaction, local versus remote site use.

The French National Library has been using a page mark-up methodology since 2001 for continuous transaction-based measurement, counting viewed pages, visitors and visits. Images and files downloads counting provides a measurement of the DL usage.

Some existing studies already showed the information that can be retrieved by servers' log analysis. In [3] and [4], Jones *et al.* propose a transaction log analysis of the New Zealand Digital Library. They report user sessions to be very short, with few and simple queries. These observations lead the authors to propose design improvements for the search interface. Similar analyses were led for other DLs, see for example the recent study by Sfakakis and Kapidakis dealing with the Hellenic National Documentation [5]. Although they provide valuable and detailed information on the use of online digital libraries, server-centric approaches fail to answer two questions: first, they have no information about the characteristics of the DL visitors (age, gender and other sociological characteristics), and second they do not know which are the contexts of DLs usage.

From a broader point of view, Brian-Kinns and Blandford gave an interesting survey of user studies for DLs [2] that shows the diversity of used methodologies, ranging from qualitative approaches to log analysis. But one can notice that the majority of cited studies deal with design (human-machine interfaces and search tools) rather than users' needs and objectives.

Our approach, which relies on a combination of three methods: user-centric data analysis, online questionnaires and interviews, gives an enhanced description of DLs uses and users. In addition, by focusing on users and uses rather on technical issues, our study adds a new point of view to the existing user studies in the field of DLs (cited in [2])

## 2    Specificities of the Users of Digital Libraries

The data provided by the online survey in March 2002 gave us an accurate vision of the characteristics of the public of Gallica. In this section, we compare them to the general portrait of French Internet users.

Table 1. Gallica users and French Internet users

|  |  | French Internet Users (from NetValue, december 2001) | BibUsages online Questionnaire (march 2002) |
|---|---|---|---|
| Men / Women |  | 58% / 42% | 69.3% / 30.7% |
| Urban |  | 81.0% | 86.4% |
| Age | Under 25 | 29.3% | 11.8% |
|  | 25-34 | 23.1% | 23.1% |
|  | 35-44 | 31.8% | 21.0% |
|  | 45-54 | 12.5% | 24.2% |
|  | More than 55 | 3.3% | 19.5% |
| Narrowband / broadband |  | 91.1% / 8.9% | 58.6% / 39.0% |

The main characteristics of the Gallica users show that they are, in comparison to French Internet users, rather senior men, with an over-representation of more than 45 year old (see Table 1). The most important difference is related to the type of Internet connection: 39% of Gallica users declare that they use a broadband access, while they are only 9% among the French Internet users population. Besides, Gallica users are mainly old Internet users: 70% of them declare that they have had an Internet access since at least 1999. In addition, their socio-professional categories reveal a high level of education and intellectual occupations (university teachers and researchers in particular, but also executives in private companies), as well as high-degree students.

# 3   Usage Data

## 3.1   Global Internet Activity

The traffic data confirmed the declarations to be found in the questionnaire concerning global usage intensity, which is very high in comparison to global French Internet users. This comparison is based on traffic data from a 4,300 people panel studied in 2002[1].

Our panel is globally speaking made up of highly active Internet users: 7.6 sessions[2] per week on average, in comparison to 2.4 sessions per week for the global population of French Internet users. The average duration of the sessions is on the other hand similar to that of the global population of French Internet users: 30 minutes for the BibUsages panel, 35 minutes for French Internet users in 2002. The difference thus exists in terms of number of sessions, and not in terms of duration of sessions.

## 3.2   Accessed Contents and Services

After 6 months of traffic capture, we collected a database containing 15,500 web sessions and almost 1,300,000 web pages (identified by their URL[3]) that were visited by the 72 users of our panel. We used a web mining platform developed at France Telecom R&D in order to analyze this database and to extract data related to the uses of certain categories of web sites.

When examining the different kinds of Web sites visited by the panel, we observed the importance of "search engines" and "cultural contents" in terms of audience (see Table 2). First, generalist portals (e.g. Yahoo) and search engines (e.g. Google) have a central place in the Web activity of our panel, and concern nearly all the users.

In addition, the panel is characterized by a very strong frequentation of the "cultural portals": digital libraries, sites proposing cultural goods for sale (e.g. Amazon) and media sites (press, radio, television) occupy a privileged place. Moreover, the sites devoted to genealogy have an important place in the uses, and reveal highly

---

[1] These data were provided by NetValue, in the context of the SensNet project involving France Telecom R&D, NetValue, Paris III University and the CNRS/LIMSI.

[2] A session is a sequence of time stamped web pages visited by a user of the panel without an interruption longer than 30 minutes.

[3] Uniform Resource Locator.

individual centres of interest; we claim that these elements have to be connected with the particular audience of the personal Web sites, which are present in 20% of the sessions, and are important sources of information for genealogical searches on Web.

**Table 2.** Global audience from our panel (period: July – December 2002)[4]

| Web site category | Number of sessions | Presence in the whole sessions | Number of users |
|---|---|---|---|
| Generalist portals | 8005 | 51.9% | 71 |
| Search engines | 4183 | 27.1% | 67 |
| Personal web sites | 3142 | 20.4% | 70 |
| Digital libraries | 1195 | 7.8% | 57 |
| Media / Newspapers | 1144 | 7.4% | 49 |
| e-business / cultural goods | 833 | 5.4% | 63 |
| Genealogy | 684 | 4.4% | 31 |
| e-business / Finance | 443 | 2.9% | 30 |
| WebMail | 439 | 2.8% | 14 |
| Media / Radio | 305 | 2.0% | 34 |
| Media / TV | 219 | 1.4% | 38 |

**Use of search engines.** Search engines occupy a very important place in the uses of the panel. During the six months of observation, 16 different search engines were used by the 72 users of our panel; Google arrives far beyond, being present in more than 75% of the sessions involving the use of a search engine, while Yahoo and Voila[5] arrive in second and third position (present in 13.7% and 11.3% of the sessions with a search engine). The meta-search engines are frequently used: 24 people used them at least once during the period, and 10 used them regularly.

Besides the usual requests addressed to search engines, related to widely used services, we notice elements which show the specificity of the panel: "bnf" (for "Bibliothèque Nationale de France", the French National Library) arrives thus in third position in the classification of requests in numbers of distinct users having addressed it. We can suppose that, for users already knowing well the BnF and Gallica Web sites, such requests are a simple and quick way to access these sites when they are not bookmarked, or when the bookmark list becomes too large to be efficiently used for site retrieval.

The request "genealogy" and its correlates show a genuine interest for this area; one finds this passion through very particular and precise requests often addressed by only one user, and it consists in proper names and place names. This observation is confirmed in the interviews:

"My personal research relates to regionalism, because I am native of [name of a town] and I love this region. Therefore I collect many things about that region, topics of genealogy and also of history and geography. [… and I create]

---

[4] Audience is both measured in terms of number of sessions and number of different users.
[5] A French search engine: http://www.voila.fr

Internet sites for archaeological or associative subjects" [Male, 47, manager, broadband Internet access]

Researches related to family memory or regional history represent important centres of interest for a significant part of the panel; in this context, Gallica appears as a source of information among others for these researches.

**Use of online DLs.** We identified 17 online digital libraries. We adopted a rather wide definition of DLs, including not only institutional libraries such as Gallica, but also associative initiatives (e.g. ABU[6]) and online revues (e.g. Revues.org), all providing text collections mainly in French. The detailed audience of these various sites (see Table 3) shows that Gallica is the most visited DL, in number of sessions as well as in number of visitors. This table also shows that the audience of other text collections is not insignificant (while our panel was composed, originally, of visitors of the Gallica site): users of the panel don't limit themselves to institutional DLs, such as Gallica, they also visit a variety of other sites providing text collections.

**Table 3.** Audience of digital libraries and online text collections

| Online digital library | Sessions | Visitors | Avg time in a session (min.) |
|---|---|---|---|
| BNF-Gallica | 822 | 54 | 21.4 |
| BNF-Other | 577 | 51 | 6.5 |
| ABU | 31 | 13 | 3.0 |
| Revues.org | 22 | 12 | 1.8 |
| Bibliothèque de Lisieux | 20 | 11 | 3.9 |
| Bibliopolis | 15 | 6 | 8.0 |
| Athena | 14 | 10 | 1.1 |
| ClicNet | 14 | 8 | 0.6 |
| Online Books Page | 10 | 4 | 1.7 |
| Electronic Text Center | 8 | 5 | 0.7 |
| BN Canada - Numérique | 5 | 3 | 1.0 |
| American Memory | 4 | 2 | 6.3 |
| Arob@ase | 4 | 3 | 0.4 |
| Berkeley DL | 3 | 1 | 7.3 |
| eLibrary | 3 | 3 | 0.5 |
| Gutenberg project | 2 | 2 | 0.8 |
| Alex Catalogue | 1 | 1 | 0.8 |
| Bibelec | 1 | 1 | 0.0 |

**Use of other categories of web sites.** We also focused on the uses of two extra categories of web sites: media sites (press, radio, TV) on the one hand and e-business sites selling cultural goods on the other. The global audience analysis already showed us that these two categories of sites have high scores in terms of audience in our panel (see Table 2 above). This seems to show a link between the visit of digital libraries on the one hand, and the sites providing "readable content" and cultural goods on the other hand. We can easily draw a parallel between the frequentation of digital libraries and the frequentation of sites offering "readable content". The use of Media/press

---

[6] « *Association des Bibliophiles Universels* » (Association of Universal Book Lovers): http://abu.cnam.fr/

sites shows high audience scores (Table 4), with a particularly intensive use of the site of the newspaper *Le Monde*.

**Table 4.** Audience of "Media / press" Web sites

| Portal | Visitors | Sessions | Nb of sessions per visitor | Avg. time per session (min.) |
|---|---|---|---|---|
| Le Monde | 37 | 719 | 19.4 | 8.1 |
| Libération | 24 | 86 | 3.6 | 3.9 |
| Les Echos | 17 | 118 | 6.9 | 5.3 |
| Nouvel Obs | 14 | 131 | 9.4 | 4.9 |
| Telerama | 14 | 107 | 7.6 | 6.3 |
| Le Figaro | 13 | 148 | 11.4 | 14.2 |
| New York Times | 6 | 81 | 13.5 | 7.7 |
| Le Point | 4 | 12 | 3.0 | 3.4 |

The frequentation of digital libraries is also closely connected to the frequentation of e-business Web sites providing cultural goods (see Table 5): the use of these sites shows the importance of bibliophilism, with an important frequentation of *Chapitre.com* and *Livre-rare-book*, two web sites devoted to bibliophilism. We also notice in this table the presence of publishers (e.g. Eyrolles, CNRS Editions...). These elements show a strong link between electronic and classical publishing: users not only seek for old books, but also visit publishers' web sites and use their catalogues, for either online or offline purchase.

**Table 5.** Audience of "e-business / cultural goods" Web sites

| Portal | Visitors | Sessions | Nb of sessions per visitor | Avg. time per session (min.) |
|---|---|---|---|---|
| Amazon | 55 | 386 | 7.0 | 4.1 |
| Fnac | 42 | 299 | 7.1 | 2.4 |
| Alapage | 29 | 107 | 3.7 | 2.2 |
| Chapitre.com | 26 | 160 | 6.2 | 9.3 |
| Livre-rare-book | 17 | 92 | 5.4 | 5.0 |
| Galaxidion | 6 | 73 | 12.2 | 6.4 |
| Librissimo | 6 | 7 | 1.2 | 4.5 |
| Numilog | 5 | 14 | 2.8 | 4.7 |
| Eyrolles | 3 | 4 | 1.3 | 1.0 |
| CNRS Editions | 2 | 8 | 4.0 | 8.6 |

### 3.3  DLs in Context: Use of Gallica

**Modalities of use.** Access to Gallica represents a significant part of the traffic of the panel, since 6.2% of the 15,500 recorded sessions include a visit of Gallica. In addition, access to Gallica involves a significant number of users: 54 panelists out of 72 visited at least once Gallica during the six-month-period.

The distribution of the intensity of use of Gallica is similar to that of Web use in general: one third of the visitors of Gallica makes more than 77% of the sessions including an access to the Gallica web site, while another third part represents 4% of these sessions only. Moreover, the most intensive users of Gallica are also intensive users of the Web: over the period, they made 400 sessions on average, for an average of 270 sessions for the other visitors of Gallica, and 150 sessions for those who never visited the site.

The 1,063 sessions including a Gallica access are overall longer than the others: 1h 01min. on average, vs. 28 minutes for the other sessions. In addition, in a session comprising an access to Gallica, the total time spent on this site itself is on average 24 minutes, that is to say almost the average duration of a session without Gallica.

Furthermore, the consultation of Gallica appears to be an activity excluding the alternate visit of other sites. In the sessions, we analyzed the alternation of the visit of the different sites. We observed that in 52% of the cases (558 sessions) navigation on Gallica occupied only one sequence, where it was not alternate with the visit of another site; and for 22% of the sessions only, we observed two distinct sequences on Gallica. "Multitask navigation" is thus seldom practiced, and navigation on Gallica tends to be a long and monolithic activity.

Within those long sequences of visit of Gallica, consultation and download of documents are the main used services (75% of the Gallica sessions), *via* the site's search engine. "Guided tours" access is less used in terms of number of sessions (only 11% of the Gallica sessions), but 30 users of the panel tried it at least once.

**Gallica in context.** The inspection of the types of sites and services visited within the "Gallica sessions" allows us to see how the use of digital libraries is articulated with other contents and services available on the Web. For that, we compared the presence of various types of sites within the Gallica sessions and in the whole sessions (see Table 6).

**Table 6.** Presence of different types of sites and services in the Gallica sessions and in the whole sessions

| | Presence in the Gallica sessions | Presence in the whole sessions | Variation of the presence in the Gallica sessions |
|---|---|---|---|
| Digital libraries | 100.0% | 7.8% | |
| e-business / cultural goods | 9.9% | 5.4% | + 82.8% |
| Search engines | 35.2% | 27.1% | + 29.7% |
| Personal Web sites | 25.7% | 20.4% | + 26.0% |
| Genealogy | 4.7% | 4.4% | + 6.0% |
| Generalist portal | 52.9% | 51.9% | + 1.8% |
| e-business / tourism | 0.8% | 0.9% | - 7.4% |
| Media / Radio | 1.3% | 2.0% | - 33.4% |
| Media / Press | 4.7% | 7.4% | - 36.6% |
| Media / TV | 0.8% | 1.4% | - 40.4% |
| e-business / Finance | 1.0% | 2.9% | - 64.0% |

We notice thus that search engines are over-represented in the Gallica sessions, where they are 1.8 times more represented than in the whole set of sessions. This important use of search engines demonstrates the importance of the use of Gallica in a context of information seeking, where a DL is considered as a source of information among others. We also notice that personal Web sites are over-represented in the sessions with Gallica, they are valuable data and text sources for very specific subjects, such as genealogy.

The use of Web sites providing cultural goods, also over-represented, seems to correspond to a task of catalogue or "testing before purchase", which is confirmed in the interviews:

> "I go on the BNF web site because [...] I guess I will be able to find something, and that I will take a little time to see some images, or some documents which I will not be able to consult otherwise, or to be sure that I will buy a book; I spoke about [an author name], I bought after having consulted the BNF a book that interested me much, for 200 €" [Male, 47, manager, broadband Internet access]

In this context, the user leafs through an old book online before purchasing it on a site specialized in bibliophilism.

Media sites are, on the contrary, less present in the Gallica sessions than in the whole traffic: if the users of Gallica are intensive consumers of online newspapers, as we have already seen (see Table 2. Global audience from our panel (period: July – December 2002)), the access to these two types of sites does not correspond to the same practices and contexts, and is done in different sessions.

**Dealing with documents.** When observing the detailed activity of users on Gallica, we notice that they often consult more than one document, and do not read these documents linearly. Only an image format (pdf) is available for the majority of the documents provided by Gallica and the document is accompanied by tables of contents in text mode which allow to search them and navigate through books. Visitors of Gallica use mainly this function to grab information in documents, and do not seem to read online, as they would do for classical books of writers. Once the information is detected, people often download the document and store it, but the interviews showed that few people read them afterwards.

The interviews allowed us to know what people do with the documents they download from online DLs. For the majority of the interviewed persons, reading on the screen is rare; screen reading is often blamed for being "tiring". It occurs in very specific contexts, where the user is mining for very specific information. If we consider the sub-division of the reading activity into sub-tasks by Adler *et al.* [1], we can say that we observed here two categories: reading to identify – "to work out which document it is (usually simply by glancing at it)" – and skimming – "getting a quick idea of the content of a document".

Printing does not often occurs, mostly because of its cost. Nevertheless, a lot of people keep downloaded documents in "personal digital libraries" focused on their personal centres of interest, and store them on CD-ROMs.

These elements lead us to consider that the status of digital documents is close to reference books, whose utility is defined by the needs of a user for a precise question at a certain time, as seen in the interviews:

> "I download [the document] and then I store it. Even, sometimes, I do not print it. But I know that it exists and then, the day when I write something,

well at this time, I will print it or I will look at it." [Female, 55, executive, narrowband Internet access]

"At the beginning I used to print, now I print less. I print what is useful, for example, when I have located [the document], I read it on screen, it is tiring but I read it on screen, and when I locate the pages which will be useful to me, then I print them." [Male, 75, retired, narrowband Internet access]

The storing of digital documents and the constitution of personal DLs can be seen as an accumulation of reference documents for possible future needs, even though they are not consulted afterwards.

## 4   Discussion

First of all, the BibUsages project increased our understanding of users of digital libraries. Digital libraries attract a public who are not necessarily regular users, but who use the service for specific research purposes: in the interviews and through traffic analysis, it was found that digital holdings allow rapid and simple access to difficult-to-find reference documents in the context of a specific research. This public seemed quite different from that of a classical library, and "professional" researchers were, comparatively-speaking, mostly absent from this group. The majority of the observed population was over forty, and for them, digital libraries represented, above all, a source of information for personal research. Among this group, Internet usage intensity was much higher than among the general French Internet user population and went hand-in-hand with the high rate of broadband Internet equipment (cable, ADSL).

The BibUsages study also made it possible to understand the different contexts of usage of digital holdings. From a global audience point of view, DL users were also large consumers of "contents-to-read" (particularly online newspapers). But if we examine more precisely the sessions where DLs were used, we notice a high correlation between DL and search-engine usage, on the one hand, and e-commerce sites selling cultural goods (such as Amazon), on the other. Two profiles emerged: that of the "non professional researcher", whose centres of interest were specific and well-defined and that of the book lover, for whom Gallica served as a "catalogue prior to purchase". In both cases, reading online and printing-out downloaded documents were seldom occurrences and reading was related to searching for targeted fragments within vast collections, bypassing whole works. In this context, the status of online documents seemed to be brought under question: while paper publications remained the primary source for works of writers, electronic publications were more closely assimilated to reference books.

Knowledge of the DL public and the contexts of usage provide some interesting implications to the project's two partners. For France Telecom, as an Internet Services Provider, there are two points worthy of mention. First of all, there is a large percentage of senior Internet user population with broadband access whose centres of interest revolve around "cultural" content in addition to the standard offer in services and communications. This atypical population among French Internet users constitutes in and of itself an interesting population to study for France Telecom, for which it is now possible to adapt the service offer by orienting it more towards search tools and "reading" content. The study also showed a relationship between commercial and non- commercial web sites. Whereas Internet players (content and access providers) perceive a dichotomy between those two categories, Internet users, themselves, move indifferently from one site to another; therefore, we ought to speak of mutual enhancement between commercial and non- commercial Web when seen in the light of actual practice.

For the French National Library, and digital libraries in general, the project enables a better understanding of its remote public and the ability to better adapt its offer. Through traffic analysis and interviews, the project revealed a strong user tendency towards downloading and a quasi-systematic use of search tools, in addition to points for ergonomic improvement. Furthermore, the BibUsages study will allow the French National Library to become more familiar with the contexts in which its digital library is visited. The user point-of-view adopted by the study provided information on the frequency of use Gallica "direct-competitors" offering online collections of texts. It also showed which types of links could be considered between Gallica and other kinds of Internet sites (booklovers' links, for ex.) and those which would not be pertinent (e.g. online newspaper sites).

Digital libraries, far from being simple digital versions of library holdings, are now attracting a new type of public, bringing about new, unique and original ways for reading and understanding texts. They represent a new arena for reading and consultation of works alongside that of traditional libraries.

# References

1. Adler, A. *et al.*: A Diary Study of Work-Related Reading: Design Implications for Digital Reading Devices. Proceedings of CHI'98, 241–248.
2. Bryan-Kinns N. and Blandford A.: A survey of user studies for digital libraries. Working paper, 2000.
3. Jones, S. *et al.*: A Transaction Log Analysis of a Digital Library. International Journal on Digital Libraries. 3-2 (2000) 152–169
4. Jones, S. *et al.*: An Analysis of Usage of a Digital Library. European Conference on Digital Libraries. (1998) 261–277
5. Sfakakis, M. and Kapidakis S.: User Behavior Tendencies on Data Collections in a Digital Library. ECDL 2002, LNCS 2458, 550–559.

# In Search for Patterns of User Interaction for Digital Libraries

Jela Steinerová

Department of Library and Information Science, Faculty of Philosophy, Comenius University Bratislava, Slovakia

**Abstract.** The paper provides preliminary results from a major study of the academic and research libraries users in Slovakia. The study is part of a larger research project on interaction of man and information environment. The goal of the research is to identify patterns of interaction of individuals and groups with information resources, derive models and information styles. The methodological model for questionnaire survey of users is described. The first results confirm the need to support user strategies, collaboration, different stages of information seeking and knowledge states, closer links with learning and problem solving, easy and flexible access, human creative processes of analysis, synthesis, interpretation, and the need to develop new knowledge organization structures.

## 1 Introduction

Ethnographical research of information seeking behaviour of users can be beneficial for the digital libraries development in several ways. One of the most significant benefits is the design of better user interfaces and overall improvement of the interaction of man and information environment. The context of our research is based on a changing paradigm of information science towards the usage of information for different user groups and over time. With regard to the information process we can identify several levels of the interaction and use of information, namely individual, group (community), domain, organizational and social levels. The inclusion of user needs and human sociocognitive features into the information process on these levels can contribute to better real-life functioning of information systems, services and products. Other benefits of deeper knowledge of user interaction with information environment can be seen in new methods of information analysis and knowledge organization. The results of our research can be used for setting further research agendas, for development of new models and prototypes of knowledge organization, and for training of both information professionals and the digital libraries users.

## 2 Background

Basic tendencies of digital libraries evolution have been formulated in many works, e.g. Borgman, 2000 [6], Troll, 2001 [28], Storey, 2002 [26], Fidel, 2000 [12]. These

T. Koch and I.T. Sølvberg (Eds.): ECDL 2003, LNCS 2769, pp. 13–23, 2003.

tendencies are related with transition from metadata to knowledge, from isolated systems to social cooperation and discovery of new links in information use, from searching to navigation and access through linked knowledge and wider contexts, from individual to collaborative information seeking and use. Many empirical studies of users (e.g. Kuhltau, 1993 [21], Ford, 2000 [13], Thomsen, 1998 [27], Burnett, 2000 [8], Hepworth, 1998 [15], Heinstrom, 2000 [14], Adkins, 2002 [1], Cole, 2000 [11], Allen, 2001 [4]) prove that individual differences in information seeking process can be identified and several cognitive styles, styles of learning and contexts can help understand the information process. We suppose that information styles are relatively constant preferences of interaction of people and information based on prototypical user needs, presentation preferences, patterns of relevance judgement, information seeking strategies, personality types, communicative and learning preferences.

In our research we would like to prove sociocognitive assumptions of information seeking and use (e.g. Allen, 1991 [3], Kuhltau, 1993 [21], Ingwersen, 1996 [18], Hjorland, 1997 [16], Jacob, 1998 [20]) in the information environment of Slovak academic and research libraries. Possible implications for theory (new models), knowledge organization and evaluation of digital libraries effectivity can be derived. It is important to take into the account such variables as types of sources, relevance judgements (Saracevic, 2000) [22], access points (Bishop, 1998) [5], different stages of information problems (e.g. Kuhltau, 1993 [21], Vakkari, 2001 [29], Bystrom, 2000 [9]) and contexts of tasks (Allen, 2001) [3]. Based on our empirical research of users we would like to identify patterns of information seeking and use and develop new models of the interaction of man and information environment. Social contexts and cognitive aspects analysed and modelled in previous works (Steinerová, 2001, 2002) [25], [23] form the starting point of the ongoing research project.

## 3 Research Questions

Our research project is aimed at identification of information seeking behaviour patterns of users in academic and research libraries based on preferences of information sources, access points, strategies and evaluation of experience. Differences between specific groups of users and patterns of information seeking styles are sought for. We suppose that at least two levels of information process emerge, namely surface and in-depth levels, and that three types of information styles can be identified (e.g. strategic, analytical, and mixed types). Perceptions of the current information seeking and perceptions of the experience after the information seeking should be identified. Other lines of our research have been directed to the use of electronic resources and the willingness of users to publish in electronic environment (these issues are not analysed in this paper).

Thus, the main research questions linked with our empirical study of users in Slovak academic and research libraries are as follows: What are the users´ perceptions of information seeking process and their position in the information environment of libraries based on constant preferences of information use? What are the perceptions of users during the information seeking process? What are the perceptions of users after the completion of information seeking?

# 4  Methodology

As a methodological tool a conceptual model for the questionnaire design has been developed (fig.1). The conceptual model identifies main characteristics of users (age, gender, languages, category, discipline) and three parts, including focus on stable user preferences (A), the course of seeking (B), and the experience after seeking (C). For identification of constant user preferences (A) we have used the criteria grouped under motivation factors (willingness to allocate time and material sources to information seeking and use, planning of strategies in information seeking), information sources (preferences of easy access, the use of formal or informal communication channels, first degree of reliability and quality control of information sources - reputation of sources).

Another groups include intellectual access (perceptions of well-arranged form, wider categories, immediate use of information can indicate surface and deeper levels of information use) and stimuli for further seeking (new ideas and contradictory information pointing to deeper information processing). Preferences from part A will be used for later analyses of information seeking styles of users.

The two following parts of the model have been separated using the sequential division of information seeking process into parts indicating perceptions in the course of seeking (B), and perceptions after the completion of the task (C) ( Kuhltau´s stages of initiation, selection, exploration, formulation, collection and presentation have been reflected).

In part B we have proposed four groups of criteria, The first group is based on perceptions of coopeation (help of librarians, preferences for independent work, cooperation with colleagues). The second group points to orientation and access points in informaton seeking (more libraries, first sources). The third group is concentrated on perceptions of qualities of sources (periodicals, indexes). The fourth group is oriented towards depth of information processing (evolution of understanding in the process of information seeking, increase of interest, and feelings in the course of seeking).

Three groups of criteria have been examined in part C. The first group indicates satisfaction with strategic planning of information seeking (need for more time, evaluation of one´s own organization of work, return to other sources). The second group concentrates on success and effects of information seeking (confirmation of knowledge as a function of information retrieval, feelings after the seeking). The third group is concerned with perceptions of relevance judgement (most relevant types of sources, criteria used for relevance judgement).

Based on the conceptual model the questionnaire has been developed and tested with students of Library and Information Science at our Department (75 subjects) and then the large-scale questionnaire survey has been designed. The statements aimed at users´ perceptions applied a 5-point Likert scale (1-almost always, 5-almost never) (Kuhltau, 1993) [21], other questions offered multiple responses. 16 selected academic and research libraries in Slovakia and 793 subjects took part in the survey. Perceptions of users have been used for testing several hypotheses. The field data have been collected, coded and analysed. The first results are produced with the use of descriptive statistics - frequency distributions, scaling and other quantitative analyses of data using SPSS v.8.0.

|  | | library | USER | region | |
|---|---|---|---|---|---|
| age | gender | languages | category | discipline | |

### A - stable preferences

| A1 motivation | A2 sources | A3 intellectual access | A4 stimuli |
|---|---|---|---|
| A1.1 time | A2.1 accessib. | A3.1 well-arranged form | A4.1 new ideas |
| A1.2 cost | A2.2 informal s. | A3.2 wider categories | A4.2 contradict.inform. |
| A1.3 planning | A2.3 renowned s. | A3.3 immediate use | |

### B - the course of seeking

| B1 percep. of cooperation | B2 orientation | B3 quality of source | B4 depth of inf. proc. |
|---|---|---|---|
| B1.1 help of libr. | B2.1 more libr. | B3.1 prof. periodicals | B4.1 understaning |
| B1.2 individ.work | B2.2 first-internet | B3.2 indexes | B4.2 increase interest |
| B1.3 cooperation | B2.3 first-catalogue | | B4.3 feelings |
| | B2.4 first-reference | | |

### C - experience after seeking

| C1 strategy | C2 success/effects | C3 relevance |
|---|---|---|
| C1.1 more time | C2.1 confirmation | C3.1 document types |
| C1.2 work organization | C2.2 feelings | C3.2 relevance criteria |
| C1.3 steps back | | |

**Fig. 1.** Conceptual model for research of information seeking behaviour of users

The data analyses proceed in several stages. The first stage identified the whole set of data using basic ethnographic characteristics. In the second stage we have analysed the above mentioned criteria from the conceptual model within the whole set of data. Basic hypotheses have been verified, the results interpreted and represented in tables and graphs. In the third stage we will analyse differences between several groups of users (men, women, younger, older users, different categories including students, teachers, researchers, managers, and different disciplines, e.g. technical sciences, social sciences, economic sciences, sciences and medicine). The fourth stage will focus on the hypothetic model of the surface and in-depth levels of the information process. Types of information seeking styles will be identified (analytic, strategic, mixed) and related to criteria from the conceptual model.

## 5  Results

The characteristics of the sample of 793 subjects include 57,3% men and 40,7% women, young people by 25 years of age cover 52,3%. Majority of subjects indicated understanding of two foreign languages, namely English and German. The third most often used foreign language is Russian. 54,6% of subjects are university students and the dominating disciplines are technical sciences (30,4%) and social sciences (28,8%). The following sequence of other disciplines has been determined: sciences and medicine, economics, arts.

The following statements have been tested in the first, second and partly third stages of the data analyses.

**Statement 1.** *Strategic aspects* of information seeeking are underestimated by users.
This statement has been confirmed. Using the conceptual model, the following criteria has been evaluated: confirmation that information seeking took the users more time than they expected (partial confirmation: 58,5%, strong confirmation: 27%), evaluation of a person´s own organization of work (many missed opportunities indicated by 44,1%, problems indicated by 22,7%), return to different sources (30,3%), return to problem definition (22,2%). As for the differences between user groups, strong confirmation of more time needed for the information seeking activity was indicated by research workers (29,2%) and students (28,6%). Younger subjects (18-25, 26-30) perceived the information seeking as more time consuming than older subjects and no major differences have been found between men and women. As for the disciplines, the time consuming problems were strongly confirmed especially by sciences and medicine and by arts. Most missed opportunities within organization of work have been indicated by students (45,5%) and managers (50%) and within disciplines by technical sciences (51%). These findings lead to the following interpretations. Users of our academic libraries need support in planning their information seeking activities (strategies). Their expectations of what can be found from sources and systems are too optimistic. Seldom can they find relevant information without recursive steps to identify further sources or to redefine the problem. It means that the support of systems or mediators in the first stages of information seeking process is still required.

**Statement 2.** The role of *collaboration* in information seeking has not been recognized properly by our users.
This statement has been confirmed. Evaluation of criteria of the use of librarians´ assistance, preferences of independent work and collaboration with colleagues indicate that user preferences are linked with the idea of information seeking as an individual activity. Many users indicate that they use the assistance of librarians seldom (mean value-3,16), they also indicate that they prefer independent work (mean-2,13) to collaboration with other colleagues (mean-2,69). The preferences of independent work confirm the need to train users in more active collaboration and cooperation and to point to collaborative features of information retrieval in digital libraries. The highest mean value of scaling in the section B has been computed for the use of support from librarians (mean-3,16), which means that traditional ways of reference work are not sufficient for our users. This is also determined culturally, as there is a lack of traditions of client-service relationships in our libraries. It means that new systems could strenghthen and actively offer the features of assistance to users with possible implications for new value-added services in the electronic environment.

**Statetment 3.** Users usually do not expect deeper effects of information seeking on their *knowledge states*.
This statement has not been confirmed. Among the evaluated criteria, the confirmation of prior knowledge during the information seeking was relevant (yes-highly:19%, yes-partly:77%), which means that the additional feature of confirmation of prior knowledge is part of information seeking. But the other criteria showed that there are strong links betweeen information seeking and the evolution of the problem understanding and formulation (mean-1,96) and that the more information users get, the more they are interested in the problem (mean-2,11). The determined feelings in the course of seeking include trust, doubts (women-17,6%) and optimism (men-22,9%). In this respect men tend to be more optimistic than women. The feelings after the completion of information seeking include satisfaction and relief. As information seeking contributes changes of knowledge states of users, we can assume that the evolution of understanding and problem statement can be supported by various knowledge organization methods in digital libraries and that these features could add value to traditional services. Our users tend to be quite optimistic in the information seeking process (their expectations are positive, they find confirmation of their knowledge, initial doubts evolve towards satisfaction and relief). This can be used for further features of new services that could contribute to the raise of interest in particular knowledge or discourse domains.

**Statement 4.** *Most relevant sources* for users in scientific communication and education are *professional journals*.
This statement has been confirmed. Professional periodicals both in traditional and electronic forms have been indicated as most relevant (mean-2,16). From the perspective of relevance judgement, most relevant document types and sources include journal articles and monographs. The use of internet search engines has also been strongly confirmed (23,3%). But the use of indexes and bibliographies

connected with deeper seeking methods has not been proved in larger scale. The criteria of relevance judgement have been rated as follows: keywords (16,5%), authors (15,8%), titles and contents (14,1%), recommended source, good reputation of source and annotations. Better training with regard to other flexible methods of access and knowledge organization would help users to conceptualize their idea of relevance judgement and efficient interaction with information sources and systems.

**Statement 5.** The methods of *first access points* in information seeking have been changing from libraries and catalogs towards internet services.
This statement has been confirmed partly. The subjects indicated that they use internet as the first source of information more often (mean-2,35) than library catalogs (mean-2,65). Seldom do they use reference works as first orientation sources (mean-2,91). However, our users still have to use more than one library for their information seeking, which happens as often as the use of internet (mean-2,35). This can be interpreted that if internet is available, then it is becoming a dominant source and first access point for information seeking. On the other hand, the pattern from the past, when it was necessary to collect information from several different specialized libraries, can still be traced within our library environment. Digital libraries could offer more effective service even in this respect. In any case library catalogs have been determined as the last solution for the access to information sources, which confirms Borgman´s often cited finding that they are difficult to use. Digital libraries and new services should provide for the ease of use and access for users on one hand, and refine the knowledge organization structures based on traditional indexing on the other hand. The support of interaction on the access side of the systems should lead to support of creativity and human dynamic knowledge evolution.

**Statement 6.** The *motivation* of users towards information seeking behaviour is rather low.
This statement has been confirmed. The criteria grouped in the evaluation of  this statement
include willingness to devote certain amount of time to information seeking and willingness to pay for relevant information. Only sometimes are our users willing to spend high amount of their time for information seeking (mean-3,01) and even less often would they like to pay for  (scientific) information. These patterns are connected with patterns of understanding of education, research and science as rather non-commercial activities that should be accessible to all who are actively involved. The communication pattern in science is also determined by the fact of simultaneous production of new knowledge based on information seeking and use. Low motivation is also proved by weak confirmation of advance planning of seeking strategies (mean-2,70). All these evaluated criteria depend on the type of information problem, on domains and other contexts, which should be taken into the account. But free sources and time savings are still strong factors that can attract users from our academic environment to services and products.

**Statement 7.** Users prefer very *simple and easy access* methods in their information seeking interactions.

This statement has been confirmed. The criterion of attractive and well-arranged form of information appealed to majority of our subjects. This criterion has been indicated as the second most frequently used within stable preferences of users (mean-2,12). Almost always and very often do they prefer good accessibility of information sources (the first top position within preferences (mean-1,72). Users also appreciate and prefer the information sources that lead to information ready for immediate use (mean-2,42), as they are probably very often under time pressure. The preferences of wider categories in knowledge organization have also been found as significant (mean-2,47). It can be concluded that digital libraries should provide for several interaction stages for their users, from simple, easy access points which provide basic orientation and navigation at the beginning of information seeking (e.g. sources, events, experts, topics, concepts), through support of problem confirmation and formulation,  to more refined content representations and support of analysis, synthesis, evaluation, presentation and production of information and knowledge.

## 6  Conclusions

The first analyses of our data point to the following patterns. Our users need more training and support at initial stages of information seeking process so that they can save time and better organize strategies of access. Support in problem formulations, conceptual understanding and overview of available sources by topics, domains and discourse communities would be helpful. It has also been confirmed that knowledge states of users are dynamic and that relevance judgements need also support and help. Evaluation of information sources by experts (reviews, refereed information) has been appreciated as the important value-added information. Wider contexts of information use (education, research, etc.) determine motivation of information seeking and this context should be incorporated into user modeling for digital libraries. Stages of user interaction need different support from mediators, the initial stage should be based on the easy and simple access.

Preliminary patterns reveal the tendency that information seeking process contributes to inspiring and creative functions of information use. Our users prefer independent work and the idea of strong individualism of  information use as an intellectual work prevail. If more cooperative features were offered to our users in digital libraries, this could support the effectivity of problem formulations, concept understanding, strategic planning, as well as exploration, selection and presentation of information in knowledge domains and discourse communities. The challenge of information science is to open traditional library functions to creative human processes of perception, analysis, synthesis and interpretation of information. New knowledge organization structures are needed to support intellectual access, learning and information use in domains and communities.

Further analyses are underway. In further stages we will concentrate on differences in gender, age, disciplines, user categories and examine groups of users mapped to strategical and analytical information seeking styles.

**Acknowledgments.** This research has been supported by the Research Grant Agency of Ministry of Education of SR, research project VEGA 1/9236/02. It has also been a part of the IST-DELOS-CEE project coordinated by NDAP and ICIMSS, Poland. The author is grateful to co-workers from the Department of Sociology, Comenius University Bratislava, namely Ms. L. Mistriková, and to selected academic and research libraries in Slovakia which have taken part in the survey.

# References

1.    Adkins, Denice, Brown-Syed, Christopher. Accommodating All Learners: Critical Inquiry and Learning Styles in the LIS Classroom. In: Proc. of 68th IFLA Council and General Conference, Glasgow, August 18–24, (2002). Code N. 047-093-E. VII. Education and Training. In: http://www.ifla.org/
2.    Albrechtsen, Hanne, Hjørland, Birger. Information Seeking and Knowledge Organization : The Presentation of a New Book. Knowledge Organization, Vol. 24 (1997), No.3, 136–144.
3.    Allen, Bryce. L. Cognitive Research in Information Science: Implications for Design. In: Williams, Martha (Ed). Annual Review of Information Science and Technology: Volume 26. Medford, NJ: Learned Information, 1991, 3–37.
4.    Allen, Bryce, Kim, Kyung-Sun. Person and Context in Information Seeking: Interactions between Cognitive and Task Variables. In : The New Review of Information Behaviour Research. Studies of Information Seeking in Context. Vol. 2, 2001. Cambridge: Taylor Graham, (2001), 1–16.
5.    Bishop, Ann P.  Measuring Access, Use, and Success in Digital Libraries. The Journal of Electronic Publishing. Vol.4 (1998), No.2.
      http://www.press.umich.edu/jep/04-02/bishop.html
6.    Borgman, Christine L. From Gutenberg to the Global Information Infrastructure. Access to Information in the Networked World. Cambridge, Mass.: The MIT Press, 2000. 324 p.
7.    Borgman, Christine L. et al. *Social Aspects of Digital Libraries*. UCLA-NSF Social Aspects of Digital Libraries Workshop : Final Report. (Nov.1996 )
      http: //Www-Lis.Gseis.Ucla.Edu/Dl/Ucla_Dl_Report.Html
8.    Burnett, Gary. Information Exchange in Virtual Communities: a Typology. In: Information Research, (2000), Vol. 5., No. 4. http://Informationr.Net/
9.    Byström, Katriina. The Effects of Task Complexity on the Relationships Between Information Types Acquired and Information Sources Used. In: The New Review of Information Behaviour Research. Studies of Information Seeking in Context. Vol. 1, 2000. Cambridge: Taylor Graham, (2000), 85–101.
10.   Cleveland, Gary.  Digital Libraries : Definitions, Issues and Challenges. - IFLA-Universal Dataflow and Telecommunications Core Programme, March 1998. 8p. Occasional Paper 8. http://www.dlib.org/dlib
11.   Cole, Charles, Kuhltau, Carol. Information and Information Seeking of Novice Versus Expert Lawyers: How Experts Add Value. In: The New Review of Information Behaviour Research. Studies of Information Seeking in Context. Vol. 1, 2000. Cambridge: Taylor Graham, (2000), 103–115.

12. Fidel, Raya; Bruce; Harry; Pejtersen, A.M.; Dumais, S.; Grudin, J.; Poltrock, S. Collaborative Information Retrieval. In: The New Review of Information Behaviour Research. Studies of Information Seeking in Context. Vol. 1, 2000. Cambridge: Taylor Graham, (2000), 235–247.

13. Ford, Nigel; Wilson, Tom; Foster, Allen; Ellis, David; Spink, Amanda. Individual Differences in Information Seeking: an Empirical Study. In: ASIS 2000. Proceedings of the 63rd ASIS Annual Meeting. Vol. 37. Chicago, Il., Nov. 12–16, 2000. Medford, Nj: Information Today, (2000), 14–24.

14. Heinström, Jannica. The Impact of Personality and Approaches to Learning on Information Behaviour. In: Information Research, , Vol. 5, (2000), No. 3. http://www.shef.ac.uk/~is/publications/infres/paper78.html

15. Hepworth, Mark. Investigating Methods for Understanding User Requirements for Information Products. In: Information Research, Vol. 4, (1998), No. 2. http:// www.shef.ac.uk/~is/publications/infres/isic/hepworth.html

16. Hjørland, Birger. Information Seeking Behaviour: What Should a General Theory Look Like? In: The New Review of Information Behaviour Research. Vol. 1, 2000. London: Taylor Graham, (2000), 19–33.

17. Hjørland, Birger. Information Seeking and Subject Representation: an Activity-Theoretical Approach to Information Science. Westport, Cn.: Greenwood Press, 1997. 213 p.

18. Ingwersen, Peter. Cognitive Perspectives of Information Retrieval Interaction: Elements of a Cognitive IR Theory. Journal of Documentation. Vol. 53, (1996) No.1, 3–50.

19. An International Research Agenda for Digital Libraries. Summary Report of the Series of Joint NSF-EU Working Groups on Future Directions for Digital Libraries Research. October 12, (1998). Eds. P. Schäuble, A.F. Smeaton. Brussels, 1998. http://www.ici.pi.cni.it/delos/nsf/brussrep.htm

20. Jacob, Elin K., Shaw, Debora. Sociocognitive Perspectives on Representation. In: Williams, Martha E.,(ed). Annual Review of Information Science and Technology: Volume 33. Medford, NJ: Learned Information, (1998), 131–185.

21. Kuhltau, Carol C. Seeking Meaning: A Process Approach To Library And Information Services. Norwood, NJ: Ablex, 1993. 199 p.

22. Saracevic, Tefko , Covi, Lisa. Challenges for Digital Library Evaluation. In: ASIS 2000. Proceedings of The 63rd ASIS Annual Meeting. Vol. 37. Chicago, Il, Nov. 12-16, (2000). Medford, Nj: Information Today, 2000, 341–350.

23. Steinerová, Jela. Kognitivne a socialne pristupy informacnej vedy. Cognitive and Social Approaches of Information Science. In: Kniznicns a informacns veda. Library and Information Science. 19. Zbornik FiFUK. Bratislava: UK, (2002), 111–128.

24. Steinerová, Jela. Human Issues of Library and Information Work. In: Information Research. Vol.6, January ( 2001), No.2. http://IinformationR.net/

25. Steinerová, Jela. Information Models of Man in Contexts of Information Society: Theoretical and Strategic Perspectives. In: Beyond the Web: Technologies, Knowledge and People. Proc. of the 29th Annual Conference of the Canadian Association for Information Science. Ed. by D. Grant Campbell. Québec : Université Laval, (2001), 200–208.

26. Storey, Tom. Moving Libraries Forward in a Digital World. OCLC Newsletter. October (2002), No. 258, 18–19.

27. Thomsen, Steve R., Staubhaar Joseph D., Bolyard, Drew M. Ethnomethodology and the Study of Online Communities: Exploring Tte Cyber Streets. In: Information Research, Vol. 4, (1998), No. 1. http://www.shef.ac.uk/~is/ publications/infres/paper50.html

28. Troll, Denise A. How And Why Are Libraries Changing? In:
    http://www.diglib.org/use/whitepaper.htm (accessed 1st July 2002).
29. Vakkari, Pertti, Pennanen, Mikko. Sources, Relevance and Contributory Information of Documents in Writing a Research Proposal: a Longitudinal Case Study. In: The New Review of Information Behaviour Research. Studies of Information Seeking in Context. Vol. 2, 2001. Cambridge: Taylor Graham,( 2001), 217–232.

# Detecting Research Trends in Digital Library Readership

Johan Bollen[1], Rick Luce[2], Somasekhar Vemulapalli[1], and Weining Xu[1]

[1] Computer Science Department, Old Dominion University, Norfolk VA 23529, USA
{jbollen,svemulap,wxu}@cs.odu.edu
[2] Research Library, Los Alamos National Laboratory, Los Alamos, NM 8754, USA
rick.luce@lanl.gov

**Abstract.** The research interests and preferences of the reader communities associated to any given digital library may change over the course of years. It is vital for digital library services and collection management to be informed of such changes, and to determine how they may point to future trends. We propose the Impact Discrepancy Ratio metric for the detection of research trends in a large digital library by comparing a reader-defined metric of journal impact to the Institute for Scientific Information Impact Factor (ISI IF) over the course of three years. An analysis for the Los Alamos National Laboratory (LANL) Research Library (RL) comparing reader impact to the ISI IF for 1998 and 2001 indicates journals relating to climatology have undergone a sharp increase in local impact. This evolution pinpoints specific shifts in the local strategies and reader interests of the LANL RL which were qualitatively validated by LANL RL management.

## 1 Introduction

The Institute for Scientific Indexing (ISI) publishes the JCR database which contains yearly citation counts for a large number of journals and the ISI Impact Factor (IF). The latter is used to assess the impact of specific journals by calculating the ratio between the number of citations to the articles which have appeared in a given journal in the two years preceeding publication of the JCR database and the total number of articles published in the given journal over that period.

The ISI IF is generally used to asses the impact of specific journals, and by proxy the quality of a researcher's publications or a departments overall publication record. It does however not capture journal impact specific to a community of Digital Library (DL) readers due to its reliance on universally defined citations. It, in other words, represents the preferences of a general group of article authors and can not be used to determine the local impact of a journal for a specific user community.

Research has for that reason focused on complementing the ISI IF with measures of reading behavior [1,2] in which download frequency is used to determine the local reader impact of a journal. Such reader impact metrics are however based on download frequencies which do not reveal structural properties in reader preferences, e.g. which journals are most central to a community's interests and how these journals relate

T. Koch and I.T. Sølvberg (Eds.): ECDL 2003, LNCS 2769, pp. 24–28, 2003.

to other journals in the collection. We therefore seek to complement the ISI IF with metrics of reader journal impact which take into account the structural features of reader preferences and their evolution over time.

As discussed in [3], we created journal relationship networks from reader article download sequences reconstructed from existing DL log files. A measure of reader journal impact, similar to Google's PageRank, was defined on the basis of the graph-theoretical structure of these networks. We used the ISI IF as an indication of journal impact in the general scientific community which can be contrasted to the generated reader journal impact values for the same journals. To detect trends in local journal impact, we define the Impact Discrepancy Ratio (IDR) which is defined as the ratio between the calculated reader journal impact and the ISI IF for a given year. The IDR reveals local deviations from general trends in journal impact as expressed by the ISI IF. IDR values are compared for the Los Alamos National Laboratory (LANL) Research Library (RL) over a period of three years (1998-2001) to detect community-specific research trends which deviate from the pattern expressed by the ISI IF in the same period.

## 2   Reader Journal Networks

We analyzed two sets of server logs which registered full-text article downloads in the LANL RL in the periods April to December 1998 and June to November 2001, each for about 35,000 downloads and 1800 unique users. We applied a methodology for the generation of reader-defined journal relationship networks [3], labeled Reader Generated Networks (RGN), which scans DL download logs for pairs of articles which have been downloaded by the same user within the same session. Journal relationship weights are updated according to the frequency by which their articles have been co-retrieved. Two RGN networks were generated from the mentioned LANL RL server logs recorded in 1998 and 2001.

The algorithm to generate RGN networks can be formalized as follows. We represent a network of journal relationship by the $n \times n$ matrix $M$ whose entries $m_{ij} \in \mathcal{R}^+$, indicate the strength of relationship between journals $v_i$ and $v_j$. We scan the DL logs for co-retrieval events which are defined as two articles in journals $v_i$ and $v_j$ being downloaded by the same user within 3600 seconds. For every co-retrieval event found in a DL log a small reinforcement value is added to the matrix entry $m_{ij}$, thereby gradually updating journal relationship weights according to the download patterns found for a given community of readers. The resulting RGN represents the implicitly expressed, communal views and perspectives of a given DL community on the relationships between a set of journals.

## 3   Reader Journal Impact Ranking

We determine reader journal impact within the generated RGN networks by calculating its PageRank value [4] which determines the impact or importance of a journal based on its context of relationships in the RGN, similar to measures of power [5] used in social network analysis. The PageRank values for each journal in the RGN networks are then normalized by the ISI IF for the same year to determine its Impact Discrepancy Ratio (IDR) value which expresses how strongly a journal's community-specific impact deviates from its general ISI IF impact.

## 3.1  Impact Discrepancy Ratio

We denote the PageRank value of a journal $i$ for year $x$ $P_{i,x}$. The ISI IF for the same journal in year $x$ is denoted $\mathrm{IF}_{i,x}$ The IDR value for a journal $i$, labeled $P'_{i,x}$, is then given by:

$$P'_{i,x} = \frac{P_{i,x}}{\mathrm{IF}_{(i,x)}}$$

and held to represent that portion of a journal's impact in a given community which cannot be explained by the more general ISI IF for the same year. The sets of high and low scoring IDR journals reveal particular research interests in the community for which article downloads have been registered in year $x$.

## 3.2  Impact Discrepancy Trend Analysis

To detect trends in the interests of a specific community of readers, we compare the IDR values of journals over a given period of time. We have registered article downloads for two subsequent years, $x$ and $x+n$, i.e. 1998 and 2003. We define the Impact Discrepancy Trend Ratio (IDTR), denoted $P^t$ for a given journal $i$ and registration years $x$ and $x+n$, as:

$$P^t_{i,x,x+n} = \frac{P'_{i,x}}{P'_{i,x+n}} = \frac{P_{i,01} \times \mathrm{IF}_{i,98}}{P_{i,98} \times \mathrm{IF}_{i,01}}$$

When $P^t \ll 1$ or $P^t \gg 1$ we find journals whose local impact has deviated strongly from their ISI IF rating over a period of time. The set of high or low IDTR scoring journals therefore indicates trends within a local DL community which deviate from the general scientific community.

# 4  Results

We calculated the Pearson's correlation between the PageRank values for the set of 292 journals which occurred in both 1998 and 2001 log files. The correlation coefficient of 0.738 ($p < 0.005$) indicated a significant stability of community-specific journal impact over a period of three years. The Pearson's correlation between 1998 and 2001 ISI IF values for the same set of journals was found to be 0.877 ($p < 0.005$).

We examined the distribution of $P^t$, i.e. IDTR, values for those journals whose $P^t \ll 1$ or $P^t \gg 1$. Table 1 lists the 10 highest scoring IDTR journals. The majority of these journals correspond to climatology, indicating that during the period 1998 to 2001 the local LANL RL impact of these journals increased significantly while their ISI IF ratings have either declined or remained stable. LANL RL management confirms these results correlate with programmatic efforts in space and atmospheric science at LANL some of which have recently received international attention, most specifically the mapping of hydrogen distribution on Mars by Laboratory scientist Bill Feldman of the Space and Atmospheric Science (NIS-1) group.

**Table 1.** Ten highest rated IDTR journals

| $P^t$ | $P'_{i,98}$ | $P'_{i,01}$ | $IF_{i,98}$ | $IF_{i,01}$ | Journal Title |
|---|---|---|---|---|---|
| 2.854 | 5.764 | 16.457 | 0.597 | 0.640 | J ARID ENVIRON |
| 2.216 | 3.097 | 6.866 | 1.111 | 1.003 | J VOLC GEOT RES |
| 2.097 | 2.486 | 5.213 | 1.384 | 1.352 | ANN BOT-LONDON |
| 1.664 | 7.058 | 11.744 | 0.937 | 1.044 | J ATMOS SOL-TERR PHY |
| 1.478 | 4.84 | 7.157 | 1.410 | 1.697 | REMOTE SENS ENVIRON |
| 1.354 | 13.862 | 18.773 | 0.826 | 1.246 | PLANET SPACE SCI |
| 1.294 | 12.105 | 15.669 | 0.902 | 0.318 | J GEOCHEM EXPLOR |
| 1.279 | 4.304 | 5.504 | 3.133 | 3.643 | APPL CATAL B-ENV |
| 1.262 | 18.000 | 22.709 | 0.286 | 0.636 | NDT&E INT |
| 1.256 | 1.562 | 1.963 | 17.085 | 14.329 | TRENDS BIOC SCI |

Table 2 lists the 10 lowest scoring IDTR journals which constitutes a more heterogeneous list of journals relating to environmental safety and biology. With few exceptions the ISI IF values for 1998 and 2001 have not changed considerably, but local LANL PageRank values have shifted considerably in the period 1998 to 2001.

**Table 2.** Ten lowest rated IDTR journals.

| $P^t$ | $P'_{i,98}$ | $P'_{i,01}$ | $IF_{i,98}$ | $IF_{i,01}$ | Journal Title |
|---|---|---|---|---|---|
| 0.079 | 31.004 | 2.440 | 00.731 | 01.252 | ECOTOX ENVIRON SAFE |
| 0.077 | 7.834 | 0.605 | 01.363 | 01.741 | CANCER LETT |
| 0.074 | 27.742 | 2.050 | 00.333 | 00.514 | OPT LASER ENG |
| 0.066 | 10.604 | 0.706 | 00.978 | 01.493 | REGUL TOXICOL PHARM |
| 0.060 | 6.597 | 0.401 | 01.516 | 02.631 | PHYSIOL MOL PLANT P |
| 0.057 | 282.171 | 16.083 | 00.042 | 00.284 | J FRANKLIN I |
| 0.050 | 183.419 | 9.195 | 00.105 | 00.391 | COMPUT IND ENG |
| 0.042 | 28.989 | 1.227 | 00.831 | 00.859 | SUPERLATTICE MICROST |
| 0.040 | 37.580 | 1.516 | 00.272 | 00.695 | J ELECTROSTAT |
| 0.035 | 10.636 | 0.370 | 00.559 | 14.000 | PROG MATER SCI |

## 5   Conclusion

We generated networks of journal relationships from reader article download sequences found in LANL RL logs registered in 1998 and 2001. PageRank values were calculated to rank journals according to their position in these networks. These values were normalized by the ISI IF to distinguish a journal's local impact from general impact in the larger scientific community. We found local reader journal impact to be less stable over a period of three years than the ISI IF which was found to be highly stable. This effect can be explained by the fact that it represents journal impact among a more general population which is less prone to swift changes than specific reader communities linked to a DL.

We detected a specific research trend pointing to an increased interest in climatology and atmospheric science at LANL relating to recent programmatic efforts in space research, most specifically mapping of hydrogen distribution on Mars. The journals for which we observed a sharp decrease of local reader impact compared to the ISI IF did not reveal any specific research trends.

Future research will focus on establishing a more coherent framework for the evaluation of journal impact in the general scientific community. At present we are comparing a metric of reader journal impact, based on reader article downloads, with a metric of journal impact based on author-citations. This situation can be improved by collecting download logs from a wide range of institutions whose populations are representative of the general scientific community. Journal impact values calculated for each specific community can then be compared to those calculated from the aggregated log samples over all institutions.

**Acknowledgments.** The authors thank Herbert Van de Sompel for his contributions to many of the ideas presented in this paper.

# References

[1] Darmoni, S.J., Roussel, F., Benichou, J., Thirion, B., Pinhas., N.: Reading factor: a new bibliometric criterion for managing digital libraries. Journal of the Medical Library Association **90** (2002) 323–327
[2] Kaplan, N.R., Nelson, M.L.: Determining the publication impact of a digital library. Journal of the American Society of Information Science **51** (2000) 324–339
[3] Bollen, J., Luce, R.: Evaluation of digital library impact and user communities by analysis of usage patterns. D-Lib Magazine **8** (2002)
[4] Brin, S., Page, L.: The anatomy of a large-scale hypertextual web search engine. Computer Networks and ISDN Systems **30** (1998) 107–117
[5] Bonacich, P.: Power and centrality: A family of measures. American Journal of Sociology **92** (1987) 1170–1182

# Evaluating the Changes in Knowledge and Attitudes of Digital Library Users

Gemma Madle, Patty Kostkova, Jane Mani-Saada, and Julius R. Weinberg

Institute of Health Sciences, City University
London, UK
g.c.madle@city.ac.uk

**Abstract.** Medical digital libraries are essentially life-critical applications providing timely access for professionals and the public to current medical knowledge and practice. This paper presents a new methodology for evaluating the impact of the knowledge within a medical digital library on users by testing their knowledge improvements and attitude changes. Using pre and post-use questionnaires we tested the impact of a small medical information website acting as an interface to the National electronic Library for Communicable Disease. The changes in user attitudes and the correlation with knowledge improvements observed indicate the potential for this methodology to be applied as a general evaluation technique of digital libraries and the impact of online information on user learning.

## 1    Introduction

Recent years have seen an explosion in the amount of health information available to patients on the Internet, but is all this newly available information making any difference to patients' behaviour? Previous usability testing of Digital Libraries (DLs) and websites has focused almost exclusively on the graphical interface issues and organisation of information within the DL or website, rather than their role in changing work practices or behaviour.

As a result of this information explosion patients are becoming better informed about their healthcare decisions, armed with endless amounts of information which they may present to their clinician [1]. It is important that we can measure the effectiveness of medical DLs and health information websites in changing patient knowledge and attitudes so that the healthcare system can exploit these resources to its best advantage.

In this paper we present our research methodology for evaluating the impact of a health information website by linking the content of the site with pre-use and post-use questionnaires testing how much users' knowledge of certain topics has changed by getting information from a digital library and how much this correlates to the change of attitude to the same topic.

Section 2 explains the background behind the evaluation, the DL involved and the Antimicrobial Resistance Website, which was used as a test bed for the research. In section 3 we describe the content structure of the Antimicrobial Resistance site and

T. Koch and I.T. Sølvberg (Eds.): ECDL 2003, LNCS 2769, pp. 29–40, 2003.

section 4 discusses the development of the pre-use and post-use questionnaires used to evaluate knowledge and attitude changes. In section 5 we present the evaluation results and also the general usability of the site. Finally, in section 6 we discuss the current status of the project, future research possibilities and in section 8 state our conclusions.

## 2    Background to the Study

This section discusses the importance of measuring the impact and usability of DLs and health information websites, how the National electronic Library for Communicable Disease (NeLCD) was involved in this research and the reasons for using the Antimicrobial Resistance website as a test bed.

### 2.1    Usability Testing of DLs

It is becoming more and more essential to address user needs and to provide evidence that the knowledge contained within a DL has an impact on the attitudes and behaviour of the users obtaining it. Until now usability evaluations of DLs have looked mainly at the graphical interface, navigation and user acceptability [2,3] rather than whether the knowledge within the DL is actually 'passed on' to the user.

For medical DLs this is of crucial importance, as they are essentially life critical applications, enabling professionals to stay up to date with current practice and empowering patients to be able to take an active role in managing their health. Recent research has shown that senior clinicians can be reluctant to allow more junior staff access to current evidence-based information, preferring instead to provide it for them or withholding it altogether [4]. This provides further support for the importance of medical DLs that are accessible to all via the Internet and their potential role in changing the culture of the health working environment and the relationships within it.

There have been studies looking at user ability to search and find specific information on the Internet [5] but there has not been enough consideration of whether the users of DLs or health information websites have actually remembered this information, whether it has had any impact on their knowledge or attitudes. Two studies investigating the effect of a video on patient knowledge and attitudes reported increases in patient knowledge after watching the video. [6,7]. But this has yet to be applied to the web environment. Van House et al [8] agree that usability studies usually only evaluate the user interface which is not sufficient evaluation for something as complex as a digital library. They believe that the library must have an impact on the user's work.

In order to test the impact of information within DLs on users knowledge and attitudes we have developed an evaluation method based on pre and post-use questionnaires. By testing user knowledge of and attitudes towards a subject before they use a DL and then when they leave the DL it is possible to measure the immediate impact of the knowledge contained within the DL on the user.

## 2.2   Antimicrobial Resistance Website

The NeLCD team has developed an ideal test bed for this research. A website aimed at the general public about Antimicrobial Resistance funded by the Department of Health provides an interface for the public into a subsection of a medical DL. This is a small enough collection of information to be suitable for this preliminary research and is aimed at providing information to the public to help reduce unnecessary prescribing of antibiotics i.e. changing their attitudes and eventual behaviour.

The DL used in this research is the NeLCD http://www.nelcd.co.uk, one of the Specialist Libraries of the National electronic Library for Health (NeLH http://www.nelh.nhs.uk). It provides an on-line, evidence-based, quality-tagged Internet portal to the best available evidence on prevention, treatment and investigation of communicable disease. In addition to providing a single point to available electronic resources on communicable diseases, the key value of the library is in a quality appraisal of all posted documents. This procedure is conducted in collaboration with all major professional societies and expert committees in the area of communicable disease in the UK.

The three major goals of the NeLH are [9]:

- To provide health care professionals and the public with knowledge and know-how to support health care related decisions
- To provide easy access to best current knowledge and know-how on the Internet
- To improve health and health care, clinical practice and patient choice.

With this in mind, in particular the first and third goals, an important consideration for the NeLCD is whether the knowledge contained within it is making any difference to the clinical practice of health professionals. It is therefore ideal to use the Antimicrobial Resistance site as a test bed for future research into the impact of the NeLCD on its users and possibly DLs in general. Although, DL evaluation methods testing knowledge and attitude changes have to be designed to match the tested DL purpose and with its aim in mind, therefore, we believe that the evaluation research needs to be clearly linked to tested DL content, although there are methodological concerns which could be generalized to all types of DLs as we will show below.

# 3   Structure of the Antimicrobial Resistance Website

As discussed in section 2 the aim of the site is to contribute to reducing inappropriate prescribing of antibiotics. It will aim to do this by changing the knowledge and attitudes of the users. As the content of the website is clearly important for the later evaluation of knowledge and attitude changes we now discuss the structure of the site including the ontology and navigation aids.

## 3.1   Content Organisation and the Ontology

To identify the scope of content for the site a search of existing 'Ask the Doctor/Expert' archives on the internet was performed to identify the most commonly asked questions about antimicrobial resistance and related issues. In addition, existing health information sites were searched to find information available on the web. Relevant current news topics were also identified.

The different areas of content were grouped into categories using MeSH headings. These categories were then subdivided into more specific groups. In an evaluation of the NHS Direct Online website (http://www.nhsdirect.nhs.uk) Nicholas et al [10] identified four broad areas of content directly related to the main reasons that people visited the site:

- To find out more about an existing condition
- To find out what to do when they think they/or another are ill
- To help avoid illness in the first place
- To find out about NHS organisations and services

Applying these findings to the NeLCD website (as it is an NHS Direct Online 'theme month' the user group can be assumed to be very similar) and assuming that people would visit the site to either learn about antimicrobial resistance, or because they want to know how it relates to the infection that they have or to know how they can help prevent it, the original MeSH categories were organized into the following three areas:

- Learn about Antimicrobial Resistance – to include Bacteria, Viruses, Fungi, Protozoa, What Makes Us Ill, Antimicrobials, Antimicrobial Resistance, Our Immune System
- Antimicrobial Resistance and Common Illnesses – to include Colds & Flu, Sore Throat, Sinusitis, Earache, Cystitis, Traveller's Diarrhoea, Malaria, HIV, Hospital Acquired Infection, Acne and Child Health
- Preventing Antimicrobial Resistance – to include Vaccination, Bioterrorism, Antibacterials and Food & Farming

Each sub-category of the three areas would have a few frequently asked questions with answers that summarized and directed the reader to the relevant evidence. In addition, links to current news articles and related quality tagged resources would allow the reader to explore the topic in more depth. The Antimicrobial Resistance site was not intended to reproduce information already present on the web, rather to provide an interface for the public to information held in the NeLCD.

Three types of item are present in the antimicrobial resistance site; *frequently asked questions*, *news items* and *other resources*. This description of documents using Dublin Core [9] will allow two methods of searching the site. A standard *full-text search* for those not sure exactly what they want and a more precise *field* search for more specific searches.

## 3.2 Navigation

The next consideration was the layout of the web pages. Navigators are important for directing a user around a site so should have an impact on the changes in knowledge and attitude. If a user cannot find knowledge within a DL how will that knowledge have any impact?

For consistency with the NeLCD the NeLH template 'wrapper page' was used as a guide for the page layout (http://www.nelh.nhs.uk/heart/heart_default.asp) along with general web design guidelines [2,3].

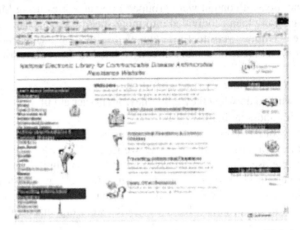

**Fig. 1.** Home Page of the NeLCD Antimicrobial Resistance Website

Figure 1 shows the home page of the antimicrobial resistance site. The navigation links to the frequently asked questions are situated on the left hand side of the page, structured as discussed previously in this paper. This menu is consistent throughout the site.

In the centre is the main content, this may be a frequently asked question, details of a recommended resource or news article, but in this case (the home page) a brief guide to the site, what is on offer and where to look for information. The electronic catalogue cards for the frequently asked questions, news articles and related resources are stored in the domino database and are dynamically generated as the item is requested by the user.

The right side of the page contains links to related news articles, resources and the 'tip of the month'. This content is dynamically generated from the Lotus Domino database each time the user requests a page and varies depending on the page selected by the user.

## 4    User Attitude Evaluation Method Based on Pre and Post Questionnaires

This section describes the methodology behind the development of the pre and post-use questionnaires to evaluate knowledge and attitude changes of the users with respect to the aim and content organisation as discussed in section 3.

The questionnaires both contain two identical questions (consisting of 7 true/false statements and 6 statements the user must rank their agreement with) and the post-questionnaire also a set of standard usability questions. The aims of the two identical sets of questions were:

- Test for changes in knowledge
- Test for changes in attitudes
- Evaluate the relationship between changes in knowledge and changes in attitude

## 4.1    Changes in Knowledge

The Oxford English Dictionary suggests that knowledge about something/or someone can be gained through information or facts.[11] To evaluate changes in knowledge about antibiotics and antibiotic resistance the user was asked to decide whether 7 statements about antibiotics were true or false. Some of the 'answers' or correct versions of the statements were more obvious in the site than others e.g. one ('People become resistant to antibiotics' True or False?) was the subject of the current tip of the month present on every page of the site.

## 4.2    Changes in Attitude

Attitude can be defined as "a psychological tendency that is expressed by evaluating a particular entity with some degree of favour or disfavour."[12] To evaluate changes in attitude the user was asked to rank their agreement with six statements on a Likert scale of 1 (strongly disagree) to 5 (strongly agree). Four of these statements were about the user's attitude to information on the site, e.g. 'Antibiotics help to reduce the duration of pain in AOM (Acute Otitis Media – a common childhood ear infection)'. The site states that 'Some children treated with antibiotics for AOM may be less likely to have pain 2-7 days after the first symptoms. But it is difficult to predict which child will benefit in this way - one study suggested that 17 must be treated for just one to benefit'. So antibiotics do reduce the duration of pain but only in one in x number of children. How the user evaluates that information will be seen in their attitude to the statement after using the site i.e. to what extent they agree or disagree with it.

The remaining two of these Likert scale statements were about the users attitudes to prescribing antibiotics for AOM, 'Doctors should prescribe antibiotics for AOM' and 'I would expect an antibiotic for me/my child if I/they had AOM'. Answers to these statements will indicate clearly the user's attitude with respect to the use of antibiotics in AOM in general and in their own situation. The level of agreement with the statements may differ between these two situations. What a user expects for themselves or their child may be very different to what they expect for the population in general.

## 4.3    Relationship between Knowledge Change and Attitude Change

It is all very well to improve people's knowledge but if this has no impact on their attitude and subsequent behaviour then in this case it would be a futile exercise. Therefore, the knowledge and attitude change evaluation, as discussed above, was designed in a complementary way to show the correlation between these variables. E.g., the knowledge questions on antibiotics were reflected in the attitude questions on AOM and a question on user learning self-assessment to indicate further correlations.

To evaluate our AR test bed these results are essential as the ultimate aim of the Antimicrobial Resistance website is to contribute to reducing inappropriate prescription of antibiotics. If people know that antibiotics are not effective treatment for certain infections as a result of using the site but would still expect one from their doctor for those infections, then the site has only half done its job.

# 5   Results

In this section we describe the user sample and discuss the changes in answers and scores observed between the pre and post-use questionnaires.

## 5.1  User Sample

The antimicrobial resistance site was tested in the Science Museum, London as part of their 'live science' program. Over a period of seven days during the two February half-term weeks 227 people took part in the study. Of these 177 completed both questionnaires. This provided a rich set of data to analyze. A paired t-test was performed to test the statistical significance of changes between pairs of questionnaires. Data available on the museum visitor population indicates that a random museum visitor is more likely to have attended university or a polytechnic, more likely to have regular internet access and less likely to be unemployed than a random member of the UK public.[13] Therefore, the sample of users in this study is not strictly representative of the whole UK population.

## 5.2  Changes in Knowledge

There was a significant change in the mean score for the true/false statements (1 for correct answer, 0 for incorrect or don't know) of users before (mean = 4.33) and after using the site (mean = 4.90 $p<0.001$). With respect to individual statements there were significant changes in the answers to four of the seven statements.

The largest change was from 9.6% of users getting the answer right to statement 1b ("People can become resistant to antibiotics") before using the site to 45.76% getting this answer correct after using the site ($p<0.001$). This reflects the visual impact of the answer to this question in the site – it was the focus of the tip of the month on the home page.

Another highly significant increase in percentage of users getting the correct answer after using the site was for statement 1c ("Antibiotics help cure most sore throats"). An increase from 57.06% to 75.14% of users answering correctly was observed ($p<0.001$). Again, the correct version of this statement was easily found in the first page about sore throats.

Smaller but still significant changes ($p<0.05$) were seen for statements 1a ("Antibiotics kill viruses") and 1e ("Antibiotic resistance can spread between bacteria"), +7.91% and +8.47% respectively. The correct versions of both of these statements were found deeper in the content of the site, within frequently asked questions, rather than as stand-alone statements.

For the remaining three true/false statements there was a slight drop in % of users getting the correct answer although none of these changes were significant. The correct versions of these statements were not so obviously explicit within the site, relying more on the user gaining an understanding of the concept of antimicrobial resistance. For each of these statements the % of users getting the correct answer before using the site was high compared to the other four statements, ranging from 73.45% to 92.09%.

## 5.3  Changes in Attitudes

With respect to changes in attitudes the most significant change (mean from 3.44 to 2.74, p<0.001) was for the statement about the duration of antibiotic course in the ear infection indicating that after using the site people were tending to neither disagree nor agree with the statement, rather than agree. The least significant change in mean score (3.12 to 2.88) was concerned with the benefit of antibiotics in reducing pain associated with this ear infection. As discussed in section 4.2, there may be benefit but it is difficult to predict so we would not expect the user to be swayed one way or the other (i.e. to agree or disagree with the statement) based on this information.

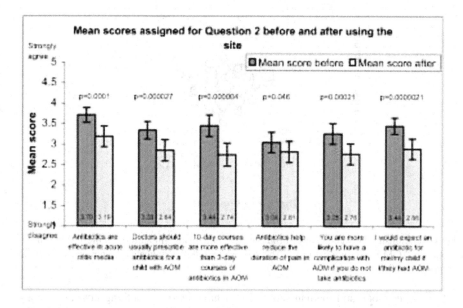

**Fig. 2.** Mean attitude scores for statements in Question Two before and after using the site. Error bars show the 95% confidence intervals for the mean.

For the two statements examining attitudes to prescribing there were significant decreases in the mean scores (i.e. levels of agreement) for both 'I would expect an antibiotic for me or my child if I/they had AOM' and 'Doctors should usually prescribe antibiotics for AOM' indicating that maybe this 'new' information the users had learned could have an impact on their potential behaviour.

## 5.4 Relationship between Changes in Knowledge and Changes in Attitudes

Comparing the actual changes in knowledge and attitude for individual users Figure 3 shows the relationship between users change in knowledge score and their change in attitude towards prescribing. 24.24% of users increased their knowledge score and decreased their attitude score (i.e. they were less likely to expect antibiotics for AOM). 10.10% of users did not change their knowledge score but decreased their attitude score. Changes in knowledge do not always equal changes in attitude, particularly when knowledge is applied to a personal situation such as the prescribing of antibiotics for AOM, so using these figures we can suggest that 34.34% of users increased their knowledge about antibiotics and resistance and allowed that knowledge to change their attitude to the prescribing of antibiotics in AOM.

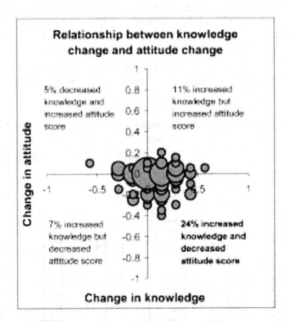

**Fig. 3.** Relationship between change in knowledge and change in attitude to prescribing of antibiotics in AOM for individual users. The size of the bubbles indicates the number of users at that point.

The mean, mode and median scores for 'I have learnt something new after using this site' were all 4 indicating that users did generally feel they had learnt from the site. This is supported by the fact that for 45.19% of users increases in knowledge scores matched the perception that they had learned from the site. In contrast 17.31% of users thought they had learned but actually decreased their knowledge score.

## 5.5  General Usability Issues

The general usability of the site was perceived by users to be good with between 70.59% and 84.97% of users agreeing or strongly agreeing with the seven usability statements.  Usability scores did not vary significantly with age, gender or self-reported confidence in using the web.  The mean usability score overall was 26.89 out of a maximum of 35 (76.83%).  Informal observation of users during the study identified a preference towards using the navigation menu on the left side of each page of the site rather than the search facility.

## 6    Related Work

As has been discussed previous evaluations of DLs and websites have focused more on the technical usability of the resources rather than their impact on learning and attitude changes.  In particular we focus this review on medical DLs as our primary concern, however, related projects to DL evaluations are also discussed.  There have been evaluations of the usability of digital libraries and health information websites.  Nicholas et al [10] evaluated the NHS Direct Online site using questionnaires.  The aim was to obtain feedback from users about the site so that future development could be based around their needs.  The study sought to identify whether users liked the site, found it useful, what they disliked, whether they easily found information or not i.e. general self-reported usability and popularity issues.

Lancaster [14] undertook an evaluation of the use of the NeLH in five public libraries in the UK with user questionnaires and focus groups with library staff.  The study found that the NeLH needs clearer navigation and more a sophisticated search facility if it is to be effectively used by public users.  The aim of the NeLH is stated on their site as:

- Our aim is to provide clinicians with access to the best current know-how and knowledge to support health care related decisions. Patients, carers and the public are welcome to use this pilot, but http://www.nhsdirect.nhs.uk/ NHS Direct Online (http://www.nhsdirect.nhs.uk) provides the best public gateway health information. [15]

While this aim states the focus of the NeLH on health care professionals rather than the public the report suggests that the NeLH is a potential source of more detailed information for the public than NHS Direct Online offers.  However, the major barrier to effective use of the NeLH in the public libraries was the ability to find information at the right level.  Lancaster suggests that there is some way to go before the knowledge gap between NHS Direct Online and the NeLH is bridged.

With respect to user behaviour, Sfakakis and Kapidakis [16] examined log files of the Hellenic National Documentation Centre Digital Library and found that users tended to use simple query structures for their searching and with experience reduced the number of operations they performed in a session.  Eysenbach and Kohler [5] found that when searching for health information consumers were successful in trying various search terms, exploring the first few hits and subsequently refining their search strategies. They also observed that users did not often remember which websites they retrieved information from or who was behind the sites. Through interviews Van House [8] et al investigated the impact of Cypress, a digital image library on the work of its users. Following user feedback and observation of user difficulties suggestions were made for redesign of Cypress.

# 7    Project Status

## 7.1  Implementation

The NeLCD antimicrobial resistance site was created using the Lotus Domino R5 platform. There are a selection of static html pages e.g. pages about the site, submenu pages. These static pages contain computed text that indicates latest news items or resources related to the current page. These news items and resources, along with the collection of frequently asked questions, are stored as documents in the Domino database. They are retrieved by the system on the fly, as and when requested by the user. Currently only full-text search is available but Dublin Core field search will be available in the near future, and it will also be possible to cross-search across the main NeLCD site.

## 7.2  Future Research

It is planned that an online evaluation of the site, similar to this evaluation with pre-use and post-use questionnaires to assess changes in knowledge and attitudes, will take place in the future. This will be supported by transaction logs to provide further information about user behaviour. In addition, more detailed mapping of the changes in answers to the site content would be useful for constructing site content e.g. how does the location or style of the answer to a question within the site affect the impact on the users' knowledge? It would be interesting to apply the methodology of this study to a larger study of the NeLCD. Knowledge and attitudes and their relationship with behaviour are difficult concepts and outcomes to measure. We recognize the limitations of this study in only testing the short-term impact of the information on the user but would argue that in this context short-term impact is important in influencing subsequent behaviour of users. However it would be valuable to investigate the long-term impact on user knowledge/attitudes perhaps by a follow-up questionnaire, say three months after completion of the pre-use and post-use questionnaires.

# 8    Conclusion

This paper shows that electronic health information resources have the potential to influence users but indicates that further research is needed to determine the most effective strategies for making information available within these resources in order to have the greatest impact

We have presented a new methodology for evaluating the users knowledge and attitude change after using DLs and informational websites that is linked strongly to the content of these resources. We have tested this methodology on a small health information website and shown that it is possible to measure the impact of the knowledge contained within the site on the users knowledge and attitudes. The results show an increase in knowledge that is linked to a decrease in attitude ranking which shows that users have changed their attitude in a right way. This has implications for future evaluations of the impact of the knowledge contained within DLs on their users.

**Acknowledgements.** We would like to thank Sabiha Foster and the 'live science' team at the Science Museum for their help with the data collection.

# References

1.  Health on the Net Foundation    "Evolution of Internet Use for health purposes", http://www.hon.ch/Survey/FebMar2001/survey.html, March 2002
2.  Nielsen J., "Designing web usability: the practice of simplicity", Indianapolis, Ind., New Riders, 1999
3.  Preece J., Rogers Y., Sharp H., "Interaction Design", John Wiley & Sons Ltd, January 2002
4.  Adams A., Blandford A., "Acceptability of Medical Digital Libraries", Health Informatics Journal, v8:no.2 (2002), pp58–66
5.  Eysenbach G., Kohler C., "How do consumers search for and appraise health information on the world wide web? Qualitative study using focus groups, usability tests and in-depth interviews, British Medical Journal v324:no.7337 (2002) pp.573–577
6.  Bauchner H., Osganian S., Smith K., Triant R., "Improving Parent Knowledge about Antibiotics: A Video Intervention", Pediatrics, v108:no.4 (2001), pp.845–850
7.  Greenberg R.S., Billet C., Zahurak M., Yaster M., "Videotape increase parental knowledge about pediatric pain management", Anesthesia & Analgesia, v89:no.4 (1999) pp.899–903
8.  Van House N.A., Butler M.H., Ogle V., Schiff L., "User centered iterative design for digital libraries: the Cypress experience", D-Lib Magazine, February 1996
9.  Weinberg J.R., Mani-Saada J., Smith K.. "The National electronic Library for Communicable Disease (NeLCD)", Poster. FIS Conference, UK, (2000)
10. Nicholas D., Huntington P., Williams P., Jordan M., "NHS Direct Online: its users and their concerns", Journal of Information Science, v28:no.4 (2002), pp305–319
11. "knowledge, n.[2]" *Oxford English Dictionary.* Ed. J. A. Simpson and E. S. C. Weiner. 2nd ed. Oxford: Clarendon Press, 1989. *OED Online.* Oxford University Press. 4 Apr. 2000. http://dictionary.oed.com/cgi/entry/00127606
12. Eagly A.H., Chaiken S., "The Psychology of Attitudes" Fort Worth, Harcourt Brace 1993
13. Burch A., "Science Museum Audience Profile: A report on the first year's data", Visitor Research Group, Science Museum London, March 2002
14. Lancaster K., "Patient Empowerment", Library & Information Update, v2:no.3 (2003), pp36-37
15. "Using NeLH" (http://www.nelh.nhs.uk/new_users.asp)
16. Sfakakis M., Kapidakis S., "User Behavior Tendencies on Data Collections in a Digital Library", ECDL 2002, LCNS 2458, pp550–559

# Towards a Role-Based Metadata Scheme for Educational Digital Libraries : A Case Study in Singapore

Dian Melati Md Ismail[1], Ming Yin[2], Yin-Leng Theng[3], Dion Hoe-Lian Goh[3], and Ee-Peng Lim[2]

[1] School of Information Technology
Temasek Polytechnic (Singapore)
0002803E@student.tp.edu.sg

[2] Center for Advanced Information Systems, School of Computer Engineering
Nanyang Technological University
Singapore 639798
{asmyin,aseplim}@ntu.edu.sg

[3] Division of Information Studies, School of Communication & Information
Nanyang Technological University
Singapore 637718
{tyltheng, ashlgoh}@ntu.edu.sg

**Abstract.** In this paper, we describe the development of an appropriate metadata scheme for GeogDL, a Web-based digital library application containing past-year examination resources for students taking a Singapore national examination in geography. The new metadata scheme was developed from established metadata schemes on education and e-learning. Initial evaluation showed that a role-based approach would be more viable, adapting to the different roles of teachers/educators and librarians contributing geography resources to GeogDL. The paper concludes with concrete implementation of the role-based metadata schema for GeogDL.

## 1   Introduction

GeogDL [12] is a Web-based digital library (DL) application containing past-year examination questions and solutions to help students prepare and revise for a Singapore national examination in geography. The geography resources in GeogDL are divided into three categories: questions; solutions and supplementary resources. In the initial version of GeogDL, these resources were described using the fifteen elements stipulated in the Dublin Core (DC) metadata element set [2] plus some user-defined ones. We made use of DC because it is more widely accepted in libraries for cataloguing online content due to its "easily understood descriptive names and single-word labels" which some librarians and para-professionals might somewhat relate to as a "simpler version of the US MARC (MAchine Readable Cataloguing) tags" [7]. However, we found that our metadata element set based on DC, extended for education with four additional elements on pedagogy, audience, duration and

T. Koch and I.T. Sølvberg (Eds.): ECDL 2003, LNCS 2769, pp. 41–51, 2003.

standards, still too restrictive to describe adequately the examination resources in GeogDL.

This paper describes our investigation to develop an appropriate metadata scheme to describe the geography examination resources in GeogDL, adhering both to international and Singapore standards on education and e-learning. Based on an initial evaluation of the metadata scheme, we proposed a refinement to the metadata scheme that adapts to the different roles of potential contributors of geography resources. The paper concludes with concrete implementation of the role-based metadata schema for GeogDL.

## 2   Metadata Schemes on Education

### 2.1   Some Metadata Schemes for Educational Resources

Although DC has been identified as the emerging resource description standard for the Internet, its simplicity is also its bane in failing to describe the more sophisticated educational resources. Attempts are made to develop a comprehensive scheme to describe adequately educational resources, among the well-known ones are : (1) Gateway to Educational Materials (GEM) [6]; (2) Instructional Management System (IMS) [14]; and (3) Shareable Content Object Reference Model (SCORM) [11].

GEM, initiated by the US National Library of Education in 1996, is a union catalogue of lesson plans and other curriculum units on the Internet, extending the DC set to a semantically rich domain-specific content representation with an additional eight elements added [6]. GEM seems more suited for teachers than students.

IMS, on the other hand, is developed to promote open specifications for facilitating online distributed learning activities such as locating and using educational content, tracking learner progress, reporting learner performance, and exchanging student records between administrative systems. The IMS Metadata specification, slightly more technical in nature than GEM, proves to be far more methodical in describing the materials to be classified [14].

SCORM is a set of specifications for developing, packaging and delivering high-quality education and training materials whenever and wherever they are needed [11]. It is a product of the U.S. Government's initiative in Advanced Distributed Learning (ADL).

### 2.2   SingCORE : Singapore-Defined Standard for Learning Systems

It is apparent from our investigation that metadata schemes need to be tailored to meet the requirements of the *specific educational systems and the countries in which the resources would mainly be used*. To support interoperability across all sectors of education and training in Australia, the EdNA Metadata Standard in Australia [3], for example, ensures that elements and element qualifiers are devised to meet the Australian education requirements.

Hence, for GeogDL to be used by schools in Singapore, its metadata scheme needs to subscribe not only to international standards but also to SingCORE [9], a Singapore-defined standard for metadata developed as part of the Singapore e-Learning Framework (SeLF).

The SingCORE framework provides a comprehensive approach to describe courseware for interoperability in different learning environments. SingCORE has eight categories proposed in IMS Learning Resource Metadata Specifications Version 1.2.2, adopting the IEEE Learning Object MetaData's conceptual model : (1) General; (2) Life Cycle; (3) Meta-Metadata; (4) Technical; (5) Educational; (6) Rights; (7) Relation; and (8) Classification. To distinguish this customized set of forty-three elements, the schema is named SingCORE – "Sing" as in "Singapore" and "CORE" to denote the most important parts.

Table 1 shows the elements identified for the eight categories and the associated elements in the SingCORE metadata set [9].

**Table 1.** SingCORE Metadata Schema

| Categories as proposed in IMS | Elements (Sub-Elements) |
|---|---|
| 1. General | Identifier, Title, Catalog Entry (Catalog, Entry), Language, Description, Keyword, Coverage, Structure, Aggregation Level |
| 2. Life Cycle | Version, Status, Contribute (Role, Entity, Date) |
| 3. Meta-Metadata | Contributor (Role, Entity, Date), Metadata Scheme |
| 4. Technical | Format, Size, Location, Requirement (Type, Name, MinVersion, MaxVersion), Installation Remarks, Other Platform Requirements, Duration |
| 5. Educational | Interactivity Type, Learning Resource Type, Interactivity Level, Semantic Density, Intended User Role, Context, Typical Age Range, Difficulty, Typical Learning Time, Description, Language |
| 6. Rights | Cost, Copyright and Other Restrictions, Description and Usage Rights, Unit Pricing |
| 7. Relation | Kind, Resource (Identifier, Description, Catalog Entry (Catalog, Entry)) |
| 8. Classification | Purpose, Taxonpath (Source, Taxon – Course (ID, Entry), Taxon – Module (ID, Entry), Taxon – Topic (ID, Entry), Taxon – Chapter/Lesson (ID, Entry)), Description, Keyword |

## 3   Development of an Appropriate Metadata Scheme for GeogDL

Ellington et. al. [4] propose four basic factors to match the natural learning processes of humans, and thus ensure the successful learning experiences of learners by: (F1) making learners *want to learn*; (F2) incorporating sufficient activities to help learners experience *learning by doing*; (F3) providing sufficient channels of *feedback* to learners; and (F4) enabling learners to *digest and relate* what they have learned to the real world.

To situate GeogDL within the context of use, an earlier study [12] was carried out on GeogDL involving designers, secondary school students and usability-trained evaluators to identify possible goals or scenarios of use prospective users might have when using GeogDL. Scenarios are beneficial in helping designers to think about possible uses of systems [1]. Four possible goals or scenarios of use with the inclusion of basic factors proposed by Ellington et. al. [4] were identified to engage learners in a successful learning experience when using GeogDL :

- *Goal #1: Practice/revision* on multiple-choice (MCQs), short structured and essay-type questions. Model answers and hints to tackle these questions should also be provided (applying F2). Feedback should be provided (applying F3).
- *Goal #2: Trend analysis.* The idea is to give information on when and what questions are being asked over the years. This would help students identify trends in the types of questions asked and the topics covered. This may increase their motivation to want to learn (applying F1).
- *Goal #3: Mock exam.* This would help students better manage their time in answering questions. To make it fun, a scoring system could be incorporated for MCQs (applying F4), while hints/model answers could be provided for structured and essay questions (applying F3).
- *Goal #4: Related links and resources.* This could include related topics, teachers' recommendations, etc., thus showing relationships of concepts, and linking concepts to the real world (applying F4).

Since the SingCORE key vocabularies, defined for the education environment in Singapore, have incorporated the IMS standards and the IEEE Learning Object Metadata's conceptual model, we decided to use SingCORE as a base to derive an appropriate metadata schema for GeogDL. To determine if the SingCORE schema is able to describe adequately geography resources in GeogDL, we interrogated the SingCORE metadata set using the above four goals.

In a detailed walkthrough of the SingCORE metadata set, we found it comprehensive but not adequate enough to support the types of resources for the four scenarios of use :

- To address Goals #1 and #2, we need metadata elements to describe the type of exam questions and record details on when the papers were examined. SingCORE metadata set does not provide for information on examination questions and resources. Hence, we suggest a pointer to an external metadata schema for examination resources under "Learning Resource Type" in the "Educational" Category in SingCORE (see Figure 1). The metadata schema for examination resources is described with new elements "Paper", "Question" and "Type" as shown in Figure 2.

  To support feedback and comments from users, enabling true essence of learning, an additional ninth category named "Annotation" would be necessary. The category would consist of a pointer to an external Annotation Metadata Schema. Annotations could take the form of free-text contribution as in forums/chats or feedback in Likert-scale ratings.

  The metadata schema for "Annotation" also addresses multiple versions, where versioning history of an annotation is kept (see Figure 3). We suggest including a "Version History Location" pointer to two more elements

"Version ID" and "Parent ID" under the "Life Cycle" category (see Figure 4), since the SingCORE metadata set does not capture versioning of resources.

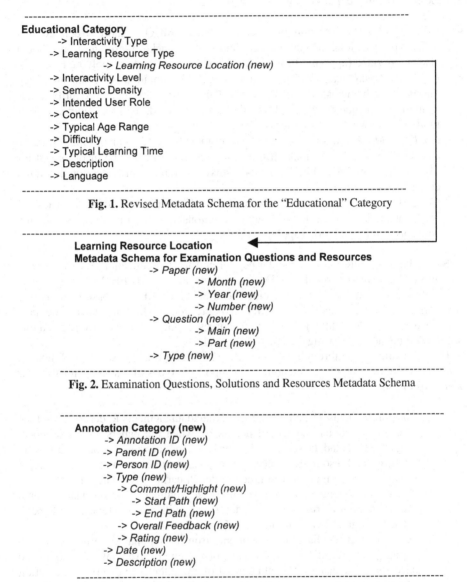

---

**Educational Category**
    -> Interactivity Type
   -> Learning Resource Type
           -> *Learning Resource Location (new)*
   -> Interactivity Level
   -> Semantic Density
   -> Intended User Role
   -> Context
   -> Typical Age Range
   -> Difficulty
   -> Typical Learning Time
   -> Description
   -> Language

---

**Fig. 1.** Revised Metadata Schema for the "Educational" Category

---

**Learning Resource Location**
**Metadata Schema for Examination Questions and Resources**
       -> *Paper (new)*
           -> *Month (new)*
           -> *Year (new)*
           -> *Number (new)*
       -> *Question (new)*
           -> *Main (new)*
           -> *Part (new)*
       -> *Type (new)*

---

**Fig. 2.** Examination Questions, Solutions and Resources Metadata Schema

---

**Annotation Category (new)**
    -> *Annotation ID (new)*
    -> *Parent ID (new)*
    -> *Person ID (new)*
    -> *Type (new)*
       -> *Comment/Highlight (new)*
          -> *Start Path (new)*
          -> *End Path (new)*
       -> *Overall Feedback (new)*
       -> *Rating (new)*
    -> *Date (new)*
    -> *Description (new)*

---

**Fig. 3.** Annotation Metadata Schema

```
-------------------------------------------------------------------------
Lifecycle Category
     -> Version History Location
     -> Version
     -> Status
     -> Contribute
         -> Role
         -> Entity
         -> Date
-------------------------------------------------------------------------
```

**Fig. 4.** Revised Metadata Schema for the "Lifecycle" Category

- To address Goal #4, we need metadata elements to describe the relationships of elements. This is addressed in SingCORE under the "Relation" category.
- Finally, we think that students' performance (Goal #3) should not be captured in the metadata set to describe resources. Instead a separate metadata schema could be used to describe users' behaviors and performance, which will not be addressed in this paper.

# 4   Initial Study and Analysis of the New Metadata Schema

Having developed the metadata scheme for GeogDL, adapted from SingCORE to support the four goals, we then conducted an initial evaluation.

## 4.1   Profiles of Subjects

Two third-year students and three lecturers from the Information Studies Programme at Temasek Polytechnic (Singapore) took part in the initial evaluation. They were familiar with general metadata standards, and would be helpful in providing feedback on the new metadata scheme developed for GeogDL. Because SingCORE is a relatively new standard approved for e-learning in Singapore, these five subjects were also not familiar with the SingCORE metadata set.

## 4.2   Protocol

A paper-based version of the SingCORE interface with the additional elements proposed for GeogDL was drawn and presented to the subjects. They were also given a sample geography examination question to be described using the metadata scheme. For each element in the metadata scheme, the subjects were asked to comment on its comprehensiveness and usefulness using a 5-point Likert-type scale. They were also asked if they needed additional help in coding the particular examination question using the metadata scheme.

## 4.3   Recommendations Towards a Role-Based Metadata Scheme

One problem highlighted was that some of the terms (jargon) used to describe elements were too difficult to understand, even to the subjects who were library-science-trained. We asked the subjects to identify those terms and changes were made to speak the users' language, for example, the element "aggregation level" was changed to "size of resource".

The subjects also commented that because they were too familiar with the DC and MARC schemes, they would prefer cataloging according to material types instead of the step-by-step entry process based on the eight categories, as proposed by SingCORE. To address this problem, GeogDL will be designed to allow input of the metadata according to the type of resources as requested by different users, determined largely by their roles.

Feedback received also showed that although the GeogDL metadata scheme contained too many elements, they thought the elements were relevant. It was, however, felt that contributors such as teachers/educators or librarians might be interested only in certain elements. Hence the metadata scheme was revised to adapt to the different roles of teachers/educators and librarians contributing geography resources to GeogDL, allowing them to see only those elements relevant to them.

Table 2 shows the revised metadata set based on roles of contributors with Column 1 stating the nine categories, and Column 2 indicating the number of elements (within brackets) in the SingCORE (S) and GeogDL (G) metadata sets. Column 3 highlights new elements added to the GeogDL metadata set to produce a more comprehensive nine categories and fifty-one elements for GeogDL. It also identifies the categories within the GeogDL metadata set relevant to the roles of contributors either as a teacher/educator or a librarian or a student, indicated under "Life Cycle" and "Meta-Metadata" categories with elements capturing role, entity and date (see Column 3, Rows 2 &3).

**Table 2.** Revised Role-Based GeogDL Metadata Set

| Category | # of Elements SingCORE (S) GeogDL (G) | Additional Elements |
| --- | --- | --- |
| 1. General | S(9); G(9) | |
| 2. Life Cycle | S(3); G(5) | Version and Parent IDs to capture versioning. Element "Contribute" describes role, entity and date. |
| 3. Meta-Metadata | S(2); G(2) | Element "Contributor/Validator" describes role, entity and date. |
| 4. Technical | S(7); G(7) | |
| 5. Educational | S(11); G(11) | More detailed info on types of resources : exam questions, solutions, resources. |
| 6. Rights | S(5); G(5) | |
| 7. Relation | S(2); G(2) | |
| 8. Classification | S(4); G(4) | |
| 9. Annotation | S(0); G(6) | Annotation, parent, person IDs, types of annotations, date, description. |

For example, the GeogDL metadata interface will be designed to trigger off customizations based on roles, for example, a bibliographic display for librarians to include only categories #1-4 and # 6-7 (see Table 2, Column 1). On the other hand, teachers/educators would be interested and able to contribute to categories #1-3, 5, 8 and 9, and hence GeogDL metadata interface will permit access only to these categories. If the categories for a resource are not complete, GeogDL will notify the respective person(s) to do so.

## 4.4     Concrete Proposal for Implementation of the Role-Based GeogDL Metadata Schema

The role-based schema of GeogDL allows contributors such as teachers/educators, librarians and students to contribute to different categories and elements of the metadata. To implement the role-based schema, an XML (Extensible Markup Language) role file is designed to contain all the roles-related information. The information will indicate the types of users, the associated tasks performed and the aspects of metadata that require their inputs.

Figure 5 shows the architecture of a role-based metadata tool in GeogDL comprising four components : (1) input/editing interface; (2) metadata tool generator; (3) GeogDL metadata schema and (4) metadata role file. For example, if a geography resource is to be input into GeogDL, based on the contributor's role, the metadata tool generator will then dynamically generate the appropriate metadata editing interface using information from the GeogDL metadata schema (#3) and the metadata role file (#4).

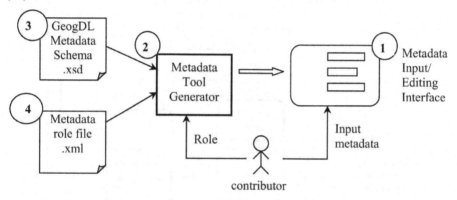

**Fig. 5.** Architecture of a Role-Based Metadata Tool in GeogDL

Figure 6 shows the role-based metadata tool in relation to the entire GeogDL architecture. Details of other components can be found in [13]. For the purpose of this paper, we will only be discussing the components relevant to metadata creation and maintenance whereby three new components are being implemented on the GeogDL interface namely : (i) Resource Input; (ii) Resource Import; and (iii) Resource Export.

For resource input, a role-editing tool allows authorized users of GeogDL to enter role-based information through a user interface with the role file automatically generated, so that the tool provides support for metadata entry and validation based on the roles of users.

GeogDL also supports import of other metadata formats to GeogDL-compliant metadata format. For example, an IMS-compliant metadata can be incorporated into GeogDL-compliant metadata via a metadata convertor tool, based on information of the IMS and GeogDL metadata schemas stored in the convertor.

Similarly, the tool also allows for conversion and export of GeogDL metadata to other established metadata formats. Presently, we are working on the conversion of two standards, IMS- and SingCORE-compliant metadata to/from GeogDL-compliant metadata. With this architecture, it would not be difficult to include conversions of other standards if necessary.

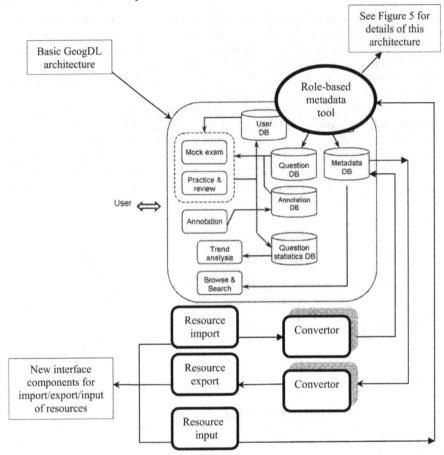

**Fig. 6.** Architecture of a Role-Based Metadata Tool in GeogDL

## 5  Related Work

Our work on deriving an appropriate metadata schema for GeogDL shares similar goals with existing DL projects employing different approaches and in different domains.

While our work has similarities with these projects, a major difference is that these DLs do not provide all the necessary features offered by GeogDL to help students to revise and prepare for a national examination in Singapore. Hence, capturing details on examination questions, sources and related resources are important. Equally important are annotations on them.

For example, the Digital Library for Earth System Education (DLESE) [10] contains elements through sharing of geography resources for various educational levels in earth system science education. A novel feature of the DL is that its contents rely entirely on users' contribution of resources, which may include maps, simulations, lesson plans, data sets, etc. Other users may then incorporate these resources into their lesson plans. Because of the complexity of geospatial educational resources, NEEDS–DLESE has adopted several metadata schemes such as DC and IMS to create a new metadata framework [8]. In contrast, GeogDL resources are mainly designed by teachers/educators for students.

A scheme closer in nature to GeogDL is the Federal Geographic Data Committee (FGDC) standard used to provide a common set of terminology and definitions for the documentation of digital geospatial data. It is, however, a rather complex standard with 119 compound elements or groups of elements hierarchically arranged to describe relationships among other elements [5].

GeogDL has special requirements which are not met by established standards such as IMS and Singapore-defined standards such as SingCORE. GeogDL derives an appropriate metadata schema based on its objectives and initial study that contributors of metadata have different roles and are capable of providing information to certain sets of elements in the metadata.

The role-based metadata tool generator allows authorised users such as teachers/educators and librarians to add and modify resources in the DL. Since each resource is associated with appropriate metadata, the tool also provides support for metadata entry and validation (see Figure 5).

## 6 Conclusion and On-Going Work

Designing any system always faces tradeoffs. One could go for simple design but not comprehensive enough to meet all requirements. In contrast, one could go for detailed and exhaustive design, but may lack practical usage. GeogDL aims to address these two areas through providing a role-based metadata schema to deal with the extensive set of elements by assigning different people to contribute to only certain elements, thus reducing the entry set of elements for each user.

Realising that there are also other resources that may not be GeogDL-compliant, a convertor is being developed to allow for conversion of GeogDL resources to IMS and SingCORE standards and vice versa, as described in Section 4.4 (see Figure 6).

More work needs to be done to further refine, test and use the metadata scheme involving different groups of authors, teachers/educators and librarians.

On-going work involves evaluating the new interface components in GeogDL to support multi-role inputs of the metadata of geography resources, as well as import/export of metadata from/to established formats to allow for wider use of resources. We believe our work have important implications on research involving DLs in education and learning systems.

**Acknowledgements.** We want to thank the teachers and students at Temasek Polytechnic (Singapore) for their invaluable feedback to the development of the metadata scheme for GeogDL. The project is partially supported by the SingAREN 21 research grant M48020004.

# References

1.  Carroll, J.: Making use: Scenario-based Design of Human-Computer Interactions. The MIT Press. (2000).
2.  Dublin Core Metadata Initiative (DCMI). http://www.dublincore.org (accessed 18 Feb 2003).
3.  Education Network Australia. http://www.ischool.washington.edu/sasutton/EdNA.html (accessed 18 Feb 2003).
4.  Ellington, H., Percival, F. and Race, P.: Handbook of Educational Technology. Kogan Page. (1995).
5.  Federal Geogrpahic Data Committee. http://www.fgdc.gov (accessed 18 Feb 2003).
6.  GEM - The Gateway to Educational Materials. http://www.geminfo.org (accessed 18 Feb 2003).
7.  Greenberg, J. (Ed.). : Metadata and organizing educational resources on the Internet. NY: The Haworth Information Press, c2000.
8.  Needs-Engineering. http://www.needs.org (accessed 18 Feb 2003).
9.  SingCORE. http://www.ecc.org.sg, (accessed 18 Feb 2003).
10. Sumner, T. and Dawe, M.: Looking at digital library usability from a reuse perspective. In Fox, E. and Borgman, C. (Eds.), Proceedings of the First ACM+IEEE Joint Conference on Digital Libraries, pp. 416–425. (2001), ACM Press.
11. SCORM. http://www.adlnet.org (accessed 18 Feb 2003).
12. Theng, Y.L. Goh, H.L., Lim, E.P., Liu, Z., Pang, L.S., Wong, B.B. and Chua, L.H.: Intergenerational Partnerships in the Design of a Digital Library of Geography Examination Resources. In Lim, E.P., Foo, S., Khoo, C., Chen, H., Fox, E., Urs, S. and Constantino, T. (Eds.), Proceedings of the 5th International Conference on Asian Digital Libraries, ICADL2002, 2555, pp. 427–439, (2002), Springer-Verlag.
13. Chua, L.H., Goh, D., Lim, E.P., Liu, Z., Ang, R.: A Digital Library For Geography Examination Resources. In Marchionini, G. & Hersh, W. (Eds.), Proceedings of the Second ACM+IEEE Joint Conference on Digital Libraries, pp. 115–116, (2002).
14. Welcome to IMS Global Learning Consortium, Inc. http://www.imsproject.org/index.html (accessed 18 Feb 2003).

# Incorporating Educational Vocabulary in Learning Object Metadata Schemas

Jian Qin[1] and Carol Jean Godby[2]

[1] School of Information Studies, Syracuse University,
Syracuse, NY 13244, USA `jqin@syr.edu`
[2] OCLC Online Computer Library Center, 6565 Frantz Road,
Dublin, OH 43017-3395, USA `godby@oclc.org`

**Abstract.** Educational metadata schemas are obligated to provide learning-related attributes in learning objects. The examination of current educational metadata standards found that few of them have places for incorporating educational vocabulary. Even within the educational category of metadata standards there is a lack of learning-related vocabulary for characterizing attributes that can help users identify the type of learning, objective, or context. The paper also discussed the problems with examples from a learning object taxonomy compiled by the authors.

## 1 Introduction

Metadata schemas are at the forefront of vocabulary control. Elements, identifiers, attributes, entities, and values used in metadata standards must employ vocabulary control of some sort in order to achieve interoperability. Yet the vocabulary issue in has deeper impact than metadata interoperability. Educational metadata schemas need to support the representation of learning objects with vocabularies that will help users judge the usefulness and relevance to their learning and instructional needs. While there are different views on learning activities and models ([4] and [12]), the metadata community realized that the schemas should reflect the educational characteristics in digital learning objects [2, 7]. But what educational characteristics should be represented and what vocabulary one should use for such representation have not been discussed in depth. As metadata schemas evolve, the vocabulary will affect not only the metadata but the learning object content structuring and encoding as well. Learning objects as the infrastructural content for educational digital libraries well justifies the significance of the vocabulary issue in learning object metadata. This paper reports preliminary findings from a study on the vocabulary used in educational metadata schemas. Our goal is to make the point that current educational metadata standards lack learning-related vocabulary, which will negatively impact the discovery and reuse of learning objects.

T. Koch and I.T. Sølvberg (Eds.): ECDL 2003, LNCS 2769, pp. 52–57, 2003.

## 2 Data

To gain insights into the use of educational vocabulary in metadata schemas, we collected data on the frequency of occurrences for all components in four metadata schemas and analyzed their frequency distributions based on vocabulary type and metadata category. The schemas under analysis included the Gateway for Educational Materials (GEM) [8], IEEE Learning Object Metadata (LOM) [12] / IMS Learning Resource Metadata Specification (IMS) [9], Educational Modeling Language (EML) [10], and Training Exchange Definition (TED) [3]. Each of the elements, attributes, entities, qualifiers, and values in these schemas was recorded as specified in a minimal instantiation of the schema, and then assigned a vocabulary type and metadata category. It should be pointed out that EML and TED were designed as XML Document Type Definitions (DTDs) and hence resulted in no occurrences in certain vocabulary types.. Vocabularies used in the Value type include those listed only in the metadata standard. External controlled vocabularies such as the one used by GEM were excluded. The general frequency distribution for each vocabulary type and schema is shown in Table 1. It should be apparent that how a schema is constructed influences the number of occurrences for a schema component. As mentioned earlier, TED is developed as an XML DTD and thus the vocabulary type "Qualifier" does not apply to it. Since all LOM/IMS components are designed as elements with predefined values for some of them, there are no attributes or other occurrences in LOM/IMS.

**Table 1.** Frequency distribution of schema components by vocabulary type

| Metadata schema | Number of occurrences by vocabulary type | | | | | |
|---|---|---|---|---|---|---|
| | Attribute | Element | Entity | Qualifier | Value | Total |
| EML | 12 | 7 | 12 | | | 31 |
| GEM | | 21 | | 64 | | 85 |
| LOM/IMS | | 90 | | | 76 | 166 |
| TED | 4 | 89 | | | | 93 |
| Total | 16 | 207 | 12 | 64 | 76 | 375 |

## 3 Findings

To find out to what extent the educational vocabulary was incorporated into these schemas, we divided all 375 occurrences of the metadata schema components into six broad categories: management, subject, descriptive, educational, rights, and technical. Among the 207 *Element* occurrences from all schemas, about one-fourth of the occurrences (51) were specified for educational metadata. The *Management*, *Descriptive*, and *Educational* categories had the largest number of occurrences (305). While the *Management* and *Descriptive* categories show conformity with Dublin Core and LOM/IMS across all schemas, the representation of educational metadata is problematic. First, the total number of occurrences (109) for the *Educational* category counted for about 29% in all occurrences (375). A detailed examination of this category revealed that there was an uneven distribution of learning-related vocabularies that authors can use to signal the types of learning, objectives, or contexts. The rest of the metadata is, essentially, overhead, which may be difficult and expensive to produce.

A second problem is that the standards present constraints for authors who intend to supply detailed educational metadata. Except for GEM's Pedagogy element, educational elements in other metadata schemes had few placeholders for values drawn from learning-related vocabulary. Table 2 shows the learning-related vocabulary obtained from the schemas included in our study. We found a lack of the terms for identifying learning objects, models, or contexts for learning objects. In the rest of this paper, we develop our proposal for an expanded vocabulary for educational metadata to fill some of these gaps.

**Table 2.** Vocabulary used in the educational elements in GEM, LOM, TED, and EML

| Category | Vocabulary used in educational elements |
|---|---|
| Assessment | Evaluation |
| Audience | IntendedEndUserRole, TypicalAgeRange, audience, teacher |
| Context | Context |
| Form | Unit-of-study, LearningResourceType, Conclusion, Content, CourseMedia, CourseSession, Image, Introduction, Presentation, ProgramSessionName, TrainingCourse, TrainingProgram, Unit, ProgramSession, UnitSession |
| General | Educational, Emphasis, SemanticDensity, CertificatesOrDiplomas, completeName, Denomination, function, location, organism, Partnership, trainingContact |
| Learning | Difficulty, InteractivityLevel, InteractivityType, TypicalLearningTime, competence, level, levelType, objective, objectives, pointDealtWith, prerequisites, subPointDealtWith |
| Pedagogy | Pedagogy, PedagogicalMethods |
| Subject | Domain |

## 4   A Vocabulary for Education Metadata

The review and analysis of metadata and educational theories and practices led us to realize that the vocabulary for educational metadata needs a high degree of term specificity and incorporation of vocabularies used in learning theories and practices. Since teachers usually work under a tight time budget, they need a more specific description about the teaching function of learning resources [6]. However, most vocabulary in traditional vocabulary systems is broad and used to represent subject domain content. The two functions of an educational vocabulary—as semantic tags for structured data or content and as predefined values for elements and attributes in metadata schemas—requires much more specific terms not for subject domains but rather, for indicating how learning objects might be useful to instructional/learning activities. Incorporating learning theories and practices into the educational vocabulary would be a prerequisite for such a vocabulary to be useful.

Before we constructed our ontology, we examined the education classes in the DDC and relevant terms in the ERIC Thesaurus. Though both resources have potentially useful terms and classes for representing learning objects, we choose to create a new vocabulary for education metadata for three reasons: 1) Most terms and classes are too broad to be used directly in metadata schemas, 2) Many new terms in the digital learning environment and learning are absent, and 3) The organization of terms and classes is not suitable for packaging the vocabulary as a knowledge base.

The educational vocabulary was generalized from sources in instructional design and technology, learning theories and practices, and traditional vocabulary tools[1]. At the time of this writing, it has the following main categories as shown in Figure 1. We used Protégé-2000 to create the vocabulary. Protégé-2000 is an Open Knowledge Base Connectivity (OKBC) compatible knowledge-base editing environment developed at Stanford University

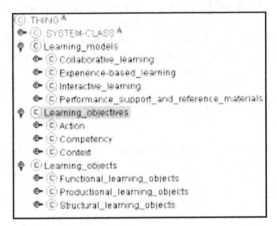

**Fig. 1.** Main categories in the educational vocabulary

(http://protégé.stanford.edu).It provides extensibility and scalability for knowledge bases without compromising system performance. Currently, the ontology contains 127 terms, or classes and subclasses, with up to four levels  A possible use of the terms in this category may be in a structured description, e.g.,

```
<Description>
    <LeaningModels>Collaborative learning—Teaming
    </LearningModels>
</Description>
```

Learning objectives are another important category in the educational vocabulary, which may be described in terms of *Action* that consists of an array of verbs matching the *Competency* [1] in analysis, application, comprehension, evaluation, knowledge, and synthesis, and *Context* such as education for creativity, for effective use of leisure, for social responsibility, etc. Categories of learning objectives may be combined to describe a learning object. For example, in the structured description mentioned above, learning objectives may be added as:

```
<Description>
 <Objective>Action—Articulate</Objective>
 <Objective>Competency—Comprehension</Objective>
```

---

```
<Objective>Context-Education for
creativity</Objective>
  <LearningModel>Collaborative learning-
Teaming</LearningModel>
  </Description>
```

It should be pointed out that the use of educational vocabulary is not intended to prescribe learning experience of users, but rather, to provide a more accurate description of learning objects so that search and selection may be more effective.

## 5  Discussion and Conclusions

The educational vocabulary presented here is a preliminary draft. More work is needed to carefully structure and map out the relationships. Nonetheless, the evidence from educational metadata schemas demonstrates a need for more learning-related vocabularies for finer representation of learning objects. A few similar efforts have been reported so far. Conlan et al [2] propose an "adaptivity" metadata element that includes terms such as "objectives," "learningstyle," "competencies.required," and "competencies.tested." The Dublin Core Education Working Group is developing vocabularies for the audience, pedagogy, and resource type categories [5]. Another project at the European Committee for Standardization (CEN/ISSS) developed a learning technologies vocabulary registry [13]. Our study took a step further and analyzed in-depth the educational vocabulary use in educational metadata schemas, which would provide useful information for building an educational vocabulary.

A unique feature in the educational vocabulary created by the authors lies in its form of ontology. Using the ontology editor Protégé, the vocabulary has the capability of defining concepts and their relationships as well as converting a portion of the ontology into XML schemas. These qualities allow the ontology to be easily expanded and incorporated in learning object metadata schemas.

Learning objects are expensive to produce. Metadata plays a key role in realizing the value invested in creating learning objects. Incorporating educational vocabulary into metadata schemas will provide more specific information on learning-related attributes and enhance their use and reuse. The lack of specific educational vocabulary in current educational metadata standards is a serious defect for further application of knowledge structures such as ontologies in learning object representation and retrieval. Incorporating educational vocabulary into learning object metadata may make metadata creation more expensive, but a practical educational vocabulary has potential for building the lexical base for knowledge mapping and automatic indexing, which may offset the cost and offer a solution to finer metadata representation.

# References

1. Bloom, B.S. (Ed.): Taxonomy of educational objectives: The classification of educational goals: Handbook I, cognitive domain. Longmans, Green New York (1956)
2. Conlan, O., Hockmeyer, C., Lefrere, P., Wade, V., Alber, D.: Extending educational metadata schemas to describe adaptive learning resources. In: Proceedings of the twelfth ACM conference on hypertext and hypermedia (2001 , Århus, none, Denmark), ACM Press, New York, USA (2001) 161–162
3. CRP Henri Tudor—CITI: Training Exchange Definition: Ted. http://hercules.xml.org/xml/schema/8dbca03a/trainingExchangeDefinition.pdf (July 2002)
4. Dodani, M. H.: The dark side of object learning: learning objects. Journal of Object Technology, 1 (Nov-Dec. 2002) 37–42
5. Dublin Core Metadata Initiative. DCMI Education Working Group. http://dublincore.org/groups/education/ (2003)
6. Fitzgerald, M. A. & McClendon, J.: The Gateway to Educational Materials: An Evaluation Study. http://www.geminfo.org/Evaluation/Fitzgerald_02.10.pdf (2002)
7. Friesen, N., Mason, J., Ward, N.: Building educational metadata application profiles. In: Proc. Int. Conf. on Dublin Core and Metadata for e-Communities 2002 (Florence Italy), Firenze University Press, 63–69
8. Gateway to Educational Materials: GEM 2.0 elements and semantics. http://www.geminfo.org/Workbench/GEM2_elements.html (2002)
9. IMS Global: IMS learning resource meta-data information model. http://www.imsproject.org/metadata/imsmdv1p2p1/imsmd_infov1p2p1.html (September 2001)
10. Koper, R.: Modeling units of study from a pedagogical perspective: the pedagogical meta-model behind EML. http://eml.ou.nl/introduction/articles.htm (2001)
11. Learning Technology Standards Committee of the IEEE: Draft standard for learning object metadata. IEEE 1484.12.1-2002. http://ltsc.ieee.org/doc/wg12/LOM_1484_12_1_v1_Final_Draft.pdf (July 2002).
12. University of Colorado at Denver. School of Education: Instructional design models. http://carbon.cudenver.edu/~mryder/itc_data/idmodels.html
13. Van Assche, F., Anido-Rifon, L., Campbell, L.M., Willem, M.: Controlled vocabularies for learning object metadata. Typology, impact analysis, guidelines and a web based Vocabularies Registry. http://www.cenorm.be/isss/LT-vocabulary/vpcrep.html (February 2003)

# Findings from the Mellon Metadata Harvesting Initiative

Martin Halbert[1], Joanne Kaczmarek[2], and Kat Hagedorn[3]

[1] Woodruff Library, Emory University, Atlanta, GA 30322, USA
mhalber@emory.edu
[2] University of Illinois, 1408 W. Gregory Dr., Urbana, IL 61801, USA
jkaczmar@uiuc.edu
[3] Digital Library Production Service, University of Michigan, Ann Arbor, MI, 48109, USA
khage@umich.edu

**Abstract.** Findings are reported from four projects initiated through funding by the Andrew W. Mellon Foundation in 2001 to explore applications of metadata harvesting using the OAI-PMH. Metadata inconsistencies among providers have been encountered and strategies for normalization have been studied. Additional findings concerning harvesting are format conflicts, harvesting problems, provider system development, and questions regarding the entire cycle of metadata production, dissemination, and use (termed metadata gardening, rather than harvesting).

## 1  Introduction

The Open Archives Protocol for Metadata Harvesting (OAI-PMH) has seen rapid adoption by online repositories since the first release of the protocol in 2001. The protocol was designed to enable many kinds of services based on a relatively simple set of six metadata dissemination mechanisms. There has been widespread anticipation that the protocol would enable a new generation of novel information discovery services. [1]

The Andrew W. Mellon Foundation fostered the adoption and exploration of the OAI-PMH through seven project grant awards in 2001 totaling US$1.5M to the following intuitions: the University of Illinois at Urbana-Champaign (UIUC), the University of Michigan, Emory University, the Southeastern Library Network (SOLINET), the University of Virginia (UVA), the Woodrow Wilson International Center for Scholars (WWICS), and the Research Libraries Group (RLG). [2] The Mellon Foundation sought through these projects to enable practical research and experimentation into services and methods of utilizing the OAI-PMH in support of scholarly communication.

This paper describes research findings from four of the seven Mellon-funded projects, specifically those of UIUC, Michigan, Emory, and SOLINET. These four institutions have developed public discovery services that aggregate metadata from many institutions. The remaining three projects were focused on applications of the OAI-PMH internal to their organizations. Their findings will not be reported here.

T. Koch and I.T. Sølvberg (Eds.): ECDL 2003, LNCS 2769, pp. 58–69, 2003.

This paper does not provide either instructions for implementing the protocol or extensive systems architecture reviews of the four projects described. Rather, the focus will be on major conclusions of these projects regarding the use of the OAI-PMH for discovery services of various kinds and directions for future research into applications of metadata harvesting.

The UIUC and Michigan projects have collaborated closely, and are reported first. The Emory and SOLINET projects were conjoined, and are reported jointly as the MetaScholar Initiative.

# 2    University of Illinois – Cultural Heritage Repository

The University of Illinois Library developed middleware tools for harvesting OAI-PMH–compliant metadata and built a Web portal through which cultural heritage resources could be discovered. This provided a basis for evaluating the potential utility of the OAI-PMH in search and discovery services, and helped identify issues that arise when implementing OAI-based services in this domain.

We developed both data provider and service provider open source tools in Visual Basic and Java which are available for download from the SourceForge Website. [3] These tools were subsequently used to create a searchable aggregation of metadata. [4] This aggregation represents a heterogeneous collection of cultural heritage materials that represent artifacts, digitized texts and images, video, sheet music, library holdings, and personal papers and manuscripts. We applied the software tools to the project in two ways. In the first instance we used the tools to provide "surrogate" data provider services for institutions interested in sharing resources but not quite prepared to provide these services themselves. In the second instance we acted as an aggregator using the service provider tools to harvest over 2 million records from across 39 institutional collections. Once harvested these records were then indexed and made searchable using the XPAT software developed and supported by the University of Michigan Library.

Our findings support the notion that the OAI-PMH is a reasonable structure for providing system interoperability among organizations or individuals interested in resource sharing and discovery. The tools are reasonably easy to install and maintain with modest ongoing support from technical staff. The service provider tools are capable of running multiple instances on one or more workstations. While the Java version of the service provider tools suffers from Java's known memory footprint issues, preliminary tests with the Visual Basic tools indicate the use of one workstation running five simultaneous harvest jobs could harvest up to ten million records in one twenty four hour period. Although the protocol seems to be a viable option for resource sharing, our Cultural Heritage Repository still encountered some distinct challenges.

## 2.1    Slow Adoption of the Protocol

Potential data providers were slow in adopting the protocol. Reasons for this slow adoption seem to be based more on available financial and personnel resources than on a lack of interest in participation. This lagging participation was addressed by hosting data via "surrogate" data provider services for interested institutions. Our data hosting allowed us to collect batch dumps of metadata records, process them to conform with the OAI-PMH, and then provide server space for them from which they could be harvested by the project's harvesting service. We believe the slow adoption by potential data providers was foreseeable. At the start of the Mellon funded projects there was not yet enough momentum behind the OAI-PMH to illicit a greater commitment from potential data providers. As the Illinois-supported surrogate data provider services are phased out only sites we can directly harvest will remain in our Cultural Heritage Repository. Providing this temporary service allowed us to work on metadata inconsistency issues early on in the project.

## 2.2    Inconsistent Applications of Metadata

A second challenge, and one faced by all data aggregators, was deciding how to manage the inconsistent application of metadata applied to data provider records. These inconsistencies are compounded when aggregating metadata records from heterogeneous collections. Various data provider communities such as libraries, museums, archives and special collections, tend to use the required Dublin Core (DC) schema differently. The DC schema is flexible, easily understood and can be used to represent a variety of resources. However it is precisely this flexibility that adds to the inconsistencies found in the metadata records we have harvested. Metadata authoring practices indicate great variances in the levels of description used. Also, as all DC elements are optional in the OAI-PMH, there is no guarantee a particular element will be found across all records. Similarly, since all DC elements are repeatable within one record, the number of occurrences could have a significant impact on the outcome of results ranking or sorting. The Illinois project team used common normalization techniques, mapping terms such as 'photo', 'picture', and 'photograph', to 'image' in the Type element. [5] We also normalized on the Date element and temporal uses of the Coverage element and continue to explore techniques for providing more usable result sets to a person searching the repository.

## 2.3    Importance of Context

The context from which some metadata records are extracted can play a significant role in the value perceived by a person whose search results have revealed these materials. Maintaining the context associated with particular records proved to be a challenge for the Illinois project. An example of records that might not be as useful when taken out of context is found in the use of finding aids used by the archival and special collection communities. Finding aids typically describe a collection rather than an individual item within a collection. The Cultural Heritage Repository received 8,730 finding aids marked up with Encoded Archival Description (EAD) from data providers. EAD is widely used in the archival and museum communities to encode metadata representing a broad spectrum of materials ranging from manuscript collections to individual photos, letters, and artifacts. The project team decided to expose as much granularity from the EAD files as possible. As such we developed algorithms to derive multiple DC metadata records, each describing an individual item, from each EAD encoded finding aid. [6] The process generated over 1,515,00 records from the original set of 8,730 finding aids. This level of granularity presented a particular challenge, as the types of records generated did not provide sufficient context for each record thereby leaving the possibility of a very unsatisfactory result set from a search. While searching discrete records embedded in an EAD finding aid may be desirable, to obtain maximum benefit, it is also imperative to provide a reference to the context of any one of these records. To this end, we developed a process that provides a link to the full EAD finding aid for each unique record, displaying the record embedded in its surrounding finding aid contextual framework. This display pops up in a separate browser window, conveniently providing a reference for the searcher to understand which archives or special collection record series generated the original record of interest. This strategy seems to make sense for displaying records aggregated from very different collections and marked up with very different metadata schemas.

## 2.4    Future Directions for Research at University of Illinois

Since the OAI-PMH allows for records with multiple metadata schemas to be harvested, providing they are minimally expressed in DC, it would not be unrealistic for service providers to harvest records in multiple formats. These records could then be served up to multiple end-user communities according to the most appropriate format for each particular group. As the OAI-PMH continues to mature, the work ahead for aggregators will focus on the delivery of services to end-users, packaging information on demand, and maintaining easy links to the contextual setting for records represented in heterogeneous repositories. The University of Illinois is engaged in some aspects of this work as it continues to extend the OAI-PMH on other grant-funded projects.

Through its National Leadership Grants (NLG) program, the Institute of Museum and Library Services (IMLS) is enabling the development of hundreds of significant new digital collections. In September 2002, IMLS awarded the University of Illinois a National Leadership Grant for a three-year research project to promote the visibility, adaptability, and interoperability of IMLS digital collections. The primary goals of the IMLS Digital Collections and Content project [7] are to:

- Create a registry of digital collections funded by the IMLS between 1998 and 2005
- Implement a search and discovery system for item-level content in these collections using the OAI-PMH.
- Research best practices for interoperability among diverse digital content and for supporting the interests of diverse user communities.

Funded by the NSF, the University of Illinois Library faculty are also working with faculty from the Department of Theoretical and Applied Mechanics (TAM) and researchers from Wolfram Research, Inc., to develop second-generation capabilities for two digital libraries to support mathematics, engineering, physics, and applied sciences education using the OAI-PMH. Metadata has been harvested from Eric Weisstein's World of Mathematics (MathWorld) Website and Wolfram Research's Mathematical Functions Website. This material is then being exposed using the OAI-PMH for inclusion in the National Science Digital Library.

# 3   University of Michigan – OAIster

OAIster, at the University of Michigan, University Libraries, Digital Library Production Service (DLPS), was one of the Mellon grant-funded projects designed to test the feasibility of using OAI-PMH to harvest digital object metadata from multiple and varied digital object repositories and develop a service to allow end-users to access that metadata. We developed a system to harvest, store, and transform this metadata, using the UIUC Java harvester and our own Java transformation tool. We utilized the capabilities of Digital Library eXtension Service (DLXS) middleware to transform the metadata into a standard format (DLXS Bibliographic Class), build indexes and make the metadata searchable through an interface using the XPAT search engine. In addition, we tested the resulting interface in-house and remotely with users in two sets of sessions.

The unique feature of OAIster is that it provides access to metadata pointing to actual digital resources. Harvested metadata that has no corresponding digital resource is not indexed in OAIster. This ensures that users can access the resource itself. OAIster can be found online at http://www.oaister.org/, with over a million records available from over 140 institutions. Because of the large number of records indexed (and growing by more than 1000 records every month), OAIster is becoming a "one-stop shopping" interface to any digital resource users might need.

As a result of this year-long project, the University of Michigan project staff encountered a number of issues that should be taken into account for future uses of OAI metadata creation and harvesting.

## 3.1   Metadata Harvesting Issues

Scheduling harvesting of metadata is challenging, as long harvesting efforts often end up overlapping, and thus cause problems with memory-intensive, concurrent processes. Specifically with the Java harvester, we would at times receive out-of-memory errors, and a harvest would fail as a result. We were unable to implement an automated solution for harvesting, as the result of time concerns, so harvesting has remained a manual, time-intensive process.

We found it quite useful to have the ability to harvest a repository completely from scratch, in addition to on an incremental basis. Because of harvester and human hiccups, records could "go missing" on a variable basis. We developed a perl script that runs on the harvester database to clean out any administrative metadata about the harvested records of a repository, allowing us to re-harvest all records from that repository.

In over 10% of the repositories currently being harvested, we have encountered XML validation errors. Some data providers have not been strict in conforming to the UTF-8 encoding standard, and our harvester fails as a result when gathering records from these repositories. If we request that the harvester gather records under loose validation, we receive "junk" records as well as normal records, although in general we receive more records than if we don't harvest using loose validation.

## 3.2    Metadata Variations

Repositories vary widely in terms of the types of records they offer. They differ in formats (e.g., text, video), academic levels (e.g., graduate student theses, peer-reviewed articles), and topics (e.g., physics, religious studies), among others. And, the repositories vary significantly in the quality of their metadata, including their use of the Dublin Core (DC) encoding format. Although all repositories must at the least encode their data in DC before being OAI compliant, institutions use certain elements more frequently, ignore other elements completely, or include namespace declarations in non-standard places, e.g., included with a DC Title tag (`<title xmlns:xsi="http://www.w3.org/2001/XMLSchema-instance">`), which ultimately means we need to create many different kinds of XSL stylesheets as part of our transformation process.

Normalization of the DC Resource Type element was our attempt to standardize some of the metadata, so that users could search more effectively using this element. The transformation tool uses a normalization table, to transform DC Resource Type values such as "Book" and "paper" to the normalized value "text," and values such as "illustration" and "Picture" to the normalized value "image." The table was manually created from a retrieval of unique DC Resource Type values among all harvested records. The resulting normalized value is placed in a new Bibliographic Class element, specifically created for this purpose. Consequently, in the interface, users are then able to limit their search to those records in which the normalized element value equals, for example, "text." Admittedly, the method we used for normalization is not perfect, since each time a new repository, with potentially different varieties of values for DC Resource Type, is added to our service, the normalization table must be created anew. The normalization of metadata will eventually require the use of a thesaurus or controlled vocabulary, and automated methods for gathering the normalization table.

## 3.3    Duplicate Metadata Records

We have encountered duplication of harvested records in two ways. We have harvested nearly every OAI-enabled data provider repository, including those that are aggregators of repositories. Because of this, we have records in our system from original repositories and from aggregator providers collecting original repositories. As an example, a search performed in OAIster for "double-well Duffing oscillator" retrieves two records, exactly the same, but one was harvested from the arXiv.org Eprint Archive repository (an original repository) and one harvested from the

CiteBase repository (an aggregator). The decision of whether or not to harvest from aggregator repositories is made more complex because these aggregators contain records that are not currently available through OAI channels, and they do not always contain all the records of a particular original repository.

Aggregator providers can be very useful for service providers who are unable to harvest certain repositories, as was the case for us in our initial attempts to harvest the arXiv.org Eprint Archive repository. However, aggregators are somewhat problematic as they can be both service providers and data providers. Providing metadata that is also being provided by the original repository complicates the issue of duplicate records. Worse, if the original repository is also a service provider, there is the danger that they could (potentially unknowingly) harvest their own data. The use of the OAI Provenance element could alleviate these problems, however it's not currently widely used by data providers and most harvesters do not have the capability to utilize it.

### 3.4   Granularity of Resources

Granularity or specificity of digital objects will become more of an issue once more metadata is available. We foresee that it will confuse the user to be able to access separate records of the scanned artwork of the Peggy Guggenheim collection, but only be able to access a single record of a book of Emily Dickinson poetry and not records for each of the poems themselves. With so many harvested records, it is not possible to manually determine the specificity of each record, and mirror that in the interface appropriately (e.g., an hierarchical display). The future of the protocol may allow more automated approaches to solving this problem, especially if the OAI Set element is more fully realized and used. (The currently defined Set element allows a data provider to indicate which groupings a record belongs to, e.g., a "low temperature physics" set.)

### 3.5   Resource Restrictions

Rights and restrictions associated with metadata, and associated with the digital objects themselves, are also an issue. For instance, in our role as data provider, we provide metadata of our own collections that contain digital objects restricted to certain communities (e.g., CIC institutions), and metadata restricted due to contractual obligations with the originator. We don't OAI enable the latter, but we do enable the former, if available.

There are issues surrounding display of metadata pointing to restricted digital objects, not the least of which is that it may confuse users if they attempt to get to a digital object and are prevented from doing so. However, there are reasons for making this metadata available. Limiting access to records because the digital objects are restricted to a certain community ends up limiting that community's total access. At DLPS, we have digital objects that fit this pattern, and we make sure to include information in records that clarifies who is able to access those objects.

The large majority of metadata that we harvest displays the DC Rights element, with values supplied by the data provider. It would be beneficial to test differing levels of restrictions and rights on digital objects with users to better answer how best to serve this metadata. Since rights information in the metadata varies widely, and currently there is no standardized method of indicating restricted digital objects (i.e., an OAI "yes/no" toggle element), testing this might inform future development of the protocol and data provider conformance.

### 3.6    Future Directions for OAIster

The University of Michigan intends to continue researching the use of OAI in a variety of ways. We expect to focus our efforts on:

- Determining a method for handling duplicate records.
- Normalizing more elements, such as DC Language.
- Providing high-level topical (or similar) browsing capabilities, perhaps drawing on the OAI Sets functionality.
- Working with UIUC on data mining research to offset issues related to metadata inconsistency.
- Targeting particular audiences within the research community.
- Collaborating with other projects that could benefit from using OAIster, e.g., giving researchers the ability to find digital objects while developing their courses online in a learning object environment.

## 4    Emory University and SOLINET – MetaScholar Initiative

Two of the projects funded by Mellon were based in Atlanta, Georgia.  The MetaArchive project, proposed by Emory University, seeks to explore how information about targeted subject collections held in small-to-medium sized library archives could be most effectively disseminated through OAI-PMH metadata harvesting services.  The AmericanSouth portal was the second Atlanta project, and was proposed by the Association of Southeastern Research Libraries (ASERL), a component of the SOLINET non-profit organization.  AmericanSouth.Org is intended to be a scholarly portal for the study of the culture and history of the American South.  These two projects were conjoined in a unified effort termed the MetaScholar Initiative in order to take advantage of complementary aspects of the two projects.  Both projects are focused on cultural research materials associated primarily with regional subject topics.  The projects have produced three portals, accessible at http://AmericanSouth.Org,   http://MetaArchive.Org,   and   http://MetaScholar.Org (containing information about the overall initiative).

During 2002 the MetaScholar Initiative installed OAI data providers at partner institutions and established a central portal infrastructure to harvest and index metadata, as well as manage contributed contextual content pieces.

**MetaArchive Project.** MetaArchive project programmers worked with archivists and technologists at institutions and archival operations of many different types and scales.  A special project focus has been on smaller college library archives, but we have also worked with large research libraries, church record repositories, university data centers, and a museum. Several dozen OAI data providers were installed during the course of the project, representing multiple archival collections.

A difference between the philosophies of the MetaScholar Initiative and many other OAI harvesting projects is that metadata for both print and online materials have been aggregated. This is because the focus of our projects is raising visibility of scholarly resources generally, regardless of access mechanisms. We are interested in studying the processes whereby institutions of multiple categories can utilize the OAI-PMH in support of information dissemination, and especially how centralized common-good technical infrastructures can be deployed to benefit smaller, underfunded archives. Archives are being selected using a collection development model, with roughly 30K records in the current MetaArchive databases. We wish to keep the MetaArchive databases small and targeted to the two subject domains of the project, papers of selected Southern political figures and religious institutions.

**AmericanSouth Project.** The AmericanSouth project has focused on a more homogenous group of nine large ASERL research libraries and their archival holdings. The majority of these archival collections are digitized materials, but online access to items cited by metadata is not a harvesting requirement for AmericanSouth any more than in the MetaArchive project. The main criteria for harvesting are scholarly value and subject domain relevance of collections as judged by a team of scholars representing different disciplines and backgrounds. This scholarly design team also provides guidance on user interface features, as well as original online content in the form of online articles and authoritative contextual subject guides.

During 2002 MetaScholar Initiative programmers collaborated with researchers at Virginia Tech to install elements of the Virginia Tech Open Digital Library software [8] at AmericanSouth and MetaArchive partner sites in order to establish OAI data provider. The MetaScholar Initiative redeployed the ARC software [9] from Old Dominion and enhanced it with additional annotation and portal features to create two experimental portals, AmericanSouth.Org and MetaArchive.Org, that combined metadata harvesting and scholarly publishing capabilities.

The MetaScholar Initiative has independently encountered and can reiterate the all the findings reported by the UIUC and Michigan projects. Without repeating their points, there are some further elaborations that MetaScholar can offer, as follows.

## 4.1    Barriers to Adopting the Protocol

THE OAI-PMH was not used, implemented, or adopted by the vast majority of libraries and archives in 2002, nor is this likely to change in 2003. This is because of a variety of barriers to adopting the protocol. This finding may appear inconsistent with the growth in numbers of OAI data providers and the simple implementation requirements of the protocol, but is nevertheless valid and significant. It is true that the numbers of OAI data providers are growing at a virtually geometric rate. [10] But despite this rapid growth in providers, the overall penetration of the protocol into the deep infrastructure of scholarly archives is still minor. Virtually no MetaScholar partners were planning on implementing the OAI-PMH before the collaboration began. Nor would the majority have been able to implement the protocol without the specialized programming assistance offered by the MetaScholar projects.

Collaborating institutions nevertheless acknowledge the clear benefits the protocol offers by enabling new means of information dissemination. The lack of priority in adopting the protocol is mainly related to the generally poor funding situation that research institutions find themselves in today, in which not only new technological initiatives, but almost any new initiatives are difficult to undertake. Where funding for new technological initiatives is available, it is primarily being expended on other fundamental infrastructural changes, mainly migrating data from obsolete or discontinued software systems (examples: mainframes, and PCs using the DOS operating system) to current digital library systems (examples: dynamic XML content management systems). These migrations are so encompassing that the technical staff available to libraries and archives are wholly occupied, and not alert to the opportunities presented by the OAI-PMH, at least in the 2002-2003 timeframe.

This finding leads us to strongly conclude that additional efforts to foster the adoption of the protocol in the library and archival communities are needed, and should be underwritten as special programs by central state and foundation funding agencies. Clearer metrics of the benefits of adopting the protocol are also needed in order to justify these expenditures.

## 4.2    Problems Associated with the Dublin Core Metadata Standard

Many of the problems reported by UIUC and Michigan (inconsistent applications of metadata, metadata variations, and granularity of resources) have also been difficulties encountered by the MetaScholar Initiative. We feel that these issues all stem inevitably from two facts: a) the primitive quality of metadata represented in the unqualified Dublin Core (UDC) format, and b) the fact that UDC is the only metadata format required by the OAI-PMH. These two facts are together problematic for services attempting to develop discovery services based on harvesting metadata using the OAI-PMH. While there is great discovery utility in being able to rapidly and easily harvest metadata from large numbers of distributed, heterogeneous systems, the search functionality in such discovery systems is compromised by unavoidable inconsistency in the metadata provided by varied sources.

**Metadata Format Collisions.** In addition to the problems identified by UIUC and Michigan, we have become deeply troubled by what we see as intractable conflicts or collisions between the approaches of groups using different metadata formats. Because MetaScholar has worked extensively with archives, we have particularly studied the problems that occur when metadata originally expressed in EAD is converted into UDC. There is a Procrustean dilemma that frequently occurs in these situations. The EAD format is primarily aimed at encoding a single finding aid document characterizing an entire collection, typically with series-level information but not usually item-level details. When converting finding aids into UDC records, the metadata wrangler in charge of the operation is often faced with two distasteful options: 1) creating a single UDC record for the entire collection (this single record must often discard much of the detail of the original finding aid in order to be of reasonable length for screen display), or 2) segmenting the series-level information into separate UDC records (that are often decontextualized by this segmentation). The UIUC and MetaScholar projects have sought middle-ground strategies in segmenting large finding aids while trying to preserve context through hyperlinks, with varying degrees of success. While this problem has been prominent initially in the case of EAD/UDC metadata collisions, we believe that similar kinds of deep metadata conflicts will likely arise as other metadata formats are increasingly harvested into discovery services. Better guidelines for consistent use of differing metadata formats are needed.

### 4.3    Metadata Gardening

While services based on metadata harvesting have been explored by several projects, we believe there is still inadequate understanding of the entire cycle of metadata production, dissemination, reprocessing, and extended uses. The MetaScholar Initiative has conceptualized this cycle as "metadata gardening" in its work with participating institutions and scholars. We think that several of the issues identified by Michigan (which MetaScholar has also encountered) including duplication of records, confusing rights restrictions, harvesting problems, and metadata variations are all examples of issues that arise when the entire cycle is not coordinated. Additional problems in this area that MetaScholar has identified are uneven representation of topics, problems in browsing across collections, and poor understanding of the value that metadata harvesting services add to scholarly communication (see below).

Without better perspective on how to coordinate the entire cycle of cultivating metadata providers, harvesting, and finally organizing metadata for discovery, we feel that these problems will continue to compromise the effectiveness of services based on metadata harvesting.

### 4.4    Interactions with Scholarly Communication

One of the primary reasons that the Mellon Foundation funded these metadata harvesting projects was to explore how the OAI-PMH could benefit scholarly communication. The MetaScholar Initiative feels that there has been relatively little direct examination of this question in any of the Mellon projects that were undertaken. A basic conviction of the MetaScholar Initiative is that simple aggregations of metadata as such are not sufficient; an associated authoritative context of some user community is always needed to make a metadata discovery service useful. Trying to understand the specific value and opportunities that may be realized by close connections of metadata services with scholarly content is an issue that the AmericanSouth scholarly design team is taking up in 2003.

### 4.5    Relationships to Other Discovery Services

There is no consensus on the relationship of metadata harvesting services with traditional library tools such as the online catalog, or newly emergent tools such as Google and other Web search engines. This issue has dismayed information service providers such as librarians at the campus level who now have yet another "one stop shopping" service to try to coherently articulate to students and other researchers. We are interested in answering the question of whether or not there are logical ways of creating federated search systems that can simultaneously query both OAI metadata aggregations as well as web search engines.

### 4.6    Future Directions for Research at Emory University and SOLINET

The MetaScholar Initiative will undertake the following projects in coming months:

- Fostering adoption of the OAI-PMH through workshops
- Examining metadata format collisions more closely
- Modeling the metadata gardening cycle
- Studying the benefits and interactions of metadata harvesting and scholarly communication
- Clarifying the relationship of metadata harvesting services and other discovery services through future testbed projects to explore the combination of metadata harvesting and web crawling

# References

1.  Lynch, C.: Metadata Harvesting and the Open Archives Initiative. ARL Bimonthly Report, Issue 217 (2001) (http://www.arl.org/newsltr/217/mhp.html)
2.  Waters, D.: The Metadata Harvesting initiative of the Mellon Foundation. ARL Bimonthly Report, Issue 217 (2001) (http://www.arl.org/newsltr/217/waters.html)
3.  SourceForge Website. (http://sourceforge.net/projects/uilib-oai/).
4.  Illinois Cultural Heritage Repository Website. (http://oai.grainger.uiuc.edu).
5.  Cole, T.W., Kaczmarek, J., Marty, P.F., Prom, C.J., Sandore, B., & Shreeves, S.L.: Now that we've found the 'hidden web' what can we do with it? The Illinois Open Archives Initiative Metadata Harvesting experience. In: Bearman, D., Trant, J. (eds): Museums and the Web 2002: selected papers from an international conference, (2002) 63–72. (http://www.archimuse.com/mw2002/papers/cole/cole.html)
6.  Prom, C.J., Habing T.G.: Using the Open Archives Initiative Protocols with EAD. In: Marchionini G., Hersch, W. (eds): JCDL 2002: Proceedings of the Second ACM/IEEE-CS Joint Conference on Digital Libraries (2002)171–180.
7.  IMLS Digital Collections and Content project (http://imlsdcc.grainger.uiuc.edu)
8.  Open Digital Libraries at Virginia Tech (http://oai.dlib.vt.edu/odl)
9.  ARC SourceForge site (http://oaiarc.sourceforge.net)
10. Van de Sompel, H., Lagoze, C.: Notes from the Interoperability Front: A Progress Report on the Open Archives Initiative. In: Agosti, M., Thanos, C.(eds): Research and Advanced Technology for Digital Libraries: 6th European Conference. Lecture Notes in Computer Science, Vol. 2458. Springer-Verlag, Berlin Heidelberg New York (2002) 150.

# Semantic Browsing

Alexander Faaborg and Carl Lagoze

Information Science, Cornell University, Ithaca, NY 14850 USA

**Abstract.** We have created software applications that allow users to both author and use Semantic Web metadata. To create and use a layer of semantic content on top of the existing Web, we have (1) implemented a user interface that expedites the task of attributing metadata to resources on the Web, and (2) augmented a Web browser to leverage this semantic metadata to provide relevant information and tasks to the user. This project provides a framework for annotating and reorganizing existing files, pages, and sites on the Web that is similar to Vannevar Bush's original concepts of trail blazing and associative indexing.

## 1 Introduction

The organization of information has been an ongoing challenge for libraries. As libraries make increasing use of Web resources to populate their collections (exemplified by the work by our colleagues in the National Science Digital Library (NSDL) [1]), digital library developers need to find effective ways to organize digital objects stored across distributed servers on the Web. Just as brick and mortar libraries built shelves for books, digital libraries need *virtual shelves* to organize the elements of their collections.

The Semantic Web effort [2] of the W3C and its collaborators is developing the tools that facilitate the organization and classification of Web resources in a manner usable to both humans and machines. A result of this effort is the Resource Description Framework (RDF) [3] that provides the syntactic and semantic building blocks for organizing Web resources. While much effort has gone into RDF and related Semantic Web standards [4], the actual user interface of the Semantic Web is rarely mentioned. We directly address this issue.

We have implemented two tools that allow users to both build and use the Semantic Web. One is a user interface for quickly generating RDF annotations that overlay a personal and sharable semantic layer on top of the underlying Web. The other is a modified Web browser that leverages this semantic layer as a means of enriching and personalizing the browsing experience, locating related information, and providing contextually relevant tasks. We believe that end-user Semantic Web tools will greatly improve the usability of the Web in future digital libraries. They will enable users to organize their individual browsing experiences and help information intermediaries, such as librarians, tailor the Web experience for their target audiences. They will help integrate the Web into digital libraries rather than make digital libraries simply catalogs of Web resources.

T. Koch and I.T. Sølvberg (Eds.): ECDL 2003, LNCS 2769, pp. 70–81, 2003.

Our work, and that of the broader Semantic Web community, helps move the Web closer to Vannevar Bush's seminal vision [5]. In 1945 Bush wrote the well-known article *As We May Think*, in which he describes the concept of blazing trails between documents. Many people consider his concept of trail blazing to be the precursor of the hypertext we find today on the World Wide Web. However, the Web in its present form falls short of Vannevar Bush's vision for a number of reasons.

First, the Web allows for only primitive trail blazing: hyperlinks under the control of the page author that have limited semantic expressiveness. Our tools allow users to overlay their own trails on top of the existing hyperlink structure. Furthermore, the expressiveness of RDF allows the user to endow these trails with rich semantic meaning.

Second, the current Web fails to realize Bush's visions of automatic processing and logic. Bush saw this logic processing as the means towards advanced capabilities such as associative indexing, in which documents immediately and automatically select other related documents. The machine-readable and semantically rich annotations created via our tools provide the foundation for agent-initiated associative indexing and other automated tasks on metadata.

It is our hope that by demonstrating semantic browsing from the perspective of end users, we will be able to establish the importance of the Semantic Web in the implementation of Web based digital libraries.

## 2    Trail Blazing Using Semantic Web Technologies

Vannevar Bush describes the concept of trail blazing as joining two documents, and "thereafter, at any time, when one of these items is in view, the other can be instantly recalled." [5] While hyperlinks provide a mechanism for joining documents on the Web, these links can only be placed on a Web page by its author, and not its readers. Our work is based on the notion that the utility of the Web as an information resource can be enriched if users themselves have the power to link together documents and otherwise annotate the Web.

One potential application of our work is in the education domain, where our NSDL project [1] has demonstrated teachers' need to weave together primary Web resources in order to make them more usable for the classroom experience [6]. For the remainder of this paper we will use an example from this domain, an imaginary high school biology teacher named Mrs. Thompson. It is important to note that our work is applicable in a variety of domains from information management inside a corporation to organizing the public Web.

Let us imagine that Mrs. Thompson, in preparation for her class, has located a Web site about the tundra biome and a Web site about the coniferous woodland biome, and she wants to guide her students to these sites. In the current Web, Mrs. Thompson might create a new document that comments on these pertinent resources intermixed with hyperlinks to them. This has a number of limitations. The first is that Mrs. Thompson's links only hook into the Web one level deep. In order to follow Mrs. Thompson's trail, her students must constantly return to her Web page and follow the next link. Related pages are not joined as in Bush's vision, but are simply referenced. It is not the case that "when one of these items is in view, the other can be instantly recalled." [5] The second limitation is that Mrs. Thompson's new Web page uses natural language to express the relationship among her chosen resources. The imprecise semantics of natural language limit the utility of her annotations to human browsing rather than machine understanding. By simply creating a new Web page, Mrs. Thompson's attempt at trail blazing does not help to organize the Web as much as it just makes it a little larger.

The challenge that Mrs. Thompson faces in making the Web useful in her teaching is to provide some level of structure and organization to her students and exploit the educational value of hypertext [7]. As described above, the current Web limits her ability to structure the Web for her students to simple pointers that then leave her students at the mercy of the Web's existing link structure, which may not be relevant to her educational goals. The standards of the Semantic Web, RDF and RDF schema, provide the building blocks for a more structured, organized, and semantically rich Web. The remainder of this section describes the utility of these Semantic Web standards in a series of progressively richer examples. In the subsequent section, we describe how our work applies these standards to enhance the Web experience.

The simplest application of the Semantic Web allows Mrs. Thompson to associate metadata with a Web page that she does not control, as illustrated in the figure below. This metadata might then be integrated into her students' Web browsing experience in a manner similar to the way Annotea [8] clients show user annotations. For instance, when browsing to a Web site about biomes in the United States Rocky Mountains, her students' Web browsers could note the pages Mrs. Thompson feels deserve a close reading as they came to them, while still allowing the students to browse freely.

The Web consists not only of pages, but the relationships between pages that are established by its navigational structure. While the meaning of these links is sometimes described by their anchor text, Mrs. Thompson may want to annotate links with information appropriate to her lesson plan and class needs, as illustrated below. For example, Mrs. Thompson would like the next page her students view after learning about the tundra to be the Web page about the coniferous woodland, because they may visit the biomes in this order on their field trip. Mrs. Thompson could annotate the hyperlink, and this information would then appear when her students viewed the tundra Web page.

The established links on the Web may not be sufficient for Mrs. Thompson's lesson goals. For example, although the links on a Web site show that the pika, a small member of the rabbit family, can be found in the tundra, she may want to create and annotate an additional link to show that this animal can also be found in the coniferous woodland. Students browsing the Web site then would be able to follow Mrs. Thompson's imposed link (shown below) as well as the established links on the Web site.

The utility of the Semantic Web comes from the fact that annotations (metadata) can be machine readable and interpretable. Concepts and taxonomies can be expressed through RDF-based ontology languages [4]. Metadata creators may then refer to the URIs of these taxonomies within their descriptions rather than using text strings. The use of these unique identifiers as references allows one of the most important types of trail blazing, the ability to automatically group disparate resources together based on their shared conceptual relationships. Vannevar Bush referred to this feature as associative indexing [5].

Mrs. Thompson may want to create her Web annotations using a subject taxonomy endorsed by the National Science Teachers Association (NSTA). Thus, instead of using strings like 'tundra' and 'pika' in her descriptions, she could use the respective URIs from the NSTA taxonomy. As we show later, this allows her students to navigate Web sites based on semantic concepts in addition to the sites' hyperlinks. When two Web pages are annotated with the same URI, associative indexing places both Web pages on the same metaphorical shelf, as illustrated below.

Because the metadata used in all of the above annotations is expressed in a machine-readable format, it can be shared between parties and merged together. For instance, because Mrs. Thompson can use URIs to associate two Web sites about animal life in the Rocky Mountains, these pages can be automatically associated with a larger set of pages also about animal life in the Rocky Mountains that have been annotated with the same URIs by other individuals. This facilitates the information environment envisioned by the NSDL where users become contributors in a dynamic collaborative environment.

In the next section we will demonstrate how these types of semantic annotations can aid in locating relevant information and improve the functionality of a Web browser, alleviating some of the frustrations users currently have with the Web. First however, we will see how a user like Mrs. Thompson can create these types of annotations with our software.

## 3    Tools to Build and Browse the Semantic Web

We have developed two applications that allow users like Mrs. Thompson to leverage the Semantic Web. Site Annotator is used to author semantic metadata about Web resources, and the Web Task Pane modifies Internet Explorer to integrate this semantic metadata into the browsing experience. Larger screen shots and additional information about these applications can be found at: http://www.cs.cornell.edu/lagoze/Projects/SemanticBrowsing/

### 3.1    Site Annotator

Site Annotator, shown above, has an address bar similar to a Web browser. When a user enters a URL into this address bar, the Web site is shown in a tree view and list view, as if the user is viewing the file system of their computer. We chose the file system metaphor because it provides an easy way to select multiple Web resources at the same time. Site Annotator is able to display

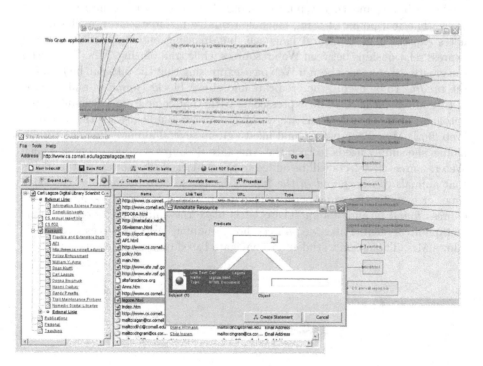

a file system view of a Web site by parsing each Web page's HTML. The file system view of a Web site is accessed through HTTP in Site Annotator and should not be confused with the Web site's actual file structure, which might be accessed through FTP. Thus, if a file exists on a Web server but none of the other files link to it, Site Annotator will not be able to find it.

The purpose of Site Annotator is to help the user author subject-predicate-object statements about Web resources. The user interface for creating a subject-predicate-object statement appears as three blocks arranged in a triangle (the foreground window in the figure above). The subject and object blocks are on the bottom of the triangle and the predicate block connects them. Web resources selected in the main window appear in the statement's subject block, which is dark green, and the statement's predicate and object blocks appear in white because they require the user's input. After the user enters information into the required predicate and object blocks and creates the statement, all three blocks turn green and the window closes. These statements can later be exported as RDF triples encoded in XML. Because of the importance of using URIs from Semantic Web ontologies when creating annotations, the application allows the user to import multiple RDF schemas through the Load RDF Schema button and reference them via URIs in their annotations.

Returning to our example of Mrs. Thompson, one of the ways she wanted to annotate the Web included leaving notes for her students to find as they browsed to particular pages. This can be accomplished by selecting the appropriate page as the subject block, selecting "has note" in the drop down list box in the predicate block, and then typing the note she wishes to leave into the object block. The real power of using machine-readable metadata however lies not in notes expressed in a natural language, but in using ontologies to group and express relationships between Web resources while trail blazing. Mrs. Thompson can create a statement about a Web page expressing that the pika can be *found in* the *tundra*. To be useful, the predicate and object blocks (*found in* and *tundra*) in this statement need to be expressed as URIs that come from a Semantic Web ontology. Many organizations are working to create ontologies for the Semantic Web [9]. If Mrs. Thompson would like to group several animals into the tundra biome, she simply needs to keep the Annotate Resource window open, and each Web resource she selects will be added to the subject block. However, statements that animals can be *found in* the *tundra* do not need to be made at the same time, or even by the same person. They simply need to use the same URIs to express *found in* and *tundra*. These URIs place the animal pages on the same metaphorical shelf. Later we will see how grouping Web resources with URIs allows Mrs. Thompson's students to navigate based on semantic concepts.

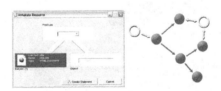

The Create Semantic Link window is similar to the Annotate Resource window, but both the subject and object files must be selected in the main window. The Create Semantic Link window allows Mrs. Thompson to create semantic associations between existing Web resources. This window resembles the basic user interface designed by Vannevar Bush when he described the concept of trail blazing: "Before him are the two items to be joined, projected onto adjacent viewing positions... The user taps a single key, and the items are permanently joined." [5] Mrs. Thompson could use the Create Semantic Link window to indicate to her students which Web page she wants them to view next, to annotate an existing hyperlink with additional information, or to create an entirely new hyperlink between Web resources. For instance, she could instruct her students that more information about the pika can be found on another Web page.

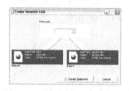 

The previous example demonstrates human intervention to create an RDF statement. There are cases however, when Site Annotator has enough knowledge to automatically generate metadata. We have been working on making Site Annotator generate RDF statements in the background while the user focuses on complex annotations like biomes. For instance, Site Annotator will automatically author semantic metadata, expressed as RDF triples, about page titles, hyperlinks, link text, and MIME types. This automatic metadata generation is only a step toward our long-term goal of identifying more complex types of relationships on the Web. Two examples include automatically detecting implicit structures in a Web site, like an article that spans multiple pages, and automatically detecting groups of files, like the structure of an image gallery.

After Site Annotator is finished generating metadata in the background and the user is finished trail blazing, the user can export the generated metadata to an RDF file by clicking the Save RDF button.

This semantic metadata can be published on the Web in a variety of ways. If the user has control of the Web site, the metadata can be placed on the server in an index.rdf file. This is functionally the opposite of a robots.txt file in that it gives parsing agents as much information as it can about the site, rather than instructing the agents to stay away. Other options include placing the semantic metadata inline with the HTML. Future changes to HTTP might provide access to the RDF metadata as part of a page request. We currently only support placing the semantic metadata in an index.rdf file, which is the simplest of these solutions.

If the user does not control the Web site, future options for sharing their metadata may include placing it in a directory service like dmoz.org, or anywhere online where a service like Google will be able to locate it. Of course, any public facility for annotating Web resources may lead to misuse and spam, so the creation of a global Semantic Web will also require a Web of Trust [10]. The Semantic Web may first emerge in controlled communities like corporate intranets and digital libraries where the reliability of metadata can be guaranteed. Users will upload RDF triples into a database or place them online to be found by a spider agent and the collection of these statements will literally form the Semantic Web. Until a Web of Trust is constructed, the public Web may only contain small discrete packets of reliable semantic metadata. However, sharing knowledge in this manner is still compelling. Imagine if an expert like Stephen Hawking could publish his personal organization of physics on the Web in an .rdf file for anyone to download.

At present, the .rdf files created by Site Annotator may be shared via email and over the Web, and then loaded in the Web Task Pane as described below. In the case of Mrs. Thompson, her students' Web browsers could be automatically set to look for semantic metadata created by her.

## 3.2   The Web Task Pane

The Web Task Pane, shown above, is a tool for semantic browsing, implemented as an explorer bar for Microsoft Internet Explorer. The user interface for the Web Task Pane is similar to the task panes found in Microsoft Windows XP and Office XP, which dynamically react to what the user is viewing. As the user browses the Web, the Web Task Pane will continually download and manipulate semantic metadata in the background, displaying information, tasks, and navigational controls in the user interface.

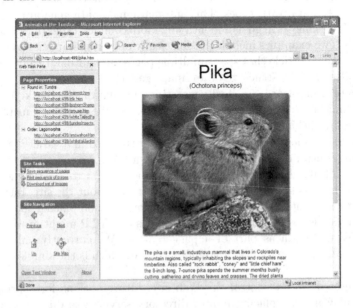

We believe that the ability to navigate based on semantic concepts can improve the overall usability of the Web. Vannevar Bush's vision noted that the human mind "operates by association. With one item in its grasp, it snaps instantly to the next that is suggested by the association of thoughts, in accordance with some intricate web of trails carried by the cells of the brain." [5] In *Hypertext and Cognition*, Jean-Francois Rouet discussed the human computer interaction involved with Web browsing, saying, "Progression in a hypertext requires active decision making on the part of the reader. In order to make coherent selections, the reader has to possess a mental representation of how the information is organized." [7] Usability on the Web breaks down when a user identifies a relationship in their mental model, but then cannot locate an appropriate hyperlink.

The first section of the Web Task Pane, Page Properties, allows the user to navigate the Semantic Web. In the above screen shot, the Web Task Pane has downloaded RDF metadata from the Semantic Web (which was created with a tool like Site Annotator) and analyzed it to learn that the pika lives in the tundra biome. It then performed associative indexing to locate other animals that also live in the tundra. Page Properties allows the user to navigate between Web resources based on semantic concepts. Allowing users to navigate on semantic concepts increases the overall density of the Web. To prevent the user from being overwhelmed with information, Page Properties contains a tree interface that the user must actively expand.

The above screen shot shows the result of associative indexing using semantic metadata, displaying links to a set of pages that are metaphorically shelved using the same predicate and subject URIs: x is *found in* the *tundra*. Other types of metadata, however, particularly those relating to a Web site's structure and files, can be used by the Web Task Pane to provide the user with a more advanced Web browser.

The second section of the Web Task Pane is called Site Tasks. The tasks that appear here are similar to tasks available in a normal Web browser like downloading or printing. Unlike current Web browsers however, these tasks go beyond the Web page the user is currently on. Often a Web browser's lack of understanding results in the user performing repetitive actions like a machine. Examples include printing each page of a multi-page article individually, or right clicking on each image in a gallery and selecting "Save As." The Web is replete with similar structures, and users perform a similar set of tasks. Because of this, the Web Task Pane is able to use semantic metadata to provide its users with contextually relevant tasks. Currently the Web Task Pane has the ability to save a sequence of pages, and download all of the images in a set. We are now in the process of expanding the number of tasks it can automate for the user based on semantic metadata.

The third section of the Web Task Pane is called Site Navigation. Here the Web Task Pane uses the same semantic metadata as the Site Tasks section, but for the purpose of providing the user with more advanced navigational controls. Providing a unified navigational interface increases Web usability because the user does not have to visually search for hyperlinks to navigate common structures on the Web. User advocate Jakob Nielsen believes that "at a minimum, Web browsers need to have better support for structural navigation." [11] The controls in the Site Navigation section include the ability to go up one level in a hierarchical structure, to view the Web site's site map, and next and previous controls for quickly navigating between resources that form a sequence.

## 4 Implementation Details

Site Annotator is a standalone Java application. Each subject-predicate-object statement the user specifies using the Annotate Resource or Create Semantic Link windows forms an RDF triple. Site Annotator integrates with the RDF visualization tool IsaViz, which was created by Xerox PARC [12], so that at any time the user can press a button and view the semantic metadata they have created graphically. To encode the statements the user creates into RDF metadata serialized in XML, Site Annotator uses the Jena API that was created by HP Labs [13].

The Web Task Pane was written in C# for the Microsoft .NET framework. It integrates with Microsoft Internet Explorer using COM interoperability. When the user loads a Web page, Internet Explorer notifies the Web Task Pane of the new URL. The Web Task Pane then attempts to locate an index.rdf file on the server containing semantic metadata. It also allows for the user to manually load .rdf files. The downloaded RDF metadata, which is serialized in XML, is manipulated using the .NET framework's implementation of DOM.

## 5 Related Work

The Mrs. Thompson example used throughout this paper is only hypothetical. However, Shipman et al. have researched the use of Vannevar Bush style trail blazing in actual classroom environments [14]. The Web Task Pane allows users to navigate based on semantic concepts, or *virtual shelves*. Carr et al. have also studied conceptual linking [15]. The Web Task Pane also provides users with richer navigation options. Preliminary work on the use of RDF for site maps has been conducted by Dan Brickley [16].

Our software applications are related to the suite of RDF tools that have been developed over the last few years. The best reference to these tools is Dave Beckett's Resource Description Framework (RDF) Resource Guide [17]. There are two RDF authoring tools in that list that are most closely related to our work: the RDF Instance Creator [18] and the IsaViz Visual Authoring Tool for RDF [12]. Site Annotator uses IsaViz for the display of RDF models.

Other Semantic Web Annotation tools include the OntoMat-Annotizer [19], the SHOE Knowledge Annotator [20], SMORE [21], MnM [22], and Trellis [23]. Semantic Web tools that extend Mozilla include the Annozilla sidebar [24], which is a client for Annotea [8], and the COHSE Annotator sidebar [25]. Semantic

Web tools that extend Internet Explorer include our work, and the work of the Annotation System project group of the National Centre for Software Technology in Bangalore [26]. The NCST's Annotate Browser explorer bar is similar to the Page Properties section of our Web Task Pane explorer bar. More information about all of the above Semantic Web Annotation tools can be found at http://annotation.semanticweb.org/tools

# 6 Conclusion

The Semantic Web is a new enough research area that most people, upon hearing the phrase "building the Semantic Web," assume the word "building" refers to its infrastructure, its syntax and protocols. We are interested in creating tools that allow end users to literally build the Semantic Web, to give it semantics. Users like Mrs. Thompson do not know about URIs, ontologies, RDF, or XML. If the Semantic Web is to become a reality, building it is going to need to be more like trail blazing with colorful blocks, and less like using XML Spy. Site Annotator, while providing a graphical interface for trail blazing with Semantic Web technologies, may still not be high-level enough for users like Mrs. Thompson. To facilitate a collaborative Semantic Web, users will need Semantic Web enabled annotation tools built into their browsers, and authors will need Semantic Web enabled tools built into their Web development software. With Semantic Web research quickly progressing, the next step in creating these applications will not be in developing their infrastructure, but in designing their user interface.

**Acknowledgments.** We would like to acknowledge the contributions of Geri Gay and Michael Spivey, who are on Alexander Faaborg's honors thesis committee. This work was supported in part by NSF Grant 9905955.

# References

1. Lagoze, C., Arms, W., Gan, S., Hillmann, D., Ingram, C., Krafft, D., Marisa, R., Phipps, J., Saylor, J., Terrizzi, C., Hoehn, W., Millman, D., Allan, J., Guzman-Lara, S., and Kalt, T.: Core Services in the Architecture of the National Digital Library for Science Education (NSDL). Presented at the Joint Conference on Digital Libraries, Portland, Oregon (2002)
2. Fensel, D., Hendler, J., Lieberman, H., Wahlster, W.: Spinning the Semantic Web: Bringing the World Wide Web to its Full Potential. MIT Press, Cambridge, Massachusetts (2003)
3. Manola, F., Miller, E.: RDF Primer. W3C Working Draft 23 January 2003 http://www.w3.org/TR/rdf-primer/
4. Dean, M., Connolly, D., van Harmelen, F., Hendler, J., Horrocks, I., McGuinness, D. L., Patel-Schneider, P. F., and Stein, L. A.: OWL Web Ontology Language 1.0 Reference. World Wide Web Consortium, W3C Working Draft 29 July 2002 http://www.w3.org/TR/2002/WD-owl-ref-20020729/
5. Bush, V. F.: As We May Think. Atlantic Monthly (July, 1945) http://www.theatlantic.com/unbound/flashbks/computer/bushf.htm

6. Dorward, J., Reinke, D., and Recker, M.: An Evaluation Model for a Digital Library Services Tool. Presented at the Joint Conference on Digital Libraries, Portland, Oregon (2002)

7. Rouet, J.-F., Levenon J., Dillon A., Spiro R.: European Association for Research on Learning and Instruction Conference, Hypertext and Cognition. Lawrence Erlbaum, Mahwah, New Jersey (1996)

8. Kahan, J., Koivunen, M.-R., Prud'Hommeaux, E., and Swick, R. R.: Annotea: An Open RDF Infrastructure for Shared Web Annotations. Presented at the Tenth International World Wide Web Conference, Hong Kong (2001)

9. Fensel, D.: OntoWeb Portal, Ontology-Based Information Exchange for Knowledge Management and Electronic Commerce (2003) http://ontoweb.aifb.uni-karlsruhe.de/

10. Khare, R., Rifkin, A.: Weaving a Web of Trust. World Wide Web Journal (1997) 77–112

11. Nielsen, J.: Designing Web Usability. New Riders, Indianapolis, Indiana (2000)

12. Pietriga, E.: IsaViz: A Visual Authoring Tool for RDF (2002) http://www.w3.org/2001/11/IsaViz/

13. Jena Semantic Web Toolkit (2003) http://www.hpl.hp.com/semweb/jena.htm

14. Shipman, F., Furuta, R., Brenner, D., Chung, C., Hsieh, H.: Using Paths in the Classroom: Experiences and Adaptations. Proceedings of the 9th ACM Conference on Hypertext (1998) 267–276

15. Carr L., Bechhofer S., Goble C., Hall W.: Conceptual Linking: Ontology-based Open Hypermedia. Proceedings of the Tenth International World Wide Web Conference, Hong Kong (2001)

16. Brickley, D.: RDF sitemaps and Dublin Core site summaries (1999) http://rudolf.opensource.ac.uk/about/specs/sitemap.html

17. Beckett, D.: Dave Beckett's Resource Description Framework (RDF) Resource Guide (2003) http://www.ilrt.bristol.ac.uk/discovery/rdf/resources/

18. Grove, M.: RDF Instance Creator, Semantic Web Research Group (2002) http://www.mindswap.org/~mhgrove/RIC/RIC.shtml

19. Handschuh, S., Staab, S., Ciravegna, F.: S-CREAM – Semi-automatic CREAtion of Metadata. Proceedings of the European Conference on Knowledge Acquisition and Management, Madrid, Spain (2002)

20. Heflin, J.: Towards the Semantic Web: Knowledge Representation in a Dynamic Distributed Environment. Ph.D. Thesis, University of Maryland, College Park, Maryland (2001)

21. Aditya, K., Parsia, B., Hendler, J., Golbeck, J.: SMORE – Semantic Markup, Ontology, and RDF Editor http://www.mindswap.org/papers/SMORE.pdf

22. Vargas-Vera, M., Motta, E., Domingue, J., Lanzoni, M., Arthur, S., Ciravegna, F.: MnM: Ontology Driven Semi-Automatic and Automatic Support for Semantic Markup. Proceedings of the 13th International Conference on Knowledge Engineering and Management, Siguenza, Spain (2002)

23. Gil, Y., Ratnakar, V.: TRELLIS: An Interactive Tool for Capturing Information Analysis and Decision Making. Proceedings of the 13th International Conference on Knowledge Engineering and Management, Siguenza, Spain (2002)

24. Annozilla (Annotea on Mozilla) (2003) http://annozilla.mozdev.org/

25. Bechhofer, S., Goble, C.: Towards Annotation using DAML+OIL. Presented at the First International Conference on Knowledge Capture, Victoria, B.C. (2001)

26. Venkatasubramani, S., Raman, R.K.V.S.: Annotations in Semantic Web. Proceedings of the Eleventh International World Wide Web Conference, Honolulu, Hawaii (2002)

# Metadata Editing by Schema

Hussein Suleman

Department of Computer Science, University of Cape Town
Private Bag, Rondebosch, 7701, South Africa
hussein@cs.uct.ac.za

**Abstract.** Metadata creation and editing is a reasonably well-understood task which involves creating forms, checking the input data and generating appropriate storage formats. XML has largely become the standard storage representation for metadata records and various automatic mechanisms are becoming popular for validation of these records, including XML Schema and Schematron. However, there is no standard methodology for creating data manipulation mechanisms. This work presents a set of guidelines and extensions to use the XML Schema standard for this purpose. The experiences and issues involved in building such a generalised structured data editor are discussed, to support the notion that metadata editing, and not just validation, should be description-driven.

## 1  Introduction

Editing of structured metadata over Web interfaces introduces complexities because of the fixed structure of standard HTML interfaces. A typical problem occurs when a metadata field is repeatable, as there is no simple way to duplicate a single field in a static HTML form. As an example of this, users may have multiple first names (e.g., Goolam Muhammad in Arabic), multiple last names (e.g., Guzman Aranda in Español) or both. In order for any metadata format to correctly capture information about individuals, there has to be flexibility in the data format as well as the input mechanism. Thus, the number of first names and last names should ideally be variable, without requiring data and providing a facility to add more fields of that type as needed.

This problem is exacerbated when there are nested metadata elements, e.g., a name element containing separate sub-elements for first and last names. If there are multiple names in addition to multiple first and last names, then the input mechanism must cater for repeatability at different levels within the metadata.

Many existing Web-based metadata tools, such as Meta builder [1] and DC-dot [2], use fixed formats for their input forms, thereby placing restrictions on the metadata format due solely to the input mechanism used. A general solution to this problem requires the creation or use of a general-purpose metadata specification language and a tool to interact with users to perform the required editing based on the specifications for metadata formats. Initial work was done in devising such a format in the Web Characterization Repository project [3].

T. Koch and I.T. Sølvberg (Eds.): ECDL 2003, LNCS 2769, pp. 82–87, 2003.

In that project, metadata formats for different types of resources (papers, tools, etc.) were specified in terms of tabular descriptions supporting only flat formats without nested elements. A similar technique was employed in the Mantis project [4] from OCLC, which used a Java applet to support modification of forms without additional server interaction. The Reggie and MetaEdit products from the MetaWeb project [5] also used Java applets and a home-grown format and XML DTDs respectively for field specification. More recently, the EPrints software [6] uses a home-grown field specification language to generate standard HTML forms when editing metadata.

With the emergence and growing popularity of the Open Archives Initiative's Protocol for Metadata Harvesting [7], an increasing number of digital library systems are using XML Schema [8] to define their metadata formats precisely. XML Schema is a declarative language to specify the format of XML files. For metadata formats encoded in XML, only a subset of the full XML Schema specification is required since metadata representations usually have a rigid structure.

It was hypothesised in this work that XML Schema can be used as the basis for a metadata description language that can drive a generalised editing process. The current trend towards writing XML Schema for existing and new metadata formats provides a ready backdrop against which to develop tools for data input to complement the schema-based validation tools used by the W3C (e.g., XSV [9]) and OAI (e.g., Repository Explorer [10]). Thus, any XML record created with such an editing tool can be validated using schema-based validation tools before being stored or processed further.

## 2   Interaction Model

In order to test this premise, the MDEdit Perl module was built to drive an editing process based on a subset of XML-Schema, augmented by elements of user interfaces. MDEdit uses plain vanilla HTML for its user interface. As a result of this, every change in the input form structure requires a client-server interaction. While this is not the most efficient operation, this approach was taken to illustrate that generalised metadata editing is still possible in the worst-case scenario where a browser has no advanced interactivity functionality. This is critical if such methods are to be employed on small form-factor devices such as PDAs and cellphones.

Fig 1 illustrates the interaction model employed by the MDEdit module. For new metadata records, MDEdit reads in the schema file and generates an HTML form from it with placeholders for minimal numbers of elements as specified by the schema. Alternatively, when a metadata record already exists, MDEdit will fill out the values already known when creating the form. Thereafter, while editing the values stored in the form, the user may request additional input elements for a single field or set of fields (as allowed by the schema). The server will then regenerate the form with additional input mechanisms inserted into the appropriate position, while still retaining all the data already entered. Finally, the user submits the form, and the server then checks that the number and type

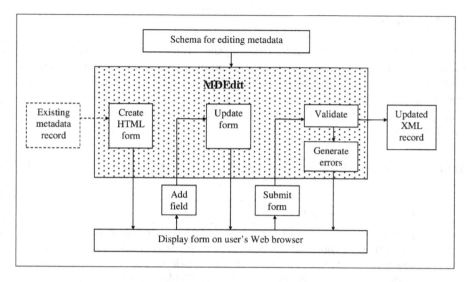

**Fig. 1.** Interaction between MDEdit, user, schema, and metadata record(s)

of each field and subfield conform to the schema. If there are errors, the form is regenerated with errors highlighted. If there are no errors, the data from the form is converted into an equivalent XML record, completing the process.

## 3 Data Types

MDEdit supports only a few data types of those available in the XML Schema standard, as these were deemed sufficient to provide input mechanisms for most popular metadata formats. The types MDEdit can operate on are:

- *string*
- *complexType*, containing a *sequence*
- *simpleType*, containing a *restriction* with *enumerations*

The following schema excerpt shows a possible general definition for names of people, with repeatability of elements at multiple levels of nesting, as discussed previously.

```
<element name="name" minOccurs="1" maxOccurs="unbounded">
  <complexType>
    <sequence>
      <element name="first"
          type="string" minOccurs="1" maxOccurs="unbounded"/>
      <element name="last"
          type="string" minOccurs="0" maxOccurs="unbounded"/>
    </sequence>
  </complexType>
</element>
```

# 4   Extensions

While XML Schema is sufficient for defining the structure of metadata, specifying the visual elements of a user interface (e.g., number of rows in a list box) requires additional information. According to the XML Schema standard, every element may have an an *appinfo* annotation containing tags specific to the application. This was exploited to define application-specific extensions, some of which are listed in Table 1.

**Table 1.** Sample of additional MDEdit schema tags to define appearance of HTML forms

| Tag | Description |
|---|---|
| <caption> | an alternate caption to use instead of the field name |
| <description> | an optional description of what the field is |
| <rows> | number of rows to use for the field display |
| <columns> | number of columns to use for the field display |
| <inputtype> | *password* – password entry box that displays * instead of characters |
| | *file* – file upload box |
| | *radio* – use radio buttons for list instead of <select> |

An example of an annotation to a schema using these extensions is as follows:

```
<element name="test" type="string">
   <annotation>
      <appinfo>
         <caption>Test Input Field</caption>
         <rows>40</rows>
      </appinfo>
   </annotation>
</element>
```

This example results is an input field in the HTML form with the text label *Test Input Field* and a text box 40 characters wide for data entry/editing.

# 5   Rendering

At each stage in the process, the internal representation of the data and type information is used to generate an equivalent HTML representation. The combination of schema type information, structural information and extensions is used to determine an appropriate and intuitive visual aspect and/or input device for each metadata field.

Fig 2 shows a typical HTML rendering of a simple annotated schema. The schema used to generate this interface can be found in [11].

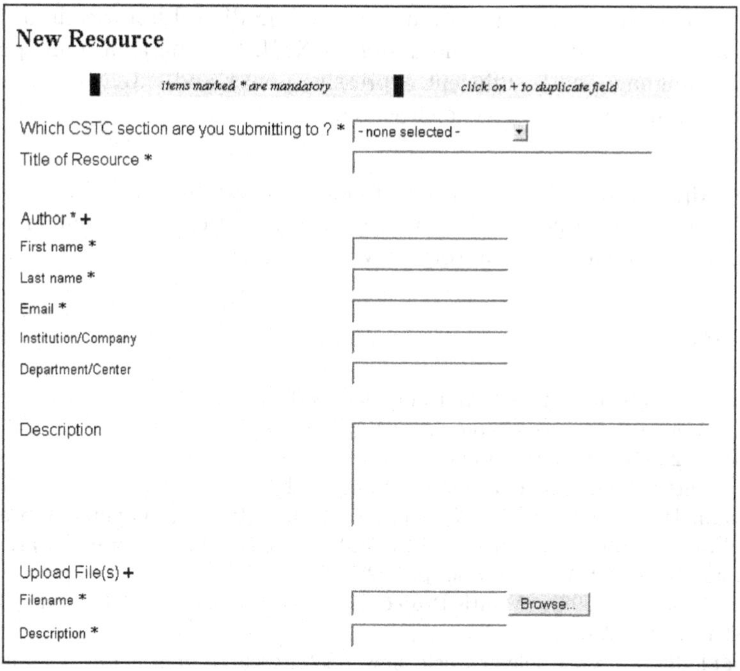

**Fig. 2.** Typical user interface generated by MDEdit

# 6   Analysis and Future Work

The MDEdit module has been used extensively while developing demonstrations of the Open Digital Library (ODL) [12] componentised model for building systems. Any loss of interactivity because of client-server communication is made up for by the generalisations possible because of the model and schema-driven nature of the tool. It has also been adopted for use on the website of the Networked Digital Library of Theses and Dissertations [13] to handle registrations of new members and addresses the problem that such registrations typically include varying numbers of individuals.

While the MDEdit tool is practically useful, it is more important as a demonstration of the principle that schema can be used to drive the process of metadata entry and editing. Various avenues remain to be explored in terms of such schema-driven metadata entry. These include:-

- extending existing tools to understand all aspects of the XML Schema specification, instead of just the subset used by MDEdit,
- investigating the feasability of serial entry drivers to create XML configuration files at a terminal, and
- using the User Interface Markup Language [14] as an intermediate representation so that the resulting interfaces can easily be retargeted to multiple devices.

While this project has implications for building digital libraries in a declarative fashion, it also vindicates the design of XML Schema as a multi-purpose descriptive language, with sufficient expressive power and extensibility to support functions beyond simple type-checking.

**Acknowledgements.** This work was funded in part by the US NSF (grant: 0002935) and was conducted while at and in conjunction with members of the Digital Library Research Laboratory at Virginia Tech.

# References

1. Vancouver Webpages (2003), Meta builder. Website
   http://vancouver-webpages.com/META/mk-metas.html
2. UKOLN (2003), DC-dot metadata editor.
   Website http://www.ukoln.ac.uk/metadata/dcdot/
3. Suleman, H., E. A. Fox and M. Abrams (2000), "Building Quality into a Digital Library", Proceedings of the Fifth ACM Conference on Digital Libraries, San Antonio, Texas, USA, June 2000, pp. 228–229.
4. Shafer, Keith E. (1998), "Mantis Project Provides a Toolkit for Cataloging", OCLC Newsletter, No. 236, pp.21–23.
   Available http://www.oclc.org/oclc/new/n236/research_mantis_project.htm
5. Distributed Systems Technology Centre (2003), The MetaWeb Project. Website
   http://www.dstc.edu.au/Research/Projects/metaweb/
6. Open Citation Project (2003), GNU EPrints 2.
   Website http://software.eprints.org/
7. Lagoze, Carl, Herbert Van de Sompel, Michael Nelson, and Simeon Warner (2002), The Open Archives Initiative Protocol for Metadata Harvesting – Version 2.0, Open Archives Initiative, June 2002. Available
   http://www.openarchives.org/OAI/2.0/openarchivesprotocol.htm
8. Fallside, David C. (editor) (2001), XML Schema Part 1: Structures and Part 2: Datatypes, W3C, 2 May 2001. Available http://www.w3.org/TR/xmlschema-1/ and http://www.w3.org/TR/xmlschema-2/
9. Thompson, Henry S., and Richard Tobin (2003), XML Schema Validator. Website http://www.ltg.ed.ac.uk/ ht/xsv-status.html
10. Suleman, Hussein (2001), "Enforcing Interoperability with the Open Archives Initiative Repository Explorer", in Proceedings of the ACM-IEEE Joint Conference on Digital Libraries, Roanoke, VA, USA, 24–28 June 2001, pp. 63–64.
11. Suleman, H. (2002), Open Digital Libraries, Ph.D. dissertation, Virginia Tech. Available http://scholar.lib.vt.edu/theses/available/etd-11222002-155624/
12. Suleman, Hussein, and Edward A. Fox (2001), "A Framework for Building Open Digital Libraries", in D-Lib Magazine, Vol. 7, No. 12, December 2001. Available http://www.dlib.org/dlib/december01/suleman/12suleman.html
13. Fox, Edward A. (2003), Networked Digital Library of Theses and Dissertations. Website http://www.ndltd.org
14. Phanouriou, Constantinos (2000), UIML: A Device-Independent User Interface Markup Language, Ph.D. dissertation, Virginia Polytechnic Institute and State University.

# Annotations: Enriching a Digital Library

Maristella Agosti and Nicola Ferro

Department of Information Engineering
University of Padua
Via Gradenigo, 6/B – 35131 Padova (PD) – Italy
{maristella.agosti, nicola.ferro}@unipd.it

**Abstract.** This paper presents the results of a study on the semantics of the concept of annotation. It specifically deals with annotations in the context of digital libraries. In the light of those considerations, general characteristics and features of an annotation service are introduced. The OpenDLib digital library is adopted as a framework of reference for our ongoing research, so the paper presents the annotations extension to the OpenDLib digital library, where the extension regards both the adopted document model and the architecture. The final part of the paper discusses and evaluates if OpenDLib has the expressive power of representing the presented semantics of annotations.

## 1 Introduction

This paper reports on a study on annotations conducted in the context of the *Technologies and Services for Enhanced Content Delivery* project, which is also known as *Enhanced Content Delivery*[1] (ECD). ECD is a research project launched by the Italian National Council of Research (CNR) in 2002 with the aim of developing methods and technologies for the enhanced delivery of contents to final users. Several academic, research, and industrial partners are participating nationwide on the project.

The final target of this research is to face in general the concept of annotation focusing on digital libraries services. General findings are then adapted to a specific digital library, such as OpenDLib, to demonstrate their use and validity.

The presentation of findings is structured as follows: Section 2 presents considerations on the semantics of the concept of annotation, this section constitutes the conceptual basis for the definition of the annotation service to be developed. Section 3 illustrates what are the aspects to be considered in annotating digital libraries. In Section 4 we briefly present OpenDLib, which is the reference digital library of ECD, Section 5 presents our proposal of extension of OpenDLib to support built-in annotations functionalities. Section 6 presents the architecture and the characteristics of the prototype annotation service. Finally, Section 7 reports some conclusions on the work.

---

[1] http://www-ecd.cnuce.cnr.it/

T. Koch and I.T. Sølvberg (Eds.): ECDL 2003, LNCS 2769, pp. 88–100, 2003.

## 2    Semantics of the Annotation Concept

The first part of the conducted study on annotations has been devoted to the analysis and understanding of the complex semantics which is behind the concept of annotation.

A lot of interesting research papers have been published over the years on this theme, see for example [7,8], where the viewpoint of understanding users' practice in annotating and of pointing out annotations patterns is addressed. Keeping in mind the previously published papers, we would like briefly to discuss the concept of annotation from a slightly different point of view, considering that the annotation is a concept which has been enriched and stratified in our cultural heritage with the passing of time.

If we look up the meaning of the following words: *annotation, gloss* and *note*, we can find that they are tightly connected with the concept of annotation itself. These words are used in order to express: explanation and clarification of words or passages of a text, therefore we can expounding on it, provide a commentary on it, and finally complete it with personal observations and ideas. We can form an opinion about the evolution and the rich semantics of the concept of annotation looking at the term gloss. The term gloss[2], at the time of the ancient Greeks, meant an obscure locution that required an additional explanation and it was also used as an explanation itself of words that were not clearly understood. While during the Middle Ages it meant an interlinear or marginal note to a biblical or juridical codex and also the collection of annotations of a glossarist; and we arrive today at its current meaning: note and annotation.

This brief description of the concept of annotation, together with the knowledge of previous research, helps us in understanding how its semantics can be complex and the role in which the concept of annotation is played out in our cultural heritage: annotations were not only a way of explaining and enriching a text with personal observations, but also a means of transmitting and sharing ideas about a concept.

We are interested in grasping and focusing our attention on three main aspects concerning the concept of annotation:

- *comprehension and study*: while studying, annotating a text is a way to investigate and understand a concept better. This process principally involves a private dimension, because the recipient of an annotation is the person who made it, although other people reading an annotated text could benefit from existing annotations;
- *interpretation and divulgation*: annotating a text could be a way of adding comments and explaining sentences of a text. The aim is to make it more comprehensible and to exchange ideas on a topic; an example could be an expert in literature who explains and annotates the Divine Comedy. This process principally involves a public dimension, because the recipients of an

---

[2] The ancient Greek word γλῶσσα (gloss) means language, idiom, spoken word, foreign or obsolete word or language.

annotation are people who are not necessarily related to the author of the annotation;

- *cooperation and revision*: a team of people could annotate a text for various purposes, as they are working on a common text or they are reviewing someone else's work; annotating a text is thus a way of sharing ideas and opinions in order to improve a text. This process principally involves a collective dimension, because the recipient of an annotation is a team of people working together on a given subject.

We can consider these three main aspects of annotation as a conceptual difference identified as *meaning of annotation*.

Even if these three main aspects of the concept of annotation are, in some way, similar to the dimensions of annotation as stated in [8], they differ because they are in fact different conceptual meanings of annotation. While dimensions of annotation are a categorization that reflects the form which they may take on.

Now that we have seen the main meanings of the concept of annotation, we have to investigate how they can appear and be represented. Basically there are three ways of representing the meaning of annotation:

- *textual sign*: is a textual materialization of the semantics of an annotation and it is expressed by a piece of text added to a document or a piece of a document;
- *graphic sign*: is the graphical materialization of the semantics of an annotation and it is expressed by a graphic mark added to a document or a piece of a document;
- *reference sign*: is the hypertextual materialization of the semantics of an annotation and it is expressed by a link between two texts.

The three basic ways, in which the meaning of annotation takes shape, can be called *sign of annotation*, keeping in mind that a sign is a formation of a meaning.

Those basic signs can be combined together to express more complex signs of annotation. For example if we take a textual sign, which is an additional explanation of a concept, it can also be combined with a type of mark, which is called a graphic sign, in order to highlight the content which it refers to, as shown in Figure 1(a). Another example could be a reference to another text, which is a reference sign, and it can be used with an arrow, which is a graphic sign. You will note that this arrow is pointing to the referred text; in addition it can be combined with a further explanation, which is a textual sign, as shown in Figure 1(b).

It is worth observing that the combination and compounding of those basic signs allows us express all the meanings of annotation, explained above: for example if a person is studying a document he simply can use a graphic sign to highlight the important content, and so the "comprehension and study" meaning of annotation can be expressed. During the revision of an article the author can use a graphic sign to delete an incorrect phrase, a textual sign is used to correct

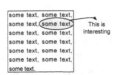
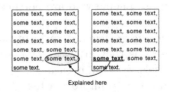

(a) Combination of a graphic and a textual sign.

(b) Combination of a reference, a graphic and a textual sign.

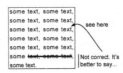

(c) Combination of basic signs to express revision.

**Fig. 1.** Combination of basic signs.

the phrase and a reference sign can be compounded with a graphic sign to indicate another piece of text justifying the correction he made, as shown in Figure 1(c). In conclusion the "cooperation and revision" meaning of annotation can be expressed in this way.

The semantic complexity of an annotation entails an intrinsic dualism between annotation as content enrichment or as a stand-alone document.

That twofold nature of the annotation is clear if we think about the process of studying a document: firstly, we can start annotating some interesting passages that require an in depth investigation, which is an annotation as content enrichment; then we can reconsider and collect our annotations and we can use them as a starting point for a new document, covering the points we would like to explain better[3], which is an annotation as a stand-alone document. In this case the annotation process can be seen as an informal, unstructured elaboration that could lead to a rethinking of the annotated document and to the creation of a new one.

---

[3] A famous annotation, which bewitched generations of mathematicians, is "I have discovered a truly remarkable proof which this margin is too small to contain", made by Fermat in the margin of Bachet's translation of Diophantus's *Arithmetica* and speaking about the famous Fermat's Last Theorem.

# 3    Annotation in the Context of a Digital Library

If we consider annotations in the context of digital libraries, this will call forth new possibilities which will enrich the semantics and expressive power of annotations. We can exploit the digital library by creating cross-linked annotations with a free flow of information between annotations and documents.

It is possible to have different layers of annotations on the same document: a private layer of annotations, which can be accessed only by the annotations author himself; a collective layer of annotations, shared by some users who are working on a document; finally a public layer of annotations, accessible to all users of the digital library. A digital library can encourage cooperative work practices, enabling the sharing of documents and annotations, also with the aid of special devices, such as XLibris [13]. Those themes are investigated and presented in detail in [7,11,9].

In the context of a digital library it is also possibile to create automatic annotations, which may help the user in approaching a document. Automatic annotations can be created using topic detection techniques to associate each annotation with its related topic, which forms the context of the annotation. In this way a document can be re-organized and segmented into topics, whose granularity can vary, and annotations can present a brief description of those topics. Then by applying automatic hypertext construction techniques, similar to those presented in [3], those pairs of topics and annotations can be linked together, proposing an alternative way of navigating the content of a digital library.

Finally, as suggested in [10,12], searching, reading and annotating a digital library can be done together with other activities, for example working with colleagues. This can also occur in a mobile context. Merging content and wireless communication can develop ubiquitous access to digital libraries, improving well established cooperative practices of work and exploiting physical and digital resources. The wireless context and the small form factor of handheld devices has challenged our technical horizons for information management and access. A detailed description of those themes can be found in [2].

On the whole this line of reasoning has two main aims:

– developing an in depth comprehension of the semantics of annotations;
– keeping in mind a list of features which a digital library should offer for supporting annotations.

# 4    OpenDLib and Its Representation of Documents

The Institute of Information Science and Technology (ISTI) of CNR of Pisa has recently designed a model of the architecture and services that enables us to design a digital library service. Based on those architectures and services a Digital Library Service System (DLSS) [1], named OpenDLib, has been developed [6].

OpenDLib is a software toolkit that can be used to create a digital library according to the requirements of a given user community, by instantiating the software appropriately and then either by loading or harvesting the content to be managed. At present OpenDLib provides a number of interoperating services that implement the basic functions of a digital library. The set of services is not fixed, but it can be extended to provide additional functionalities. To gain further information on the system and the ongoing project, the Web site of OpenDlib can be consulted[4].

The documents that can be used in OpenDLib have to conform to its document model. This model has been named *Document Model for Digital Library* (DoMDL) and it has been illustrated in [5,4]. DoMDL has the power to represent structured, multilingual and multimedia documents.

DoMDL is based on the following entities, which have been defined in [4]:

- *document*: represents the more general aspect of a document, i.e. the document as a distinct intellectual creation;
- *version*: represents a specific edition of the distinct intellectual creation, i.e. an instance along the time dimension;
- *view*: models a specific intellectual expression of an edition of a document. A view excludes physical aspects that are not integral to the intellectual perception of a document. The entity View is specialized in two sub-entities: Metadata and Content. The former view perceives a version through the conceptualizations given by its metadata representations; the latter is the view of the document content. Content has two sub-entities: Body, and Reference. The Body entity represents a view of the document content that can be either perceived as a whole or as the aggregation of other views. A Reference entity represents a view which is equal to the one that has already been registered and does not need to be explicitly stored;
- *manifestation*: models the physical formats under which a document is disseminated.

DoMDL becomes a central starting point for the research that has to be conducted on an annotation service, since it becomes the document reference model in consideration, therefore DoMDL has been investigated and analysed. We have developed and sketched an example of DoMDL, that can help in understanding its main features.

In Fig. 2 the example of DoMDL for a document of thesis type is shown. We can observe that:

- we have a document, called "Thesis";
- this document has two versions, one is called "Draft", the other is called "Final". The final version has some bibliographic metadata, represented in the view named "Bibdata". This view has a manifestation, which refers to the file dcq_final.xml, and this is actually where the bibliographic records for the thesis are stored;
- the draft version of the thesis is organized into parts and chapters, represented respectively by the views "Parts" and "Chapters". There are two

---

[4] http://www.opendlib.com/

parts, "Part 1" and "Part 2". We can see that "Part 1" contains two chapters "Chapter 1" and "Chapter 2", that are the same chapters contained in the view "Chapters". So we do not have to duplicate these views, but we put a *reference* in the view "Parts" to the views "Chapter 1" and "Chapter 2" contained in the view "Chapters". The view "Chapter 2" has many different manifestations, i.e. `chapter2.ps`, `chapter2.tex` and `ftp://.../chapter2.pdf`, and some metadata, represented by the view "Metadata Chapter 2" and stored in the manifestation `dc_chapter2.xml`;

– the final version of the thesis is organized into chapters, view "Chapters", and we can notice that the second chapter, view "Chapter 2", has not changed from the draft version, so we can make a *reference* to its manifestation `chapter2.tex`.

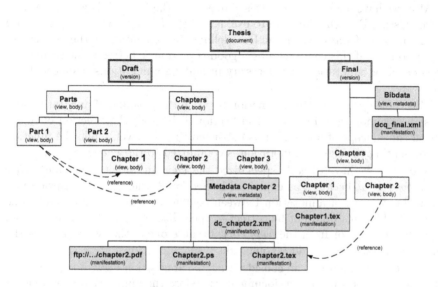

**Fig. 2.** Example of DoMDL.

## 5  The Annotation and the OpenDLib Digital Library

According to the constructs of DoMDL, annotations are modelled in two levels: the first level is representing the annotation as another kind of view, so the DoMDL is extended, containing not only a *metadata view* and a *body view* but also an *annotation view*; the second level is representing the annotation as a *manifestation*.

This extension of the model is consistent with the approach taken in defining the DoMDL, preserving the way of representing the structure of a document and of its metadata. So the DoMDL comes out seamlessly extended and this way of extending the DoMDL could be used as an example of transparent addition of new features to the DoMDL.

Furthermore the actual content of an annotation can be stored in the *Repository*, which is the storage service of OpenDLib, and can be modelled in the same way as any other manifestation of a document. This means that also annotations can benefit from all those features, such as delivering, dissemination, transcoding, that standard documents of OpenDLib benefit from. This extension also maintains the possibility of creating *references* in order to avoid the duplication of information.

Finally this choice of representing and storing annotations give us the possibility of exploiting the search functionalities already implemented in OpenDLib. Indeed the annotation is seen as any other part of the structure of a document in OpenDLib. Therefore it can be searched as any other document in OpenDLib.

After we have made sure that this extension of the DoMDL is well integrated in the existing DoMDL, we have to evaluate if the DoMDL offers us a powerful enough means of representing and modelling the semantics of the concept of annotation and if this choice can be a good compromise between the richness of the concept of annotation and necessity of making annotations manageable by a software.

This choice preserves the distinction between the meaning of annotation and the sign of annotation, introduced in Section 2, because the function of representing the concept of annotation is entrusted to *view* level, while the function of representing the sign of annotation is committed to the *manifestation* level.

Note that we have directly specialized the *view* and not the *metadata view* or the *body view*, because, as explained in Section 2, there is an intrinsic dualism in the concept of annotation between content enrichment and stand-alone document. Thus it would not be correct to specialize the annotation either from the *metadata view* or from the *body view*, because one of the two aspects of the concept of annotation would be omitted.

On the other hand we can consider that the annotation view models the link between an annotation and a document, therefore the annotation view renders the annotation as content enrichment, while the annotation manifestation renders the annotations as stand-alone document. This is not contrary to what has been explained above, because the annotation view is neither a metadata nor a body view, which would have forced the annotation to be either a content enrichment or a stand-alone document, but only maintains the possibility of having a link between an annotation and a document.

Furthermore many of these annotation manifestations can be included in the same annotation view and this renders the compounding of signs of annotations, which is the basic mechanism in order to express the meaning of annotation, illustrated in Section 2.

Finally this representation of annotation allows us to easily manage both threads of annotations, i.e. an annotation made in response or comment to another annotation, because we simply nest an annotation view into another, as it is naturally done with DoMDL, and sets of annotation, i.e. a bundle of annotations on the same passage of text, because we simply put all the annotation views in the view of the passage of text or the annotation they refer to.

So we can conclude that this extension to the DoMDL fairly represents the semantic of an annotation, discussed in Section 2.

Figure 3 reports an example of the extended DoMDL. We can observe that:

- we have added an annotation to the whole final version, represented by the view named "Annotation 1", whose content is stored in the manifestation ann1_final.xml.
- also "Chapter 2" as an annotation, represented by the view named "Annotation 2" and stored in the manifestation annotation2.xml, but this annotation is shared with "Chapter 1", so we can put a *reference* to it.
- on "Annotation 2" there is a "discussion thread", because there is another nested annotation, represented by the view named "Annotation 3" and stored in the manifestation annotation2.xml. Notice that by means of the *reference* also "Chapter 1" is linked to the "discussion thread" on "Annotation 2".

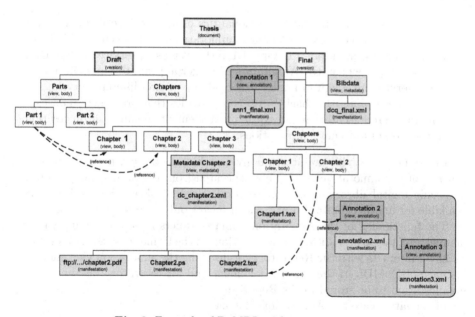

**Fig. 3.** Example of DoMDL with annotations.

## 6   OpenDLib Architecture and Annotation Service

The OpenDLib architecture has been introduced in [6,4], the reader interested in gaining an in depth understanding of the architecture is invited to refer to those papers. Since we work to develop a prototype annotation service for extending the OpenDLib digital library, we have choosen to extend its architecture as depicted in Figure 4 where the general architecture of this service is shown.

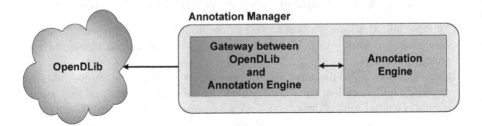

**Fig. 4.** Architecture of the Annotation Service in OpenDlib.

The service has been named *Annotation Manager* and it is organized in two blocks:

- *gateway*: this server provides functionalities of mediator between the back-end server, which creates and manages annotations, and the OpenDLib federation. From the standpoint of OpenDLib this is a usual service of OpenDLib and so, on the whole, the Annotation Manager appears to OpenDLib as an usual service, although in reality it is made up of two different servers;
- *annotation engine*: this back-end server provides the core functionalities of annotation representation, annotation management and annotation creation, in the case of automatic annotations.

Please note that this architecture gives us high flexibility, because the core features of the annotation service are separated from the actual integration in a specific digital library. This architectural decision allows the service to be available for another digital library, which means only creating a new gateway.

The functioning of the Annotation Manager differs if we are dealing with a manual annotation or a automatic annotation. In the former case the Annotation Manager interacts with the Repository for inserting the annotation view into the instance of DoMDL of the desired document and for returning the annotation manifestation to be stored in the Repository.

In the latter case the Annotation Manager:

- requests and receives the manifestation of a document from the *Repository*;
- elaborates and indexes the received document and creates the annotation, representing it with an annotation view and an annotation manifestation;
- returns to the Repository the annotation view to be inserted into the DoMDL and the manifestation of the annotation.

The annotation view is going to contain all data that are necessary to link the annotation view itself, stored in the Repository, with the information about the annotation, stored in the Annotation Manager. It needs to be noted that the last item of the previous list is also the same as the manual annotation case.

The annotation creation process is shown in Fig. 5(a) and the relationships between the different objects are show in Fig. 5(b).

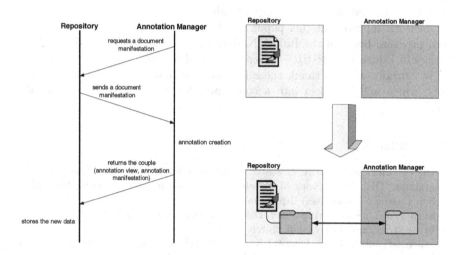

(a) Annotation creation process.

(b) The *Repository* and the *Annotation Manager* before and after the creation of an annotation.

**Fig. 5.** Creation and management of annotations.

A final remark: the chosen way of inserting the annotation service in the architecture of OpenDLib is a good choice, because it enables all of the features described in Section 3 to be feasible. Furthermore it is flexible enough to be extended in supporting particular apparatuses, such as XLibris, and handheld devices.

# 7   Conclusion

We have presented in this paper our findings on a general study on annotations and on relevant aspects of designing and developing an innovative service for annotating a digital library. The work is conducted in the context of the ECD national ongoing project which is due to be completed by the end of 2004. By then the final annotation service is going to be released.

**Acknowledgements.** Sincere thanks are due to Massimo Melucci, of the Department of Information Engineering of the University of Padua, for the time he spent with the authors in discussing the aspects related to annotations and their automatic construction.

The authors wish to thank Fausto Rabitti, co-ordinator of ECD activities related to the area of the ECD project devoted to digital libraries for his support. Daniela Castelli and Pasquale Pagano, of ISTI of CNR of Pisa, deserve a special thanks, because they have spent their time in introducing to the authors all of necessary and relevant aspects of OpenDLib.

The work reported in this paper has been conducted in the context of a joined program between the Italian National Research Council (CNR) and the Ministry of Education (MIUR), under the law 449/97-99.

The authors wish to thank the anonymous reviewers for their useful comments, which will be taken into account also for future developments of the work.

# References

[1] Digital Libraries: Future Research Directions for a European Research Programme. DELOS Network of Excellence Brainstorming Workshop, June 2001, San Cassiano (Dolomites), Italy. Online
http://delos-noe.iei.pi.cnr.it/activities/researchforum/
Brainstorming/, last visited March 14, 2003.

[2] M. Agosti and N. Ferro. Chapter X: Managing the Interactions between Handheld Devices, Mobile Applications, and Users. In E. P. Lim and K. Siau, editors, *Advances in Mobile Commerce Technologies*, pages 204–233. Idea Group, Hershey, USA, 2003.

[3] M. Agosti and M. Melucci. Information Retrieval Techniques for the Automatic Construction of Hypertext. In A. Kent and C.M. Hall, editors, *Encyclopedia of Library and Information Science*, volume 66, pages 139–172. Marcel Dekker, New York, USA, 2000.

[4] D. Castelli and P. Pagano. A Flexible Repository Service: the OpenDLib solution. In J. Á. Carvalho, A. Hübler, and A. A. Baptista, editors, *Proc. 6th International ICCC/IFIP Conference on Electronic Publishing (Elpub 2002)*, pages 194–202. Verlag für Wissenschaft und Forschung, Berlin, 2002.

[5] D. Castelli and P. Pagano. Foundations of a Multidimensional Query Language for Digital Libraries. In M. Agosti and C. Thanos, editors, *Proc. 6th European Conference on Research and Advanced Technology for Digital Libraries (ECDL 2002)*, pages 251–265. Lecture Notes in Computer Science (LNCS) 2458, Springer, Berlin, 2002.

[6] D. Castelli and P. Pagano. OpenDLib: a Digital Library Service System. In M. Agosti and C. Thanos, editors, *Proc. 6th European Conference on Research and Advanced Technology for Digital Libraries (ECDL 2002)*, pages 292–308. Lecture Notes in Computer Science (LNCS) 2458, Springer, Berlin, 2002.

[7] C. C. Marshall. Annotation: from Paper Books to the Digital Library. In R. B. Allen and E. Rasmussen, editors, *Proc. 2nd International Conference on Digital Libraries (DL 97)*, pages 233–240. ACM Press, New York, 1997.

[8] C. C. Marshall. Toward an ecology of hypertext annotation. In R. Akscyn, editor, *Proc. ACM Conference on Hypertext and Hypermedia: links, objects, time and space—structure in hypermedia systems*, pages 40–49. ACM Press, New York, 1998.

[9] C. C. Marshall and A. J. B. Brush. From Personal to Shared Annotations. In L. Terveen and D. Wixon, editors, *Proc. Conference on Human Factors and Computing Systems (CHI 2002) – Extended Abstracts on Human factors in Computer Systems*, pages 812–813. ACM Press, New York, 2002.

[10] C. C. Marshall, G. Golovchinsky, and M. N. Price. Digital Libraries and Mobility. *Communications of the ACM*, 44:55–56, 2001.

[11] C. C. Marshall, M. N. Price, G. Golovchinsky, and B.N. Schilit. Introducing a Digital Library Reading Appliance into a Reading Group. In N. Rowe and E. A. Fox, editors, *Proc. 4th International Conference on Digital Libraries (DL 99)*, pages 77–84. ACM Press, New York, 1999.

[12] C. C. Marshall and C. Ruotolo. Reading-in-the-Small: A Study of Reading on Small Form Factor Devices. In W. Hers and G. Marchionini, editors, *Proc. 2nd ACM/IEEE-CS Joint Conference on Digital Libraries (JCDL 2002)*, pages 56–64. ACM Press, New York, 2002.

[13] B. N. Schilit, M. N. Price, and G. Golovchinsky. Digital Library Information Appliances. In I. Witten, R. Akscyn, and F. M. III Shipman, editors, *Proc. 3rd International Conference on Digital Libraries (DL 98)*, pages 217–226. ACM Press, New York, 1998.

# Identifying Useful Passages in Documents Based on Annotation Patterns

Frank Shipman[2], Morgan Price[1], Catherine C. Marshall[3], and Gene Golovchinsky[1]

[1]FX Palo Alto Laboratory
3400 Hillview Avenue, Building 4, Palo Alto, CA 94304
gene@fxpal.com

[2]Department of Computer Science, Texas A&M University
College Station, TX 77843-3112
shipman@cs.tamu.edu

[3]Microsoft Corporation
1 Microsoft Way, Redmond, WA 98052
cathymar@microsoft.com

**Abstract.** Many readers annotate passages that are important to their work. If we understand the relationship between the types of marks on a passage and the passage's ultimate utility in a task, then we can design e-book software to facilitate access to the most important annotated parts of the documents. To investigate this hypothesis and to guide software design, we have analyzed annotations collected during an earlier study of law students reading printed case law and writing Moot Court briefs. This study has allowed us to characterize the relationship between the students' annotations and the citations they use in their final written briefs. We think of annotations that relate directly to the written brief as *high-value annotations*; these annotations have particular, detectable characteristics. Based on this study we have designed a mark parser that analyzes freeform digital ink to identify such high-value annotations.

## 1   Introduction

We read for many reasons: we read for fun; we read for general knowledge; and we read with a particular task in mind. When we read for fun, we seldom annotate; but when we read material crucial to a particular task, our annotations may cover its pages. In fact, a diary study of reading found that over a quarter of the writing that occurs during work-related reading is in the form of annotations, marks on top of existing documents [1]. Annotations may perform a variety of functions; for example, they may emphasize a particular point in the document, express a reaction, compare the text to other texts, record a related idea, or generate action items.

We are investigating methods for identifying important passages in an annotated document; as O'Hara and Sellen suggest, these passages may then be used in related activities such as writing or re-reading the document [6]. Just as readers use the table of contents, indices, and document structure to orient themselves during a first pass through the material, their annotations may be used for orientation during re-reading.

T. Koch and I.T. Sølvberg (Eds.): ECDL 2003, LNCS 2769, pp. 101–112, 2003.

In a past study, we examined how law students read and annotated printed source materials to prepare for a Moot Court competition, a venue in which the students argue hypothetical cases. The previous study used the results of interviews and observations to characterize the students' general reading and annotation practices [5]. At the conclusion of that study, we collected the law students' written legal briefs and the case law they printed from the legal information services to do their legal research; we used this material informally at the time to verify what the students had said in interviews about their annotation practices. In this study, we focus in greater detail on these extensive materials to better understand how the students' annotations contributed to the text of the briefs they wrote for Moot Court. The next section presents the study method and identifies specific types of annotation marks and their frequency near passages later used in the written brief. Based on these patterns, we have designed and developed a mechanism to identify, categorize, group, and rank annotations. We describe this mechanism, the mark parser, which was integrated into XLibris [8], and discuss how it can support readers in using their high-value annotations in subsequent writing tasks.

## 2    Relationship between Annotation and Use

Legal briefs are written arguments that present one side's point of view in a legal case within the context of legal precedent. In the US, legal precedent is set by cases, published accounts of the facts and outcomes of legal rulings. Thus, students' writings refer to many prior cases — pointing out the similarities to and differences from the current case — to bolster their arguments. These references are in the form of quotations and citations.

Analysis of the students' legal briefs and the corresponding annotated court cases can yield insight into how different types of annotation were used to identify potential quotations and citations. Students used their annotations in other ways, such as reusing the structure of an argument, but in this analysis we focus on the connection between annotated passages, and quotations and citations used in the briefs. Reuse of references to annotated passages in writing is a conservative estimate of the utility of the annotations.

We spent a three month period observing the complete Moot Court process, from the initial period of instruction through the students' research and writing to the final mock courtroom presentation of competing oral arguments. During this period of time, we conducted a series of in-depth semi-structured contextual interviews of nine of the students who participated in the competition and the two faculty members and two third year law students who organized it. After the competition had ended, we collected the students' completed legal briefs and the printed-out cases they had read and annotated while they were doing their research. In [5] we mainly relied on field notes from the observations, full transcriptions from the interviews, and a set of digital photos to report important qualitative findings about legal research as it is conducted in this kind of heterogeneous information environment; we also describe how we used these findings to redesign an evolving tablet computer-based e-book prototype, XLibris. The earlier study thus forms a backdrop for the more detailed investigation of the particular aspect of the law students' practice we discuss here: how readers – the law students – used their annotated source materials – the printed cases – in a writing task, composing a legal brief.

The study described in this paper is based on materials collected from seven students. The documents include each student's final brief and the printed cases the student read in preparing the brief. Each student wrote approximately 20 double-spaced pages and used from 46 to 105 legal references/citations. In addition to gathering and printing cases from the two online legal information services, Westlaw and Lexis, the students used textbooks, books in the library, and read online. As a consequence not all of the cases the students read and cited were available for our study. Thus our analysis is limited to the collection of those cases printed out on loose paper. According to the data gathered in our earlier interviews, these were generally the most recent cases and, for most students, were the most highly cited and relevant cases. Table 1 summarizes the number of documents collected, the number of citations in the student's brief, and the number of those citations that were to collected documents.

**Table 1.** Number of collected source documents and the percentage of student citations to them.

|   |   | Brief 1 | Brief 2 | Brief 3 | Brief 4 | Brief 5 | Brief 6 | Brief 7 |
|---|---|---------|---------|---------|---------|---------|---------|---------|
| A | # of collected source documents | 16 | 11 | 20 | 13 | 21 | 10 | 27 |
| B | Total # of citations | 54 | 59 | 46 | 46 | 105 | 67 | 99 |
| C | Citations to collected source documents | 36 67% | 45 76% | 32 70% | 46 100% | 80 76% | 23 34% | 94 95% |

## 2.1   From Citation to Source

The first detailed analysis of the documents identified the types of marks associated with passages that were subsequently used in the writing of the legal brief. In this analysis we looked at all citations in a brief and went back to locate the cited passage to see if and how it was annotated. For example, one brief included the statement:

> "The court in Vernonia stated that the 'most significant element' of the case was that the drug testing program 'was undertaken in furtherance of the government's responsibilities, under a public school system, as guardian and tutor of children entrusted to its care.' Vernonia, 515 U.S. at 664."

This citation comes from the annotated passage shown in Figure 1. We take a passage to be the identifiable region with which an annotation is associated.

Table 2 shows the number of citations in each brief that refer to documents collected in the study and the number of those citations where the passage in the original document was marked in a particular way. Places where a cited passage was marked in more than one way, such as with highlighter and a comment, have been included in the value for all applicable rows (e.g. highlight, comment, and multiple mark types). The

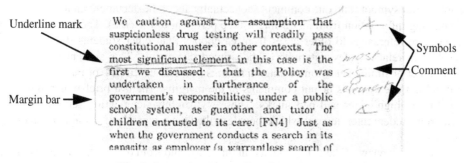

**Fig. 1.** Annotations on section of case document.

rows starting with "highlight" are all subsets of the "marked in any way" set and indicate how many marks of that type were used. For example, the citation of the passage in Figure 1 is included in five counts for this brief: Marked in any way, Comment, Underline, Symbol, and Margin bar. These types of marks are based on opaque digital ink; highlights are similar to underlines using translucent ink and circles are looped text in either opaque or translucent ink — the bottom of a circle can be seen at the top of Figure 1.

**Table 2.** Number of citations and types of annotation on cited passages for each student.

|  | Brief 1 | Brief 2 | Brief 3 | Brief 4 | Brief 5 | Brief 6 | Brief 7 |
|---|---|---|---|---|---|---|---|
| Citations to collected source documents (row C in Table 1) | 36 | 45 | 32 | 46 | 80 | 23 | 94 |
| Unmarked | 8 | 8 | 27 | 5 | 78 | 10 | 26 |
| Marked in any way | 28 | 37 | 5 | 41 | 2 | 13 | 68 |
| Highlight | 27 | 1 | 0 | 35 | 0 | 10 | 43 |
| Comment | 3 | 14 | 0 | 11 | 1 | 0 | 23 |
| Symbol | 8 | 4 | 0 | 7 | 1 | 0 | 5 |
| Underline | 1 | 5 | 4 | 1 | 0 | 2 | 5 |
| Circle | 0 | 17 | 0 | 5 | 0 | 1 | 0 |
| Margin bar | 0 | 14 | 1 | 0 | 0 | 0 | 18 |
| Multiple mark types | 12 | 18 | 0 | 17 | 0 | 0 | 25 |

We can characterize the varying annotation styles of the seven students by looking at their papers and by the data in Table 2 above. The first brief writer used highlighters and symbols to code the documents as he read them. The second brief writer did not use highlighter, but instead used circles or margin bars and wrote comments in the margins of the documents. The third writer made few marks — 22 total passages across 20 cases. The fourth writer frequently combined highlighting and comments in the margin for areas of particular interest. The fifth writer made very few marks on the papers: four symbols and one comment (not actually about the document annotated but containing information from an on-line source pertinent to the case). The sixth writer used more references to older cases from casebooks than other students did, which resulted in relatively few citations to the printed documents. This student used the highlighter or similar selection-oriented markings (underlines, circles, or margin bars), but did not use symbols or put comments in the margins. The last brief writer annotated using highlighter and pen marks. These stylistic characterizations confirm the data from student interviews in which they described their general annotation practices (see [5]).

From our review of the data collected in this study and from other related studies of annotation [4, 6, 9], we have observed clear stylistic differences in how people annotate. Some people prefer to highlight; some underline or circle; and some use margin bars, comments, and symbols. Despite all these differences, we can distinguish two general categories of annotators: those for whom annotation is a common practice (the "happy highlighters," students 1, 2, 4, and 7), and those for whom it is the exception (the "meager markers," students 3 and 5). Note that student 6 falls in between these two categories; in practice the two categories are actually stereotypes at the extremes of a continuum.

## 2.2   From Source to Citation

We now look at how frequently the students created single and multiple annotations for a passage. Table 3 summarizes readers' annotations of the source materials.

**Table 3.** Documents, pages, passages marked, and passages multimarked per student.

|  | Brief 1 | Brief 2 | Brief 3 | Brief 4 | Brief 5 | Brief 6 | Brief 7 |
|---|---|---|---|---|---|---|---|
| # source documents (row A in Table 1) | 16 | 11 | 20 | 13 | 21 | 10 | 27 |
| # marked documents | 15<br>*94%* | 11<br>*100%* | 2<br>*10%* | 13<br>*100%* | 2<br>*10%* | 7<br>*70%* | 22<br>*81%* |
| total # of pages in marked documents | 279 | 178 | 36 | 331 | 78 | 231 | 608 |
| # pages with marks | 148<br>*53%* | 98<br>*55%* | 8<br>*22%* | 102<br>*31%* | 3<br>*4%* | 69<br>*30%* | 219<br>*36%* |
| # marked passages | 552 | 325 | 22 | 311 | 5 | 159 | 688 |
| passages marked per page marked | 3.73 | 3.32 | 2.75 | 3.05 | 1.67 | 2.30 | 3.14 |
| # multimarked passages | 83 | 59 | 1 | 75 | 0 | 10 | 172 |
| % of marked passages multimarked | 15% | 18% | 5% | 24% | 0 | 6% | 25% |

The happy highlighters annotated (marked in any way) between 81 and 100% of their source documents; by contrast, two of the meager markers only annotated 10%

while student 6 annotated 70% of her source documents. Among the 1741 total pages of marked-up source documents, there were 647 marked pages with annotations on 2062 passages. Again, the happy highlighters marked a higher percentage of pages in their documents and had more passages marked per page than the meager markers. Where the happy highlighters really stood apart was in the use of multiple marks for a single passage. They had between 59 and 172 such passages in their source materials where the other students had between 0 and 10.

## 2.3  Discussion

One confounding factor in this analysis is we do not know how many times each document was read and whether the students annotated the documents during the first or a subsequent reading. While the annotations were still next to cited passages, it is possible the students remarked the passages while writing the brief; thus any mechanism we designed based on our analysis would apply only to re-reading or re-use of the materials for a similar task. However, during interviews with the students, they described re-reading key cases while they were outlining or writing. One student reported that she would go over her annotations during a second reading pass and put an asterisk by the important ones [5].

A second issue is whether the results from this specific annotation task can be generalized to inform the design of annotation systems. In particular, do people generally annotate heavily enough to imply value in algorithms for locating high-value annotations? While the writing task was different, O'Hara and Sellen's subjects describe annotation practices similar to those seen here [6].

# 3   Annotation Patterns and Useful Passages

In spite of the students' stylistic idiosyncrasies, this study indicates that there may be some simple methods for using mark grouping and type information to select passages that were relatively likely to be used in the students' writing task.

As a first pass, we look at the how selecting passages with any mark at all or just those passages that are multimarked might have helped these students. To do this we compare the measures of recall and precision for these two passage selection criteria. First, we define recall and precision measures based on percent of passages cited in the students' briefs that were annotated with any mark in the source materials. Second, we define recall and precision measures based on percent of passages cited in the students' briefs that were annotated in the source materials with multiple marks of different types, such as margin bar and comment, or circled passage and highlighted phrase. In the following discussion we refer to such sets of marks as multimarks. These measures were chosen to allow us to compare the relative utility of these criteria for sparse marking patterns, as well as for dense marking patterns (our so-called meager markers and happy highlighters). Table 4 summarizes these measures across all of the briefs.

By comparing the frequencies of cited passages that were annotated, we can evaluate different algorithms for locating useful passages based on annotation. For briefs 1,

**Table 4.** Recall and precision rates for passages with any mark and passages with multiple marks

|  | Happy Highlighters | | | | | Meager Markers | |
|---|---|---|---|---|---|---|---|
|  | Brief 1 | Brief 2 | Brief 4 | Brief 7 | Brief 6 | Brief 3 | Brief 5 |
| Mark recall | 78% | 82% | 89% | 72% | **56%** | **16%** | **3%** |
| Mark precision | 5% | 11% | 13% | 10% | **8%** | **23%** | **20%** |
| Multimark recall | **33%** | **40%** | **37%** | **27%** | 0% | 0% | 0% |
| Multimark precision | **14%** | **31%** | **23%** | **15%** | 0% | 0% | -- |

2, 4, and 7 (the happy highlighters), 14%, 31%, 23%, and 15% of the passages with multiple marks were cited by students. This is the precision score for using multiple marks on a passage as a selection criterion. For students 3 and 5 (the meager markers), 23% and 20% of the passages marked in any way were later cited. It is evident that the happy highlighters and meager markers achieve comparable precision scores with multimarks and single marks, respectively. But student 6, who was in between the happy highlighters and the meager markers in annotation practice, ends up with only an 8% precision rate when using marks for retrieval and 0% when using multimarks.

Figure 2 presents another view of the precision and recall figures for cited passages in each brief. Precision percentage is calculated as the percent of marked or multimarked passages actually cited. The table shows that to maximize precision, we should use multimarks when they are sufficiently frequent (i.e. the ratio from Table 3 exceeds 0.1). In Table 4, bold indicates the initial method best suited for selecting useful passages. The choice of single vs. multiply marked passages makes these heuristics sensitive to the readers' predisposition to marking.

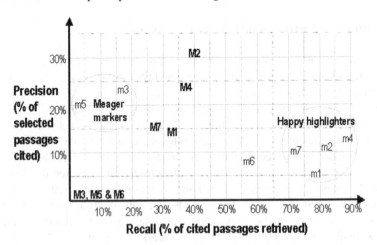

**Fig. 2.** Precision and recall graph for selecting any mark (m) versus selecting multimarks (M) for the seven students.

Figure 2 shows the two clusters of students ("happy highlighters" and "meager markers") with the selection methods performing significantly different for the two groups. This clustering has led us to develop a simple annotation-style user model for determining the appropriate selection and emphasis criteria.

On one hand, the precision and recall rates are seemingly low, raising questions of their ultimate utility. These rates may be explained by the fact that the students' marks are not universally geared toward writing. On the other hand, detecting these patterns presents an opportunity to implement the annotation-based facilities we describe in this paper. It may be that these rates are sufficient to implement useful functionality, and will serve to reinforce this aspect of annotative practice.

In some cases, e.g. briefs 1, 6, and 7, our mark/multimark selection heuristic yields too many potentially important passages; and therefore is insufficiently selective for our purposes. Thus, while selecting multimarks first and then marks is likely to provide some benefit, further discrimination is required. One way to improve our heuristic is to develop a method of ranking the marked passages. We discuss such a method in the next section.

## 4    Grouping, Typing, and Computing the Emphasis of Annotation Marks

Based on the analysis of annotation and citation patterns in legal briefs, we found a common set of base annotation types. There are two main categories of annotation types: selection marks such as highlighting, underlining, circling, and margin bars that identify a document passage, and interpretative marks such as comments and symbols that respond to the content. Of course, the roles of these two classes of marks are not completely distinct, since the act of selecting text out of a body is an interpretive act and marginalia naturally select text nearby as the focus of attention.

These observations led us to design and implement a mark parser that identifies structure and emphasis in pen stroke information of a reading appliance like XLibris [8]. The mark parser categorizes groups of marks into annotation types and constructs a passage-based grouping of annotations to identify high-emphasis sections of the document.

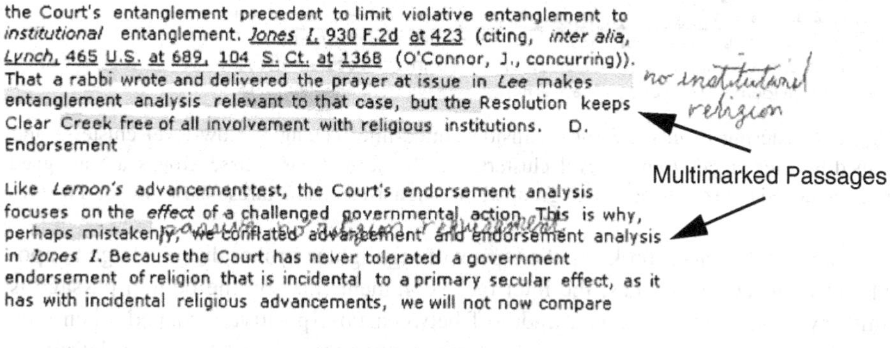

**Fig. 3.** Multimarked text from XLibris.

To illustrate how the parser works, we will use the text and annotations from Figure 3. In this example our goal is to detect that the red ink marks are comments attached to the same passage as the neighboring highlighter marks. This would mark the two passages as multimarked and provide relative weightings of perceived emphasis (emphasis values) for comparing these and other marked passages.

The mark parser consists of a three-pass process of grouping, typing, and ranking the relative importance of reader marks. The first pass of the parser clusters the time-ordered marks into low-level groups based on time, distance, and pen type. This combines the individual pen strokes into clusters that are considered a single annotation.

The parser's first pass uses a function of temporal and spatial distance to determine breaks in the grouping of marks similar to that in Dynomite [2]. The algorithm includes pen-type differences (i.e., highlighter vs. ink) in computing the temporal and spatial gaps within the stroke sequence, since highlighters and pens are used differently in annotation. Practically, XLibris data demonstrates that temporal gaps between related marks (such as those strokes constituting a written annotation) are larger when using the pen than the highlighter. We speculate that readers may reflect more when they write interpretive comments and symbols than when they simply highlight a passage. The first stage of the parser also groups pen strokes that represent contiguous, but spatially distinct marks such as multi-line comments. This process results in a one or two level hierarchical clustering of marks into groups, as shown in the dotted and dashed regions in Figure 4. The dashed lines in Figure 4 indicate the results of this first stage. The dotted line regions are the results of the temporal and spatial clustering when multiple clusters are grouped together as being part of a single mark.

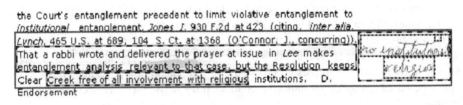

**Fig. 4.** Clustering results are shown inside dotted-line rectangles (low-level clusters) and dashed-line rectangles (higher-level clusters). In the second pass, these groups are assigned types, attached to text passages, and grouped into higher-level structures (shown as solid lines).

Note that the parser broke up the top set of highlighter strokes due to a large temporal gap between the strokes; the interlinear comment (ink) on the bottom passage is similarly broken up. There is a trade-off between false-positive (grouped when they should not be) and false-negative (not grouped when they should be) when defining a boundary in spatial/temporal clustering. Because the later passes of the mark parser combine clusters into higher-level structures, we have adopted a conservative strategy that produces more clusters. These smaller clusters are likely to be grouped in subsequent passes of the mark parser.

The second pass categorizes the mark clusters into annotation types using the pen type, the number of component marks, and the size and shape of the extent of the cluster. In the example in Figure 4, the six higher level clusters (shown in dashed-line rectangles) include three highlight annotations and three comment annotations.

Stroke types are based on pen type, the number of overlapping words, and the stroke's shape. For example, clusters composed of five or more pen marks (as opposed to highlighter marks) are considered comments. When the clusters are categorized, emphasis values are also assigned; the emphasis values are heuristic assessments of the relative importance of the annotation types.

There are three basic emphasis values assigned to the mark clusters. These values are based on two design guidelines. First, initial emphasis values were selected so that passages with a combination of mark clusters would be ranked higher than or equal to passages marked with only one cluster. Second, marks that are more precise in indicating focused attention are assigned higher emphasis values than those that are just rough indications of interest. So for the area highlight and area circle marks, the emphasis value is low (10). More focused selection marks — underline, margin bar, highlight, and circle — are assigned an intermediate value (15). Interpretive marks (comments, symbols, and callouts) are given a high emphasis value (20). In our example, the three comment clusters have an emphasis value of 20, while the three highlighter clusters have emphasis values of 15.

The third pass of the mark parser groups the mark clusters with passages from the source text. Text passages are associated with individual strokes by identifying the sentence nearest the stroke, with some preference for sentences next to the marks (thus a greater horizontal gap is allowed relative to the vertical gap). Any textual overlap between the passages associated with mark clusters will cause them to be grouped into a multimark cluster, creating the highest-level entities in the resulting parse tree. The highlighter and comments are attached to the same sentences in the text in the above example so the two passages are correctly recognized as multimarks, shown by solid rectangles, in Figure 4.

Emphasis values of these multimark clusters are the sum of the emphasis values of the component clusters. Thus, our two marked passages in the example above have emphasis values of 50 and 55 for the top and bottom passages respectively.

As the example illustrates, there is ample opportunity for misrecognition in the parsing process. Stroke clustering, attaching type information, and grouping passages with clusters are heuristic but the overall results match the desired outcome. Because lower levels of the parse may contain incorrect sub-groupings, it is important to design uses for the recognized structure that do not rely on precise clustering results.

## 5    Using the Results of the Mark Parser

The motivation for the mark parser was to locate areas of high emphasis that could help focus a reader's attention in re-reading a document or in performing a related task

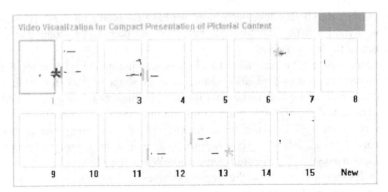

**Fig. 5.** Emphasis marks in XLibris's thumbnail overview of a document

such as writing. The mark parser has been integrated into XLibris to aid in locating valuable passages. XLibris readers often navigate to particular sections of a document using the thumbnail overview. By indicating annotation type and emphasis in this view, the user's attention will be directed to high-emphasis passages. Figure 5 shows the current use of color and icon shape to bring attention to particular passages in the document. This has similarities to Graham's depiction of computer-generated annotations in thumbnails [3] although XLibris' additions are based on the reader's own interactions with the document.

Color and icon are varied according to the emphasis value and type of the annotations. Color is used to indicate the relative emphasis of marked passages. Passages with high emphasis values (above 49) appear in red; those with medium values (between 35 and 49) appear in orange; and the others over the threshold (between 23 and 34) appear in yellow. The two icons used in the overview represent information about the type of the annotations on the emphasized passage. Asterisks are put next to annotations including interpretive marks such as comments, symbols, and callouts. An emphasized passage with only selection marks (highlighters, underlines, margin bars, and circles) is marked by a tab or exaggerated margin bar on the side of the page. Currently, we only use the two icons but this can be extended to convey more of the annotation type information to the user.

## 6   Summary

Our study of the law students' materials reinforced our past findings on the idiosyncratic nature of annotation practices. Within the variety of annotation styles, however, students could be grouped based on whether annotation is a common activity or whether it is the exception. On one hand, students who annotated sparsely were more likely to cite any passage they had annotated. On the other hand, those who annotated frequently were more likely to cite any passage with multiple marks.

A precision/recall analysis of using selection criteria based marked and multimarked passages indicated potential for such metrics but also pointed out the need for a more refined scheme for comparing marked passages.

This analysis led to the design of the mark parser. The mark parser uses location, time, and pen type information to cluster strokes into annotations. It then uses clusters' location, size, shape, pen information, and stroke information to categorize them into one of the following annotation types: comment, symbol, callout, highlight, circle, margin bar, or underline. Finally, the mark parser groups annotation clusters together based on the passage of the document to which the annotation refers. Relative emphasis values are associated with the annotation clusters and with the passage-based groups of annotations. By using the clustering and grouping heuristics in conjunction with the assessment of the relative value of the reader's annotations, we can identify which marks are likely to represent high-value annotations.

Initial experience running the mark parser on XLibris annotations gathered during an earlier study of a reading group [4] indicates that it correctly identifies the majority of high-level annotations, although lower-level structures in the parse include some noise due to the heuristic nature of the process. As an example of how the parse results can be used to help readers in their subsequent activities, we implemented a thumbnail-based document overview that indicates where the high-value annotations are and allows the reader to navigate directly to them. This application exemplifies how the mark parser results enable functionality and user interface improvements supporting reading-related activities, such as writing and collaboration, for systems supporting a combination of freeform and other annotations [7].

# References

1. Adler, A., Gujar, A., Harrison, B.L., O'Hara, K., and Sellen, A. A Diary Study of Work-Related Reading: Design Implications for Digital Reading Devices, in Proceedings of CHI '98 (April 1998), ACM Press, 241-248.
2. Chiu, P. and Wilcox, L. A Dynamic Grouping Technique for Ink and Audio Notes, in Proceedings of UIST '98 (November 1998), ACM Press, 195-202.
3. Graham, J. The Reader's Helper: A Personalized Document Reading Environment, in Proceedings of CHI '99 (May 1999), ACM Press, 481-488.
4. Marshall, C.C., Price, M.N., Golovchinsky, G., and Schilit, B.N. Introducing a digital library reading appliance into a reading group, in Proceedings of ACM Digital Libraries '99 (August 1999), ACM Press, 77-84.
5. Marshall, C.C., Price, M.N., Golovchinsky, G., and Schilit, B.N. Designing e-Books for Legal Research, in Proceedings of JCDL 2001 (June 2001), ACM Press, 41-49.
6. O'Hara, K. and Sellen, A. A comparison of reading paper and on-line documents, in Proceedings of CHI '97 (March 1997), ACM Press, 335-342.
7. Phelps, T. and Wilensky, R. Multivalent Annotations, in Proceedings of the 1997 European Conference on Digital Libraries (September 1997), Springer, 287-303.
8. Schilit, B.N., Golovchinsky, G., and Price, M.N. Beyond Paper: Supporting Active Reading with Free Form Digital Ink Annotations, in Proceedings of CHI '98 (April 1998), ACM Press, 249-256.
9. Wolfe, J.L. Effects of Annotations on Student Writers, in Proceedings of ACM Digital Libraries 2000 (June 2000), ACM Press, 19-26.

# Others Also Use: A Robust Recommender System for Scientific Libraries

Andreas Geyer-Schulz, Andreas Neumann, and Anke Thede

Institute for Information Engineering and Management,
Division for Information Services and Electronic Markets,
Department of Economics and Business Engineering,
Universität Karlsruhe (TH), D-76128 Karlsruhe, Germany
{geyer-schulz, neumann, thede}@em.uni-karlsruhe.de
http://www.em.uni-karlsruhe.de/

**Abstract.** Scientific digital library systems are a very promising application area for value-added expert advice services. Such systems could significantly reduce the search and evaluation costs of information products for students and scientists. This holds for pure digital libraries as well as for traditional scientific libraries with online public access catalogs (OPAC). In this contribution we first outline different types of recommendation services for scientific libraries and their general integration strategies. Then we focus on a recommender system based on log file analysis that is fully operational within the legacy library system of the Universität Karlsruhe (TH) since June 2002. Its underlying mathematical model, the implementation within the OPAC, as well as the first user evaluation is presented.

## 1 Introduction

Pure digital libraries as well as almost all of today's traditional scientific libraries are equipped with electronic library management systems. With the addition of digital library services traditional institutions are being converted to hybrid libraries offering both paper books and journals on location and electronic delivery of digital documents. The underlying digital catalog systems and OPACs of all types of libraries are a very promising application area for recommender systems as value-added services. This is due to the problem that scientists and students are more and more incapable of efficiently finding relevant literature in conventional database oriented catalog systems and heavily rely on peers for recommendations [21].

In long discussions with librarians and computer scientists we have identified the following obstacles for the deployment of recommender technology:

- In general librarians are concerned about the privacy of library users: The "reading" history of users must be protected.
- Current public library systems support millions of users. Under rigorous budget restrictions all system changes increasing system load would require additional investment in IT-equipment or reduce the service-level and stability of these systems.
- Traditional library systems deal with an amount of data which is at least one order of magnitude higher than in commercial environments. Only comprehensive internet search engines are larger.

T. Koch and I.T. Sølvberg (Eds.): ECDL 2003, LNCS 2769, pp. 113–125, 2003.

In this paper we present a strategy to overcome these obstacles. We first review in the next section current work in digital library research. In Sect. 3 we present the scalable architecture of a distributed recommender system operated by the university library of the Universität Karlsruhe (TH) which distributes load. In Sect. 4 we address the question of privacy and data volume by adapting Ehrenbergs's repeat-buying theory for anonymous session data and restricted local updates of low complexity. We compare this method with several other currently available recommender technologies. Section 5 shows the evaluation of this recommender system.

## 2   Related Work in Digital Library Research

Much work has been done in the field of digital libraries to support the users' process of search information extraction. An example is the Stanford Digital Library Project [18] within the scope of which the system Fab [6,7] was developed. Fab is a combination of a content-based and a collaborative recommender system that filters web pages according to content analysis and creates usage profiles for user groups with similar interests.

Another example is PADDLE [19], a system dealing with the information overload caused by the mass of documents in digital libraries by introducing customization and personalization features. Furthermore the UC Berkeley Digital Library Project [30] offers users to build personalized collections of their documents of interest. Recommendation services for digital libraries and their evaluation methods are discussed by Bollen and Rocha [8]. The virtual university of the Wirtschaftsuniversität Wien [13,28] offers a collection of categorized web links and is equipped with many different recommendation and personalization services. Other projects deal with the problem of information overload and intelligent systems for information retrieval in digital libraries like e.g. query relevance feedback [27,25] and information alert systems [4,12].

Many commercial sites have proved that a variety of different value-added services can successfully be added to digital library applications. In fact, online bookstores not offering at least some of these services are not supposed to have a stake in the future. Amazon.com is the most sophisticated of them, offering many different types of recommendation services. But others like bol.com jumped on the bandwagon of recommendations as well, thus achieving a broader bandwidth of information about documents than a book store clerk can possibly provide.

In contrast to digital libraries, no related work can be found in the field of traditional scientific libraries although these are up to date still the ones offering the broadest and largest variety of literature. Current digital library projects are compared to traditional ones often specialized and comprise less documents and in addition are focused on different types of documents like web pages not present in traditional libraries.

## 3   An Architecture for Distributed Recommender Services for Digital and Hybrid Library Systems

The architecture of the recommender system operated by the university library of the Universität Karlsruhe (TH) is shown in Fig. 1 (a previous version of this architecture can be found in [16]). The architecture is based on an agency of software agents which belong to three system layers. The layers are the legacy library system, the recommender

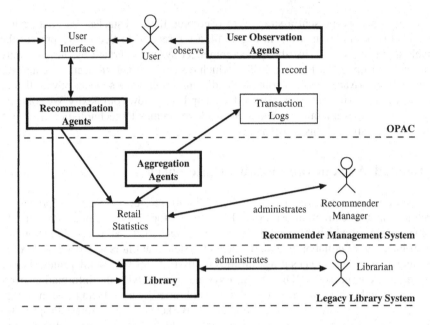

**Fig. 1.** An Architecture for a Library with Recommender Services

management system, and the online public access catalog. The legacy library system corresponds to the meta-data management system, the recommender management system to the broker management system, and the OPAC to the business-to-customer interface in the generic version of this architecture, see Geyer-Schulz et al. [14]. Arrows represent the interactions between persons, software agents, and information stores in Fig. 1. The direction of the arrows shows who starts an activity, a name near an arrow describes the activity, unlabeled arrows are simple information request.

The university library system constitutes a legacy library whose information objects are described by the library's traditional MAB format [10] for books and journals which is the German meta-data standard representation.

As we can see from Fig. 1 the interface of the legacy library system consists of a single method for retrieving meta-data by a unique object key. This implies that the recommender system and the OPAC of the legacy library system are completely independent from the database technology used in this layer. In the absence of a standard interface for external applications the recommender system is integrated into the web-interface of the OPAC. As a consequence, the recommender management system level and the OPAC are more tightly coupled. As we describe in the next section, the recommender service is based on transaction log data from observed user behavior. We compare a library to an information market in which selecting an information object (e.g. clicking on a link) is considered as a purchase of this object. More specifically, in the library environment inspection of detailed entries indicates interest in a certain document and is regarded as an equivalent to a purchase. The reason for this is the cost of following an additional link for the user, measured by the time spent for this activity. For privacy reasons lending data were not used in this project. However, even if it is possible to use lending data, the

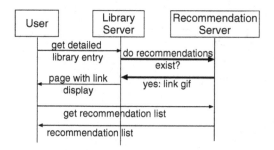

**Fig. 2.** Message Trace for Detailed View and Recommendation Request

service degree of the library has to be investigated. In our project because of the high degree of non-availability of books (above 50 %) lending data is severely biased.

As shown in Fig. 1 the recommender service at the library of the Universität Karlsruhe (TH) is implemented by means of three software agents. These independently acting agents gather information (user observation agent), process empirical data (aggregation agent), and generate the recommendation lists and pass them to the users (recommendation agent).

Figure 2 shows the message trace triggered by a user who requests a detailed view of a book (see Fig. 3) and then visits the list of recommendations for this book (see Fig. 4). Recommendation lists are precomputed during off-peak time within the incremental update process and are stored in HTML format on the recommendation server to optimize for fast HTTP answers and to reduce load on the library server. Analysis of the operation of the recommendation service during the last six months showed that the library server executed sixteen thousand additional HTTP requests on the busiest day which is an almost negligible overhead. These additional requests are marked by bold arrows in Fig. 2.

Currently the recommendation server resides on a standard PC with a 1.2 GHz AMD Athlon processor and 1,5 GB main memory, running Mandrake Linux (Kernel Version 2.4.17). The software agents are implemented in Perl (5.6) using MySQL as the underlying database system.

The user interface is shown in Figures 3 and 4. In Fig. 3 the detailed inspection page of documents including author (Lazinger, Susan S.), title (Digital Preservation and Metadata), publisher, keywords etc. is presented. The link to the recommendations can be found in the darker bar on the right side (Empfehlungen (Others also use ... )). It appears only if recommendations do exist for the specific document. Clicking on this link displays the recommendation page for this book shown in Fig. 4. The individual recommendations are listed in descending order. The number of co-purchases with "Digital Preservation and Metadata" is indicated in brackets. The system is operational at www.ubka.uni-karlsruhe.de.

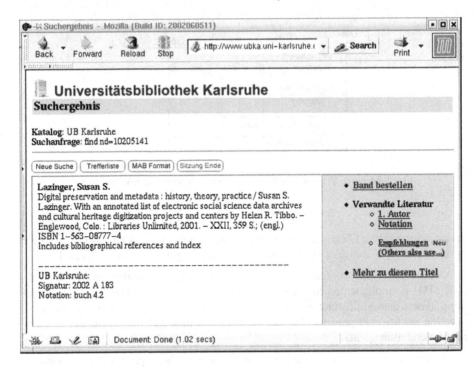

**Fig. 3.** Detailed View of Documents

# 4  Adapting Ehrenberg's Repeat-Buying Theory for Libraries

Ehrenberg´s repeat-buying theory as used in consumer panel analysis successfully describes the empirical regularity for the repeat-buying behavior of consumers for certain classes of non-durable consumer products like soaps, coffee, and toothpaste.

This section is, therefore, structured as follows: in Sect. 4.1 we introduce Ehrenbergs's classic repeat-buying theory for consumer panel analysis, in Sect. 4.2 we describe the modifications necessary to make this theory applicable in the context of scientific libraries. Finally, in Sect. 4.3 we compare this approach with related recommender methodologies.

## 4.1  Ehrenberg's Repeat-Buying Theory for Consumer Panel Analysis

Consumers purchasing non-durable consumer products make two basic decisions: the choice of a certain product class (purchase incidence) and the choice of a certain brand. Ehrenberg's main contribution is that the regularities of repeat-buying behavoir are captured to a high degree by concentrating on the purchase incidence process of a single brand as opposed to brand switching behavior. Repeat-buying theory was originally targeted towards the analysis of consumer panels. A consumer panel is a representative sample of consumers who report this purchases completely and faithfully to a marketing research company. The report of a consumer is his purchase history which is structured

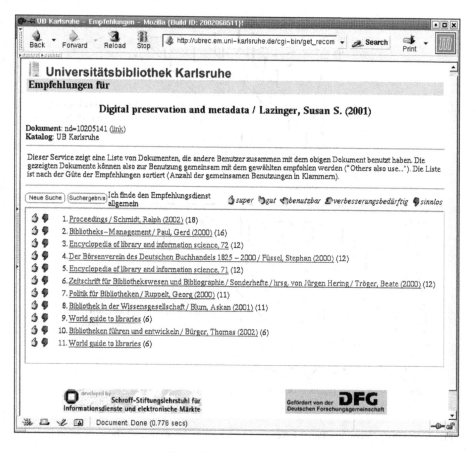

**Fig. 4.** Recommendation List

in market baskets which contain all products bought in a single trip to a store (purchase incidence).

In consumer panel analysis the stochastic process for a single brand is coded as a sequence of discrete binary variables, the purchase occasions, at which the consumer purchased the product (coded as 1). Such a process is shown for product $x_1$ and user $i$ by the lower left process in Fig. 5. Note, that the number of items purchased as well as package sizes are ignored. Consumer panel analysis is carried out in distinct time periods (1-week, 4-week, quarterly) which nicely link to established marketing reporting practices.

By arguing that consumers purchase products independently, because of e. g. restocking items only as necessary, Ehrenberg ([11], p. 128) postulated the following stochastic process model of compound Poisson form for the description of stationary purchasing behavior over a sequence of equal periods of time:

1. Purchases of a specific consumer are regarded as independent drawings from a Poisson distribution.

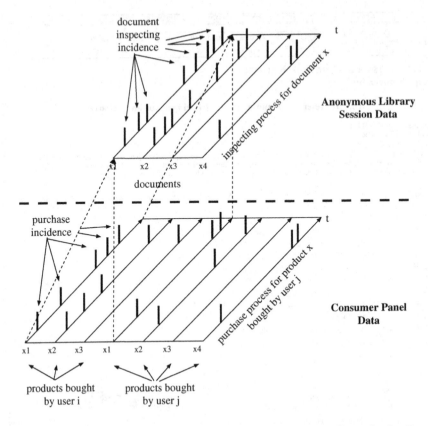

document
inspecting
incidence

Anonymous Library
Session Data

x1   x2   x3   x4

documents

purchase
incidence

Consumer Panel
Data

x1   x2   x3   x1   x2   x3   x4

products bought
by user i

products bought
by user j

**Fig. 5.** Adapting Consumer Panel Purchase Incidences to Anonymous Library Session Data

2. The average purchase rates of consumers differ in the long run, they follow a Gamma-distribution with exponent $k$ and mean $m$.

These assumptions lead directly to a negative binomial distribution (NBD) with exponent k and mean $m = ak$ for the probability of observing a consumer with $r$ purchase occurrences in the observation period:

$$P_r = \int_0^\infty \frac{e^{-\frac{\mu}{a}}\mu^{k-1}}{a^k \Gamma(k)} \frac{e^{-\mu}\mu^r}{r!} d\mu = (1+a)^{-k}\frac{\Gamma(k+r)}{\Gamma(r+1)\Gamma(k)}\left(\frac{a}{1+a}\right)^r \quad (1)$$

with variance $\sigma^2 = m\left(1 + \frac{m}{k}\right)$.

In day-to-day marketing practice this theory successfully predicts which proportion of buyers of a product buy it also in the next period and which not, how often repeat-buyers buy in each period, and what the influence of light, medium, and heavy buyers is on the purchases of the next period. For a more recent survey see [29]. In addition, Ehrenberg suggests that this model with its strong independence structure explains the regularities in markets and thus can be used as a filter to discover non-random deviations from regular market behavior. It is this last usage which we will exploit in the next section by using repeat-buying theory to account for random co-occurrences of products and thus to identify deviations as interesting recommendations.

## 4.2 Ehrenberg's Repeat-Buying Theory for Anonymous Market Basket Analysis

In this section we apply consumer panel analysis in the context of a scientific library in order to identify non-random co-occurrences of inspecting document details as recommendations for library users. In this context we interpret "purchase occasion" as a "detailed document inspection" and "market baskets" as "user sessions" within a library's OPAC.

Next, let us consider the top level of Fig. 5. The main difference to the lower level of Fig. 5 is that the identity of a library's user (a consumer) is not observed, we analyze a stream of anonymous market baskets (user sessions). The advantage of this in a library setting is that the privacy of the users is respected. All analysis is based on statistical aggregates. The purchase process for product $x_1$ in Fig. 5 is – as illustrated by the dotted arrows from users $i$ and $j$ – the aggregate purchase process for both users. As in the analysis of telephone systems where the aggregated process of incoming calls is traditionally modelled as a Poisson process, the aggregate process of inspecting document details must follow a Poisson distribution according to the superposition theorem for Poisson processes [26].

In addition, with anonymous library users, the share of never-users in the population is unknown. If we consider the NBD-model in (1), this implies that a class of zero-buyers is unknown and that the integration should start at a small $\delta > 0$ – we have a truncated integral without a zero-class. Chatfield has proved [11] that the resulting distribution with $q = \frac{a}{1+a}$ is

$$P_r = c \int_\delta^\infty \frac{e^{-\mu}\mu^r}{r!} \frac{e^{-\frac{\mu}{a}}}{\mu} d\mu = \frac{-q^r}{r \ln(1-q)}, \quad r \geq 1 \qquad (2)$$

which is the logarithmic series distribution (LSD) with mean $w = \frac{-q}{(1-q)\ln(1-q)}$ and variance $\sigma^2 = \frac{w}{(1-q)} - w^2 = \frac{-q\left(1+\frac{q}{\ln(1-q)}\right)}{(1-q)^2 \ln(1-q)}$. The parameter $q$ of a LSD distribution is easily estimated from the mean purchase frequency $w$ of buyers, it does not depend on non-buyers and thus the estimation can be efficiently carried out without taking the whole sample into account. Note that $\sigma^2 > w$ should hold for LSD distributions (see [20]).

Self-selection [24] is crucial in identifying homogeneous library user segments. A library user segment is a set of anonymous users with common interest shown by inspecting the same document. The self-selection constraint is that the search cost of a user is so high that a user is willing only to inspect the detailed information of documents which are of interest to him. The higher the users value their time, the more effective is the self-selection constraint in this context. Inspection of the detailed information of a document signals genuine interest in the document. The self-selection constraint enforces the credibility of this signal. Furthermore, when the self-selection constraint holds, we can rely on this signal, because it will not be in the interest of users to fake interest. In addition, the self-selection constraint ensures that the recommendations are presented only to interested users since only those visit the detailed information page where recommendations are offered.

For giving recommendations we now consider document pairs. For some fixed document $x$ in the set $X$ of all documents of the library we look at the purchase frequency of pairs $(x, i)$ with $i \in X \setminus \{x\}$. For our recommender services for document $x$ we need the conditional probability that document $i$ has been inspected under the condition that document $x$ has been inspected in the same session. Because of the independence assumption it is easy to see [13] that the conditional probability $p_r(i \mid x)$ is again Poisson distributed.

The occurrence of repeat-purchases in a library setting on the aggregate level is best explained by the way research is done at a university. Today research is organized as a communication-intensive team-effort including university teachers and students. Repeat purchases on the aggregate level are now triggered by several informal word-of-mouth processes like e. g. the tutoring of students in a seminar, the recommendations given in various feedback an review processes etc. In addition, in each term a significant part of library users change as new students enter and graduates leave the university. A third effect which triggers repeat-purchases is the complementary nature of the net of science: e. g. several independent application-oriented research groups in marketing research, telecommunications, statistics, and operations research apply Poisson-processes in their field of study. For each of these segments we can identify the purchase histories as follows [13]: For each document $x$ the purchase history for this segment contains all sessions in which $x$ has been inspected. For each pair of documents $(x, i)$ the purchase history for this segment contains all sessions in which $(x, i)$ has been inspected. The stochastic process for the segment $(x, i) - n$ library users which have inspected document $x$ and another document $i$ follows a Poisson distribution. Assuming that the parameters $\mu$ of the segments' Poisson distributions follow a truncated $\Gamma$-distribution, Chatfield's argument can be repeated and the probability of $r$ inspections of document pairs $(x, i)$ is a LSD distribution shown in (2).

A recommendation for a document $x$ simply is an outlier of the LSD-model – that is a document $y$ that has been used more often in the same session as could have been expected from independent random choice acts. A recommendation reveals a complementarity between documents. A detailed description of the algorithm for computing recommendations is given in [15].

As Fig. 6 shows, the framework described in the previous chapter holds for the Lazinger example. The observed frequency distribution $f(x \text{ obs})$ corresponds to the ranking by decreasing number of repeated co-purchases in Fig. 4. Recommendations are the outliers, i. e. products that have been bought together more often than expected by the stochastic model. More specifically, an LSD-model with a robust mean of 1.848 and a parameter $q = 0.675$ passes a $\chi^2$-goodness-of-fit test at $\alpha = 0.01$ ($\chi^2 = 6.234$ which is below 10.828, the critical value at $\alpha = 0.01$).

## 4.3   Related Methodologies for Recommender Systems

Different methodologies have been used in the past for generating recommendations based on collaborative filtering. One of the first systems was GroupLens [22] for recommending usenet news based on user ratings of single news articles and user correlation coefficients. Using regression models is a model based possibility for recommending items based on user attributes as well as product attributes and expert ratings [3,23]. A very popular method are association rules [1,2] and its variants [9,5] which are used

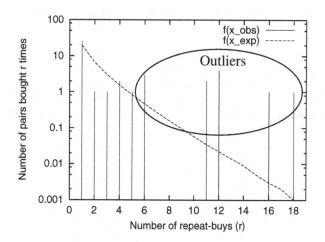

**Fig. 6.** Logarithmic Plot of the Frequency Distribution of "Digital Preservation and Metadata" by Lazinger

to find correlated product groups from market basket data. applying traditional recommender approaches is difficult in a library context. The main two reasons for this are the large number of documents in scientific libraries (10 to 100 million) and the anonymity of users. The number of documents exceeds the number of articles of retailers considerably, even Amazon.com is one order of magnitude smaller.

Collaborative filtering methods suffer from the anonymity of user data and inherently high update complexity of correlation coefficients. In addition the expressiveness of linear product moment correlation coefficients is severely limited. The calculation effort for updating these coefficients is $O(n^2)$ in the number of documents in a library which is simply computationally expensive.

The main advantage of regression models is that different data sources can be integrated in their model equations. However, in a library context the only legal data source is anonymous usage data. This means that in library context for each document for which recommendations are desired a model must be selected out of $2^{n-1}$ possible models. In practice the model selection problem is considerably simplified by pruning all variables with a correlation coefficient of zero. However in the context of a library this still implies the automatic model selection of $n$ models and their estimation. The currently fastest regression methods still require the inversion of the model's covariance matrix. Both model selection and model estimation require a high computational overhead.

Association rules have the advantage that no model assumptions are made and that they can thus be applied to data of any kind of structure. But they are not very well suited for very large scale data, because of the necessity of making a priori assumptions on thresholds as e. g. support and confidence. In addition both of these parameters depend on total sample size and thus all parameters must be recomputed with every update. For a library context the fact that thresholds are not robust over longer periods of time and must be continuously readjusted to ensure high recommendation quality is severe disadvantage. The requirement of continuous data analysis for the successfull operation

**Table 1.** Detailed results for observation period 2001/01/01 to 2003/03/13

| $q$ undef. | no $\chi^2$ (< 3 classes) | Sign. $\alpha = 0.05$ | Sign. $\alpha = 0.01$ | Not sign. | $\sum$ |
|---|---|---|---|---|---|
| 695.108 | 298.493 | 16.576 | 20.976 | 28.943 | 1.060.096 |
| (0) | (125.575) | (16.440) | (18.788) | (26.289) | (187.092) |

$\sum$ (before the data rows, leftmost column)

($n$) denotes $n$ lists of recommendations. Total number of recommendations: 1.983.908

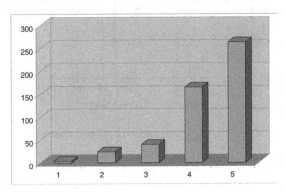

**Fig. 7.** Opinions of users about the recommendation service: dispensable (1) – super (5)

of a recommender system is unacceptable for most libraries. A detailed comparison can be found in [17].

The current implementation features incremental updates of market baskets with a complexity of $O(n^2)$ in time and space with $n$ the number of items updated. Only for updated market baskets the LSD-models are re-estimated. Since the upper bound is reduced by a reduction of the update period this improves the scalability of the algorithm. Simple association rule algorithms compute market baskets essentially in the same way. However, the advantage of this algorithm is that the only parameter for the LSD estimation, the mean, can be computed for updated market baskets only and does not depend on global values like support and confidence. In addition, the performance of the LSD model is very robust and thus suited for day-to-day operations.

## 5    Evaluation

The statistical results for the sample data of the 23 libraries hosted by the library of the Universität Karlsruhe (TH) are summarized in Table 1. From the 15 million documents contained in the combined library catalog 1,060,096 have been inspected by users together in a session with at least one other document. For 187,092 of these products lists of recommendations with a total of 1,983,908 entries have been generated. The coverage of the recommendersystem is 187,092/15mill=1.25 %. However, in the observation period 2001/01/01–2003/03/13 users inspected 1,717,503 documents, for 655,828 of these recommendations were available. This is a coverage of 38.18 % of the documents actually in use.

For testing user acceptance we inserted a five item Likert scale into the user interface (see Fig. 3). The possibilites where 'dispensable' (1), 'needs improvement' (2), 'usable' (3), 'good' (4), and 'super' (5). In the period 2003-02-07 – 2003-05-19 we collected a total of 496 votes the distribution of which can be seen in Fig. 7. The mean is 4.33 with a standard deviation of 0.88. The usage of the service can be inferred from the web server log data. On the one hand we can calculate the number of detailed library pages being visited and whether a link to a recommendation page was displayed and we see how many recommendation pages where visited each day. From the above results we can infer that among the people visiting the recommendation service a very high percentage is very satisfied or satisfied with the availability and the quality of such a service. Recommendations were used 118.83 times on average per day with an increasing trend throughout the observation period.

**Acknowledgement.** We gratefully acknowledge the funding of the project "Scientific Libraries in Information Markets" by the Deutsche Forschungsgemeinschaft within the scope of the research initiative "$V^3D^2$" (DFG-SPP 1041).

# References

1. R. Agrawal, T. Imielinski, and A. Swami. Mining association rules between sets of items in large databases. In P. Buneman and S. Jajodia, editors, *Proc. ACM SIGMOD Int. Conf. on Management of Data*, volume 22, Washington, D.C., USA, Jun 1993. ACM, ACM Press.
2. R. Agrawal and R. Srikant. Fast algorithms for mining association rules. In *Proc. 20th Very Large Databases Conf., Santiago, Chile*, pages 487–499, Sep 1994.
3. A. Ansari, S. Essegaier, and R. Kohli. Internet recommendation systems. *Journal of Marketing Research*, 37:363–375, Aug 2000.
4. A. Apps and R. MacIntyre. Prototyping Digital Library Technologies in zetoc. In M. Agosti and C. Thanos, editors, *Research and Advanced Technology for Digital Libraries*, volume 2458 of *LNCS*, pages 309–323. Springer, Sep 2002.
5. Y. Aumann and Y. Lindell. A statistical theory for quantitative association rules. In U. Chaudhuri and D. Madigan, editors, *Proc. 5th ACM SIGKDD int. conference on Knowledge Discovey and Data Mining, San Diego, California*, pages 261–270, New York, 1999. ACM, ACM press.
6. M. Balabanovic. An adaptive web page recommendation service. In *Proc. 1st Int. Conf. on Autonomous Agents*, Marina del Rey, California, Feb 1997.
7. M. Balabanovic and Y. Shoham. Fab: Content-based, collaborative recommendation. *Communications of the ACM*, 40(3):66–72, Mar 1997.
8. J. Bollen and L. M. Rocha. An adaptive systems approach to the implementation and evaluation of digital library recommendation systems. In J. Borbinha and T. Baker, editors, *Proc. 4th Eur. Conf. on Digital Libraries*, volume 1923 of *LNCS*, pages 356–359. Springer, 2000.
9. S. Brin, R. Motwani, and C. Silverstein. Beyond market baskets: Generalizing association rules to correlations. In J. M. Peckman, editor, *Proc. ACM SIGMOD Int. Conf. on Management of Data, Tucson, Arizona*, volume 26, pages 265–276, New York, NY 10036, USA, May 1997. ACM Press.
10. Die Deutsche Bibliothek. MAB: Maschinelles Austauschformat für Bibliotheken. http://www.ddb.de/professionell/mab.htm.
11. A. S. C. Ehrenberg. *Repeat-Buying: Facts, Theory and Applications*. Charles Griffin & Company Ltd, London, 2 edition, 1988.

12. N. Fuhr et al. Daffodil: an integrated desktop for supporting high-level search activities in federated digital libraries. In M. Agosti and C. Thanos, editors, *Research and Advanced Technology for Digital Libraries*, volume 2458 of *LNCS*, pages 597–612. Springer, 2002.

13. A. Geyer-Schulz, M. Hahsler, and M. Jahn. A customer purchase incidence model applied to recommender services. In R. Kohavi et al., editor, *Proc. WebKDD – Mining log data across all customer touchpoints*, volume 2356 of *LNAI*, pages 25–47, Berlin, 2002. Springer-Verlag.

14. A. Geyer-Schulz, M. Hahsler, and M. Jahn. Recommendations for virtual universities from observed user behavior. In W. Gaul and G. Ritter, editors, *Classification, Automation, and New Media*, volume 20 of *Studies in Classification, Data Analysis, and Knowledge Organization*, pages 273–280, Heidelberg, 2002. Springer-Verlag.

15. A. Geyer-Schulz, M. Hahsler, A. Neumann, and A. Thede. Behavior-based recommender systems as value-added services for scientific libraries. In H. Bozdogan, editor, *Statistical Data Mining and Knowledge Discovery*. Chapmann & Hall / CRC, 2003.

16. A. Geyer-Schulz, M. Hahsler, A. Neumann, and A. Thede. An integration strategy for distributed recommender services in legacy library systems. Studies in Classification, Data Analysis, and Knowledge Organization, Heidelberg, 2003. Springer-Verlag. To appear.

17. A. Geyer-Schulz, M. Hahsler, and A. Thede. Comparing association-rules and repeat-buying based recommender systems in a B2B environment. Studies in Classification, Data Analysis, and Knowledge Organization, Heidelberg, 2003. Springer-Verlag. To appear.

18. The Stanford Digital Libraries Group. The stanford digital library project. *Communications of the ACM*, 38(4):59–60, April 1995.

19. D. Hicks, K. Tochtermann, and A. Kussmaul. Augmenting digital catalogue functionality with support for customization. In *Proc. 3rd Int. Conf. on Asian Digital Libraries*, 2000.

20. N. L. Johnson, A. W. Kemp, and S. Kotz. *Univariate Discrete Distributions*. Wiley Series in Probability and Mathematical Statistics. J. Wiley, 2nd edition, 1993.

21. R. Klatt et al. Nutzung und Potenziale der innovativen Mediennutzung im Lernalltag der Hochschulen, 2001. BMBF-Studie, http://www.stefi.de/.

22. J. Konstan et al. Grouplens: Applying Collaborative Filtering to Usernet News. *Communications of the ACM*, 40(3):77–87, Mar 1997.

23. A. Mild and M. Natter. Collaborative filtering or regression models for internet recommendation systems? *Journal of Targeting, Measurement and Analysis for Marketing*, 10(4):304–313, Jan 2002.

24. P. Milgrom and J. Roberts. *Economics, Organization and Management*. Prentice-Hall, Upper Saddle River, 1 edition, 1992.

25. I. Papadakis, I. Andreou, and V. Chrissikopoulos. Interactive search results. In M. Agosti and C. Thanos, editors, *Research and Advanced Technology for Digital Libraries*, volume 2458 of *LNCS*, pages 448–462. Springer, Sep 2002.

26. T. Rolski et al. *Stochastic processes for insurance and finance*. J. Wiley, Chichester, 1999.

27. G. Salton and C. Buckley. Improving retrieval performance by relevance feedback. *Journal of the American Society for Information Science*, 41(4):288–297, 1990.

28. Virtual university of the Wirtschaftsuniversität Wien. http://vu.wu-wien.ac.at/.

29. U. Wagner and A. Taudes. Stochastic models of consumer behaviour. *European Journal of Operational Research*, 29(1):1–23, 1987.

30. R. Wilensky et al. Reinventing scholarly information dissemination and use. Technical report, University of California, Berkeley, 1999.
http://elib.cs.berkeley.edu/pl/about.html.

# Cross-Lingual Text Categorization

Nuria Bel[1], Cornelis H.A. Koster[2], and Marta Villegas[1]

[1] Grup d'Investigació en Lingüística Computacional Universitat de Barcelona, 08028
- Barcelona, Spain. {nuria,tona}@gilc.ub.es
[2] Computer Science Dept., University of Nijmegen, Toernooiveld 1, 6525ED
Nijmegen, The Netherlands. kees@cs.kun.nl

**Abstract.** This article deals with the problem of Cross-Lingual Text
Categorization (CLTC), which arises when documents in different languages must be classified according to the same classification tree. We describe practical and cost-effective solutions for automatic Cross-Lingual
Text Categorization, both in case a sufficient number of training examples is available for each new language and in the case that for some
language no training examples are available.
Experimental results of the bi-lingual classification of the ILO corpus
(with documents in English and Spanish) are obtained using bi-lingual
training, terminology translation and profile-based translation.

## 1 Introduction

Text Categorization is an important but usually rather inconspicuous part of
Document Management and (more generally) Knowledge Management. It is used
in many information-providing institutions, either in the form of a hierarchical
mono-classification ("where does this document belong in our topic hierarchy")
or as a multi-classification, assigning zero or more keywords to the document,
with the purpose of enhancing and simplifying retrieval.

Automatic Text Categorization techniques based on manually constructed
class profiles have shown that a high accuracy can be achieved, but the cost
of manual profile construction and maintenance is quite high. Automatic Text
Categorization systems based on supervised learning [16] can reach a similar
accuracy, so that the (semi)automatic classification of monolingual documents
is becoming standard practice. Now the question arises how to deal efficiently
with collections of documents in more than one language, that are to be classified
according to the same Classification Tree.

This article describes the cross-lingual classification techniques developed in
the PEKING project [1] and presents the results achieved in classifying the ILO
corpus using the LCS classification engine.

In the following two sections we relate our research to previous research in
Cross-Language Information Retrieval, describe the ILO corpus and our experimental approach. In section 4 we establish a baseline for mono-lingual classification of the ILO corpus, using different classification algorithms (Winnow

---

[1] http://www.cs.kun.nl/peking

T. Koch and I.T. Sølvberg (Eds.): ECDL 2003, LNCS 2769, pp. 126–139, 2003.

and Rocchio). In sections 5 and 6 we propose three different solutions for cross-language classification, implying increasingly smaller (and therefore less costly) translation tasks. Then we describe our main experiments in multi-lingual classification, and compare the results to the baseline.

# 2   Previous Research

When we embarked on this line of research, we did not find any publications addressing the area of Cross-Lingual Text Categorization as such. On the other hand, there is a rich literature addressing the related problem of Cross-Lingual Information Retrieval (CLIR).

Both CLIR and CLTC are based on some computation of the similarity between texts, comparing documents with queries or class profiles. The most important difference between them is the fact that CLIR is based on queries, consisting of a few words only, whereas in CLTC each class is defined by an extensive profile (which may be seen as a weighted collection of documents).

In developing techniques for CLTC, we want to keep in mind the lessons learned in CLIR.

## 2.1   Cross-Lingual Information Retrieval

CLIR is concerned with the problem of a user formulating a query in one language in order to retrieve documents in several (other) languages. Two approaches can be distinguished:

1. translation-based systems either translate queries into the document language or languages, or they translate documents into the query language
2. Intermediate representation systems transfer both queries and documents into some language-independent representation, be it a thesaurus, some ontological representation or a language-independent vector space model.

It is important to notice that all current approaches have inherent problems. Translation of documents into a given language for a large number of documents is a rather expensive approach, especially in terms of time demands. Using thesauri or ontological taxonomies requires the availability of parallel or comparable corpora, and the same is required by interlingual vector space techniques.

To collect and process this material is time consuming, but more crucially, these techniques based on statistical approaches reduce accuracy when not enough material is available.

The less expensive approach is to translate the queries. The most widely used techniques for translating queries proceed by first identifying content words (simple or multi-word units such as compounds) and then supplying all possible translations. These translations can be used in normal search engines, reducing the development costs.

In [12], the effect of the *quality* of the translation resource is investigated. Furthermore it compares the effects of pre- and post-expansion: A query consisting of a number of words is expanded, either before or after translation (or both), with related words from the lexicon or from some corpus.

The expansion technique in the paper is a form of *pseudo relevance feedback*: using either the original query or its translated version and retrieving documents in the same language, the top 25 retrieved documents were taken as positive examples. From those, a set of 60 weighted query terms was composed including the original terms. This amounts to a combination of query expansion and term re-weighting.

The effect of degrading the quality of the linguistic resources turned out to be gradual. Therefore, it is to be expected that the effect of upgrading the resources should be gradual too. Weakness of the translation resources can be compensated for by query expansion.

In another recent paper[10] the use of Language Modeling in IR ([2,7]) is extended to bi-lingual CLIR. For each query $Q$ a *relevance model* is estimated consisting of a set of probabilities $P(w|R_Q)$ (the probability that a word sampled at random from a relevant document would be the word $w$).

In monolingual IR this relevance model is estimated by taking a set of documents relevant to the query. In CLIR, we need a relevance model for both the source language and the target language. The second can be obtained using either a parallel corpus or a bi-lingual lexicon giving translation probabilities.

The paper provides strong support for the Language Modeling approach in IR, in spite of the simplicity of the language models used (unigram). In using more informative representations (linguistically motivated terms) the effect should possibly be even larger.

## 2.2   Cross-Lingual Text Categorization

Cross-lingual Text Categorization (CLTC) or Cross-lingual classification is a new research subject, about which no previous literature appears to be available. Still, it concerns a practical problem, which is increasingly felt in e.g. the documentation departments of multinationals and international organizations as they come to rely on automatic document classification. It is also manifest in many Search Engines on the web, which rely on a hierarchical classification of web pages to reduce search complexity and to raise accuracy: how should they combine this hierarchy with a classification on languages?

We shall distinguish two practical cases of CLTC:

- **poly-lingual training**:
  One classifier is trained on labeled documents written in different languages (or possible using different languages within one document).
- **cross-lingual training**: Labeled training documents are available only in one language, and we want to classify documents written in another language.

Most practical situations will be between these two extremes. Our experiments will show that the following is a feasible scenario:

> An organization, which already has an automatic classification system installed, wishes to extend this system to classify also documents in other languages. In order to ease the transition, some documents in those other languages are provided, either in untranslated form but manually supplied with a class label, or in translated form and without such a label. With limited manual intervention, a bootstrap of the system can be performed, so that documents in all those languages can be classified automatically in their original form by a single poly-lingual classifier.

By means of a number of experiments, we shall test the following hypotheses:

- **poly-lingual training**: simultaneous training on labeled documents in languages A and B will allow us to classify both A and B documents *with the same classifier*
- **cross-lingual training**: a monolingually trained classifier for language A plus a translation of the most important terms from language B to A allows to classify documents written in B.

### 2.3   Lessons from CLIR for CLTC?

In CLTC, for performing translations we shall have to use similar linguistic resources as in CLIR. Since our resources are less than ideal, should we compensate by implementing pre- and post-expansion? In CLTC, the role of the queries (with which test documents are compared) is played by the class profiles, which are composed from many documents; this may well have the same effect as explicit expansion of the documents or the profiles with morphological variants and synonyms. In fact, a class profile can be seen as an approximative (unigram) Language Model for the documents in that particular class.

## 3   The Experimental Procedure

All experiments were performed with Version 2.0 of the Linguistic Classification System LCS developed in the PEKING project[2], which implements the Winnow and Rocchio algorithms. It makes sense to compare those two algorithms, because we expect them to show qualitative differences in behaviour for some tasks. In Rocchio a class profile is essentially computed as a centroid, a weighted sum of the train documents, whereas Winnow[5,6] by heuristic techniques computes (just like SVM)an optimal linear separator in the term space between positive and negative examples.

In the experiments we have used either a 25/75 or a 50/50 split of the data for training and testing, as stated in the text, with 12-fold or 16-fold cross-validation. Our goal is to compare the effect of different representations of the

---

[2] www.cs.kun.nl/peking

data rather than to reach the highest accuracy, and keeping the train sets small is good for performance (the cross-validation experiments are computationally very heavy). As a measure of Accuracy we have used the *micro-averaged F1 value.*

Although the ILO corpus is mono-classified (precisely one class per document) we allowed the classifiers to give 0-3 classes per document (which gives an indication of the Accuracy in multi-classification). Multi-classification gives more room for errors, and therefore has a somewhat lower Accuracy than Mono-classification.

For each representation, we first determined the optimal tuning and term selection parameters on the train set. The optimal parameter values depend on the corpus and on the document representation; their tuning is known to have an important effect on the Accuracy (see e.g. [8]), and without it the results from different experiments are hard to compare.

## 3.1   The ILO Corpus

The ILO corpus is a collection of full-text documents, each labeled with one classname (mono-classification) which we have downloaded from the ILOLEX website of the International Labour Organisation[3]. ILOLEX describes itself as "a trilingual database containing ILO Conventions and Recommendations, ratification information, comments of the Committee of Experts and the Committee on Freedom of Association, representations, complaints, interpretations, General Surveys, and numerous related documents".

The languages concerned are English, Spanish and French. From ILOLEX we extracted a bi-lingual corpus (only English and Spanish) of documents labeled for classification.

Although in the actual database every document has a translation, in constructing our corpus the documents were selected according to rough balance, avoiding total symmetry of documents in terms of language, that is, we have included some documents both in English and Spanish, and some in only one language. Some statistics of the ILO corpus:

1. the English version consists of 2165 documents. It comprises (after the removal of HTML tags) 4.2 million words, totalling 27 Mbytes. The average length of a document is 1942 words, and the document length varies widely, between 39 and 38646 words.
2. the Spanish version consists of 1590 documents. It comprises (after the removal of HTML tags) 4.7 million words, 30 Mbytes. The document length ranges from 117 to 7500 words. Most of the documents are around 2000 words.

The corpus is mono-classified into 12 categories, with a rather varying number of documents per category:

---

[3] http://ilolex.ilo.ch:1567/Spanish/index.htm

| class name | # docs English | # docs Spanish | class description |
|---|---|---|---|
| 02 | 123 | 74 | Human rights |
| 03 | 397 | 86 | Conditions of employment |
| 04 | 299 | 71 | Conditions of work |
| 05 | 22 | 23 | Economic and social development |
| 06 | 414 | 448 | Employment |
| 07 | 279 | 278 | Labour Relations |
| 08 | 85 | 81 | Labour Administration |
| 09 | 98 | 86 | Health and Labour |
| 10 | 156 | 148 | Social Security |
| 11 | 81 | 20 | Training |
| 12 | 131 | 154 | Special prov. by category of persons |
| 13 | 108 | 121 | Special prov. by Sector of Econ. Act. |
| Total: | 2165 | 1590 | |

## 4 The Mono-lingual Baseline

In order to establish a baseline with which to compare the results of cross-lingual classification, we first measured the Accuracy achieved in mono-lingual classification of the Spanish and English documents in the ILO corpus.

We also compared the traditional keyword representation with one in which multi-word terms were contracted into a single term (normalized keywords).

### 4.1 Monolingual Keywords

The original documents were minimally preprocessed: de-capitalization, segmentation into words and elimination of certain special characters. In particular, no lemmatization was performed. The results (25/75 shuffle, 12-fold cross-validation) are as follows:

| algorithm | representation | language | Accuracy | |
|---|---|---|---|---|
| | | | Multi 0:3 | Mono 1:1 |
| Winnow | keywords | English | .840±.013 | .865±.007 |
| Rocchio | keywords | English | .823±.010 | .800±.010 |
| Winnow | keywords | Spanish | .768±.014 | .790±.015 |
| Rocchio | keywords | Spanish | .755±.007 | .764±.013 |

The Accuracy on the Spanish documents is significantly lower than on the English documents (according to Steiner's theorem for a Pierson-III distribution with bounds zero and one, $a \pm b$ and $c \pm d$ are different with risc $< 3\%$ when $| a - c | > \sqrt{b^2 + d^2}$, see page 929 of [1]), which is due not only to language characteristics but also to the fact that fewer train documents are available. In mono-classifying the English documents, Winnow is significantly more accurate than Rocchio.

Figure 1 shows *learning curves* for the English documents, one for Winnow and one for Rocchio. (The learning curves for the Spanish documents are not given here, because they look quite similar.)

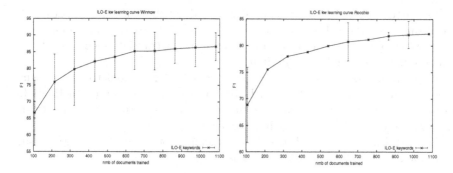

**Fig. 1.** Learning curves for English, Winnow and Rocchio

Using a 50/50 split of the English corpus, a classifier was trained in 10 epochs (= stepwise increasing subsets of the train set) and tested with the test set of 50% of the documents. This process was repeated for 16 different shuffles of the documents and the results averaged (16-fold cross-evaluation). The graphs show the Accuracy as a function of the number of documents trained, with error bars.

Notice that Winnow is on the whole more accurate than Rocchio, but that the variance is much larger for Winnow than for Rocchio.

### 4.2 Lemmatized Keywords

Using the same pre-processing but in addition lemmatizing the noun and verb forms in the documents, the results are as follows:

| algorithm | representation | language | Accuracy Multi 0:3 | Mono 1:1 |
|---|---|---|---|---|
| Winnow | lemmatized keywords | English | .845±.008 | .863±.006 |
| Rocchio | lemmatized keywords | English | .797±.012 | .817±.012 |
| Winnow | lemmatized keywords | Spanish | .768±.012 | .788±.015 |
| Rocchio | lemmatized keywords | Spanish | .759±.010 | .758±.017 |

In distinction to the situation in query-based Retrieval, in Text Categorization the lemmatization of terms does not seem to improve the Accuracy: although lemmatization enhances the Recall of terms, it may well hurt Precision more (see also [15]). In Text Categorization the positive effect of the conflation of morphological variants of a word is small: If two forms of a word are both important terms for a class, then they will both obtain an appropriate positive weight for that class provided they occur often enough, and if they don't occur often enough, their contribution is not important anyway.

### 4.3 Linguistically Motivated Terms

The use of n-grams instead of single words (unigrams) as terms has been advocated for Automatic Text Classification. Experiments like those of [11,4], where only statistically relevant n-grams were used, did not show better results than the use of single keywords. For our experiment in CLTC the extraction of multi-word terms was required in order to be able to find proper translation equivalents, i.e. "trade union" vs. "sindicato" in Spanish.

In addition, for the monolingual experiments, we wanted to test to what extent linguistically motivated multi-word terms (for a survey on methods for automatic extraction of technical terms see [3]), rather than just statistically motivated ones, could make any improvement.

For Spanish, we extracted these Linguistically Motivated Terms (LMT) using both quantitative and linguistic strategies:

- A first list of candidates was extracted using Mutual Information and Likelihood Ratio measures over the available corpus
- The list of candidates was filtered by checking it against the list of well formed Noun Phrases that followed the patterns N+N, N+ADJ and N+prep+N.

This process ensured that all Spanish multi-words were both linguistically and statistically motivated and resulted in 303 bigrams (N+ADJ), and 288 trigrams (N+de+N mainly).

For want of a better term, we shall use the term *normalized* for a text in which important multi-word expressions have been contracted into one term (e.g. 'software_engineering' or 'Trabajadores_migrantes').

The list of English multi-word expressions was built from the multi-words present in the bilingual database (see section 6.1), that is, those resulting from the translation of Spanish terms and LMT's.

Training and testing on normalized documents gave the following results:

| algorithm | representation | language | Accuracy | |
|---|---|---|---|---|
| | | | Multi 0:3 | Mono 1:1 |
| Winnow | normalized keywords | English | .840±.013 | .867±.011 |
| Rocchio | normalized keywords | English | .824±.010 | .829±.011 |
| Winnow | normalized keywords | Spanish | .762±.013 | .800±.013 |
| Rocchio | normalized keywords | Spanish | .769±.010 | .779±.010 |

For English, the normalization has no effect, for Rocchio on Spanish there is a barely significant improvement. For Winnow there is no effect.

Even when using linguistic phrases rather than statistical phrases, document normalization seems to make no significant improvement to automatic classification (see also [9,8]).

## 4.4  Comparing the Learning Curves

In order to faciltiate their comparison, figure 2 shows, for each combination of language and classification algorithm, the learning curves (50/50 split, 10 epochs, 16-fold cross-validation) for each of the three document representations.

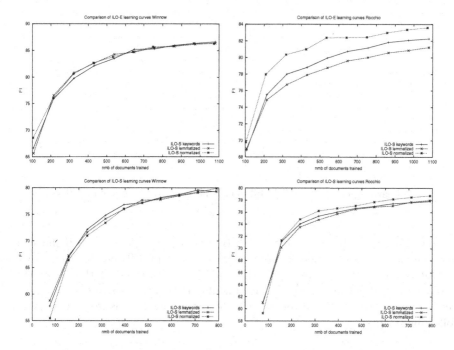

**Fig. 2.** Learning curves (English and Spanish, Winnow and Rocchio)

For Winnow, the representation chosen makes no difference. Rocchio gains somewhat by normalisation, especially for English, whereas lemmatization has a small negative impact. Observe also that lemmatization and normalization do not improve the classification accuracy for small numbers of training documents, where it might be expected that term conflation would be more effective.

Since Winnow is the most accurate algorithm, we are more interested in its behaviour than in that of Rocchio, and therefore we may ignore the influence of lemmatization and normalization implied in the translation processes in the following sections.

## 5   Poly-lingual Training and Testing

In this section we shall investigate the effect of training on labeled documents written in a mix of languages. Since we have a bi-lingual corpus, we shall restrict ourselves (without loss of generality) to the bi-lingual case. The bi-lingual training approach amounts to building a single classifier from a set of labeled train documents in both languages, which will classify documents in any of the two trained languages, without translating anything and even without trying to find out what language the documents are in. We exploit the strong statistical properties of the classification algorithms, and use no linguistic resources.

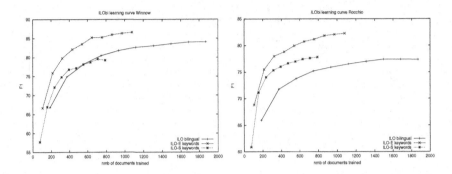

**Fig. 3.** Learning curves (English, bilingual and Spanish, Winnow and Rocchio)

The 2167 English and 1590 Spanish ILO documents (labeled with the same class-labels) were combined at random into one corpus. Then this corpus was randomly split into 4 train sets each containing 15% (563) of the documents and a fixed test set of 40% of the documents, a train set of size comparable to the above experiments, and tested with the remaining 40% as test set, with the following results:

| algorithm | representation | language | Accuracy | |
|---|---|---|---|---|
| | | | Multi 0:3 | Mono 1:1 |
| Winnow | keywords | English and Spanish | .785±.013 | .811±.014 |
| Rocchio | keywords | English and Spanish | .739±.009 | .758±.014 |

Using the Winnow classifier, the Accuracy achieved for the mixture of Spanish and English documents lies after 563 train documents above that for Spanish documents alone. But at this point only about 225 Spanish documents have been trained, so that it is quite surprising that the Accuracy is so high.

In graph 3 the learning curve for bi-lingual training (50/50 split, 16-fold cross-validation) is compared with those for the Spanish and English mono-lingual corpora.

Again, keeping in mind the number of documents trained in each language, the curve for bi-lingual classification with Winnow is nicely in the middle. Although the vocabularies of the two languages are very different, Winnow trains a classifier which is good at either. Rocchio on the other hand is quite negatively impacted. It attempts to construct a centroid out of all documents in a class, and is confused by a document set that has two very different centroids.

As an afterthought, we tested how well an English classifier understands Spanish, by training Winnow mono on 2164 English documents and testing on 1590 Spanish documents, without any translation whatsoever. We found an Accuracy of 10.75%! In spite of the difference in vocabulary, there are still some terms shared, probably mostly non-linguistic elements (proper names, abbreviations like ceacr, maybe even numbers) which are the same in both languages.

# 6    Cross-Lingual Training and Testing

For Cross-Lingual Text Categorization, three translation strategies may be distinguished. The first two are familiar from Cross Language Information Retrieval (CLIR):

- **document translation:** Although translating the complete document is workable, it is not popular in CLIR, because automatic translations are not satisfactory and manual translations are too expensive
- **terminology translation:** constructing a terminology for each of the relevant domains (classes), and translating all domain terms. It is expected that these include all or most of the terms which are relevant for classification.
- **profile-based translation:** translate only the terms actually occurring in the class profiles (Most Important Terms or MIT's).

Translation of the complete document (either manually or automatically) has not been evaluated by us, since it costs much more effort than the other approaches possibility, without promising better results. Our experiments with the other techniques are described below.

## 6.1    The Linguistic Resources

We know from Cross-Lingual Information Retrieval applications that existing translation lexica are very limited. In order to enlarge their coverage it is also possible to extract translation equivalences from aligned corpora. but both approaches show some drawbacks [14]. While bi-lingual dictionaries and glossaries provide reliable information, they propose more than one translation per term without preference information. Aligned corpora for very innovative domains, such as technical ones, offer contextualized translations, but the errors introduced by statistical processing of texts in order to align them are considerable.

Our translation resources were built using a corpus-driven approach, following a frequency criterion to include nouns, adjectives and verbs with a frequency higher than 30 occurrences in the bilingual lexicon. The resulting list consisted of 4462 wordforms (out of 4.619.681 tokens) for Spanish and 5258 (out of 4.609.670 tokens) for English.

## 6.2    Terminology Translation

In the approach based on terminology translation, these resources were used as follows:

1. training a classifier on all 2167 normalized English documents
2. using this classifier to classify the 1590 pseudo-English (Spanish) documents.

Our experiments (training on subsets of 25% of the English documents, testing on all pseudo-English documents, 12-fold cross-validation, and similarly for Spanish) gave the following results:

| algorithm | representation | language | Accuracy | |
|-----------|----------------|----------|----------|----------|
| | | | Multi 0:3 | Mono 1:1 |
| Winnow | keywords | English and pseudo-English | .696±.051 | .792±.012 |
| Rocchio | keywords | English and pseudo-English | .592±.025 | .709±.012 |
| Winnow | keywords | Spanish and pseudo-Spanish | .552±.062 | .617±.062 |
| Rocchio | keywords | Spanish and pseudo-Spanish | .538±.045 | .589±.029 |

Winnow's mono-classification of pseudo-English documents after training on English documents is quite good (as good as when training and testing on Spanish keywords), but when translating English documents to pseudo-Spanish the result is not good (which is only partly explained by the lower number of train examples). Rocchio is in all cases much worse than for monolingual classification.

Both algorithms are much worse in multi-classification. A closer look at the classification process shows why: the test documents obtain very low and widely varying thresholds. Without forcing each document to obtain one class, 25% of the pseudo-English documents and nearly 50% of the pseudo-Spanish documents are not accepted by Winnow for any class. We have violated the fundamental assumption that train- and test-documents must be sampled from the same distribution, on which the threshold computation (and indeed the whole classification approach) is based. In the pseudo-English documents most English words from the train set are missing, and therefore the thresholds are too high. Furthermore, the many synonyms generated as a translation for a single term in the original distort their frequency distribution. This thresholding problem can be solved by filtering the words in the english train set and using a validation set to set the thresholds (not tried here).

In spite of the thresholding problem, terminology translation is a viable approach for cross-lingual mono-classification.

## 6.3  Profile-Based Translation

Why don't we ask the classifier what terms it would like to find? When using an English classifier on Spanish terms, we should need for each English term in the profile a list of only those terms in Spanish that can be translated to that English term – including morphological variation, spelling variation and synonymy. We need a translation for only the terms actually occurring in the profile, and not for any other term (because it would not contribute anything).

Our previous research [13] has shown that, using a suitable Term Selection algorithm, a surprisingly small number of terms per class (40-150) gives optimal Accuracy. All other terms can safely and even profitably be eliminated. Based on this observation, we have investigated the effect of translating *only* towards the words occurring in the class profiles, performing the following experiment:

1. we determined the best 150 terms in classifying all English documents with Winnow, and combined the results into a vocabulary of 923 different words (out of 22000)
2. a translation table from Spanish to English was constructed, comprising for each English word in the vocabulary those Spanish words that may be translated to it

3. a classifier was trained on all English documents but using only the words in the vocabulary
4. this classifier was tested on all Spanish documents, translating only the Spanish terms having a translation towards a word in the vocabulary.

The resulting accuracy when using profile-translation (training a classifier on English documents and classifying with it Spanish documents in which just the profile words have been translated) gave the following results:

| algorithm | representation | language | Accuracy | |
|---|---|---|---|---|
| | | | Multi 0:3 | Mono 1:1 |
| Winnow | keywords | profile translation Eng/Spa | .605±.071 | .724±.035 |
| Rocchio | keywords | profile translation Eng/Spa | .681±.048 | .730±.019 |

Taking into account that the best accuracy achieved in the mono-classification of Spanish documents was .775, that no labeled Spanish documents were needed and that the required translation effort is very small, an Accuracy of .724 in cross-lingual classification is not bad. On this corpus, Rocchio does as well as Winnow in mono-classification and even significantly better in multi-classification.

## 7    Conclusion

Cross-lingual Text Categorization is actually easier than Cross-lingual Information Retrieval, for the same reason that lemmatization and term normalization have much less effect in CLTC than in CLIR: the law of large numbers is with us. Given an abundance of training documents, our statistical classification algorithms will function well, even in the absence of term conflation, which is the CLTC equivalent of expansion in CLIR. We do not have to work hard to ensure that all linguistically related forms or synonyms of a word are conflated: If two equivalent forms of a word occur frequently enough to have an impact on classification, they will also do so as independent terms.

We have found viable solutions for two extreme cases of Cross-Lingual Text Categorization, between which all practical cases can be situated. On the one hand we found that *poly-lingual training*, training one single classifier to classify documents in a number of languages, is the simplest approach to cross-lingual Text Categorization, provided that enough training examples are available in the respective languages (tens to hundreds), and the classification algorithm used is immune to the evident disjointedness of the resulting class profile (as is the case for Winnow but not for Rocchio).

At the other extreme, when for the new language no labeled train documents are available it is possible to use *terminology translation*: find, buy or construct a translation resource from the new language to the language in which the classifier has been trained, and translate just the typical terms of the documents. Finally, it is possible to translate only the terms in the class profile. Although the accuracy is somewhat lower, this *profile-based translation* provides a very cost-effective way to perform Cross-lingual Classification: in our experiment an average of 60 terms per class had to be translated.

In a practical classification system, the above techniques can be combined, by using terminology translation or profile-based translation to generate examples for poly-lingual training and then bootstrap the poly-lingual classifier (with some manual checking of uncertain classifications).

# References

1. M. Abramowitz and Irena A. Stegun (1970), Handbook of Mathematical Functions, 9th edition.
2. A. Berger and J. Lafferty (1999), Information Retrieval as statistical translation, Proceedings ACM SIGIR'99, pp. 222–229.
3. Cabré, M.T., R. Estopà and J. Vivaldi (2001), Automatic Term Detection: A review of current systems, In: *Recent Advances in Computational Terminology*, John Benjamins, Amsterdam.
4. M.F. Caropreso, S. Matwin and F. Sebastiani (2000), A learner-independent evaluation of the usefulness of statistical phrases for automated text categorization, A. G. Chin (Ed.), *Text Databases and Document Management: Theory and Practice*, Idea Group Publishing, Hershey, US, pp. 78–102.
5. I. Dagan, Y. Karov, D. Roth (1997), Mistake-Driven Learning in Text Categorization. *Proceedings of the Second Conference on Empirical Methods in NLP*, pp. 55–63.
6. A. Grove, N. Littlestone, and D. Schuurmans (2001), General convergence results for linear discriminant updates. Machine Learning 43(3), pp. 173–210.
7. Djoerd Hiemstra and F. de Jong (1999), Disambiguation strategies for cross-language Information Retrieval, Proceedings ECDL'99, Springer SLNC vol 1696 pp. 274–293.
8. Cornelis H.A. Koster and Marc Seutter (2002), Taming Wild Phrases, Proceedings 25th European Conference on IR Research (ECIR'03), Springer LNCS 2633, pp 161–176.
9. Leah S. Larkey (1999), A patent search and classification system, Proceedings of DL-99, 4th ACM Conference on Digital Libraries, pp. 179–187.
10. V. Lavrenko, M. Choquette and W. Bruce Croft (2002), Cross-Lingual Relevance Models, Proceedings ACM SIGIR'02, pp. 175–182.
11. Lewis, D.D. (1992), An evaluation of phrasal and clustered representations on a text categorization task. Proceedings ACM SIGIR'92.
12. Paul McNamee and James Mayfield (2002), Comparing Cross-Language Query Expansion Techniques by Degrading Translation Resources, Proceedings ACM SIGIR'02, pp. 159–166.
13. C. Peters and C.H.A. Koster, Uncertainty-based Noise Reduction and Term Selection in Text Categorization, Proceedings 24th BCS-IRSG European Colloquium on IR Research, Springer LNCS 2291, pp 248–267.
14. Philip Resnik, Douglas W. Oard, and Gina-Anne Levow (2001), Improved Cross-Language Retrieval using Backoff Translation, Human Language Technology Conference (HLT), San Diego, CA, March 2001.
15. E. Riloff (1995), Little Words Can Make a Big Difference for Text Classification, Proceedings ACM SIGIR'95, pp. 130–136.
16. F. Sebastiani (2002), Machine learning in automated text categorization. ACM Computing Surveys, Vol 34 no 1, 2002, pp. 1–47.

# Automatic Multi-label Subject Indexing in a Multilingual Environment

Boris Lauser[1] and Andreas Hotho[2]

[1] FAO of the UN, Library & Documentation Systems Division,
00100 Rome, Italy
boris.lauser@fao.org
http://www.fao.org
[2] University of Karlsruhe, Institute AIFB,
76131 Karlsruhe, Germany
hotho@aifb.uni-karlsruhe.de

**Abstract.** This paper presents an approach to automatically subject index full-text documents with multiple labels based on binary support vector machines (SVM). The aim was to test the applicability of SVMs with a real world dataset. We have also explored the feasibility of incorporating multilingual background knowledge, as represented in thesauri or ontologies, into our text document representation for indexing purposes. The test set for our evaluations has been compiled from an extensive document base maintained by the Food and Agriculture Organization (FAO) of the United Nations (UN). Empirical results show that SVMs are a good method for automatic multi- label classification of documents in multiple languages.

## 1 Introduction

The management of large amounts of information and knowledge is of ever increasing importance in today's large organizations. With the ease of making information available online, especially in corporate intranets and knowledge bases, organizing information for later retrieval becomes an increasingly difficult task. Subject indexing is the act of describing a document in terms of its subject content. The purpose of subject indexing is to make it possible to easily retrieve references on a particular subject. It is the process of extracting the main concepts of a document, representing those concepts by keywords in the chosen language and associating these keywords with the document. In order to be unambiguous and carry out this process in a more standardized way, keywords should be chosen from a controlled vocabulary.

The AGROVOC[1] thesaurus, developed and maintained by the Food and Agricultural Organization[2] (FAO) of the United Nations (UN), is a controlled vocabulary developed for the agricultural domain. The FAO manages a vast amount of documents and information related to agriculture. Professional librarians and indexers use the AGROVOC thesaurus as a controlled vocabulary to manually index all documents

---

[1] [http://www.fao.org/agrovoc].

[2] [http://www.fao.org].

T. Koch and I.T. Sølvberg (Eds.): ECDL 2003, LNCS 2769, pp. 140–151, 2003.
© Springer-Verlag Berlin Heidelberg 2003

and resources managed by FAO's information management system. They are allowed to assign as many labels as necessary to index a document. In the following we call the automatic assignment process of suitable keywords to the documents the *multi-label* and *multi-class*[3] classification problem. This process is applied to resources in all the official FAO languages and herewith constitutes a *multilingual* problem. The cost of labour for professional indexers and the increase in growth in available electronic resources has resulted in a backlog of resources that are not indexed. Automatic document indexing could be particularly useful in digital libraries such as the ones maintained at the FAO to make more resources available through the system.

This paper presents an approach to use binary support vector machines (SVM) for automatic subject indexing of full-text documents with multiple labels. An extensive test document set has been compiled from FAO's large quantity of resources in which *multi-label* and *multilingual* indexing have been evaluated. Motivated by our text clustering results with background knowledge (cf. [7]), we have further analyzed the integration of domain specific background knowledge in the form of the multilingual AGROVOC thesaurus for performance improvement. With the evaluated results we will reason the integration of background knowledge with SVMs to be a promising approach towards (semi-) automatic, multilingual, multi-label subject document indexing.

The paper is outlined as follows: The next section introduces the reader to automatic text categorization, in particular support vector machines and the multi-label classification problem. Section 3 gives a brief introduction to ontologies and their representation. In Section 4, we explain in detail the compilation of the used test document set and the evaluation settings followed by a discussion of the results. We conclude by suggesting promising future possibilities for subject indexing of multilingual documents.

## 2 Automatic Text Categorization

Text categorization is the process of algorithmically analyzing a document to assign a set of categories (or index terms) that succinctly describe the content of the document [11]. Various methods from different communities have been applied in automatic text categorization approaches, such as classical IR based classifiers, statistical learning classifiers, decision trees, inductive rule learning, expert systems or support vector machines (SVM). More comprehensive surveys of algorithms used for automatic classification can be found in [11], [1], and [12]. One application of text categorization is document indexing, in which several keywords taken from a controlled vocabulary such as a thesaurus or an ontology are assigned to a document in order to describe its subject. Support vector machines have been shown to outperform other approaches [1]. In this research, we therefore use an SVM-based approach to be applied to the multi-label classification problem as described in the following sections in accordance with the definitions given in [12]:

---

[3] In the following we only use the term multi-label.

## 2.1 The Classification Problem

**Multi-Label Classification Problem.** In a multi-label classification problem, each document can be assigned an arbitrary number $m$ (multiple labels) of $n$ (multiple) possible classes. We have a set of training documents $X$ and a set of classes $C = \{c_1,...,c_n\}$. Each document $x_i \in X$ is associated with a subset $C_i \subseteq C$ ($|C_i| = m$) of relevant classes. The task is to find the most coinciding approximation of the unknown target function $\Phi : X \times C \rightarrow \{true, false\}$ by using a function $\overline{\Phi} : X \times C \rightarrow \{true, false\}$, typically called a classifier or learned model. $\overline{\Phi}$ reflects the unknown but "ideal" assignment of documents to classes.

In the single-label case, only one class is assigned. The binary classification problem is a special case of the single-label problem and can be described as follows:

**Binary Classification Problem.** Each of the documents $x_i \in X$ is assigned to only one of two possible classes $c_i$ or its complement $\hat{c}_i$.

There are different alternatives towards multi-label document indexing as carried out in the FAO. In this research we adopted the approach of transforming a multi-label classification problem into $|C|$ independent problems of binary classification. This requires that categories be stochastically independent, that is, for any $c_i, c_k$ the value of $\Phi(x_i, c_i)$ does not depend on the value of $\Phi(x_i, c_k)$ and vice versa. In the case of document indexing at the FAO, this is a reasonable assumption.

## 2.2 Binary Support Vector Machines

Vapnik first introduced support vector machines (SVM) in 1995 [5]. They have been applied to the area of text classification first by Joachims in 1998 [8]. In support vector machines, documents are represented using the vector space model:

**Vector Space Model.** A document $x_i$ is transformed into a $d$-dimensional feature space $\mathbb{R}^d$. Each dimension corresponds to a term (word, also referred to as feature). The values are the frequencies of the terms in the document. A document is represented by its word-vector of term frequencies,

$$\vec{x}_i = (tf(x_i, t_1),..., tf(x_i, t_{|T|})) ,$$

where $T$ is the set of terms that occur at least once in at least one document in the whole set ($|T| = d$) and the $tf(x_i, t)$ represent the term frequency of term $t \in T$ in document $x_i$.

There are a wide variety of weights and ways to choose a term/feature. A more detailed discussion can be found in [12]. In this case, terms (or later concepts from the ontology) are chosen as features and the standard *tfidf* (Term Frequency Inverse Document Frequency) measure is used as term weight calculated as

$$tfidf(x_i, t) = \log(tf(x_i, t) + 1) * \log\left(\frac{N}{df(t)}\right),$$

where $tf(x_i, t)$ is the frequency of term $t$ in document $x_i$ and $N$ is the total number of documents (|X|) and $df(t)$ (document frequency) is the number of documents, a term $t$ occurred in.

A binary SVM tries to separate all the word vectors of the training document examples into two classes by a hyper plane, maximizing the distance of the nearest training examples. Therefore, it is also referred to as the maximum margin hyper plane. A test document is then predicted by the SVM by determining, on which side of the hyper plane its word vector is. A very good and detailed introduction to SVM and document representations is provided in [14].

## 2.3  Related Approaches

A different approach described in [10] uses a Bayesian classifier together with a document mixture model to predict multiple classes for each document. This approach takes into consideration all classes at the same time as opposed to splitting the whole problem into a number of binary classifiers.

A recently taken similar approach towards multi-label classification using binary classifiers is discussed in [6]. The difference to our approach is that these algorithms can be applied in online settings, where the examples are presented one at a time, as opposed to the batch setting used with support vector machines.

## 3  Background Knowledge in Form of Ontologies

Apart from solving the multi-label problem, the additional incorporation of background knowledge as provided by domain specific ontologies is the second focus of this work. Since ontologies have been defined many times, we will abstain from giving a formal definition of domain ontologies in favour of introducing the main aspects in a short example. The underlining formal definition, used representation and notions in this work are in accordance with [3]. This is also the basis of our implementation in the KAON Framework[4]. Figure 1 shows a very small extract of the AGROVOC thesaurus, represented as an ontology. Refer to [9] for a detailed discussion of converting the AGROVOC thesaurus into an ontology. An ontology is basically a tree-ordered hierarchy structure of concepts as shown in Figure 1.

Each concept in the picture (drawn as a rectangle) has lexical entries (labels, synonyms) attached to it. The picture only shows the English labels of the concepts. The important fact for our purposes – explained in more detail in section 4 – is that a

---

[4] [http://kaon.semanticweb.org/].

concept itself is actually language independent and internally represented by a URI[5] (Uniform resource identifier). Every concept has a super concept, e.g. "supply balance" is the super concept of "stocks". The highest concept is "root". In addition to the tree structure, an ontology can have arbitrary lateral relationships, as shown here with a 'related term' relationship. As opposed to simple thesauri, ontologies allow for many types of relationships, making it a more expressive instrument of abstract domain modelling.

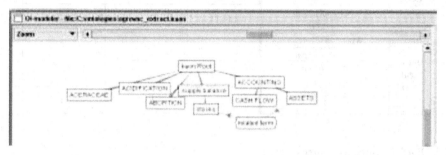

**Fig. 1.** Small ontology extract

# 4   Evaluation

## 4.1   The Test Document Set

To evaluate this research, a set of training and test documents has been compiled from the agricultural resources of the FAO. Journals, proceedings, single articles and many other resources constitute an extremely heterogeneous test set, differing substantially in size and descriptive content of its documents. The metadata elements of the resources contain a subject element in addition to others such as title, URL, etc. Subject indexing is carried out using keywords from the AGROVOC thesaurus which provides over 16607 potential document descriptors to choose from. A maximum of 6 primary descriptors, describing the most important concepts of a resource, can be used to index a document. Additionally, an indefinite number of secondary descriptors can be chosen, as well as geographic descriptors (for example country information). Only the primary descriptor associations have been considered in this evaluation. Metadata information about FAO documents is stored in any of the three languages English, French and Spanish. The test sets have been compiled with the requirement of having at least 50 documents for each class. Table 1 shows an overview of the so compiled test sets in the 3 different languages.

---

[5] See also [http://www.w3.org/Addressing/].

**Table 1.** Compiled multi-label test document set in 3 languages

| | | English (en) | French (fr) | Spanish (es) |
|---|---|---|---|---|
| Total | # Documents | 1016 | 698 | 563 |
| | # Classes | 7 | 9 | 7 |
| Class Level | Max ($\frac{\#documents}{class}$) | 315 | 214 | 179 |
| | Min ($\frac{\#documents}{class}$) | 108 | 58 | 58 |
| | Avg ($\frac{\#documents}{class}$) | 145,14 | 77,56 | 80,43 |
| Document level | Max ($\frac{\#labels}{document}$) | 3 | 3 | 3 |
| | Min ($\frac{\#labels}{document}$) | 1 | 1 | 1 |
| | Avg ($\frac{\#labels}{document}$) | 1,25 | 1,40 | 1,42 |

## 4.2  Performance Measures

The common notions of precision and recall from the Information Retrieval (IR) community have been applied to measure performance of the conducted tests [12]. The initial document set $X$ (pre-classified by human indexers) is split into a training document set $X_{Tr}$ and a test document set $X_{Te}$, so that $X = X_{Te} \cup X_{Tr}$. The corpus of documents is pre-classified, i.e. the values of the function $\overline{\Phi}$ are known for every pair $(x_i, c_i)$. The model is built with the training set and evaluated with the test set.

Precision and recall are measured for each class and calculated from four different numbers according to Table 2.

**Table 2.** Contingency table for class $c_i$

| Class $c_i$ | | Expert judgements | |
|---|---|---|---|
| | | YES | NO |
| Classifier judgements | YES | TP$_i$ | FP$_i$ |
| | NO | FN$_i$ | TN$_i$ |

TP$_i$ (true positives) is the number of documents correctly assigned to class $c_i$. FP$_i$ (false positives), FN$_i$ (false negatives) and TN$_i$ (true negatives) are defined accordingly.

Overall performance is measured by summing up the values over all classes, and calculates precision and recall according to the micro-averaging approach [12] to:

$$Precision_{micro} = \frac{\sum_{i=1}^{|C|} TP_i}{\sum_{i=1}^{|C|} (TP_i + FP_i)} \qquad Recall_{micro} = \frac{\sum_{i=1}^{|C|} TP_i}{\sum_{i=1}^{|C|} (TP_i + FN_i)}$$

Precision is an indicator of how many of the predictions were actually correct. On the other hand, recall is an indicator of how many of the pre-classified documents have also been predicted, i.e. it provides an indication of how exhaustive the predictions were. Clearly, both figures must be measured to be able to draw a conclusion on performance.

### 4.3 Evaluation Criteria and Setup

Within this research work, three different test settings have been carried out:

**Single-label vs. multi-label classification**. The first evaluation focused on the comparison of single-label classification vs. multi-label classification. For this purpose, a second set of documents has been compiled from the document set shown in Table 1. This time, however, only the first primary descriptor assigned to the document was used, assuming that this is the most important descriptor for the respective document. One binary support vector machine is trained for each unordered pair of classes on the training document set resulting in $(m*(m-1))/2$ support vector machines. Each document of the test set is then evaluated against each SVM. A binary SVM votes for the better class amongst the two it can choose from. A score is associated with each class calculated based on the number of votes for the respective class. The score is > 0 if more than 50% of a class's SVMs have voted for this class. In the single-label case, the class with the best score is assigned to a document. In the multi-label case, we introduced a score-threshold. All classes with a score greater than the score threshold were assigned to a document. Obviously, the number of assigned labels varies with the chosen score threshold.
Because the English document sets provide the most extensive test sets., they have been chosen for this first evaluation, The number of training examples per class has been varied from 5 up to 100. The number of test examples has been held at a constant rate of 50 test documents per class. In case of the multi-label test set, the score threshold has been varied between 0 and 0.6.

**Multilingual classification**. The second evaluation has been motivated by the idea that support vector machines basically operate independently of languages and document representations. The simplest possible scenario is a classifier that, given an arbitrary document, decides for one of the 3 classes (English, French or Spanish). A very simple document set has been compiled out of the single-label document sets that have been compiled for the previous evaluation, each pre-classified to its corresponding language class (English, French, Spanish) respectively. Each class contains more than 500 documents. The classifier has been trained varying the number of training documents per class between 5 and 200, leaving the number of test documents at a constant rate of 100 test documents per class.

**Integration of domain-specific background knowledge**. The third and last evaluation tests the effect of integrating the domain specific background knowledge provided by the AGROVOC ontology. The integration of background knowledge is accomplished by extending the word vector of a document with related concepts, extracted from the domain ontology by using word-concept mappings and exploring concept relationships. The necessary steps to integrate the background knowledge are more formally outlined in Hotho et. al. [7]. In our evaluation, we varied two parameters: the **concept integration depth**, i.e. the maximum depth up to which super concepts and related concepts of a term are included; and the **concept integration mode**, for which 3 possible options exist:

 - Add all concepts found in the ontology to the word vector (**add**)
 - Replace all words in the word vector with corresponding concepts (**replace**)
 - Consider only the concepts found in the ontology, i.e. for each document, create
   a word-vector only consisting of the domain specific concepts (**only**)

The idea behind this integration is to move the word vector of a document towards the specific domain and topic it represents, therefore making it more distinguishable from other word vectors. Domain specific background knowledge bares a certain potential to accomplish this task, in a way that it only contains the concepts, which are descriptive for the domain.

In our test case, the AGROVOC thesaurus has been pruned to reflect the domain of the compiled document sets. Pruning in this case means the extraction of only the relevant concepts for a specific domain, thus resulting in an ontology/thesaurus significantly smaller in size. The algorithm used here has been applied in other domains [13] and adapted within the project at the FAO [9].

We evaluated the integration of the pruned AGROVOC on the English document set for the single-label case. Apart from variation of the number of training and test examples per class and all possible concept integration modes, the concept integration depth has been varied from 1 to 2, 1 meaning that only matching concepts have been considered.

## 4.4 Results

**Single-label vs. multi-label classification.** For each parameter variation, 15 independent test runs have been conducted. In each run the document set has been split into an independent training and test set. Performance measures have been averaged over all 15 runs respectively.

In the single-label case, precision and recall are always the same and the calculation of both values is not needed. The precision values ranged from 47% (5 training examples per class) to 67% (100 training examples per class). In case of multi-label classification, both precision and recall have been calculated, since here they differ from each other substantially. Keeping the score threshold low implies that many labels – assumingly too many – get assigned to each test document. This results in low precision, because many of the classifications are wrong. However, in that case recall is high because most of the test documents get assigned the labels of the classes they are pre-classified to. Table 3 shows the development of precision and recall depending on the score threshold exemplary for the English set with 50 training examples per class. By raising the score threshold, fewer labels get assigned to each document. In our test cases, precision could go up to as much as 45% and recall plummeted to as low as 76%. In order to make these contradictory effects comparable with the single-label classification, the so-called breakeven value has been computed as the average mean of precision and recall, assuming that both measures are rated equally important.

**Table 3.** Results of multi-label classification with the English language test set. Development of precision and recall depending on the score threshold.

| Score Threshold | Measure | 50 Training Ex. |
|---|---|---|
| 0.0 | Precision | 0.2727 |
| | Recall | 0.9329 |
| | Breakeven | 0.6028 |
| 0.1 | Precision | 0.2754 |
| | Recall | 0.9350 |
| | Breakeven | 0.6052 |
| 0.3 | Precision | 0.3412 |
| | Recall | 0.8721 |
| | Breakeven | 0.6066 |
| 0.5 | Precision | 0.4492 |
| | Recall | 0.7618 |
| | Breakeven | 0.6055 |
| 0.6 | Precision | 0.4539 |
| | Recall | 0.7702 |
| | Breakeven | 0.6121 |

Figure 2 shows all the results in one chart. The Spanish and French multi-label test sets have been additionally evaluated regarding language behaviour of the classifier. The breakeven values are shown depending on the training examples used for building the SVMs. Multi-label classification has shown overall worse performance than the single-label case. However, taking into account the higher complexity of the multi-label problem, the difference comparing the overall results between the two approaches is reasonable. Regarding performance of different languages, we can already infer from the multi-label results that languages different from English seem to perform equally well.

The breakeven values displayed here have been achieved with the overall superior configuration of a score threshold of 0.1. Raising the threshold further always resulted in similar breakeven values. No clear statement can be made on the use of varying the score threshold beyond that value. It depends on the intended goal of applying the classifier. If the classifier is used to help a human indexer by suggesting a large set of possible index terms from which the indexer can choose, then it is clearly advantageous to have a high recall, suggesting most of the 'good' terms amongst others. If, however, the automatic classifier is used without human support, it becomes more necessary to limit the risk of assigning wrong labels and aim for high precision. In the latter case, a higher score threshold should be chosen.

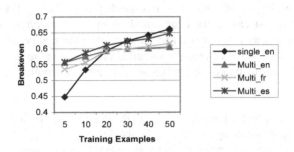

**Fig. 2.** Results single-label vs. multi-label classification

**Multilingual classification**. The application of the scenario described in section 4.3 resulted in almost 100% precision in all test runs. This clearly shows that support vector machines are able to distinguish almost perfectly between languages.

**Integration of domain-specific background knowledge**. The integration of the pruned AGROVOC ontology was only able to show a slight increase in precision in the case of adding concepts to the word-vector and replacing words with their respective concepts. However, the performance gains did not show any significance. Figure 3 shows the results for the evaluation runs with 10 and 50 training examples per class. The leftmost values (ontology integration depth 0) display the results without ontology integration as reference. The remainder of the values belongs to each variation in integration mode (*add, replace, only*) and depth (*1* meaning that only the concepts which matched the label have been considered, whereas *2* means that also the direct super- sub- and related concepts have been considered).

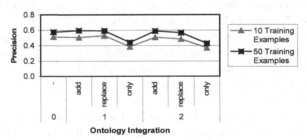

**Fig. 3.** Results of ontology integration with the English single-label test document set.

In the case of totally replacing the word-vector of a document (concept integration mode *only*), the overall results even slightly decreased. This effect leads to the assumption that the used ontology misses domain specific vocabulary needed to unambiguously define the content of the domain documents. Considering our description of subject indexing made above, a document's content should be described by leaving out all non-domain-specific concepts.

# 5  Conclusion and Outlook

Our results clearly show that SVMs behave robustly across different languages. The fact that no significant performance differences between the languages have been found in the multi-label case[6] indicates that SVMs can be applied to classify documents in different languages. SVMs seem to be especially applicable to the complex case of assigning multiple labels to a document. The inferior results of multi-label indexing compared to the single-label case are clearly explained by the increased complexity of the task. Among human classifiers, multi-label subject indexing is an inconsistent task; opinions vary from person to person and there is no single correct assignment of labels to a document regarding the type and number of chosen labels. Taking this phenomenon (also known as indexer-indexer inconsistency [4]) into consideration, the results found can even be interpreted as equally good. This is a rather optimistic hypothesis and since the two cases are not directly comparable, further research and evaluation are needed in order to confirm it. These results combined with the fact that the integration of background knowledge did not show any significant performance losses – except in the case of total replacement of a document's word-vector – leads us to an interesting conclusion for further research and evaluation. In the FAO (and most probably in many other environments), English resources heavily outweigh the availability of resources in other languages. As clearly shown in our results, the quality of SVMs strongly correlates with the number of used training examples. A desired scenario is therefore to be able to train the classifier with documents in one language only (i.e. English), and be able to use it to classify documents in other languages. This can be achieved by replacement of a document's word-vector by using only the concepts found in the multilingual domain specific background knowledge. AGROVOC is available online in 5 different languages and has been translated into many others. A document's word-vector thus becomes language independent and the resulting classification should be the same. With respect to the lower performance in case of replacing a document's word-vector with its domain-specific concepts only, future research should be applied towards testing the exhaustiveness of the AGROVOC ontology used here. On the other hand, the AGROVOC is a more generic thesaurus, used for the whole agricultural domain. Subsets of the documents used in this research are assumingly more specific to certain domains. It would therefore be especially of interest to re-evaluate the settings used in this test set by using a document set limited to a very specific domain and a suitable domain specific ontology.

Moreover, especially in multinational organizations and environments like that provided at the FAO, more and more documents are actually multilingual, containing parts written in different languages. The integration of background knowledge as described above obviously has potential in showing robust behaviour towards those kinds of documents.

---

[6] This result could be confirmed with further test runs conducted on the document sets compiled for single-label classification.

In conclusion, the results shown here are preliminary steps towards a promising option to use support vector machines for automatic subject indexing in a multilingual environment. Future research should exploit different other domains, in order to prove or confute the findings made here.

**Acknowledgements.** We express our gratitude to the FAO of the UN, Rome for the funding of our work. We especially thank all our colleagues there for their substantial contribution in requirements analysis and the compilation of the test document sets.

# References

1. Aas, K.; Eikvil, L.: Text Categorization: a survey. Technical Report #941, Norwegian Computing Center. 1999.
2. Berners-Lee, T.; Fielding, R.; Irvine, U.C.; Masinter, L.: Uniform Resource Identifiers (URI): Generic Syntax. IETF Request for Comments: 2396. [Online: http://www.ietf.org/rfc/rfc2396.txt]. August 1998.
3. Bozsak, E.; Ehrig, M.; Handschuh, S.; Hotho, et al: KAON -- Towards a Large Scale Semantic Web. In: Bauknecht, K.; Min Tjoa, A.; Quirchmayr, G. (Eds.): Proc. of the 3rd Intl. Conf. on E-Commerce and Web Technologies (EC-Web 2002), 2002, 304–313.
4. Chung, Y.; Pottenger, W. M.; Schatz, B. R.: Automatic Subject Indexing Using an Associative Neural Network, in: Proceedings of the 3 rd ACM International Conference on Digital Libraries (DL'98), pp. 59–68. ACM Press, 1998.
5. Cortes, C.; Vapnik, V.: Support-Vector Networks. In Machine Learning, 20(3):273–297, September 1995.
6. Crammer, K.; Singer, Y.: A new family of online algorithms for category ranking. In Proceedings of the 25th annual international ACM SIGIR conference on Research and development in information retrieval, pp. 151–158. Tampere, Finland. 2002.
7. Hotho, A.; Staab, S. and Stumme, G. (2003). Text clustering based on background knowledge (Technical Report 425), University of Karlsruhe, Institute AIFB. 36 pages.
8. Joachims, T.: Text categorization with Support Vector Machines: Learning with many relevant features. In Machine Learning: ECML-98, Tenth European Conference on Machine Learning, 1998. pp. 137–142. [http://citeseer.nj.nec.com/article/joachims98text.html].
9. Lauser, B.: Semi-automatic ontology engineering and ontology supported document indexing in a multilingual environment. Internal Report. University of Karlsruhe, Institute of Applied Informatics and Formal Description Methods. 2003.
10. McCallum, A.: Multi-label text classification with a mixture model trained by em. AAAI'99 Workshop on Text Learning. 1999.
11. Ruiz, M. E.; Srinivasan, P.: Combining Machine Learning and Hierarchical Structures for text categorization. In Proceedings of the 10th ASIS SIG/CR Classification Research Workshop, Advances in Classification Research–Vol. 10. November 1999.
12. Sebastiani, F.: Machine learning in automated text categorization. Tech. Rep. IEI-B4-31-1999, Consiglio Nazionale delle Ricerche, Pisa, Italy. 1999.
13. Volz, R.: Akquisition von Ontologien mit Text-Mining-Verfahren. Technical Report 27, Rentenanstalt/Swiss Life, CC/ITRD, CH-8022 Zürich, Switzerland, ISSN 1424–4691. 2000.
14. Witten, I.; Frank, E.: Data Mining, Practical Machine Learning Tools and techniques with Java implementations. Morgan Kaufmann. 1999.

# Automatic Induction of Rules for Classification and Interpretation of Cultural Heritage Material

S. Ferilli, F. Esposito, T.M.A. Basile, and N. Di Mauro

Dipartimento di Informatica
Università di Bari
via E. Orabona, 4 - 70125 Bari - Italia
{ ferilli, esposito, basile, nicodimauro}@di.uniba.it

**Abstract.** This work presents the application of incremental symbolic learning strategies for the automatic induction of classification and interpretation rules in the cultural heritage domain. Specifically, such experience was carried out in the environment of the EU project COLLATE, in whose architecture the incremental learning system INTHELEX is used as a learning component. Results are reported, proving that the system was able to learn highly reliable rules for such a complex task.

## 1 Introduction

Many important historic and cultural sources, which constitute a major part of our cultural heritage, are fragile and distributed in various archives, which still lack effective and efficient technological support for cooperative and collaborative knowledge working. The IST-1999-20882 project COLLATE (Collaboratory for Annotation, Indexing and Retrieval of Digitized Historical Archive Material) aims at developing a WWW-based *collaboratory* [7] for archives, researchers and end-users working with digitized historic/cultural material (URL: http://www.collate.de). The chosen sample domain concerns a large corpus of multi-format documents concerning rare historic film censorship from the 20's and 30's, but includes also newspaper articles, photos, stills, posters and film fragments, provided by three major European film archives. In-depth analysis and comparison of such documents can give evidence about different film versions and cuts, and allow to restore lost/damaged films or identify actors and film fragments of unknown origin. All material is analyzed, indexed, annotated and interlinked by film experts, to which the COLLATE system aims at providing suitable task-based interfaces and knowledge management tools to support individual work and collaboration. Continuously integrating valuable knowledge about the cultural, political and social contexts into its digital data and metadata repositories, it will provide improved content-based functionality to better retrieve and interpret the historic material.

Supported by previous successful experience in the application of symbolic learning techniques to classification and understanding of paper documents [4,6, 9], our aim is learning to automatically identify and label document classes and

T. Koch and I.T. Sølvberg (Eds.): ECDL 2003, LNCS 2769, pp. 152–163, 2003.

significant components, to be used for indexing/retrieval purposes and to be submitted to the COLLATE users for annotation. Combining results from the manual and automatic indexing procedures, elaborate content-based retrieval mechanisms can be applied [2]. The challenge comes from the low layout quality and standard of such a material, which introduces a considerable amount of noise in its description. As regards the layout quality, it is often affected by manual annotations, stamps that overlap to sensible components, ink specks, etc. As to the layout standard, many documents are typewritten sheets, that consist of all equally spaced lines in Gothic type.

Our proposal, supported by successful experiments reported in this paper, is to exploit symbolic (first-order logic) learning techniques, whose high level representation can better manage the complexity of the task and allows the use of different reasoning strategies than pure induction with the objective of making the learning process more effective and efficient.

The following section introduces and describes the classes of documents that were considered for the experiments. Then, Section 3 presents the system INTHELEX along with its features, and Section 4 shows experimental results. Lastly, Section 5 draws some conclusions and outlines future work directions.

## 2   Documents

This Section aims at briefly describing the documents that were taken into account for the research described in this paper. The COLLATE repository, set up by the film archives DIF (Deutsches Filminstitut, Frankfurt am Main), FAA (Film Archive Austria, Vienna) and NFA (Národni Filmový Archiv, Prague), includes a large collection of several thousands comprehensive documents concerning film culture, and focuses on documents related to censorship processes (see Figure 1). The importance of censorship for film production distribution lies mainly in the fact that it is often impossible to identify a unique film. Often, there are lots of different film versions with cuts, changed endings and new inter-titles, depending on the place and date of release. Exactly these differences are documented in censorship documents and allow statements about the original film. They define and identify the object of interest. Often they provide the only source available today for the reconstruction of the large number of films that have been lost or destroyed. Censorship documents support this restoration process by identifying and structuring the film fragments. They allow to put together film fragments from various copies in order to obtain a correct reconstruction. Each Country developed its own censorship history embedded in the political history. The collection is complemented by further documents like press articles, correspondence, photos, etc.

The sample document reported in the upper-left part of Figure 1 is an **Application Form** belonging to NFA. This kind of documents was required for applying to get the permission to show a film from a production or distribution company. This was common practice mainly in Czechoslovakia. The consequence of this application was the examination by the censorship office. The "application

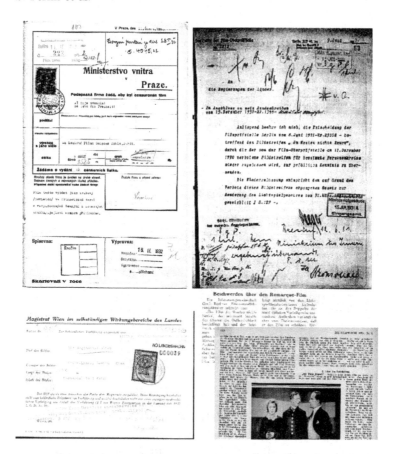

**Fig. 1.** Sample COLLATE documents

form" could be a source for information like: *Name of applicant* (production or distribution company), *title of the film, year of production, length* (before censorship), *brief content, information about earlier examinations,* etc. It was usually accompanied by a list of intertitles or dialogue list. Indeed, the applicant was obliged to enclose a list of intertitles or, in case of sound films, a list with the beginnings of the dialogues. These lists served to check whether a film shown in the cinema was the same as the one examined by the censorship office.

As regards the document shown in the upper-right side of Figure 1, it is an instance of **Censorship Decision**. This kind of documents are about the decision whether a film could or could not – and in which version – be distributed and shown throughout a Country. The Censorship Decision is often a protocol of the examination meeting and is issued by the censorship office. It provides information such as: *film title, participants in the examination, notices on content, juridical legitimization for the decision, legal motivation, conditions for permission* (for example cuts, change of title, etc.), *reference to previous de-*

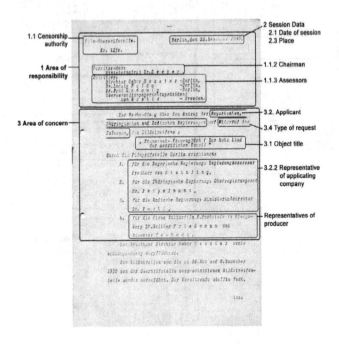

**Fig. 2.** Sample COLLATE Document Text Structure

*cisions, costs for the procedure.* For instance, Figure 2 shows the first page of one such document, with the interesting items already annotated by the experts. Indeed, it is noteworthy that almost all documents in the COLLATE collection are multipage, but generally just the first page contains information of interest.

The lower-left part of Figure 1 reports an example of **Registration Card**, a certification that the film had been approved for exhibition in the present version by the censoring authority. The registration cards were given to the distribution company which had to pay for this, and had to enclose the cards to the film copies. When the police checked the cinemas from time to time, the owner or projectionist had to show the registration card. Such cards constitute a large portion of the COLLATE collection, mainly provided by FAA and DIF, and are an important source for film reconstruction. They are a source for the following information: *Film title, production company, date and number of examination, length* (after censoring), *number of acts, brief content, forbidden parts, staff.*

The last documents in Figure 1 represent **Articles** from the contemporary film press, newspapers or magazines. They are necessary to reconstruct the context of a film, since they enlighten the reception background. One may also find debates and details on censorship there, because the press of every political direction watched closely the results of the examination.

# 3   The Learning Component

The need of automatically labelling the huge amount of documents in the COL-LATE repository, along with their significant components, suggested the use of a learning system to learn rules for such tasks from a small number of selected and annotated sample documents. In particular, the complexity of the domain and the need for the rules to be understandable by film experts, led to the choice of symbolic first-order learning.

INTHELEX (INcremental THEory Learner from EXamples) is a learning system for the induction of *hierarchical* logic theories from examples [5]: it learns theories expressed in a first-order logic representation from positive and negative examples; it can learn simultaneously *multiple concepts*, possibly related to each other (recursion is not allowed); it retains all the processed examples, so to guarantee validity of the learned theories on all of them; it is a *closed loop* learning system (i.e. a system in which feedback on performance is used to activate the theory revision phase [1]); it is *fully incremental* (in addition to the possibility of refining a previously generated version of the theory, learning can also start from an empty theory); it is based on the *Object Identity assumption* (terms, even variables, denoted by different names within a formula must refer to different objects).

INTHELEX incorporates two refinement operators, one for generalizing hypotheses that reject positive examples, and the other for specializing hypotheses that explain negative examples. It exploits a (possibly empty) previous version of the theory, a graph describing the dependence relationships among concepts, and an historical memory of all the past examples that led to the current theory. Whenever a new example is taken into account, it is stored in such a repository and the current theory is checked against it.

If it is positive and not covered, generalization must be performed. One of the definitions of the concept the example refers to is chosen by the system for generalization. If a generalization can be found that is consistent with all the past negative examples, then it replaces the chosen definition in the theory, or else another definition is chosen to be generalized. If no definition can be generalized in a consistent way, the system checks if the exact shape of the example itself can be regarded as a definition that is consistent with the past negative examples. If so, it is added to the theory, or else the example itself is added as an exception.

If the example is negative and covered, specialization is needed. Among the theory definitions involved in the example coverage, INTHELEX tries to specialize one at the lowest possible level in the dependency graph by adding to it positive information, which characterize all the past positive examples and can discriminate them from the current negative one. In case of failure on all of the considered definitions, the system tries to add negative information, that is able to discriminate the negative example from all the past positive ones, to the definition related to the concept the example is an instance of. If this fails too, the negative example is added to the theory as an exception. New incoming observations are always checked against the exceptions before applying the rules that define the concept they refer to.

Another peculiarity in INTHELEX is the integration of multistrategy operators that may help in the solution of the theory revision problem by preprocessing the incoming information [6], according to the theoretical framework for integrating different learning strategies known as Inferential Learning Theory [8]. Namely, deduction is exploited to fill observations with information that is not explicitly stated, but is implicit in their description, and hence refers to the possibility of better representing the examples and, consequently, the inferred theories. Conversely, abduction aims at completing possibly partial information in the examples (adding more details), whereas abstraction removes superfluous details from the description of both the examples and the theory. Thus, even if with opposite perspectives, both aim at reducing the computational effort required to learn a correct theory with respect to the incoming examples.

To ensure uniformity of the example descriptions, INTHELEX requires the observations to be expressed only in terms of basic predicates that have no definition. Nevertheless, combinations of these predicates might identify higher level concepts that is worth adding to the descriptions in order to raise their semantic level. For this reason, INTHELEX exploits deduction to recognize such concepts and explicitly add them to the examples description. For doing this, it can be provided with a Background Knowledge, supposed to be correct and hence not modifiable, containing (complete or partial) definitions in the same format as the theory rules.

Abduction was defined by Peirce as hypothesizing some facts that, together with a given theory, could explain a given observation. Abducibles are the predicates about which assumptions (*abductions*) can be made: They carry all the incompleteness of the domain (if it were possible to complete these predicates then the theory would be correctly described). Integrity constraints (each corresponding to a combination of literals that is not allowed to occur) provide indirect information about them. The proof procedure implemented in INTHELEX starts from a goal and a set of initial assumptions and results in a set of consistent hypotheses by intertwining *abductive* and *consistency derivations*.

The exploitation of abstraction concerns the shift from the language in which the theory is described to a higher level one. Abstraction takes place at the world-perception level, and then propagates to higher levels, by means of a set of operators. An abstraction theory contains information for performing the shift specified by such operators, that allow the system to replace a number of components by a compound object, to decrease the granularity of a set of values, to ignore whole objects or just part of their features, and to neglect the number of occurrences of some kind of object. In INTHELEX the abstraction theory must be given, and the system automatically applies it to the learning problem at hand before processing the examples.

## 4    Experimental Results

INTHELEX was considered a suitable learning component for the COLLATE architecture based on its previous successful application to different kinds of

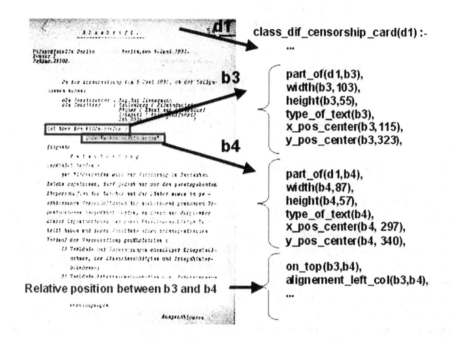

**Fig. 3.** An example of processed document

documents, indicating a good generality of the approach. Moreover, many of its features met the requirements imposed by the complexity of the documents to be handled. In addition to being a symbolic (first-order logic) incremental system, its multistrategy capabilities seemed very useful. For instance, abduction could make the system more flexible in the absence of particular layout components due to the typist's style, while abstraction could help in focusing on layout patterns that are meaningful to the identification of the interesting details, neglecting less interesting ones. Experimental results, reported in the following, confirm the above expectations.

The COLLATE dataset for INTHELEX consisted of 29 documents for the class faa_registration_card, 36 ones for the class dif_censorship_decision, 24 for the class nfa_cen_dec_model_a and 13 for the class nfa_cen_dec_model_b. Other 17 reject documents were obtained from newspaper articles. Note that the symbolic method adopted allows the experiment supervisor to specifically select prototypical examples to be included in the learning set. This explains why theories with good predictiveness can be obtained even from few observations.

The first-order descriptions of such documents, needed to run INTHELEX, were automatically generated by the system WISDOM++ [3]. Starting from scanned images, it is able to identify in few seconds the layout blocks that make up a paper document and to describe them in terms of their size (height and width, in pixels), position (horizontal and vertical, in pixels from the top-

```
pos_left(X):-
    x_pos_centre(X,Y), Y >= 0, Y =< 213.
pos_center(X):-
    x_pos_centre(X,Y), Y >= 214, Y =< 426.
pos_right(X):-
    x_pos_centre(X,Y), Y >= 427.
```

**Fig. 4.** Abstraction rules for horizontal block position

left corner), type (text, line, picture and mixed) and relative position (horizontal/vertical alignment between two blocks, adjacency). It is not a domain-specific system, since it has already been used to process several other kinds of documents, such as commercial letters and scientific papers. Figure 3 shows an example of a document and its description.

Since the inductive procedure embedded in INTHELEX is not able to handle numeric values (such as the number of pixels in the document descriptions provided by WISDOM++), a change of representation in the description language was necessary, such that final observations were made up of symbolic attributes only. The abstraction operator was used for breaking numeric values into intervals represented by symbolic constants (*discretization*), by providing the system with an Abstraction Theory containing rules that encode such a language shift. Figure 4 shows the rules of the Abstraction Theory that are in charge of discretizing the horizontal position of a layout block in a document.

The complexity of the domain is confirmed by the description length of the documents, that ranges between 40 and 379 literals (144 on average) for class faa_registration_card, between 54 and 263 (215 on average) for class dif_censorship_decision; between 105 and 585 (269 on average) for class nfa_cen_dec_model_a and between 191 and 384 literals (260 on average) for class nfa_cen_dec_model_b. It is worth noting that the description length after the abstraction process on numeric features doesn't change (increase/decrease) with respect to the original one, since each numeric value is now represented by a corresponding symbolic value.

Each document was considered as a positive example for the class it belongs, and as a negative example for the other classes to be learned; reject documents were considered as negative examples for all classes. Definitions for each class were learned, starting from the empty theory, and their predictive accuracy was tested according to a 10-fold cross validation methodology, ensuring that each fold contained the same proportion of positive and negative examples. Table 1 reports the experimental results, averaged on the 10 folds, of the classification process in this environment as regards number of clauses that define the concept ($Cl$), number of performed generalizations ($lgg$), Accuracy on the test set (expressed in percentage) and Runtime (in seconds).

As regards the rules learned by the system, Figure 5 shows a definition for the classification of documents belonging to dif_censorship_decision class. An explanation of the concept according to this rule is "a document belongs to

```
class_dif_cen_decision(A) :-
    image_lenght_long(A), image_width_short(A),
    part_of(A, B), type_of_text(B),
    width_medium_large(B), height_very_very_small(B),
    pos_left(B), pos_upper(B),
    part_of(A, C), type_of_text(C),
    height_very_very_small(C),
    pos_left(C), pos_upper(C),
    on_top(C, D), type_of_text(D),
    width_medium_large(D), height_very_very_small(D),
    pos_left(D), pos_upper(D).
```

**Fig. 5.** Example of learned definition

this class if it has long length and short width, it contains three components in the upper-left part, all of type text and having very short height, two of which are medium large and one of these two is on top of the third". Two remarks are worth for this class: first, the features in this description are common to all the learned definitions in the 10 folds, which suggests that the system was able to catch the significant components and explains why its performance on this class is the best of all; second, starting with descriptions whose average length was 215, the average number of literals in the learned rules is just 22.

Each document is composed by blocks whose labels regard the role they play in it. For instance, in one of the three blocks appearing in the rule in Figure 5 the experts recognized a "session_data" item. The curiosity of checking the correctness of such a guess was one of the motivations to run additional experiments aimed at learning definitions for the semantic labels of interest for each document class. Indeed, different document classes have different labels. As regard the first class of documents, **faa_registration_card**, the domain experts provided the following labels characterizing the objects belonging to it (in square brackets the number of items in the document dataset): *registration_au* [28+], *date_place* [26+], *department* [17+], *applicant* [11+], *reg_number* [28+] , *film_genre* [20+], *film_length* [19+], *film_producer* [18+], *film_title* [20+]. Like in the classification step, each example is positive for the label(s) it belongs to, and negative for all the others. Again, a 10-fold cross-validation was applied, and the results were averaged (see Table 2).

**Table 1.** Statistics for Document Classification

|        | Cl   | Lgg  | Accuracy | Runtime |
|--------|------|------|----------|---------|
| DIF    | 1.00 | 7.50 | 99.17    | 17.13   |
| FAA    | 3.50 | 9.70 | 94.17    | 334.05  |
| NFA_A  | 2.80 | 7.30 | 93.92    | 87.71   |
| NFA_B  | 1.70 | 5.40 | 97.56    | 92.05   |

**Table 2.** Statistics for Understanding FAA

|  | Cl | Lgg | Accuracy | Runtime |
|---|---|---|---|---|
| registration_au | 5.6 | 12.5 | 91.43 | 3739.366 |
| date_place | 6.9 | 13.5 | 86.69 | 7239.625 |
| department | 1.9 | 6.6 | 98.95 | 118.625 |
| applicant | 2 | 4.5 | 97.89 | 93.993 |
| reg_number | 5.1 | 14.4 | 91.95 | 4578.208 |
| film_genre | 4 | 8.4 | 93.02 | 2344.899 |
| film_length | 5.5 | 9.9 | 90.87 | 3855.391 |
| film_producer | 4.9 | 10.4 | 94.05 | 4717.17 |
| film_title | 5.4 | 11.1 | 89.85 | 4863.084 |

The labels specified for class dif_censorship_decision were: *cens_signature* [35+], *cert_signature* [35+], *object_title* [36+], *cens_authority* [36+], *chairman* [36+], *assessors* [36+], *session_data* [36+], *representative* [49+]. Table 3 shows the results of a 10-fold cross-validation run on this dataset.

**Table 3.** Statistics for Understanding DIF

|  | Cl | Lgg | Accuracy | Runtime |
|---|---|---|---|---|
| cens_signature | 2.2 | 11.6 | 98.32 | 1459.883 |
| cert_signature | 2.2 | 7.6 | 98.31 | 176.592 |
| object_title | 5 | 15.2 | 94.66 | 3960.829 |
| cens_authority | 2.9 | 12.1 | 97.64 | 2519.45 |
| chairman | 4.6 | 13.8 | 93.10 | 9332.845 |
| assessors | 4.6 | 15 | 94.48 | 12170.93 |
| session_data | 2.5 | 8.6 | 97.68 | 1037.96 |
| representative | 5.6 | 20.7 | 92.98 | 13761.958 |

Finally, class nfa_cen_dec_model_a was characterized by these labels, almost all different from the others: *dispatch_office* [33+], *applic_notes* [18+], *no_censor_card* [21+], *film_producer* [20+], *no_prec_doc* [20+], *applicant* [22+], *film_genre* [17+], *registration_au* [25+], *cens_process* [30+], *cens_card* [26+], *delivery_date* [16+]. Again, a 10-fold cross-validation was applied, whose averaged results are reported in Table 4.

The reported outcomes reveal that INTHELEX was actually able to learn significant definitions for both the document classes and the layout blocks of interest for each of them. Indeed, the predictive accuracy is always very high, reaching even 99.17% in one case and only in 2 cases out of 32 falling below 90% (specifically, 86.69% and 89.85%). It is very interesting to note that the best accuracy is obtained by a theory made up of only one clause (that we may state has perfectly grasped the target concept), and coincides with the best runtime (classification for class DIF). The learned rules show a high degree of understandability for human experts, which was one of the requirements for the

**Table 4.** Statistics for understanding (Model A)

|  | Cl | Lgg | Accuracy | Runtime |
|---|---|---|---|---|
| *dispatch_office* | 6.8 | 13.9 | 94.28 | 13149.31 |
| *applic_notes* | 2.5 | 5.7 | 98.81 | 231.05 |
| *no_censor_card* | 5.3 | 11.2 | 95.47 | 8136.796 |
| *film_producer* | 4.9 | 9.6 | 93.98 | 5303.78 |
| *no_prec_doc* | 4.6 | 11 | 93.97 | 5561.14 |
| *applicant* | 6.7 | 11.5 | 93.66 | 15588.15 |
| *film_genre* | 2.8 | 6.9 | 98.53 | 684.35 |
| *registration_au* | 4.1 | 12.5 | 94.64 | 5159.74 |
| *cens_process* | 4.8 | 10.8 | 98.51 | 4027.90 |
| *cens_card* | 5.6 | 11.8 | 94.62 | 3363.86 |
| *delivery_date* | 4 | 9.1 | 95.515 | 3827.34 |

experiment. As expected, the classification problem turned out to be easier than the interpretation one (that is concerned with the semantics of the layout blocks inside documents). This is suggested by the tendential increase in number of clauses, performed generalizations and runtime from Table 1 to Tables 3, 2 and 4. Such an increase is particularly evident for the runtime, even if it should be considered that the high predictive accuracy should ensure that few theory revisions can be expected when processing further documents. Scalability should be ensured, since we expect that very few documents will generate theory revision. Moreover, symbolic representations allow the expert to properly choose the training examples so that few of them are sufficient to reach a correct definition.

## 5   Conclusions and Future Work

This paper proposed the application of symbolic (first-order logic) multistrategy learning techniques to induce rules for automatic classification and interpretation of cultural heritage material. Experimental results prove the benefits that such an approach can bring. Specifically, the chosen domain comes from the EU project COLLATE, concerned with film censorship documents dating back to the 20s and 30s. The learning component is the incremental system INTHELEX, whose performance on such a task proved very interesting.

Future work will concern finding better and more tailored ways of exploiting the features provided by INTHELEX in order to tackle in a still more efficient and effective way the problems raised by the low layout quality typical of cultural heritage documents. In particular, being able to handle numeric/probabilistic features could provide important support for this aim.

**Acknowledgements.** This work was partially funded by the EU project IST-1999-20882 COLLATE "Collaboratory for Annotation, Indexing and Retrieval of Digitized Historical Archive Material".

# References

[1] J. M. Becker. Inductive learning of decision rules with exceptions: Methodology and experimentation. B.s. diss., Dept. of Computer Science, University of Illinois at Urbana-Champaign, Urbana, Illinois, USA, 1985. UIUCDCS-F-85-945.

[2] H. Brocks, U. Thiel, A. Stein, and A. Dirsch-Weigand. Customizable retrieval functions based on user tasks in the cultural heritage domain. In P. Constantopoulos and I.T. Sølvberg, editors, *Research and Advanced Technology for Digital Libraries*, number 2163 in LNCS, pages 37–48. Springer, 2001.

[3] F. Esposito, D. Malerba, and F.A. Lisi. Machine learning for intelligent processing of printed documents. *Journal of Intelligent Information Systems*, 14(2/3):175–198, 2000.

[4] F. Esposito, D. Malerba, G. Semeraro, N. Fanizzi, and S. Ferilli. Adding machine learning and knowledge intensive techniques to a digital library service. *International Journal on Digital Libraries*, 2(1):3–19, 1998.

[5] F. Esposito, G. Semeraro, N. Fanizzi, and S. Ferilli. Multistrategy Theory Revision: Induction and abduction in INTHELEX. *Machine Learning Journal*, 38(1/2):133–156, 2000.

[6] S. Ferilli. *A Framework for Incremental Synthesis of Logic Theories: An Application to Document Processing*. Ph.D. thesis, Dipartimento di Informatica, Università di Bari, Bari, Italy, November 2000.

[7] R.T. Kouzes, J.D. Myers, and W.A. Wulf. Collaboratories: Doing science on the internet. *IEEE Computer*, 29(8):40–46, 1996.

[8] R. S. Michalski. Inferential theory of learning. developing foundations for multistrategy learning. In R. S. Michalski and G. Tecuci, editors, *Machine Learning. A Multistrategy Approach*, volume IV, pages 3–61. Morgan Kaufmann, San Mateo, CA, U.S.A., 1994.

[9] G. Semeraro, S. Ferilli, N. Fanizzi, and F. Esposito. Document classification and interpretation through the inference of logic-based models. In P. Constantopoulos and I.T. Sølvberg, editors, *Research and Advanced Technology for Digital Libraries*, number 2163 in LNCS, pages 59–70. Springer, 2001.

# An Integrated Digital Library Server with OAI and Self-Organizing Capabilities

Hyunki Kim, Chee-Yoong Choo, and Su-Shing Chen

Computer and Information Science and Engineering Department,
University of Florida, Gainesville, Florida 32611, USA
{hykim, cc3, suchen}@cise.ufl.edu

**Abstract.** The Open Archives Initiative (OAI) is an experimental initiative for the interoperability of Digital Libraries (DLs) based on *metadata harvesting*. The goal of OAI is to develop and promote interoperability solutions to facilitate the efficient dissemination of content. At present, however, there are still several challenging issues such as metadata incorrectness, poor quality of metadata, and metadata inconsistency that have to be solved in order to create a variety of high-quality services. In this paper we propose an integrated DL system with OAI and self-organizing capabilities. The system provides two value-added services, cross-archive searching and interactive concept browsing services, for organizing, exploring, and searching a collection of harvested metadata to satisfy users' information needs. We also propose a multi-layered Self-Organizing Map (SOM) algorithm for building a subject-specific concept hierarchy using two input vector sets constructed by indexing the harvested metadata collection. By using the concept hierarchy, we can also automatically classify the harvested metadata collection for the purpose of selective harvesting.

## 1 Introduction

The Open Archives Initiative (OAI) [1], [2] is an experimental initiative for the interoperability of Digital Libraries based on *metadata harvesting*. The goal of OAI is to develop and promote interoperability solutions to facilitate the efficient dissemination of content. The Open Archives Initiative Protocol for Metadata Harvesting (OAI-PMH) [2] provides an application-independent interoperability framework. OAI-PMH requests are expressed as Hypertext Transfer Protocol (HTTP) requests such as HTTP GET or POST methods. All responses to OAI-PMH requests must be well-formed eXtensible Markup Language (XML) instance documents.

In the OAI framework, there are two classes of participants: data providers and service providers [2]. Data providers adopt the OAI technical framework as a means of exposing the content of metadata. The requirement for metadata interoperability is addressed by requiring that all OAI data providers supply metadata in a common format – the Dublin Core Metadata Element Set (DCMES) [3]. Service providers harvest metadata from data providers using the OAI-PMH and use the metadata as the basis for building value-added services. These archives would then act as a federation

T. Koch and I.T. Sølvberg (Eds.): ECDL 2003, LNCS 2769, pp. 164–175, 2003.

of repositories, by indexing documents in a standardized way so that multiple collections could be searched as though they form a single collection [1].

At present, however, there are still several challenging issues in order to create a wide variety of high-quality services. These issues are metadata incorrectness (e.g. XML encoding or syntax errors), poor quality of metadata, and metadata inconsistency. One of challenging problems for service providers originates from metadata inconsistency and variability among OAI archives [4], [5]. This is because OAI uses the simple (unqualified) Dublin Core that uses no qualifiers as the common metadata set to encourage metadata suppliers to expose Dublin Core metadata according to their own needs at the initial stage [1]. The Dublin Core metadata standard consists of fifteen elements and each element is optional and repeatable. It provides a semantic vocabulary for describing the information properties. Content data for some elements may be selected from a controlled vocabulary, a limited set of consistently used and carefully defined terms, and data providers try to use controlled vocabularies in several elements. But controlled vocabularies are only widely used in some elements not relating to the content of item, such as type, format, language, and date elements, among OAI archives [5]. Without basic terminology control among data providers, metadata inconsistency and variability can profoundly degrade the quality of service providers.

Since most cross-archive search services are based on keyword search technology in Information Retrieval, cross-archive keyword search of metadata that is harvested often results in a relatively low recall (only a proportion of the relevant documents are retrieved) and poor precision (only a proportion of the retrieved documents are relevant). Users sometimes cannot exactly articulate their information needs. Thus, a better mechanism is needed to fully exploit structured metadata [6].

In this paper we propose an integrated DL system with OAI and self-organizing capabilities. This system provides two valued-added services, cross-archive searching and interactive concept browsing, to provide powerful methods for organizing, exploring, and searching collections of metadata harvested to satisfy users' information needs. We also propose a multi-layered Self-Organizing Map (SOM) algorithm for building a subject-specific concept hierarchy using two input vector sets constructed by indexing the harvested metadata collection. We can also automatically classify the harvested metadata collection for the purpose of selective harvesting.

## 2  Related Work

We discuss related work on federated searching and document clustering approaches in this Section.

### 2.1  Federated Searching

There are two ways to implement a coherent set of digital services across heterogeneous digital repositories: a distributed searching approach and a harvesting approach

[5]. Distributed searching has been widely researched as the method for federating DLs. Distributed searching is cast in three parts – database selection, query processing, and results merging [8]. An experimental study on the distributed searching shows that distributed searching in a large number of heterogeneous nodes does not easily provide a federated search service, since the federated system is vulnerable to its weakest component [9].

In the harvesting approach, distributed searching can be emulated after harvesting metadata from repositories and a building cross-archive search on the metadata harvested [7]. Thus, data is duplicated and cross-archive searching does not always provide fresh data. Good retrieval performance, however, can be achieved in the harvesting approach compared to that of distributed searching regardless of a number of nodes. Liu et al. [5] introduced a federated searching interface, which allow users to search and select specific fields with data constructed from the metadata harvested, and an interactive searching interface for the subject field to solve the problem of metadata variability.

## 2.2  Document Clustering

Document clustering is used to group similar documents into a cluster [10]. Document clustering methods are in general divided into two ways: hierarchical and partitioning approaches [11]. The hierarchical clustering methods build a hierarchical clustering tree called a *dendrogram*, which shows how the clusters are related.

There are two types of hierarchical clustering: agglomerative (bottom-up) and divisive (top-down) approaches [11]. In agglomerative clustering, each object is initially placed in its own cluster. The two or more most similar clusters are merged into a single cluster recursively. A divisive clustering initially places all objects into a single cluster. The two objects that are in the same cluster but are most dissimilar are used as seed points for two clusters. All objects in this cluster are placed into the new cluster that has the closest seed. This procedure continues until a threshold distance, used to determine when the procedure stops, is reached.

Partitioning methods divide a data set into a set of disjoint clusters. Depending on how representatives are constructed, partitioning algorithms are subdivided into $k$-means and $k$-medoids methods. In $k$-means, each cluster is represented by its centroid, which is a mean of the points within a cluster. In $k$-medoids, each cluster is represented by one data point of the cluster, which is located near its center. The $k$-means method is minimizing the error sum of squared Euclidean distances whereas the $k$-medoids method is instead using dissimilarity. These methods are either minimizing the sum of dissimilarities of different clusters or minimizing the maximum dissimilarity between the data point and the seed point.

Partitioning methods are better than hierarchical ones in the sense that they do not depend on previously found clusters [11]. On the other hand, partitioning methods make implicit assumptions on the form of clusters and cannot deal with the tens of thousands of dimensions [11]. For example, the k-means method needs to define the number of final clusters in advance and tends to favor spherical clusters. Hence, statistical clustering methods are not suitable for handling high dimensional data, for reducing the dimensionality of a data set, nor for visualization of the data. A new approach to addressing clustering and classification problems is based on the connectionist, or neural network computing [11], [12], [13], [14], [15], [16], [17]. The self-organizing map that is an artificial neural network algorithm is especially suitable for data survey because it has prominent visualization and abstraction properties [11], [13], [14], [15], [16].

## 3   Concept Harvest Employing the SOM

To improve retrieval efficiency and effectiveness, data mining and machine learning have been widely researched. One of the most prominent neural networks for cluster analysis is the Self-Organizing Map [11], [12], [13], [14], [15], [16], [17].

The Self-Organizing Map [17] is an unsupervised-learning neural network algorithm for the visualization of high-dimensional data. In its basic form it produces a similarity graph of input data. It converts the nonlinear statistical relationships between high-dimensional data into simple geometric relationships of their image points on a low-dimensional display, usually a regular two-dimensional grid of nodes. The SOM may be described formally as a nonlinear, ordered, smooth mapping of the high-dimensional input data manifolds onto the elements of a regular, low-dimensional array. The SOM, thereby, compresses information while preserving the most important topological and/or metric relationships of the primary data elements on the display. It may also be thought to produce some kind of abstraction. These two characteristics of visualization and abstraction can be utilized in a number of ways in complex tasks such as process analysis, machine perception, and data mining [17].

### 3.1   The Data

For the following experiments we harvested a collection of 19,559 metadata elements from 5 OAI registered data providers. The harvested metadata describes either electronic theses and dissertation materials or technical reports in scientific fields. Table 1 shows statistical figures related to the metadata harvested.

**Table 1.** Statistical Figures for the number of harvested records.

| OAI Repository ID | Repository Name | Number of Harvested Records |
|---|---|---|
| caltechcstr | Caltech Computer Science Technical Reports | 358 |
| LSUETD | LSU Electronic Thesis and Dissertation Archive | 324 |
| HKUTO | Hong Kong University Theses Online | 8,598 |
| | M.I.T. Theses | 6,830 |
| VTETD | Virginia Tech Electronic Thesis and Dissertation Collection | 3,449 |

## 3.2  Preprocessing: Noun Phrase Extraction and Construction of Document Input Vectors

DCMES describes content, intellectual property, and instantiation of the resource [18]. Coverage, description, type, relation, source, subject, and title elements are used to describe the content of the resource. Especially, description, title, and subject elements give the account, name, and topic of the content of the resource, respectively. We consider these three elements important to be indexed for the clustering of metadata by employing the Self-Organizing Map.

To produce a concept hierarchy employing the SOM, documents must be represented by a set of features. We use full-text indexing to extract a list of terms and then weight these terms using the vector space model in Information Retrieval [10], [19]. In the vector space model, documents are represented as term vectors using the product of the term frequency (TF) and the inverse document frequency (IDF). Each entry in the document vector corresponds to the weight of a term in the document. We use a normalized TF x IDF term weighting scheme, the Best fully weighted scheme [19], so that longer documents are not unfairly given more weight and all values of a document vector are distributed in the range of 0 to 1. Thus, a weighted word histogram can be viewed as the feature vector describing the document [20].

During preprocessing we made two input vector sets for the SOM: subject and description feature vectors. The Subject input vector constructed by indexing the subject elements of the metadata collection was used to construct a subject-specific top-tier concept map. The description input vector built by indexing the title and description elements of the metadata collection was used to build a sub-layer concept hierarchy after constructing the top-tier concept map.

The preprocessing procedure is divided into two stages: noun phrase extraction, and term weighting. In the noun phrase extraction phase, we first took the description, subject, and title elements from the database and tokenized these elements based on the Penn Treebank tokenization scheme to detect sentence boundaries and to separate extraneous punctuations from the input text. We then automatically assigned part of speech tags to words reflecting their syntactic category by employing the rule-based part of speech tagger [21], [22]. After recognizing the chunks that consist of noun phrases and chunking them from the tagged text, we extracted noun phrases.

We then counted occurrences of all terms in the whole corpus for each input set. From the corpus constructed by indexing the title and description elements, we eliminated some terms occurring less than the frequency threshold (in this experiment less than 10 times) and common terms by consulting a list of 903 stop words. Finally, we weighted the indexed terms using the Best fully weighted scheme and assigned corresponding term weights to each document. Thus, the weighted term vector can be used as the input vector of the SOM.

We identified 1,674 terms by indexing the subject elements in the 13,427 metadata set. We also indexed 1,871 terms from the description and title elements of metadata set, after removing 142,388 terms, which were either common terms or terms having a low term frequency. Although all documents of the metadata set had the title elements, 6,072 and 15,344 documents did not have the subject and description elements, respectively.

### 3.3  Construction of a Concept Hierarchy

We then constructed a concept hierarchy by extending the multilayered SOM algorithm [15], permitting unlimited layers of SOM, with two input vector sets. The vector size of the subject feature vector was 1,674 and the vector size of the description feature vector was 1,871. The SOM defines a mapping from the input data space onto a usually two-dimensional array of nodes. Every node $i$ is represented by a model vector, also called *reference vector*, $m_i = [m_{i1}, m_{i2}, ..., m_{in}]$, where $n$ is input vector dimension.

The following algorithm describes how to construct a subject-specific concept hierarchy using two different input vector sets for Dublin Core metadata.

1. *Initialize network by using the subject feature vector as the input vector*: Create a two-dimensional map and randomly initialize model vectors $m_i$ in the range of 0 to 1 to start from an arbitrary initial state.

2. *Present input vector in sequential order*: Cyclically present the input vector $x(t)$, the weighted input vector of a $n$-dimensional space, to all nodes in the network. Each entry in the input vector corresponds to the weight of a noun phrase in the document. Zero means the term has no significance in the document or it simply does not exist in the document.

3. *Find the winning node by computing the Euclidean distance for each node*: In order to compare the input and weight vectors, each node computes the Euclidean distance between its weight vector and the input vector. The smallest Euclidean distance identifies the best-matching node, chosen as the winning node for that particular input vector. The best-matching node, denoted by the subscript c, is

$$\|x - m_c\| = \min_i \{\|x - m_i\|\} \ . \tag{1}$$

4. *Update weights of the winning node and its topological neighborhoods*: The update rule for the model vector of node $i$ is

$$m_i(t+1) = m_i(t) + \alpha(t)h_{ci}(t)[x(t) - m_i(t)], \tag{2}$$

where t is the discrete-time coordinate, $\alpha(t)$ is the adaptation coefficient, and $h_{ci}(t)$ the neighborhood function, a smoothing kernel centered on the wining node.

5. *Repeat steps 2-4 until all iterations have been completed.*

6. *Label nodes of the trained network with the noun phrases of the subject feature vectors*: For each node, determine the dimension with the greatest value and label the node with a corresponding noun phrase for that node and aggregate nodes with the same noun phrase into groups. Thus, a subject-specific top-tier concept map is generated.

7. *Repeat steps 1-6 by using the description feature vector as the input vector for each grouped concept region*: For each grouped concept region containing more than $k$ documents (e.g., 100), recursively create a sub-layer SOM by repeating steps 1-6 and using the description feature vector as the input vector.

For each input vector set, we generated a concept hierarchy using the SOM, limiting the maximum level of hierarchy to 3. We built a 20 x 20 SOM and presented each subject feature vector 100 times to the SOM. We then recursively built the sub-layer concept hierarchy by training a new 20 x 20 SOM with a new input vector. The new input vector was dynamically constructed by selecting only a document feature vector contained in the concept region from the upper-level feature vector. We identified 49 concept regions from the top-level SOM.

## 4  System Overview

The proposed integrated DL system is designed to serve both as a data and service provider. The architecture of the system consists of three main components as shown in Fig. 1: the harvester, the data provider, and a set of the service providers. The harvester that issues OAI-PMH requests to archives and collects metadata encoded in XML from archives supports selective and automatic harvesting. Although the harvester component can be viewed as a part of a service provider, we have distinguished it to better clarify the importance of this component in the integrated DL architecture. The data provider can expose harvested metadata, reformat harvested metadata to other metadata formats, and correct erroneous metadata before it is exposed to service providers. The service providers provide two value-added services, cross-archive searching and interactive concept browsing, to users.

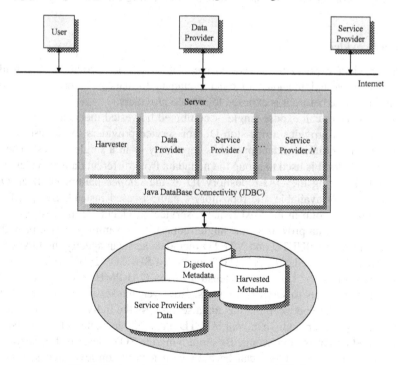

**Fig. 1.** System Architecture of the Integrated DL System

## 4.1 Harvester

The harvester harvests metadata from various OAI-PMH compliant archives. The web accessible graphical user interface that is password protected allows the administrator to harvest metadata from a data provider. In this step the administrator can selectively harvest metadata based on (1) the date the metadata was added or modified, (2) the metadata prefix (a string to specify the metadata format in OAI-PMH requests), (3) the archive predefined set, and (4) the individual records. The latter parameter for selective harvesting allows the administrator to specify which records are worth harvesting and digested into the integrated DL.

The harvester component also has the capability to do automatic harvesting on a timely basis (daily, weekly or monthly). This service is controlled by the administrator based on how often new metadata is inserted, and the rate the metadata is updated for a given data provider. In the automatic harvesting, only newly added or updated metadata from the original data provider is requested and digested into the integrated DL. Automatic harvesting based on statistical data gathered from the data providers is currently being investigated. Such statistical data would be useful for automatic adaptation harvesting without human intervention and it is also needed to minimize the problem of propagation change [24], [25]. Propagation change happens when the harvester waits a certain amount of time between harvest operations; and thus becomes out of synchronization with the data provider that it is harvesting. This problem is further propagated to the next harvester harvesting the previously stated harvester.

## 4.2 Data Provider

The data provider exposes the harvested metadata to service providers. It can also reformat the harvested metadata to other metadata formats and correct erroneous metadata if possible before it is exposed to service providers.

The data provider can expose single or combined harvested metadata sets to service providers. This provides a one-stop DL for service providers to harvest various metadata sets from different data providers separately or in a single request. The *set* field in the OAI-PMH is used to group the metadata from different data providers into different sets by using the OAI repository ID as the *setSpec* parameter. If an OAI repository ID is not available, the repository's name is used instead. By specifying more than one set group in the OAI request, service providers can harvest metadata sets from different data providers in a single request. For example, service providers who want to harvest LSUETD and VTETD metadata sets can specify the OAI-PMH set parameter as "set=LSUETD,VTETD" (or "set=LSUETD%2CVTETD" after encoded for transmission). This is an extension of the OAI-PMH in our part to serve integrated metadata sets to service providers. However, the service provider will not be able to differentiate between the metadata sets unless the individual record identifiers are descriptive enough (e.g., oai:VTETD:etd-11). Metadata sets can also be grouped, based on terms or concepts. By employing the SOM described in Section 3, hierarchical organization of sets can be built with tens of top-level nodes, each of which is itself a set. One example is to group the metadata sets into different top-level subject-specific domains such as "Chemical Engineering" or "Civil Engineering". Each top-level set may have sub-layer sets of the sub-subjects or related subjects such as "Computer Science" and "Algorithm."

When necessary, metadata digested into the DL can be converted to other metadata formats before being exposed to service providers. For example, metadata harvested from VTETD as Dublin Core can be reformatted to MAchine-Readable Cataloging (MARC) format on the fly before being exposed to service providers. This allows the service providers to focus their services on the metadata harvested instead of having to build harvesters for different metadata formats.

We are also able to expose metadata sets from data providers that have metadata XML syntax or encoding errors. Not all data providers strictly implement the OAI-PMH as with our experiments. By relaxing our harvesting approach, we are able to obtain metadata sets from these data providers and correct the syntax or encoding errors where possible before the metadata is exposed to service providers.

### 4.3  Service Providers

Service Providers use the metadata harvested via the OAI-PMH as a basis for building value-added services [2]. Our service providers provide cross-archive searching and interactive concept browsing services to users.

### Cross-Archive Search

The cross-archive search provides users with a way to search on part or all of the archived metadata from the archives harvested.

**Fig. 2.** Cross-archive Search Interface

The search service is based on full-text search on the DC elements from the harvested metadata collection. A simple, keyword-based search is provided as shown in Fig. 2, where the title and description metadata elements from all harvested archives are queried. The resulting records returned are ranked based on the relevance to the user's query term.

We also provide an advanced search for users who want more refined results for their search process. The query fields provided are based on DC elements and users can sort the resulting records based on the results relevance to the query term, the date the record was created or updated, and the original archive name. Boolean operators (AND/OR) can be used with the query fields. Users are also provided with the option to choose the archives that they want to query on. The result set from the search process can be further refined with the filter elements. Fig. 3 shows the search result page.

**Fig. 3.** Search Result Page

**Fig. 4.** Browsing of the Concept Hierarchy

**Interactive Concept Browsing**

After training the SOM and inserting data of the concept hierarchy into the database, we built an interactive user interface for organizing and browsing the harvested metadata. We represented the concept hierarchy as a tree structure to help users find a set of documents and locate good starting points for searching.

Fig. 4 shows the user interface. The concept tree shown on the left pane displays the clustered information space. When the user clicks on a concept label, the associated document set is displayed on the right pane. Users can see more detailed information of a document by clicking on the title of a document shown on the right pane.

## 5  Problems Encountered

The problem of metadata variability limits the effectiveness of our data provider component as well as our services offered. Some metadata harvested do not have the title and description elements and the date, type and format elements show great variation among archives. This problem usually occurs due to the use of unqualified DC [23].

Many data providers could not be harvested due to various reasons: connection refused, service temporarily unavailable, and XML encoding errors at the data provider server. Some registered data providers only contain a few metadata records. These data providers might be experimental OAI archives.

Metadata quality offered by data providers is also questionable. Different archives present different metadata qualities and even a single archive might have different metadata qualities for their records. This is due to the subjective interpretation of the records by the metadata authors. Metadata quality affects the usefulness and value of services offered on top of the metadata.

Metadata synchronization between data provider and service provider is very important [5], [25]. Our system can selectively harvest metadata from data providers. However, the SOM processing for new or modified metadata is not feasible, since we have to recalculate input vectors of SOM and retrain the SOM with new input vectors.

## 6  Conclusions

We have proposed the integrated DL system architecture with OAI and self-organizing capabilities. The proposed DL system can serve both as a data provider and service provider. To provide the users with powerful methods for organizing, exploring, and searching collection of harvested metadata, we combined cross-archive searching with interactive concept browsing services.

We have also proposed the multi-layered Self-Organizing Map algorithm for building a subject-specific concept hierarchy using two input vector sets constructed by indexing the harvested metadata collection. The generated concept hierarchy can be used for two purposes: building an interactive concept browsing service and automatic classification of harvested metadata for the purpose of selective harvesting.

## References

1.  Lagoze, C. and Sompel, H. Van de: The Open Archives Initiative: Building a low-barrier interoperability framework. In *Proceedings of the First ACM/IEEE Joint Conference on Digital Libraries*, Roanoke, VA (2001) 54–62
2.  Lagoze, C. and Sompel, H. Van de: The Open Archives Initiative Protocol for Metadata Harvesting. Open Archives Initiative (2001)
3.  Dublin Core Metadata Initiative.: Dublin Core Metadata Element Set, Version 1.1: Reference Description. (1999), http://www.dublincore.org/documents/1999/07/02/dces/.
4.  Sompel, H. Van de, Krichel, T., and Nelson, M. L.: The UPS Prototype: an experimental end-user service across e-print archives. In *D-Lib Magazine,* Vol. 6, No. 2 (2000)

5.  Liu, X., Maly, K., Zubair, M., Hong, Q., Nelson, M. L., Knudson, F., and Holtkamp, I.: Federated Searching Interfaces Techniques for Heterogeneous OAI Repositories. In *Journal of Digital Information*, Vol. 2, Issue 4 (2002)
6.  Chen, S.: *Digital Libraries: The Life Cycle of Information*. Better Earth Publisher, 1998.
7.  Chen, S. and Choo, C.: A DL Server with OAI Capabilities: Managing the Metadata Complexity. In *Joint Conference on Digital Libraries (JCDL'2002)*, Portland, OR. 2002.
8.  Powell, A. L., French, J. C., and Callan, J.: The Impact of Database Selection on Distributed Searching. In *Proceedings of the 23rd Annual International ACM SIGIR Conference on Research and Development in Information Retrieval*, ACM (2000) 232–239
9.  Powell, A. L. and French, J. C.: Growth and Server Availability of the NCSTL Digital Library. In *Proceedings of 5th ACM Conference on Digital Libraries* (2000) 264–265
10. Baeza-Yates, R. and Ribeiro-Neto, B.: *Modern Information Retrieval*. ACM Press and Addison Wesley (1999)
11. Vesanto, J., and Alhoniemi, E.: Clustering of the Self-Organizing Map. In *IEEE Transactions on Neural Networks*, Vol. 11, Issue 3 (2000) 586–600
12. Chakrabarti, S.: Data mining for hypertext: A tutorial survey. In *ACM SIGKDD Explorations*, Vol. 1, Issue 2, January (2000) 1–11
13. Chen, H., Schuffels, C., and Orwig, R.: Internet Categorization and Search: A Self-Organizing Approach. In *Journal of Visual Communication and Image Representation*, Vol. 7, No. 1 (1996) 88–102
14. Kohonen, T.: Self-Organization of Very Large Document Collection: State of the Art. In *Proceedings of ICANN98, the 8th International Conference on Artificial Neural Networks*, Skovde, Sweden (1998)
15. Roussinov, D., and Chen, H.: A Scalable Self-Organizing Map Algorithm for Textual Classification: A Neural Network Approach to Thesaurus Generation. *Communication Cognition and Artificial Intelligence*, Vol. 15, No. 1–2 (1998) 81–111
16. Dittenbach, M., Merkl, D., and Rauber, A.: The Growing Hierarchical Self-Organizing Map. In *Proceedings of the International Joint Conference on Neural Networks (IJCNN 2000)*, Vol. 6 (2000) 15–19
17. Kohonen, T.: *Self-Organizing Maps*. 3rd Edition, Springer Verlag, Berlin, Germany (2001)
18. Hillmann, D.: Using Dublin Core. Dublin Core Metadata Initiative Recommendation (2001) http://www.dublincore.org/documents/2001/04/12/usageguide/.
19. Salton, G., and Buckley, C.: Term-Weighting Approaches in Automatic Text Retrieval. *Information Processing and Management*, Vol. 24, No. 5 (1988) 513–523
20. Kohonen, T., Kaski, S., Lagus, K., Salojärvi, J., Honkela, J., Paatero, V., and Saarela, A.: Self Organizing of a Massive Document Collection. *IEEE Transactions on Neural Networks*, Vol. 11, No. 3, May (2000)
21. Brill, E.: A Simple Rule-based Part of Speech Tagger. In *Proceedings of the 3rd Conference on Applied Natural Language Processing*, Trento, Italy (1992)
22. Brill, E.: Some advances in transformation-based part of speech tagging. In *Proceedings of the 12th National Conference on Artificial Intelligence*, Seattle, WA (1994)
23. Liu, X., Maly, K., Zubair, M., and Nelson, M. L.: Arc - An OAI Service Provider for Digital Library Federation. In *D-Lib Magazine*, Vol. 7, No. 4, April (2001)
24. Suleman, H. and Fox, E. A.: Beyond Harvesting: Digital Library Components as OAI Extensions. Technical report, Virginia Tech Dept. of Computer Science, January (2002)
25. Liu, X., Brody, T., Harnad, S., Carr, L., Maly, K., Zubair, M., and Nelson, M. L.: A Scalable Architecture for Harvest-Based Digital Libraries - The ODU/Southampton Experiments. In D-Lib Magazine, Vol. 8, No. 11, November (2002)

# YAPI: Yet Another Path Index for XML Searching

Giuseppe Amato[1], Franca Debole[1], Pavel Zezula[2], and Fausto Rabitti[1]

[1] ISTI-CNR, Pisa, Italy,
{G.Amato,F.Debole,F.Rabitti}@isti.cnr.it
http://www.isti.cnr.it
[2] Masaryk University, Brno, Czech Republic,
zezula@fi.muni.cz
http://www.fi.muni.cz

**Abstract.** As many metadata are encoded in XML, and many digital libraries need to manage XML documents, efficient techniques for searching in such formatted data are required. In order to efficiently process path expressions with wildcards on XML data, a new path index is proposed. Extensive evaluation confirms better performance with respect to other techniques proposed in the literature. An extension of the proposed technique to deal with the content of XML documents in addition to their structure is also discussed.

## 1 Introduction

Efficient management of metadata is an important issue in Digital Library systems. Simple flat solutions to metadata collections such as the Dublin Core cannot be applied to complex metadata models requested by advanced multimedia digital libraries. These complex metadata models often include nested structures, hierarchies, multiple views, and semistructured information, which cannot efficiently be handled by techniques based on a simple term inversion or by application of the relational databases. Instead, efficient technology for the management of such data should be developed.

Recently, several interesting trends to processing complex metadata by means of XML structures have been observed. Specifically, new generation digital libraries, such as ECHO [1] or OpenDlib [5], have chosen to encode their supported metadata with XML. Recent standards, for instance the MPEG-7 [8], require to encode metadata in XML. Moreover, some digital libraries consider XML documents as their native format of documents.

The obvious advantage of encoding metadata in XML is that they can easily be exported and imported. They can also be easily read by human user in their raw format. In addition to the documents' content, XML documents contain explicit information on their structures. However, efficient management of large XML document repositories is still a challenge. Searching for information in an XML document repository involves checking structural relationships in addition to content predicates, and the process of finding structural relationships has been

T. Koch and I.T. Sølvberg (Eds.): ECDL 2003, LNCS 2769, pp. 176–187, 2003.
© Springer-Verlag Berlin Heidelberg 2003

recognized as the most critical for achieving the global efficiency. Several XML query languages, as for instance XPath [6] and XQuery [7], are based on the use of path expressions containing optional wildcards. This poses a new problem, given that traditional query processing approaches have been proven not to be efficient in this case.

The aim of this paper is to propose a path index, that is an index structure to support evaluation of containment relationships for XML searching. The proposed index is able to efficiently process path expressions even in the presence of wildcards, and experiments have shown an evident superiority of our technique with respect to other approaches. An extension of the path index to deal with the content of elements or the value of attributes is also discussed.

The paper is organized as follows. Section 2 surveys the basic concepts, and Section 3 presents the idea of the path index. Section 4 discusses how the path index can be extended to also deal with content. Section 5 presents a comparative evaluation of the proposed technique. Section 6 concludes the paper.

## 2   Preliminaries

In this section we briefly discuss some general concepts, necessary for the rest of the paper. We first introduce the inverted index as an access structure typically used for efficient text document retrieval. Then, we survey a technique for processing partially specified query terms.

### 2.1   Inverted Index

Efficient text retrieval is typically supported by the use of an *inverted index* [9]. This index structure associates terms, contained in text documents, with items describing their occurrence. An item can be just a reference to a text document containing the term or it might contain additional information, such as the location of the term in the text or the term frequency. An inverted index consists of two main components: a set of *inverted file entries* or *posting lists*, each containing a list of items corresponding to the associated term; and a *search structure* that maps terms to the corresponding posting lists. The set of terms indexed by the search structure, that is the set of terms contained in the whole text collection, is called the *lexicon*.

In order to search for text documents containing a specific term, the search structure is used first to obtain the posting list. Then the posting list is used to get the qualifying items.

### 2.2   Partially Specified Query Terms

A technique for processing partially specified query terms (queries with wildcards) in text databases was proposed in [3]. This technique is based on the construction of a *rotated* (or *permuted*) *lexicon*, consisting of all possible rotations of all terms in the original lexicon.

Let us suppose that our original lexicon includes the term `apple`. The rotated lexicon will contain the terms `apple^`, `pple^a`, `ple^ap`, `le^app`, `e^appl`, `^apple`, where `^` is used as the string terminating character. The rotated lexicon is alphabetically ordered by using the sort sequence `^`, `a,b,c,...` and it is inserted in an inverted index using a search structure that maintains the rotated lexicon ordered. This can be obtained, for instance, by using a $B^+$-Tree. Rotated versions of all terms in the original lexicon are mapped to the posting list associated with the original term.

By using the ordered rotated lexicon, query patterns A, *A, A*B, A*, and *A* (A, and B are sub-terms that compose the entire query term, and * is the wildcard) can be processed by transforming the query according to the following transformation rules:

I) A transforms to ^A; II) *A transforms to A^*; III) A*B transforms to B^A*; IV) A* transforms to ^A*; V) *A* transforms to A*.

Then the transformed query terms are used to search in the rotated lexicon. For example, suppose that our original lexicon contains `apple`, `aisle`, `appeal`, `employ`, `staple`. Figure 1 shows the obtained rotated lexicon, ordered alphabetically. Now consider the following queries: `apple`, `*ple`, `app*`, `*pl*`, and `a*le`. Figure 1 also shows how they are transformed and how the transformed query terms are matched against the rotated lexicon. For instance, the query `*pl*` is transformed into `pl*`, that matches the entries `ple^ap`, `ple^sta`, `ploy^em` corresponding to the terms `apple`, `staple`, `employ` of the original lexicon.

A drawback of this technique is the memory overhead due to the rotation. In fact, an average memory overhead observed in [12] is about 250%. A memory reducing variant of this method is discussed in [2]. The memory overhead is reduced by representing the rotated lexicon as an array of pointers, one for each position in the original lexicon. This array of pointers is sorted accordingly to the rotated form of each term. By using this technique, [12] reports the memory overhead of about 30%.

## 3    Rotated Path Index

Wildcards are also frequently used in XPath expressions. In many systems these expressions are processed by multiple *containment joins* [11,4], which can be very inefficient in case of long paths or element names with many occurrences. We propose an alternative approach that exploits the rotated lexicon technique. In this way, typical XPath expressions, containing wildcards, are processed efficiently even in presence of long paths and high frequency of element names.

An XML document can be seen as a flat representation of a tree structure. For example, see Figure 2 for a portion of an XML document and its tree representation. In the figure, white nodes represent XML elements, and black nodes represent the XML content. Additional node types can be used to represent elements' attributes – in our example we omit them for the sake of simplicity.

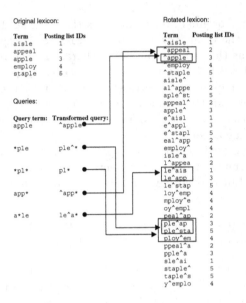

**Fig. 1.** The original lexicon, the rotated lexicon, and some queries processed on the rotated lexicon

To identify specific elements in an XML document, nodes of the tree are also associated with a unique identifier, which we call *element instance identifier*, assigned with a preorder visit to the tree. In the remainder of this paper, XML document of Figure 2 and the corresponding tree representation will be used as a running example to explain the technique that we propose.

A simple possibility of indexing the structure of XML documents is to use an inverted index to associate each pathname, appearing in an XML document, with the list of its occurrences. For instance, in our example, the path /people/person/address is associated with a posting list containing element instance identifiers 8 and 16. This approach has some similarity to text indexing, considering that the paths play the role of terms and the names of elements play the role of characters. In text retrieval systems, each term is associated with the list of its occurrences. Here each path is associated with the list of elements that can be reached following the path. By analogy to the terminology used in text retrieval systems, we call *path lexicon* and *element lexicon*, respectively, the set of pathnames and the set of element names occurring in an XML document repository.

By exploiting this analogy, our proposal is to use the rotated lexicon technique from Section 2.2 to build a *rotated path lexicon*. In this way, we are able to efficiently process common path expressions containing wildcards, with no need of containment joins. We call the *rotated path* a path generated through the rotation. Note that names of attributes can also be indexed by using this technique. In fact, they can be considered as children of the corresponding elements and

```
<people>
   <person>
      <name>
         <fn>John</fn>
         <ln>Smith</ln>
      </name>
      <address>St. Mary Street, Boston
      </address>
      ...
   </person>
   <person>
      <name>
         <fn>Bill</fn>
         <ln>McCulloc</ln>
      </name>
      <address>Queen Street, S.Francisco
      </address>
      ...
   </person>
   ...
</people>
```

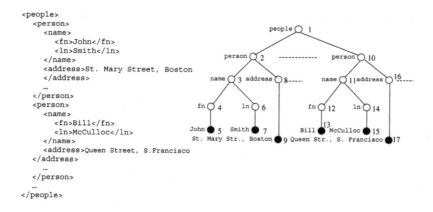

**Fig. 2.** An example of XML data and its tree representation

managed similarly to the elements. The character @, accordingly to the XPath syntax, is added in front of attribute names to distinguish them from elements.

XPath uses two different types of wildcards. One is // and stands for any descendent element or self (that is 0 or more optional steps). The other is * and stands for exactly one element[1] (that is exactly one step). Let $P$, $P1$, and $P2$, be *pure path expressions*, that is path expressions containing just a sequence of element (and attribute) names, with no wildcards, and predicates. In addition to pure path expressions, the rotated path lexicon allows processing the following path expressions containing wildcards: $//P$, $P1//P2$, $P//$, and $//P//$[2]. This is obtained by using the query translation rules discussed in Section 2.2.

With a small additional computational effort, we can also process paths $*P$, $P1*P2$, $P*$, and $*P*$. The idea is to use again the query translation rules and filter out paths whose length is not equal to the length of the query path. Other generic XPath expressions can be processed by decomposing them in sub-expressions, consistent with the patterns described above, and combining the obtained results through containment joins.

To reduce the storage space required for the rotated path lexicon, each element name is encoded by an unique identifier (not to be confused with element instance identifiers introduced before) implemented, for instance, as an integer. Thus, pathnames are represented as *encoded pathnames* consisting of sequences of encoded elements, instead of strings. A specific identifier is reserved for the *path terminating element*. The number of entries in the rotated path lexicon is $\#PL \times (avg\_PL\_len)$, where $\#PL$ is the cardinality of the path lexicon and $avg\_PL\_len$ is the average length of paths in the path lexicon, including the ter-

---

[1] In text retrieval systems * is typically used to substitute any sequence of characters, as we said in Section 2.2, so the XPath correspondent is // rather than *.

[2] To be precise, note that P// and //P// alone are not syntactically valid XPath expression. In fact, they should be completed as P//node() and //P//node(), for instance. In this paper, we simplify the notation by omitting the node() function.

| Element lexicon: | Encoded element lexicon | | Rotated path lex. | Posting list ID: |
|---|---|---|---|---|
| *Term. element* | 0 | | /0/1 | 1 |
| people | 1 | | /0/1/2 | 2 |
| person | 2 | | /0/1/2/3 | 3 |
| name | 3 | | /0/1/2/3/4 | 4 |
| fn | 4 | | /0/1/2/3/5 | 5 |
| ln | 5 | | /0/1/2/6 | 6 |
| address | 6 | | /1/0 | 1 |
| | | | /1/2/0 | 2 |
| | | | /1/2/3/0 | 3 |
| | | | /1/2/3/4/0 | 4 |
| | | | /1/2/3/5/0 | 5 |
| | | | /1/2/6/0 | 6 |

| Path lexicon | Encoded path lexicon | Posting lists: | /2/0/1 | 2 |
|---|---|---|---|---|
| /people | /1/0 | 1->{1} | /2/3/0/1 | 3 |
| /people/person | /1/2/0 | 2->{2,10} | /2/3/4/0/1 | 4 |
| /people/person/name | /1/2/3/0 | 3->{3,11} | /2/3/5/0/1 | 5 |
| /people/person/name/fn | /1/2/3/4/0 | 4->{4,12} | /2/6/0/1 | 6 |
| /people/person/name/ln | /1/2/3/5/0 | 5->{6,14} | /3/0/1/2 | 3 |
| /people/person/address | /1/2/6/0 | 6->{8,16} | /3/4/0/1/2 | 4 |
| | | | /3/5/0/1/2 | 5 |
| | | | /4/0/1/2/3 | 4 |
| | | | /5/0/1/2/3 | 5 |
| | | | /6/0/1/2 | 6 |

**Fig. 3.** Element lexicon, path lexicon, rotated path lexicon, and posting lists relative to XML example in Figure 2.

minating element. In our example $\#PL$ is 6, $avg\_PL\_len$ is $3.8\bar{3}$, so the number of entries in the rotated path lexicon is 23. Note that the number of element instances affects only the size of posting lists. To illustrate, Figure 3 shows the element lexicon, the path lexicon, and the rotated path lexicon, obtained from our example, along with their respective encoding. The posting list, associated with each pathname in the example, is also shown.

**Example.** Suppose the XPath expression //person/name//. The element name identifiers associated with person and name are 2 and 3, respectively, and the encoded query is //2/3//. According to the query translation rules, this query is processed by searching the rotated lexicon for /2/3//. Rotated paths that qualify for this query are /2/3/0/1, /2/3/4/0/1, and /2/3/5/0/1, corresponding to path names /people/person/name, /people/person/name/fn, and /people/person /name/ln. By merging their posting lists, we decide elements relevant to this XPath expression as those associated with the element instance identifiers {3, 4, 6, 11, 12, 14}.

## 4   Indexing XML Data Structures and Their Content

Suppose the XPath expression /people//name[fn="Bill"]/fn. This returns all fn elements that are children of a name element, and that are descendants of a people root element, whose content is exactly the string Bill. To process this query, content predicates, in addition to structural relationships, should be separately verified. This can be inefficient since either the access to the document, in case of non indexed content, or additional containment joins, in case of indexed content, are required. However, the rotated path index technique can be extended in such a way that content predicates and structural relationships can be handled simultaneously. In the following, two different implementation directions are discussed.

## 4.1  Structure+Content Queries by Extending the Path Index

Content of an element can be seen as a special child of the element so it can also be included as last element of a path. We add a special character $<$[3] in front of the content string to distinguish it from name of elements and attributes. For instance, `Bill` will be `<Bill`, and the path from the root to the content is `/people/person/name/fn/<Bill`. In Section 3, we proposed a similar technique to index names of attributes.

Suppose $P/<cont$ is a pathname, where *cont* is the content and $P$ the path from the root. The posting list associated with $P/<cont$ (and its rotations) contains the list of elements reachable via $P$ that have content *cont*. This is a subset of the posting list associated with $P$.

Of course, it does not make sense to index content of all elements and attributes. The database administrator can decide, tacking into account performance issues, which elements and attributes should have their content indexed.

Suppose in our example that we decide to index the content of elements `fn`. In this case, pathnames `/people/person/name/fn/<Bill` and `/people/person/na me/fn/<John` are added to the path lexicon. The rotated path lexicon is also updated with the corresponding rotated paths. The corresponding posting lists are $\{4\}$ and $\{12\}$. Note that in this example the posting lists contain just one element. However, if several persons whose first name is `Bill` occur, the corresponding posting lists would be larger.

By using this extension, our original XPath expression can simply be processed by a single access to the path index as:

1. let $R_1 = pathIndexSearch(/people//name/fn/<Bill)$;
2. return $R_1$

and we are able to process XPath expressions that contain equality predicates on specific elements or attributes, with just one access to the path index.

## 4.2  Structure+Content Queries by Indexing Posting Lists

Another possibility to support efficient processing of path expressions with predicates on content is to organize the element instance identifiers of posting lists by using specific access methods. For instance, each posting lists corresponding to frequently searched elements can be indexed with a different $B^+$-Tree that uses content of elements as keys. This implies that elements satisfying a predicate can be efficiently retrieved from these posting lists. This idea is illustrated in Figure 4.

---

[3] We use $<$ as flag since content of an element or attribute cannot start with it.

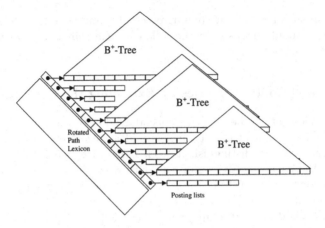

**Fig. 4.** Some posting lists are indexed by a dedicate B$^+$-Tree, so content predicates on elements of these posting lists can be processed efficiently.

In this approach, a path expression can be processed in two steps. First, the path index is searched to find the posting lists satisfying the structural part. Then, the obtained indexed posting lists are searched through the associated access method, using the content predicate. Posting lists that are not indexed should be searched checking the content of each element.

Our query example `/people//name[fn="Bill"]/fn` can be processed with just two index accesses as:

1. let $R_1 = pathIndexSearch(/people//name/fn)$;
2. let $R_2 = contentIndexSearch(R_1,"Bill")$;
3. return $R_2$

where we suppose that the posting list $R_1$ associated with `/people/person/na me/fn` is indexed with a B$^+$-Tree, so it can be searched as a content index.

The advantage of this technique is that all predicates supported by the access method used to index the posting list, such as $<$, $>$, $\leq$, $\geq$, and $=$, in case of B$^+$-Tree, can be processed efficiently.

## 5   Experiments

The path index was implemented by using BerkeleyDB. Specifically, the search structure was implemented as a B$^+$-tree with multiple keys, so posting lists are automatically managed by BerkeleyDB. Elements in posting lists contain, in addition to the element instance identifier, the start and the end position of the corresponding element – start and end positions are, respectively, the positions of the start and the end tags of elements in XML documents. In this way, containment joins can still be used to process queries that are not compliant to the supported path expressions.

**Table 1.** Number of files, occurrences of specific elements, and total number of elements in the three generated datasets.

|  | Small Dataset | Medium Dataset | Large Dataset |
|---|---|---|---|
| # XML files | 430 | 4300 | 43000 |
| `<article>` occurrences | 430 | 4300 | 43000 |
| `<prolog>` occurrences | 430 | 4300 | 43000 |
| `<authors>` occurrences | 405 | 4037 | 40432 |
| `<author>` occurrences | 10047 | 98523 | 989752 |
| `<contact>` occurrences | 10047 | 98523 | 989752 |
| `<email>` occurrences | 9224 | 90729 | 910420 |
| # total elements | 625726 | 5684115 | 56505321 |

We compared our path index with the containment join according to the implementation from [11]. Accordingly, an *Element Index* was used that associates each element with its (start,end) position and the containment join was implemented as the Multi Predicate MerGe JoiN (MPMGJN). The element index was developed as a $B^+$-tree with multiple keys in BerkeleyDB.

Retrieval of the posting list associated with a key (a rotated path in case of the path index, an element name in case of the element index) was implemented with the bulk retrieval functionality, provided by the BerkeleyDB. Everything was implemented in Java, JDK 1.4.0 and run on a PC with a 1800 GHz Intel pentium 4, 512 Mb main memory, EIDE disk, running Windows 2000 Professional edition with NT file system (NTFS).

We have used a benchmark from XBench [10] to run our experiments. Specifically we have used the Text Centric Multiple Documents (TC/MD) benchmark whose Schema diagram is shown in Figure 5. This benchmark simulates a repository of text documents similar to the Reuters news corpus or the Springer Digital library. It consists of numerous relatively small text-centric documents with explicit structure description, looseness of schema and possibly recursive elements. We have modified the XBench Perl scripts to be able to control the number of generated XML files. Then, we have generated three different datasets with increasing size, to test the scalability of the path index with increasing number of elements. Statistics of the three generated datasets can be seen in Table 1.

We have run the experiments using various path expressions based on the query patterns supported by the path index. We have coded query names as Q<*p*><*l*>, where <*p*> takes values between 1 and 4, in correspondence of the query pattern tested, <*l*> indicates the length of the path expression, in terms of number of element names, and can be L(ong) or S(hort). Table 2 details the test queries, while the number of occurrences in the datatses of the element names that we have used in the queries is reported in Table 1. We have processed Q1<*l*> and Q2<*l*> both with path index and containment join. The other queries, Q3<*l*> and Q4<*l*>, were only processed with the path index, since processing them with the containment join only is not possible.

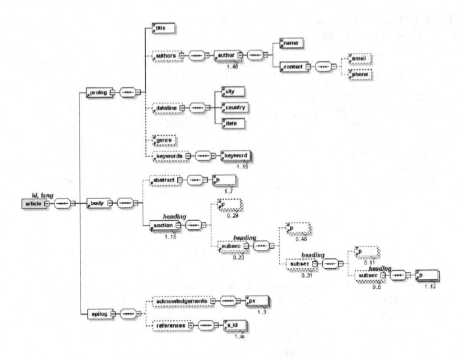

**Fig. 5.** Schema Diagram of the used benchmark

Performance comparison between path index and containement join is shown in Table 3 were the processing time, expressed in milliseconds, and the number of elements retrieved by each query is reported. Processing time includes access to the path index and retrieval of the posting lists. In case of containment join, processing time includes access to the element index and execution of the join algorithm (which also include retrieval of the needed posting lists).

The experiments we have performed have shown an evident superiority of the path index with respect to the containment join. The difference in performance can be justified by observing that the dominant cost is due to the retrieval of the posting lists. In fact, the cost of accessing the search structures is negligible. However, while in case of the path index just the final posting lists should be retrieved, the containment join has to retrieve a posting list for each element name specified in the path expressions, in order to join them. Thus as expected, performance of the path index is practically independent on the length of the path expression, while performance of the containment join degrades with longer path expressions. This is evident when the size of the intermediate posting lists, corresponding to the number of occurrences of the intermediate element names specified in the query, is large. The path index does not need to access these huge posting lists since it directly accesses the posting lists associated with entire paths that match the query. As a consequence, the path index has also the property of better scaling when the number of XML elements, and consequently

**Table 2.** Queries used for the experiments

| Query | Pattern | XPath expression |
|-------|---------|------------------|
| Q1L | //P | //authors/author/contact/email |
| Q1S | | //contact/email |
| Q2L | P1//P2 | /article/prolog//contact/email |
| Q2S | | /article//email |
| Q3L | P// | /article/prolog/authors/author// |
| Q3S | | /article/prolog// |
| Q4L | //P// | //authors/author// |
| Q4S | | //author// |

**Table 3.** Performance comparison. Time is expressed in milliseconds.

| Query | Dataset | Path index | Cont. join | #Retr. el |
|-------|---------|-----------|-----------|-----------|
| Q1L | Small | 19 | 86 | 9224 |
| | Medium | 75 | 612 | 90729 |
| | Large | 1079 | 62601 | 910420 |
| Q2L | Small | 19 | 81 | 9224 |
| | Medium | 75 | 421 | 90729 |
| | Large | 1074 | 48268 | 910420 |
| Q3L | Small | 106 | | 46269 |
| | Medium | 906 | - | 454239 |
| | Large | 5056 | | 4562725 |
| Q4L | Small | 106 | | 46269 |
| | Medium | 906 | - | 454239 |
| | Large | 5020 | | 4562725 |
| Q1S | Small | 19 | 53 | 9224 |
| | Medium | 75 | 194 | 90729 |
| | Large | 1100 | 25686 | 910420 |
| Q2S | Small | 19 | 36 | 9224 |
| | Medium | 75 | 132 | 90729 |
| | Large | 1092 | 3351 | 910420 |
| Q3S | Small | 267 | | 53119 |
| | Medium | 590 | - | 521753 |
| | Large | 5435 | | 5242441 |
| Q4S | Small | 105 | | 46269 |
| | Medium | 904 | - | 454239 |
| | Large | 4982 | | 4562725 |

the size of posting lists associated with elements names, increase. In our experiments, this is particularly evident for queries Q1L, Q2L, and Q1S, where, using the large dataset, performance of the containment join becomes more than one order of magnitude worse than the path index.

# 6    Conclusions

We have proposed a path index that supports efficient processing of typical
path expressions containing wildcards. The proposed index structure can be
easily extended to also support path expressions containing content predicates
in addition to constraints on structural relationships. Extensive evaluations have
demonstrated the superiority of our approach to the previously proposed techniques.

# References

1. Giuseppe Amato, Claudio Gennaro, and Pasquale Savino. Indexing and retrieving
   documentary films: managing metadata in the ECHO system. In *4th Intl. Workshop on Multimedia Information Retrieval December 6, Juan-les-Pins, France, in
   conjunction with ACM Multimedia*, 2002.
2. G. Gonnet anf R. Baeza-Yates. *Handbook of data structure and algorithms.*
   Addison-Wesley, Reading, Massachussets, second edition, 1991.
3. P. Brately and Y. Choueka. Processing truncated terms in document retrieval
   systems. *Information Processing & Management*, 18(5):257–266, 1982.
4. Nicolas Bruno, Nick Koudas, and Divesh Srivastava. Holistic twig joins: Optimal
   XML pattern matching. In *Proceedings of the 2002 ACM SIGMOD International
   Conference on Management of Data*, pp. 310–321, Madison Wisconsin, USA, June
   2002. ACM, 2002.
5. Donatella Castelli and Pasquale Pagano. Opendlib: A digital library service system.
   In Maristella Agosti and Constantino Thanos, editors, *6th European Conference,
   ECDL 2002, Rome, Italy, September 16–18, 2002, Proceedings*, volume 2458 of
   *LNCS*, pages 292–308. Springer, 2002.
6. World Wide Web Consortium. XML path language (XPath), version 1.0, W3C.
   Recommendation, November 1999.
7. World Wide Web Consortium. XQuery 1.0: An XML query language. W3C Working Draft, November 2002.
   http://www.w3.org/TR/xquery.
8. N. Day and J.M. Martnez. Introduction to MPEG- 7 (v4.0). working document
   N4675, 2002. Available at:
   http://mpeg.telecomitalialab.com/working documents.htm.
9. Gerald Salton and Michael J. McGill. *Introduction to Modern Information Retrieval.* McGraw-Hill Book Company, 1983.
10. Benjamin Bin Yao, M. Tamer Özsu, and John Keenleyside. XBench – a family
    of benchmarks for XML DBMSs. Technical Report TR-CS-2002-39, University of
    Waterloo, December 2002.
    http://db.uwaterloo.ca/~ddbms/projects/xbench/index.html.
11. Chun Zhang, Jeffrey F. Naughton, David J. DeWitt, Qiong Luo, and Guy M.
    Lohman. On supporting containment queries in relational database management
    systems. InWalid G. Aref, editor, *ACM SIGMOD Conference 2001: Santa Barbara,
    CA, USA*, Proceedings. ACM, 2001.
12. Justin Zobel, Alistair Moffat, and Ron Sacks-Davis. Searching large lexicons for
    partially specified terms using compressed inverted files. In Rakesh Agrawal, Seán
    Baker, and David A. Bell, editors, *19th International Conference on Very Large
    Data Bases, August 24–27, 1993, Dublin, Ireland, Proceedings*, pages 290–301. Mor-
    gan Kaufmann, 1993.

# Structure-Aware Query for Digital Libraries: Use Cases and Challenges for the Humanities*

Christopher York, Clifford Wulfman, and Greg Crane

Perseus Project
Tufts University,
Medford, MA 02155, U.S.A.

**Abstract.** Much recent research in database design focuses on persistence models for semistructured data similar to the SGML and XML that humanities digital libraries have long used to encode digital editions of texts. Structure-aware querying promises to simplify the design of such digital repositories by allowing them to store and query texts using a single, unified information model. Using content the Perseus Project has acquired over the past ten years as a test case, we describe the advantages and delimit the problems in managing structure-aware queries over multiple or ambiguous schemas, evaluate the place of markup in digital libraries where much content is automatically generated, and examine the uses for structure-aware query in a system that stores both semistructured content and graph-structured metadata.

## 1 Introduction

Much recent research in database design focuses on persistence models for semi-structured data similar to the SGML and XML that humanities digital libraries have long used to mark up electronic editions of texts [5], [7], [8]. From the Perseus Project's perspective, such databases differ from other persistence options primarily in offering indices over a set of primitive relations (e.g. ancestry and sibling predicates) that path languages such as XPath [4] can then query— much as text management systems offer indices over a set of primitive relations (e.g. stemming and tokenization) that full-text engines can then query. The Perseus document-management system, described in [10], uses relational databases to warehouse data harvested from SGML/XML documents stored in a filesystem. To add new functionality to its user interface, one must first write code to harvest data from the document store, design an appropriate relational schema to warehouse it and, finally, write user-interface code to access the data warehouse. Structure-aware querying offers the possibility to index and retrieve document fragments directly, thus easing the task of building new interface components and exposing more of the rich markup that characterizes documents in Perseus' repository for use in user queries. However, the DTDs,

---

* A grant from the Digital Libraries Initiative Phase 2 (NSF IIS-9817484) provided support for this work.

T. Koch and I.T. Sølvberg (Eds.): ECDL 2003, LNCS 2769, pp. 188–193, 2003.

metadata formats, and user requirements for Perseus' digital library fit uneasily in the paradigm of boolean query over XML datagrams that guides the design of XQuery [3], the dominant path-based query language. Indeed, any path-based query language presupposing a one-to-one relationship between a semantic concept and its syntactic expression in markup must be supplemented by a data-integration layer to be of practical use in querying documents that conform to permissive or heterogeneous schemas. To illustrate the problem, we will examine Perseus' use cases for structure-aware query, how our data model affects requirements for query language functionality, and, finally, how several data-integration strategies would interact with structure-aware query facilities in Perseus' digital repository.

## 2   Use Cases

Structure-aware querying could be used in three different areas of the Perseus document-management system: metadata retrieval, markup harvesting and presentation, and user-directed document retrieval.

*Metadata retrieval.* The majority of queries to Perseus' repository retrieve document metadata rather than actual content, primarily to determine title, author, collection membership, and other simple bibliographic information for users browsing the library. As described in [10], Perseus' document-level metadata are represented in the Resource Description Framework's XML format using Dublin core fields. Dublin core's isPartOf and isVersionOf relations tie metadata about document instances, text versions, and collections to each other. Because metadata queries typically join properties for a number of RDF resources—for example, locating titles and authors for each edition of a text in a given collection—we cannot use XPath 1.0 to query the RDF in XML form, for it cannot express joins on element content. Moreover, although it would be possible to query Perseus metadata via a path language with joins if one first transformed the RDF to a canonical XML-based triples format [9], the resulting XML would be only very shallowly semistructured, thus obviating the usefulness of a path-based query language. Hence, because of the mismatch between RDF's graph-centric data model and XML's semistructured data model, we determined that structure-aware querying is an inappropriate access method for Perseus metadata.

*Markup harvesting and presentation.* Fragments of content markup are harvested from XML documents at several places in the system. Extended bibliographic information from a document tagged in the Text Encoding Initiative's DTD, for example, are gathered for display in a list of collection contents; similarly, lists of all place- or person-names mentioned in a document are needed for display in mapping and timeline tools. In most cases, the information retrieved supplements or refines a query on the RDF metadata for a document or collection. For example, given a document's title and author, RDF metadata queries might yield the document's unique id; after then locating the XML content from the id, a structure-aware query could return all of the placeName elements within it. Similarly, requests for fragments of XML documents will depend on an earlier metadata query; for example, the XPath query document('2000.01.0038.xml')//.[@type='chapter'][@part= 'N'][@n='4'] will return Chapter 4 of Booth's *Life and Labour of the People of London* given the document id. Because such queries merely identify an element or set of elements in the markup and do not require joining, sorting, or composing sets of elements, a simple path language like XPath 1.0 can cover Perseus' retrieval needs in this area.

*User-directed document retrieval.* For advanced users familiar with the DTDs of documents in the system, structure-aware querying offers the possibility of supplementing full-text retrieval with structural constraints on the surrounding markup. For example, one would like to enable users familiar with the TEI to issue queries such as document(*)//(#)[//persName contains 'Georgia'] to retrieve document fragments containing markup that indicates the word 'Georgia' was used as a person's name rather than as a place name. As Fuhr and Großjohann [6] note, however, such functionality requires operators for relevance-weighted search in place of boolean ones, as well as DTD-specific information on what constitutes the relevant fragment of markup containing each search hit (identified above with (#)). Users are also likely to want support for data types and 'semantic relativism': the former would, for example, enable searches for documents where //publicationDate is later than August 17, 1982; the latter would allow markup as diverse as <doc publicationDate='October 27, 1983'>... and <publicationDate>October 27, 1983</publicationDate> to match such a query.

# 3   Challenges for Structure-Aware Retrieval

Turning from use cases for structure-aware retrieval to its place in digital library architecture, it becomes clear that three problems confront humanities repositories deploying path-based querying:

*Permissive and heterogeneous DTDs.* Complex DTDs like that of the TEI frequently give encoders multiple ways of encoding the same semantics. For example, editors using the TEI can tag temporal concepts using any of <date>, <time>, <dateRange>, <timeRange>, <dateStruct> or <timeStruct>; likewise, locations might call for <address>, <name type='place'>, <placeName> or <rs type='place'>. While unfettered flexibility gives encoders a nuanced language in which to express complex textual semantics, it is ill-suited to the needs of users and client code accessing documents. Users of digital editions are more likely to care about retrieving markup by semantics (e.g. "find documents containing references to 'Tufts' as an organization") than about the syntactic distinction between <rs type='organization'>Tufts</rs> and <orgName>

Tufts</orgName>. Not only will many DTDs have more than one way to tag a given concept, a living digital library is likely to have documents from a number of different DTDs, each with an idiosyncratic element set. The primary challenge for structure-aware querying in such a repository is to balance semantic access to its data—thus integrating diverse tagging strategies—with syntactic access to the markup of specific documents, for those concepts where the library's DTDs legislate a canonical XML form.

*Integration with automatically generated markup.* Most of the markup in Perseus' document-management system was produced by hand, but a significant portion was automatically generated by information-extraction algorithms tuned to identify place names and dates in running text [11]. While many constructs used by information-extraction routines to annotate text— such as feature-level language analysis, named-entity recognition, and certainty metrics—can be represented using the TEI, such annotations are both ubiquitous and easily regenerated. If stored in XML, the resulting texts are so highly tagged as to be unreadable by humans and sufficiently large to defy conventional XML processing. Storing these annotations separately, as standoff markup on a human-produced XML file, is the only viable solution. For clients and users of structure-aware queries, however, it would be advantageous for automatically produced standoff markup to *appear* as though it were stored in XML. One could then query the repository for document(*)//placeName[. contains 'Athens'] and receive appropriate results whether the markup is human-produced and stored in the XML source document, or automatically generated and stored as standoff markup.

*User familiarity with DTDs.* Finally, user-directed document retrieval using structured queries presumes that users will be familiar both with the DTDs and the markup practices of a given text repository. In the case of the TEI, with some 600 elements and a specification that covers two large volumes, this means that only advanced users will attempt structure-aware queries. Nevertheless, much of the markup in a document repository is of significant interest to advanced users with correspondingly diverse search requirements; for example, a Greek text with feature-level linguistic markup will be of use to historical linguists, students of Greek, and textual critics. Digital library interfaces for cultural heritage content will, therefore, need to balance ease-of-use for novice users with the need to expose markup via structure-aware query to advanced users.

## 4    Data Integration for Structure Aware Query

There are several ways to address the challenges presented to document repositories by the need for structure-aware querying. Past data-integration practice at Perseus has been to translate equivalent markup into a Perseus-specific set of database fields which are then accessed by the user interface [10]. While this solution effectively bridges multiple markup strategies for similar concepts, it limits the markup that reaches the user to fields in Perseus' canonical set. As a result, much existing markup is unused by web interfaces and inaccessible to everyday users. Implementing structure-aware query on top of this system is not possible, because only a very small subset of the available documents' structure is indexed. Several other options exist, however, each with advantages and disadvantages:

*Translate markup to a data-integration DTD.* Extending Perseus' existing data-integration approach, one could define a canonical DTD in which any construct appearing in a variety of forms in repository documents is mapped to a single, unambiguous representation. This amounts to producing a view over semistructured data throughout the repository, much as described in [1] and [2]. Users and client applications could then issue structure-aware queries over the documents in canonicalized form. Such an approach has disadvantages: clients must use the system's proprietary data-integration DTD, and the repository's developers must produce it. Hence, although the markup-translation approach achieves the goal of exposing data from multiple and permissive DTDs to structural queries, the requirement that clients and users learn a proprietary DTD when others, such as the TEI, have wide public acceptance makes semistructured views a less viable option than others for Perseus.

*Harvest semantic metadata from the repository.* As mentioned previously, Perseus' metadata is stored using RDF-embedded Dublin core. An alternate approach to the semistructured data-integration problem is to harvest markup from repository documents, integrate it with an existing ontology, and allow client interfaces and users to access the resulting metadata using standard RDF query languages. This solution, like the previous one, requires users and interface programmers to access a separate data-integration representation, but it has the virtue that other digital libraries are likely to adopt a standard metadata ontology as well. However, this approach requires digital library implementers to create a well-defined mapping between the DTDs their library uses and standard ontologies, and to maintain the structure-aware queries that implement the mapping.

*Expand syntactic queries to account for ambiguity.* A final approach to the semistructured data-integration problem would expand all structure-aware queries before executing them. In such a system, clients and users could formulate queries assuming that the repository's markup conforms to a standard format such as the TEI; provided appropriate translations are available, a query such as `document(*)/.[//placeName='Tufts']` would expand to match not only `<placeName>Tufts</placeName>` but also `<name type='place'>Tufts</name>`. Such a system would, in effect, implement semistructured views via query rewriting, with the variation that fragments within a single document could appear in multiple forms simultaneously. The system would, however, be of limited use to programmatic clients, for it would of necessity return results in the document's original representation—which the client code might not be able to process.

## 5   Future Work

Work on Perseus' legacy content reveals several overarching requirements for a structure-aware query system: repository architectures need to handle multiple DTDs and copious offset markup, and even among documents conforming to a single DTD and without offset markup, tagging strategies are quite diverse. Structure-aware querying offers the promise of simplified access to repository contents, but the semistructured data-integration problem caused by the diversity of tagging in humanities digital libraries requires solutions that reach beyond the domain of indexing path-based primitives. Future work at Perseus will investigate a hybrid approach that harvests semantic metadata from the repository for query by user interface clients while providing syntactic query expansion for advanced users who wish to issue structure-aware searches directly.

## References

1. Abiteboul, S., McHugh, J., Rys, M., Vassalos, V., and Wiener, J. Incremental Maintenance for Materialized Views over Semistructured Data, in *Proceedings of the 24th International Conference on Very Large Data Bases (VLDB 1998)*, 38–49.
2. Aguilera, V., Cluet, S., Milo, T., Veltri, P., and Vodislav, D. Views in a Large-Scale XML Repository. VLDB *11 (3)* (2002), 238–255.
3. Boag, S., Chamberlin, D., Fernandez, M.F., Florescu, D., Robie, J., Simeon, J., and Stefanescu, M. XQuery 1.0: An XML Query Language. W3C Working Draft (2002). http://www.w3.org/TR/xquery.
4. Clark, J., and DeRose, S. XML Path Language (XPath) 1.0. W3C Recommendation (1999). http://www.w3.org/TR/xpath.
5. Fiebig, T., Helmer, S., Kanne, C.-C., Moerkotte, G., Neumann, J., Schiele, R., and Westmann, T. Anatomy of a Native XML Base Management System. VLDB *11 (4)* (2002), 292–314.
6. Fuhr, N., and Großjohann, K. XIRQL: A Query Language for Information Retrieval in XML Documents, in *Proceedings of the 24th Annual International Conference on Research and Development in Information Retrieval (2001)*, 172–180.
7. Jagadish, H.V., Al-Khalifa, S., Chapman, A., Lakshmanan, L.V.S., Nierman, A., Paparizos, S., Patel, J.M., Srivastava, D., Wiwatwattana, N., Wu, Y., and Yu, C. TIMBER: A Native XML Database. VLDB *11 (4)* (2002), 274–291.
8. McHugh, J., Abiteboul, S., Goldman, R., Quass, D., and Wisdom, J. Lore: A Database Management System for Semistructured Data, *ACM SIGMOD International Conference on Management of Data (SIGMOD 1997)* SIGMOD Record *26 (3)* (1997), 54–66.
9. Robie, J., Garshol, L.M., Newcomb, S., Fuchs, M., Miller, L., Brickley, D., Christophides, V. and Karvounarakis, G. The Syntactic Web: Syntax and Semantics on the Web. Markup Languages: Theory and Practice *3 (4)* (2001), 411–440.
10. Smith, D.A., Mahoney, A. and Rydberg-Cox, J.A. Managing XML Documents in an Integrated Digital Library. Markup Languages: Theory and Practice *2 (3)* (2000), 205–214.
11. Smith, D., and Crane, G. Disambiguating Geographic Names in a Historical Digital Library, in *Proceedings of the 5th European Conference on Digital Libraries (ECDL 2001)*, 127–136.

# Combining DAML+OIL, XSLT, and Probabilistic Logics for Uncertain Schema Mappings in MIND

Henrik Nottelmann and Norbert Fuhr

Institute of Informatics and Interactive Systems, University of Duisburg-Essen,
47048 Duisburg, Germany, {nottelmann,fuhr}@uni-duisburg.de

**Abstract.** When distributed, heterogeneous digital libraries have to be integrated, one of the crucial tasks is to map between different schemas. As schemas may have different granularities, and as schema attributes do not always match precisely, a general-purpose schema mapping approach requires support for uncertain mappings. In this paper we present one of the very few approaches for defining and using uncertain schema mappings. We combine different technologies like DAML+OIL, probabilistic Datalog (since DAML+OIL—as similar ontology languages—lacks rules) and XSLT for actually transforming queries and documents. This declarative approach is fully implemented in the project MIND (which develops methods for retrieval in networked multimedia digital libraries). However, as DAML+OIL lacks some important features, the proposed approach is only a stepping stone for an integrated solution.

## 1 Introduction

Federated digital libraries (DLs) integrate a large number of legacy DLs; so they give users the impression of one coherent, homogeneous library. MIND [15] is such a system for heterogeneous and non-co-operative multimedia libraries. Heterogeneity appears in different forms: In MIND, differences in query languages, communication protocols and document models are solved by DL-specific wrappers.

Libraries also differ in the document structure (schemas). Users cannot deal efficiently with this semantic heterogeneity and therefore should only know one system-wide or personalised standard schema. In MIND, the standard schema is defined ontologically and independent from the sources. Then, queries are transformed from the standard schema into the DL schemas, and documents vice versa.

In contrast to most of the approaches available so far, MIND explicitly supports uncertain schema mappings. Schemas may have different granularity, and schema attributes do not always match precisely (e.g. authors and editors vs. the more general attribute creators). So creators cannot be mapped onto authors precisely but only with a specific probability. Systems with purely deterministic mappings fail in such settings.

In MIND, we model MIND documents and queries in DAML+OIL (the forthcoming standard ontology language) so that we can extend our approach to nested structures fairly easy. As DAML+OIL lacks rules, we specify schema mappings in probabilistic Datalog. The rules are then converted into XSLT stylesheets for transforming the DAML+OIL models. XSLT implementations are available for all major programming languages, so our approach can be used easily in other projects. DAML+OIL schema definitions,

T. Koch and I.T. Sølvberg (Eds.): ECDL 2003, LNCS 2769, pp. 194–206, 2003.

pDatalog rules and the resulting XSLT stylesheets can be stored in textual files, so it is very easy to update the mappings when a schema is changed (without recompiling code). We are aware that there are many open questions, so this work should be considered a stepping stone.

The rest of this paper is structured as follows. The next section gives a survey of other approaches for handling heterogeneous schemas. Section 3 introduces the MIND document model. In section 4 we model MIND documents and queries in DAML+OIL. Section 5 describes how schema mappings are expressed in probabilistic logics. Section 6 summarises the major ideas presented in this paper and gives an outlook on future research.

## 2   Related Work

Mappings between heterogeneous schemas have been studied for quite a while, but only one of the existing approaches allows for uncertain mappings.

In the field of federated databases, two approaches are distinguished: In "local as view" (LaV), the source schemas are defined as views (mappings) over a fixed global schema. This makes it easy to add a new source, but query transformation has exponential time complexity. In contrast, the global schema is defined as a view over local schemas in the "global as view" (GaV) approach. Here, query transformation can be reduced to rule unfolding, but the global view has to be modified whenever a new source is added.

The BGLaV approach [20] combines the advantages of both worlds. The global schema is specified ontologically and independent from the sources, the source schema models the documents returned by the source, and mappings are defined by relational algebra expressions. This approach has polynomial time complexity for query transformation (like GaV) while adding new sources is fairly simple (like LaV), and is used in an extended form in MIND.

A framework for dealing with heterogeneous OSM schemas is presented in [1]. OSM models contain objects, their relationships and a predicate calculus for expressing constraints. As in BGLaV, the global schema is defined ontologically and independent from the source schemas. Interaction with an administrator is assumed (however not required) for setting up deterministic mappings between objects (and relations, respectively). These mappings can model specialisation/generalisation relationships, and string processing operators are provided.

The GaV system Demetrios [6] follows a different approach with SQL as query language for both the user and the sources. The SQL extension FRAQL is used for defining mappings from the source relations onto global relations. FRAQL allows e.g. for accessing metadata, restructuring tables and converting values.

TSIMMIS [3] is one of the early systems integrating heterogeneous digital libraries. Schema mappings are defined in a textual format with actions which are executed when a corresponding template matches a query.

MARIAN [10] shares some common aspects with our approach. Attributes can be mapped onto others with simple rules, specified with the declarative 5S language. Uncertain mappings are possible by weighting the mapping rules. In contrast to the wrapper based system MIND, MARIAN uses a harvesting approach: It periodically downloads all documents from an information source and stores them in a local index. Thus, MAR-IAN has to transform documents into a standard schema only once, and does not require query transformations at all.

With the growing popularity of XML, mappings between different DTDs are also investigated. Due to the deterministic nature of XML, uncertainty is not supported by any of these approaches.

A tree-grammar-based approach for inducing integrated views (XML-QL templates which can be used for stating user queries) for XML data with heterogeneous DTDs is presented in [11]. Type trees derived from the source DTDs are converted into a tree automaton. States belonging to similar types are merged to obtain a minimised integrated view.

LSD [5] uses a machine learning approach for finding matching elements. Different classifiers (e.g. naive Bayes, kNN, county name recogniser) are trained on pairs of XML documents (one corresponding to the global schema, the other one corresponding to one of the local schemas), where an administrator has to identify matching elements. After this training phase, the classifiers are combined and applied to different source schemas.

Cupid [13] is a generic schema matching algorithm for detecting matching schema elements (not restricted to DTDs or XML Schemas). Cupid discovers matchings based on names (by using linguistic techniques, e.g. a thesaurus), data types, constraints and schema structure.

None of the approaches described in this section aside from MARIAN (whose harvesting approach is incompatible with MIND) addresses the problem of uncertain mappings: Either a mapping between attributes of different schemas is deterministic, or it is ignored. However, since information retrieval has to deal with uncertainty and vagueness anyway, we think that uncertain mappings should be supported for retrieval in digital libraries, and thus was integrated within MIND.

## 3   MIND Document Model

MIND adopts the document model presented in [8] with only slight modifications.

Like in database systems, data types with comparison operators are explicitly modelled. However, vagueness of query formulations is one of the key concepts of Information Retrieval. Thus, it is crucial that comparison operators have a probabilistic interpretation (as proposed in [7]). Vagueness is required e.g. when a user is uncertain about the exact publication year of a document or the spelling of an author name. These comparison operators are called "vague predicates". For a specific attribute value the vague predicate yields an estimate of the probability that the condition is fulfilled from the user's point of view — instead of a Boolean value as in DB systems.

**Definition 1 (Data types).** *A data type $D$ is a pair $(dom(D), pred(D))$, where $dom(D)$ is the domain (all possible values) and $pred(D) = \{p_1, \ldots, p_n\}$ is the set of (vague) predicates. Each predicate is a function $p_i : dom(D) \times dom'(D, p_i) \rightarrow [0, 1]$, and $dom'(D, p_i)$ is the domain of all possible comparison values (values in a query) for that predicate $p_i$. The set of all data types is denoted by $\mathcal{D}$.*

In most cases we have $dom'(D, p_i) = dom(D)$. On the other hand, the predicate *isIn* of the data type *Year* has a pair of year numbers (a time period) as comparison value: $dom'(Year, isIn) = dom(Year) \times dom(Year)$. In addition, some of the predicates may be Boolean (like =), i.e. the mapping is restricted to the set $\{0, 1\}$.

MIND employs a linear document model. Different parts of documents are specified by named and typed attributes:

**Definition 2 (Schema).** *A schema $S$ is a set of schema attributes $\{A_1, \ldots, A_n\}$. A schema attribute $A$ is a pair $(dt(A), pred(A))$ of a data type $dt(A) \in \mathcal{D}$ and a subset $pred(A) \subseteq pred(dt(A))$ of supported predicates. For brevity, we write $dom(A) = dom(dt(A))$.*

*Example 1.* In the remainder of this paper, we will use the schemas

$S_1 := \{au = (Name, \{equals\}), da = (DateISO8601, \{=\}), ti = (Text, \{contains\})\}$,

$S_2 := \{author = (Name, \{equals, soundslike\}), editor = (Name, \{equals, soundslike\})$,
$\qquad date = (DateEN, \{same, vague - same\}), title = (Text, \{contains\})\}$.

Here, valid values of *DateISO8601* are "2003-03-10" or "2003-12-24"; values of *DateEN* are "03/10/03" or "12/24/03".

A document is an instance of a specific schema, assigning values to attributes:

**Definition 3 (Document).** *A document $d$ is a pair $(S, att)$ of a schema $S = schema(d)$ and a set of document attributes $att = \{a_1, \ldots, a_n\}$. A document attribute $a$ is a triple $(w, A, v)$ of a schema attribute $A \in S$, a value $v \in dom(A)$ and a probabilistic weight $w \in [0, 1]$ specifying the probability that $v$ is a correct value of $A$.*

In most cases, the weight of a document attribute equals 1 (which can then be left out). It can be less than 1 for expressing uncertainty about the correct value (e.g. if the year of creation for an artefact is only approximately known).

A schema attribute can be used by more than one document attribute (e.g. for multiple authors), and schema attributes can be left out completely.

*Example 2.* These are the representations of the same document according to the two schemas defined above:

$d_1 := (S_1, \{(au, "N.\ Fuhr"), (au, "J.\ Callan"), (au, "B.\ Croft"), (au, "J.\ Lafferty")$,
$\qquad (da, "2001-01-01"), (ti, "Language\ Models\ and\ ...")\})$,

$d_2 := (S_2, \{(author, "N.\ Fuhr"), (editor, "J.\ Callan"), (editor, "B.\ Croft")$,
$\qquad (editor, "J.\ Lafferty"), (date, "01/01/01"), (title, "Language\ Models\ and\ ...")\})$.

These examples show that $S_2$ is more specific than $S_1$ as it distinguishes between authors and editors but $S_1$ puts both in the attribute *au*.

**Definition 4 (Query).** *A query q is a pair $(S, cond)$ of a schema $S = schema(q)$ and a set of query conditions $cond = \{c_1, \ldots, c_n\}$. A query condition c is a tuple $(w, A, p, v)$ of a probabilistic weight $w \in [0, 1]$ specifying the importance of this condition, a schema attribute $A \in S$, a predicate $p \in pred(A)$ and a comparison value $v \in dom'(S, p)$.*

*Example 3.* These queries corresponding to the two schemas should return documents $d_1$ and $d_2$, respectively:

$q_1 := (S_1, \{(0.8, au, equals, \text{``Fuhr''}), (0.2, da, =, \text{``2001''})\}),$

$q_2 := (S_2, \{(0.8, author, soundslike, \text{``Fuhr''}), (0.2, date, vague - same, \text{``2001''})\}).$

## 4   Modelling Documents and Queries in DAML+OIL

In the previous section we described the linear, flat document model used within the MIND project. We plan, however, to extend our model to nested structures. The most promising candidate for expressing nested schemas and documents is the RDF Schema extension DAML+OIL [4] which has the power to become the standard ontology language

RDF [12] is developed in the context of the Semantic Web as a specification language for objects and their properties via statements of the form "subject predicate object" (also called triples). The subject of the statement is an RDF object, the predicate is a property, and the object of a statement is another RDF object or a literal (a value, e.g. a string or a number). The vocabulary (object classes, properties) can be defined with the schema specification language RDF Schema (RDFS for short) [2]. DAML+OIL enriches RDFS with more advanced primitives: E.g. the range of a property can be specified w.r.t. the domain (in RDFS, it can only be specified globally). As there will never be one single standard ontology, schema mapping remains a crucial issue in the DAML+OIL world.

Thus, we decided to map the MIND document model onto DAML+OIL, i.e. that MIND schemas[1]) are modelled as DAML+OIL schemas. However, the DAML+OIL language has two restrictions we have to face:

1. DAML+OIL employs XML Schema for modelling data types. XML Schema is designed to define documents, not queries. The major difference is that the former simply store values (unary data type predicates) whereas queries compare two values (binary data type predicates). In contrast to approaches like $\mathcal{SHOQ}(\mathbf{D_n})$ [16], XML Schema (and thus, DAML+OIL), only support unary data type predicates.
2. DAML+OIL does not support the concept of uncertainty. However, in our document model document attribute values and query conditions can be weighted probabilistically.

These problems can be solved in two different ways: We can extend the language by allowing n-ary data type predicates (i.e., allowing properties for daml:DataType subclasses and their instances), and by attaching a probabilistic weight to every statement.

---

[1] With "schema", we mean MIND schemas in this paper, not DAML+OIL schemas.

We disregarded this alternative, as it contradicts the efforts of establishing a standard ontology language, and existing DAML+OIL and RDF tools would not work any more.

So we followed solutions which remain within the RDF world: As DAML+OIL data types only have a restricted expressiveness, we model MIND data types as classes in DAML+OIL (subclasses of mind:DT) instead of DAML+OIL data types directly. Every instance of a MIND data type class has a property mind:value; the range is a DAML+OIL data type. Search predicates are modelled by a property mind:pred with the domain mind:DT and the range mind:Predicate.

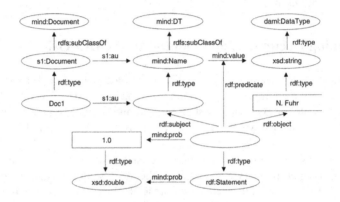

**Fig. 1.** Documents in DAML+OIL

Furthermore, reification (statements about statements) is used for supporting uncertainty. Statements can have a property mind:prob which specifies the probability that this statement is correct. Reification is supported by RDFS, but DAML+OIL tools cannot give any semantics to such triples. However, we will later see that we don't use DAML+OIL tools directly, so we think that this extension does not introduce additional problems.

Examples for documents and queries are shown in figures 1 and 2. The first "level" introduces some common concepts used in the MIND document model, the second row defines the MIND schema $S_1$ and a concrete data type. The lower part models one specific document. The document attribute *au* is modelled by anonymous instances of mind:Name and rdf:Statement (reification). Queries are modelled in a similar way.

## 5   Heterogeneous Schemas

As pointed out above, in heterogeneous environments queries have to be transformed from the standard schema to the DL schema, and documents from the DL schema to the standard schema. In MIND, the standard schema is defined ontologically and independently from the libraries, and the DL schemas represent the structure of library documents (similar to BGLaV, but in contrast to LaV or GaV).

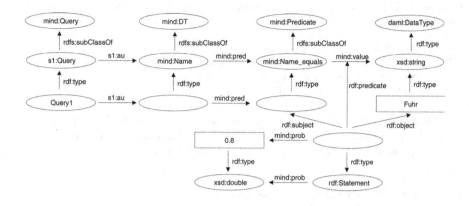

**Fig. 2.** Queries in DAML+OIL

For these transformations, rules (stating the relationships between attributes of the two different schemas) are required. DAML+OIL does not support rules (besides properties like rdfs:subClassOf which could be viewed as rules). DAML-L is intended to add rules to DAML+OIL, but this language is not yet completed.

In MIND we decided to map parts of DAML+OIL models onto probabilistic Datalog. This probabilistic Horn clause logic provides a powerful and flexible rule mechanism. The rules are then automatically converted into XSLT stylesheets which operate on XML serialisations of DAML+OIL models (documents and queries).

### 5.1 Probabilistic Datalog

Datalog [18] is a variant of predicate logic based on function-free Horn clauses. Negation is allowed, but its use is limited. Rules have the form

```
father(X,Y) :- parent(X,Y) & sex(X,male).
```

where father(X,Y) is the head literal of the rule (with predicate father and variables X and Y). The right part forms the body, a conjunction of literals ("subgoals") parent(X,Y) and sex(X,male). Negated literals start with an exclamation mark. Variables like X start with an uppercase character, constants like male with a lowercase character. Thus the rule states that X is the father of Y if it is a male parent.

Facts are rules with empty body and only constants in the head literal:

```
sex(peter,male). sex(mary,female). 0.9 parent(peter,mary).
```

In probabilistic Datalog (pDatalog for short) [9], every fact can have a probabilistic weight (if it is left out, the weight equals one). In the same way, rules also can be weighted. If more than one rule is formulated for the same head predicate, we have to know $Pr(p|\neg r_1 \wedge \neg r_2)$, $Pr(p|r_1 \wedge \neg r_2)$, $Pr(p|\neg r_1 \wedge r_2)$ and $Pr(p|r_1 \wedge r_2)$. This is equivalent to the situation in probabilistic inference networks where a link matrix with the same conditional probabilities has to be given.

*Example 4.* The following rules state that two documents are semantically related iff they have the same author or are linked together:

```
sameauthor(D1,D2) :- author(D1,A) & author(D2,A).
0.5 related(D1,D2) :- link(D1,D2) & !link(D1,D2).
0.2 related(D1,D2) :- !link(D1,D2) & link(D1,D2).
0.7 related(D1,D2) :- link(D1,D2) & link(D1,D2).
```

This rule set with $2^{n-1}$ rules for $n$ original rules cannot be evaluated in general, but the $2^{n-1}$ probabilities and the $n$ original rules can be transformed into a new set of $n$ certain rules with $2^{n-1}$ additional uncertain weights [19,14].

## 5.2   Mapping DAML+OIL onto pDatalog

For our purpose, a simple, straight-forward mapping of parts of a DAML+OIL model onto probabilistic Datalog is sufficient:

**Definition 5 (Mapping DAML+OIL onto pDatalog).** *Every DAML+OIL class is mapped onto a unary pDatalog predicate with the same name (where the namespace prefix and the local name are concatenated with a "#"). Instances of a DAML+OIL class are facts referring to that predicate.*

*Every property is mapped onto a binary pDatalog predicate with the same name. Statements "s p o" with subject s, predicate p (the property) and object o are mapped onto facts p(s,o). If the statement is weighted, this is regarded as the fact's probabilistic weight.*

As we deal with text (including brackets, punctuations and whitespace), we allow strings in quotation marks as constants as well.

The statements (triples) depicted in figures 1 and 2 are converted into the following pDatalog facts:

```
s1#au(doc1,x1). mind#name(x1). mind#value(x1,"N. Fuhr").

s1#au(query1,xx1). mind#name(xx1). mind#pred(xx1,xx2).
mind#name_equals(xx2). 0.8 mind#value(xx2,"Fuhr").
```

For every document attribute we have three facts with an auxiliary constant (x1), for every query condition even five facts with two auxiliary constants (xx1 and xx2). This is due to the problem that DAML+OIL does not support binary data type predicates in DAML+OIL for modelling query. However, pDatalog supports n-ary predicates, so we can define shortcuts:

```
s1#au(doc1,"N. Fuhr").

0.8 s1#au_equals(query1,"Fuhr").
```

The first fact can be obtained by

```
s1#au(D,V) :- s1#au(D,X) & mind#name(X) & mind#value(X,V).
```

This model can be used for retrieval in pDatalog. We need one rule for every predicate which combines corresponding query conditions, document attribute values and a pDatalog "implementation" of the search predicate:

```
s1#result(Q,D)  :- s1#au_equals(Q,V1) & s1#au(D,V2) &
                   mind-dt#name_equals(V2,V1).
s1#result(Q,D)  :- s1#da_eq(Q,V1) & s1#da(D,V2) &
                   =(V2,V1).
s1#result(Q,D)  :- s1#ti_contains(Q,V1) & s1#ti(D,V2) &
                   mind-dt#text_contains(V2,V1).

?- s1#result(query1,D).
```

The last line retrieves the result of query query1; with the document base used so far, this is document doc1 (with probability $0.8 \cdot equals("N.Fuhr","Fuhr") = 0.8$).

### 5.3  Schema Mapping Rules

In this subsection, schema $S_2$ is the standard schema and $S_1$ is the DL schema. Then, we have to map document attribute S1#au onto document attributes S2#author and S2#editor with probabilities 0.7 and 0.3, respectively (the probabilities are fictious). These "mapping rules" can be expressed by these pDatalog rules:

```
s2#title(D,V)  :- s1#title(D,V).
0.7 s2#author(D,V)  :- s1#au(D,V).
0.3 s2#editor(D,V)  :- s1#au(D,V).

s1#title_contains(D,V)  :- s2#title_contains(D,V).
0.7 s1#au_equals(Q,V)  :- s2#author_equals(Q,V) & !s2#editor_equals(Q,V).
0.3 s1#au_equals(Q,V)  :- !s2#author_equals(Q,V) & s2#editor_equals(Q,V).
1.0 s1#au_equals(Q,V)  :- s2#author_equals(Q,V) & s2#editor_equals(Q,V).
```

The first block defines schema mapping rules for documents, the rules of the second block can be used for query transformation. As we want to transform queries from the standard schema into the DL schema, we have DL schema attributes in the head and standard schema attributes in the bodies for query rules. The probabilities decrease the weights of the created $S_2$ document attributes and the created DL schema conditions, respectively.

In some cases, string processing is required, too, e.g. for transforming *DateISO8601* date values into *DateEN* value when we map S1#da onto S2#date. For this we introduce some new (predefined) string processing predicates:

**Definition 6 (Built-in predicates).** *For string processing, the deterministic built-in string processing predicates* $starts\text{-}with(B,C)$, $concat(A,B,C,D)$ *(also possible with more arguments to be concatenated),* $substring\text{-}after(A,B,C)$, $substring\text{-}before(A,B,C)$ *and* $substring(A,B,C,D)$ *can be used with the obvious meanings, e.g.:*

$$concat(A,B,C) \Leftrightarrow A \text{ is concatenation of } B \text{ and } C.$$

*In addition, pDatalog provides the binary predicates* = *and* <> *(for all constants, e.g.* =("A","B")*) and* >, >=, < *and* <= *(only for numbers).*

In some cases comparison values also have to be transformed. Due to the inverted direction for query rules (with the DL schema in the head), the transformed comparison value can be computed easily.

For other application areas, however, this approach is not feasible. If we want to perform retrieval in heterogeneous libraries, we need query rules with the same direction as for document rules. In our example, this means that $S_2$ attributes have to be used in the rule heads, and $S_1$ attributes must appear in the body. For retrieval involving schema mapping, we can formulate the following rules for our example schemas:

```
0.7 mapping(author,au).
s2#author(D,V)  :- s1#au(D,V) & mapping(author,au).
s2#author_equals(Q,V) :- s1#au_equals(Q,V) & mapping(author,au).
s2#author_soundslike(Q,V) :- s1#au_equals(Q,V) & mapping(author,au).

s2#result(Q,D) :- s2#author_equals(Q,V1) & s2#author(D,V2) &
                  mind-dt#name_equals(V2,V1).
s2#result(Q,D) :- s2#author_soundslike(Q,V1) & s2#author(D,V2) &
                  mind-dt#name_soundslike(V2,V1).
```

The additional fact `0.7 mapping(author,au).` is required; if we weight the document and query mapping rules directly by 0.7, the weight is considered twice in the results.

## 5.4   Transforming Queries and Documents with XSLT

In federated DL systems, wrappers are used for querying the underlying libraries. Thus, we cannot directly retrieve DL documents with probabilistic Datalog. Of course the pDatalog rules could be evaluated for transforming queries and documents. We use a more general approach: DAML+OIL models are serialised in XML. XSLT is a well-established technology for transforming an XML document into other textual formats, e.g. another XML document (mapping between different DTDs or transforming the content), an HTML document (for creating web pages) or simple text. XSLT processors are freely available for a large number of programming languages.

The XSLT stylesheets are created based on the pDatalog rules. The mapping is straight-forward, but space precludes us from explaining it in detail. The transformation of pDatalog rules into XSLT is done once after the mapping rules are set up, and can be performed completely automatically. We obtain one stylesheet for transforming documents and another one for transforming queries.

Then, documents are transformed in three steps (see figure 3):

1. The documents (internal objects, referring to the DL schema) are converted into DAML+OIL and serialised in XML.
2. The resulting XML document is transformed into another XML document by the document transformation XSLT stylesheet. The resulting XML document is also a serialisation of a DAML+OIL model, corresponding to the standard schema.
3. The resulting XML document is parsed and converted to new internal objects.

Queries are transformed in a similar way.

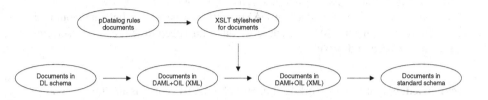

**Fig. 3.** Document transformation process

## 6 Conclusion

In this paper we proposed a declarative approach for defining and handling uncertain schema mappings implemented in MIND. We start from a linear document model and convert it into DAML+OIL (the forthcoming ontology standard). Later this will allow us to extend our approach to documents with a nested structure (see below). Weights are modelled with reification (for schema mappings, we need weights only for specific cases, we do not weight the rdfs:subClassOf property). As rules cannot be expressed directly in DAML+OIL yet, we applied probabilistic Datalog for specifying schema mapping rules. As these rules and the stylesheets derived from them can be kept in text files, adding or modifying the schema mapping rules is very easy and does not require any new program code.

However, our approach raises a number of questions: DAML+OIL data types (which use XML Schema data types) do not support n-ary data type predicates, so we cannot model MIND data types and their search predicates directly in DAML+OIL. In addition, uncertainty is not supported by DAML+OIL. We overcome this problem by using reification, which is available in RDFS but not in DAML+OIL (so DAML+OIL tools are not able to assign semantics to these triples). The third problem is the lack of rules (the DAML-L language which adds rules to DAML+OIL is still not released). Thus, we mapped DAML+OIL onto pDatalog and used its rule and inference mechanism. However, it would be more pleasant to have an integrated framework which allows for stating rules and uncertain facts directly in DAML+OIL. Although this would lead to further incompatibilities, it might be worth extending the language itself by at least binary data type predicates, uncertainty and probabilistic rules.

In addition, we plan to learn the schema mapping rules. Rule candidates can be found by investigating the schema definitions, e.g. two attributes having the same name are good matching candidates, and attributes with the same data type might also match if different names are used. However these rules are not always correct, e.g. if the attributes *title* and *location* both have the data type *Text*. Thus, the candidates have to be verified with documents in both schemas. Although in general we do not have DL documents in the standard schema at this stage, we often have schema mapping rules for other libraries which have some overlap with the DL under consideration. Documents occurring in both DLs then can be used for improving the schema mapping rules.

Finally, we plan to extend schema mappings towards schemas with deeper structure. The ultimate goal would be to specify mappings between arbitrary DAML+OIL models, but this poses problems as we cannot specify properties for data types (see section 4). One solution would be to extend the DAML+OIL language; another one would be to restrict the approach to DAML+OIL descriptions with a deep structure but a form similar to the one we used in this paper.

**Acknowledgements.** This work is supported by the EU commission under grant IST-2000-26061 (project MIND).

# References

[1]   J. Biskup and D. W. Embley. Extracting information from heterogeneous information sources using ontologically specified target views. *Information Systems*, 28(3):169—212, 2003.

[2]   D. Brickley and R. Guha. RDF vocabulary description language 1.0: RDF Schema, w3c working draft. Technical report, World Wide Web Consortium, Apr. 2002.

[3]   S. Chawathe, H. Garcia-Molina, J. Hammer, K. Ireland, Y. Papakonstantinou, J. Ullman, and J. Widom. The TSIMMIS project: Integration of heterogeneous information sources. In *16th Meeting of the Information Processing Society of Japan*, pages 7–18. Tokyo, Japan, 1994.

[4]   D. Connolly, F. v. Harmelen, I. Horrocks, D. L. McGuinness, P. F. Patel-Schneider, and L. A. Stein. DAML+OIL (march 2001) reference description. Technical report, World Wide Web Consortium, 2001. http://www.w3.org/TR/daml+oil-reference.

[5]   A. Doan, P. Domingos, and A. Y. Halevy. Reconciling schemas of disparate data sources: A machine-learning approach. In *SIGMOD Conference*, 2001.

[6]   M. Endig, M. Hoding, G. Saake, K.-U. Sattler, and E. Schallehn. Federation services for heterogeneous digital libraries accessing cooperative and non-cooperative sources. In *Kyoto International Conference on Digital Libraries*, pages 314–321, 2000.

[7]   N. Fuhr. A probabilistic framework for vague queries and imprecise information in databases. In *Proceedings of the 16th International Conference on Very Large Databases*, pages 696–707, Los Altos, California, 1990. Morgan Kaufman.

[8]   N. Fuhr. Towards data abstraction in networked information retrieval systems. *Information Processing and Management*, 35(2):101–119, 1999.

[9]   N. Fuhr. Probabilistic Datalog: Implementing logical information retrieval for advanced applications. *Journal of the American Society for Information Science*, 51(2):95–110, 2000.

[10]  M. A. Goncalves, R. K. France, and E. A. Fox. MARIAN: Flexible interoperability for federated digital libraries. In P. Constantopoulos and I. T. Soelvberg, editors, *Research and Advanced Technology for Digital Libraries*, volume 2163 of *Lecture Notes in Computer Science*, pages 173–186, Berlin et al., 2001. Springer.

[11]  E. Jeong and C.-N. Hsu. Induction of integrated view for XML data with heterogeneous DTDs. In Paques et al. [17], pages 151–158.

[12]  O. Lassila and R. R. Swick. Resource description framework (RDF) model and syntax specification. W3C recommendation, World Wide Web Consortium, Feb. 1999. http://www.w3.org/TR/1999/REC-rdf-syntax-19990222/.

[13]  J. Madhavan, P. A. Bernstein, and E. Rahm. Generic schema matching with cupid. In *Proc. 27th VLDB Conference*, pages 49–58, 2001. http://www.research.microsoft.com/~philbe/CupidVLDB01.pdf.

[14]  H. Nottelmann and N. Fuhr. Learning probabilistic Datalog rules for information classification and transformation. In Paques et al. [17], pages 387–394.

[15] H. Nottelmann and N. Fuhr. MIND: An architecture for multimedia information retrieval in federated digital libraries. In *Proceedings of the DELOS-Workshop on Interoperability in Digital Libraries*. DELOS-Network of Excellence on Digital Libraries, 2001.

[16] J. Z. Pan and I. Horrocks. Semantic web ontology reasoning in the $\mathcal{SHOQ}(\mathbf{D_n})$ description logic. In *Proc. of the 2002 Description Logic Workshop (DL 2002)*, 2002.

[17] H. Paques, L. Liu, and D. Grossman, editors. *Proceedings of the 10th International Conference on Information and Knowledge Management*, New York, 2001. ACM.

[18] J. D. Ullman. *Principles of Database and Knowledge-Base Systems*, volume I. Computer Science Press, Rockville (Md.), 1988.

[19] B. Wüthrich. On the learning of rule uncertainties and their integration into probabilistic knowledge bases. *Journal of Intelligent Information Systems*, 2:245–264, 1993.

[20] L. Xu and D. Embley. Combining the best of global-as-view and local-as-view for data integration. submitted for publication, http://www.deg.byu.edu/papers/PODS.integration.pdf.

# Digitometric Services for Open Archives Environments

Tim Brody, Simon Kampa, Stevan Harnad, Les Carr, and Steve Hitchcock

Intelligence, Agents, Multimedia Group
University of Southampton, UK
{tdb01r, srk, harnad, lac, sh94r}@ecs.soton.ac.uk

**Abstract.** We describe "digitometric" services and tools that add value to open-access eprint archives using the Open Archives Initiative (OAI) Protocol for Metadata Harvesting. Celestial is an OAI cache and gateway tool. Citebase Search enhances OAI-harvested metadata with linked references harvested from the full-text to provide a web service for citation navigation and research impact analysis. Digitometrics builds on data harvested using OAI to provide advanced visualisation and hypertext navigation for the research community. Together these services provide a modular, distributed architecture for building a "semantic web" for the research literature.

## 1 Introduction

In this paper we describe digitometric tools that apply and extend the Open Archives Initiative Protocol for Metadata Harvesting (OAI-PMH) as a means of building user services for the scientific and scholarly literature.

The services described in this paper touch on a number of digital library topics: infrastructure, accessing legacy data, harvesting, online archiving, online publication, open access, scientometrics, and linking. This covers both the use of existing data through discovery and conversion, and building new data through processing and analysis.

As authors increasingly use eprint archives (built using free tools such as Southampton's eprints.org [6]) to maximise their research impact - by maximising user access to and usage of their research through open-access - this resource is becoming an important tool for researchers. With open-access and an OAI-PMH interface any service can harvest metadata from an eprint archive and provide added-value, from simple cross-archive searching, through to advanced user interfaces and analytic tools.

The first part of this paper provides background about the OAI-PMH. We introduce the Celestial tool [4] (a cache/gateway for the OAI-PMH) and Citebase [5] (an end-user service that applies citation-analysis to existing OAI-PMH compliant eprint archives). We then analyse Citebase's database, and summarise the findings of a user survey conducted by the Open Citation Project [7]. Finally we introduce some of the new directions arising out of this work - creating a knowledge environment built on the OAI-PMH.

T. Koch and I.T. Sølvberg (Eds.): ECDL 2003, LNCS 2769, pp. 207–220, 2003.

## 2   Open Archives Initiative

The Open Archives Initiative [13] Protocol for Metadata Harvesting (OAI-PMH) is designed to address the need to expose metadata - titles, authors, abstracts etc. - from research literature archives in a structured form. An XML protocol built on the HTTP standard, OAI-PMH is in effect a CGI interface to databases. Based on 6 commands (or "verbs" in OAI parlance) OAI-PMH allows metadata to be incrementally harvested by *service providers* (the HTTP client) from *data providers* (the HTTP server).

There are 62 OAI-registered publicly accessible data providers (plus another 98 unregistered ones), exposing around two million records covering research literature (e.g. arXiv.org), music manuscripts (e.g. Library of Congress), theses, and others. Some service providers have been developed or adapted to make use of OAI-PMH, that allow users to search both commercial abstract databases and the freely available abstracts from public data providers (e.g. Scirus [25]). In the USA OAI-PMH is being used to build a large-scale distributed library system, NSDL [14].

The OAI-PMH allows the transfer of *metadata records* encoded in XML. To be OAI-compliant a data provider must expose their records in Dublin Core, but they can expose their data in any format that can be encoded in XML. The metadata records that describe a single entity form an *item*, identified by a unique *identifier*.

The OAI-PMH is being used to transfer sizeable amounts of data - in the case of http://arXiv.org/ some 230,000 metadata records (Figure 1 shows the increase in records for all OAI archives cached by 'Celestial' – see next section). As the number of OAI-PMH sites increases, and the size of the data provider databases grows (Figure 2), there is a growing need to build scalable infrastructures to support the transfer of data from data providers to service providers (a many to many relation). Caching is a useful method to distribute the load within such distributed systems using tools like Celestial.

## 3   Celestial

Celestial is software that supports the caching of metadata from OAI archives, gateways between legacy (1.0 and 1.1) and current (2.0) OAI implementations, and attempts to correct incorrectly implemented OAI archives.

In a distributed environment caching moves processing and network load away from the source and closer to the target (Figure 3). As OAI archives are often small and low-performance, reducing the load on them can be important – especially where the OAI-PMH interface may be seen to interfere with other services. To support the caching of OAI responses Celestial acts as an *OAI cache/proxy*. Working at the application-level it harvests records from data providers using the OAI-PMH, and re-exposes them to service-providers through its own OAI-PMH interface. Celestial is able to make a complete copy of an OAI archive, including all the metadata records, and set memberships associated with an item. Should the data provider become unavailable, Celestial is able to act as a surrogate.

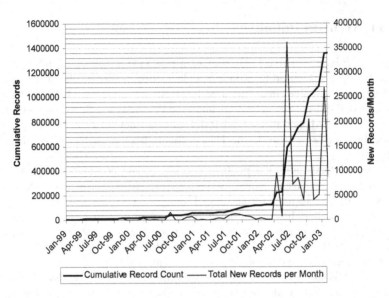

**Fig. 1.** Celestial attempts to harvest records from 161 OAI archives. Each OAI record harvested contains a datestamp (when the OAI record was created or last updated). A histogram of these datestamps plots the growth of OAI records over time. This figure shows the number of new OAI records per month (*thin blue line*) and the cumulative number of records (*thick black line*). The peaks in new records shows when large, new archives come online and expose a large back-catalog of pre-existing records. ("Record" usually – but not always – means a full-text paper.)

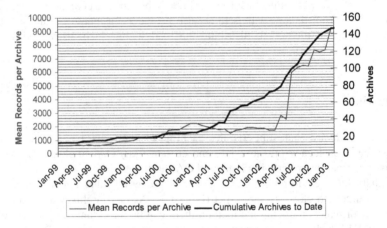

**Fig. 2.** A rough estimate of when OAI archives have come online can be calculated by taking the earliest datestamp from that archive. This shows the cumulative number of available OAI archives (*thick black line*), and the mean number of records in those archives (*thin red line*). Note that both the number of archives and the number of records in those archives is increasing.

By using the incremental, datestamp-based harvesting ability of OAI-PMH, Celestial only harvests those records that are new or have changed from a data provider. By comparison an HTTP cache would have to query all records to determine whether they had altered from a prior harvest.

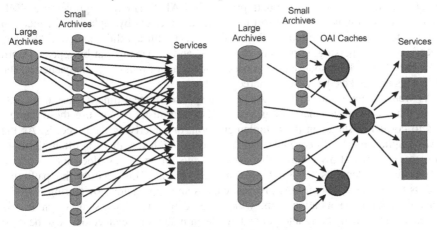

**Fig. 3.** Non-aggregated vs. Aggregated OAI harvesting.

Celestial is designed to provide as high performance as possible. It achieves this by trading storage space for performance. A significant overhead with any XML-based application is generating the XML tag structures. To avoid this Celestial stores the OAI header and metadata as XML. When generating a response Celestial prints the raw data, and only needs to generate XML tags for the OAI protocol components (e.g. the request header, and flow-control tokens).

OAI-PMH flow-control is handled using stateless cursors. Celestial assigns each record a datestamp and unique identifier. These two values are joined to form an index into the record list. As a harvester retrieves records Celestial moves a cursor along this index, and at the end of a partial list Celestial provides the harvester with the current cursor (the datestamp plus unique identifier), and an encoding of the original request (which might include a set or datestamp filter) in the OAI-PMH resumption token. Given a resumption token Celestial can jump straight to the end of the previous partial list by using the index key.

If new records are added to Celestial during a harvest they will be returned at the end of the harvest, as the new record's datestamp will be greater than any previous records. This makes the resumption tokens generated by Celestial stateless, as no changes can occur that would make the result set inconsistent.

OAI archives that have not upgraded to 2.0 have been removed from the official OAI-compliant list (and hence unlikely to be included in new OAI services). As Celestial provides an OAI 2.0 (the current version) interface to harvesters, but can itself harvest from version 1.0, 1.1 or 2.0, it acts as an *OAI gateway* between non-upgraded data providers and upgraded service providers. In OAI 2.0 each record has the set membership of that record. To provide the set hierarchy to OAI 2.0 harvesters Celestial inverts the set membership exported by an OAI 1.x archive. For OAI 1.x this set membership is found by exhaustively querying each set, building up the set membership for each item.

Often data providers will export records from sources that are not Unicode-based. If a data provider does not convert and check these records before exporting them, bad characters can appear in the data provider's OAI-PMH export, preventing XML parsing. Celestial makes a best-effort to correct these errors by replacing the location of bad characters (as reported by the XML parser) with a valid character, "?". The process of XML parsing, correcting characters, and re-parsing can be repeated until either the OAI-PMH response can be parsed or the act of replacing encroaches on the XML tags and makes the response unrecoverable.

As well as attempting to fix OAI-PMH responses in real-time, Celestial records errors that occur during harvesting. An archive administrator can use these harvest logs to correct mistakes in their implementation, or underlying data records. As the OAI-compliance tests do not make a full harvest of archives, this can often highlight problems (e.g. with flow-control) that the OAI registration process does not.

Celestial implements the OAI provenance schema. This records the path that records have taken through OAI proxies, caches and aggregators, by storing with the metadata record the location from which the record was harvested, when it was harvested, and whether any alterations have been made. Provenance data can be used by service providers to "de-dup" the same record, if the service harvests from multiple sources.

A promising possibility for Celestial is as a tool for exposing any data source via an OAI-PMH interface. Out of the box, Celestial only supports getting data via OAI. It is relatively easy, however, to create a system that would insert records directly into Celestial's back-end database, which can then be served through the OAI-PMH interface.

While Celestial is a distinct, freely-downloadable software package, at Southampton University [3] a mirror of Celestial hosts a copy of the metadata from 161 different OAI archives (OAI-registered archives (including the OAI-registered eprints.org archives), plus any unregistered eprints.org installations found, and active archives registered with the Repository Explorer [9]).

The Celestial mirror is used within Southampton by Citebase Search. As a developing service Citebase often needs to completely re-harvest its metadata, and using a local mirror avoids repeatedly making very large requests to source archives.

## 4 Citebase Search

Citebase, more fully described by Hitchcock et al. [1], allows users to find research papers stored in open access, OAI-compliant archives - currently arXiv (http://arxiv.org/), CogPrints (http://cogprints.soton.ac.uk/) and BioMed Central (http://www.biomedcentral.com/). Citebase harvests OAI metadata records for papers in these archives, as well as extracting the references from each paper. The association between document records and references is the basis for a classical citation database. Citebase is best viewed as a kind of "Google for the refereed literature", because it ranks search results based on the number of references to papers or authors (although it is not – currently – using a hub-authority graph algorithm to rank). Citebase contains 230,000 full-text eprint records, and 6 million references (of which 1 million are linked to the full-text).

Citebase was developed as part of the JISC/NSF Open Citation Project, which ended December 2002. As part of the project report a user survey [23] was conducted on Citebase. This was used both to evaluate the outcomes of the project, and to help guide the future direction of Citebase as an ongoing service. The report found that "Citebase can be used simply and reliably for resource discovery. It was shown tasks can be accomplished efficiently with Citebase regardless of the background of the user."

Primarily a user-service, Citebase provides a Web site that allows users to perform a meta-search (title, author etc.), navigate the literature using linked citations and citation analysis, and to retrieve linked full-texts in Adobe PDF format. Citebase also provides a machine interface to the citation data it collects through its own OAI-PMH interface using the Academic Metadata Format (AMF) [10], a new XML format for scholarly literature. As part of the development of Citebase we have looked at the relationship between citation impact ("how many times has this article been cited") and web impact ("how many times has this article been read").

Citation-navigation provides Web-links over the existing author-generated references. First, wherever possible, Citebase links each reference cited by a given article to the full-text of the article that it cites (if it is in the database). This fan-in ("citations-from") and fan-out ("citations-to") then provides the user with links to all articles (in the database) that have cited a given article, as well as to all articles that have been co-cited alongside (hence are related to) the given article. This allows the user to navigate back in time (articles referred-to), forward in time (cited-by), and sideways (co-cited alongside).

Citebase provides information about both the citation impact and usage impact of research articles (and authors), generated from the open-access pre-print and post-print literature that Citebase covers. The citation impact of an article is the number of citations to that article. The usage impact is an estimate of the number of downloads of that article (so far available for one arXiv.org mirror only).

## 4.1  Citebase's Web Interface

The front-end of Citebase is a meta-search engine. This allows the user to search for articles by author, keywords in the title or abstract, publication (e.g. journal), and date of publication. After generating a search, Citebase allows the results to be ranked by 6 criteria: citations (to the article or authors), Web hits (to the article or authors), date of creation, and last update. The by-author ranking is calculated as the mean number of citations or hits to an author (e.g. total citations divided by total papers to author "Hawking, S"). A per-article author-impact is then calculated by taking the mean author-impact of all the named authors. Citebase currently uses only the family name and the first initial to identify authors; as these services develop it is hoped that algorithms (to be developed in collaboration with the Institute for Scientific Information, ISI) for recognizing and distinguishing authors with the same or similar names will improve this metric.

From the meta-search users can either choose to view an abstract page, or jump directly to a cached full-text PDF (if available) for each matching article.

The abstract page displays a full meta-record (title, authors, abstract, rights etc.), the articles cited by the current article, articles that have cited the current article, and articles co-cited alongside the current article. In addition to listing the citing articles, Citebase provides a summary graph of citations and downloads (e.g. see Figure 4). This provides a visual link between the citation and web impacts.

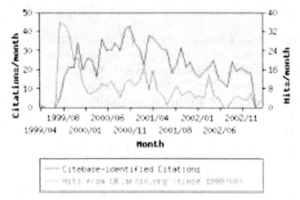

**Fig. 4.** The Citebase abstract page displays a histogram of citations to and downloads of the current article over time. This particular article shows the burst of downloads that articles receive soon after they are deposited, which then drops to either nothing (if the paper achieves little impact), or continues at a lower level. The citation impact of an article peaks after a delay of between 3 months to a year (depending on the speed of the publication cycle) before slowly dropping as the paper gets older and less relevant.

When viewing a cached full-text PDF, Citebase overlays reference links within the document, so a user can jump from viewing a full-text to the abstract page of a cited article.

Like the archives it harvests from, Citebase provides an OAI-PMH interface to the data that it contains. Along with re-exposing the Dublin Core metadata (title, author, abstract), Citebase provides records in the Academic Metadata Format (AMF) [10]. AMF encapsulates the relationships within the scholarly research: between authors, articles, organisations, and publications. Other services can harvest this enhanced metadata from Citebase to provide a reference-linked environment, or perform further analysis (or they can be harvested by the source archives to enhance their own data).

## 4.2  Analysing Citebase's Database

Since the creation of Garfield's science citation index [21,22] researchers have analysed the "citation web" to look for patterns in the growth and direction of scholarly research – most often to determine how the ISI Journal Impact Factor is related to a particular subset of the research literature. With the research literature moving online a new metric for impact can be measured: web hits – an indicator of how much an article has been accessed.

Web hit data can be subject to inaccuracies and noise. For example, if an arXiv paper is referenced by Slashdot [12] it will receive many hits from casual users (the "Slashdot effect"), which probably do not reflect true impact on other researchers. Citebase filters Web logs by removing known Web crawlers (e.g. Googlebot), then only counting one hit from one location per day. This is probably an over-correction, for although it removes most "unwanted" hits, it also excludes valid hits from users who may be sharing a single machine, or Web proxy.

Given the success of the arXiv.org online archive, it is not surprising that citation-impact and usage-impact (measured from the UK arXiv.org mirror) are related. The effect is probably bi-directional: the more something is cited, the more it is read as researchers follow citations, and the more something is read, the more likely it is to be cited as researchers cite what they have read. (We are teasing apart these two effects, as they probably have different time-constants, citation-to-reading being a short-latency effect, occurring soon after the time the citing article appears, and reading-to-citation being a longer-latency effect, requiring the reader to first write a paper of his own.) As researchers use the Web more, and the amount of literature available online increases, these trends are likely to grow (Table 1). It is the few, very high-impact articles, for which the correlation between citation and web impact is highest (Table 1). In order to analyse the correlation between citation and web impact a Web tool "Correlation Generator" [24] was created that allowed various parameters to be altered, and a correlation to be generated on-the-fly.

**Table 1.** High Energy Physics (HEP) is the longest established and most comprehensive of the subject areas within arXiv. It is the best example of what a completely open-access corpus would look like. While the other subject areas covered by arXiv are incomplete they provide a comparison for partial-coverage. The articles contained in the entire archive ("All") and HEP were separated into quartiles (of size $n$) according to their citation impact (Q4 is highest impact quartile, Q1 lowest). The correlation $r$ was then found between the citation impact and usage impact of the articles contained within each quartile. HEP shows the highest correlation, with .5 for the highest citation impact quartile.

| *All* | *r=.27, n=219328* |
|---|---|
| Q1 (lo) | r=.26, n=54832 |
| Q2 | r=.18, n=54832 |
| Q3 | r=.28, n=54832 |
| **Q4 (hi)** | **r=.34**, n=54832 |

| *hep* | *r=.33, n=74020* |
|---|---|
| Q1 (lo) | r=.23, n=18505 |
| Q2 | r=.23, n=18505 |
| Q3 | r=.30, n=18505 |
| **Q4 (hi)** | **r=.50**, n=18505 |

The correlation between citation and usage impact is highest at the high end of the citation impact spectrum. Low impact articles disappear into obscurity, little read and little cited, while a few high impact articles continue to be read and cited for longer periods of time. But regardless of whether a article is destined for obscurity or fame, it still gets a burst of Web impact soon after it is first released on the web (probably coming from users who are following that topic either through the arXiv's automatic daily/weekly new-paper alerting service or through regular active browsing of new contents).

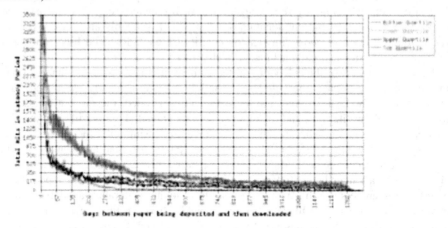

**Fig. 5.** The bi-directional influence of citation and usage impact is a cycle: an article is written, archived, "advertised" by an alerting service, read, and perhaps eventually (after several months) cited by a new article, a new "advertisement" that loops back to make it read more again, etc. An important article, destined for higher citation impact, will already have been read more; it will also continue to be read more over time than a low citation impact article (as users loop back to it from citations appearing in newer articles). Dividing the arXiv.org articles into citation-impact quartiles, a histogram of hit data for each quartile can be plotted against the time delay between the article being deposited and later downloaded (the "hit latency"). While all 4 quartiles show a large number of downloads within the first few days of being available, higher impact (*top line*) show double the hit rate over a longer period of time.

## 5   Digitometric Services for OAI

Scholarly research consists of systematic investigation, gathering the empirical, theoretical, and scholarly information relevant to a particular research field. These disparate activities include detective work - becoming proficient in a field and understanding its present and past literature's landscape. This is a continuous task that requires a scholar's constant and full attention.

The Digitometric Framework provides advanced services over research metadata collected from various OAI-compliant archives. The Framework exposes an open and extensible interface where services are attached to enable researchers to better investigate and understand their research field. Basic visualisations (e.g. bar charts of papers/author) to advanced visualisations (e.g. co-citation maps), knowledge services (e.g. identifying the most prominent researchers), and hypertext linking of different research artifacts have been implemented and added as services.

The experimental Digitometric software consists of a back-end database to store metadata harvested from OAI archives, software to interact with the database and provide the base functionality of the framework, and several interchangeable and extensible modules representing each of the analysis and visualization services. Harvested metadata are analysed, enhanced (e.g. adding data for visualisations), and converted into a native format for use in the framework.

Initially, the database was populated with the entire collection of papers in the arXiv.org archive. This provided a large database to create and explore detailed visualisations of the research landscape.

## 5.1  Visualising Research

The Digitometric services can be used to dynamically visualise different aspects of research metadata. For example, users can retrieve basic graphs illustrating the highest publishing authors or the citation network of a particular publication (Figure 6).

### Citation Network

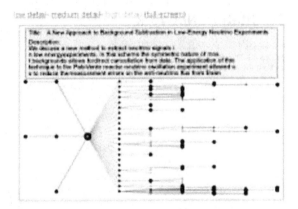

**Fig. 6.** A dynamically generated citation network. The current article is shown in the middle (a single red dot), while articles that have cited the current article are linked by blue lines (and articles that have cited those), and articles that the current article has cited are linked by red lines (and articles cited by those article).

More interestingly, co-citation maps can be dynamically generated and displayed. Two papers are co-cited when a third paper cites them both. Co-citation analysis therefore relates bibliographic data based on co-citation strengths (i.e. the number of times two papers are cited together). The premise is that similar papers, for example papers that discuss or raise the same issue or methodology, are frequently co-cited. When co-citation values are used as proximity measures in visualisations where papers that are frequently co-cited are plotted near each other, the resulting graph enables "research fronts" (speciality fields) to be identified. Research fronts will usually emerge around a few seminal (or core) papers that are heavily co-cited [20]. These graphs can be evaluated, for example, to determine how a particular idea has influenced a field. In this case, several clusters may arise around the corresponding publication, each containing papers that share a common interpretation or understanding of the idea. Furthermore, researchers could analyse the clusters over different time periods to understand how research "hot-spots" have changed and been absorbed into the corpus.

Co-citation analysis has been criticised [16,19] for over-simplifying of the citation link, for technical problems (e.g. inaccurate citations), and for focusing only on citations when other factors (e.g. social/political motivation behind the citation) should be taken into consideration. However, Garfield [17] nevertheless notes that co-citation provides a useful and predictive perspective on scholarly material when used cautiously and wisely. He shows convincingly how he has uncovered important historical links between research fronts using co-citation analysis that scholars had previously overlooked [18].

Users of the Digitometric services can retrieve a co-citation map at any time and even use a particular publication as the launch point for navigating the co-citation space. Different variables are set to define the accuracy, size and co-citation threshold to be used, each having a significant bearing on the time required to construct the maps.

## Co-Citation Network

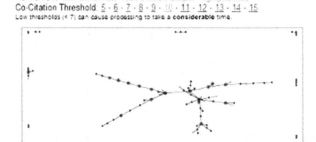

**Fig. 7.** A co-citation map embedded within the Digitometric user interface. The nodes on the map represent individual publications. By hovering with the mouse pointer over a node, the user can generate details (title, author, abstract) in the information box. The arcs between the nodes represent a co-citation relationship. A cluster of related publications (perhaps around a project, or theorem) are evident in the centre of the map. Four distinct paths emanate out of this indicating the possibility of specialty fields arising out of the main cluster.

### 5.2  Knowledge Questions

Digitometrics can also analyse the metadata and infer new facts. Such capabilites are central to the Semantic Web initiative. For example, based on the citation patterns between papers, the most significant papers and prominent researchers can be detected. The contributions to a particular line of research or researcher can be mapped by analysing and displaying co-authorship patterns (Figure 9). With further high quality metadata available, researchers can raise increasingly subtle questions about the direction and time-course of developments in their research field, such as how perspectives have changed and how a particular methodology has affected a research area.

**Fig. 8.** A full-sized co-citation map with a lower co-citation threshold resulting in more nodes being included. Several clusters (research fronts) are evident, in particular the large cluster towards the bottom right of the map. Researchers may get a better understanding of their research landscape by exploring these clusters and the relationships between them. Different colours are also used to indicate which nodes have been recently highly cited, paving the way for up-and-coming (or dying) research fronts to be identified. There are also several occurrences of 5 or 6 nodes emanating sequentially out of a single node, indicating a sequence of papers being published that address a common problem or theme.

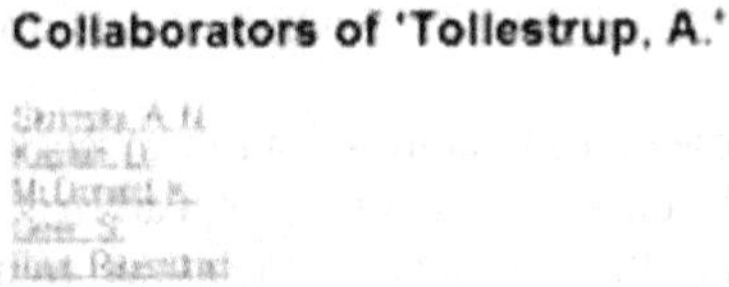

**Collaborators of 'Tollestrup, A.'**

Skinner, A. H.
Kaplan, D.
McDonald, K.
Carer, S.
Hunt, Balestricci

**Fig. 9.** The collaborators for a researcher "Tollestrup, A" are calculated and presented by analysing co-authorship patterns.

## 5.3  Hypertext Navigation

Digitometrics enables complete hypertext linking between different research artifacts (e.g. researcher, publication, project, organisation, publication medium, text). When a service is offered for a particular artifact (e.g. collaboration lists among researchers, co-citation maps for literature) these are available to authors, researchers, or evaluators (Figure 10).

**PERSON**

Services

tale Abe. Surrexork

Publications

Newadotive conditions, entices and its significance for local research
Towards Non additive Quantum information Theory
Enforcing uncertainty relation for power law wave packets
Nonadditive measures and quantum entanglement of a class of mixed states of N-th system
Entropic uncertainty relation with and its evaluation
Implications of form invariance to the Structure of Nonextensive
Entropy
Quantum entanglement inferred by the principle of maximum Tsallis entropy
Nonadditivity of Tsallis entropies Inconsistencies
Microscopical basis

Fig. 10. Typical information screen for a researcher. This illustrates the metadata gathered for a particular researcher, including a list of all their known publications, plus the collaboration measure is offered as a service (Figure 9).

# 6 Conclusion

As the coverage of the open-access archives increases so will the technology to process and parse the online corpus, to provide hypertext-navigation (between articles, authors, institutions, and collections), and to provide real-time analysis ("digitometrics") of the research world, for example to improve the accuracy and breadth of research assessment.

The potential benefit for research literature – and research itself - through open-access, distributed archives is only beginning to appear. Authors maximise their research impact by maximising the visibility of their work, and at the same time provide a huge resource to build services on. Celestial, Citebase, and Digitometric Services demonstrate some of this potential – even with the limited amount of literature available now.

# References

1.  Hitchcock, S. et al: "Open Citation Linking: The Way Forward". D-Lib Magazine, Vol. 8, No. 10, October 2002 (available at http://www.dlib.org/dlib/october02/hitchcock/10hitchcock.html)
2.  Liu, X., Brody, T. et al: "A Scalable Architecture for Harvest-Based Digital Libraries" D-Lib Magazine, Vol 8, No. 11, November 2002 (available at http://www.dlib.org/dlib/november02/liu/11liu.html)
3.  University of Southampton Celestial Mirror http://celestial.eprints.org/cgi-bin/status
4.  Celestial http://celestial.eprints.org/
5.  Citebase Search http://citebase.eprints.org/
6.  EPrints.org http://software.eprints.org/
7.  Open Citation Project http://opcit.eprints.org/

8. Open Archives Initiative http://www.openarchives.org/

9. Repository Explorer http://www.purl.org/NET/oai_explorer

10. Academic Metadata Format http://amf.openlib.org/doc/ebisu.html

11. Dublin Core http://dublincore.org/

12. Slashdot http://www.slashdot.org/

13. van de Sompel, H., Lagoze, C.: "Notes from the Interoperability Front: A Progress Report on the Open Archives Initiative" ECDL 2002, in LNCS 2458, pp. 144–157

14. Lagoze, C., Arms, W., Gan, S., Hillmann, D., Ingram, C., Krafft, D., Marisa, R., Phipps, J., Saylor, J., Terrizzi, C., Hoehn, W., Millman, D., Allan, J., Guzman-Lara, S., Kalt, T. (2002) "Core Services in the Architecture of the National Digital Library for Science Education (NSDL)" Proceedings of the second ACM/IEEE-CS joint conference on Digital libraries 201-209 http://arxiv.org/abs/cs.DL/0201025

15. AKT reference http://www.hyphen.info/

16. Edge, D.: "Why I am not a co-citationist?", Society for Social Studies of Science Newsletter, 2, pp13–19, 1977.

17. Garfield, E.: "Scientists should understand the limitations as well as the virtues of citation analysis", The Scientist, 7 (14), p12, 1993.

18. Garfield, E., Sher, I., and Torpie, R.: "The use of citation data in writing the history of science, Institute for Scientific Information", Philadelphia, 1964. (available from: http://www.garfield.library.upenn.edu/papers/useofcitdatawritinghistofsci.pdf)

19. MacRoberts, M. and MacRoberts, B.: "Problems of citation analysis: a critical review", Journal of the American Society for Information Science, 40 (5), pp342–349, 1989.

20. Small, H.: "Co-Citation in the Scientific Literature: A New Measure of the Relationships Between Two Documents", Journal of the American Society for Information Science, 24, pp265–269, 1973.

21. Harnad, S., Carr, L.: "Integrating, navigating, and analysing open Eprint archives through open citation linking (the OpCit project)" Current Science, Vol 59, No. 5, September 2000 (available from http://tejas.serc.iisc.ernet.in/~currsci/sep102000/629.pdf)

22. Garfield, E.: "Citation Indexes for Science: A New Dimension in Documentation through Association of Ideas" Science, Vol. 122, No. 3159, pp108–111, 1955 (available from http://www.garfield.library.upenn.edu/papers/science_v122(3159)p108y1955.html)

23. Hitchcock, S., Wookeu, A. et al: "Evaluating Citebase, an open access Web-based citation-ranked search and impact discovery service" 2002 (available from http://opcit.eprints.org/evaluation/Citebase-evaluation/evaluation-report.html)

24. Citebase Correlation Generator http://citebase.eprints.org/analysis/correlation.php

25. "Scirus, for scientific information only" http://www.scirus.com/about/

# Search Engine-Crawler Symbiosis: Adapting to Community Interests

Gautam Pant, Shannon Bradshaw, and Filippo Menczer*

Department of Management Sciences
The University of Iowa, Iowa City IA 52242, USA
{gautam-pant,shannon-bradshaw,filippo-menczer}@uiowa.edu

**Abstract.** Web crawlers have been used for nearly a decade as a search engine component to create and update large collections of documents. Typically the crawler and the rest of the search engine are not closely integrated. If the purpose of a search engine is to have as large a collection as possible to serve the general Web community, a close integration may not be necessary. However, if the search engine caters to a specific community with shared focused interests, it can take advantage of such an integration. In this paper we investigate a tightly coupled system in which the crawler and the search engine engage in a symbiotic relationship. The crawler feeds the search engine and the search engine in turn helps the crawler to better its performance. We show that the symbiosis can help the system learn about a community's interests and serve such a community with better focus.

## 1 Introduction

General purpose search engines have typically used exhaustive crawlers to build and update large collections of documents. The cost of crawling and indexing the collections is amortized over millions of queries received by the search engines. However, the large size, the dynamic nature and the diversity of the Web warrant more focused solutions that allow for direct and indirect collaboration amongst Web searchers of similar interests. Such solutions may be more scalable and distributable while being effective and efficient. They may also lead to new ways of searching that are hard to imagine with the centralized exhaustive approach followed by the current search engines.

Web communities with focused interests can be found in many professional and casual settings. For example, a set of software engineers at their workplace may have very focused interests. It would not be surprising if most of their queries to search engines on a given day were around a narrow topic. In fact, a small collection of Web pages (say, 50,000 pages) may satisfy most of their needs for a short period of time. However, it is non-trivial to identify a small focused collection, out of a much larger Web, that is representative of a community's

---

* Current affiliation: School of Informatics and Computer Science Department, Indiana University. Email: fil@indiana.edu

T. Koch and I.T. Sølvberg (Eds.): ECDL 2003, LNCS 2769, pp. 221–232, 2003.

interests. It is also important to tweak the collection with time so that it remains focused on the current interests of the community. Given that we have such a collection for a community, a search engine that indexes it may be able to better serve the community. For example, owing to the small size of the collection, the search engine can be kept extremely fresh by crawling on a daily or weekly basis. In addition, more sophisticated information retrieval, text mining and visualization tools may be applied that are not as efficient and/or effective for a much larger corpus. Also, such a system can provide collaboration opportunities between the users.

If the purpose of a search engine is to have as large a collection as possible to serve the general Web community, a close integration between the crawler and the other components of the engine may not be necessary. The main goal of the crawler is to keep the coverage and freshness of the search engine index high, and this task is not informed by user interactions. For this reason, the crawler and the rest of the search engine typically have little or no communication between them. Some search engines may use crawlers that focus their crawl using heuristics similar to those used by the search engine to rank the documents [1]. But they do not closely integrate the crawling algorithm with the search engine.

In this paper we discuss a particular Web searching model in which a *topical* or *focused* crawler and a search engine engage in a mutually beneficial relationship in order to cater to a particular community of users. Specifically, the goal is to incrementally refine a collection on a broad set of topics in order to focus the collection on the set of topics relevant to the community. The flexibility of the model allows for adaptation to drifting interests in the community.

## 2    Symbiosis between Search Engine and Crawler

The search engine-crawler[1] symbiotic system could live on a large server or a desktop machine. It could be serving a single user or a set of users. The system tightly couples a search engine and a crawler to learn from the user queries given to the search engine in the recent past. A learning process, involving search engine-crawler symbiosis, is used to prepare a focused collection that may be better suited for queries in the near future. The process is repeated on a daily or a weekly basis. The queries serve as an approximation for the interests of a set of users. We can use all or a sample of the recent queries as *representative* requests. These representative queries are used to capture a focused set of Web documents for answering the queries in the near future — each representative query is used as a learning opportunity.

A topical crawler picks one representative query at a time and queries the search engine using it. The search engine responds with the top N_HITS URLs that satisfy the query and also all the URLs that have a link to the top URLs. This gives the crawler a *seed set* of URLs. The crawler then crawls up to MAX_PAGES starting from the seed set, using the representative query to guide

---

[1] Note that for the rest of the paper, we use the term "search engine" to refer to all of the search engine components other than the crawler.

itself. After MAX_PAGES are crawled on a query, the search engine indexes the new pages retrieved. The crawler queries the search engine again, with the same representative query, and the steps mentioned above repeat. This search engine-crawler loop may continue up to MAX_ITER iterations or until some convergence level (based on a threshold THETA) is achieved in the seed sets from two consecutive iterations. The new pages from the last iteration are added to a new collection. The iterations are repeated for all of the representative queries. At the end, the current index is deleted and the new collection is used to create a new index. The new index is used by the search engine to answer the queries until the entire process repeats.

```
new_collection = ();
foreach query (representative_queries) {
    repeat (MAX_ITER or until intersect(old_seed_set, seed_set) > THETA) {
        old_seed_set = seed_set;
        seed_set = search_engine(query, N_HITS);
        new_pages = crawler(query, seed_set, MAX_PAGES);
        index(new_pages);
        new_collection = add(new_collection, new_pages);
    }
}
clear_index();
index(new_collection);
```

**Fig. 1.** Pseudo-code of symbiotic process between search engine and crawler

The idea is that through this symbiotic process, the crawler can exploit an existing search engine index in order to obtain a focused collection for the search engine that may better satisfy future user queries.

A pseudo-code illustrating this symbiotic process is shown in Figure 1. The parameters MAX_PAGES, MAX_ITER, THETA and the number of representative queries are fixed based on resource availability. For example, if the system runs on a desktop used by a single user, then we may index a few thousand pages. On the other hand, if the system runs on a large server with many users, it may be desirable to index millions of pages. Once we fix the maximum number of pages to be indexed (MAX_IN_INDEX), MAX_PAGES can be derived as follows:

$$\text{MAX\_PAGES} = \frac{\text{MAX\_IN\_INDEX}}{|\text{representative\_queries}|}$$

where |representative_queries| is the number of representative queries. Parameters such as MAX_ITER and THETA are influenced by available disk space since they lead to a temporary increase in size of the index before the new collection is ready. The number of queries that are used as representative queries may be based on the amount of time taken by iterations for a single query. One may like to restrict the total time taken by all of the representative queries to, say, 12 hours (off peak hours of a day). At the end of the process shown in Figure 1, the new collection to be indexed must be of a size less than or equal to MAX_IN_INDEX.

Hence, we maintain an upper bound on the size of the index used by the search engine to answer user queries.

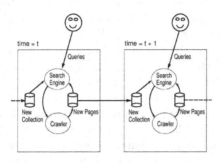

**Fig. 2.** Creation of a new index from an old one

Another way of looking at the process is through its temporal sequence. The pseudo-code shown in Figure 1 may be repeated at regular intervals to create new collections to cater to future queries. Figure 2 shows that the index at time $t$ is used by the process described in Figure 1 to create a new index for time $t + 1$. The scale of time $t$ could be a day, a week or a month based on the need for index freshness, the time available, and the maximum size of the collection (MAX_IN_INDEX).

## 3   Implementation

Currently, the search engine-crawler symbiosis is implemented using a search engine called Rosetta [5,4] and a Naive Best-First crawler [14,15]. Both the search engine and the crawler were not built specifically for this application. They have been used before for independent searching [5] and crawling [14,15] tasks. We want to demonstrate the use of the symbiotic model by picking an off-the-shelf search engine and a generic topical crawler.

### 3.1   Rosetta

While the architecture we describe here is not wedded to any one type of indexing or retrieval system or for that matter any particular approach to crawling, the Rosetta search engine is particularly well-suited to this architecture. Rosetta is based on an indexing technique called Reference Directed Indexing (RDI) [5]. This technique is designed around the idea that for any topic, the community of Web users interested in that topic find and identify an ever-evolving body of useful information and do so in such a way that their findings can be leveraged to help the less well-informed find what they need. Rosetta uses hyperlinks and the contexts in which they are created as the basis for indexing and retrieving documents. While many authors have introduced a variety of ways to use link information in search systems [6,7], Rosetta's approach is novel in the way it uses the combined evidence of multiple references to a document to both determine the popularity of that document and to isolate the words that best identify why it is popular, and therefore, the queries for which it is most relevant. As an example we consider www.mayura.com, the Web site of Mayura software. Mayura is a drawing program for the Microsoft Windows platform that allows one to easily draw from scratch or import, modify and export images in a variety of formats. A comparative analysis of the text in the immediate vicinity of each link to www.mayura.com yields the following terms among those most frequently used in reference to this document: *Mayura, PageDraw, drawing program, Windows, export, PDF, EPS*. Many Web authors who have found this tool useful have referenced its homepage. In doing so they indicate not simply that Mayura Draw is useful in the abstract, but that it is useful for a very specific set of reasons, among them those identified by the terms listed above. Different referrers to a document tend to emphasize many of the same features of that document. As a result some of their terms naturally overlap. If many referrers use a particular term in reference to a document, it is quite likely that searchers will use that term in queries for the information the document contains. Rosetta indexes each document in its collection incrementally as it discovers references to these documents in pages gathered by the crawler. The RDI technique is something like a voting mechanism which uses terms found in the immediate vicinity of a hyperlink to a document. It treats each referring page as a voter permitted one vote for each index term used in reference to a document. Continuing with the Mayura example, the following lists the top 10 index terms extracted for www.mayura.com from the four referring pages. The number of votes indicates the number of pages that use each term in the immediate vicinity of a link to www.mayura.com.

| TERM | VOTES |
|---|---|
| Mayura Draw | 4 |
| drawing program | 4 |
| format | 4 |
| illustrations | 3 |
| Windows | 3 |
| PDF | 3 |
| EPS | 3 |
| ... | ... |

Rosetta uses the number of votes for a term as a measure of term frequency in a weighting metric similar to TFIDF [19]. In other work [5], we have found that the combined evidence from multiple contexts in which a document has been referred is an extremely accurate identifier of good index terms for a document, much better in fact, than measures of word use within the document itself [4]. In addition, inherent in the model is a measure of relative importance among all documents indexed by the same terms. The number of votes an index term receives indicates not only the relative value of that term in association with a particular document, but also the number of referrers that have chosen to direct their readers to that document versus another.

## 3.2   Naive Best-First Crawler

The Naive Best-First crawler uses the cosine similarity between a page and the query to score the URLs in the page. This similarity measure is based on simple term frequency, however common terms are conflated using a standard stemming algorithm [18]. The *crawl frontier* with unvisited URLs is kept as a priority queue based on the score. Every time the crawler needs to fetch a page, it picks the best one in the queue. In our previous evaluation studies, we have found the Naive Best-First crawler to be a strong competitor among other algorithms for short crawls of a few thousand pages, on general crawling tasks [14,15].

The crawler can have a number of threads that share a single crawl frontier. Each thread picks the best URL to crawl from the frontier, fetches the corresponding page, scores the unvisited URLs within the page and adds the URLs to the frontier at appropriate positions. We allow the crawler to spawn as many as 75 threads and the maximum size of the frontier is set to 10,000. In order to avoid inundating any Web server with requests, the frontier enforces the constraint that every batch of $D$ URLs fetched from it are from $D$ different server host names ($D = 50$). Due to the multi-threaded nature of the crawler and the enforced ethics the crawler does not follow a strict best first order. Also, the multiple threads make the crawler behave like a Best-N-First crawler where $N$ is related to the number of threads. Best-N-First crawler is a generalized version of Naive Best-First crawler that picks $N$ best URLs to crawl at a time [17]. We have found Best-N-First (with $N = 256$) to perform well, especially when performance is measured through recall of relevant pages [15].

## 4   Evaluation

We want to investigate the use of search engine-crawler symbiosis in capturing community interests. The initial collection for the search engine may be generated by using the bookmark files of the users and doing a Breadth-First crawl until a certain number of pages (MAX_IN_INDEX) have been retrieved.

### 4.1   Community and Queries

We used a portion of the Open Directory Project[2] (ODP) as the basis for this simulation. In particular, we used the "Business/E-commerce" category to simulate a community. This category, being only two levels deep in the hierarchy of ODP topics, is sufficiently broad to enable the simulation of a community of people with many shared interests and many individual interests as well. From "Business/E-commerce" we used the root category and all sub-categories that have at least 10 external URLs. We assume that our fictitious community's interests lie within the categories selected. As seed URLs used to begin the simulation we selected as many as five URLs at random from each of the included categories.

[2] http://dmoz.org

In bootstrapping a search engine for a real community such URLs might be acquired from the Web browser bookmarks of members of that community or from a pool of URLs listed on a community resource page of some kind. Throughout the rest of the paper we will refer them as *bookmark* URLs.

Having selected the bookmark URLs, we then collected a pool of queries to represent the individual inquiries of our community during a period of one work week (five days). ODP editors include a brief summary of each URL listed within a given category. We used these summaries to derive phrases that simulate user queries. We first split the summaries into tokens using a set of stop words as delimiters, keeping only tokens with 2, 3, or 4 words for further processing. Next, we manually filtered the tokens to remove those that were incoherent groups of words representative of the type of errors made by such a shallow parsing technique. This process left us with nearly 1200 queries. The queries thus obtained form the *query pool* for the simulation to follow. Finally, we associated each query with the ODP category from which it was derived. This knowledge was not made available to the system, but was used to provide an understanding of the context of the query during the evaluation phase.

## 4.2   Simulation

We simulated 5 days of the search engine-crawler system at work. The initial collection was created for day 1 using a Breadth-First crawl that retrieved MAX_IN_INDEX $= 100,000$ pages from the Web starting from the bookmark URLs. To simulate a day of usage we randomly picked 100 queries from the query pool. At the end of each simulated day, we ran the symbiotic process described in Section 2 using all 100 queries to create a new index for the next day. For this simulation we set the MAX_PAGES (maximum pages per query iteration) parameter to 1000 pages, the maximum number of iterations is MAX_ITER $= 3$, and the number of top URLs used as seeds for each iteration, N_HITS $= 25$. Owing to the small MAX_ITER, we do not check for convergence in the current simulation.

In real-world use such a process may run during the off-peak hours (overnight) so that the new index is ready before the next morning. In fact, the implemented system using the Rosetta search engine and the Naive Best-First crawler takes around 11 hours to complete the process of shifting from the old index to a new one (Figure 2) using a 1Ghz pentium III IBM Thinkpad running the Windows 2000 operating system. Note that the current Rosetta implementation has foregone some parallelization and other optimizations for ease of implementation. Hence, we can speed up the process even further after some optimization.

## 4.3   Performance Metrics

The purpose of this technology is to incrementally refine a collection on a broad set of topics in order to focus the collection on the set of topics relevant to a particular community. To test the degree to which the system meets this objective we measured the relative performance as it progressed through the five days of simulation. We chose to treat the system as a black-box, and measure the performance of the search engine in response to queries from each of the five days, because this is the way an end-user experiences the merits of the system.

To judge the search engine results for hundreds of queries over 5 days would be a time consuming task. Hence, we decided to use only a sample of the daily queries for our evaluation. Twelve test subjects evaluated five to ten queries randomly selected from the 100 (20 per day) sample queries used in the evaluation. The test subjects are graduate students in a class on information technology; they were awarded extra credit for participating in the study. We asked the subjects to determine the relevance of the top ten search results for each query based on the context in which the query originated. As we mentioned earlier, the context for each query was provided as the category in the ODP from which the query was drawn. The subjects were asked to browse the relevant category in order to acquire an understanding of the meaning of each query. This step is important because no real-world user submits a query to search engine unless a specific set of circumstances has motivated the need for information. Note that the search results for the same query on two different days in this evaluation were going against two different indexes. We maintained the indexes as they existed on each of the five days and submitted the queries sampled from that day against that day's index. To avoid manual bias in evaluation, we hid any information that would have indicated on which day the query originated.

Based on the binary relevance assessments obtained from the subjects, we computed the precision $P$ among the top 10 hits returned by the search engine for each query. We average this performance measure over the sample queries for each day, and plot the mean performance over time.

In addition to the black-box approach mentioned above, we want to evaluate the quality of the collections created by the crawler. We would like to quantify a new collection's ability to satisfy the queries to follow. Note that precision $P$ is not only affected by the collection quality but also by the quality of the indexing and the ranking mechanism. Here, we want to isolate the quality of the collection as it was created by the crawler. This also gives us an idea about the performance of the crawler. A way to measure a new collection's quality is by calculating the average cosine similarity between the pages in the collection and a representation (centroid) of the queries submitted on the corresponding day. To represent a day's queries, we simply concatenate them. Note that the collection is created before the queries are submitted to the system (see Figure 2). We measure the average cosine similarity between the collection and the queries as follows:

$$S(\mathcal{C}, q) = \frac{1}{|\mathcal{C}|} \sum_{p \in \mathcal{C}} \frac{v_q \cdot v_p}{\| v_q \| \cdot \| v_p \|}$$

where $\mathcal{C}$ is a collection of pages for a particular day, $q$ is the concatenated query text for the same day, $v_q$ and $v_p$ are TFIDF [19] based vector representations of the concatenated queries and the page respectively, $v_q \cdot v_p$ is the inner product of the two vectors, and $\| v \|$ is the Euclidean norm of the vector $v$.

## 4.4   Results

We first present the results of the study in which we measure search engine performance across five days of simulation using the metric $P$ defined in Section 4.3. Figure 3 (a) depicts the five values for $P$ as judged by our test subjects, averaged over 20 queries per day. For the initial collection the system retrieved approximately 3.5 relevant documents among the top ten search results on average.

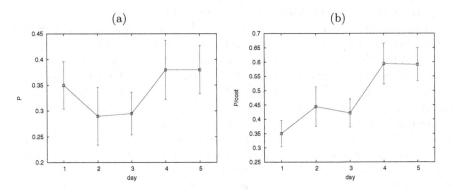

**Fig. 3.** (a) P over five days of simulation (b) The ratio of precision to cost of gathering and maintaining the collection for each day of the simulation. The error bars correspond to ±1 standard error.

Performance dropped slightly on the second and third days of the simulation. As a reason for this we speculate that initially, the system may have overfit its collection to the set of queries from day one and possibly day two. We have seen this type of behavior before in other work on systems that learn the interests of their users [16]. Finally, this evaluation suggests that after the initial decline in performance, $P$ improves to a level greater than that found with the initial collection. However, statistical significance of this preliminary result does not allow for a definitive confirmation; further experiments are required, both with more extensive evaluations (more queries) and over a longer period of time.

While not significant in terms of $P$, this result is perhaps stronger than it may first appear, because the system achieves this level of $P$ with a collection that is over one-third smaller than the collection from the first day of the simulation. The size of the collection decreases from approximately 100,000 pages on the first day to approximately 65,000 pages on the fifth day. This is due to the crawler becoming more focused as a result of its interaction with the search engine. More specifically, as the crawler explores regions of the Web near the search results for a query, it finds many URLs encountered in crawls for other queries as well. Because we do not store the same URL in a collection more than once, any redundancy in the information gathered for a day results in a reduction in the size of the collection. While this may also negatively affect generalization performance during the initial phase of the symbiotic process (Figure 3 (a)), it affords

(a)                                              (b)

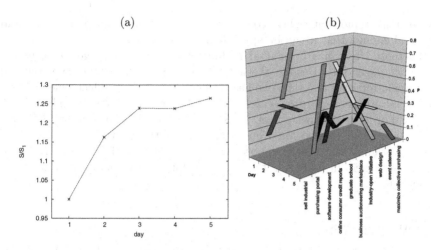

**Fig. 4.** (a) Relevance of the collection as a whole to the queries submitted on each of the five days (b) Performance on queries that occurred on more than one day.

significant efficiency gains in terms of saved disk space, crawling and indexing time, and bandwidth. To quantify such gain, we look at the ratio of average precision over the relative size of the collection or *cost*. The cost of a collection is equal to the size of the collection divided by MAX_IN_INDEX (100,000 pages). The plot in Figure 3 (b) indicates that from a perfomance/cost perspective, the symbiotic system can lead to substantial benefits.

Next, we measured the cosine similarity, $S(\mathcal{C}, q)$, between the collection for a given day and the queries for that day. Figure 4 (a) plots the ratio of $S(\mathcal{C}, q)$ to $S_1(\mathcal{C}, q)$ for day one. Over time, the crawler with the help of the search engine, is able to fetch pages that are lexically more similar to the queries of the day. The error bars on the plot are extremely small and hence not clearly visible. Hence, we find significant improvement in collection quality over the simulation period.

On further analysis, we found that 10 queries appeared more than once in the manually evaluated set of queries. We plotted the metric $P$ for each of the repeating queries against the days on which they appeared (Figure 4 (b)). We noticed that for most of the queries the value of $P$ improved with time. In particular, there are queries for which no result was found the first time they appeared, but on subsequent occurrence the system found several relevant results. On average the system found 4.5 more relevant results for repeating queries between the first and the last time they were submitted to the system.

## 5   Related Work

The large size and the dynamic nature of the Web has prompted many different efforts to build focused search engines [10,12]. While we too attempt to build a focused search engine, our approach is adaptive to the changing interests of the user(s). Furthermore, it tightly couples the search engine and the crawler, and is general enough that it can be applied to any topic.

Referential text has been used to find Web sites [9], categorize pages [2] and crawl pages [11]. Despite the active use of referential text for variety of information retrieval tasks, no one has yet demonstrated the effectiveness of this technique for general-purpose search. There is a large and growing body of work on topical or focused crawlers (e.g.,[11,8,13]). Such crawlers use variety of lexical and/or link-based cues within Web pages to guide their path.

Our work also relates to collaborative filtering [3] since the queries submitted by the users, help in preparing the collection for similar queries by other users in the future.

## 6    Conclusions

The purpose of the symbiotic system we describe here is to incrementally refine a broad collection in order to bring into focus the set of topics relevant to a particular community. While more experimentation is needed to make any strong claims about the benefits to end users, the work presented here demonstrates that in a short amount of time, the type of symbiotic system we have developed can eliminate much of the irrelevant information from an initial collection and thereby achieve the desired focus. It is important to note that the system, though it learns from the behavior of its users, does so implicitly, requiring no effort beyond the type of simple searches they are already doing.

One obvious extension to the work is to integrate the crawler and the engine further. For example, the crawler's best first strategy could be based on TFIDF similarity rather than just TF. A generic crawler does not have the luxury of an IDF index because the collection is not yet available. In our model however the collection indexed by the engine in the previous iteration can be used by the crawler in the current iteration to generate IDF weights that can improve its link scores. In addition, the crawler could tap into the more global information available to the search engine — such as good hubs and multiple contexts. On a different note, the proposed symbiotic model can be distributed on a larger Peer-to-Peer (P2P) search system which can bring in added opportunities for identifying and connecting communities of users.

**Acknowledgments.** We acknowledge the contributions of Padmini Srinivasan, Kristian Hammond and Rik Belew in related projects. Thanks go to the students who volunteered to help in the evaluation. This work is funded in part by NSF CAREER Grant No. IIS-0133124 to FM.

## References

1. A. Arasu, J. Cho, H. Garcia-Molina, A. Paepcke, and S. Raghavan. Searching the Web. *ACM Transactions on Internet Technology*, 1(1), 2001.

232    G. Pant, S. Bradshaw, and F. Menczer

2. G. Attardi, A. Gullí, and F. Sebastiani. Automatic Web page categorization by link and context analysis. In *Proceedings of THAI-99, 1st European Symposium on Telematics, Hypermedia and Artificial Intelligence*, 1999.
3. M Balabanović and Y Shoham. Content-based, collaborative recommendation. *Communications of the ACM*, 40(3):67–72, 1997.
4. S. Bradshaw and K. Hammond. Automatically indexing documents: Content vs. reference. In *Sixth International Conference on Intelligent User Interfaces*, San Francisco, CA, January 14–17 2002.
5. Shannon Bradshaw. *Reference Directed Indexing: Indexing Scientific Literature in the Context of its Use*. PhD thesis, Northwestern University, 2002.
6. S. Brin and L. Page. The anatomy of a large-scale hypertextual Web search engine. *Computer Networks*, 30(1–7):107–117, 1998.
7. S. Chakrabarti, B. Dom, P. Raghavan, S. Rajagopalan, D. Gibson, and J. Kleinberg. Automatic resource compilation by analyzing hyperlink structure and associated text. *Computer Networks*, 30(1–7):65–74, 1998.
8. S. Chakrabarti, M. van den Berg, and B. Dom. Focused crawling: A new approach to topic-specific Web resource discovery. *Computer Networks*, 31(11–16):1623–1640, 1999.
9. N. Craswell, D. Hawking, and S. Robertson. Effective site finding using link anchor information. In *Proc. 24th Annual Intl. ACM SIGIR Conf. on Research and Development in Information Retrieval*, 2001.
10. C.L. Giles, K.D. Bollacker, and S. Lawrence. Citeseer: an automatic citation indexing system. In *Proceedings of the third ACM conference on Digital libraries*, 1998.
11. M. Hersovici, M. Jacovi, Y. S. Maarek, D. Pelleg, M. Shtalhaim, and S. Ur. The shark-search algorithm — An application: Tailored Web site mapping. In *WWW7*, 1998.
12. A.K. McCallum, K. Nigam, J. Rennie, and K. Seymore. Automating the construction of internet portals with machine learning. *Information Retrieval*, 3(2):127–163, 2000.
13. F. Menczer and R. K. Belew. Adaptive retrieval agents: Internalizing local context and scaling up to the Web. *Machine Learning*, 39(2–3):203–242, 2000.
14. F. Menczer, G. Pant, M. Ruiz, and P. Srinivasan. Evaluating topic-driven Web crawlers. In *Proc. 24th Annual Intl. ACM SIGIR Conf. on Research and Development in Information Retrieval*, 2001.
15. F. Menczer, G. Pant, and P. Srinivasan. Topical web crawlers: Evaluating adaptive algorithms. *To appear in ACM Trans. on Internet Technologies*, 2003. http://dollar.biz.uiowa.edu/~fil/Papers/TOIT.pdf.
16. F. Menczer, W.N. Street, N. Vishwakarma, A. Monge, and M. Jakobsson. IntelliShopper: A proactive, personal, private shopping assistant. In *Proc. 1st ACM Int. Joint Conf. on Autonomous Agents and MultiAgent Systems (AAMAS)*, 2002.
17. G. Pant, P. Srinivasan, and F. Menczer. Exploration versus exploitation in topic driven crawlers. In *WWW02 Workshop on Web Dynamics*, 2002.
18. M. Porter. An algorithm for suffix stripping. *Program*, 14(3):130–137, 1980.
19. G. Salton and M.J. McGill. *Introduction to Modern Information Retrieval*. McGraw-Hill, 1983.

# Topical Crawling for Business Intelligence

Gautam Pant and Filippo Menczer*

Department of Management Sciences
The University of Iowa, Iowa City IA 52242, USA
{gautam-pant,filippo-menczer}@uiowa.edu

**Abstract.** The Web provides us with a vast resource for business intelligence. However, the large size of the Web and its dynamic nature make the task of foraging appropriate information challenging. General-purpose search engines and business portals may be used to gather some basic intelligence. Topical crawlers, driven by richer contexts, can then leverage on the basic intelligence to facilitate in-depth and up-to-date research. In this paper we investigate the use of topical crawlers in creating a small document collection that helps locate relevant business entities. The problem of locating business entities is encountered when an organization looks for competitors, partners or acquisitions. We formalize the problem, create a test bed, introduce metrics to measure the performance of crawlers, and compare the results of four different crawlers. Our results underscore the importance of identifying good hubs and exploiting link contexts based on tag trees for accelerating the crawl and improving the overall results.

## 1   Introduction

A large number of business entities — start-up companies and established corporations — have a Web presence. This makes the Web a lucrative source for locating business information of interest. A company that is planning to diversify or invest in a start-up would want to locate a number of players in the area of business. The intelligence gathering process may involve manual efforts using search engines, business portals or personal contacts. Topical crawlers can help in extracting a small but focused document collection from the Web that can then be thoroughly mined for appropriate information using off-the-shelf text mining, indexing and ranking tools.

Topical crawlers, also called focused crawlers, have been studied extensively in the past [6,7,3,10,2]. In our previous evaluation studies of topical crawlers, we found a similarity based Naive Best-First crawler to be quite effective [11,12, 18]. However, the Naive Best-First crawler made no use of the inherent structure available in an HTML document. We also studied algorithms that attempt to identify the context of a link using a sliding window and a distance measure based on number of links separating a word from a given link. However, such approaches

---

* Current affiliation: School of Informatics and Computer Science Department, Indiana University. Email: fil@indiana.edu

T. Koch and I.T. Sølvberg (Eds.): ECDL 2003, LNCS 2769, pp. 233–244, 2003.
© Springer-Verlag Berlin Heidelberg 2003

often performed no better than variants of the Naive Best-First approach [12, 18]. In this paper we consider a crawler that identifies the context of a link using the HTML page's tag tree or Document Object Model (DOM) representation.

The problem of locating business entities on the Web maps onto the general problem of Web resource discovery. However, it has some features that distinguish it from the general case. In particular, business communities are highly competitive. Hence, it is unlikely that a company's Web page would link to a Web page of its competitor. A topical crawler that is aware of such domain level characteristic may utilize it to its advantage.

We evaluate our crawlers over millions of pages across 159 topics. Based on the number of topics and the number of pages crawled per topic, our evaluations are the most extensive in the currently available topical crawling literature.

## 2   The Problem

Searching for URLs of related business entities is a type of business intelligence problem. The entities could be related through the area of competence, research thrust, comparable nature (like start-ups) or a combination of such features. We start by assuming that a short list of URLs of related business entities is already available. However, the list needs to be further expanded. The short list may have been generated manually with the help of search engines, business portals or Web directories. An analyst may face some hurdles in expanding the list of relevant URLs. Such hurdles could be due to lack of appropriate content in relevant pages, inadequate user queries, staleness of search engines' collections, or bias in search engines' ranking. Similar problems plague information discovery using Web directories or portals. The staleness of a search engine's collection is highlighted by the dynamic nature of the Web [9]. Cho and Garcia-Molina [4] have shown, in a study with 720,000 Web pages and spanning over 4 months, that 40% of the pages in the .com domain changed every day. Hence, it is reasonable to complement traditional techniques with topical crawlers to discover up-to-date business information.

Since our focus is on studying the effect of different crawling techniques, we do not investigate the issue of ranking. We believe that ranking is a separate task best left until a collection has been created. In fact, many different indexing, ranking or text mining tools may be applied to retrieve information from the collection. Our goal is to find ways of crawling and building a small but effective collection for the purpose of finding related business entities. We measure the quality of the collection at various points during the crawl through precision-like and recall-like metrics that are described next.

## 3   The Test Bed

For our test bed, we need a number of *topics* and corresponding lists of related business entities. The hierarchical categories of the Open Directory Project

(ODP)[1] are used for this purpose. ODP provides us with a categorical collection of URLs that are manually edited and not biased by commercial considerations. Hence, we can find categories that list related business entities as judged by humans. To begin with, we identify categories in the ODP hierarchy that end with any of the following words: "Companies," "Consultants," or "Manufacturers." These categories serve as topics for our test bed. We collect only those categories that have more than 20 unique external URLs and we skip categories that have "Regional," "World" and "International" as a top-level or sub-category. After going through the entire RDF dump of ODP, 159 such categories are found. Next, we split each category's external URLs into two disjoint sets — *seeds* and *targets*. The set of seeds is created by picking 10 external URLs at random from a category. The remaining URLs make up the targets. The seeds are given to the crawlers as starting links while the targets are used for evaluation. The *keywords* that guide the crawlers are created by concatenating all the alphanumeric tokens in the ODP category name leaving out the most general category (Science, Arts etc.). We also concatenate the manual descriptions of the seeds and the targets and create a master *description* that would serve as another source for evaluations. An example of a topic with corresponding keywords, description, seeds and targets as extracted from an ODP category is shown in Table 1.

Each crawler is provided with a set of keywords and the corresponding seeds to start the crawl. A crawler is then allowed to crawl up to 10,000 pages starting from the seeds. The process is repeated for each of the 159 topics in the test bed. As a result, we may crawl more than one and a half million pages for one crawler alone. We use the following precision-like and recall-like measures to understand the performance of the crawlers:

- **Precision@N**: We measure the precision for a crawler on topic $t$ after crawling $N$ pages as:

$$precision@N_t = \frac{1}{N} \cdot \sum_{i=1}^{N} sim(d_t, p_i) \qquad (1)$$

where $d_t$ is the description of the topic $t$, $p_i$ is a crawled page, and $sim(d_t, p_i)$ is the cosine similarity between the two. The cosine similarity is measured using a TF-IDF weighting scheme [17]. In particular, the weight of a term $k$ in a given page $p$ is computed as:

$$w_{kp} = \left(0.5 + \frac{0.5 \cdot tf_{kp}}{\max_{k' \in T_p} tf_{k'p}}\right) \cdot \ln\left(\frac{|C_t^*|}{df_k}\right) \qquad (2)$$

where $tf_{kp}$ is the frequency of the term $k$ in page $p$, $T_p$ is the set of all terms in page $p$, $C_t^*$ is the set of pages crawled by all the crawlers for topic $t$ at the end of the crawl, and $df_k$ is the number of pages in $C_t^*$ that contain the term $k$. After representing a topic description ($d$) and a crawled page ($p$)

---

[1] http://dmoz.org

as a vector of term weights ($v_d$ and $v_p$ respectively), the cosine similarity between them is computed as:

$$sim(d,p) = \frac{v_d \cdot v_p}{\| v_d \| \cdot \| v_p \|} \qquad (3)$$

where $v_d \cdot v_p$ is the dot (inner) product of the two vectors. Note that the terms used for cosine similarity, throughout this paper, undergo stemming (using Porter stemming algorithm [15]) and stoplisting.

For a given $N$, we can average $precision@N_t$ over all the topics in the test bed to get the *average precision@N*. The latter can be plotted as a trajectory over time, where time is approximated by increasing values of crawled pages ($N$).

- **Target recall@N**: In the absence of a known relevant set, we treat the recall of the targets as an indirect indicator of actual recall (Figure 1). The *target recall@N_t* for a crawler on a topic $t$ can be computed at various points ($N$) during the crawl:

$$target\ recall@N_t = \frac{\mid T_t \cap C_t^N \mid}{\mid T_t \mid} \qquad (4)$$

where $T_t$ is the set of targets for topic $t$, and $C_t^N$ is the set of $N$ crawled pages. Again, we can average the recall (*average target recall@N*) at various values of $N$ over the topics in the test bed.

The above evaluation metrics are a special case of a general evaluation methodology for topical crawlers [18]. We will perform one-tailed t-tests to understand, in statistical terms, the benefit of using one crawler over another. The null hypothesis in all such tests will be that the two crawlers under consideration perform equally well.

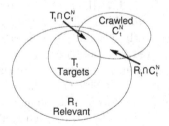

**Fig. 1.** $\mid T_t \cap C_t^N \mid / \mid T_t \mid$ as an estimate of $\mid R_t \cap C_t^N \mid / \mid R_t \mid$

## 4    Crawlers

We evaluate the performance of four different crawlers. Before we describe the crawling algorithms, it is worthwhile to illustrate the general crawling infrastructure that all the crawlers use.

**Table 1.** A sample topic - keywords, description, seeds, targets

| keywords | description | seeds | targets |
|---|---|---|---|
| Gambling Equipment Manufacturers | Gemaco Cards Manufacturer of promotional and casino playing cards in poker, bridge ... R.T. Plastics Supplier of casino value, roulette, poker and tournament chips ... | http://www.gemacocards.com/ http://www.rtplastics.com/ http://www.ally.com/ http://www.amtote.com/ http://www.pokerchips.com/ ... | http://www.agtco.com/ http://www.cartamundi.com/ http://www.barcrest.co.uk/ http://www.ilts.com/ http://www.ballygaming.com/ http://www.tcsgroup.com/ http://pidcgroup.com/ ... |

## 4.1 Crawling Infrastructure

The crawlers are implemented as multi-threaded objects in Java. Each crawler has many (possibly hundreds) threads of execution sharing a single synchronized *frontier* that lists the unvisited URLs. Each thread of the crawler follows a *crawling loop* that involves picking the next URL to crawl from the frontier, fetching the page corresponding to the URL through HTTP, parsing the retrieved page, and finally adding the unvisited URLs to the frontier. Before the URLs are added to the frontier they may be assigned a score that represents the estimated benefit of visiting the page corresponding to the URL. Some of the crawlers utilize the tag tree structure of the Web pages. They first *tidy*[2] the HTML page and then use an XML parser to obtain relevant information from the DOM structure. Tidying an HTML page includes both insertion of missing tags and reordering of tags in the page. The process is necessary for mapping the content of a page onto a tree structure with integrity, where each node has a single parent. We also enclose all the text tokens within <text>...</text> tags. This makes sure that all text tokens appear as leaves on the tag tree. While this step is not necessary for mapping an HTML document to a tree structure, it does provide some simplifications for the analysis. Figure 2 shows a snippet of an HTML page that is subsequently cleaned and converted into convenient XML format before being represented as a tag tree.

The current crawler implementation uses 75 threads of execution and limits the maximum size of the frontier to 70,000. Only the first 10KB of a Web page are downloaded. Note that during a crawl of 10,000 pages, a crawler may encounter more than 70,000 unvisited URLs. However, given that the average number of outlinks on Web pages is 7 [16], the maximum frontier size is not very restrictive for a crawl of 10,000 pages. Being a shared resource for all the threads, the frontier is also responsible for enforcing certain ethics that prevent the threads from accessing the same server too frequently. In particular, the frontier tries to enforce the constraint that every batch of $D$ URLs picked from it are from $D$ different server host names ($D = 50$). The crawlers also respect the Robot Exclusion Protocol.[3]

---

[2] http://www.w3.org/People/Raggett/tidy/
[3] http://www.robotstxt.org/wc/norobots.html

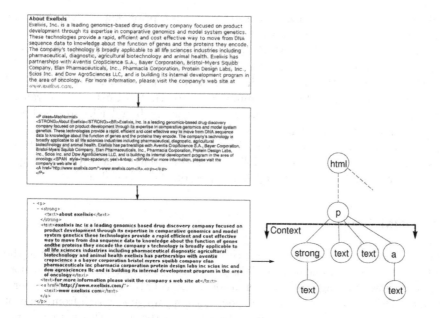

**Fig. 2.** An HTML snippet (top) whose source (center) is modified into a convenient XML format (bottom). The tag tree representation of the HTML snippet is shown on the right.

## 4.2  Breadth-First Crawler

Breadth-First is a baseline crawler for our experiments. The crawl frontier is a FIFO queue. Each thread of the crawler picks up the URL at the front of the queue and adds new unvisited URLs to the back of it. Since the crawler is multi-threaded, many pages are fetched simultaneously. Hence, it is possible that the pages are not fetched in an exact FIFO order. In addition the ethics enforced in the system, that prevent inundating a Web server with requests, also make the crawler deviate from strict FIFO order. The crawler adds unvisited URLs to the frontier only when the size of the frontier is less than the maximum allowed.

## 4.3  Naive Best-First Crawler

The Naive Best-First crawler treats a Web page as a bag of words. It computes the cosine similarity of the page to the given keywords and uses it as a score ($link\_score_{bfs}$) of the unvisited URLs on the page. The URLs are then added to the frontier that is maintained as a priority queue using the scores. Each thread picks the best URL in the frontier to crawl, and inserts the unvisited URLs at appropriate positions in the priority queue. The $link\_score_{bfs}$ is computed using Equation 3. However, the keywords replace the topic description, and the vector representation is based only on term frequencies. A TF-IDF weighting scheme is problematic during the crawl because there is no a priori knowledge about the distribution of terms across crawled pages.

As in the case of the Breadth-First crawler, a multi-threaded version of Naive Best-First crawler with ethical behavior does not crawl in an exact best first order. Due to multiple threads it acts like a Best-N-First crawler where $N$ is related to the number of simultaneously running threads. Best-N-First is a generalized version of the Naive Best-First crawler that picks $N$ best URLs to crawl at a time. We have found certain versions of the Best-N-First crawler to be strong competitors in our previous evaluations [14,12,18]. Note that the Naive Best-First crawler and the crawlers to follow keep the frontier size within its upper bound by retaining only the best URLs based on the assigned scores.

## 4.4  DOM Crawler

Unlike the Naive Best-First crawler, the DOM crawler tries to make use of the structure that is available in an HTML page through its tag tree representation. Figure 2 shows the tag tree representation of an HTML snippet. In its general form, the DOM crawler treats some node that appears on the path from the root of the tag tree to a link as an *aggregation node* of the link. All the text in the sub-tree rooted at the aggregation node is then considered a context of the link. In the current implementation of the DOM crawler we have set the immediate parent of a link to be its aggregation node. While the choice of the parent as the aggregation node may seem arbitrary, we note that it is no more arbitrary than picking up $W$ words or bytes around a hyperlink and treating them as the link's context as has been done before [7,1]. In an ideal situation we would like to identify the optimal aggregation node for a given page and topic. This problem is being studied [13] but it is beyond the scope of this paper. In our example from Figure 2, all the text (at any depth) under the <p> paragraph tag forms a context for the link http://www.exelixis.com. After associating a link with its context, the crawler computes the cosine similarity between the context and the given keywords. The measure is called the *context_score*. In addition, the crawler computes the cosine similarity between the page in which the link was found and the keywords, which corresponds to $link\_score_{bfs}$. The final $link\_score_{dom}$ associated with a link is computed by:

$$link\_score_{dom} = \alpha \cdot link\_score_{bfs} + (1 - \alpha) \cdot context\_score$$

where $\alpha$ weighs the relative importance of the entire page content vs. the context of a link. It is set to 0.25 to give more importance to the *context_score*. The frontier is a priority queue based on $link\_score_{dom}$. In practice, due to the reasons mentioned for the other crawlers, the individual pages are not fetched in the exact order of priority.

Note that the Naive Best-First crawler can be seen as a special case of the DOM crawler in which the aggregation node is set to the root of the DOM tree (the <html> tag), or where $\alpha = 1$.

## 4.5   Hub-Seeking Crawler

The Hub-Seeking crawler is an extension of the DOM crawler that tries to explore potential hubs during its crawl. Since the seed URLs are assumed relevant to the topic, the crawler determines that a page that links to many of the *seed hosts* is a good hub. Seed hosts are fully qualified host names for Web servers, such as www.igt.com, of the seed URLs. A page points to www.igt.com if it points to any page from the host. The crawler assigns a *hub_score* to each page based on the number of seed hosts it points to. It then combines the *hub_score* with the *link_score*$_{\text{dom}}$ to get a *link_score*$_{\text{hub}}$ for each link on a given page. We would like *hub_score* to have the following properties:

- It should be a non-negative increasing function for all values of $n \geq 0$, where $n$ is the number of seed hosts.
- It should have extremely small or zero value for $n = 0, 1$ (to avoid false positives). The score for $n = 2$ should be relatively high as compared to the average *link_score*$_{\text{dom}}$. The event that a page points to two different business entities in the same area is relatively unlikely and hence must be fully exploited.
- The scores must lie between 0 and 1 so that they can be compared against *link_score*$_{\text{dom}}$.

While there is an infinite number of functions that satisfy the above properties, we use the one described in Figure 3.

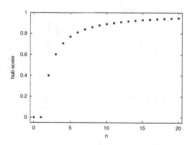

**Fig. 3.** Hub scores based on $hub\_score(n) = \frac{n \cdot (n-1)}{1+n^2}, n = 0, 1, 2, \dots$.

Note that the Equation in Figure 3 relies on the fact that the seed URLs are relevant. It is *ad hoc* and lacks the sophistication of methods such as Kleinberg's algorithm [8] to identify hubs and authorities. However, it is easy to compute in real time during the crawl using the link information from a single page. The *link_score*$_{\text{hub}}$ that is used to prioritize the frontier queue is calculated as:

$$link\_score_{\text{hub}} = max(hub\_score, link\_score_{\text{dom}}). \qquad (5)$$

## 5   Performance

Figures 4 (a) & (b) show the performance of all the crawlers described above on the test bed. We note that on average the Hub-Seeking crawler performs better than the DOM Crawler which in turn performs better than the Best-First crawler for most part of the 10,000 page crawls. The baseline Breadth-First crawler performs the worst as expected. The above observation is true for both of the performance metrics described in section 3. We note that the performance of the Hub-Seeking crawler is significantly better than the Naive Best-First crawler on *average target recall*@10000 (Figure 4 (b)). In fact a one tailed t-test to check the same generates a p-value of 0.004. While the Hub-Seeking crawler outperforms the Best-First crawler even on the *average precision*@10000 metric (Figure 4 (a)), a corresponding one tailed t-test gives a p-value of 0.105. Hence, the benefit is not as significant for precision. However, this means that while building a collection that is at least as topically focused as the one built by the Naive Best-First crawler, the Hub-Seeking crawler will harvest a greater number of the relevant pages of other business entities in the area.

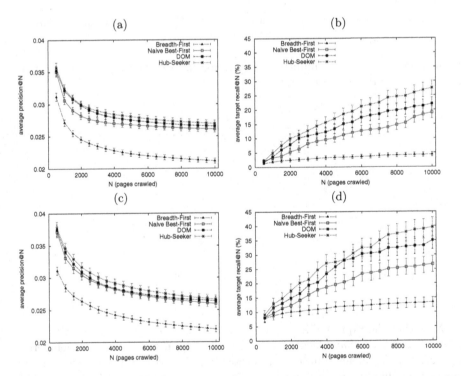

**Fig. 4.** Performance of the crawlers: (a) *average precision*@$N$ and (b) *average target recall*@$N$ using the ODP links as seeds; (c) *average precision*@$N$ and (d) *average target recall*@$N$ using the augmented seeds. The error bars correspond to ±1 standard error.

# 6   Improving the Seed Set

A search engine can assist a topical crawler by sharing the more global Web information available to it. We use the Google API[4] to automatically find more effective seeds for the crawler. The Hub-Seeking crawler assumes that a page that points to many of the seed hosts is a good hub. We use a similar idea to find good hubs from a search engine in order to better seed the crawl. Using the Google API, we find the top 10 back-links of all the test bed seeds for a topic. We then count the number of times a back-link repeats across different seeds. The count is used as a *hub_score*. The process is repeated for all the 159 topics in the test bed. Only the top 10 back-links in accordance with the *hub_score* are kept for each topic. If the count for a back-link is less than 2 then the link is filtered out. Also, to make sure that the problem is non-trivial, we must avoid hubs that are duplicates of the ODP page that lists the seeds and the targets. For this purpose, we do not include any back-link that is from the domain dmoz.org or directory.google.com (a popular directory based on ODP data). Furthermore, to screen unknown ODP mirrors, any back-link page that has higher than 90% cosine similarity to the the topic description is filtered out. A back-link page is first projected into the space of terms that appear in the topic description, and then the cosine similarity is measured in a manner similar to the Naive Best-First crawler. The projection is necessary to ignore extra text (in addition to the ODP data) that may have been added by a site. Due to the filtering criterion and limited results through the Google API, it is possible that we do not find even a single hub for certain topics. In fact, out of the 159 topics, we find hubs for only 94 topics. We use the hubs thus obtained along with the original test bed seeds to form an *augmented seed* set. The augmented seeds are used to start the crawl for each of the 94 topics.

Figures 4 (c) & (d) show the performance of the four crawlers using the augmented seed set. We first notice that the order of performance (on both metrics) among the crawlers remains the same as that for the original seeds. However, the performance of the DOM crawler in addition to the Hub-Seeking crawler is significantly better than the Naive Best-First crawler on *average target recall@10000* (Figure 4 (d)). One tailed t-tests to verify the same yield p-value of 0.024 for the DOM crawler and 0.002 for the Hub-Seeking crawler. Another important observation to make is that all the crawlers better their performance as compared to the experiments using the original seeds for most part of the 10000 page crawls (cf. Figure 4 (a),(b) and Figure 4 (c),(d)). However, *average precision@N* plots (with augmented seeds) show steeper downhill slopes leading to slightly poorer performance towards the end of the crawls for all but the Breadth-First crawler (Figure 4 (c)). The benefit of augmented seeds is more prominent when we look at *average target recall@N* plots (cf. Figure 4 (b) and (d)). We perform one-tailed t-tests to check the hypothesis that the availability of augmented seeds (that include hubs) significantly improves the performance of the crawlers based on *average target recall@10000*. We find that for all the crawlers the null hy-

---

[4] http://www.google.com/apis/

pothesis (no difference with augmented seeds) can be rejected in favor of the alternative hypothesis (performance improves with augmented seeds) at $\alpha = 0.015$ (in most cases even lower) significance level. We conclude that there is strong evidence that the availability of "good" hubs during the crawl does improve the performance of the crawlers. By providing the hubs, the search engine assists the crawlers in making a good start that affects their overall performance.

## 7    Related Work

Various facets of Web crawlers have been studied in depth for nearly a decade (e.g.,[6,7,3,10]). Chakrabarti et al. [3] used a distiller within their crawler that identified good hubs using a modified version of Kleinberg's algorithm [8]. As noted earlier we use a much simpler approach to identify potential hubs. Moreover, the authors did not show any strong evidence of the benefit of using hubs during the crawl. In a more recent work Chakrabarti et al. [2] used the DOM structure of a Web page in a focused crawler. However, their use of DOM trees is different from the present idea of using the aggregation node to associate a link to a context. In particular, their method uses the DOM tree in a manner similar to the idea of using text tokens in the "vicinity" of a link to derive the context. In contrast, the aggregation node explicitly captures the tag tree hierarchy by grouping text tokens based on a common ancestor.

Measuring the performance of a crawler is a challenging problem due to the non-availability of relevant sets on the Web. Nevertheless, researchers use various metrics to understand the performance of topical crawlers (e.g.,[5,3,11]). A study by Menczer et al. [11] on the evaluation of topical crawlers looks at a number of ways to compare different crawlers. A more general framework to evaluate topical crawlers is presented by Srinivasan et al. [18].

## 8    Conclusions

We investigated the problem of creating a small but effective collection of Web documents for the purpose of locating related business entities by evaluating four different crawlers. We found that the Hub-Seeking crawler that identifies potential hubs and exploits the intra-document structure significantly outperforms the Naive Best-First crawler based on estimated recall. The Hub-Seeking crawler also maintains a better estimated precision than the Naive Best-First crawler. Since Web pages of similar business entities are expected to form a competitive Web community, recognizing neutral hubs that link to many of the competing entities is important. We do see a positive effect in performance through identification of hubs both at the start of the crawl and during the crawl process.

In the future we would like to explore the performance of the Hub-Seeking crawler on more general crawling problems. As noted earlier, the issue of finding the optimal aggregation node is being investigated [13].

**Acknowledgments.** Thanks to Robin McEntire, Valdis A. Dzelzkalns, and Paul Stead at GlaxoSmithKline for their valuable suggestions. This work has been supported in part through a summer internship by GlaxoSmithKline R&D to GP, and by the NSF under CAREER grant No. IIS-0133124 to FM.

# References

1. S. Chakrabarti, B. Dom, D. Gibson, J. Kleinberg, P. Raghavan, and S. Rajagopalan. Automatic resource list compilation by analyzing hyperlink structure and associated text. In *WWW7*, 1998.
2. S. Chakrabarti, K. Punera, and M. Subramanyam. Accelerated focused crawling through online relevance feedback. In *WWW2002*, Hawaii, May 2002.
3. S. Chakrabarti, M. van den Berg, and B. Dom. Focused crawling: A new approach to topic-specific Web resource discovery. In *WWW8*, May 1999.
4. J. Cho and H. Garcia-Molina. The evolution of the web and implications for an incremental crawler. In *VLDB 2000*, Cairo, Egypt.
5. J. Cho, H. Garcia-Molina, and L. Page. Efficient crawling through URL ordering. *Computer Networks*, 30(1–7):161–172, 1998.
6. P. M. E. De Bra and R. D. J. Post. Information retrieval in the World Wide Web: Making client-based searching feasible. In *Proc. 1st International World Wide Web Conference*, 1994.
7. M. Hersovici, M. Jacovi, Y. S. Maarek, D. Pelleg, M. Shtalhaim, and S. Ur. The shark-search algorithm — An application: Tailored Web site mapping. In *WWW7*, 1998.
8. J. Kleinberg. Authoritative sources in a hyperlinked environment. *Journal of the ACM*, 46(5):604–632, 1999.
9. S. Lawrence and C.L. Giles. Accessibility of information on the Web. *Nature*, 400:107–109, 1999.
10. F. Menczer and R. K. Belew. Adaptive retrieval agents: Internalizing local context and scaling up to the Web. *Machine Learning*, 39(2–3):203–242, 2000.
11. F. Menczer, G. Pant, M. Ruiz, and P. Srinivasan. Evaluating topic-driven Web crawlers. In *Proc. 24th Annual Intl. ACM SIGIR Conf. on Research and Development in Information Retrieval*, 2001.
12. F. Menczer, G. Pant, and P. Srinivasan. Topical web crawlers: Evaluating adaptive algorithms. *To appear in ACM Trans. on Internet Technologies*, 2003. http://dollar.biz.uiowa.edu/~fil/Papers/TOIT.pdf.
13. G. Pant. Deriving Link-context from HTML Tag Tree. In *8th ACM SIGMOD Workshop on Research Issues in Data Mining and Knowledge Discovery*, 2003.
14. G. Pant, P. Srinivasan, and F. Menczer. Exploration versus exploitation in topic driven crawlers. In *WWW02 Workshop on Web Dynamics*, 2002.
15. M. Porter. An algorithm for suffix stripping. *Program*, 14(3):130–137, 1980.
16. S. RaviKumar, P. Raghavan, S. Rajagopalan, D. Sivakumar, A. Tomkins, and E. Upfal. Stochastic models for the Web graph. In *FOCS*, pages 57–65, Nov. 2000.
17. G. Salton and M.J. McGill. *Introduction to Modern Information Retrieval*. McGraw-Hill, 1983.
18. P. Srinivasan, F. Menczer, and G. Pant. A general evaluation framework for topical crawlers. *Information Retrieval*, Submitted, 2003. http://dollar.biz.uiowa.edu/~fil/Papers/crawl_framework.pdf.

# SozioNet: Networking Social Science Resources

Wolfgang Meier, Natascha Schumann, Sue Heise, and Rudi Schmiede

Department of Sociology,
Darmstadt University of Technology,
Darmstadt, Germany,
sozionet@ifs.tu-darmstadt.de

**Abstract.** SozioNet[1] forms part of a forthcoming national social science information portal, which is currently being developed by the German Infoconnex[2] initiative. Inspired by successful examples like MathNet[3] or SOSIG[4], SozioNet provides access to freely available web resources with relevance to social science. It is based on a network of social science institutions and scientists, to agree on and establish common metadata standards. SozioNet implements a general infrastructure for the creation of semantically rich metadata, and for the harvesting and retrieval of relevant resources with a domain specific focus.

## 1 Introduction

Infoconnex represents a joint effort to integrate existing information services and ongoing activities related to education, social science and psychology. In addition to the other activities coordinated by the initiative, SozioNet concentrates on freely available web resources with relevance to German social science. It thus complements the already existing information services available to social scientists, including, for example, the Virtual Library of Sociology[5]. The project is funded by the German Federal Ministry of Education and Research and was launched in spring 2002. However, the basic idea for the project already goes back to 1998.

SozioNet has been greatly inspired by such successful projects as MathNet, Phys-Net and SOSIG. Although obliged to its predecessors, SozioNet differs from them in several aspects, concerning basic concepts, technology and standards, for example, by the use of ontologies and current semantic web standards like DAML [12] or OWL [4]. This paper presents an overview of the project, the metadata schemes and the standards used in SozioNet. We then introduce the general infrastructure for metadata creation and resource harvesting. Finally, the paper takes a closer look on some of the innovative aspects implemented in two of the core components: the user-interface for metadata creation and the harvesting component. The user-interface offers a personalized wizard for metadata creation with distinguishing features like automatic summarization of existing metadata, and the management of metadata records in persistent collections. It is

---

[1] http://www.sozionet.org
[2] http://www.infoconnex.de
[3] http://www.mathnet.org
[4] http://www.sosig.ac.uk
[5] http://www.vibsoz.de

T. Koch and I.T. Sølvberg (Eds.): ECDL 2003, LNCS 2769, pp. 245–256, 2003.

build on top of state-of-the-art technologies like Apache's Cocoon and the forthcoming XForms standard. The harvesting component is based on a highly configurable pipeline concept, which reverses the pipelines introduced by Cocoon, while building upon the same component framework.

Unlike other scientific communities, the social sciences have not yet established a (living) pre-print culture. However, many institutions have begun to make working papers, project reports or dissertations available on the web. Other web-sites provide or collect materials dedicated to specific subjects, and increasingly, individual scientists start to publish their work results.

But, searching for these resources can be a rather tedious task: most resources are somewhere hidden on faculty servers, project pages or individual homepages, all implementing their own specific site structure, web design and search facilities. Also, common web-wide search engines are usually based on the algorithmic processing of arbitrary contents and fail to address the needs of a given scientific community.

A digital library that focusses on a specific scientific domain can help to improve this situation, given that the players involved agree on common standards with respect to formal requirements, metadata sets, metadata quality and classification rules. In particular, implementing common metadata standards is a central prerequisite for a DL dedicated to a given discipline. Researchers or students should be able to browse and search resources by domain specific categories and concepts taken from established classifications or thesauri.

At the same time, a strong commitment to open standards is required to ensure that valuable resources can be accessed and reused from contexts outside the community. The RDF Resource Description Framework [7] and related standards provide a well-established foundation for metadata interchange. Moreover, the ongoing efforts to establish standards for the "Semantic Web" will enable individual resources to be connected to a rich web of information objects.

Like MathNet and PhysNet, SozioNet is based on the principle of self-organization: social scientists and scientific institutions are encouraged to publish relevant resources and institutional information on the web, using the metadata standards established by the project. SozioNet provides tools to help authors create semantically rich metadata. The project also implements a general infrastructure to harvest the relevant resources from the web, and to search through these resources with a domain specific focus.

Besides providing access to common resources like working papers or project reports, SozioNet also aims to improve the visibility of social science institutions. Similar to the concepts first introduced by MathNet, institutions are motivated to create a so-called SozioNet page, which summarizes important institutional information on a standardized, additional web page. When browsing through different institutional homepages, users have constantly to adapt to a variety of web designs, site structures or navigation facilities. The SozioNet page will provide an additional, standardized entry-point into the web site, and will be dynamically generated from machine-readable metadata. To summarize, SozioNet aims to

- provide access to freely available web resources with relevance to social scientists
- build up a network of social science institutions to agree upon and establish common standards for the publication of scientific resources on the web

- improve the quality of web searches by concentrating on a given scientific domain
- improve the visibility of social science institutions and the resources and services they provide

Currently, in March 2003, 13 institutions have signed a cooperation agreement to participate in the development of SozioNet. This includes social science faculties as well as independent research institutes not directly affiliated to an university. While some faculties are just starting to make their resources available through SozioNet, there are also many institutions which have been publishing larger volumes of social science materials for a much longer period of time. This includes, for example, the German Youth Institute in Munich or the Social Science Research Center in Berlin. These institutions host a considerable amount of relevant materials. They usually have their own content management and publishing workflow. SozioNet has thus to meet the requirements of both, small university institutes and independant research institutions with pre-existing, possibly large collections of resources.

The remaining sections are organized as follows: The following section introduces the metadata schemes used in SozioNet and the backing ontology model. Section 3 provides a brief overview of the general architecture. Finally, section 4 will have a closer look at two central components: the user interface for metadata creation and management, and the harvesting component.

## 2 Metadata Schemes

As outlined above, it is vital for SozioNet that all players involved agree on a common basis for the creation of semantically rich metadata. This process can build upon existing standards like, for example, Dublin Core. However, there are additional aspects, which are specific to the social science domain. These domain specific aspects should be made transparent to the end user and to software agents accessing the resource.

All metadata in SozioNet is encoded in RDF [7]. RDF provides a simple language for expressing metadata and is commonly used to embed structured metadata into documents. RDF just defines a basic model and a serialization syntax. It does not specify a vocabulary. Vocabulary semantics, expressed in the form of RDF schemas, have to be defined by the communities using RDF. In addition to the RDF core standard, RDF schemas ensure the validity and data integrity of a given RDF data set, thus defining a specific vocabulary [2].

The benefits introduced by the RDF and RDF schema standards can not be over-estimated. In particular, they enable metadata designers to rely on standardized and well-known schemas for the common elements of the metadata model, which can be clearly separated from domain specific vocabularies in a way that is transparent to users and software agents.

In the context of the W3C's semantic web initative, the foundations provided by RDF and RDF schema have been further extended. RDF schema defines modelling primitives for classes, properties, the relationships between classes and properties, and restrictions. The DARPA Agent Markup Language (DAML) extends this basic vocabulary by introducing a still limited set of additional language elements and useful distinctions [12].

It also clarifies many aspects that have been intentionally left open in the RDF schema standard.

From our point of view, DAML ontologies are usually easier to read and understand than comparable schemas written without the help of DAML. Also, tools like Hewlett Packard's Jena [8] offer direct support for this standard, for example, to create instances of a DAML class or to introspect the class hierarchy starting at a given instance. DAML will be superseded by the W3Cs Web Ontology Language (OWL), which is available as a working draft ([4], see also [9] for a discussion of the relationship between OWL and RDF).

SozioNet uses metadata in two main areas: first, participating social science institutions have agreed to enhance common resources like working papers, lecture notes, educational materials etc. with high-quality metadata. Second, RDF metadata is also at the core of the SozioNet secondary homepage, which provides information about the institution, faculty staff, research fields, educational focus, and so on.

*Example 1.*
```
<rdf:RDF>
  <sn:ResearchPaper rdf:about="http://www.zeitschriftarbeit.de
      /docs/2-2000/wolf.PDF">
  <dc:title>Das Netzwerk als Signatur der Epoche</dc:title>
  <dcq:abstract>Der Aufsatz beinhaltet ...</dcq:abstract>
  <dc:language>DE</ dc:language>
  <dcq:IMT>application/pdf</dcq:IMT>
  <dcq:created>1999-07-14</dcq:created>
  <dc:publisher>Landesinstitut Sozialforschungsstelle
  Dortmund</dc:publisher>
  <dc:creator>Wolf, Harald</dc:creator>
  <dc:subject rdf:resource="http://www.sozionet.org/1.0
      /classification#10220"/>
  <dc:subject rdf:resource="http://www.sozionet.org/1.0
      /classification#1080404"/>
  <dc:subject rdf:resource="http://www.sozionet.org/1.0
      /thesaurus#soziologische_Theorie"/>
  </sn:ResearchPaper>
</rdf:RDF>
```

A (shortened) sample metadata record for a working paper is shown above. For common web resources, most metadata properties are taken from the Dublin Core element set and the Dublin Core qualifier scheme.

A closer look at the example reveals several domain specific aspects. In particular, the SozioNet metadata scheme is backed by an ontology. The ontology defines, for example, different document classes like working paper, dissertation or lecture note. It also models the relationships between different object types and includes references to the classification and the thesaurus. The ontology basically defines a shared vocabulary for the SozioNet domain, containing concepts which are not covered by simple Dublin Core or other common schemas. Such domain specific schemes are defined in the SozioNet namespace.

Another important part of the ontology models the social science classification and thesaurus. Both are well established in German social science and are constantly maintained and enhanced by the Social Science Research Centre in Bonn. For SozioNet, the classification as well as the thesaurus are also defined as ontologies. The metadata record thus links directly to the definition of the corresponding term using an RDF reference in the subject property. This is a powerful feature of the implementation of the ontology.

Since classification and thesaurus are themselves defined in RDF and linked to the metadata record, it becomes possible for a software agent to explore the structure of the classification or thesaurus, and to navigate through the classification terms or descriptors connected to the current item. This is supported by RDF-related tools like, for example, Jena [8].

Currently, the base ontology as well as the classification and thesaurus are defined as DAML ontologies. We are prepared to migrate our metadata schemes to OWL, once this working draft is approaching a stable state.

The base ontology is extended by further object types which are part of the SozioNet homepage. This includes, for example, institutional information, information on faculty members or educational focus. The ontology model for these items has been largely influenced by existing proposals[6]. The draft also uses many properties from the vCard standard for general contact information.

In a future perspective, the different information objects should interconnect to a web of recombinable information items. For example, the creator property in a given metadata record could directly link to a personal description of the author on his homepage. However, implementing such features would require an additional standardization of personal homepages (as in MathNet's Persona Mathematica). As all participating institutions should be involved in the standardization process, we currently concentrate on common web resources. Additional information objects will be included in the future.

Embedding RDF into HTML or XHTML documents is still an open issue. It is a common practice to include the RDF into an XML comment. However, this contradicts the basic concepts of XML. The revised version of the RDF/XML syntax specification follows a proposal of the Dublin Core Initiative [1]: the RDF metadata should be saved into an auxiliary file, which is linked from the HTML document header. SozioNet supports this recommendation. Authors should not directly embed their metadata into HTML. Best practice should be to provide a separate file containing only the metadata.

## 3    Architecture

The self-organization of social science institutions and scientists plays an important role in the SozioNet concept. Storing resources to a centralized server system would clearly contradict this principle. All materials will thus remain under the control of the publishing institution or individual, who are responsible for making the resource available and are also responsible for the generation of high-quality metadata, using the standards established in the project.

---

[6] For a list of example ontologies refer to http://www.daml.org/ontologies

## 3.1 Metadata Creation and Harvesting

As indicated in figure 1, SozioNet provides web-based tools for the creation of metadata records (see section 4). These tools are mainly intended for institutions, which have not yet established their own publishing procedures or for individual authors, who would like to create metadata for a limited set of materials. The generated metadata records should either be directly embedded into the source document, or preferably, stored as an auxiliary file in the same server context as the referenced resource. SozioNet gathers the

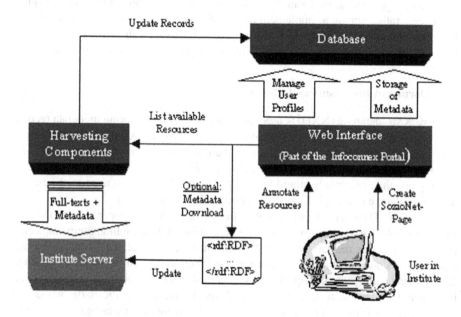

**Fig. 1.** Architecture Overview

available resources through a harvesting component (see the left side of figure 1), which will be described in more depth below. The harvester will periodically scan through all web-addresses known to the system, extracting metadata and indexing the fulltext-content of the resource.

However, the basic harvesting scenario has some known limitations: first, harvesting an entire faculty web site will necessarily include a large number of irrelevant resources without value to social science. Second, faculty members may not have direct access to the webserver, so updated documents have to be forwarded to the person responsible, which may take some time. Finally, the harvester will not recognize document updates immediately, but only during the next scheduled harvesting run.

SozioNet thus implements a hybrid solution: Metadata records entered through the SozioNet tools are stored in a central database. The harvester is just responsible for updating these records if it finds newer versions on the corresponding web site, and for indexing the fulltext content of the referenced resource. Alternatively, the location of new resources can be entered directly into the harvester's database. These resources will be included into the scheduled gathering process. The harvester will thus not scan entire web sites, but only those locations which are known to contain relevant resources. This is in concept similar to the strategy implemented by SOSIG, i.e. the URLs in the manual created catalogue are used to initiate a gathering process, which tries to find additional resources to include.

Since several institutions run their own content management system or digital library, the harvester requires additional support to periodically retrieve metadata records from these existing systems.

The OAI protocol is well-suited for this task [6]. Furthermore, OAI data providers are usually rather simple to implement on top of existing systems. In this scenario, the harvester obtains metadata records conforming to SozioNet standards through OAI. It then only needs to access the referenced documents to fulltext-index their content.

## 3.2  Document Processing and Storage

A native XML database (NXD) is used as storage backend for storing metadata records and (optionally) fulltext contents. As outlined above, the database just represents a temporary data store. The harvester compares the database contents to the metadata descriptions it gathers from the web. If a newer record is found for the same resource, it will replace the one already stored in the db. The database is also used to store other temporary data, e.g. user profiles, thesaurus and classification data.

Using a NXD has a number of benefits: first, it allows the developer to think in XML from A to Z. All components in SozioNet are based on XML, including, for example, the project's web pages, the harvester and the metadata tools. Second, the database provides a schema-less document store, i.e. arbitrary document types can be mixed in the same database collection without requiring modifications to some underlying storage model. For example, RDF metadata records may differ in domain specific parts, while still conforming to SozioNet standards. It is also very likely that our metadata schemes will evolve over time, so documents may follow different versions of the same scheme.

Finally, XML is increasingly accepted in the social sciences not only as a standard for document authoring, but also for the exchange of valuable research data and research results. Since the project builds on XML database technology, SozioNet is able to integrate and search XML based data sets. Participating institutions are encouraged to extend the use of XML on basis of the already existing XML document types.

SozioNet currently uses eXist[7], an open source native XML database system, featuring index-based query processing, tight integration with other open source components (like Apache's Cocoon), simple deployment, and support for a variety of common standards as, for example, the XML:DB API for database access [5]. Particularly useful for SozioNet, eXist also offers query language extensions for index-based keyword searches, queries on the proximity of terms, or regular expression based search patterns. Despite its relatively short history, eXist has already been successfully used in a number of commercial and non-commercial projects. However, since database access is provided through established standard interfaces, SozioNet components do not depend on this particular NXD implementation.

---

[7] http://exist-db.org

The fulltext content of a resource is fetched by the harvester and indexed in a separate process. As will be described in more depth below, the harvester transforms HTML documents into well-formed XML by passing them to an HTML normalizer. The HTML normalizer closes open tags, adds missing elements or quotes attributes to generate a well-formed XML output stream. The output is then forwarded to one or more transformation steps.

Storing the now well-formed XHTML without modifications does not make much sense: while the HTML standard basically encourages authors to explicate the document structure, most HTML creators tend to misuse the corresponding tags for formatting purposes. For example, section headings or tables are very often used as layout elements and thus loose their structural meaning.

As a result, queries on the document structure - as offered by the XML database - may produce rather poor results when applied to heterogeneous HTML documents. In SozioNet, HTML documents are thus transformed into a simplified XML document type, which tries to preserve the basic document structure, e.g. section headings, paragraphs or links. The same applies to other document formats like PDF. However, PDF contains even less structural information, so the benefits are limited. Thus, as an alternative to storing the document's fulltext-content as XML, the harvester also supports fulltext-indexing of the content by forwarding it to Apache's Lucene.

### 3.3  Search Facilities

Currently, metadata search facilities are also implemented on top of the XML database. This is not an ideal solution, since RDF/XML is just one serialization form of RDF and it is always possible to represent the same given RDF data set by different XML documents. To be correct, the database just deals with the XML serialization of RDF and not with the underlying RDF data model itself.

To leverage the full power of RDF, one needs a tool which is able to work directly on the basic RDF triple model. Several tools are available, for example, Hewlett-Packard's Jena [8] or Sesame [3]. However, most tools tested in the project lacked some required features, e.g. efficient keyword searches in strings, and there have been some doubts with respect to scalability and performance. Also, the automatic reasoning capabilities built into many tools are not really a requirement at the current stage of development. Thus, for the time being, we decided to offer metadata search facilities on basis of XML. We are still prepared to switch to a specialized RDF search engine if required by future developments.

## 4  SozioNet Components

This section will have a closer look at some of the core components of SozioNet. However, most components are still rapidly evolving and will have to be covered by separate papers later on.

## 4.1   Metadata Creation

While some institutions have already defined their own publishing workflow, it seems that most sociologists have no experience with metadata creation. It is thus vital to support metadata creators with proper tools, which do not require any knowledge of metadata formats and only a minimal knowledge of the underlying standards. In SozioNet, we thus developed a reusable interface for metadata editing, called MetaWizard. It offers some outstanding features:

- Based on a server-side implementation of the forthcoming XForms W3C standard, allowing forms to span multiple screens. Uses a model-view-controller architecture.
- Personalized user interface: each user has a home-collection, containing the metadata records he created. Records entered through previous sessions can be revised or removed at any time.
- Existing metadata, e.g. META tags in HTML, is preserved by summarizing the referenced resource at the start of a new editing session.

As described above, entered metadata records are stored in a native XML database. The interface is fully personalized, i.e. every user has his own user profile and home collection, to which created records are assigned. User authentication is done by the database.

Users may either create new records, or delete or edit records they have entered during a previous editing session. Metadata creators are encouraged to download the created metadata and to store it on their institution's webserver, but they are not obliged to do so.

When creating new metadata records, the harvester will try to retrieve the web page at the location specified by the user. This feature has been inspired by the DC Dot service[8]. If the page is readable, it will be passed to a summarizer to extract existing metadata. The extracted data is then filled into the following web forms and reviewed by the user. This summarizing feature works very well, for example, if the web page already contains Dublin Core or other common metadata fields in HTML META tags. Of course, existing RDF metadata conforming to SozioNet standards is also recognized, making it possible to upload hand-edited files. However, if no metadata is found in the document, the results of the summarizing process will be limited: in many cases, only the title and a few fields from the HTTP header, including content language, modification date and mime type, can be extracted (for a more sophisticated approach to automatic metadata extraction from social science resources see [10] and [11]).

The user-interface has been implemented on top of Apache's Cocoon[9]. Cocoon offers a rich application server environment for the development of XML based applications. In particular, current versions of Cocoon come with XMLForms, a server-side implementation of the new XForms standard, which provides a powerful technology for the definition of user interfaces. Contrary to simple HTML forms, XMLForms may span over multiple screens and support a model-view-controller separation. Cocoon handles the session management and the transformation of XML pages into HTML. The developer can thus concentrate on the processing logic, which is defined by the means of so called actions.

---

[8] http://www.ukoln.ac.uk/metadata/dcdot/
[9] http://xml.apache.org/cocoon

The backing model is implemented as a set of Java beans, which are automatically transformed into RDF/XML by a Java-to-XML mapping tool. This way, we can easily adapt to different metadata models and keep the interface highly configurable.

## 4.2  Metadata Harvesting

Harvesting web resources is supported by quite a number of different software tools. For example, the open source Harvest software[10] is wide-spread and used in many projects, including MathNet and PhysNet.

Harvest makes a basic distinction between gatherers and brokers. A gatherer is used to recursively scan web locations and to retrieve the resources it finds through a number of supported protocols. The gatherer will forward the pages it finds to so-called summarizers, which are responsible for extracting metadata records, filtering contents, and so on. Based on the gathered data, brokers provide the intended retrieval functionality, usually through external retrieval engines. Though Harvest is highly configurable, SozioNet has slightly different requirements:

1. All metadata will be encoded in RDF. The harvester should thus be able to extract RDF metadata records and, even more important, it should maintain the basic structure of the RDF data.
2. We expect a growing portion of documents to be in XML. The harvester should recognize XML documents and pass them directly to the XML-enabled database to preserve the structural information contained in the XML.

While the second requirement can be easily met by XML-aware summarizers, the first is not so easy to deal with: the original Harvest software stores metadata internally in a format called SOIF. SOIF is a simple, hierarchical format, while RDF records can describe an arbitrary complex graph structure. Converting RDF to SOIF thus implies a possible loss of information and an undesirable reduction of complexity.

Several extensions to Harvest respond to this problematic, replacing the SOIF data store by an RDF triple store[11]. However, additional difficulties showed up during our experiments: for example, the existing, XML-based gatherers failed to process HTML pages which were not valid XML. Also, the installation process was fairly difficult, making it hard to redistribute the software to partner institutions.

As a result, SozioNet is currently using its own harvester, based on a variety of freely available open source tools and backed by a simple, yet powerful component model. The harvester is entirely based on XML and related standards as, for example, SAX (the Simple API for XML).

The basic idea behind the software could be described as follows: take the core paradigm of Apache's Cocoon and apply it to a harvesting scenario. The core paradigm of Cocoon is the pipeline. Each pipeline starts with a generator, producing an XML stream, which is passed through an arbitrary number of transformation steps. At the

[10] http://harvest.sourceforge.net

[11] see the CAP7 Gatherer Component developed in the project CARMEN (http://http://www.mathematik.uni-osnabrueck.de/projects/carmen/AP7/), which uses CARA (http://cara.sourceforge.net) as an RDF triple store

end of the cascaded pipeline, a serializer writes the generated XML stream to whatever output format is desired, e.g. HTML or PDF.

Now, instead of transforming the source XML into the desired output format, the SozioNet harvester does it the other way around, i.e. the input could be a PDF, Word, HTML or XML document, but the output will always be XML. In the cascaded pipeline, the generator is responsible for reading the source document and for producing an XML stream, which is forwarded to the transformation steps. Depending on the type of input document, different serializers are selected: for example, HTML documents are first passed to one of the available HTML normalizers. The normalizers will try to transform the document into well-formed XML, e.g. by adding missing tags, closing opened elements or quoting attributes.

Transformers manipulate their input XML stream, for example, to extract existing metadata, summarize the document, or copy the stream to one or more sub-pipelines, each having a different function. In the basic scenario, two sub-pipelines are used: one to extract metadata from the incoming XML stream, another to prepare and index the fulltext content of the document. Transformers will often be based on XSL, i.e. most of the summarizing functionality provided by the original Harvest software is replaced by XSL stylesheets. Finally, serializers will consume the incoming XML stream and forward the result to the XML database or the fulltext indexer.

The basic concept is similar to the plug-in pipelines implemented in the Greenstone DL software [13]. However, our pipelines rely entirely on XML processing standards like SAX for streaming XML or XSL for transformations.

Multiple pipelines may be defined in the configuration file. The harvester will select the correct pipeline by looking at the mime-type of the source. Currently, there are pipelines and generators for XML/XHTML, non well-formed HTML and PDFs.

The SozioNet harvester not only benefits from the core paradigm of Cocoon, it is also based on exactly the same component framework, called Avalon. Avalon is the driving force behind the configurable pipelines. It implements a framework based on roles and contracts. Each component has a role, for example, in case of the harvester: generator, transformer or serializer. New components can be added through a configuration file or at runtime, by registering them with a component manager or a component selector. The framework usually cares about the configuration of components and provides a general contract for the methods called in each component.

As a result, the harvester is highly configurable. New components may be added at any time by implementing the Java interface for the desired role and registering the created Java class through the configuration file.

# 5    Conclusion

The SozioNet project complements and extends already existing information services available to social scientists in Germany. It will provide state-of-the art solutions using current and future web standards, thus ensuring that the resources collected can be maintained and accessed in the future.

# References

1. Beckett, D. (Ed.): RDF/XML Syntax Specification (Revised). W3C Working Draft 23 January 2003. http://www.w3.org/TR/rdf-syntax-grammar
2. Brickley, D., Guha, R. V.: RDF Vocabulary Description Language 1.0: RDF Schema. W3C Candiate Recommendation. http://www.w3.org/TR/rdf-schema/
3. Broekstra, J., Kampman, A., van Harmelen, F.: Sesame: A Generic Architecture for Storing and Querying RDF and RDF Schema. In Horrocks, I., Hendler, J. (Eds.): The Semantic Web – ISWC 2002. Proceedings of the First International Semantic Web Conference, Sardinia, Italy, June 9–12, 2002.
4. Dean, M., Schreiber, G. (Eds.): Web Ontology Language (OWL) Reference Version 1.0. W3C Working Draft 21 February 2003. http://www.w3.org/TR/owl-ref/
5. Meier, W.: eXist Native XML Database. In Chaudri, A. B., Rashid A., Zicaro R. (Eds.): XML Data Management. Native XML and XML-Enabled Database Systems. Addison-Wesley, Boston MA, 2003.
6. Lagoze, C., Van de Sompel, Nelson, M., Wagner, S. (Eds.): The Open Archives Initiative Protocol for Metadata Harvesting. Protocol Version 2.0 of 2002-06-14. http://www.openarchives.org/OAI/openarchivesprotocol.html
7. Lassila, O., Swick, R. R. (Eds.): Resource Description Framework (RDF) Model and Syntax Specification. W3C Recommendation 22 February 1999. http://www.w3.org/TR/1999/REC-rdf-syntax-19990222/
8. McBride, B.: Jena: A Semantic Web Toolkit. IEEE Internet Computing Online. November, 2002. http://dsonline.computer.org/0211/f/w6jena.htm
9. Patel-Schneider, P. F., Fensel, D.: Layering the Semantic Web: Problems and Directions. In Horrocks, I., Hendler, J. (Eds.): The Semantic Web – ISWC 2002. Proceedings of the First International Semantic Web Conference, Sardinia, Italy, June 9–12, 2002.
10. Strötgen, R.: Meta-data Extraction and Query Translation. Treatment of Semantic Heterogeneity. In Agosti, M., Thanos, C. (Eds.): Research and Advanced Technology for Digital Libraries. Proceedings of the 6th European Conference, ECDL, 2002, Rome, Italy.
11. Strötgen, R., Kokkelink, S.: Metadatenextraktion aus Internetquellen: Heterogenitätsbehandlung im Projekt Carmen. In Schmidt, R. (Ed.): Information Research & Content Management: Orientierung, Ordnung und Organisation im Wissensmarks; 23. Online-Tagung der DGI, Frankfurt am Main, 2001.
12. van Harmelen, F., Patel-Schneider, P. F., Herrocks, I. (Eds.): Reference Description of the DAML+OIL (March 2001) Ontology Markup Language. http://www.daml.org/2001/03/reference.html
13. Witten, I. H., Bainbridge, D., Paynter, G., Boddie, S.: Importing Documents and Metadata into Digital Libraries: Requirements Analysis and an Extensible Architecture. In Agosti, M., Thanos, C. (Eds.): Research and Advanced Technology for Digital Libraries. Proceedings of the 6th European Conference, ECDL, 2002, Rome, Italy.

# VASCODA: A German Scientific Portal for Cross-Searching Distributed Digital Resource Collections

Heike Neuroth[1] and Tamara Pianos[2]

[1] Göttingen State and University Library (SUB), Platz der Göttinger Sieben 1,
37073 Göttingen, Germany
neuroth@mail.sub.uni-goettingen.de
http://www.sub.uni-goettingen.de

[2] German National Library of Science and Technology (TIB),
Welfengarten 1b, 30167 Hannover, Germany
Tamara.Pianos@tib.uni-hannover.de
http://www.tib.uni-hannover.de/

**Abstract.** The German information science community - with the support of the two main funding agencies in Germany - will develop a scientific portal, vascoda, for cross-searching distributed metadata collections. In platitudinous words, one of the services of vascoda is going to be a "Google"-like search for the academic community, an easy to use, yet sophisticated search-engine to supply information on high-quality resources from different media and technical environments. Reaching this objective requires considerable standardisation activity amongst the main players to harmonise the already existing services (e.g. regarding metadata, protocols, etc.). The co-operation amongst the participants including both of the funding agencies is creating a unique team-work situation in Germany thus strengthening the information science community.

## 1 Introduction

Vascoda [1] is a new portal for scientific information going online in August 2003. It will be a central access point covering all fields of science from Anglo-American Culture to Wood-Technology. The portal will allow interdisciplinary searches as well as complex navigation and browsing. Access to all types of documents will be possible: born-digital as well as digitised and print materials can be obtained either free of charge or through pay-per-view options. The service will include full-texts, link-collections, databases, subject-specific search engines and more. The portal is also a nucleus in the creation of a German Digital Library.

Two of the most important sponsors of subject-information in Germany, the BMBF and the DFG are working together to make this portal a reality and to benefit from a combined portal instead of sponsoring two or more competing access points.

More than thirty German institutions – with co-operation partners world wide – are working together to offer users an actual one-stop-shop for all scientific information.

T. Koch and I.T. Sølvberg (Eds.): ECDL 2003, LNCS 2769, pp. 257–262, 2003.

The partners of this project are libraries as well as information centres and other institutions providing quality academic information.

The first release is going to be realised through the co-operation between the network of subject-based Virtual Libraries and the Electronic Journals Library (EZB) as well as the Information Alliance. Together these institutions will make it possible to combine the search for information and the access to full-text documents.

While a search through Google or other search engines usually generates a handful of hits useful for academic or other high-standard research accompanied by countless links of no use, the new portal will only index quality material overcoming the limits of standard search engines indexing webpages regardless of their subject and quality. Vascoda allows access to quality information only, thus creating a collection of trustworthy sources for its users. The quality is guaranteed through human selection of the sources with a tight selection policy. Some partners also co-operate with scientists from their respective subject-fields to ensure the quality of the documents. Also, vascoda is not going to be limited to supplying internet resources but grants access to all types of documents and information relevant for scientific research, e.g. through the integration of library OPACs etc.

The vascoda server will be a third party, creating a resource discovery broker service based on digital resources selected and described by individual institutions, mainly libraries. In this sense vascoda takes the place of a multidisciplinary broker service based on the co-operation between Virtual Libraries, Electronic Journals Library, and the Information Alliance covering different subject areas like Physics, Engineering, Earth Sciences, Mathematics, History, Literature, Social Sciences etc. The target user-group is going to be the higher education and academic research community. The broker pilot will not be restrictive in terms of collections, resources, granularity, subject areas, language of resources/metadata, etc. Cross-searching facilities in the pilot system will be based on a common set of metadata elements and probably main subject classes. Mappings from the local sets of metadata elements to the common vascoda metadata set are necessary for cross-searching.

## 2  Digital Resource Collection

The combined services of the Electronic Journals Library (EZB), of the Virtual Libraries and the Information Alliance are going to grant direct access to many different types of digital documents like dissertations, databases, bibliographies, journals, full-texts etc. Together, the three players will make it easy to obtain trustworthy quality information through searching and browsing options. An easy and convenient access for users to all types of documents in all academic fields is the most important aim of this project.

The single subject-specific entry points will be the fundamental components of this interdisciplinary service. The partners' single services have to be standardised in order to provide complex cross-searching and browsing.

## 2.1  Virtual Libraries

The individual Virtual Libraries (VLibs), under the roof of the Subject-Based Virtual Library [2] offer access to information and documents relevant for research in a specific field of study. Not only the searching but also the delivery of documents stored and scattered around the world will be integrated by these Virtual Libraries. The VLib-AAC [3] e.g. is an interdisciplinary research library for scholars and students of Anglo-American Culture. It has a single interface that merges traditional library media (books, journals, etc.) and electronic resources to a seamless information gateway. This is achieved by integrating the library OPAC and databases with a collection of internet resources.

So far, most individual Virtual Libraries offer different subsections for searching different collections like databases, websites, journals etc. In the long run, the different collections will be integrated by metasearches.

## 2.2  Electronic Journals Library

The Electronic Journals Library "Elektronische Zeitschriftenbibliothek" EZB, a joint initiative of 213 German libraries, offers a quality collection of academic journals through granting fast, structured and standardised access to scientific and academic full text journals. At the moment (May 2003), the EZB contains 15,002 titles, among them 1,762 online-only journals, covering all scientifically relevant subjects. 4,829 journals are offered free-of-charge by the publishing institution. Additionally, participating libraries can offer full text access for their users to most of the journals they subscribe to. Through this joint initiative, the number of journals only available by pay-per-view is limited immensely. Integrating this service into the joint portal will allow access to the valuable licence information held by the EZB.

## 2.3  The Information Alliance

The Information Alliance focuses on providing digital full-texts, published materials and grey literature. Partners of the Information Alliance are information centres and specialised libraries. Together, they make an effort to combine the search results of databases with the electronic full-texts provided either by publishers, grey-literature- or preprint-servers etc. The Information Alliance consists of the following single services: GetInfo, EconDoc, Medpilot, and infoconnex.

# 3  Concept – Metadata and Architecture

An agreement on a set of core metadata is necessary for the realisation of cross-searching distributed metadata collections. The development of a metadata model (vascoda Application Profile) that would allow the user to perform multidisciplinary research simultaneously in several high quality metadata collections will be of prior importance. An important feature is the stock taking and evaluation of the metadata formats used by all partners, which will result in the formulation of a core set of metadata for cross-searching the distributed metadata collections. In a final step all partners have to map their local metadata elements according to a common metadata format provided by vascoda and defined in a specific Application Profile. In general this process is called normalisation of metadata.

The vascoda metadata model will consider experiences and developments that have emerged from the context of the MetaLib project [4] where an extensive survey of all Virtual Libraries partners' metadata formats was done via a questionnaire [5]. 14 Virtual Libraries answered the questionnaire, therewith covering subject fields like history, psychology, economics and others. Besides gathering information about document types, search language, cataloguing rules, thesauri and classification systems one main goal was the analysis of all metadata elements used by partners and whether these elements are based on the Dublin Core Metadata Element Set [6]. The result of this survey was the recommendation of a metadata core set (VLib Application Profile [7]).

For the definition of such a core set the following aspects need to be considered:
- which metadata elements are supported by each partner
- semantic definition of each element (including refinements and encoding schemes)
- syntactic definition of each element (rules, codes, standards, etc.)
- cataloguing rules, e.g. for creator, description etc.
- repeatability of elements
- form of obligation of each element (e.g. mandatory, recommended, optional)
- language qualifier (for title, description, subject) to inform about the language of the metadata
- which administrative elements are necessary for the technical realisation of the common broker service (e.g. acronym and URL of each partners' service)

The VLib Application Profile will probably be the basis of the vascoda Application Profile. Especially the metadata formats brought in by the Information Alliance partners need to be strongly considered. These partners will not provide such a detailed set of metadata as the Virtual Libraries. The realisation of a first step basic search (release 1, see below) across the metadata elements like "Title", "Creator", "Subject" is not likely to cause major difficulties. Only more sophisticated search functions like "Wildcard-Search" could be limited as some Virtual Library partners cannot support this function for technical reasons.

Going one step further and trying to develop an advanced search where single metadata elements are cross-searchable requires a detailed analysis of the new partners' (EZB and partners of the Information Alliance) services. To offer a search e.g. for "Creator" a couple of agreements are needed. If for example searching across first and last names simultaneously was not allowed, cataloguing rules for the element "Creator" would need to be discussed.

A major advantage has been the VLib partners' quick agreement on the internationally known Dublin Core metadata format that is going to serve as an interchange format between their own metadata formats and the vascoda metadata core set. Using

Dublin Core metadata elements including refinements, qualifiers and controlled vocabulary systems guarantees a maximum of standardisation and interoperability and allows future co-operation with other information providers.

To ensure interoperability the core set was established and will be developed further according to international norms and standards. The Library of Congress for example developed and now maintains a Metadata Object Description Schema (MODS [8]) which is also considered in the Dublin Core Library Application Profile [9].

A standard template for describing each metadata element will consider current developments done by the European Standardisation Agency CEN/ISSS in the ISSS WS-MMI-DC "Dublin Core Application Profile Guidelines" [10].

Partners agreed to use HTTP [11] and SOAP [12] technology for developing the first release with basic search functions. Partners of the Information Alliance already developed a first test version for cross-searching their distributed services. FIZ Karlsruhe is now going to develop the technical framework for the search engine. At the moment the VLib partners are examining their ability to support the required protocols.

## 4  Outlook

The first release of vascoda will include a simple search over the digital information resources provided by the Information Alliance and by the subject-based Virtual Libraries (Subject Gateways) combined with links to information and resources provided by the EZB. In addition there will be links to all the other services provided by the three main players. The first release will be published in August 2003 to present first results at the IFLA 2003 conference in Berlin.

The second release will offer complex search and browsing options that can be realised through a standardisation of metadata and possibly a joint cataloguing database for internet resources.

Enhanced subject access is considered to be one of the key services offered by portals. Thus an important part of the vascoda service is going to be the provision of subject browsing service across the distributed metadata collections. The participating partners, therefore, will investigate ways that would enable the user to browse across a single subject hierarchy covering the content of all participating services.

In order to accomplish subject cross-browsing between all distributed metadata collections of the participating services, the different local classification systems need to be mapped to a common classification system. The Vlib partners already agreed to use the Dewey Decimal Classification (DDC) as the common browsing system. Some partners will have to map their local classification system to DDC while other partners already use the DDC to catalogue their resources.

This task will comprise some theoretical investigations especially regarding the two other main players (EZB and the Information Alliance), a certain check of existing similar approaches (e.g. Renardus [13]), development of guidelines to ensure a standardised way of mapping activities and finally the mapping effort itself.

# 5  Co-operation

World-wide, information specialists and scientists are working on gateways and portals to create access points to quality information. The Resource Discovery Network (RDN [14]), the Renardus service or science.gov [15] to name just a few – already offer an impressive service. In some fields their aims are similar to vascoda's and in some others their objectives differ. Exchanging knowledge and experiences with these and other networks is going to be crucial for developing a high-quality product such as vascoda to guarantee its future connectivity with other international products. Mutual exchange and learning from each other enhances everybody's ability to make the most of their respective resources as well as saving time, money and manpower by sharing technologies and knowledge thus drawing on already existing developments. An important precondition for these goals is to anticipate standardisation activities with regard to their interoperability with other information broker and portals on a maximum level.

# References

1.  Vascoda: http://www.vascoda.de/ URLs of partners and sponsors can be found here.
2.  The Subject-Based Virtual Library - A Co-operation of German Virtual Libraries, http://www.virtuellefachbibliothek.de/VLibEnglHome.htm
3.  Virtual Library of Anglo-American Culture, http://www.sub.uni-goettingen.de/vlib/
4.  Metadata Server, http://www2.sub.uni-goettingen.de/
5.  Vlib Fragebogen, http://www2.sub.uni-goettingen.de/metacore/fragebogen/
6.  Overview of documentation for DCMI Metadata Terms, http://www.dublincore.org/usage/documents/overview/
7.  Vlib Application Profile, Version 1.0: 2001-10-05 http://www2.sub.uni-goettingen.de/metacore/empfehlungen/core_set.pdf
8.  Metadata Object Description Schema (MODS), http://www.loc.gov/standards/mods/
9.  DC Library Application Profile, http://www.dublincore.org/documents/2002/09/24/library-application-profile/
10. Metadata Dublin Core (MMI-DC) Workshop, http://www.cenorm.be/isss/Workshop/MMI-DC/
11. HTTP – Hypertext Transfer Protocol, http://www.w3.org/Protocols/
12. XML Protocol Working Group, http://www.w3.org/2000/xp/Group/
13. Renardus, http://www.renardus.org/
14. Resource Discovery Network, http://www.rdn.ac.uk/
15. Government Science Portal, http://science.gov/

# Scenario-Based Generation of Digital Library Services

Rohit Kelapure, Marcos André Gonçalves, and Edward A. Fox

Department of Computer Science
Virginia Tech
Blacksburg, VA 24061, USA
{rkelapur,mgoncalv,fox}@vt.edu

**Abstract.** We describe the development, implementation, and deployment of a new generic digital library generator yielding implementations of digital library services from models of DL "societies" and "scenarios". The distinct aspects of our solution are: 1) approach based on a formal, theoretical framework; 2) use of state-of-the-art database and software engineering techniques such as domain-specific declarative languages, scenario synthesis, componentized and model driven architectures; 3) analysis centered on scenario-based design and DL societal relationships; 4) automatic transformations and mappings from scenarios to workflow designs and from these to Java implementations, 5) special attention paid to issues of simplicity of implementation, modularity, reusability, and extensibility. We demonstrate the feasibility of the approach through a number of examples.

## 1 Introduction

With the increasing amount of information being created digitally or converted to digital formats and made available through Digital Libraries (DLs), there is greater demand for building tailored DL services to attend the preferences and needs of diverse communities. However, construction and adaptation of such services takes significant effort when not assisted by methodologies, tools, and environments that support the complete life cycle of DL development, including requirements gathering, conceptual modeling, rapid prototyping, and code generation/reuse. With current systems these activities are only partially supported, generally in an uncorrelated way that may lead to inconsistencies and incompleteness. Moreover, such existing approaches are not buttressed by comprehensive and formal foundations and theories. In this paper we describe a new generic DL generator based on the 5S (Streams, Structures, Spaces, Scenarios, Societies) formal framework [1] , focusing on support for two key aspects of DLs: "societies" and "scenarios" [2]. The first relates to support for users, user communities, collaboration, agents, resource manager routines, and other similar entities. The latter relates to services, workflow, and other descriptions and implementations of DL functionality. The principal contribution of our work is the development, implementation, and deployment of a generic DL generator that can be used by DL designers to semi-automatically produce tailored DL services from models of societies and scenarios. By doing this the generator attempts to bridge the gap between DL models and system implementation, i.e., between concept and execution, therefore partially validating the formal theory of 5S. We demonstrate the feasibility of this approach and substantiate our claims by providing two examples that illustrate the features of the generator. This paper is

T. Koch and I.T. Sølvberg (Eds.): ECDL 2003, LNCS 2769, pp. 263–275, 2003.

organized as follows. Section 2 describes our approach and development environment. Section 3 is the core of the paper and details examples, architecture, and implementation of our digital library generator. The "Examples" subsection focuses on extensibility and reusability. Section 4 deals with related work, while Section 5 concludes the paper.

## 2    Approach

Our objective is to cover the whole process of DL development, from requirements to analysis, analysis to design, design to implementation. We aim to generate "tailored" DL software satisfying the particular requirements of specific DL societies. The basic idea is to develop models, languages, and tools able to capture the rich set of DL requirements and properties of particular settings and to automatically convert these "patterns" into different representations by properly "compiling", transforming, and mapping models in different levels and phases of the DL development process. The assumption is that automatic transformations and mappings diminish the risk of inconsistency and increase productivity. This view will be supported by:

1. Having a model based approach that allows the DL designer to describe: 1) the kinds of multimedia information the DL supports (Stream Model); 2) how that information is structured and organized (Structural Model); 3) different logical and presentational properties and operations of DL components (Spatial Model); 4) the behavior of the DL (Scenario Model); and 5) the different societies of actors and managers of services that act together to carry out the DL behavior (Societal Model) [3]. We have organized and formalized these and other DL notions into the 5S (Streams, Structures, Spaces, Societies, Scenarios) framework. This formal framework provides a foundation for the DL generator.
2. Using a domain-specific language based on 5S, 5SL, for declarative specification and automatic generation of DLs. Domain specific languages enable applications to be programmed with domain abstractions, thereby allowing compact, clear, and machine-processable specifications to replace detailed and abstruse code [4].
3. Using scenario based design for defining the behavior of a system. Scenarios keep design discussion focused on user activities; more specifically, they keep design discussion focused on the level of task organization that actors experience in their tasks. In 5S, we envision scenarios as sequences of events that modify states of a computation in order to accomplish some functional requirement. We use scenarios to describe the behavior of DL services and societal interactions.
4. Implementing a code generator that allows a DL designer to provide a modeling specification in terms of scenarios and societies. This generates implementations using precise transformations/mappings. The generated DL makes use of well defined components that each carry out key DL functions interacting with one another using lightweight protocols. We draw heavily upon work with the Open Archives Initiative Protocol for Metadata Harvesting (OAI-PMH) [1] and Open Digital Libraries (ODL [2, 3]), so generation can occur atop a number of DL toolkits (initially two).

We adopt an approach shown to be highly effective in other areas of computing: develop powerful theories and (meta)models (i.e., 5S); use them to develop formal specifications (i.e., 5SL), and generate tailored systems from those specifications (using 5SLGen). We explain the approach in the context of the classical software engineering process (see Fig. 1). During requirements gathering (see 1 in Fig. 1) the DL designer captures all "societal" conditions and capabilities to which the DL must conform. 5S provides a common ground terminology and domain model that is close to the DL world and furnishes precisely defined concepts so that the resulting description is understandable by end users. The role of the DL expert is to design a metamodel for DLs based on 5S, which will be used for modeling the DL. In the analysis phase (see 2 in Fig. 1), the requirements are formally captured in 5SL. The DL designer must be aware of functional requirements — what services a community needs and what form of interaction these services should have with the users of the DL: publishers, searchers, and administrators. Modeling such a complex system using only an XML-based language requires a great deal of knowledge of the 5S theory and language syntax. Accordingly, we introduced 5SGraph [5], a visual modeling tool that helps designers to model a DL instance without knowing the theoretical foundations and the syntactical details of 5SL. The focus of the design phase (see 3 in Fig. 1) is to produce models that are closer to the implementation and the target architecture, but still preserve the structure of the system as captured by the analysis model. 5SLGen produces design models from 5SL models by transforming higher-level 5SL concepts into object-oriented classes and workflows. This transformation involves scenario analysis and scenario synthesis. Finally in the implementation phase (see 4 in Fig. 1), 5SLGen uses the produced design models to generate running DL services by integrating components from pools, mapping models to specific target platforms and languages (e.g., Java, Perl), and compiling and producing new components and subsystems. This digital library generator, 5SLGen, is the focus of this paper.

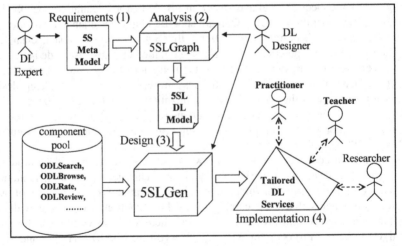

**Fig. 1.** Overview of the architecture for DL modeling and generation

# 3    The 5SLGEN Digital Library Generator

## 3.1    Model

We envision the services exposed by a DL to be either of the composite or elementary type. Elementary services provide the basic infrastructure for the DL. Examples include collecting, indexing, rating, and linking.    Composite services can be composed of other services (elementary or composed) by reusing or extending them. For example, a relevance feedback service extends the capabilities of a basic search service while a lesson plan building service can use already existing searching, browsing, and binding services to find and organize relevant resources.

The problem of composability of services has been studied recently, mainly in the Web community [6, 7]. However, DL services are restricted to certain specific types with constrained inputs and outputs, therefore making the problem more manageable and possible to be treated with domain specific techniques. Figure 2 shows a model for the services exposed by the tailored DL produced by 5SLGen. The model defines composite services recursively as an aggregation of other services, composite or elementary. Elementary services do not rely on other services to fulfill their responsibilities while composite services act like umbrella structures that bring together other services, which collaborate to implement certain functionality. The application logic of a composite service is described by a workflow, i.e., a combination of control and data flows that mirror the behavior defined in the services scenarios, including invocations of other services. Statecharts [8] and Petri nets [9] are possible notations for formally representing workflows. In our implementations we chose statecharts to represent the workflow of a service [10]. Statecharts represent a compact way of describing the dynamic aspects of the system. Statecharts connect events and states. When an event is received, the system leaves its current state, initiates the actions specified for the transition, and enters a new state. The next state depends on the current state as well as the event.

The distinct aspects of this model are: 1) the combination of an explicit workflow and service aggregation to support composite services; 2) the emphasis on scenario-based modeling of services and the automatic generation of workflows from them; and 3) the role of the service manager (a societal member) as the binding point for societal relationships, scenario interactions, and spatial visualizations. From an architectural and implementation point of view, point 1 becomes significant, since combining a small set of basic DL services (like searching and browsing) from a pool of DL components should allow a designer to model and generate most digital libraries (at least from the behavioral point of view) with a minimum amount of coding. The only situations when coding is unavoidable are, for example, when a specific behavior of a composite service (e.g., Rocchio based expansion of a query in relevance feedback) is not defined by any component in the core pool or cannot be reused (e.g., due to incompatibility of interfaces).

More importantly, the model also shows how the 5 'Ss' help when defining all components of a real, implemented DL. Services are implemented as components taken from the pool or automatically generated from the scenarios and their interactions/relationships. Service managers define the context or functionality of the service in terms of its operations and the data it expects, and are associated with a spatial (presentational) model of a user interface. It is interesting to notice the connections between the service manager roles and the classical Model-View-Controller (MVC) architecture of user interfaces [11], which explicitly separates functionality, behavior, and presentation and has helped facilitate the development of user interfaces that are modular and extensible. Service managers and actors communicate through streams (e.g., protocols) and structures (e.g., structured streams such as metadata specifications and digital objects). Finally the model provides the basic architectural underpinnings for the creation of DL generators, as described in Section 3.3.

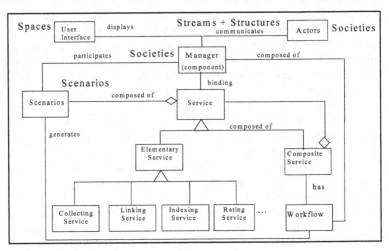

**Fig. 2.** DL Service Composition Model or Pattern

## 3.2   Examples

In this section we present examples of two services, a Relevance Feedback Search service and a Lesson Plan Building service, implemented using 5SLGen. The services exposed follow the model explained in Figure 2, and illustrate reusability and extensibility.

### 3.2.1   Extensibility: A Relevance Feedback Service

Scenario 1: Relevance feedback is a well known technique to improve quality of search services. A relevance feedback service extends a basic search service by allowing the user to choose from the results of a search the documents that are relevant. The selected relevant documents are then used by the Relevance Feedback Manager to construct an expanded query (using the Rocchio method, for example), which is then run to retrieve the next set of documents to be presented to the user.

Figure 3 shows the relationship between the relevance feedback service and the search service (left part) and describes the relevance feedback scenario in terms of a UML sequence diagram (middle part). A sequence diagram focuses on the time ordering of events between members of societies. These members appear along the top margin of a dashed line that represents a timeline. Events can be associated with actions that the service managers perform to provide a given functionality. For the sake of brevity we do not show the corresponding 5SL modeling in XML; the interested reader is pointed to [5SL] for syntactic details. The <<extends>> relationship specifies that an instance of a relevance feedback search service includes the behavior of a search service and adds specific events, subject to specific conditions (e.g., the set of relevant documents cannot be empty). The scenario shows that all the events associated with the basic search scenario occur in the relevance feedback scenario, with the addition of the expandQuery event and synchronous response. The statechart for the Relevance Feedback Manager derived from the scenario is shown in the figure too. There are only two states: the system transitions from the default to the "expanded query" state after reception of the expandQuery event (if the condition is true) and immediately transitions back to the default state where it can receive other requests.

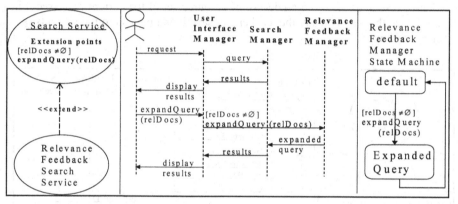

**Fig. 3.** Relationships between services for relevance feedback

### 3.2.2    Reusability: Lesson Plan Building Service

Scenario 2: A lesson plan aggregates specific educational metadata and correlated resources (e.g., papers, simulations) available in the Computing and Information Technology Interactive Digital Educational Library (CITIDEL, www.citidel.org) into a coherent package useful for some CS teaching activity. A specific service manager called VIADUCT supports this service, which can be used only by teachers registered with CITIDEL. To build a lesson plan, the teacher uses the information-seeking services of CITIDEL (i.e., searching and browsing) to look for relevant resources to a specific lesson, chooses among those using any subjective criteria (e.g., by relevance, by date), assembles a number of the chosen resources together using a binder service, and associates descriptive metadata such as typical DC-based ones like author, identifier, language – as well as specific ones such as topic area, target audience, and time required for the whole lesson plan object. The teacher has to explicitly publish the lesson plan to allow students to view it. To allow a select group of people to view the lesson plan, the teacher saves the plan, returns to the main VIADUCT user information page, re-opens the project, and gives the project URL to whomever she wishes.

Figure 4 shows that the lesson plan building (LPB) service includes three other services: Searching, Browsing, and Binding, as well as the main scenario of the LPB service. Figure 5 presents the statechart generated from scenario synthesis of the main scenario with other related scenarios of this service (not shown for brevity). The teacher starts the construction of a new lesson plan from the main menu (see 1 in Fig. 5). The lesson plan edit page allows the teacher to fill out basic metadata about the plan and organize a number of related resources together (see 2 in Fig. 5). To locate relevant resources the teacher can either search or browse (see 3 and 4 in Fig. 5) the collection according to some criteria and sorting order. Having the results of an initial search/browse activity the user can either: 1) search for a similar document (see 5 in Fig. 5); 2) browse a particular entry for details (see 6 in Fig. 5); 3) perform another search (see 7 in Fig. 5); or 4) select a number of items to put in her binder (see 8 in Fig. 5). If the user chooses the latest option the binder is shown and she can transfer a number of resources from the binder to the resource set of the current plan (see 9 in Fig. 5). Once the plan is ready the teacher can save it and publish to the students (see 10 and 11 in Fig. 5).

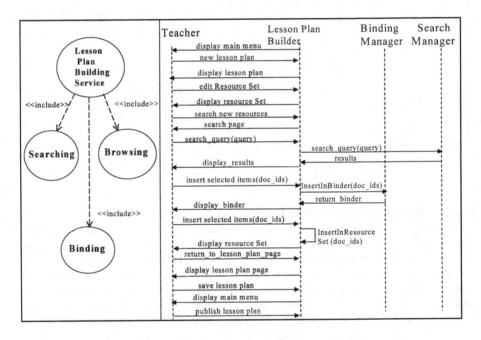

**Fig. 4.** Relationships between the services for the lesson plan in VIADUCT

## 3.3  5SLGen Architecture and Implementation

The architecture of 5SLGen is shown in Figure 6. The generated system is organized around the idea of a clean separation between service managers, that implement operations and carry data; views, for displaying all or a portion of the data; and controllers, for handling events that affect the data or the view(s) [11]. The functionality of elementary services such as searching, browsing, etc., is provided by a component. The ODL project has exploited the conceptual framework provided by the OAI-PMH to develop a pool of components that communicate through a family of lightweight protocols, using XML as the data interchange mechanism. As the implementation of the component can be in any language, in order to use them on a particular platform or with a specific language we need to define wrappers that translate foreign operations on the component to their native operation. We have defined such Java wrappers for ODL components that expose the functionality of the component through a Java interface. Each wrapper talks to its component using the extended semantics of the OAI-PMH. Any component that follows the ODL protocols can be included in the component pool, by defining a wrapper that exposes its functionality in Java. The standard semantics of the OAI-PMH protocol thus enables the composition of heterogeneous components with the wrappers acting as a bridge between the protocol implementation and the target platform.

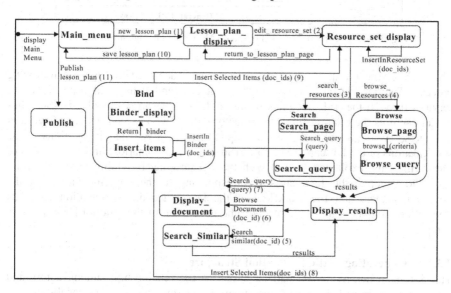

**Fig. 5.** Statechart diagram of the VIADUCT system

In the context of 5SLGen, the service managers either are represented by one or more component wrappers or are generated from the 5SL-Societies model. The generated service managers may contain skeletal code for operations and capabilities not defined in any component of the pools; this code needs to be provided by the designer. The controller maps onto the workflow of the system generated from the 5SL-Scenarios model. The view corresponds to the user interface presentation. The DL designer binds the presentation elements with the service managers to complete the implementation of the generated DL services.

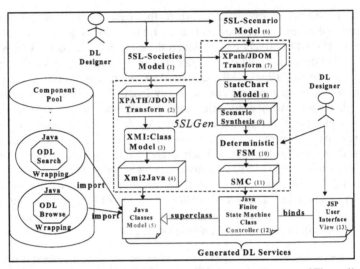

**Fig. 6.** Architecture of 5SLGen based on MVC (expanding part of Figure 1)

This architecture for the generated DL services is achieved through the following process: The DL designer captures the structural and behavioral aspects of DL services through the 5SL-Societies model and 5SL-Scenarios model. 5SL-Societies model captures the relationships among actors (those who use services) and services managers, whereas 5SL-Scenarios capture their dynamic interactions. The specifications of the DL captured in 5SL (Societies and Scenarios) undergo a series of transformations (explained below) with the DL designer providing input at certain stages to generate the Java classes corresponding to the implementations of the service managers and the workflow of the DL. Once the presentation elements (views) are coupled with the controller, the generation of the tailored DL service is complete.

### 3.3.1    Generating Static Contextual Structure

The 5SL-Societies model is realized based on the relationships among actors and service managers and the set of operations that define the services' capabilities. In order to generate Java classes from the 5SL-Societies model we have chosen an intermediate step of transforming (see 2 in Figure 6) the 5SL-Societies XML Model into a XMI [13] representation model (see 3 in Figure 6) using the JDOM and XPATH XML APIs. XMI is an XML based industry standard to enable easy interchange of metadata between modeling tools and between tools and metadata repositories. Many CASE tools serialize UML diagrams to XMI. Generation of XMI files for the 5SL-Societies model enables the exchange of the 5S-Societies model among various UML modeling tools supporting modeling as well as forward and reverse engineering. Moreover, existing freeware tools (see 4 in Figure 6) enable the generation of Java code from the serialized XMI Model (XMI2Java). We use an open source XMI2Java implementation to generate Java classes that implement the service managers (see 5 in Figure 6) for the generated DL.

### 3.3.2 Generating Dynamic Behavior

The 5SL-Scenarios model is used to capture the dynamic behavior of services (e.g., see Figures 3 and 4) as scenarios. In order to describe the whole behavior of a DL service, a great multitude of scenarios is required to capture the complete set of possible societal interactions. Scenarios can contain other scenarios and in many cases are only small variations of others. This requires an approach for scenario integration in order to capture the whole behavior of the system. Also, in order to be able to generate an implementation from the scenarios, the level of abstraction needs to be reduced to a more concrete model in terms of computational actions and change of states that occur during scenario execution. These problems can be addressed by generating a statechart model (see 8 in Figure 6) from the scenarios (see 6 in Figure 6). The mapping from scenarios to statecharts is performed according to the following rules: For any object in a sequence diagram, incoming arrows represent events received by the object and they become transitions (see Section 3.1). Outgoing arrows are actions and they become actions of the transitions leading to the states. The intervals between events become states. The object starts in the default state specified in the 5SL-Societies model [14]. This transformation (see 7 in Figure 6) is achieved by parsing the 5SL-Scenarios modeled in XML with the JDOM and XPATH XML APIs [15, 16] and implementing the rules mentioned above.

Again, since scenarios represent partial descriptions of the system behavior, an approach for scenario composition is needed to produce a more complete specification of the service. As each scenario is mapped to a statechart we synthesize the statecharts derived in the previous step to perform scenario composition. The statecharts are synthesized (see 9 in Fig. 6) according to the following rules [14]: 1) if a transition is common to the two statecharts, it is taken only once into the final statechart; 2) if at a certain moment in time either one or another scenario is executed, the statecharts are combined with sequential (object can be in only one state) sub-states within a composite state; and 3) if two scenarios are executed at the same time they are combined with concurrent sub-states (object can be in more than one state) within a composite state.

A statechart extends a traditional finite-state machine (FSM) with notions of hierarchy and concurrency. A FSM represents a mathematical model of a system that attempts to reduce the model complexity thereby providing a powerful manner to describe the dynamic behavior of systems and components. The synthesized statechart (Figures 3 and 5) generated using the above rules represents the FSM/workflow for the DL service (see 10 in Fig. 6). To generate code from the FSM we have extended an open source state machine compiler (see 11 in Fig. 6) that compiles the annotated FSM to generate code (Java classes — see 12 in Figure 6) for the controller of the DL services. Before compilation the FSM is annotated by providing component specific implementation details from the DL designer (see Fig. 6).

There are many techniques of implementing state machines; the most common implies some sort of switch or if-then-else statements for implementing state dependent behavior; however this solution is not scalable; therefore we chose to implement FSM using the state design pattern from [17]. The state pattern localizes state-specific behavior in an individual class for each state, and puts all the behavior for that state in a single state object eliminating the necessity for a set of long, look-alike conditional statements. In the context of 5SLGen, when the service manager class receives an event, it delegates the request to its state object, which provides the appropriate state specific behavior.

The lesson plan building and relevance feedback service have been implemented using the above generation process. Manual intervention is required for: first annotating the FSM with component specific implementation details, and second providing the views for the data. Building on current work, we plan to implement a fully functional and automatic version of 5SLGen before the conference starts. When functional, this will amount to a total of about 2000 lines of code.

## 4  Related Work

The first work to advocate a goal-oriented requirements analysis approach for digital libraries is [18], but that work does not propose any development tool or environment. The closest approach to our DL generator is the collection services and plug-in architecture of Greenstone [19]. However their architecture covers only portions of the Stream and Structural models of 5S with little support for modeling and generation of customized DL services (other than basic searching and browsing).

While much attention has been paid to DL architectures and systems, very few works tackle the problem of integrated DL design, conceptual modeling, and requirements gathering. Examples of work on DL architectures and systems include: monolithic systems (e.g., Greenstone[19], MARIAN[20]), componentized architectures (e.g, ODL[12], OpenDlib[21]), agent-based architectures (e.g., UMDL[22]), and layered architectures (e.g., Alexandria[23]). Our declarative/generative approach should be generalizable for any of those systems/architectures by taking some or all of those systems as part of our component pools. There is no reason why those systems and their components can not be incorporated into our component pools, given that they export clear, reusable software interfaces with accessible entry points.

Most research done in the area of code generation from requirements has not been directed towards specific domains such as DLs. Most CASE tools do not address issues raised by research in scenario-based requirements analysis and design such as scenario generation, management of scenario descriptions, analysis and integration of scenarios, and bridging the gap between scenario descriptions and software designs and implementation [2]. We have attempted to tackle the above problems and to bridge the model system gap through the 5S framework.

## 5  Conclusions and Future Work

We have presented a new digital library generator capable of producing running versions of DL services from models of DL scenarios and societies and pools of components. Automatic mappings from 5SL societies and scenarios models to code have helped diminish the risk of inconsistency and incompleteness in implementations of DL services. Code generation on the basis of the 5S metamodel supports our claim for a model driven architecture. Research problems such as scenario synthesis and scenario generation have been tackled by implementing an algorithm for scenario synthesis and modeling scenarios with 5SGraph. The implementation of DLs with simple Web Service-like components, instead of monolithic software, facilitates extensibility and reusability. The architecture of the generated DL services is based on a clear separation between model, behavior, and presentation. This separation provides for clarity of design, extensibility, and modularity of generated code. Future work will aim especially to reduce the amount of manual intervention needed from the designer. For example, the state machine compiler (SMC) responsible for generation of Java code from the annotated state machine does not support parameterized events/actions which requires manual modification of the FSM. In the current implementation of 5SLGen the DL designer determines the component to be used for the service. We envision that the components used in 5SLGen will eventually be implemented as web services. Thus the mapping described above can be determined programatically using the WSDL [7] document exposed by the web service. We are modifying SMC to support these capabilities. Also we are investigating (semi-) automatic (rather than manual) ways of generating the user interface from the 5S-Spaces model and connecting them with the controller classes. Finally, once all those issues are solved we plan to connect the generation tool with the 5SGraph modeling tool to yield a complete CASE tool for DLs based on the 5S metamodel.

# References

1.  M. A. Goncalves, E. A. Fox, L. T. Watson, and N. A. Kipp, "Streams, Structures, Spaces, Scenarios, Societies (5S): A Formal Model for Digital Libraries," Virginia Tech, CS Dept. TR-03-04, 2003. http://eprints.cs.vt.edu:8000/archive/00000646/ (re-submitted after revision from an earlier version, for publication in ACM Transactions on Information Systems)
2.  J. M. Carroll, *Scenario-based design: Envisioning work and technology in system development*. New York: John Wiley and Sons, 1995.
3.  M. A. Goncalves and E. A. Fox, "5SL – A Language for Declarative Specification and Generation of Digital Libraries," in *Proceedings JCDL'2002*, Portland, OR: ACM, 2002.
4.  D. S. Batory, C. Johnson, B. MacDonald, and D. v. Heeder, "Achieving extensibility through product-lines and domain-specific languages: a case study," *TOSEM*, vol. 11, pp. 191–214, 2002.
5.  Q. Zhu, "5SGraph: A Modeling Tool for Digital Libraries," Virginia Tech CS Dept., Masters Thesis, 2002. http://scholar.lib.vt.edu/theses/available/etd-11272002-210531/
6.  M. H. Burstein, J. R. Hobbs, O. Lassila, D. Martin, D. V. McDermott, S. A. McIlraith, S. Narayanan, M. Paolucci, T. R. Payne, and K. P. Sycara, "DAML-S: Web Service Description for the Semantic Web," International Semantic Web Conference, 2002.
7.  F. Curbera, M. Duftler, R. Khalaf, W. Nagy, N. Mukhi, and S. Weerawarana, "Unraveling the Web Services Web: An Introduction to SOAP, WSDL, and UDDI," *IEEE Internet Computing*, vol. 6, pp. 86–93, 2002.
8.  G. Booch, I. Jacobson, J. Rumbaugh, and J. Rumbaugh, *The Unified Modeling Language User Guide*: Addison-Wesley Pub Co, 1998.
9.  W. Reisig, *Petri nets: an introduction*: Springer-Verlag, New York, Inc., 1985.
10. D. Harel, "Statecharts: A Visual Formalism for Complex Systems," *Science of Computer Programming*, vol. 8, pp. 231–274, 1987. http://citeseer.nj.nec.com/harel87statecharts.html

11. F. Buschmann, R. Meunier, H. Rohnert, P. Sommerlad, and M. Stal, *Pattern-Oriented Software Architecture: A System of Patterns*, vol. 1: John Wiley & Son Ltd., 1996.

12. H. Suleman and E. A. Fox, "A Framework for Building Open Digital Libraries," *D-Lib Magazine*, vol. 7, 2001. http://www.dlib.org/dlib/december01/suleman/12suleman.html

13. OMG, "OMG-XML Metadata Interchange (XMI) Specification, v1.2": OMG, 2002, pp. 268. http://cgi.omg.org/docs/formal/02-01-01.pdf

14. S. Vasilache and J. Tanaka, "Synthesizing Statecharts from Multiple Interrelated Scenarios," Zheng Zhou, China, 2001.

15. J. Hunter, "JDOM 1.0"Java Community Process, 2001. http://jcp.org/en/jsr/detail?id=102#4

16. W3C, "XML Path Language (XPath) Version 1.0", J. Clark and S. DeRose, eds., 1999. http://www.w3.org/TR/xpath

17. E. Gamma, R. Helm, R. Johnson, and J. Vlissides, *Design Patterns*, 1st edition ed: Addison-Wesley Pub. Co., 1995.

18. D. Bolchini and P. Paolini, "Goal-Oriented Requirements Specification for Digital Libraries," *Lecture Notes in Computer Science*, vol. 2458, pp. 107–115, 2002.

19. I. H. Witten, R. J. McNab, S. J. Boddie, and D. Bainbridge, "Greenstone: A Comprehensive Open-Source Digital Library Software System," in *Proceedings of the Fifth ACM Conference on Digital Libraries: DL '00, June 2–7, 2000, San Antonio, TX*. New York: ACM Press, 2000, pp. 113–121.

20. M. A. Gonçalves, R. K. France, and E. A. Fox, "MARIAN: Flexible Interoperability for Federated Digital Libraries," in *Procs of the 5th European Conference on Research and Advanced Technology for Digital Libraries*. Darmstadt, Germany: 2001, pp. 161–172.

21. D. Castelli and P. Pagano, "OpenDLib: A Digital Library Service System," ECDL 2002, Rome, Italy, 2002.

22. P. Weinstein and G. Alloway, "Seed Ontologies: growing digital libraries as distributed, intelligent systems," in *Second ACM International Conference on Digital Libraries, Philadelphia, PA*. New York: ACM Press, 1997.

23. J. Frew, M. Freeston, N. Freitas, L. Hill, G. Janée, K. Lovette, R. Nideffer, T. Smith, and Q. Zheng, "The Alexandria Digital Library Architecture," *IJODL*, vol. 2, pp. 259–268, 2000.

# An Evaluation of Document Prefetching in a Distributed Digital Library

Jochen Hollmann[1], Anders Ardö[2], and Per Stenström[1]

[1] Department of Computer Engineering
Chalmers University of Technology
412 96  Göteborg, Sweden
{joho,pers}@ce.chalmers.se,

[2] Department of Information Technology
Lund University
Box 118
221 00 Lund, Sweden
anders@it.lth.se

**Abstract.** Latency is a fundamental problem for all distributed systems including digital libraries. To reduce user perceived delays both caching – keeping accessed objects for future use – and prefetching – transferring objects ahead of access time – can be used. In a previous paper we have reported that caching is not worthwhile for digital libraries due to low re-access frequencies.

In this paper we evaluate our previous findings that prefetching can be used instead. To do this we have set up an experimental prefetching proxy which is able to retrieve documents from remote fulltext archives before the user demands them. Using a simple prediction to keep the overhead of unnecessarily transfered data limited, we find that it is possible to cut the user perceived average delay a factor of two.

## 1  Introduction

Within the last decade, almost all major academic publishers have built up Digital Libraries (DL) which offer fulltext archives of conference and journal articles in electronic form. This has given the research community better accessibility to articles from conferences and journals. Some university libraries have integrated the bibliographic databases from various publishers into a single point of access, so that the users can effectively search many fulltext archives at once. DTV's Article Database Service DADS [1,2] is such a system which implements a large amalgamated index database covering many publishers, searchable through a gateway which redirects fulltext requests to the publishers fulltext servers. This avoids the cost of huge replicated archives as well as many copyright issues. As a result, digital libraries are realized as a distributed information system.

Transferring documents from remote servers distributed around the world suffers from the latency of networks and servers. While increasing network and

T. Koch and I.T. Sølvberg (Eds.): ECDL 2003, LNCS 2769, pp. 276–287, 2003.

server bandwidth can partly mitigate its impact, the latency time for an unloaded infrastructure is still significant.

Standard techniques to hide latency are *caching* and *prefetching*, and have been applied to computer systems [3] as well as to web-based systems [4]. Caching works by keeping a copy of previously accessed data close to the consumer for future re-use and is thus useful for frequently accessed objects. Unfortunately almost all accessed articles in digital libraries are accessed with very low frequencies. This is the reason why caching does not work well for DL as we observed in a previous study [5].

Prefetching, transferring a data object ahead of access time, can be applied even if the data objects are accessed only once. If perfect knowledge of future accesses would exist, it would be possible to transfer data objects sufficiently in advance so that a local copy would be available close to the user; thus, hiding almost all of the latency. In reality it is impossible to have perfect knowledge about future accesses; hence, a critical issue for prefetching is to establish a good predictor.

Digital article libraries can organize document accesses as a two-step process. First the bibliographic record is shown, then the user can proceed to access the fulltext from the remote server. In a previous study [6] we found that a good prediction can be made if a prefetch is issued when the article abstract is viewed. In this study, the goal is to see whether such a prefetching approach works under real-world conditions by evaluating it in the context of real users.

The specific research questions addressed by this research are: How much of the network and server latency can be hidden? How much does the network traffic increase by superfluous and unnecessary prefetch requests? Finally, how long should we keep prefetched documents in the cache, before we decide that the user will not access them in the future?

To answer these questions we have set up an experimental gateway which implements the proposed prefetching scheme. We have made this system available to all members of our university during almost half a year and logged their activities, as well as the document transfers. By analyzing the resulting user access log files and comparing them to a simulated environment without prefetching, we show the effects of prefetching. We were able to cut the average latency the user experiences by a factor of two. We have also found that this increases the number of document transfers by less than a factor two.

As for the rest of this paper, in Section 2 we describe our digital library system followed by the experimental setup in Section 3, before introducing the evaluation method in the next section. In Section 5 we show our results. Section 6 gives an overview of prefetching mainly in the area of the World Wide Web. Finally we summarize and conclude.

## 2   Distributed Digital Library for Articles

The aim of every library is to make a large collection of publications easily accessible to the readers. To achieve this, libraries used to build up an archive as well as an index to enhance searching for a particular publication. With the shift to digital libraries, libraries have stopped collecting periodicals and instead provide licenses to directly access remote fulltext archives offered as a service from most publishers.

While many libraries also rely on web interfaces provided by publishers, some have built their own gateways to access these fulltext archives. Figure 1, taken from our previous paper [6], shows the architecture of such an approach. In an academic environment the university library would typically run a gateway service which has access to an index database and the remote fulltext servers provided by publishers. The gateway may have a document cache to serve some document requests locally.

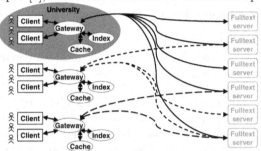

**Fig. 1.** Architecture of a distributed digital library. Adapted from [6]

## 2.1   The DADS System

For the study in this paper we have used DTV's Article Database Service DADS [1,2] as an implementation of the above architecture. DADS was developed with the aim of providing the user with a single point of access to all research related literature by merging the index databases of all major publishers into a single super-database.

The DADS user interface is implemented as a web application. Users interact with the DADS system using a standard web browser, which displays dynamically generated web pages. This implements a user model for the search process shown in Figure 2 (adapted from our previous paper [6]). A user normally starts in the state *search* by providing keywords which should appear within the bibliographic record, for example in the title, the abstract or the authors name. Normally the user wants to reduce the number of hits to a manageable amount. This brings them to the *refine* state. From both states, the user can move on to the *hit list* state, where up to 10 articles are shown. Selecting one of those articles brings them to the *show record* state, where they can view the bibliographic record including the abstract.

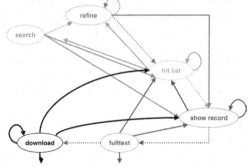

**Fig. 2.** User model during a search session. Adapted from [6]

If the users decide that they want to fetch the whole article, they proceed to the *download* state. To do so, the user has to pass through the *fulltext* state, which offers different delivery methods. A paper copy can be ordered from the library for all articles, while online copies in PDF format are only available for a large but limited subset of the indexed articles. A more detailed description and analysis of the user model can be found in our previous paper [6].

## 2.2   Prefetching

We extended the DADS system by a prefetching component. This was accomplished by adding a file area on the gateway machine as a fulltext cache. We also changed the gateway to manage the prefetch cache in the following way:

- In the state *show record* we check if the corresponding document can be found in the cache. If not, a lock for this document is acquired first before fetching the document from the publishers fulltext archive is started. Locking avoids the occurrence of concurrent prefetches as well as the delivery of incomplete documents to the clients. When the transfer is completed the lock is removed.

- In the state *download* we deliver the paper directly from the cache if it exists and is not locked. If it is locked, we create a dynamic page telling the user that prefetching is in progress and program the user's browser to poll the download page with a short delay again. If it is neither locked nor existing – which is an error condition – we start the actions of the *show record* state and program the user's browser as above.

These two changes are sufficient to implement a simple prefetching strategy.

## 2.3   The Aim of This Study

Given the above system, the overall question is if it allows most of the latency to be hidden. Furthermore we want to find out how large the overhead in terms of increased network traffic is. Particularly we are interested in the following issues:

- The percentage of documents that can be served by prefetched documents from the cache. This critically depends on the time between viewing the abstract and requesting the document.

- How many of the documents are prefetched, but never accessed by the user? Compared to the useful prefetches this gives a measure for the overhead introduced by our scheme.

- Prefetched documents not picked up by the user can potentially pollute the (limited) cache. To avoid this, there should be a strategy for when a document should be considered useless and evicted from the cache.

# 3    Experimental Setup

In order to evaluate our method of prefetching we have set up a DADS gateway at Chalmers University of Technology in Gothenburg, Sweden. The gateway was available to all members of the university, approximately 8000 students and 2000 employees. In order to attract as many potential users as possible on campus, the prefetch experiment was announced in the library newsletter to all departments. It was also promoted as a top link on Chalmers libraries front page. Our volunteer users had not used DADS before, but all users had access to the fulltext archives before by using each publishers web interface. We conducted the prefetch experiment from March 1 until August 15, 2002.

We implemented the gateway using a retired commodity PC running Linux on a Pentium processor with 166MHz and 64MB of RAM. The machine had a disk with 1.6GB used for storing the OS, the gateway and the cache for prefetched documents. Our low cost solution did not have the index database available locally. Instead it connected to the remote index database of the original DADS system in Copenhagen, Denmark. While this inevitably slowed down the navigation interface slightly, it was hardly noticeable, because of the good network connection to Copenhagen, Denmark (14 hops, typical round trip time 17ms, measured bandwidth 1.5MBit/sec). It did not have any influence on the timing behavior we wanted to observe, because this is given by the users and not by the gateway.

We did not implement any cleanup strategy for prefetched documents, neither for those delivered to the user nor for those which were never requested. Instead we kept all prefetched documents in the cache. Only once did we have to clean the cache due to the limited disk space; but again this had no influence on the timing behavior for our measurements.

The navigation interface was stripped down to offer only searching (standard DADS does also include browsing). We configured the interface to search only for articles with fulltext available by default, but did not remove the possibility of searching even for articles without an online fulltext copy. We made this decision because we wanted the users to consider the system as useful as possible, in order to attract as many people as we could. Nor did we remove the *fulltext* page (see Figure 2). While we removed the option to order a printout copy from the library, we still gave the users two alternatives. The first was to download the article from our cache, the second to download the article from the publishers web site. This intermediate step did influence the timing behavior of the user, because the user needed to click on one more hyper link, but we think that the effects were in the range of a second, because the user did proceed quickly.

This decision has the following advantages. Firstly the user could compare our prefetching gateway with the publishers server to experience the difference in speed. Secondly, in case our prefetcher had problems, the users could still get the documents from the publishers fulltext server. And in fact these issues came up, mainly due to the access protection strategies used by some publishers.

# 4    Evaluation Method

In order to analyze the transfer time, start and end points of each document transfer have to be logged. On a per document basis, the prefetch transfer time $PTT$ is defined as the transfer time from the fulltext server to the gateway. Similarly, the client transfer time $CTT$ is defined as the transfer time from the gateway to the client. Note that CTTs are only available for documents requested by the users. Additionally, we define the download time $DT$, which is the user observed delay. Also, the publisher of each document is available.

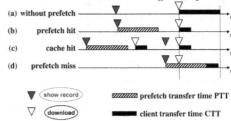

Fig. 3.  Occurrence of events

## 4.1    Classification of Events

For our analysis, we apply the following scheme shown in Figure 3. The download requests from the client are used as time alignment in the following cases:

(a). The figure shows the DT, when fetching directly from the fulltext server. This DT is equal to the PTT in all other cases assuming that the gateway has approximately the same network distance as the clients.

(b). In the case of a successful prefetch, the gateway can prefetch the whole article from the fulltext server before the client requests it. This is possible because the *show record* in the above example occurs long enough in advance. When the client transfers the document from the gateway cache later, the experienced DT will be reduced to CTT due to the local access hiding latency.

(c). Because no cache cleanup strategy is implemented, there may be cases where the document can be served from the cache avoiding another prefetch of the same document. Even in this case the download time is reduced.

(d). In this case our prefetching strategy failed. The time frame from *show record* to the actual *download* is too short to transfer the complete document. In our implementation this delays the transfer to the client. This can potentially lead to an increased DT. In the worst case DT is the sum of PTT and CTT. Streaming the data through the proxy instead of waiting for the prefetch would avoid this, but we decided against it in favor of a simple clean implementation.

Using the above event classification scheme, we can classify all of the download events in our traces into one of the categories (b) to (d) (see Figure 3).

|  | all publishers | $E$ only | $I$ only |
|---|---|---|---|
| Prefetch hits: | 70.46% | 84.17% | 66.53% |
| Prefetch misses: | 14.93% | 3.89% | 15.04% |
| Cache hits: | 14.60% | 11.94% | 18.51% |
| Overhead: | 78.63% | 63.06% | 69.41% |
| not used/used: | 530/674 | 198/314 | 236/340 |
| Average download time |  |  |  |
| with prefetching : | 2.21s | 1.16s | 3.19s |
| without prefetch : | 4.94s | 2.13s | 7.30s |

**Fig. 4.** Field test prefetch statistics

## 4.2   Comparison to Non-prefetching Systems

In order to evaluate our particular configuration it is necessary to compare it to other possible setups. A simulation of alternatives, based on the time stamps available from the traces, is a simple way to do this while preserving the timing behavior of the users. Additionally we need the assumption that the PTT equals the DT without prefetching in place. This is reasonable, because both the client and the gateway are very close to each other compared to the network distance from the fulltext servers.

To simulate a system without prefetching, we move the PTT of case (b) on the time line to the download event, hence transforming it into case (a). This will create a new end point for the DT.

An important part of the analysis is the increase in document transfers, which is caused by prefetched documents not requested by the user later on. We define the overhead introduced by dividing the number of prefetched documents by the number of downloaded documents.

To do this we keep the state on a per document basis. Once a document is prefetched it is useless until it is requested by the user, where it becomes useful.

During our analysis we have found that only two large international publishers were heavily used, while the remaining publishers in our experiment experienced less than 100 download requests each. We have therefore decided to present our results for Publisher $E$ and $I$ as well as for all publishers together. This is especially interesting as $Es$ fulltext archive is approximately 10 times faster than $Is$ archive, both in bandwidth and round trip time. (E: 16 ms round trip, 200 Kbytes/s, 2.3 million articles; I: > 120 ms, 1-30 KBytes/s, 1 million articles). The difference mainly comes from the fact that $Es$ archive is located close by in Europe, while $Is$ archive is located in North America.

## 5   Results

In the first analysis we want to be convinced that our simple prefetching scheme works. Table 4 shows the results. The most important observation is that we get a considerable amount of prefetch hits. Not surprisingly, the prefetch hit rate is a lot higher for the fast $E$ source than the slow $I$ server. Obviously the opposite applies for the prefetch misses.

The 10-20% hit rate due to caching is about equal for all three cases and shows what would be achievable by a pure caching strategy. As for the traffic overhead due to prefetching, we introduce a factor of less than two.

The analysis of average download times shows that it is possible to shorten the download time a factor of two consistently in all cases. Considering that this result could be still improved by overlaying the download phase with the prefetching phase for all hits during prefetch, this result is really encouraging. Hence we conclude that one solution to the latency problem in the domain of digital libraries is prefetching.

This leaves us with one question to answer. How long should we keep pre-fetched documents in the cache before we decide that they are not going to be used?

To answer this question, we have analyzed the time between the *show record* and the *download* state, where available. Figure 5 shows the cumulative distribution during the first hour after an abstract was shown on a logarith-

mic scale. We have also included our previous findings [6] marked *original DADS*, where the users moved less quickly to the document download. Hence our assumption that the users proceed quickly through the *fulltext* state is sound. Also we can clearly see that in almost all cases it is sufficient to keep the article for an hour. If it is not downloaded by then, we can almost be certain that this prefetch wasted only bandwidth. Note that this fig-

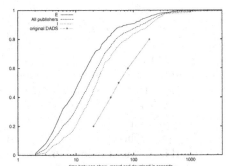

**Fig. 5.** CDF for timing between viewing the abstract and downloading the document

ure does not show the timing between subsequent accesses to the same document.

Hence the conclusion is that we do not have to keep articles for more than one hour, which allows the cache size to be limited.

Considering these results, we should modify our strategy as follows:

- We keep the strategy to fetch an article into the cache, when the user views the abstract.
- If no download occurs during the first hour, we discard the article.
- If a download occurs within an hour, we remove the article with the download.

Note that this approach will eliminate the cache hits, as articles are always removed from the cache on the first download.

# 6   Related Work

An alternative to prefetching is traditional caching, which not only reduces the latency but also reduces the data transferred. Since in digital libraries the articles are neither modified by the clients nor updated on the servers, this seems to be an ideal approach at first glance. Unfortunately caching requires multiple accesses to the same document in order to work. In a previous study [5] we have shown that this is not the case for 85% of the accessed documents, when not considering re-accesses from the same client. So even with prefetching it does not make sense to keep once accessed articles in the cache for the future. Apart from the small latency gain and the costs, this can also involve copyright issues.

Hence for distributed digital libraries we propose to use document prefetch only, a topic not studied before to the best of our knowledge. The closest area of research is prefetching in the World Wide Web. See Lee [4] for a quick overview of both caching and prefetching and Duchamp[7] for a more in depth overview of the early work done.

Two main categories of different approaches can be found in the literature. The most popular approach is to use proxy or server log analysis in order to predict future accesses of the clients [7,8,9,10,11,12,13,14]. However building up a probabilistic model in one way or the other requires that the candidates for prefetching have been accessed many times before. As we have just seen in the case of caching above, we are missing this property, at least at the university level. Hence, these methods are not applicable to digital libraries.

The second approach in web prefetching is to extract the hyperlinks contained in web documents and prefetch based on those links. As a result, this approach is not limited to pages previously accessed by a particular client or other users.

Eden et al. [15] proposed to let the user mark links, which can be prefetched by the client ahead of time, claiming that this would not increase the amount of data transfered, while still reducing the latency by a factor of three. While extremely simple, it is unrealistic to assume, that the users would be willing to mark all interesting links as well as that they would always follow all of their own hints. Hence, approaches which do not involve the user will be more realistic.

Chinen and Yamaguchi [16] analyzed a web proxy based implementation, where the proxy is placed close to the user in the same way as our gateway. Their proxy uses the first 10 links encountered in the parsed web pages to fetch the linked pages including a maximum of ten images. Their analysis showed in one configuration a 64% hit rate reducing the average latency from 15 to 6 seconds by increasing the traffic by a factor of 2.5.

The work of El-Saddik et al. [17] improved this scheme by ranking the included links according to the words in the link description text, which is compared to the description texts clicked by the user earlier. The underlying reasoning is similar to ours in the way that they try to get information about the intention of the user.

They use a maximum of 15 prefetched web documents per web page and found a lot of generated network traffic: 10 times the amount using the Chinen and Yamaguchi approach and 4.29 times the amount than using their own approach, in both cases compared to the amount of traffic without prefetching. The more recent work of Davison [18] is quite similar to their approach. Ibrahim [19] also implemented a similar approach using a neural network targeting news web sites. The neural network is used to learn about the interests of a particular user using keywords in the anchor text. They report a low waste rate of 20% to 30%.

WebCompanion [20] by Klemm takes another approach. It selects the pre-fetched links by the quality of the network connection. Klemm also proposes a name resolutions cache, used to find the web servers.

Cohen and Haim [21] proposed setting up just the network connection to the server in advance instead of prefetching the documents themselves. This is done by doing the name resolution early and establishing the TCP/IP connection. They also force the web servers to be warmed up for the imminent request by asking for the document size. Hence the server has to access the file system. Their techniques are clearly applicable in our case, and could have yielded additional gains. In fact, we know the publisher's servers in advance and could use (multiple) persistent connections to the few fulltext server to speed up transfer times even more.

Foxwell and Menasce [22] studied the effects of prefetching for web search engines. They reported only 14% latency reduction for their best example. This was achieved by prefetching the top eight matching documents of all queries, with a maximum average hit ratio of 35%.

Our prefetching approach is much simpler compared to the above approaches [16,17,18,19,20]. Instead of limiting the potential documents or using a selection scheme to prefetch the highly likely pages, our users give us the information which document is most likely to be accessed for free by moving to the *show record* state. With this information we achieve similar latency reductions with lower overhead, when compared with current web prefetch methods. Typical values are 50% latency reduction with 150% increase in network traffic [17,20], while we achieved the same reduction with less than 80%.

This navigation scheme is possible due to the structure of having biblio-graphic information available from the index database corresponding to the full-text articles. The Web in its current form does not offer this structure, hence it is much harder to build a prefetching system. It is interesting to see that old fashioned ways of organizing information, as in traditional libraries, still have their value in the fast moving digital world.

# 7   Conclusions

We have set up a prefetching experiment for fulltext servers from major academic publishers. The results from the experiment show that we could reduce the average experienced download time to 1/2 using a simple scheme. At the same time the additional introduced document transfers accounted for less than half of all transfers. We also found that holding articles for a maximum of one hour in the cache is sufficient.

These encouraging results, as compared to web prefetching, are attributable to the well-structured user model digital article libraries provide. By keeping the user "busy" with reading the bibliographic record, including the abstract, we have enough time to prefetch the article in most cases. Because the user has already selected this particular article at that time from a hit list, we experience the extremely high likelihood that they will proceed to download the article – in our case from a prefetch cache close to the user.

**Acknowledgments.** We are grateful to Prof. Dr. Ulrich Rüde and Dr. Graham Horton from the institution of system simulation at the Friedrich-Alexander-Universität, Erlangen-Nürnberg, Germany for providing us with infrastructure and a magnitude of insights how to gather and analyze relevant data.

We would also like to thank the following publishers for allowing us to prefetch fulltext articles from their fulltext servers: Elsevier, IEEE, ABI, Academic Press, IOP, Springer, Emerald, Kluwer Academic Publishers, RSC and IPG. Special thanks go to Silke Struve and David Ashby for proof-reading. This research is supported by the NORDUnet2 initiative.

# References

1. Ardö, A., Falcoz, F., Nielsen, T., Shanawa, S.B.: Integrating article databases and full text archives into a digital journal collection. In Nikolaou, C., Stephanidis, C., eds.: Proceedings of the Second European Conference on Research and Advanced Technology for Digital Libraries, ECDL'98. Volume 1513 of Lecture Notes in Computer Science., Springer-Verlag (1998) 641–642
2. Sandfær, M., Ardö, A., Falcoz, F., Shanawa, S.: The architecture of DADS - a large digital library of scientific journals. In: Online Information 99, Proceedings. (1999) 217–223
3. Hennessy, J., Patterson, D.: Computer Architecture: A Quantitative Approach. second edn. Morgan Kaufmann Publishers Inc. (1996)
4. Lee, D.C.: Methods for web bandwidth and response time improvement. In Abrams, M., ed.: World Wide Web - Beyond the Basics. Prentice Hall (1998)
5. Hollmann, J., Ardö, A., Stenström, P.: Prospects of caching in a distributed digital library. Technical Report 03-04, Department of Computer Engeneering, Chalmers University of Technology, S-41296 Göteborg, Sweden (2003)
6. Hollmann, J., Ardö, A., Stenström, P.: Empirical observations regarding predictability in user access-behavior in a distributed digital library system. In: Proceedings of the 16th International Parallel and Distributed Processing Symposium, Fort Lauderdale, FL, USA, IEEE (2002) 221–228
7. Duchamp, D.: Prefetching hyperlinks. In: Proceedings of the Second USENIX Sysmposium on Internet Technologies and Systems, Bolder, CO, USA, USENIX (1999) 127–138
8. Padmanabhan, V.N., Mogul, J.C.: Using predictive prefetching to improve world wide web latency. ACM SIGCOMM Computer Communications Review **26** (1996) 22–36
9. Markatos, E.P., Chronaki, C.E.: A top 10 approach for prefetching the web. In: Proceedings of INET'98 Conference, Geneva, Switzerland (1998)

10. Palpanas, T., Mendelzon, A.: Web-prefetch using partial match prediction. In: Proceedings of the 4th International Web Caching Workshop (WCW'99), San Diego, CA, USA (1999)
11. Sarukkai, R.R.: Link prediction and path analysis using markov chains. Computer Networks **33** (2000) 377–386
12. Yang, Q., Zhang, H.H., Li, T.: Mining web logs for prediction models in www caching and prefetching. In: 7th ACM SIGKDD International Conference on Knowledge Discovery and Data Mining KDD'01. (2001)
13. Wu, Y.H., Chen, A.L.P.: Prediction of web page accesses by proxy server log. World Wide Web **5** (2002) 67–88
14. Chen, X., Zhang, X.: Coordinated data prefetching by utilizing reference information at both proxy and web servers. In: Proceedings of the 2nd ACM Workshop on Performance and Architecture of Web Servers (PAWS-2001), Cambridge, MA (2001)
15. Eden, A.N., Joh, B.W., Mudge, T.: Web latency reduction via client-side prefetching. In: IEEE International Symposium on Performance Analysis of Systems and Software, Austin, TX, USA, IEEE (2000) 193–200
16. Chinen, K., Yamaguchi, S.: An interactive prefetching proxy server for improvement of www latency. In: The Seventh Annual Conference of the Internet Society (INET 97), Kuala Lumpur, Malaysia (1997)
17. El-Saddik, A., Griwodz, C., Steinmetz, R.: Exploiting user behaviour in prefetching www documents. In: Proceedings of 5th International Workshop on Interactive Distributed Multimedia Systems and Telecommunication Service (IDMS98). Volume 1483 of Lecture Notes in Computer Science., Oslo, Norway, Springer-Verlag (1998) 302–311
18. Davison, B.D.: Predicting web actions from html content. In: Hypertext 2002: Proceedings of the Thirteenth ACM Conference on Hypertext and Hypermedia, ACM (2002) 159–168
19. Ibrahim, T., Xu, C.Z.: Neural nets based predictive prefetching to tolerate www latency. In: Proceedings 20th IEEE International Conference on Distributed Computing Systems. (2000) 636–643
20. Klemm, R.: Webcompanion: a friendly client-side web prefetching agent. IEEE Transactions on Knowledge and Data Engineering **11** (1999) 577–594
21. Cohen, E., Kaplan, H.: Prefetching the means for document transfer: A new approach for reducing web latency. In: Nineteenth Annual Joint Conference of the IEEE Computer and Communications Societies INFOCOM 2000. Volume 2., IEEE (2000) 854–863
22. Foxwell, H., Menasce, D.A.: Prefetching results of web searches. In: Proceedings of the 1998 24th International Conference for the Resource Management and Performance Evaluation of Enterprise Computing Systems, CMG. Part 2. Volume 2., CMG (1998) 602–609

# An Architecture for Online Information Integration on Concurrent Resource Access on a Z39.50 Environment

Michalis Sfakakis[1] and Sarantos Kapidakis[2]

[1] National Documentation Centre / National Hellenic Research Foundation,
48 Vas. Constantinou, GR-11635 Athens, Greece
msfaka@ekt.gr
[2] Archive and Library Sciences Department / Ionian University,
Plateia Eleftherias, Paleo Anaktoro, Corfu 49100, Greece
sarantos@ionio.gr

**Abstract.** The lack of information integration, by the existing online systems, for resource sharing in a distributed environment, impacts directly to the development and the usage of dynamically defined Virtual Union Catalogues. In this work we propose a design approach for the construction of an online system, able to improve the information integration when a Dynamic Resource Collection is used, by taking into account the restrictions imposed by the network environment and the Z39.50 protocol. The main strength of this architecture is the presentation of de-duplicated results to the user, by the gradual application of the duplicate detection process in small received packets (sets of results), as the data packets flow from the participating servers. While it presents results to the user, it also processes a limited amount of data ahead of time, to be ready before the user requests them.

## 1 Introduction

The development of Union Catalogues has impacted resource sharing, giving the users the ability to access information, describing library content from one central point. The first implementations of Union Catalogs were based on the centralized model, due to technology limitations. In our days, the current technology, combined with the implementation of the Z39.50 protocol [1], enables the implementation of Union Catalogues based on the distributed model. Independently of the Union Catalogue underlining implementation model, the consistent searching and indexing, the consolidation of records and the performance and management are the main functional requirements that they have to conform to [7].

Until now, all of these functional requirements are satisfied well, in Union Catalogs implemented according to the centralized model, remaining open issues for virtual Union Catalogs, dynamically defined from distributed resources [2, 6, 7]. The local autonomy and control of the participating systems [7], plus the ability of the user to define his/her own virtual collections from a common interface [11], necessitates the design and the implementation of systems based on the distributed model.

T. Koch and I.T. Sølvberg (Eds.): ECDL 2003, LNCS 2769, pp. 288–299, 2003.

The development and the implementation of the Z39.50 protocol gave the challenge to the library community, not only to have a standard model for their system development, but also to focus on higher levels of interoperability after solving the lowest level of system interoperability [8, 9]. Higher levels of interoperability include the consistent searching and indexing of the distributed resources and are mainly affected by the local implementation of standards and associated profiles of the Z39.50 protocol [3, 4, 10].

Networks, computer systems and interoperability improvements, give the base for approaches to design online, real time systems according to the distributed model. The current implementations of the systems that build dynamically defined virtual Union Catalogues, mix the result sets but do not merge them, by applying duplicate detection procedures, to avoid performance issues. When some implementations try to approach the problem, the consolidation of records is based on some coded data (e.g. ISBN, ISSN, LC number, etc.), when they exist. The result set merging (consolidation of records) is a requirement identified by user studies [11] and has to be improved by the systems proposed to support multi database searching in any environment, networked or not. A deep solution to this problem requires the retrieval of all the results, which probably could only be implemented in offline circumstances.

The problem of the information integration in a distributed environment is not a new one, and mainly appears in two variations. When applied in the development of centralized Union Catalogues or in collection creation by harvesting techniques, the challenge is to make high quality duplicate detection and merging on large amount of data offline, without serious time restrictions. In contrast, when applied in virtual Union Catalogues, dynamically defined from distributed resources, the challenge is to make good quality duplicate detection, on medium to small amount of data online and present them to the user in real time.

This work proposes a system architecture for online use, built on the distributed search model, for improving the consolidation of records without performance penalties, taking into account the Z39.50 protocol futures. The main strength of this architecture is the presentation of de-duplicated results to the user, by the gradual application of the duplicate detection process in small received packets (sets of results), as the data packets flow from the participating servers. While it presents results to the user, it also processes a limited amount of data ahead of time, to be ready before the user requests them.

In this work, we use the Z39.50 protocol because it is widely used in the area of libraries and also due to its complexity, the different levels of support for relevant facilities and the varieties of the existing implementations. Most of the proposed architecture is protocol-independent and could be applied equally well for other client/server information retrieval protocols, responding in real time, even if they provide partial results each time or they timeout on inactivity.

The rest of the paper organized as follows: section 2 describes the problems for the online information integration from concurrent resource access and the way that it works in a distributed Z39.50 environment. Section 3 describes the practices of the currently used systems. Section 4 describes the architecture of the proposed system and finally section 5 concludes the paper and presents a number of interesting issues arrived from this work for further development and research.

## 2 Problem Description

The Z39.50 protocol is based on the client/server model. The client (origin) sends an init request to the server (target) and if the server accepts the request, it starts a new session (a Z-association). The init respond, sent by the server to the client, includes information about the server characteristics (e.g. protocol version, supported services, etc.). For every Z-association, the server holds a search history (i.e. the result sets for the performed queries), which includes the last result set or more, depending on the support of the named result sets by the server. During the session, the client can request data from any result set included in the search history. The search history stays alive during the session, while either the origin or the target, via the close service, can abruptly terminate the session. The protocol defines that one 'close-reason' of the session is the 'lack of activity', which means that the server can close (timeout) the session when the client does not send a request for a period of time. The timeout period is server dependent.

The termination of the communication between the Z39.50 client and server costs the loss of the previously issued results and their arrangements (duplication detection or sorting). The client, in order to be able to continue the process from the termination point, has to reconnect to the timed out server, re-execute the query and finally request the rest of the data. Two problems are issued by the session reactivation: The first is the performance overhead. The second is that there is no guarantee that the new result set will be identical with the previously working one. This means that, in order to have consistent results, we have to retrieve all the data from the beginning of the result set and to reapply the whole process.

Depending on the implementation level of the Z39.50 protocol by the server, some servers could implement, in their resources, the duplicate detection service [12], the sort service or none of them. In a distributed concurrently accessed environment, this means that when a user defines a virtual collection of databases (resources), some databases could belong to a server which implements neither the duplicate detection service nor the sort service, which is the majority of the current Z39.50 implementations. Additional interoperability issues are the variations in the implementation level of the supported duplicate detection or sort service and the differences in the applied duplicate detection algorithms.

The duplicate detection problem occurs, in different forms, in a number of disciplines whenever the integration of information is required. In the area of libraries, from the late of 70s, during the development of centralized union catalogues, one approach to the problem was the automatic detection of duplicate monographic records [5]. The differences in semantic models and formats used for the metadata encoding, as well as their quality and consistency, are crucial issues affecting the overall effectiveness and the quality of the de-duplication process. Usually, after the identification of the related records by the duplicate detection process, the next step is the merging of the duplicates in a union record. According to the Z39.50 duplicate detection model [12], the duplicates are clustered in 'equivalence classes', by applying the matching criteria to a specific portion of each record. A representative record is selected for every equivalence class, which is also retained and arranged (sorted) by a combination of the values from some parameters.

A Z39.50 client which communicates concurrently with a number of disparate Z39.50 servers has to deal with the heterogeneity in the way it receives the resulting data (e.g. some results do not includes duplicates, others are only sorted and others are received in a server depended manner). Even at the best case, when the client receives de-duplicated results from all the servers, it also has to de-duplicate them. The client, also, has to take care of the differences between the timeouts and the performances of the participating servers. Finally the client has to perform all its operations and responds to the user in real time, or at least with limited delays.

Due to the complexity and the expensiveness of the duplicate detection algorithms, high-quality consolidation process for large amounts of records can be applied mostly in offline environments [7]. In an online environment (web based or not), where the user in most cases does not retrieve all his results at once but progressively in small packets, expecting the results promptly, we can only afford to apply quality de-duplication process on small number of records to create the sets of unique records to present. To do this, we have to invent heuristics to save processing time, even by sacrificing some accuracy in the duplicate detection process. One possible way to achieve this could be by applying the de-duplication process in the first waves of data sets that arrive from the servers, during the first times we present data to the user. This approach postpones the problem of comparing large amounts of records – if needed at all – to later steps, during the time the user is reading the presented data.

## 3  Practices of the Currently Used Systems

The majority of the current implementations of the Z39.50 servers support the basic services of the protocol (e.g. Init, search, present and scan). A small number of servers support the sort service and a minority of them supports the duplicate detection service. The lack of the implementation for the duplicate detection service is due to the late specification and acceptance of the service by the protocol and also due to its implementation complexity. This situation impacts to the efficiency of the clients, when they concurrently access multiple resources from different Z39.50 servers.

At the Z39.50 client side, the current implementations, when they give the ability to the user to access multiple resources, they work dispatching the requests from the user, sequentially or in parallel, to the participating systems, and after receiving the responses, they start to presenting the results sequentially back to the user. At the first presentation step, some systems, usually the web based, display a specific number of results from every resource, or a specific number of results from one resource (the first selected). After the first presentation step, they also give the ability to the user to request results from a specific resource. Other systems start downloading the results sequentially from each server. The user is able to read the received data, but the client has to download all the results in order to accomplish the duplicate detection process. The last approach is forbidden in online interactive environments, especially for large amounts of data, due to response time and timeout issues.

In the most common case, there is not uniformity in the structure and the content of the received result sets from the servers. Finally, in any case, the problem of the de-duplication and integration of the information from all the resources, which depends on the client's functionality, may involve less or more work, but it exists. Due to performance issues, the majority of the existing clients do not make any integration of the received information, by a duplicate detection process, or they make primitive approaches based on some coded data (e.g. ISBN, ISSN, LC number, etc.).

# 4   System's Architecture Description

In a distributed resource environment, we have a set $R$ of $r$ participating resources (i.e. $r = |R|$), available from a set $S$ of $s$ servers (i.e. $s = |S|$). Every server from $S$ could be accessed remotely via the network and could publish more than one resource from $R$. When the retrieval of the distributed resources accomplished by an online system, the system displays the results in steps, by generating *Presentation Sets* with a small number of results. The maximum number $p$ of the results that every *Presentation Set* $P$ will contain is defined by negotiation of the user and the system.

The user interacts with the system by first defining the desired collection of resources. This action, in a more advanced system, could be automatically accomplished by the system, using the appropriate metadata describing the content of the resources, or by both in cooperation. Then the user sends a search request. He could also specify the desired number of records (e.g. 25), which the system will include in each *Presentation Set* response. If the number of records, which satisfies the user's request, is greater than the defined number of records for display, then the user could subsequently request the remaining *Presentation Sets*.

Two major critical points coexist in an online distributed system, which accesses concurrently resources via the network and integrates the information, by applying duplicate detection procedures for the results returned by the participating systems. The first is the performance of the network links and the availability of the resources. The second is the complexity and the expensiveness of the duplicate detection algorithms, for presenting to the user only once each record that is multiply located in the resources.

In our proposed system, the duplicate detection process is applied using each received set of data from the servers and comparing them against the previously processed results - which are sorted and do not contain duplicates. We incrementally compare and eliminate the duplicate records in every metadata record presentation. When it is possible, we use the appropriate services supported by the servers (e.g. duplicate detection or sort) in order to get data in more processed condition and consequently to apply more specialized and efficient algorithms. Also, during the time the user is reading a set of results, the system prepares the next sets of unique records for display, by requesting a small portion of the remaining data from the servers and applying the duplicate detection process. We do not apply the duplicate detection algorithm in one shot, to all metadata records that belong to a specific query result. The benefits of this approach are that we avoid downloading large amounts of data from the participating systems over the network and we apply the duplicate detection algorithm to a small number of records in the first steps.

The system consists of the *Request Interface*, the *Data Integrator* and the *Resource Communicator* modules. The *Data Integrator* is composed by a number of interacting components, in order to accomplish the information integration for the data arrived from the *Resource Communicator* module. The interaction between the modules and the components is accomplished either by synchronous data transmissions using queues or by messages. Fig. 1 outlines System's modules, components and their interactions. The rectangles represent the modules, the ellipses represent the components, the solid lines represent data transmissions and the dashed lines represent control message transmissions. The ellipsis with the double lines indicates that, in an expanded architecture, multiple instances of the component could run on different CPUs and communicate by shared memory, for increasing the overall response time.

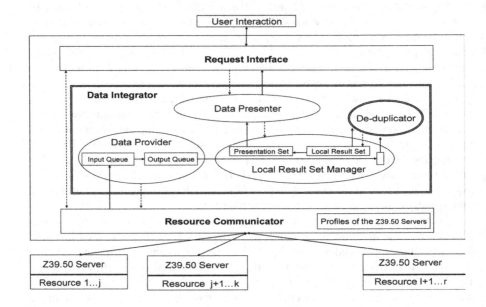

**Fig. 1.** System's modules, components and their interactions

### 4.1  Modules, Components, and Interactions

The three modules from which the proposed system is composed of are the *Request Interface*, the *Data Integrator* and the *Resource Communicator*. Their description and their interactions are:

- The *Request Interface* receives every user request (search or present) and dispatches it to the appropriate internal modules, waiting for (at most *p*) records (i.e. the *Presentation Set*) to display. When the module receives the de-duplicated results from the *Data Integrator* module, it sends them to the user and waits for further commands.

- The *Resource Communicator* accesses the resources, using the appropriate communication protocols (e.g. Z39.50), and sends them the appropriate commands to retrieve data from them, according to the user request, which is sent by the *Request*

*Interface* module. It also takes into account the services that the servers support and their differences in the timeout and the performance, from the *Profiles of the Z39.50 Servers*. If a server supports the duplicate detection or the sort service, it requests from the server to use them. The module does not retrieve all the resulting records from every resource, but every time it only retrieves at most *p* (actually, there can be a different *p* per resource, but to simplify the description we assume it is the same, and is the number of records the *Request Interface* waits for displaying). By this approach, the *Resource Communicator* avoids downloading vast amounts of data from the network and in every 'request data step' it retrieves at most *p* records from every resource. When the module receives a result set from a resource, it sends it to the *Data Integrator* module for the de-duplication process. The *Resource Communicator* starts its action when it receives a search request by the *Request Interface* module and sends messages to it when access control is in effect by a server or a resource, or when a server is not available.

- The *Data Integrator* receives the data sets from the Resource Communicator, makes the information integration by applying the duplicate detection process and manages the processed unique records to be ready for presentation to the user. When the first *Presentation Set* with non-duplicate records is accomplished, it sends it to the *Request Interface*. Subsequently, it prepares the next *Presentation Set* and waits for commands for possibly different sets from the *Request Interface*.

All the components or modules of the system accomplish their actions working in parallel, unless they wait for input (data or control message transmission) from another component or module.

The *Data Integrator* module accomplishes its goal by the interaction of the four internal components, *Data Provider, Local Result Set Manager, De-duplicator* and *Data Presenter*. Their description is:

- The *Data Provider* receives data from the *Resource Communicator* module and subsequently sends them, one at a time, to the appropriate component, which will further process them. The *Data Provider* is using internally two queue structures and guarantees to be able to receive data from the *Resource Communicator* at any time, even without prior request and also to always provide enough data for processing. The first task ensures that the *Resource Communicator* will be able to retrieve data from the resources in emergency conditions (i.e. some servers are close to timeout their connection), or due to slow performance from any server. For the control of the second task, when the number of data contained in the *Data Provider* is less than a threshold, the *Data Provider* sends a 'request data' message to the *Resource Communicator*.

- The *Local Result Set Manager* holds and arranges (e.g. sorts) the de-duplicated records in its internal *Local Result Set* structure. The first task of the *Local Result Set Manager* is the activation of the duplicate detection component (i.e. *De-duplicator*) for all the incoming records. It also prepares the *Presentation Set*, using the presentation set queue, by copying the *p* records (i.e. the number of requested records for display) from the *Local Result Set* structure. When the number of the existing records in the *Local Result Set* is less than *p*, an 'end of data' is appended into the Presentation Set queue.

- The *De-duplicator* receives a record from the *Local Result Set Manager* and accomplishes the duplicate detection process. It compares the record with all the records, appropriately ordered, in the *Local Result Set* Structure. After the comparison process, it sends the results from the process (i.e. the set of records that this record belongs to, or none, if the record does not match with any set) to the *Local Result Set Manager*, which then places the record in the right position in the *Local Result Set*. The *Local Result Set Manager* sends all incoming records to the *De-duplicator*.

- The *Data Presenter* is used for the interaction with the *Request Interface* module. It dispatches the received requests for data, from the *Request Interface*, to the *Local Result Set Manager* and returns the unique records (if any) back to the *Request Interface* module. When the *Data Presenter* dispatches the present request for $p$ records to the *Local Result Set Manager*, it waits (blocked by reading) for the Presentation Set queue to be filled with the requested number of records. Finally, it also monitors the system timeout on the connection with the user (i.e. no request for data from the *Request Interface* module for a period of time), closing the session.

## 4.2  Accomplishing a Search Request

The system starts its action when the user submits a search request and the *Request Interface* module receives the request. The following steps describe the functions, the flow of data and control messages transmissions performed by the modules of the system.

When the *Request Interface* module receives a search request, from the user interface subsystem, the following actions take place:

1  The *Request Interface* module sends a 'request data' message for $p$ records to the *Data Integrator* module and then waits for (at most $p$) records from it.

2  The *Request Interface* module, also, forwards the search request including the number $p$, to the *Resource Communicator* module and continues monitoring for user requests.

3  The *Resource Communicator* module waits for messages from the *Request Interface* and when it receives a new search request, it concurrently starts the following sequences of steps for every server:

3.1  The *Resource Communicator* module interprets the search request to the appropriate message format for the server, sends it to the server and waits for its reply.

3.2  When the reply is received from the server, it adds the number of records (hits) found, for the user request in the server's resources. If the replies from all the servers have arrived, it sends the sum to the *Request Interface* module.

3.3  If the server supports either the duplicate detection service or the sort service, it also request to de-duplicate or sort its results, after its initial response to the search request.

3.4  Requests a number of records (e.g. $p$) from every server, which replied on its last request.

3.5  When a result set arrives, it sends the data to the *Data Integrator module*.

3.6  It waits for further commands, but if there is no communication with the server for a period close to its timeout, the procedure jumps to step 3.4.

4 The *Data Integrator* module de-duplicates part of the data sent by the *Resource Communicator* and prepares the *Presentation Set*. When *p* unique records are found, the module sends them to the *Request Interface* module. If at any time the number of records available for de-duplication is less than a threshold (e.g. 5*p*), the *Data Integrator* module sends a 'request data' message to the *Resource Communicator* module, which subsequently repeats the steps 3.4 and 3.5 for each server.

Here are some comments and clarifications for the steps described previously. The *Request Interface* module sends the requested number *p* to the *Resource Communicator* module in order to make known how many records (how big the *Presentation Set* is) the user expects to retrieve from every system response. The *Resource Communicator* module can use it to calculate the number of records that will request from the servers (step 3.4). The number of requested records could be different for every server and could be greater or less than *p*. The *Resource Communicator* module calculates the number of records to request, using the characteristics for every server, from the *Profiles of the Z39.50 servers*, and the number of results found in every resource. When a server has slow performance the number of requested records could vary to avoid long waiting time. Also, the number of requested records could be small, when the server has a short timeout period. In this case the *Resource Communicator* avoids the session reactivation by often requesting data from it. In contrast, the number of requested records could be big, when the number of results is big and the server has fast performance and fast network links.

The *Resource Communicator* starts its action when it receives a search request by the *Request Interface* module (step 3) and sends messages to it if access control is in effect by a server or a resource. The message could be sent to the *Request Interface* module before contacting the server (step 3.1), if the *Profiles of the Z39.50 servers* contain the appropriate information, or after the step when a server or a resource is challenged by access control. Also, the *Resource Communicator* informs the *Request Interface* when a server is down. If the *Resource Communicator* knows that the server will not be available for a period of time, from the *Profiles of the Z39.50 servers*, the module sends the message before the step 3.1. In any other case it sends the message after this step. A critical decision of the *Resource Communicator*, for the overall system performance, is to understand that a server is down and to continue the interaction with the other modules, with the results from the other available resources. For this decision, the *Profiles of Z39.50 servers* could help if they contain information about the response time of each server and the unavailability history.

At step 3.2, the *Resource Communicator* module calculates the number of hits found for the user's request and returns it to the *Request Interface* module (which is performed once for every search request). This number is not actually accurate, because the system has not accomplished yet the record de-duplication. This information is very essential to the user (and is expected by the Z39.50 protocol), in order to decide for an alternative, more specific request. Even at the best case, when all servers support the duplicate detection service, this number is only somehow closer to the real one. The only way to calculate the precise number of hits found by the servers is to retrieve and de-duplicate all the data from all the resources, which is forbidden in online environments

The sequence of steps from 3.1 through 3.6, used for search and retrieve the resources of a server, is performed in parallel with the corresponding steps of other servers. Also the *Resource Communicator* module could skip step 3.3 and go directly to step 3.4, for a server that supports neither the duplicate detection nor the sort service.

The *Resource Communicator* module, in order to avoid the session reactivation, which is imposed by the existence of the timeout form a server, could request data from a resource, at any time, independently of the existence of a 'request data' message. The module derives the information concerning the timeout period of a server from the *Profiles of the Z39.50 servers.*

Finally at step 4, where the *Data Integrator* module prepares the *Presentation Set*, the module could request data from the *Resource Communicator* module, not only when the number of current de-duplicated results is less than $p$, but also when it is less than a threshold. This action utilises the time the user is reading the data and the system prepares the data for the next *Presentation Set.*

### 4.2.1 Data Integrator Internal Description

After the explanation of the search request execution progress, we further analyze how the internal components of the *Data Integrator* module perform the functions, the data transmissions and the flow of control message transmissions, when the module is activated, as described in steps 1 and 4 at section 4.2. The *Data Integrator* module consists of four internal components, as we already described, and interoperates with both the other modules. The first message that the *Data Integrator* receives, through its *Data Presenter* component, comes from the *Request Interface* module (step 1). The *Data Presenter* instructs all components to flush any data from previous requests and informs the *Local Result Set Manager* that it is expecting $p$ records. Initially all the components in the module are in an idle state, waiting for data to process. Regardless of this, the module actually starts its action immediately after the first record written, by the *Resource Communicator* module (step 3.5), to the *Data Provider* component. From this point, the *Data Integrator* module starts working in parallel with the other modules.

When the *Resource Communicator* module writes the first record to the *Data Provider*, the following actions take place inside the *Data Integrator* module:

1  The *Data Provider* starts to transfer data from its input queue to its output queue possibly by rearranging them, for example in an order that optimizes the initial processing time. If the number of data contained in it is less than a threshold (e.g. 5$p$), the *Data Provider* sends a 'request data' message to the *Resource Communicator.*

2  While the *Local Result Set Manager* has less than a threshold (e.g. 3 $p$) unique record, it tries to read from the *Data Provider* and for every record found, it calls the *De-Duplicator* to compare the record.

2.1  The *De-Duplicator* compares the record with the records in the *Local Result Set* and then sends the results back to the *Local Result Set Manager.*

2.2  The *Local Result Set Manager* receives the results from the duplicate detection process and arranges the record into the *Local Result Set.*

2.3  If the number of new unique records in the *Local Result Set* becomes $p$, it copies the $p$ new unique records into the *Presentation Set* and activates the *Data Presenter.*

3  When the *Presentation Set* is filled with (the *p*) records, the *Data Presenter* component dispatches the records to the *Request Interface* module and waits to receive the next 'request data' message from it. If the component does not receive any request during its predefined timeout period, it terminates the system.

As we have already reported, every component works in parallel with the others, when it requires no input from another component.

One of the activities of the *Data Integrator* module is to request data from the *Recourse Communicator*, when the already retrieved data are not enough to complete the *Presentation Set* and to prepare at least the next one. On the other hand, when enough records (for the next possible request) have been de-duplicated, some components of the *Data Integrator* will be in an idle state mode, releasing the CPU and avoiding downloading more records from the resources with no apparent reason (e.g. if a server is close to timeout the connection). This behavior is affected by two thresholds; the first concerns the number of records in the *Data Provider* and the second concerns the number of the de-duplicated records in the *Local Result Set* which makes the *Local Result Set Manager* to stop reading records from the *Data Provider*, leaving the *De-duplicator* inactive.

The *Local Result Set Manager* keeps two orderings of the records in the *Local Result Set* (step 2.2). The first, sorts the records in order to support the *De-Duplicator* to apply duplicate detection algorithms efficiently. The second arrangement facilitates easy location of the non-presented records to the user in a sorted way. This ordering is different, especially if some newly de-duplicated unique records are placed before elements already presented to the user.

### 4.3  Accomplishing a Present Request

As we described in section 4.2, the system starts its action when the user submits a search request. After this, the user could request from the system to retrieve another *Presentation Set*. In this case, the *Data Presenter* requests the records from the *Local Result Set Manager* in the *Data Integrator* module, and waits until the *Data Integrator* has found the requested records, performing the steps of section 4.2.1. When the requested number of records is available in the *Local Result Set*, it fills the *Presentation Set* with the records and performs step 3 of section 4.2.1.

## 5  Conclusions and Future Research

The online duplicate detection process (as a part of the information integration) from resources accessed concurrently in a network environment, is a requirement identified by user studies and is challenged by a number of issues relevant to the performance of the participating servers and their network links, plus to the complexity and the expensiveness of the duplicate detection algorithms. These issues make inefficient any approach to the application of the information integration in online environments, especially when large amounts of data must be processed. In our system we do not try to integrate all the results from all the recourses at once. We attack this problem by retrieving a small number of records from the participating resources (independently if they provide de-duplicated or sorted results), we apply the duplicate detection process on these records and we create a presentation set of unique records to display to the user. In cases were the user query results to large amount of records, he usually does not retrieve all the results anyway, but reforms its query.

From this work, a number of interesting points arrives for future development and research. A better approximation for the number of records satisfying the search request, possibly using the Z39.50 facilities and preview statistics, is a critical point for assisting the user to decide how more specific he must be when re-expressing his request. Another point of interest is how to extend the system to derive priorities for the servers and their resources, based on supported features, performance statistics from previous accesses and other parameters, and at the same time to take into account user defined priorities possibly based on the importance of the content of the resources. Another interesting problem is a selection or an adaptation to a good de-duplication algorithm for different record completeness and different provision of records by the servers (e.g. all sorted, none sorted, all de-duplicated, none de-duplicated, etc.). Also, an approximation method for the number of requested records from a server, using its characteristics (e.g. performance) and the number of results found in its resources is another issue to solve. Finally an implementation of the proposed system and its performance evaluation will show points for further system improvement and extensions for other services.

# References

1.  ANSI/NISO: Z39.50 Information Retrieval: application service definition and protocol specification: approved May 10, 1995.
2.  Coyle, Karen. The Virtual Union Catalogue: A Comparative Study. D-Lib Magazine vol. 6:num. 3 (March 2000).
3.  Dunsire, Gordon. Joined up indexes: interoperability issues in Z39.50 networks. 68th IFLA Council and General Conference, August 18–24, 2002.
4.  Gill, Tony and Miller Pall. Re-inventing the Wheel? Standards, Interoperability and Digital Cultural Content. D-Lib Magazine vol. 8:num. 1 (January 2002)
5.  Hickey, Thomas B. and Rypka, David J. Automatic detection of duplicate monographic records. Journal of Library Automation, 12:2 (June 1979), pp. 125–142.
6.  Lunau, Carrol & Turner, Fay. Issues Related to the Use of Z39.50 to Emulate a Centralized Union Catalogue. Prepared for the ARL Access Committee, National Library of Canada, April 1997. http://www.nlc-bnc.ca/resource/vcuc/ezarl2.htm.
7.  Lynch, Clifford A. Building the Infrastructure of Resource Sharing: Union Catalogs, Distributed Search, and Cross-Database Linkage. Library Trends 45:3 (Winter 1997), pp. 448–461.
8.  Lynch, C., Garcia-Molina H., "Interoperability, Scaling, and the Digital Libraries Research Agenda: A Report on the May 18-19, 1995", IITA Digital Libraries Workshop, August 22, 1995. http://www-diglib.stanford.edu/diglib/pub/reports/iita-dlw/.
9.  Moen, W. E. Mapping the Interoperability Landscape for the Networked Information Retrieval, JCDL 2001, June 24–28, 2001, Roanoke, Virginia, USA.
10. Moen, W. E. Improving Z39.50 Interoperability: Z39.50 Profiles and Testbeds for Library Applications. 67th IFLA Council and General Conference, August 16–25, 2001.
11. Payette, S. D. and Rieger, O.Y. "Z39.50 the User's Perspective", D-Lib Magazine, April 1997.
12. 13. Z39.50 Duplicate Detection Service (adopted by the Z39.50–1995 Amendment 2). http://lcweb.loc.gov/z3950/agency/amend/dedup.html

# The ADEPT Concept-Based Digital Learning Environment

T.R. Smith, D. Ancona, O. Buchel, M. Freeston, W. Heller, R. Nottrott,
T. Tierney, and A. Ushakov

The Alexandria Digital Earth Prototype Project, University of California, Santa Barbara
smithtr@cs.ucsb.edu
http://www.alexandria.ucsb.edu

**Abstract.** We describe the design and application of a Digital Learning Environment (DLE) that is integrated with the collections and services of the Alexandria Digital Library (ADL). This DLE is in operational use in undergraduate teaching environments. Its design and development incorporate the assumption that deep understanding of both scientific phenomena and scientific methods is facilitated when learning materials are explicitly organized, accessed and presented at the level of granularity of appropriate sets of scientific concepts and their interrelationships. The DLE supports services for the creating, searching, and displaying: (1) knowledge bases (KBs) of strongly structured models of scientific concepts; (2) DL collections of information objects organized and accessible by the concepts of the KBs; and (3) collections of presentation materials, such as lectures and laboratory materials, that are organized as trajectories through the KB of concepts.

## 1 Introduction

Digital library and knowledge representation technologies, together with web technology, provide a natural basis for creating and using *digital learning environments*. Through its use of structured metadata, whether human or machine created, digital library (DL) technology supports *disciplined access* to both learning materials and any digital information objects used in their creation. Knowledge representation (KR) technology supports the *organization of content* of learning materials during their creation and presentation. Web technology supports *services* facilitating the creation, structuring, and presentation of learning materials within digital learning environments (DLEs.)

We describe an operational DLE that is based on the three technologies. It consists of three classes of DL collections and associated services that are integrated into the Alexandria Digital Library (ADL.) The DLE supports the creation, use, and re-use of learning materials in different fields of science and in various learning environments, including classroom, laboratory, and self-guided environments. The DLE is being developed as part of the Alexandria Digital Earth Prototype (ADEPT)[1] and is currently in operational use for teaching Physical Geography to undergraduate students at University of California, Santa Barbara (UCSB).

T. Koch and I.T. Sølvberg (Eds.): ECDL 2003, LNCS 2769, pp. 300–312, 2003.

The ADEPT DLE is based on the assumption that learning materials for scientific disciplines can, and perhaps should, be primarily organized for access and presentation in terms of *objective scientific concepts and their interrelationships* (see, for example, [2]). Objectively definable concepts provide the fundamental ``granules'' of knowledge from which scientists create their symbolic representations of phenomena. The concept-based organization of scientific knowledge provides a natural granularity and structure for the presentation of learning materials.

Such granularity is characteristically reflected in the manner in which scientific knowledge is organized and represented in learning materials such as lectures, textbooks, and laboratory manuals. These materials are typically structured around a *sequence* of some selected set of concepts that is augmented with additional information. A simple example is that of a lecture initially constructed as an (indented) list of concepts, and then embellished with textual annotations and graphic illustrations of the concepts and their interrelationships. We note that presentations may also be structured around trees, graphs, or even hyper-graphs of concepts.

The costs, however, of creating conceptually integrated learning materials for non-digital learning environments are high, as illustrated in the development of a new textbook. Furthermore, a thorough integration of several sources of learning material at the conceptual level is highly constrained by time costs and printing technology, with ``formal'' representation of concepts typically being relegated to glossaries of concept terms and definitions at the ends of textbooks.

DLEs offer two advantages over purely print-based learning environments. The first is the richness and diversity of the learning materials that may be accessed from both local and networked sources, including DLs. The second is the emerging availability of KR and Web technologies for integrating such materials at the level of scientific concepts. In particular, KR and Web technologies allow us to extend relatively simple examples of concept KBs, such as thesauri, gazetteers, and ontologies, into more informative representations of concepts and their interrelationships. We may create digital KBs of information about concepts for use in organizing learning materials for presentation. The ADEPT DLE takes advantage of such technologies in support of its basic assumption concerning the conceptual organization of science learning materials.

A further premise underlying the ADEPT DLE is that learning in any domain of science is enhanced through an understanding of the nature and organization of the (sometimes alternative) sets of concepts that may be employed in representing both the phenomena and methodologies of that domain [3]. Such understanding involves (1) the choice of concepts used in representing some phenomenon; (2) the representation and semantics of each of the concepts; (3) the interrelationships among the concepts; and (4) the way in which the concepts are used in representing scientific phenomena.

In this paper, we describe an operational DLE that is based on the preceding ideas. We first provide an overview of the DLE in terms of its three classes of collections and their associated creation and presentation services. We then discuss each of these collections and associated services, including: (1) collections of information objects that illustrate some aspect of a concept, or relationship between concepts, and that may be accessed in terms of structured metadata that refers to the concept; (2) a KB of knowledge about concepts that may be used to organize and augment learning presentation materials; and (3) collections of re-usable learning presentation materials. We also summarize some outcomes of an ongoing evaluation of the DLE as well as continuing developments.

A demonstration version of the ADEPT DLE may be accessed at http://www.alexandria.ucsb.edu/learning/demos

## 2  The ADEPT DLE

The goal of the Alexandria Digital Earth Prototype (ADEPT) DLE is to employ and extend DL-based collections and services for the creation and presentation of learning materials that are organized in terms of scientific concepts and that may themselves be accessed and re-used. As illustrated in Figure 1, the DLE involves three classes of collections. The first contain typical DL items, such as images, maps, texts, and animations, that may be used in illustrating or representing some concept or interrelationship between concepts. A satellite image may, for example, exemplify the concept of a *watershed*. Such items, which we term information objects, are characterized by structured metadata and may be viewed as part of ``regular'' DL collections. Their value in the creation of learning materials is greatly enhanced by a metadata field which identifies the concept(s) to which the item is related. This field supports a simple form of content-based search for materials that are illustrative of a given concept and its use.

|  | Collection of DL Objects | KB of Concepts | Collection of Presentations |
|---|---|---|---|
| **Create/Edit Services** | ADN Metadata Input | Concept Input/Edit | Presentation Composer |
| **Search Services** | ADL Middleware Search | KB Search | Presentation Search |
| **Display Services** | ADEPT Client(s) | Concept Display | Presentation Display |

**Fig. 1.** Collections and Services of the ADEPT DLE

A second class of collections are characterized by items representing systematic knowledge about each of the concepts used in characterizing some domain of scientific knowledge. An example would be the knowledge of the concept of *watershed*, such as how the concept may be represented and its relations to other concepts. These knowledge bases (KBs) of concepts may be viewed as generalizations of thesauri and gazetteers. Their value for the construction of learning materials follows from their modular and re-usable nature.

A third class of collections are characterized by items that are best described as *presentation materials*, such lecture, laboratory, or self-guided presentations. We may view them as created around a skeleton of concepts that characterize a domain of knowledge about a phenomenon. The items are fleshed out with annotations about the concepts and their interrelationships as well as with illustrative items selected from both the regular DL and KB collections. A lecture on *watersheds*, for example, might contain annotations about the relationships among the *streams* that make up the *stream network* of a *watershed*, together with images of exemplary *networks* and information from the KB on how to represent *stream networks* and their interrelationships. Such learning materials may be characterized by their own metadata, stored as DL collections, accessed for learning purposes, and employed in creating new learning materials.

Each class of collection is supported by a suite of web-based services for item-level *creation, search*, and *display*. These services include browser-based support for item creation for all three classes of collections, including: (1) a form-based service for creating item-level metadata in the ``regular'' DL collections which includes a field for associated concept information; (2) a form-based service for creating structured knowledge about the concepts in the KB; and (3) a service for creating presentation materials constructed about a skeleton of concepts, together with annotations and illustrative items ``dragged'' from the other collections.

There are also services for *search* and *display,* including a service that displays interactive graphical representations of the concepts forming the skeleton of presentation materials. In Figure 2, we present a video frame of a classroom showing, from left to right, displays of the skeleton of concepts of a lecture, the lecture presentation materials, and an illustrative item from the associated DL collection. The contents of this figure are described below.

**Fig. 2.** A Classroom Presentation. Left to Right: the Knowledge Window, the Lecture Window and the Collection Window

The three collections and associated services are supportable at either the server side or the client side.

## 2.1 Collections of Illustrative Information Objects

The ADL Project has developed a operational DL supporting distributed, persistent collections of digital information objects characterized by item- and collection-level metadata. Middleware search services are made interoperable over catalogs based on different metadata standards with the use of "search buckets" [4]. This infrastructure supports ADEPT DLE collections of web-viewable information objects, such as maps, images, videos, and texts, that an instructor may wish to integrate into learning materials. In the context of the ADEPT DLE, such objects may be viewed as illustrating a scientific concept or relationship between concepts.

Collection of items are cataloged using the Alexandria/DLESE/NASA (ADN) joint metadata framework [5]. The ADN framework, built on version 1.2 of the IMS metadata standard, has 10 sections covering standard and specialized bibliographic fields such as file format, usage rights, educational standards, relations to other records, geospatial, temporal, and *related concepts*. The metadata field for *related concepts* supports item-level search in terms of concepts that characterize phenomena represented in the item. Concepts represented in the scientific concept KB of an ADEPT DLE (see below) automatically appear in the controlled vocabularies of the catalog.

ADEPT collections of illustrative items are essentially metadata records for items with URLs providing access to the items themselves. Collections are currently implemented as MySQL DBs with PHP interfaces for adding and editing object metadata. The database is capable of outputting XML records that validate against the schema suite describing the ADN. The actual objects are stored in a web accessible location on the server with references in the form of URLs stored in the database. Once an instructor has selected some object for inclusion in learning materials, there is no further need to access the database.

Information for standard library fields (title, description, author) is keyed-in manually or in some cases (author) controlled by authority records when multiple records containing the same data are present. Geospatial data may either be hand-entered or may be created and entered using the Alexandria map-browser interface, inverting its primary function as a search/display tool. The map-browser is embedded into the metadata creation form, recording the bounding box drawn upon it and inserting this into the appropriate field for the metadata record.

The database of object metadata is searched using the ADL middleware. Queries may be expressed that search for specific information in multiple metadata fields, and may employ the ADEPT map-browser interface for visual designation of geospatial search parameters.

The display of the items in the object collection is currently implemented through a web browser using a standard set of installed plug-ins.

## 2.2 Knowledge Bases of Scientific Concepts

ADEPT has developed a *strongly structured model* (SSM) of scientific concepts represented in terms of a frame-based KR system with slots and attribute-value fillers.

This SSM extends significantly the typically thesauri-like definitions of concepts that have traditionally been used in library environments [6,7]. Such extensions are motivated by the work of various scientific groups in constructing detailed, objective models of the concepts underlying their domains, such as the MatML Working Group of the National Institute of Standards and Technology (NIST, concepts relating to substances of Materials Science [8]) and the Chemical Abstracts Service Registry [9,10] of the American Chemical Society (ACS, concepts relating to chemical substances.)

The KB of SSMs of concepts serves users of the DLE as a source for: (1) "reference" information about concepts in terms of relatively complete descriptions of the concepts required in a given context; (2) creating graphic displays of the "concept spaces" that may be used in representing given phenomena; (3) creating modular, "reusable" presentation material concerning a given concept and its relationships to other concepts; and (4) metadata for classifying DL collections of learning objects in terms of the concepts represented in the item. Important *elements* of an SSM include:

- **terms:** simple (linguistic) representations denoting a concept;
- **descriptions:** of the concept in natural language;
- **historical origins:** of the concept in natural language;
- **examples:** of prototypical examples of the concept;
- **defining operations:** objective descriptions of procedures, such as measurement procedures, that define the semantics of the concept;
- **hierarchical relations:** thesaurus-like relations such as *isa* and *part-of;*
- **scientific classifications:** represents a concept in terms of regions in some n-dimensional geometric or topological space (*Igneous Rocks* , for example, may be represented as regions in a space characterized by chemical and mineral composition);
- **scientific representations:** of a concept given in terms of specialized scientific languages (e.g., graphical, mathematical, or Computational) from which useful information may be derived using syntactic procedures;
- **properties:** of a concept, typically given in terms of other concepts (such as the *Elevation* of a *Watershed*);
- **causal relations:** of one concept to others;.
- **co-relations:** of one concept to other.

Web-based services support the input, access, and editing of SSMs of concepts within a browser environment. Creation of a concept SSM is form-based at the level of choosing which of the above *concept elements* to define. Creation of individual elements, such as *properties*, is supported by a word-like editor that, although simple, supports mathematical and tabular formatting and the creation of links to other materials. These services are implemented in PHP (server-side) and JavaScript (client-side).

Figure 3 illustrates the form for the concept entry tool, together with an edit window opened on a concept element.

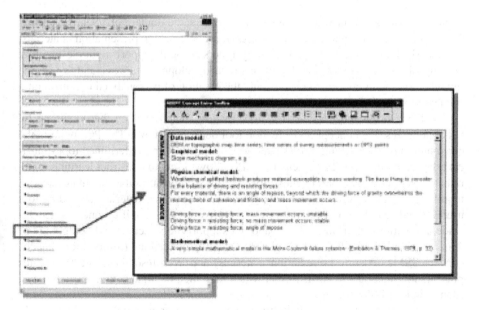

**Fig. 3.** The concept entry tool

Representations of the SSMs may be accessed in both visual and textual forms, with the former illustrating interrelationships among concepts and providing "global" views of the structure of the concept space. Textual forms allow DLE users to browse and link to the contents of SSMs.

We have implemented a KB of concepts as a centralized MySQL DB with thin client access through a web browser that supports the creation, access, and display of concepts. An extensive relationship structure has been implemented to allow for interaction between different concept types. In response to queries the DB, which supports adherence to a defined XML structure, returns an XML document by way of a PHP script.

A KB that currently holds approximately 1200 concepts from the domain of Physical Geography has been created by "domain experts" using these input tools.

## 2.3  Collections of Presentation Materials

Central to the ADEPT DLE are services that support the creation, search, and display of collections of *learning presentation materials* such as lecture, laboratory, and self-organized study materials. These services support users in incorporating items from other DLEs and collections into presentation materials.

Experience with presentation materials such as lectures or textbooks, whether traditional or not, indicates that instructors vary significantly in the way in which they structure and format presentation materials. In particular, there is variation in the choice of the underlying framework of concepts for describing and explaining phenomena, even though instructors may draw on the same domain of scientific knowledge. This suggests that creation services for constructing presentation materials, particularly if they are to be re-usable by others, should support a simple modular decomposition of materials that facilitates: their development, access, and re-use; the flexible creation of concept skeletons; and the creation of personalized organizational frameworks and formatting.

We have developed a web-based *presentation composer* (PC) that is similar to, but generalizes, the concept SST creation tool described above. The PC supports the quasi-automatic structuring of presentation materials in terms determined to a significant degree by the user. In particular, the PC allows users to construct learning materials that: (1) possess a variable level of granular composition that facilitates access, modification, and re-use; (2) organize presentation learning materials according to a user-defined template and/or around a structured set of scientific concepts; (3) include annotations of arbitrary form; and (4) support the selection and "dragging" of items from other sources, including different DLE collections (information objects, concept SSMs, existing presentation materials) and Web resources. The PC creates presentation materials in XML format which may then be organized in various ways, such as indexed file structures.

The PC supports the creation of structured presentation materials at two levels. At the highest level, a drop-down menu on the presentation browse page supports the creation, editing, and organization of basic granules from which presentations are constructed. At the second level, word-like edit windows support the creation of content within the granules, similar to that of the concepts SSMs. There is also a "meta-level" at which the user may create a presentation template that contains personalized classes of granules for different presentation types.

A given class of granule is characterized by a heading and any characteristic content that an instructor wishes to have appear whenever a granule is edited or displayed. Granule headings that we, for example, have created for structuring lecture presentation materials for the Physical Geography course include:

- *Topic, Subtopic, Subsubtopic;*
- *Phenomena, Observational Procedure, Fact*
- *Concept, Model, Theory*
- *Hypothesis/Evaluation, Question/Answer, Statement/Derivation, Comment*

as well as other and "blank" headings. Granule headings and associated material that the user may wish to include, are first created at the meta-level in a "template" file created by the same PC in a recursive application.

At the top level of creation, the PC supports various operations on the granules as units, including their relocation and indentation within the current or other presentations. The PC also supports the creation of *structure* among selected granules for use in displays of the presentation materials. An important example of such structuring operations is in creating *graphical representations of the conceptual structure of a presentation*.

In our current, personalized applications of the PC, we employ the heading *"Concept"* to introduce a concept, associated information, and links from the concept name to the SSM of the concept. A PC *conceptualization* operation allows users to associate a given concept occurring in a presentation (such as *Stream Velocity*) with other concepts occurring in the presentation (such as *Depth, Slope, Roughness*), so creating a network structure among the concepts. Since the output of the PC is represented in XML, it is straightforward at presentation time for display services to locate the "tags" for the *concept* heading and to structure the various concept terms into a graph for display.

At the second, or granule, level of presentation a word-like edit window, similar to that of the concept SSM input service, allows the user to enter and format arbitrary materials. When initially opened the granule edit window contains the personalized heading, together with optional content that is automatically part of a granule, or is blank. The user may then create arbitrarily formatted material within the edit window.

Current *display services* for presentation materials support different views of the materials that may be employed simultaneously during presentations. Two important classes of views include: (1) representations of the full presentation materials in various formats, including a single browser page, a collapsible outline of HTML droplets, or sequences of powerpoint-like slides; and (2) representations of views of organizational and conceptual frameworks of the materials as interactive graphs.

The first class of views is provided by XSL transformations of the underlying XML in which presentations are represented. The XSL is used in specifying content, positioning, and style sheet for font, colors, spacing, etc. We illustrate, in Figure 4, a browser view of a portion of a lecture presentation for a course in Physical Geography. This figure indicates various granule headings, annotation materials, and links to other information objects using thumbnail icons.

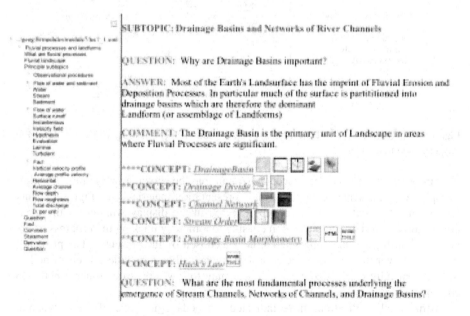

**Fig. 4.** The Lecture Window – Illustration of a Lecture from the Physical Geography Class

The second class of display services makes use of the facilities within the PC for creating structure among the presentation granules. Suppose, for example, that a user has created a *conceptualization* (or network of relationships) among the *concepts* of a presentation. We may then create graphical representations of this *conceptualization* (or concept space) using a 2D Java applet that is based upon a forced springs algorithm [11] although it is designed for the easy addition of new graphing algorithms. We show in Figure 5 the output of a Java applet representing a *conceptualization* of the concept *Mass Movement* employed in lecture presentations for the domain of Physical Geography.

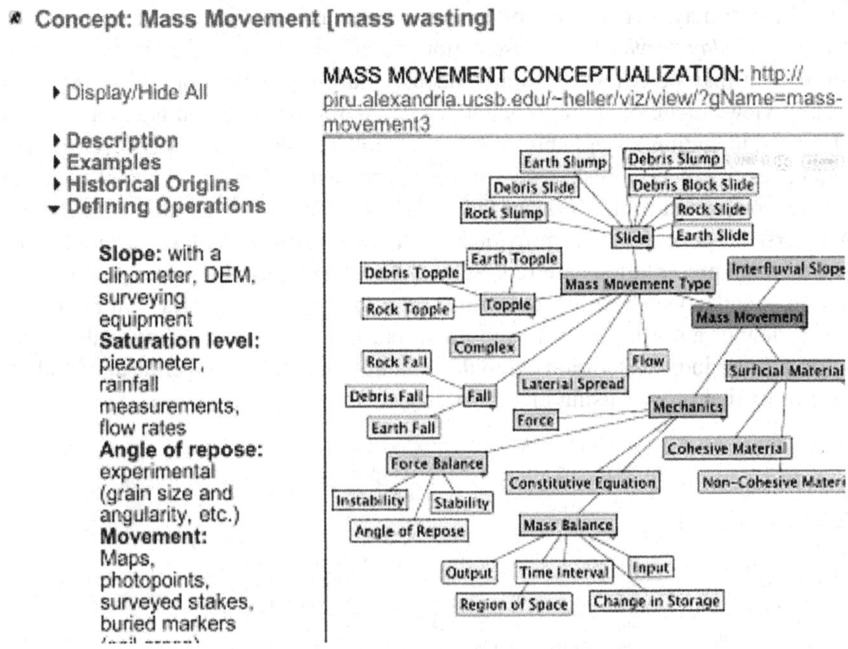

**Fig. 5.** Visual Presentation of the Concept Space - the Concept of *Mass Movement* from the Physical Geography Course

During a presentation, the conceptualization may be shown as a dynamic graph in a display window separate from the main presentation materials (see Figure 2). This display may be centered on a concept selected in the display window of the main presentation materials and be used in quasi-autonomously tracking the progress of the presentation through the conceptual structure chosen by the presenter. The presenter has control over the number of relationship levels visible, may hide subsets of nodes, may dynamically reorganize the graph, and may follow links from concept nodes to concept SSMs.

Instructional applications have indicated the pedagogic value of these dynamic representations of the conceptual structure, or *conceptualization,* of presentation materials. In effect, such conceptualizations provide, for a given concept, an answer to the question: "What other concepts, selected perhaps from the KB of concepts, might be of value in explaining or understanding this concept?" As an example, a reasonable answer for the concept of *Stream Velocity* might be *Roughness, Slope,* and *Depth*, since these are concepts that enter into elemental scientific representations of the concept. Such conceptualizations typically expand into a network and have value in providing students with incrementally-constructed but global views of the conceptual structure of the learning materials.

We note the many other applications of our second class of views, including views of the presentation content in terms of topical structure or methodological approaches and views of other relationships between concepts, such as standard, thesauri-type relationships.

## 3 Application, Evaluation, and Plans

The first application of the ADEPT DLE was focused on preparing presentation materials for relatively large classes of UCSB undergraduate students in the domain of Physical Geography. Three collections were created for this application: (1) an ADL collection involving item level metadata of over 1000 items of heterogeneous material illustrating various concepts in the knowledge domain; (2) a KB of over 1200 SSMs of the concepts employed in explaining the phenomena and methodology of the domain; and (3) a collection of lecture and laboratory presentations. The ADL collection contains such items as maps, images, figures, and animations. All presentation materials for both lectures and laboratories were made accessible over the web to students in the classes.

The actual presentation of *lecture* materials involved the use of three projector screens driven from a single computer. A frame from a video taken during a lecture is shown in Figure 2. The center screen shows the main presentation materials; the left screen shows a graphical representation of part of the conceptual structure of the lecture; and the right screen shows an illustrative item from the information object collection. The left screen is also used in showing information from the concept SSTs in the concept KB.

We note that three screens are not inherent in the design of the DLE, and that a presenter may prefer to use one, two, or even four screens. A presenter may control the displays from any of the presentation windows, although in the UCSB application, primary control resides in the main presentation window.

The design, implementation, and evaluation of ADEPT DLE involves an incremental process during which evaluative information obtained from class applications is employed in redesign and redevelopment. Data for ongoing evaluation of the efficacy of the DLE in undergraduate education is provided by: (1) monitoring of presentation sessions, including the videoing and audio-taping of each lecture; (2) responses to questionnaires answered by students; (3) informal and formal course evaluations by UCSB's Instructional Development; and (4) formal testing of the performance of students by members of the ADEPT evaluation team.

The formal testing involves students taking a sequence of cognitive tests at different times during a term, with comparisons being made with students in other introductory courses. These tests include: (1) a graph comprehension test; (2) a science text comprehension test; (3) a hypothesis generation test; (4) a scientific reasoning test; and (5) scientific attitudes assessment. The current results from the evaluation process are encouraging and will be the subject of a forthcoming paper.

Although in operational use, the ADEPT DLE is a system under constant development. Current development activities include: (1) augmentations of the services for collection creation, search, and display, especially in the direction of graphically-based services; (2) creation of an interface that provides unified access to the DLE; (3) support for "active learning objects" embedded in presentation items, and especially variable-parameter simulation models; and (4) support for XML databases.

Applications of the DLE are currently being created for other Geography courses at UCSB and other universities. Future applications are being planned for other domains of science.

Finally we note that the ADEPT DLE faces two significant issues of a nontechnical nature that typify the development of any DLE. The first is the issue of intellectual property rights and copyright. We are addressing these issues with a combination of seeking copyright permissions, finding materials without copyright restrictions, and using protected access and limiting access to materials to students in the classes. The second issue is the development of domain-specific KBs of concept representations. Based on the referenced examples of concept KBs developed by NIST and ACS, we believe that there is a great potential for domain-specific communities to develop both SSMs and KBs of concept.

**Acknowledgements.** The work described herein was partially supported by the NSF-DARPA-NASA Digital Libraries Initiative and the NSF NSDL initiative under NSF IR94-11330, NSF IIS-9817432, DUE-0121578, and UCAR S02-36644.

# References

1. Alexandria Digital Library Project Homepage. (2002) http://www.alexandria.ucsb.edu
2. Marshall, B., Zhang, Y., Chen, H., Lally, A., Shen, R., Fox, E., Cassel, L.N.: Convergence of Knowledge Management and E-Learning: the GetSmart Experience. Proceedings. 2003 Joint Conference on Digital Libraries, May 27–31, 2003, Rice University, Houston, Texas. IEEE Computer Society, Los Alamitos, CA. (2003) 135–146
3. Mayer, R., Smith, T.R., Borgman, C.L.: Digital Libraries as Instructional Aids for Knowledge Construction. Educational Technology. (2002)
4. Janee, G., Frew, J.: The ADEPT Digital Library Architecture. Proceedings of the Second ACM/IEEE-CS Joint Conference on Digital Libraries (JCDL ' 02), Portland, OR, July 14–18, 2002. IEEE Computer Society, Los Alamitos, CA. (2002)
5. ADEPT/DLESE: ADN Joint Metadata Content Model. (2001) http://www.dlese.org/Metadata/

6.    Smith, T.R., Zeng, M.L.: The ADEPT Knowledge Team: Structured Models of Scientific Concepts for Organizing, Accessing, and Using Learning Materials. In: Challenges in knowledge representation and Organization for the 21st century. Integration of Knowledge Across Boundaries: Proceedings of the Seventh International ISKO Conference, 10-13 July 2002, Granada, Spain. (2002) 232–239

7.    Smith, T.R. Zeng, M.L., ADEPT Knowledge Team: Structured Models of Scientific Concepts as a Basis for Organizing, Accessing, and Using Learning Materials. University of California Santa Barbara, Department of Computer Science Technical Report 2002–04 (2002)

8.    NIST: MatML: eXtensible Markup Language for Materials Property Data. Version 3.0 Schema. Prepared by E.F.Begley on behalf of the MatML Working Group. (2003). http://www.matml.org/downloads/MatMLv30.pdf

9.    CAS: Chemical Abstracts Service Homepage. http://www.cas.org.

10.   Weisgerber, D.W.: Chemical Abstracts Service. Chemical Registry System: History, Scope, and Impacts. Journal of the American Society for Information Science, 148(4) (1997) 349–360.

11.   Ancona, D.: Visual Explorations for the Alexandria Digital Earth Prototype. Second International Workshop on Visual Interfaces to Digital Libraries, JC DL, Portland, Oregon, (2002)

# A User Evaluation of Hierarchical Phrase Browsing

Katrina D. Edgar[1], David M. Nichols[1], Gordon W. Paynter[2],
Kirsten Thomson[1], and Ian H. Witten[1]

[1] Department of Computer Science, University of Waikato, Hamilton, New Zealand
{kde2, dmn, kthomson, ihw}@cs.waikato.ac.nz
[2] University of California, Riverside, CA, USA
paynter@ucr.edu

**Abstract.** Phrase browsing interfaces based on hierarchies of phrases extracted automatically from document collections offer a useful compromise between automatic full-text searching and manually-created subject indexes. The literature contains descriptions of such systems that many find compelling and persuasive. However, evaluation studies have either been anecdotal, or focused on objective measures of the quality of automatically-extracted index terms, or restricted to questions of computational efficiency and feasibility. This paper reports on an empirical, controlled user study that compares hierarchical phrase browsing with full-text searching over a range of information seeking tasks. Users found the results located via phrase browsing to be relevant and useful but preferred keyword searching for certain types of queries. Users' experiences were marred by interface details, including inconsistencies between the phrase browser and the surrounding digital library interface.

## 1 Introduction

The central mission of any digital library service is to make information readily available to users. In practice, people generally seek information by directed search, or serendipitous browsing, or some combination of the two. Typical search interfaces, like those found in digital libraries and Internet portals, allow users to enter queries and retrieve sets of relevant documents. Typical browsing interfaces, often presented via the now-ubiquitous Web hypertext browser, help users navigate between resources in an unplanned, undirected manner; new resources are discovered along the way. Between these extremes lies a wide range of interactive interfaces based on both manually-generated and automatically-created information and supporting varying levels of user knowledge and direction.

Effective information-seeking schemes embody mechanisms that prevent users from drowning in information. Most digital libraries let users browse lists of document metadata such as titles and authors (e.g. [19]). As collections grow, however, raw metadata rapidly becomes too voluminous to scan effectively [15]. The standard solution is to provide a topic-oriented hierarchy—such as a library classification scheme—that permits users to drill down from broad groups of items to more manageable subsets. Hierarchical classification schemes have been refined over decades into invaluable search tools, and are universally used in traditional libraries as the ba-

T. Koch and I.T. Sølvberg (Eds.): ECDL 2003, LNCS 2769, pp. 313–324, 2003.

sis for the logical and physical organization of library holdings. Clearly, high-quality classification information should be used wherever it is available to assist users in their browsing activities.

But manual classification is costly. In many digital library or Web-based document collections, accurate subject categories do not exist, and are not feasible to produce. Machine-readable subject thesauri are useful tools for exploring document collections topically, but in many cases digital library documents are not tagged with thesaurus metadata. The problem may ultimately be solved by automated hierarchical classification, an active research topic with some promise for the future (e.g. [4, 10, 11]). Today, however, alternative access mechanisms are sorely needed.

One alternative to manual classification is to automatically create a subject browser that resembles a thesaurus but is based on the occurrence of interesting phrases in documents rather than authoritative subject classifications. We call this strategy *hierarchical phrase browsing* because it allows users to browse through the phrases that occur in a large document collection, examining the terminology that is actually used in the documents, exploring the context in which phrases are used, and retrieving information based on the presence or absence of phrases. Lexical inclusion—whether one phrase occurs as a sub-phrase of another—provides a natural, intuitive, foundation for the hierarchy.

This paper documents the first formal user evaluation of a hierarchical phrase browsing interface based on automatically generated phrases. We focus on a particular browsing tool whose evolution has been described in the literature [13, 15]. Section 2 outlines related work and describes how phrase browsing differs from conventional search and browsing techniques. We then briefly sketch the operation of the target system, *Phind* (for "phrase index"), from a user perspective. The experimental conditions are detailed in Section 4 and the findings presented in Section 5. Finally we discuss how our findings might influence the design of future phrase browsing interfaces for digital libraries.

## 2   Hierarchical Phrase Browsing

By *hierarchical phrase browsing* we refer to any means of exploring the terminology used in a large document collection, independent of the particular documents in which terms occur, and based on words and phrases extracted automatically from the target documents themselves. Although lexically based, these phrases constitute a plausible, easily-understood, hierarchical, topic-oriented structure for the information in the collection. Several such phrase browsing interfaces are described in the literature, but none have been subjected to rigorous user evaluation. Previous research has concentrated on system description [1, 7, 15, 18], the quality of assigned index terms [14, 17] and evaluation for efficiency [2]; the contribution of this paper is to describe how users actually interact with a phrase browsing interface.

Gutwin *et al.* [7] describe an interface that lets users explore relationships between keyphrases extracted from all documents in a collection. In a small user evaluation, they found evidence that "a phrase-based approach to indexing and presentation offers better support for browsing tasks than traditional query engines" because it provides "a different level of information that is more appropriate for some kinds of tasks, and is certainly not detrimental in others." More specifically, they found that the interface performed best when the initial query is general, since a broader range of possible extensions becomes available; that phrase quality was a significant factor; that some legitimate topics are not well-represented as phrases; and that despite the convenience of the interface, some participants lacked confidence in its results. These results have spurred research into keyphrase quality [8, 9] and the development of new phrase extraction methods [5].

Others have evaluated automatically-extracted phrases and phrase hierarchies. Sanderson and Croft [16] describe a method for deriving phrase hierarchies based on phrase co-occurrence, called *subsumption hierarchies*, which are presented to users through standard menu systems, and evaluated by asking human subjects to identify the relationship between pairs of phrases. They conclude that the hierarchies "emulate some of the properties of manually generated subject hierarchies." In a later evaluation, Lawrie and Croft [12] compare subsumption hierarchies to other hierarchies by estimating the number of selections a user must make to browse from the top of a hierarchy to a relevant phrase, and observe large differences. Paynter *et al.* [14] compare automatically-extracted phrases (generated by Phind, the same system studied in the present paper) with a manually-created subject thesaurus, and discovered enough overlap to consider using the extracted phrase set as a source of suggestions for the thesaurus maintainers. Wacholder *et al.* [17] describe a *dynamic text browser* system for navigating index terms extracted from documents with natural language processing techniques, and evaluate it based on three criteria: index term coherence, coverage of document content and usefulness. None of these evaluations attempts to assess the user's experiences with a phrase browsing interface.

# 3   An Interface for Hierarchical Phrase Browsing

The Phind phrase browsing interface is part of the Greenstone digital library software [19]. Greenstone is a complete system for creating, managing, and distributing digital library collections that is freely available from the New Zealand Digital Library Project (*http://nzdl.org*). Phind browsers can be added to any Greenstone collection, and applied to any combination of the documents' text and metadata fields.

## 3.1   Using Phind

Fig. 1 shows Phind in use with a Greenstone collection called *FAO on the Internet*, described in more detail in Section 4. The user enters an initial term in the search box at the top. On pressing the 'Search' button, the upper panel appears. This shows the phrases at the top level in the hierarchy that contain the search term—in this case, the word *forest*. The list is sorted by phrase frequency; on the right is the number of times a phrase appears, and preceding that is the number of documents in which it appears.

**Fig. 1.** Browsing for information about *forest* using Phind

The results are initially limited to the first ten phrases because many of the phrase lists are very large. The total number of phrases appears above the list: in this case 10 phrases are displayed of an available 1632 top-level phrases that contain the term *forest*. At the end of the list is an item that reads 'get more phrases' (displayed in a distinctive color). Clicking it downloads a further ten phrases, which will be accumulated in the browser window so that the user can scroll through all phrases that have been downloaded so far.

The lower panel in Fig. 1 appears when the user clicks one of the phrases in the upper list. In this case the user has clicked *sustainable forest* (which is why that line is highlighted in the upper panel), causing the lower panel to display phrases that contain the text *sustainable forest*. The text above the lower panel shows that the phrase *sustainable forest* appears in 36 larger phrases, and in 258 documents.

If one continues to descend through the phrase hierarchy, longer and more specific phrases will be found. The page holds only two panels, and when a phrase in the lower panel is clicked the contents of that panel move up to the top panel to make way for the phrase's expansion in the lower panel. In Fig. 2, for example, the user has expanded *sustainable forest management*, and begun scrolling through its expansions.

The interface not only presents the expansions of the phrase, it lists the documents in which the phrase occurs. Each panel shows a phrase list followed by a document list. The first ten document titles are loaded immediately, and become visible when the list is scrolled. In the lower panel of Fig. 2, the user has scrolled down so that the first six document titles are visible. Document titles are easily distinguished on the screen because they appear in a different color from phrases. On the black-and-white rendition in Fig. 2 they are distinguished by the absence of a "document" count, because this, by definition, is equal to 1 for the phrase in question (otherwise the document would appear not under the phrase itself but under an expansion of it.) Only the first ten document titles are downloaded, and (as with phrases) users can 'get more documents' by clicking on a special entry at the end of the list (which would become visible if the panel were scrolled down a little more).

**Fig. 2.** Expanding on *sustainable forest*

Clicking on a document title opens that document in a new window. In fact, in Fig. 2 the user has clicked on *Unasylva 182 * Sustainable forest management* (that is why its line is highlighted), which displays the document in a new window. As Fig. 2 indicates, that document contains 20 occurrences of the phrase *sustainable forest management*. Greenstone will optionally underline each occurrence of the phrase in the document text.

### 3.2  Extracting Phind Phrases

Underlying the Phind user interface is a hierarchy of phrases that appear in the document collection. In their evaluation of a hierarchical keyphrase interface, Gutwin *et al.* [7] observed that the user experience is affected by phrase set quality, and by topics that are not well-represented by a browsable phrase. For this reason, the Greenstone version of Phind is based on a completely new phrase extraction scheme that eschews highly selective phrase sets, and instead creates a hierarchy from every repeated phrase in the document collection (with some caveats). As an example, consider the following paragraph from a document in the *FAO on the Internet (1998)* collection, which is annotated with parentheses to show the phrase structure:

The capacity of the (Desert Locust) for (rapid multiplication) and ((long-distance) migration) ((under [favourable) conditions]) results in highly (variable population) levels over (space and time). Periodically, major population ((upsurges and [plagues) develop]), usually following a sequence of (good rains) which favour reproduction. Such (upsurges and plagues) are interspersed by (periods of (relative inactivity)) called recessions during which ((Desert [Locust) populations]) may remain at very (low levels) for a number of years.

We use the term "phrase hierarchy" to describe the subphrase relationship, though it is not a tree structure; square brackets appear in the above excerpt to indicate non-nested phrases. In Phind, a "phrase" is defined as a sequence of words that occurs more than once in the text. To include *every* such phrase would clutter the interface with trivial phrases, so we add three further conditions to the definition. Phrases must not contain *phrase delimiters*, must neither begin nor end with a *stopword*, and must be *maximal-length*.

The first two restrictions are purely syntactic. If the text were treated as an undifferentiated stream of words, many of the phrases extracted from it would cross syntactic boundaries. To take an extreme example, the last word of one document and the first word of the next are unlikely to form a meaningful two-word phrase. For this reason, we impose the constraint that phrases may not include delimiters. Delimiters are defined as the end of documents, the end of sentences, and any punctuation characters. In practice, we tune the punctuation rule to account for common (and language-dependent) usage: in English, for example, neither the apostrophe in *don't* nor the hyphen in *language-dependent* are interpreted as phrase boundaries. We also mandate that stopwords (like *the, of,* and *for*) may not appear at the beginning or end of a phrase to avoid trivial expansions like *the capacity* or *locust for*.

The requirement that phrases are maximal-length sequences is more complex. A phrase is maximal-length if it occurs in more than one context, where by "context" we mean the words that flank the phrase where it appears in the text. Phrases that are not maximal-length—ones that are flanked by the same words wherever they appear—are expanded to encompass the identical context. In the FAO collection, for example, the phrase *forest industries strategy* occurs only in the longer phrase *forestry industries strategy study*, so the latter term is displayed at the top level of the hierarchy in place of the former. On the other hand, the phrase *sustainable forest* occurs in many different contents—ten examples can be seen in the lower pane of Fig. 1.

The three conditions are carefully chosen to provide a phrase structure that covers all the topics appearing in the documents and which makes the phrase/subphrase relationship both simple and obvious. This phrase structure allows an interface to clearly situate a user in the hierarchy, yet it remains simple enough to be generated for large collections with limited computational resources.

# 4 Study Description

The user evaluation assessed the usability and utility of the Phind phrase browsing interface. The goals of the evaluation were threefold: (i) to determine the value of using Phind to browse a topic as a way of learning what a collection has about that topic; (ii) to determine whether Phind is better than keyword searching in terms of ease of locating specific information held within a collection and ease of navigation; and (iii) to assess the participants' subjective acceptance of Phind's interface.

The study was conducted during February 2003 at the University of Waikato Usability Laboratory. Each session involved only one participant, who performed two tasks during a single session. Because the study was comparative, we used a within-subject design: each participant worked with both the phrase browsing interface and keyword searching. The design was counter-balanced by randomizing the order of the tasks to reduce the effect of transfer learning.

There were twelve participants in the study. All were students (seven graduates) who were nearly evenly split between computing and management disciplines. All but one of the participants typically used computers for more than an hour a day, all were familiar with Internet keyword searching but only nine had previously used a digital library. Three-quarters of the participants were male.

The study used the FAO Collection within Greenstone; it comprises the Web site of the Food and Agriculture Organization (FAO) of the United Nations, in a version that was distributed on CD-ROM in 1998. This is not an ordinary, informally-organized Web site. The mandate of the FAO is to distribute agricultural information internationally, and the information included is controlled, giving it more of the characteristics of a typical digital library collection. With 21,700 Web pages, as well as around 13,700 associated files (image files, PDFs, etc.), it corresponds to a medium-sized collection of approximately 140 million words of text. The Web site (*http://www.fao.org*) has since grown to many times this size, but we use the 1998 version as it was selected by editors at the FAO, and contains no dynamic content.

Each participant was asked to complete seven tasks that involve locating information, understanding content, and recognizing and using elements and functions. Participants were asked to complete a variety of information searching tasks with both the usual Greenstone keyword searching and the Phind interface. Participants were not given any explicit training but were prompted with help during their first task. The study included both exploratory questions, e.g.:

–'find out more about national forest programmes in different countries'

and specific retrieval tasks, e.g.:

–'where can golden apple snails be found?'
–'what was the locust numbers situation during May in Kuwait?'
–'what does APFSOS stand for?'

The participants used a browser to access the FAO Collection on the New Zealand Digital Library Web server. The Phind interface is a presented as a Java applet within Greenstone. Participants' interactions were recorded on video and they were also asked to complete questionnaires before and after the tasks, and a final comparison questionnaire.

# 5  Results

The analysis of the session video recordings and the participants' questionnaires yielded an abundance of data; we present the main findings here in terms of task performance, general usability of the Phind interface and usability problems discovered in the interface.

## 5.1  Task Performance

Most participants (10 out of 12) indicated in their questionnaire that they had found the results returned by Phind to be *clear and easy to understand*. Similarly, 10 out of 12 indicated that Phind's results were *relevant and useful to the query*. For both these questions the participants rated Phind to be clearly superior to keyword searching.

*Exploratory Questions.* The participants were generally positive about performing exploratory tasks in Phind. These tasks gave rise to positive feedback regarding the way the system is set out and subphrases are presented.

Some participants spent in excess of 10 minutes completing these questions. Its exploratory nature meant they were prepared to keep going almost indefinitely, finding out more detailed information than was required. Most participants used this time to explore the interface, and some asked questions regarding the actions that occurred. This period exposed many of the usability issues reported in Section 5.3.

Most users followed the same paths through the top level of the hierarchy on multiple occasions (e.g. *Forest*, then *national forest*, then *national forest programmes*), before following different avenues with more specific phrases, which suggests that many participants were unaware of the function of the navigation buttons.

*Specific Retrieval Tasks.* The participants had difficulties using phrase browsing to complete the specific retrieval tasks that involved multiple topics, e.g. 'what are the most widely planted pines for timber and pulp production in the southern United States?' and 'What was the locust numbers situation during May in Kuwait?' Of the 12 participants who attempted these two questions with Phind, four gave up, five gave the wrong answer and only three found the correct answer. In stark contrast, these two tasks were successfully completed by 11 of the 12 participants who used keyword searching.

## 5.2  The Phind Interface

Users readily accepted the idea of phrase browsing; in the summary questionnaire two thirds of participants listed the concept of Phind as the *element or feature that they liked the most*. Comments included: "The way you filter through the results to narrow it down" and "The idea of it – takes the work out of searching for you."

Three-quarters of the participants commented on Phind's inability to search on more than one term. All participants tried at least one multi-term search in Phind.

*Being able to search on only one term* appeared in the summary questionnaires of three participants as an element or feature that they disliked most. Comments included: "You should be able to put more than one word" and "Confusing when I was searching for two different topics."

## 5.3  Phind Usability Issues

Analysis of the participants' interactions, particularly in response to the exploratory questions, identified a range of usability problems in the Phind user interface.

*Two Window Display.* The use of two windows was problematic for some participants. Three participants minimized the document window instead of closing it, which meant that when they clicked on a document link, Phind opened the document in the hidden window. This was not apparent to the participants, who received no indication at all that the document had opened. All three of these participants had to be prompted repeatedly that their document could be found in the other window.

*Results Panels.* Five participants had problems with the relationship between Phind's two result panels. For example, one thought that the lower panel was always a subsection of the upper one. Three thought that the phrases would remain in the upper panel and the documents would remain in the bottom one. Confusion arose when these participants investigated a second phrase link from the top screen and ended up with the results of their two phrase links being displayed and their list of phrases in the history.

*Title Display.* The titles of the returned documents are centered in the display space (see Fig. 2 above for an example). However, when the document title exceeds the width available it is truncated at both ends, and users have no means to scroll horizontally. Half the participants commented negatively on this truncated display. Often the displayed portion of the title is insufficient to indicate a document's topic. Comments included: "It would be nice if you could read at the sides" and "How are you going to know what's contained in a paper if you can't see the title?"
    At the phrase link level of the hierarchy the same truncation occurs, but with slightly different results. This is because phrase links are aligned on the search term that they contain, rather than on the text as a whole.

*User Feedback from Requests.* Five participants found it frustrating that there was no feedback after a request to indicate that processing was occurring. Impatient participants often clicked a link several times while waiting for Phind to load the next results page. To prevent this re-occurring, some participants were eventually told verbally that Phind was indeed processing their request.

*Navigation.* The navigation provided by Phind was underused. Five of the twelve participants did not use the 'Previous' or 'Next' buttons at all. One did not appear to understand the 'Previous' button and listed "not being able to go back" as one of the *elements or features that they most disliked about Phind* in their summary question-naire. Of the seven participants who did use the navigation buttons, two participants first had to enquire, "Is there a way to go back?" We also observed that few partici-pants followed the 'get more phrases' and 'get more documents' links, suggesting that their function was poorly understood by some participants.

## 5.4  Summary

Although two-thirds of the participants liked the concept behind Phind, only a quarter named it as the search method they preferred overall. The two main reasons appear to be difficulties with multi-term topics and queries, and assorted usability issues with the interface.

# 6  Discussion

Users readily accepted the phrase browsing concept, despite several shortcomings in the Phind interface, and were able to understand the results. In this sense, the interface is a success.

However, three quarters of the users preferred the keyword searching over phrase browsing overall. Despite liking the Phind interface, the participants found many problems. The main functional problem was Phind's inability to perform multi-word queries. Another problem is Phind's unfamiliarity: with a new interface like Phind, a learning period is required, and the limited verbal help we provided is unlikely to match the experience of our participants already had with keyword searching. On the other had, this unfamiliarity may lend an aspect of novelty value to its appeal.

The study showed that the issue of locating a starting point for a phrase browsing interaction was problematic. In providing a text box for a user to enter a term the in-terface suggested that any terms could be entered; as in, say, a web search engine. A common result of this is the zero-hit response as the user's terms did not exist as a phrase in any of the documents. However this behaviour contrasts sharply with browsing once the user has entered the phrase hierarchy, where *all* options displayed are actual phrases from the texts.

The study clearly implies that the Phind interface should be refined to distinguish specific interface effects from more general phrase browsing issues. Although the us-ability issues were individually small, they clearly had a significant impact on the participants' experiences. In this regard the study reinforces existing usability studies of digital library use. In particular, we observed two previously-reported design is-sues: "working across boundaries" in the different paradigms of browser-based key-word searching vs. the Java-based Phind interface; and "blind alleys" when Phind us-ers attempted multi-term phrase queries [3]. 'Boundary' related problems included inconsistent experiences with the opening of windows leading to lost documents, lack of feedback during query evaluation, unfamiliar navigation tools, and problems un-derstanding the relationship between frames and result sets.

Phind is implemented as a Java applet within the Greenstone digital library, which is otherwise HTML-based. Several issues appear to have arisen because Phind was originally developed as a stand-alone application connecting to a customised server [13] and was only relatively recently ported to the hypertext environment. We hope that by making Phind more consistent with Greenstone's usual behaviour, and with the users' usual expectations of Web site design, these problems will be resolved.

However, there is an alternative perspective. It is attractive to consider re-casting Phind as an interface in which it is impossible to express zero-hit queries [6]. If the initial word were selected from a list of the actual vocabulary of the document collection instead of being freely typed, users could drill into the contents of the collection simply by clicking on words and phrases to reveal ever longer ones. This pulls the implementation strategy away from HTML and firmly into a more reactive interface, revealing a tension between trying to conform with existing search interface paradigms and pushing the envelope of reactive interfaces.

There are clearly usability issues with the Phind interface, but the participants' reactions to phrase browsing are encouraging. In addition to interface design work, a larger longitudinal study would be interesting to examine whether these positive reactions transfer from the usability laboratory to everyday information searching.

## 7 Conclusion

Although hierarchical phrase browsing systems have existed for some time, there appears to be little research on users' experiences with this style of interaction. This study compared a stable, familiar search interface with a novel hierarchical phrase browsing system. The upshot was that although the participants preferred the search interface, they could see the potential advantages of phrase browsing.

Through its universal adoption in Internet search engines, the keyword search paradigm dominates information retrieval today. Phrase browsing interfaces promise something more—an interaction with greater structure that offers improved support for users' exploration of document collections.

## References

1. Anick, P., Tiperneni, S.: The Paraphrase Search Assistant: Terminological Feedback for Iterative Information Seeking. In Proceedings of the 22nd Annual International ACM SIGIR Conference on Research and Development in Information Retrieval. Berkeley, CA, USA (1999) 153–159
2. Bahle, D., Williams, H.E., Zobel, J.: Efficient Phrase Querying with an Auxiliary Index. In Proceedings of the ACM-SIGIR Conference on Research and Development in Information Retrieval. Tampere, Finland (2002) 215–221
3. Blandford, A., Stelmaszewska, H., Bryan-Kinns, N.: Use of Multiple Digital Libraries: A Case Study. In Proceedings of the First ACM/IEEE-CS Joint Conference on Digital Libraries. Roanoke, VA, USA (2001) 179–188

4. Dolin, R.: Pharos: A Scalable, Distributed Architecture for Locating Heterogeneous Information Sources. PhD Thesis, University of California, Santa Barbara, Santa Barbara, CA, USA (1998)
5. Frank E., Paynter G.W., Witten I.H., Gutwin C., Nevill-Manning C.G.: Domain-specific Keyphrase Extraction. In Proceedings of the International Joint Conference on Artificial Intelligence. Stockholm, Sweden (1999) 668–673
6. Greene, S., Tanin, E., Plaisant, C., Shneiderman, B., Olsen, L., Major, G., Johns, S.: The End of Zero-Hit Queries: Query Previews for NASA's Global Change Master Directory. International Journal of Digital Libraries 2(2-3) (1999) 79–90
7. Gutwin C., Paynter G., Witten I.H., Nevill-Manning C., Frank, E.: Improving Browsing in Digital Libraries with Keyphrase Indexes, Journal of. Decision Support Systems 27(1-2) (1999) 81–104
8. Jones S., Paynter G. W.: Automatic Extraction of Document Keyphrases for Use in Digital Libraries: Evaluation and Applications. Journal of the American Society for Information Science and Technology 53(2) (2002) 653–677
9. Jones S., Paynter G. W.: An Evaluation of Document Keyphrase Sets. Journal of Digital Information 4 (1) (2003)
10. Koller, D., Sahami, M.: Hierarchically Classifying Documents Using Very Few Words. In Proceedings of ICML-97: the 14th International Conference on Machine Learning. Nashville, TN, USA (1997) 170–178
11. Larson, R. R.: Experiments in Automatic Library of Congress Classification. Journal of the American Society for Information Science 43(2) (1992) 130–148
12. Lawrie, D., Croft, W. B.: Discovering and Comparing Hierarchies. In Proceedings of Recherche d'Informations Assistee par Ordinateur (RIAO) Conference. Paris, France (2000) 314–330
13. Nevill-Manning, C.G., Witten, I.H., Paynter, G.W.: Browsing in Digital Libraries: A Phrase-based Approach. In Proceedings of the Second ACM International Conference on Digital Libraries. Philadelphia, PA, USA (1997) 230–236
14. Paynter, G.W., Witten, I.H., Cunningham, S.J.: Evaluating Extracted Phrases and Extending Thesauri. In Proceedings of the Third International Conference on Asian Digital Libraries. Seoul, Korea (2000) 131–138
15. Paynter, G.W., Witten, I.H, Cunningham, S.J., Buchanan, G.: Scalable Browsing for Large Collections: A Case Study. In Proceedings of the Fifth ACM Conference on Digital Libraries, San Antonio, TX, USA (2000) 215–223
16. Sanderson, M. Croft, W. B.: Deriving Concept Hierarchies from Text. In Proceedings of the 22nd Annual International ACM SIGIR Conference on Research and Development in Information Retrieval, Berkeley, CA, USA (1999) 206–213.
17. Wacholder, N., Evans, D.K., Klavans, J.L.: Automatic Identification and Organization of Index Terms for Interactive Browsing. In Proceedings of the First ACM/IEEE-CS Joint Conference on Digital Libraries. Roanoke, VA, USA (2001) 126–134
18. Wacholder, N., Nevill-Manning, C.: Workshop 2: the Technology of Browsing Applications. In Proceedings of the First ACM/IEEE-CS Joint Conference on Digital Libraries. Roanoke, VA, USA (2001) 483
19. Witten, I.H., Bainbridge, D.: How to Build a Digital Library. Morgan Kaufmann, San Francisco, CA, USA (2003)

# Visual Semantic Modeling of Digital Libraries

Qinwei Zhu[1], Marcos André Gonçalves[1], Rao Shen[1], Lillian Cassell[2], and
Edward A. Fox[1]

[1]Department of Computer Science
Virginia Tech
Blacksburg, VA 24061, USA
{qzhu,mgoncalv,rshen,fox}@vt.edu

[2]Villanova University
Villanova, PA 19085-1699
lillian.cassell@villanova.edu

**Abstract.** The current interest from non-experts who wish to build digital libraries (DLs) is strong worldwide. However, since DLs are complex systems, it usually takes considerable time and effort to create and tailor a DL to satisfy specific needs and requirements of target communities/societies. What is needed is a simplified modeling process and rapid generation of DLs. To enable this, DLs can be modeled with descriptive domain-specific languages. A visual tool would be helpful to non-experts so they may model a DL without knowing the theoretical foundations and the syntactic details of the descriptive language. In this paper, we present a domain-specific visual DL modeling tool, 5SGraph. It employs a metamodel that describes DLs using the 5S theory. The output from 5SGraph is a DL model that is an instance of the metamodel, expressed in the 5S description language. Furthermore, 5SGraph maintains semantic constraints specified by the 5S metamodel and enforces these constraints over the instance model to ensure semantic consistency and correctness. 5SGraph enables component reuse to reduce the time and effort of designers. 5SGraph also is designed to accommodate and integrate several other complementary tools reflecting the interdisciplinary nature of DLs. Thus, tools based on concept maps to fulfill those roles are introduced. The 5SGraph tool has been tested with real users and several modeling tasks in a usability experiment, and its usefulness and learnability have been demonstrated.

## 1 Introduction

The interest from non-experts who wish to build digital libraries (DLs) is strong worldwide. However, since DLs are complex systems, it is difficult to create and tailor them to satisfy specific needs and requirements of target communities (for generality, referred to herein as "societies"). What is needed is a simplified modeling process involving descriptive domain-specific languages [1], and rapid generation of DLs. In such languages, models are made up of elements representing concepts, rules, and terminology that are part of the domain world, as opposed to the world of code or of generic modeling languages (e.g., UML [2]). A visual tool should be helpful to

T. Koch and I.T. Sølvberg (Eds.): ECDL 2003, LNCS 2769, pp. 325–337, 2003.

non-experts so they may model a DL without knowing the theoretical foundations and the syntactic details of the descriptive languages.

Thus, we present a domain-specific visual modeling tool, 5SGraph, aimed at modeling DLs. 5SGraph is based on a metamodel that describes DLs using the 5S theory [3]. The output from 5SGraph is a DL model that is an instance of the metamodel, expressed in the 5S description language (5SL) [4]. 5SGraph presents the metamodel in a structured toolbox, and provides a top-down visual building environment for designers. The visual proximity of the metamodel and instance model facilitates requirements gathering and simplifies the modeling process. Furthermore, 5SGraph maintains semantic constraints specified by the 5S metamodel and enforces these constraints over the instance model to ensure semantic consistency and correctness. 5SGraph enables component reuse, to reduce the time and efforts of designers. 5SGraph also is designed to be flexible and extensible, able to accommodate and integrate several other complementary tools (e.g., to model societal relationships, scenarios, or complex digital objects), reflecting the interdisciplinary nature of DLs. 5SGraph has been tested with real users and several modeling tasks in a usability experiment [5] and its usefulness and learnability have been demonstrated.

This paper is organized as follows. Section 2 provides background on theory, language, and approach. Section 3 describes 5SGraph: its design, functionality, key features, and visualization properties. Section 4 presents design, measures, and results of a usability experiment to evaluate the tool. Section 5 covers semantic modeling of DL constructs with concept maps. Section 6 concludes the paper.

## 2  Background

Recognizing the difficulties in understanding, defining, describing, and modeling complex DLs, and building upon work launched in 1999 [7], Gonçalves, Fox, et al. have proposed and formalized the 5S (Streams, Structures, Spaces, Scenarios, and Societies) theory of DLs [3]. The many definitions in [3] unambiguously specify key characteristics and behaviors of DLs. This enables automatic mapping from 5S models to actual implementations as well as the study of qualitative properties of these models (e.g., completeness, consistency, etc.) [6].

In order to model a DL, a designer has to describe:  1) the kinds of multimedia information the DL supports; 2) how that information is structured and organized; 3) different logical and presentational properties and operations of DL components; 4) the behavior of the DL; and 5) the different societies of actors and managers of services that act to carry out the DL behavior. To accommodate these, Gonçalves and Fox proposed 5SL, for declarative specification and generation of DLs based on 5S [4]. It is a high-level, domain-specific language, which: 1) raises the level of abstraction in DL specification and modeling by offering abstractions for the domain at hand; and 2) shows how DL design issues may be combined in a coherent framework that enriches, extends, and customizes classical models for databases, information retrieval, and hypertext.   5SL is an XML realization of the 5S model, addressing interoperability and reuse in its design. Table 1 summarizes, for each of the 'S' models: the formal definition and the objective of the model.

**Table 1.** 5S/5SL overview.

| Model | Formal definition | Objective within 5SL |
|---|---|---|
| **Streams** | Sequences of arbitrary types | Describe properties of the DL content such as encoding and language for textual material or particular forms of multimedia data |
| **Structures** | Labeled directed graphs | Specify organizational aspects of the DL (e.g., structural /descriptive metadata, hyper-texts, taxonomies, classification schemes) |
| **Spaces** | Sets of objects and operations on those objects that obey specific constraints | Define logical and presentational views of several components |
| **Scenarios** | Sequences of events that modify states of a computation in order to accomplish some functional requirement | Detail the behavior of the DL services |
| **Societies** | Sets of communities and relationships (relations) among them | Define managers, responsible for running DL services; actors, that use those services; and relationships among them |

Table 2 shows the set of concepts/primitives and sub-languages and notations used in the implementation of each 'S' model within 5SL.

**Table 2.** 5SL primitives and implementation.

| Model | Primitives | 5SL implementation |
|---|---|---|
| **Streams Model** | Text; video; audio; picture; software program | MIME types |
| **Structures Model** | Collection; catalog; hypertext; document; metadata; organization tools | XML and RDF schemas; Topic maps ML (XTM) |
| **Spaces Model** | User interface; index; retrieval model | MathML, UIML, XSL |
| **Scenarios Model** | Service; event; condition; action | Extended UML sequence diagrams; XML serialization |
| **Societies Model** | Community; service managers; actors; relationships; attributes; operations | XML serialization |

## 3    The 5SGraph Modeling Tool

### 3.1  Functionality

With 5SL, a DL designer does not need to be an expert in software engineering or information science. The designer only needs to have a clear conceptual picture of the needed DL and be able to transform the conceptual picture to 5SL files. This greatly reduces the burden on designers, speeds up the building process, and increases the quality of the DLs built. However, 5SL has its own problems and limitations:

1. The designer must understand 5SL well enough to be able to write a 5SL file and to correctly use it to express his/her ideal digital library.

2. The 5SL file, which describes a DL, consists of five sub-models (Stream model, Structural model, Spatial model, Scenarios model, and Societal model). Although all of the five sub-models are expressed in XML, they use different sets of concepts and have different semantics. Thus, the 5SL specification is compatible and extensible, because many existing standard formats can be used within the 5SL language. Yet, to build one DL, the designer needs to understand the five or more different semantic specifications that are required to express the system.

3. When large and complex digital libraries are to be built, it is very hard even for experts to manually write those XML files without any assistance from a tool.

4. It is very difficult to obtain the big picture of a DL just from a huge set of XML files. This may cause trouble for maintenance, upgrade, or even understanding of an existing system.

5. A number of semantic constraints exist between (inter-model constraints) and within (intra-model constraints) the sub-models. Designers need extra effort to ensure consistency in the whole model.

Reflecting on the above mentioned disadvantages of 5SL, we consider the following four functions of a modeling tool based on the 5S/5SL framework to be essential: To help DL designers to 1) understand the 5S model quickly and easily; 2) build their own DLs without difficulty.; 3) transform their models into complete, correct, and consistent 5SL files automatically; 4) understand, maintain, and upgrade existing DL models conveniently.

Accordingly, our 5SGraph modeling tool supports these functions as it provides an easy-to-use graphical interface. It automatically generates desired 5SL files for the designer. Since visualization often helps people understand complex models, 5SGraph is able to load and graphically display DL metamodels. The visual model shows the structure and different concepts of a DL and the relationship among these concepts. 5SGraph also provides a structured toolbox to let the designer build a DL by manipulation and composition of visual components (see Figure 1). The structured toolbox provides all the visual components of the metamodel, and shows the structural relationships among these components. The visualization thus provides guidance while the designer is building the model. The designer only needs to deal with a graphical interface and pull visual components together. It is not required to memorize the details of the syntax and semantics of 5SL. Cognitive load is reduced. Typing effort and typing errors are reduced. Furthermore, correctness and consistency can be automatically guaranteed by 5SGraph; thus it yields correct and consistent 5SL XML files according to the visual model built by the designer. As such, 5SGraph eliminates the disadvantages of working with raw 5SL.

The concept of metamodel is very important to assure flexibility. The metamodel describes a generic DL. The model for a specific DL is an instance of the metamodel, which in our case is a domain-specific metamodel, i.e., specific to the domain of building DLs. Since the 5S framework is still under development, it is expected that more changes and additions will be made in the future, especially to 5SL. Fortunately, when given a new metamodel, the tool can be used with future versions of the 5S model as well.

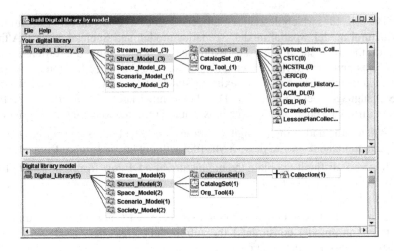

**Fig. 1.** 5SGraph sample interface with structured toolbox (bottom part) and workspace (upper part); figure shows modeling of collections for the CITIDEL project (www.citidel.org).

## 3.2 Key Features

Some of the major features of the tool include:

- Flexible and extensible architecture

5SGraph is a domain-specific modeling tool. Thus, the model is made up of elements that are part of the domain world, not the whole entity world. 5SGraph is tailored to accommodate a certain domain metamodel: for 5S. Methods that are appropriate only to 5S can be used to optimize the modeling process. Reuse in such a specific domain is realistic and efficient, because the models in that domain have many characteristics in common.

The 5SL language extensively uses existing standards. The reason is that the specification of a DL involves many sub-domains, and there are various standard specifications for each sub-domain. There also are many well-developed tools for those sub-domains. For example, metadata is an important element in 5S. Several existing metadata editors can be used to view and edit metadata. Another example concerns the scenario part of 5S. A specific scenario can be modeled and described by UML sequence diagrams, so existing UML modeling tools can be used for this purpose [8].

The 5SGraph tool should not "re-invent the wheel". Therefore, the tool is designed to be a super-tool, which means it provides an infrastructure based on the 5S model and calls existing tools as needed. In the interest of brevity, however, except for our new work that is discussed in Section 5, this paper focuses on how 5SGraph helps with modeling a DL, rather than on how 5SGraph calls other tools to create customized components.

• Reuse of components and sub-models

In 5SGraph, component reusability means that components designed in one user model can be saved and reused in other user models. Reusability saves time and effort. There are components that are common for different DL systems. For example, many DLs share the same data formats, and the same descriptive metadata standards. The components representing the Stream Model or the metadata in the Structural Model can be built once and reused in different DLs. When a new component is needed, the user does not need to build a component from scratch. He/she loads a similar component and spends relatively less time by making minor changes to customize the loaded component (see Figure 2).

Of course, not all components are designed to be reusable. A reusable component should be self-contained and independent.

• Synchronization between the model and the metamodel

There are two views in the tool. One is for the toolbox (metamodel); the other is for the user model. These two views are related through the type/instance relationships between components in the toolbox and components in the user model. When a user selects an instance component in the workspace (user model), 5SGraph is able to synchronize the view of the toolbox by showing a visible path from the root to the corresponding type of selected component (see Figure 1). The convenience of synchronization is that: 1) The user does not need to manually search all the components in the toolbox to find the correct type component; and 2) The tool helps the user focus on the most important relationships of the type components. The child components that can be added to the current component are within easy reach.

• Enforcing of semantic constraints

Certain inherent semantic constraints exist in the hierarchical structure of the 5S model. These constraints in 5S are divided into two categories. Value constraints specify the range of possible values of an element, while association constraints define the relationships among different components. Examples of such constraints include:

1. The streams used in the definition of a digital object (document) are predefined in the Stream Model.
2. A collection consists of different kinds of documents. A catalog describes a collection, since a catalog collects all the administrative or descriptive metadata that apply to the digital objects in the collection. A catalog, therefore, is dependent on a collection.
3. The services that the actor (a member of the Society Model) uses or a manager (another member of the Society Model) runs can be drawn only from the services already defined in the Scenario Model.

The 5SGraph tool is able to manage these constraints. For example, an actor only can use services that have been defined in the Scenario Model. This is specified in the metamodel, where the SubNodes part of actor contains the Datatype 'Services' (not shown in the figure), which means only existing instances of Services can become child nodes of an actor. The declaration of an actor, Teacher, is shown in Figure 3(a). In order to associate actors with the services they use, the designer browses back to the Scenario Model to select services:   metadata search, multi-scheme browsing, profile filtering, browsing, cataloging, focused crawling, lesson plan building, and lesson plan customized browsing (this one with four scenarios: unordered and ordered browsing, guided path, and slide show — as supported by the VIADUCT manager). When the designer browses back to Actor in the Scenario Model in the metamodel, he/she finds that the created set of services are automatically added into the metamodel under the node "Actor" (see Figure 3(b), structured toolbox), allowing him/her to connect the defined services with the actors that use them. In the example, Learner is connected to all but two services (focused crawling, run by the "crawlifier" manager, and lesson plan building, used only by teachers).

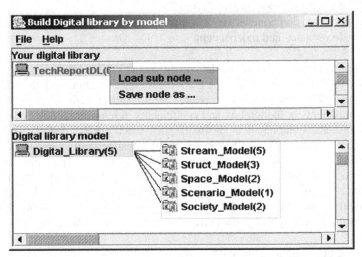

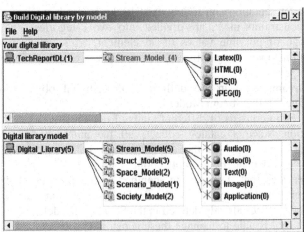

**Fig. 2.** Reuse of models before and after loading.

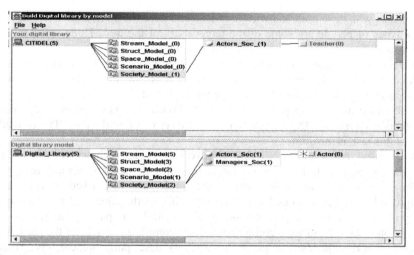

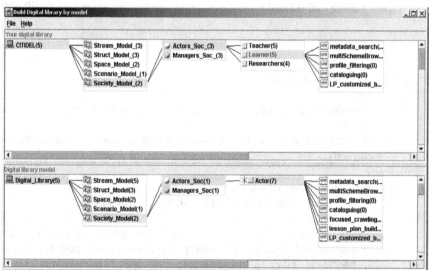

**Fig. 3.** Enforcing semantic constraints in the CITIDEL system. See (top) teacher as actor and (bottom) learner services.

## 4 Evaluation

We conducted a pilot usability test regarding 5SGraph. The questions to be answered were: 1) Is the tool effective in helping users build DL models based on the 5S theory? 2) Does the tool help users efficiently describe DL models in the 5S language? 3) Are users satisfied with the tool? Participants of this preliminary test included seventeen volunteers from a graduate level Information Storage and Retrieval class, or from the DL research group of Virginia Tech.  We choose participants who have basic knowledge of DLs and have the motivation to create DLs. These types of people are some of the target users of the tool. Three representative tasks with different levels of difficulty were selected:

*Task 1*: build a simple model of a Technical Report Digital Library using reusable model components. The difficulty level of this task is low. Its purpose is to help the participants to get familiar with 5S and the 5SGraph tool.

*Task 2*: finish an existing partial model of CITIDEL (Computing and Information Technology Interactive Digital Educational Library, www.citidel.org). The difficulty level of this task is medium.

*Task 3*: build a model of NDLTD (Networked Digital Library of Theses and Dissertations, www.ndltd.org) from scratch. The difficulty level of this task is high.

The procedures were as follows: 1) the participant was asked to read some background documents about 5S and the modeling methodology; 2) the participant was given an introductory presentation on 5SGraph; 3) the participant was given a description of task 1 and we recorded how he/she completed it; 4) after the participant finished each task, he/she was given the next task description immediately; 5) after the participant finished all the tasks, he/she was given a questionnaire form to fill out.

## 4.1  Measures

We use the following test measures:
- Effectiveness
  - ○ Completion rate: percentage of participants who complete each task correctly.
  - ○ Goal achievement: extent to which each task is achieved completely and correctly.
- Efficiency
  - ○ Task time: time to complete each task.
  - ○ Closeness to expertise: minimum task time divided by task time.
- Satisfaction
  Satisfaction is measured using a subjective 10-point bipolar rating scale, where 1 is the worst rating and 10 is the best rating. After each participant finishes all three tasks, he/she is given a questionnaire and asked to rate the overall learnability, effectiveness, and satisfaction based on his/her observation.

## 4.2  Results

- Effectiveness: The high completion rate and the high goal achievement rate demonstrate the effectiveness of 5SGraph (see Table 3).
- Efficiency: Most participants finish tasks in less than 20 minutes (see Figure 4); the generated 5SL files are very accurate.
- Closeness to Expertise reflects the learnability of the tool (see Table 3, Figure 5). There are three observations, which have been confirmed statistically (t test: 0.05).

a.  Observation 1: the mean Closeness to Expertise in task 2 is significantly greater than that in task 1.
b.  Observation 2: the mean Closeness to Expertise in task 3 is significantly greater than that in task 1.
c.  Observation 3: the mean Closeness to Expertise in task 3 is not significantly different from that in task 2.

**Table 3.** Overall Performance Results for Three Tasks

|  | Task 1 | Task 2 | Task 3 |
|---|---|---|---|
| Completion Rate (%) | 100 | 100 | 100 |
| Mean Task Time (min) | 11.3 | 11.4 | 15.1 |
| Mean Closeness to Expertise | 0.483 | 0.752 | 0.712 |
| Mean Goal Achievement (%) | 97.4 | 97.4 | 98.2 |

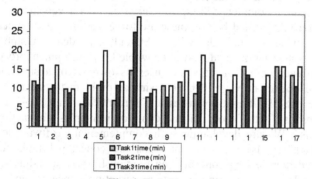

**Fig. 4.** Task Time

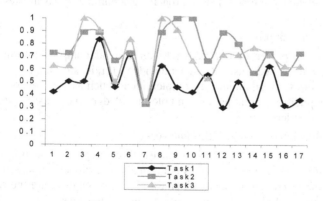

**Fig. 5.** Closeness to Expertise

It appears that the tool is easy to learn and use. A short task such as task 1 is enough for users to become familiar with the tool. User proficiency is quite close to expert performance level after they use the tool the first time. In fact, there are some participants (#9 and #10) with good computer skills who achieved a completion speed very close to the expert's in tasks 2 and 3. Observation 3 indicates that users have similar performance in tasks 2 and 3. The reason may be that users have become highly familiar with the tool after task 1. The remaining difference between the participants and the expert may be due to other factors, e.g., familiarity with the tasks, typing speed, reading speed, and skill in using computers.

The average rating of user satisfaction is 9.1 and the average rating of tool usefulness is 9.2. From these numbers, it appears that our participants are satisfied with the tool and consider it useful for building DLs based on 5S.

## 5  Semantic Modeling of Digital Libraries with Concept Maps

5SGraph can already capture many DL conceptual properties and inter-model constraints, but a number of explicit inter- and intra-model relationships and properties (e.g., relationships among actors and service managers, between managers and their defined operations, the temporal order of events in scenarios) still need to be captured to create a complete 5SL specification useful for generation of a final DL implementation. As argued before, these are to be captured using external "plugin" software tools, which can be called within 5SGraph as needed. 5SGraph thus acts like a "conductor" that organizes and guides the whole DL development process.

However if each complementary tool uses its own set of abstractions, graphical notations, and operations we will have a similar problem to one mentioned before regarding the use of different syntaxes and semantics within the 5SL sub-models. What is desired is a set of tools that use common principles, abstractions, notations, and operations. We are developing such complementary software tools based on "Concept Maps" (CMs) [9]. Concept maps are conceptual tools for organizing knowledge and representing concepts and relationships as node-link diagrams. The nodes are labeled with descriptive text, representing concepts, and the links are labeled with relationship types. This approach has a number of advantages including:

1.  Simplicity and intuitiveness

CMs harness the power of our vision to understand complex information "at-a-glance". They have been used to generate ideas (brain storming, etc.), to design complex structures, to communicate complex ideas (such as concepts of DLs), to aid learning by explicitly integrating new and old knowledge, and to assess understanding or diagnose misunderstanding.

2.  Natural integration with the 5S framework

The underlying model of a CM is a labeled directed graph, which in terms of 5S defines exactly a "Structure". Besides being natural to model DL structures such as metadata formats and classification schemes, CMs also can capture the relationships of the Societies Model. Moreover, with few extensions (e.g., multilabels in relationships to express dynamic scenario events[1], enumeration of labels to simulate temporal sequencing) they can be used to model scenarios.

---

[1] In more formal terms, to extend CMs to be multigraphs.

3.    Amenability to formalization

The basic notions of concepts and relationships are more amenable to formalization in terms of precise constructs (such as semantic networks, topic maps, and ontologies) than the notions of higher level but more ambiguous and informal design models such as UML class and sequence diagrams [10, 11]. In harmony with the formal nature of 5S, this can be used to formally prove properties of the final 5SL model such as correctness and completeness.

Figure 6 shows a CM modeling of a portion of the society sub-model of the CITIDEL system (www.citidel.org). That model shows a teacher interacting with a lesson plan building manager to create instructional material for students. The lesson plan builder is composed of three managers for other services: Searching, Browsing, and Binding. All the operations defined in those managers are incorporated by the Builder, which also can define its own operations. Operations have parameters and return types. Different colors are given to different types of concepts (i.e., actors, service managers, operations) based on different level of hierarchical importance.

We used the CM editor of the GetSmart system developed by the Artificial Intelligence Lab at the University of Arizona [12] to produce the maps. GetSmart can export a map into a tailored XML format. We have extended GetSmart to extract the hierarchical information embedded in the Societal CMs and produce the corresponding 5SL-Society XML file that then can be incorporated or imported by 5SGraph. We plan to implement similar extensions for the other 'S's.

## 6    Conclusions and Future Work

A domain-specific visual modeling tool (5SGraph), built for the purpose of modeling and building DLs based on the 5S model, is presented in this paper. This work on 5SGraph is an important part of a large project that aims at rapid DL design and generation based on a formal theoretical framework. Such generation may be facilitated if designers are able to describe their DLs using domain-specific description languages as the first step, but such advantages can be compromised if the language is too complex. 5SGraph reduces the difficulties of this step for digital librarians. To the best of our knowledge, there has been no other similar modeling tool in this area developed for this purpose.

Having recently decoupling the current concept map editor from GetSmart to become a stand-alone tool, we can use it to incorporate the necessary extensions and constraints to complement the design of other 'S' models. We will integrate the stand-alone tool with 5SGraph, improve its interface and interactions mechanisms, use it in educational settings to teach about DLs, and perform more tests, especially with more librarians as participants.

**Acknowledgments.** Thanks are given for the support of NSF through its grants: IIS-9986089, IIS-0002935, IIS-0080748, IIS-0086227, DUE-0121679, DUE0121741, and DUE-0136690. The second author is supported by CAPES.

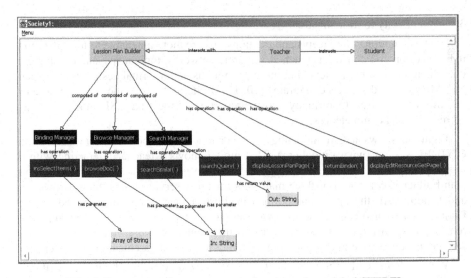

**Fig. 6.** Concept map for a component of society sub-model of CITIDEL.

# References

1. Kieburtz, R.B. et al.: A Software Engineering Experiment in Software Component Generation, Proc. of 18th Int. Conf. on Software Engineering, pp. 542–553, Berlin, 1996.
2. Booch, G., Rumbauth, J., and Jacobson, I.: The Unified Modeling Language User Guide, Addison-Wesley, Reading, Massachusetts, USA (1999)
3. Gonçalves, M. A., Fox, E. A., Watson, L.T., and Kipp, N.: Stream, Structures, Spaces, Scenarios, Societies (5S): A Formal Model for Digital Libraries, Virginia Tech CS Tech. Rep., TR-03-04, http://eprints.cs.vt.edu/archive/00000646 (re-submitted after revision from an earlier version, for publication in ACM Transactions on Information Systems)
4. Gonçalves, M. A., Fox, E. A.: 5SL – a language for declarative specification and generation of digital libraries. JCDL 2002: 263–272, Portland, Oregon (2002)
5. Zhu, Q.: 5Sgraph: A Visual Modeling Tool for Digital Libraries. Master Thesis. Virginia Tech. http://scholar.lib.vt.edu/theses/available/etd-11272002-210531/ (2002)
6. Gonçalves, M. A. Digital Libraries: formal theory, language, design, generation, quality, and evaluation. PhD Dissertation proposal. CS Dept., Virginia Tech, 2003.
7. Fox, E. A., From Theory to Practice in Digital Libraries: 5S and Educational Applications (NDLTD, CSTC), Workshop on Digital Libraries, Albuquerque NM, July 7–9, 1999.
8. Tigris.com, ArgoUML:    design tool with cognitive support. http://argouml.tigis.org (2002)
9. Novak, J.D.: Learning, creating, and using knowledge: concept maps as facilitative tools in schools and corporations, Lawrence Erlbaum and Associates: Mawah, NJ (1998)
10. Gaines, B.R., Shaw, M.L.G.: Concept maps as hypermedia components, International Journal of Human-Computer Studies, vol. 41, pp. 59–107 (1995)
11. Eden, A. H.: A Theory of Object-Oriented Design, Journal of Information Systems Frontiers, Vol. 4. No. 4, pp. 179–191 (2002)
12. Marshall, B., Zhang, Y., Chen, H., Lally, A., Shen, R., and Fox, E.: Convergence of knowledge Management and E-learning: The GetSmart Experience, JCDL'03, Houston, Texas, May 27–31 (2003)

# Connecting Interface Metaphors to Support Creation of Path-Based Collections

Unmil P. Karadkar, Andruid Kerne, Richard Furuta, Luis Francisco-Revilla,
Frank Shipman, and Jin Wang

Center for the Study of Digital Libraries and Department of Computer Science
Texas A&M University
College Station, TX 77843-3112, USA

**Abstract.** Walden's Paths is a suite of tools that supports the creation and presentation of linear hypermedia paths—targeted collections that enable authors to
reorganize and contextualize Web-based information for presentation to an audience. Its current tools focus primarily on authoring and presenting paths, but
not on the discovery and vetting of the materials that are included in the path.
CollageMachine, on the other hand, focuses strongly on the exploration of Web
spaces at the granularity of their media elements through presentation as a streaming collage, modified temporally through learning from user behavior. In this paper
we present an initial investigation of the differences in expectations, assumptions,
and work practices caused by the differing metaphors of browser based and CollageMachine Web search result representations, and how they affect the process
of creating paths.

## 1 Introduction

Collections of digital materials are significant communicative artifacts in digital libraries,
both for collections established by a formal organization [5], but also for collections kept
for the purpose of organizing materials into an individual's personal information space
[16]. Collection building and management software, like VKB [13], Hunter Gatherer
[10], or Collector [16], which aids end-users in creating digital library collections [16],
support various structures for user collections; for example, bookmark lists and file
systems support tree-like structures, VKB supports stacks, lists and composites, while
the Collector uses Greenstone-specific storage and access structures. Our own system,
Walden's Paths [11], supports linear paths of items, perhaps the easiest form to create,
understand, and convey to others.

Hypertext-based paths have a long history, beginning with Bush's memex [1], and
including Trigg's Guided Tours and Tabletops [15], and Zellweger's Scripted Documents
and Active Paths [17]. In Walden's Paths, paths are collections of World-Wide Web
material used to communicate information from path authors to path readers. Earlier we
reported on use of paths in an educational setting, where teachers used paths to express
curricular concepts and achieve academic goals [3,11]. These path authors relied on
Web search engines to locate relevant information. They devoted exhaustive time to
searching and locating pages for inclusion in the paths, following every link that was

T. Koch and I.T. Sølvberg (Eds.): ECDL 2003, LNCS 2769, pp. 338–349, 2003.

**Fig. 1.** The Path Server, the path viewing interface

even remotely interesting to explore the information it contains. Unfortunately, keyword-based searches do not return pages that may use conceptually similar but syntactically different terms. Further, the authors' understanding of their problem space is emergent—as they add information to their paths, they get a better sense of additional pages that must be included in the path, resulting in modification of the original search. Consequently, the traditional search engine sometimes became cumbersome. This led us to explore alternative work practices for collection creation.

CollageMachine [6,7,8] addresses some of the above issues. It starts with a user-specified seeding (for example, search terms or Web addresses) that reflects the user's interests and retrieves matching information from Web. It then extracts information elements from these pages and streams them to a continuously evolving canvas to build an active collage. It also crawls the space and presents information from linked pages. Users may participate in the creation of the collage by interacting with elements that they like and cut those they dislike. It supports emergent behavior by learning from user actions. However, user interaction is not necessary as the collage continues to evolve even when a user takes a break to do other tasks. Such a tool provides the opportunity for a very different work practice during collection creation—one where the user is actively engaged in managing existing resources while at the same time peripherally monitoring CollageMachine for potential additions to the collection.

In this paper we explore the effects of using CollageMachine as an information forager for creating paths. We present the observations of a preliminary study and discuss how these inform the system architecture for co-use of the path authoring tool with CollageMachine. We specifically focus on the practices of experienced Web searchers and how these result in behavioral expectations from CollageMachine.

We introduce Walden's Paths and CollageMachine in the next two sections. Section 4 presents our observations of users who developed paths using CollageMachine and Google [4] to locate information. Sections 5 and 6 discusses our observations, their implications for system design, and research directions for the future.

## 2  Walden's Paths

Walden's Paths [11] facilitates use of Web-based information collections, where the collection author usually is not the Web page author. This is achieved through paths: Web-based, linear meta-documents (documents whose contents are other documents). In implementation, paths consist of a sequence of *stops*, each of which presents a Web page and an annotation. Annotations, therefore, aid path authors in providing a rhetorical structure that recontextualizes Web-based information from possibly disparate sources.

Readers may view paths via the Path Server using recent versions of standard Web browsers with the interface shown in Figure 1. The stop's Web page, as it would be displayed without the mediation by Walden's Paths, is displayed at the bottom. The annotation or contextualizing text added by the path's author is at top right. The top left portion contains the controls for navigating along the path. Readers may view the stops on the path in order by clicking on the "Next" and "Back" arrows or they may jump to any stop on the path by scrolling to and clicking on the corresponding "paw." Readers can follow links on pages at any time to freely examine the information space. While the reader is browsing off the path, the controls are replaced by one that links back to the last page visited on the path, thus providing an easy way to return to the path.

The process of path authoring starts with concept development. Authors need to begin by forming a sense of what they want to communicate, who the intended audience is, and how Web resources will be involved. Then, more specifically, they must [12]: Locate promising Web sites; Browse and evaluate materials at these sites; Select information elements for use in the path; Develop an outline for the presentation; Place and order stops within the sections of the path; and Write the introductory text and annotate the stops. This list is not intended to imply that steps must be followed a strict order or that all of them will be carried out in all authoring situations. For example, a path author who uses his own Web pages does not need to search for or evaluate the materials. However, when information is retrieved from the Web via search tools, the author must ascertain its veracity and relevance to ensure the integrity of the path. The current Walden's Paths authoring tools support only the last three steps, assuming that authors will use separate search engines and Web browsers in carrying out the first three tasks.

The PathAuthor is a stand-alone Java application. Figure 2 shows a snapshot taken during path authoring. This shows the interface used to create and edit the path specification. This interface displays information about the path as a whole, i.e., the path title and list of stops in the path, and includes controls for reordering the stops by shifting them up or down. The Path Preview feature enables authors to get a reader's view of the path without requiring them to connect to the Path Server. The PathAuthor also

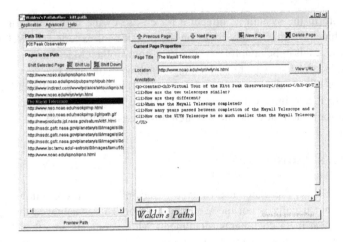

**Fig. 2.** The PathAuthor

contains controls for working at the page level. An author may create new stops, delete the currently active stop, or edit the contents of the current stop. The active stop may be changed by clicking on the desired stop in the stop list or by using the "Previous" or "Next" stop buttons. For each stop, the author may provide a title, the Web location, presumably retrieved from a Web search engine, and the contextualizing text for this Web page. The URL of a Web page can be dragged from a browser and dropped into the PathAuthor "Location" field, copy and pasted, or typed in directly.

Finding resources traditionally has relied on Web search engines, e.g., Google [4]. These use the now familiar keyword and result list metaphor, where users provide the keywords or key phrases of interest and the search engine responds with a list of links to Web pages. Inherent in the metaphor is the temporal separation of query and result—search engines perform a one-time search for the specified keywords and preferences and return the list of matching pages leaving the user to browse through these, opening pages that may seem interesting or relevant. Returned results do not initiate a behavior without user action. The transaction unit is a Web page, thus the search engines can be said to work at page granularity. In contrast, CollageMachine embodies a continuous browsing metaphor at the granularity of information elements.

## 3   CollageMachine

CollageMachine [6,7,8] is a generative Web visualization tool that encourages Web space exploration. New ideas emerge through open-ended processes of exploration with preinventive representations [2]. The result list metaphor for interaction with Web search results is effective when one knows what one is looking for and how to specify it. However, in cases where either the goal or effective keywords are still in formation, the need to click through many links becomes a burden. The visual combinations of information elements that CollageMachine generates afford exploratory interaction.

**Fig. 3.** Collage session seeded with Web pages from the NSF Digital Libraries Initiative Phase 2.

CollageMachine affords browsing not at the Web page level but at the finer-grained level of media elements—components of pages such as images, chunks of text, videos, sounds, etc. Collaging begins with a set of seeds, in the form of Web addresses. Seed addresses may be entered directly, may result from search queries, or may be dragged from pages being viewed in a Web browser. Seeds may be specified at any time, either initially or during the course of a session. CollageMachine uses the seeds to download pages and then breaks them down into their constituent media elements, maintaining internally a model of their referential hypermedia graph structure. The media elements are presented to the user in a dynamically evolving collaged presentation that updates continuously as the hypermedia graph structure is traversed. Figure 3 displays a snapshot of an ongoing collage session. In the figure, the cursor is positioned over an image element in the upper left hand corner. In this rollover state, CollageMachine displays metadata about the image, and also about the container of its origin.

CollageMachine provides means for the user to affect its presentation. The design tools (see Figure 3, bottom center) enable the viewer to perform operations such as cutting, dragging, and resizing of collage elements. Elements can be dragged both within the collage but also out to other applications, such as traditional Web browsers. (As an accelerator, when the Web page tool is active, clicking on an element opens the

**Fig. 4.** Authoring paths while browsing with CollageMachine

contextualizing Web page in a traditional browser window.) The design tools allow the viewer to express interest, or disinterest, in displayed elements. A model of user interests is built from these actions. Interest is propagated from the initial element to related ones by spreading activation [9]. When the user interacts with a collage element, this affects the program's determination of related material, modifying the subsequent choices of elements to present.

This model of interests serves as the basis for all of the program's collage-making operations. Automatic browsing can get noisy quickly if the program's procession is purely random since beyond the initial seeds there is no a priori knowledge of which hyperlinks are relevant. The model also guides decisions about the sizes and shapes of new media elements that enter the collage, and which already visible elements to cover.

Collage works by creating new assemblages of found objects. These new formations can challenge our internal representations, and thus stimulate the formation of new ones. CollageMachine is designed to support mixed-attention use; that is, sometimes one gives it full attention: interacting with the compositions by grabbing elements of interest that show up, and engaging in expressive collage design. At other times, the user can let the evolving collage slip into the ambient periphery, while giving attention to other activities. This supports creative processes such as divergent thinking and incubation [2] that can lead to the emergence of new ideas. It is the process of going away and returning that helps create new internal structures of representation that enable insight. Peripheral sensing of the evolving stimulus of the collage facilitates incubation.

## 4    Pilot Study

To gain an understanding of the differences in the processes, expectations and practices caused by the use of different information-finding metaphors we conducted a pilot study, observing users as they created paths using resources discovered with CollageMachine and with Google.

The user pool consisted of seven individuals with at least a baccalaureate degree, most with a master's degree, in a variety of science and social science related fields. All had some teaching experience, as graduate teaching assistants or as teachers in local school districts. They were conversant with browsing and searching on the Web. None had worked with either Walden's Paths or CollageMachine before the evaluation; however, some were familiar with Walden's Paths at a conceptual level.

The users were randomly assigned to one of two pools. One pool searched the Web with CollageMachine to locate resources for paths, while the other searched with Google. Since CollageMachine uses Google to convert queries into an initial set of Web pages, the tasks differ only in the paradigms for presenting and browsing results.

We requested two-hour time slots from the users, but informed them that the tasks were not timed and that they could take as long as they wanted to accomplish them. Most users actually took closer to three hours in completing the tasks. We observed the users while they worked, but did not interrupt with questions or comments. Since we wanted to understand the problems faced by users, we answered their questions, either conceptual or operational, at any time during the path authoring session.

The users first answered a demographic questionnaire and received a brief introduction to the study tools. We then asked each user to author two paths, the first on a topic that we selected that was unfamiliar to them and the second on a topic of their choice that they might teach in a class. Because CollageMachine emphasizes the visually appealing aspects of Web pages, we ensured that the topics we selected were visually rich, for example, French painting, introduction to architecture, and tourism in Africa. In both tasks, the users were left free to choose the length and the nature of the path.

We displayed the PathAuthor on the left and the search tool on the right so that initially none of the applications was completely obscured by another. Figure 4, a screen captured from a user session, displays the unmodified position of these applications along with the Web page display of one of the collage elements. The PathAuthor and CollageMachine were instrumented to generate logs of user actions and we captured all screen activity to get the overall context of the actions. The screen capture was especially important, as we were not able to obtain logs of user interaction with Google. After authoring the paths, users completed a post-activity questionnaire. Finally, we asked them about their experience with the tools and shared some of our observations to get their inputs in a free-form audio-recorded interview.

Users displayed an active interest in learning the tools. During the short training provided, they asked questions to clarify concepts and operations. While CollageMachine's concepts evoked some initial surprise, they liked the variety of operations that could be performed. They especially liked the grab tools and used positive as well as negative grabs to try and guide CollageMachine to objects that interested them. Some users (but not all) discovered CollageMachine's contextualizing metadata as they let the mouse hover over the media elements and used this feature to avoid visiting sites whose names did not interest them. At other times, users were taken by the visual appeal of the elements and while the element was clearly orthogonal to the topic of their path, decided to visit the containing pages out of curiosity. A user who was creating a path on 17th century painting could not resist the urge to visit a page that contained a picture of a little boy in a modern firefighter's suit.

As in an earlier study [3], users seemed to grasp the concepts of paths and the process of creating paths quickly, getting off to a running start with the PathAuthor once its features were explained. Users created paths that were diverse in length (between three and twelve stops long) that varied substantially in focus as well as nature. Some created paths to aid classroom-teaching sessions for specific topics, e.g., Mitochondrial DNA, Basic Concepts in Ecology, and Leatherback turtles. Others developed paths that provided an overview and resources for a semester-long course (Introduction to Robotics). Yet others developed resource lists that targeted a variety of audiences, including a resource list for Chinese Recipes.

Users who searched with Google were familiar with the metaphor, the process, the interface, and the interaction. However, CollageMachine users, who were exposed to a completely novel information location paradigm, took some time to adjust to the tools, typically taking more time to create the first path than to create the second, both being of comparable lengths. The paths created with CollageMachine tended to use more pages from a Web site than those created with Google. This could be because CollageMachine not only explores Web pages returned by the keyword search, but also crawls to pages linked from them. The linked pages may not contain the user-specified search terms, but may explicate a topic related to the path. Thus, CollageMachine was aiding users by assuming some of the responsibility for "browsing" off of the initial search results.

As expected when confronted with a tool supporting an alternative work practice, CollageMachine users tended to judge the software based on expectations more appropriate of a search engine. Some of the users were confused by the initial delay in viewing results while CollageMachine was mining pages and extracting elements for display and feared that it had not found anything of interest or that they had specified incorrect query terms. Others thought that the element display delay wasted their time. One user felt that Google was better because it presented her with multiple Web pages at a time that matched the search criteria and she could choose to go to a particular page or Web site and ignore the ones that did not interest her. Many comments regarding CollageMachine focused on the relevance of the search results returned. As the elements in the Web pages were displayed out of context, users had some trouble putting them back in the context without having to view the page that contained each image or chunk of text. Pages that were more descriptive or illustrative generated more elements for display and the users had little control over the decision to display these. The users expected CollageMachine to reflect the grab cues depicting their interest instantly and not display additional elements from these pages.

One of the features we expected to be of use remained virtually unused. We showed users that dragging a collage element into the location bar of the PathAuthor copied the location of the Web container of the element into the location bar. Instead, users preferred to click on CollageMachine elements, bringing up the enclosing page in a Web browser, and then drag the location of relevant pages from the *browser* into the PathAuthor's location bar. It appears that they were interested in knowing the original context of the elements in the Web pages before deciding whether to include it in their paths.

## 5  Discussion

Users requested additional features in the PathAuthor and CollageMachine. Users requested a work area in the PathAuthor where they could store pages that seemed interesting for possible future use. While the users who searched with Google were reasonably certain that they could find the page again if needed, users of CollageMachine were anxious to save the pages that they had found, lest they could not reach it later.

Drag-and-drop semantics in the realm of collage elements raise questions. One user wished to drag an element (not the Web page containing it) into the PathAuthor, thus making the stop point to the image. This raises the question of what drag-and-drop semantics should be when applied to collage elements. A collage element, unlike text in browsers or a Web location, is a complex entity. The element is represented by an interface (the image or text), points to its container, and accepts certain actions from the user, such as clicking on it to open its containing Web page. Further, the interface that the element presents is a sample, rather than a complete representation of the element—for example an image may be scaled or text abstracted. When an author drags an element from CollageMachine into the PathAuthor, the action may have several possible interpretations. The user may wish to include the Web page that contains the displayed element or, equally possible, may wish to include the image itself, or indeed the abstracted form. Thus the simple action of dragging an element may have multiple connotations.

CollageMachine uses indeterminacy—that is, structured randomness—in the selection of elements for creating the collage [7]. The path authors tended to express that there was not enough connection between their design actions in the collage space, and the results of what media CollageMachine retrieved and displayed. This was hinted at via comments about the unpredictable nature of the elements that CollageMachine would show. They were also concerned about CollageMachine not acting on their grab directives in a predictable manner. This indicates both that CollageMachine users need richer tools for expressing their intentions, and, more fundamentally, that the program's model of the user's intentions must be more effective in representing the user's intentions based on their expressive actions, and making selection and composition decisions based on these expressions. When there is the right level of structure, the indeterminacy will effectively serve to create openness and variation.

The users who participated in the evaluation were conversant with the traditional Web search/results paradigm, and unfamiliar with CollageMachine. This is reflected in their expectations of CollageMachine as well as their work practices. The authors interacted with the browser as much as possible, treating CollageMachine as a search interface alone, using it simply as an area to look for interesting pages, quite akin to the lists of search results returned by Google. We expect that as users become familiar with the collage browsing metaphor, they may exhibit more collage-centric behaviors.

Some users feared that if they did not devote their attention to the developing collage, they might miss out on information, causing their paths to be less effective. Similarly, some users expressed the need to stop the developing collage when they were working with the PathAuthor. Again, this is an issue of paradigm familiarity that we expect would diminish with further experience.

Some users were not comfortable dealing with the recontextualization that results as CollageMachine deconstructs Web pages and assembles their constituent media elements. A media element's original context can be important in determining if it fits in a path intended for a specific set of readers. Users demonstrated their interest in the element's context by viewing the containing Web pages for elements that interested them. One user, who had not yet discovered collage element rollover state, commented about the lack of element context: "I saw an interesting picture, viewed and added the page to my path. The next few pictures gave me the same page again and again...." CollageMachine's display of multiple images from a relevant page confused this user who, from past experience with Web search engines, assumed that they must all be from unique pages. Viewing the rollover information would have alerted the user that these images came from a single page. Enhancing the notion of context in CollageMachine, as well as better communication of its operational model, would help here.

# 6   Conclusion

We observed that authors who started with a sketchy notion and were flexible regarding the contents of their paths appreciated CollageMachine. On the other hand, authors who mentally crystallized the flow and contents of their paths before starting were frustrated by lack of a deterministic response to their specific queries. Due to its structured indeterminacy, CollageMachine presents itself as an attractive option for path authors when they are flexible about the contents of the paths they create within their domain of interest. CollageMachine may serve as a more suitable foraging tool for paths that have fewer constraints. A few examples include paths that do not target specific grade levels or age groups, and paths that are not rhetorically intense, for example, resource lists. CollageMachine may also serve as an effective tool to explore the authoring space for a particular topic before deciding the structure of the path. As an exploration tool, the author may seed a collage with general query terms and let the collage develop for a while, with periodic interjection to keep the collage from wandering too far off topic. Most importantly, mixed-mode environments, in which different tools for the presentation and building of collections are available concurrently, will let users match interface metaphors to the mental models and activity at hand.

The integration of CollageMachine and PathAuthor raises fundamental issues about the activity of collection building. Collection building is a creative process. In this, it differs markedly from well-defined tasks, such as simply looking up train schedules, stock prices or API specifications (though links to all of these materials may end up in a collection). Browsing/searching for something known is essentially an information location activity. Collection building is a kind of authoring, a process of formation that draws from intuition.

Although path authors start with a certain sense of what they are looking for, this sense is likely to evolve through the course of path formation. What is found in the process influences the sense of what is being looked for. External factors, such as feedback from independent sources, may also influence the evolution of concept and path formation; indeed it may modify the very definition of the path's subject. Incubation [14] refers to the way mental models evolve when one is not directly working on concept and strategy formation. Sometimes, insight comes when we go away and return. One explanation is that new inputs create new perspective that allows our internal representations to re-form. Return after absence can thus be part of the evolution of insight. In short, feedback both from the authoring process itself, and from other processes, including internal cognitive ones, and communication with other sources, all have an effect. Tools that intend to support collection building need to consider the different processes that are involved, and support them.

Another aspect that arises is that users do not necessarily have a strong sense of the issues involved in collection-building, even though they have great need to keep track of stuff they encounter while browsing. Their exposure to tools for collection building is limited. Typical users have exposure to browsers, and their favorites mechanisms. They have word processors, into which elements can be dragged. As Schraefel points out [10], word processors are particularly weak for collection building. The problem is that while they support the collection of media elements, they don't automatically enable keeping track of the Web page container from which each element is drawn. The connections of elements to their contextualizing containers are essential.

The observations of the authoring process with CollageMachine and Google has begun to provide us with insight into issues that path authors encounter with respect to the tools and their operation, as well as their cognitive processes. Authors' practices are shaped both by their current tools, but also by their past experiences. The features of existing tools create expectations for newer tools to fulfill. The users were familiar with drag-and-drop as well as the copy-paste actions and these posed no problems for them. On the other hand, they were familiar with exploring search results via resource lists and shifting gears to browse search results via temporal collages did not map easily to their expectations. The users were aware of this fact and expressed that they could get used to browsing collages with some practice. This highlights needs in three overlapping areas: communicating with users, understanding and addressing the conceptual and usability issues that arise in the new environment, and reconciling the expectations of authors with the expectations of the tools. Paradigms do not shift all at once. Users will gain perspective on collection-building through exposure to a rich set of metaphors. Design needs to be based on a combination of the needs that users articulate now, and from developers' imaginations [8] of how practice can be transformed.

The pilot study focused on observing how users create paths and understanding their motivations, needs, and practices. We intend to enhance the PathAuthor and CollageMachine by developing the features requested by the authors and modifying the existing tools to better suit the motivations and work practices of the authors. We also intend to test the authoring of paths with users who are familiar with CollageMachine and train other users to work effectively with it. The work practices of the authors and changes after training, if any, will yield further clues about the facets of the collection building process.

The "search, examine, then add" practice of collection building has developed as people became comfortable with search engines over the last decade. While the study reinforces the fact that users tend to take new tools and fit them into existing work practices, it also provides examples of other forms that collection building might take. In the end, path authors and other collection builders should have tools supporting a variety of work practices, including both directed search and peripheral browsing. Towards this end, we will build environments in which users can choose different interface metaphors to support their changing cognitive processes and continue to identify cognitive, semantic, interface design, usability, and architectural issues that arise in the process of connecting metaphors during collection building.

**Acknowledgements.** We thank the users who participated in the pilot study. This material is based upon work supported by the National Science Foundation under grant numbers DUE-0085798, DUE-0121527 and IIS-0219540.

# References

1. V. Bush. As we may think. *The Atlantic Monthly*, pages 101–108, Aug. 1945.
2. R. Finke, T. Ward, and S. Smith. *Creative Cognition*. MIT Press, Cambridge MA, 1992.
3. R. Furuta, F. Shipman, C. Marshall, D. Brenner, and H. Hsieh. Hypertext paths and the World-Wide Web: Experiences with Walden's Paths. In *Proceedings of Hypertext'97*, pages 167–176. ACM Press, Apr. 1997.
4. Google. http://www.google.com/ (accessed January 2003).
5. Institute of Museum and Library Sciences. A framework of guidance for building good digital collections. http://www.imls.gov/pubs/forumframework.htm (accessed January 2003).
6. A. Kerne. *CollageMachine: A Model of Interface Ecology*. Ph.D. dissertation, New York University, 2001.
7. A. Kerne. CollageMachine: Interest-driven browsing through streaming collage. In *Proceedings of Cast01, Living in Mixed Realities*, pages 241–244, Sept. 2001.
8. A. Kerne. Concept-context-design: A creative model for the development of interactivity. In *Proceedings of the ACM Creativity and Cognition Conference*, pages 192–199, 2002.
9. G. Salton and C. Buckley. On the use of spreading activation methods in automatic information retrieval. In *Proceedings of SIGIR 1988*, pages 147–160, 1988.
10. M. Schraefel, Y. Zhu, D. Modjeska, D. Wigdor, and S. Zhao. Hunter Gatherer: Interaction support for the creation and management of within-Web-page collections. In *Proceedings of WWW 2002*, May 2002.
11. F. Shipman, R. Furuta, D. Brenner, C. Chung, and H. Hsieh. Guided paths through Web-based collections: Design, experiences, and adaptations. *Journal of the American Society of Information Sciences (JASIS)*, 51(3):260–272, Mar. 2000.
12. F. M. Shipman, R. Furuta, and C. C. Marshall. Generating Web-based presentations in spatial hypertext. In *Proceedings of International Conference on Intelligent User Interfaces*, pages 71–78. ACM Press, Jan. 1997.
13. F. M. Shipman, H. Hsieh, R. Airhart, P. Maloor, J. M. Moore, and D. Shah. Emergent structure in analytic workspaces: Design and use of the visual knowledge builder. In *Proceedings of Interact 2001*, pages 132–139, July 2001.
14. S. M. Smith and S. E. Blankenship. Incubation and the persistence of fixation in problem solving. *American Journal of Psychology*, 104:61–87, 1991.
15. R. H. Trigg. Guided tours and tabletops: Tools for communicating in a hypertext environment. *ACM Transactions on Office Information Systems*, 6(4):398–414, Oct. 1988.
16. I. H. Witten, D. Bainbridge, and S. J. Boddie. Power to the people: end-user building of digital library collections. In *Proceedings of the first ACM/IEEE-CS joint conference on Digital libraries*, pages 94–103, June 2001.
17. P. T. Zellweger. Scripted documents: A hypertext path mechanism. In *Proceedings of the Second ACM conference on Hypertext*, pages 1–26, Nov. 1989.

# Managing Change in a Digital Library System with Many Interface Languages

David Bainbridge, Katrina D. Edgar, John R. McPherson, and Ian H. Witten

Department of Computer Science, University of Waikato,
Hamilton, New Zealand.
davidb@cs.waikato.ac.nz
Phone (+64) 7 838 4407, fax (+64) 7 858 5095

**Abstract.** Managing the organizational and software complexity of a comprehensive open source digital library system presents a significant challenge. The challenge becomes even more imposing when the interface is available in different languages, for enhancements to the software and changes to the interface must be faithfully reflected in each language version. This paper describes the solution adopted by Greenstone, a multilingual digital library system distributed by UNESCO in a trilingual European version (English, French, Spanish), complete with all documentation, and whose interface is available in many further languages. Greenstone incorporates a language translation facility which allows authorized people to update the interface in specified languages. A standard version control system is used to manage software change, and from this the system automatically determines which language fragments need updating and presents them to the human translator.

**Keywords:** Digital library interfaces, multilingual systems, interface architecture, version control system.

## 1  Introduction

As the capabilities of distributed digital libraries increase, managing organizational and software complexity becomes a key issue. How can collections and indexes be updated without impacting queries currently in progress? When users are offered a choice of languages to communicate with the system, how does the software cope with all the versions of the text that is displayed? With multimedia collections, how can search engines for searching various media types be accommodated within a uniform, extensible software framework? How can several user interface clients for the same collection co-exist? How do these clients learn about new collections that are created at other library sites?

This paper focuses on the problem of multilingual interfaces. The Greenstone digital library software is a comprehensive system that is widely used internationally [5], and is freely available under the GNU General Public License. Dozens of collections are hosted at the New Zealand Digital Library site[1] where the

---

[1] http://nzdl.org

T. Koch and I.T. Sølvberg (Eds.): ECDL 2003, LNCS 2769, pp. 350–361, 2003.

software originates, in a variety of languages and spanning a variety of media formats: text, images, video, audio and music. Many international sites offer further collections. Indeed, the Greenstone mailing list has active members from over forty different countries.

Greenstone is distributed by UNESCO in a trilingual version (English, French, Spanish), complete with all documentation (several hundred pages) in each language. These three language interfaces include all installation instructions, readme files, installer dialogue, on-line help, user interface components, and documentation. The interface is also available in a large number of other languages: Arabic, Chinese, Dutch, German, Hebrew, Indonesian, Italian, Māori, Portuguese, Russian, and Turkish. Other languages, such as Hindi, Kannada, Tamil, Czech, Vietnamese, and Nepalese, are in various stages of development. In addition, Greenstone is a growing system: new facilities and subsystems are constantly being developed and added. As a result, language interfaces run the risk of rapidly become seriously outdated.

The problem of maintaining an evolving multilingual digital library software system is severe—particularly when the software is open source. No single person knows all interface languages; no single person knows about all modifications to the software—indeed there is likely no overlap at all between those who translate the interface and those who develop the software. Currently, Greenstone has about twenty interface languages and there are around 600 linguistic fragments in each interface, ranging from single words like *search*, through short phrases like *search for*, *which contain*, *of the words*, to sentences like *More than ... documents matched the query*, to complete paragraphs like those in the on-line help text. Maintaining the interface in many different languages is a logistic nightmare.

This paper describes the software structure that we have developed to cope with this challenge. We begin by showing some examples of the translation facility to demonstrate its operation. Then we describe the technical infrastructure that provides the underlying functionality. This requires an understanding of the Greenstone macro language—the backbone to the multilingual delivery mechanism—and consequently we give an overview to this also. The translation facility is not specific to macro files, however; it can be adapted to any language management technique—such as Java resource bundles—that records for each language and each item of text to be displayed a pair comprising a language independent label and a language dependent value.

## 2   Translator Demonstration

The Greenstone translation facility helps users to perform three kinds of task:

- translate the interface into a new language,
- update an existing language interface to reflect new Greenstone facilities,
- refine an existing language interface by correcting errors.

An initial screen, part of which is shown in Figure 1, explains this to users on entry, accompanied by some further information. At the bottom of the page, the

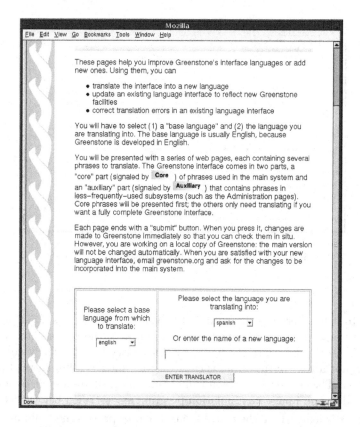

**Fig. 1.** Part of the translation facility's opening page.

user selects (a) a "base language" and (b) the language they are translating into. The base language is usually English, because this is what is used to develop Greenstone and so it is the most up-to-date interface. However, users are free to select other base languages if they prefer.

Having selected the two languages, users press the "enter translator" button. After a short pause, a page containing phrases to translate appears—generally the first of many such pages. Roughly fifteen phrases appear per page, but the number is contextually reduced for long textual items (which can run to several paragraphs in the case of help text).

## 2.1   Updating an Existing Language Interface

In Figure 2 the user has begun to update the Spanish language interface, using English as the base language. On the left are the base language phrases, and on the right are boxes into which translated versions can be entered. Two kinds of phrases appear: ones that are missing from the Spanish version, and ones whose Spanish translation is outdated because the English version has been edited more

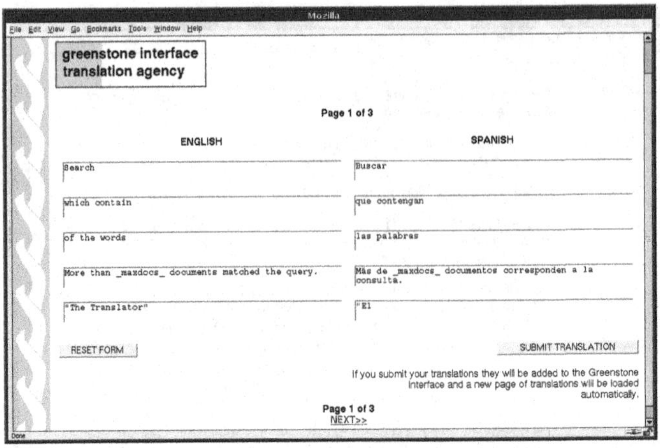

**Fig. 2.** Translating English phrases to Spanish.

recently. In the latter case the outdated translation appears as a visual cue. In the figure the user has methodically worked through the phrases and is in the process of entering text into the final box. This entry is particularly noteworthy since it is not a text phrase from the Greenstone interface but instead appears on a button. The translated version will be automatically rendered, on a colored background, by an image manipulation program as described below (Section 3).

When satisfied with all the translations, the user presses the "submit" button shown at the bottom of the page; then the next page in the sequence is generated. Pressing "submit" also commits the changes to the Greenstone system. Changes to the interface take place immediately: users can see their new translations in context by accessing (or reloading) appropriate pages in Greenstone. However, these changes are not made automatically to the public Greenstone site, nor are they automatically committed to the master software repository. Instead, to guard against error and misuse, they take effect in a special replica of the Greenstone site used for translation. If Greenstone encounters any phrases that have not been translated, the fall-back strategy is to render them in the default language for the site, usually English.

If desired, users can reset the page to its initial settings, or proceed to the next page without committing any changes. When satisfied with the entire translation, users notify the administrator of the central Greenstone repository through email of the change. There, issuing a single command fully integrates the changes into the officially released version of the software. If it suits, since each page is saved when it is submitted, a user need not translate all phrases in one sitting. Moreover, when they return to the service the sequence of pages is regenerated, which means that only the outstanding phrases are shown.

Greenstone distinguishes between phrases that are used in the main system—for instance, search, browsing and help pages—and phrases in less-frequently-used subsystems—for instance the Collector used to help build new collections [5], the site administration pages through which usage statistics and logs are viewed, and the translator service itself—for this too needs translating! For well-maintained language interfaces such as Spanish and French, only one or two pages of new translation requests are generated when new features are added. However, some less-used language interfaces contain translations only for the core phrases that appear in the main system.

## 2.2  Adding New Languages

New languages are added in the same way that existing ones are updated, except of course that no existing translations appear in the right-hand column. A total of 68 pages of translations are generated, averaging 9 phrases each (600 in total). About half of these (35 pages, 360 phrases) pertain to the core Greenstone system.

## 2.3  Text Handling

Because of the multilingual nature of Greenstone, attention must be given to character encoding issues. There are many different character encoding schemes in use today—as an example, the code 253 means "capital Y with an acute accent" (Ý) in the standard Western character set (International Organization for Standardization (ISO) standard 8859-1) while the same code corresponds to "a dot-less lower-case i" (ı) in the standard Turkish character set.

All text in Greenstone, including the macro files, is handled internally using Unicode (UTF-8) [4]. Unicode is an ISO standard providing every character in every language with a unique number. For example, in Unicode, a Western Y with acute accent has the code 253 while a Western dot-less i has the code 305. Greenstone supports any character set that can be mapped onto Unicode, which includes the majority of sets currently in use world-wide.

Modern browsers allow Unicode text to be entered into web forms. Unfortunately there is no standard way of forcing a browser to upload information in Unicode—or even to check what character set it uses to submit text fields. Some browsers always submit forms encoded in the user's default character set. However, major browsers generally submit forms using the same character set that is used for the current page, so in practice if pages are sent out with Unicode specified, returned text is usually encoded the same way.

## 2.4  Refining a Language Interface

Sometimes phrases in an existing language interface need to be refined. For example, a typographical error may have been overlooked when entering a phrase, or seeing a phrase in its actual interface context may suggest a better form of expression.

To accommodate this requirement users need to be able to locate an existing phrase and update its translation. One solution is to provide a complete list of all phrases in the language, not just the empty or outdated ones presented in Figure 2. The user could scan through this list to locate the desired phrase and correct or revise it. However, given the number of pages and phrases involved this would be a tedious and impractical task.

A more effective strategy is to allow users to locate a given phrase by searching for it, and then receive from the system a page that translates that one phrase. Interestingly, this idea can be implemented by making the set of phrases into a multilingual digital library collection. Within Greenstone, this special collection is designed as follows. Treat each language as a document and each phrase as a section within it. For each document, store its language as metadata and use this as a discriminator to form subcollections. Finally, set the collection to be a "private" (rather than a "public") one to prevent it from appearing on the site's home page. It can still be accessed by a URL that includes the collection name explicitly.

In Figure 3(a) the user is seeking macros in the Spanish language interface that contain the term *autor*. There are five matching items. The user is interested in the fifth, and clicks the page icon to the left of this entry. The result, in Figure 3(b), shows a pseudo-rendered version of the text. Basic HTML formatting of the text (such as the heading) is carried out, but other text phrases embedded in this text phrase are not expanded and appear in their raw form flanked by underscores (_) to indicate that they should not be translated (for example _textreadingdocs_ in Figure 3(b)). Figure 3(c) shows the page for translating this same phrase. It is brought up by clicking on the "Translate" link in Figure 3(a). The new translation is entered into the right-hand box, or the existing one altered by editing the contents of that box—just as in Figure 2.

## 3   Greenstone Macros

Language interface independence in Greenstone is achieved using a simple macro language. Figure 4 shows an artificially-constructed excerpt to illustrate the syntax through which macros are defined and used. Macro definitions comprise a name, flanked by underscores, and the corresponding content, placed within braces ({ ... }).

Macros are grouped together into *packages*, with lexical scoping, and an inheritance scheme is used to determine which definitions are in effect at any given time. This allows global formatting styles to be embedded with the particular content that is generated for a page. For example, typical pages contain a _header_ .... _content_ .... _footer_ sequence. Figure 4 shows a baseline page defined in the "Globals" package, which, in fact, is never intended to be seen. It is overridden in the "query" package below to generate a page that invites the user to enter search terms and perform a query.

Macros can include parameters interposed in square brackets between name and content. Such parameters are known as "page parameters" because they control the overall generation of a page. They are expressed as $[x = y]$, which gives parameter $x$ the value $y$. Two parameters of particular interest are $l$, which

(a)

(b)

(c)

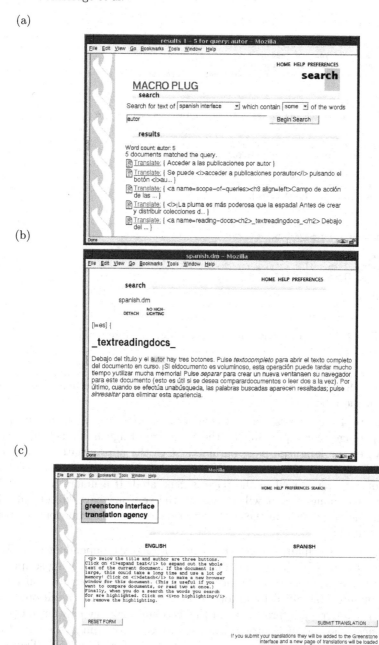

**Fig. 3.** Various screen shots of the translation interface: (a) seeking Spanish phrases that use the term *autor*; (b) pseudo-rendered version of the fifth text phrase in (a); (c) translation page for the fifth text phrase in (a).

```
package Globals

_header_  { The New Zealand Digital Library Project }
_content_ { Oops. If you are reading this then an error
            has occurred in the runtime system. }
_footer_  { Powered by <a href="www.greenstone.org">Greenstone</a>. }

package query

_content_ { _If_(_cgiargqb_ eq "large",_largequerybox_,_normalquerybox_)
   ... }

# ... the macro descriptions for _largequerybox_, _normalquerybox_,
#  and other nested macros are omitted for brevity

_header_ [l=en] {Begin search }
_header_ [l=fr] {Démarrer la recherche }
_header_ [l=es] {Iniciar la búsqueda}

# ... and so on

# Images containing language-dependent text

## "HELP" ## top_nav_button ## chelp ##
_httpiconchelp_ [l=en,v=1] {_httpimg_/en/chelp.gif}
_httpiconchelp_ [l=en,v=0] {HELP}

# ... and so on
```

**Fig. 4.** Excerpt of macro file syntax to demonstrate main features.

determines what language is used, and $v$, which controls whether or not images are used in the interface.

In Figure 4 three versions of the macro _header_ are defined within the "query" package, corresponding to the languages English, French and Spanish. They set the language page parameter $l$ to the appropriate two-letter international standard abbreviation (ISO 639), enabling the system to present the appropriate version when the page is generated. If a macro has no definition for a given language, it will resolve to the version given without any language parameter—which, in the current Greenstone implementation, is English (though it needn't be).

Greenstone uses many images that contain language-dependent text. These are created by the GNU image manipulation program GIMP, using scripting to automate the image generation process. Macro files use a specially constructed form of comment (signified by a double hash, ##) to convey additional information for a progressing program—in this case an image generation script. An example near the end of Figure 4 generates an icon containing the text *HELP* and places it in the file *chelp.gif* in subdirectory *en* (for "English"). The image generation script parses the comment to determine what type of image to generate, what text is to be placed on it, and where to put the result; automatically generates the image; and stores it in the language-specific directory appropriate to the $l$ page parameter (if any).

A precedence ordering for evaluating page parameters is built into the macro language to resolve conflicting definitions. Also included are conditional state-

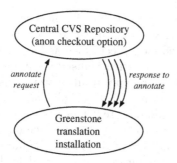

**Fig. 5.** Relationship between the central repository and translation installation.

ments—an example can be seen in the _content_ macro of Figure 4, which uses an "If" statement, conditioned by the macro _cgiargqb_, to determine whether the query box that appears on the search page should be the normal one or a large one. The value of _cgiargqb_ is set at runtime by the Greenstone system (the user can change it on a "Preferences" page). Many other system-defined macros have values that are determined at runtime: examples include the URL prefix where Greenstone is installed on the system, and the number of documents returned by a search.

Figure 4 is artificial in both content (to demonstration the salient features of the macro language) and layout (for expository convenience). In reality, all English text phrases are stored together in the file *english.dm*, with French phrases in *french.dm* and so on (the suffix *.dm* denotes a macro file). Package names serve to lexically scope the phrase definitions. And in fact there are two files for each language, for example *english.dm* and *english2.dm*, which contain the core Greenstone phrases and those used in auxiliary subsystems respectively, so that the translation facility can differentiate between these two classes.

## 4    Software Infrastructure

To help manage software developed by a disparate network of people and promote an open software philosophy, Greenstone utilizes the concurrent versioning system CVS [1]. Version control is used not just for source code, but also for images, configuration files, and—importantly for this application—the macro files themselves. Macro files define the user interface in a language-independent manner, and also contain the language fragments that flesh out the interface for each particular language. A key insight was that this same mechanism could be used to manage the maintenance of multilingual text. A few customized scripts generate form-based web pages through which the different language interfaces are updated.

A commonly used technology that supports the localization of text in software projects is the *gettext* programming interface [2]. Essentially the technique is a based around a message catalog where a message identifier is paired with a language identifier to retrieve a particular text fragment. Although *gettext* is for software developers, individual projects such as KDE have developed graphical tools, such as KBabel,[2] to assist their translators in managing the fragments of language specific text. For our application, however, using the existing macro framework in conjunction with CVS has significant advantages. Changes take effect in the interface immediately; text files are used rather than binary ones; macros can be spread across arbitrary files, and one macro can reference others.

More in keeping with the Greenstone macro file infrastructure and functionality is the structured, parameterized syntax used by FirstSearch to generate (amongst other things) language independent Web pages [3]. The techniques described in this paper, therefore, are equally applicable to this system.

## 4.1   Generating the Translation Pages

Figure 5 illustrates a Greenstone installation in which someone is translating or updating a language interface. Requests are sent to the central repository of the Greenstone software, using CVS's *anonymous checkout* option. These requests retrieve the definitive version of each phrase. The *annotate* feature of CVS details for each line in a file when it was last edited, and by whom (amongst other things). This makes it easy for the translation utility to determine which language fragments have been outdated by subsequent alterations to the base language fragments.

Before beginning translation, the user selects the base and target languages using the page in Figure 1. When this page is submitted, a script is activated that performs the steps shown in Figure 6. First, the definitive versions of all text fragments in the two chosen languages are retrieved. Each stream is parsed and built into an associative array, indexed by macro name, that records the date of the most recent edit. These two arrays, one for each language, are analyzed to determine which macro entries in the translation language have never been translated before or whose translation is now out of date. The differences are transferred to a third associative array, also indexed by macro name, which records the content of the base language macro and the target language macro (if present).

From this information a series of pages is generated for the translator. Certain features of the text fragments (for example, length in characters) are used to decide how many phrases to place on each page. The name of the file containing the macro is used to determine whether it is one of the core set of phrases, or forms part of an auxiliary subsystem.

## 4.2   Updating the Repository

One of the central features of CVS is the ability to update one's local copy of the software; that is, to merge any changes made to the central repository into

---

[2] http://i18m.kde.org/tools/kbabel/

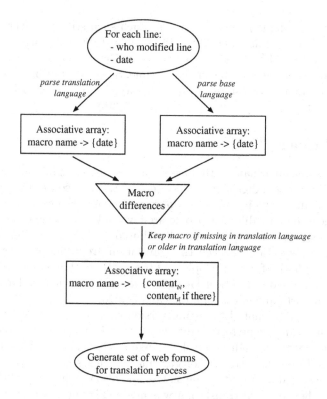

**Fig. 6.** Determining which macros to present for translation.

the local version, while maintaining any local changes that are not in the main version. Conversely, it would be easy to fully automate the system by arranging that changes in the language macros are automatically committed into the main CVS repository (by trusted users). However, we have chosen not to do this—at least until we gain more experience with the system. Instead, the updated macro files are manually installed by the administrator of the central Greenstone site, who inspects them before committing them to the repository.

## 4.3   Searching for Text Phrases

As discussed in Section 2.4 (and illustrated in Figure 3), the Greenstone system itself is used to enable the language phrases to be searched. This is supported by creating a standard digital library collection using the macro files as the input documents. Greenstone uses an extensible scheme of "plugins" to import documents into the system, and a special plugin was written to process macro files. In Greenstone, a configuration file controls which language interfaces are to be offered at any particular site, and this file is parsed to locate the macro files that contain language-specific strings. Each such string is given *Language* metadata based on the filename, using the standard ISO 639 language code.

Appropriate translation pages are generated directly by the search mechanism. The process for generating these is simple. Since the user has signaled that they definitely want to translate this phrase, there is no need to check it against the repository to determine whether it is out of date.

## 5  Conclusions

We have presented a mechanism that assists in creating and maintaining multiple language interfaces to a digital library system, in an open-source environment in which the system and its interface are constantly evolving. The problem is a difficult one because many different people are involved—language translators and software developers—who are widely distributed geographically. Furthermore, there is little intersection between the translation group and the development group, in terms both of actual people and the skill sets they possess. Moreover, much of the work involved in translating interfaces is essentially volunteer labor, which is notoriously difficult to organize and control.

The key insight is that the existing version control system used to manage software change can also be recruited to assist with language maintenance. Once a human translator has indicated what language is being considered, and the base language from which translations are made, the system can work out what fragments are new and need to be translated, and also which fragments have been altered since their original translation was made. These can then be presented on a web form for the translator to process. Changes to the interface take place immediately so that the result can be reviewed in context. Two interesting self-referential twists are that the digital library mechanism itself can be used to enable translators to search for specific phrases, and that the interface to the translation system itself can be presented for translation using precisely the same mechanism.

The upshot is that translators are insulated from technical details of how the software is organized, and software developers are insulated from linguistic considerations of how to translate or modify natural language phrases in the interfaces they build and maintain.

## References

1. P. Cederqvist. *CVS – Concurrent Versions System*, 1.11.3 edition, December 2002.
2. U. Drepper, J. Meyering, F. Pinard, and B. Haible. *GNU gettext tools*. Free Software Foundation, Inc., Boston, MA, USA, 0.11.2 edition, April 2002.
3. G. Perlman. Achieving universal usability by designing for change. *IEEE Internet Computing*, 6(2):46–55, 2002.
4. Unicode Consortium. *The Unicode Standard, Version 3.0*. Addison Wesley, Reading, MA, USA, 2000.
5. I. H. Witten and D. Bainbridge. *How to Build a Digital Library*. Morgan Kaufmann, San Francisco, CA, USA, 2003.

# A Service for Supporting Virtual Views of Large Heterogeneous Digital Libraries

Leonardo Candela, Donatella Castelli, and Pasquale Pagano

Istituto di Scienza e Tecnologie dell'Informazione "Alessandro Faedo"
Consiglio Nazionale delle Ricerche
Area della Ricerca CNR di Pisa
Via G. Moruzzi, 1 - 56124 PISA - Italy
{candela, castelli, pagano}@isti.cnr.it

**Abstract.** This paper presents an innovative type of digital library basic architectural service, the *Collection Service*, that supports the dynamic construction of customized virtual user views of the digital library. These views make transparent to the users the real DL content, services and their physical organization. By realizing the independency between the physical digital library and the digital library perceived by the user the Collection Service also creates the conditions for services optimization. The paper exemplifies this service by showing how it has been instantiated in the CYCLADES and SCHOLNET digital library systems.

## 1 Introduction

This paper presents an innovative type of digital library (DL) basic architectural service, the *Collection Service* (CS), that supports the dynamic construction of virtual user views of the DL. These views make transparent to the users the real DL content, services and their physical organization.

The CS has its roots in the experience that we accumulated when developing the ERCIM Technical Reference Digital Library (ETRDL)[1]. This DL, which became operational in 1998, was designed as the "European branch" of the NC-STRL DL [2]. ETRDL provided access to a technical document collection of eight national publishing institutions working in the area of computer science and applied mathematics. One of the objectives was to permit *localization*, i. e. to satisfy the specific requirements for functionality of each participating institution in the management and access of their documents. In order to achieve this objective, we partitioned the whole information space into subsets, called *collections*. Two macro collections NCSTRL and ETRDL were created, plus a separate collection for each publishing institution. Access to the ETRDL DL followed a "by collection" paradigm. A common User Interface listed the collections available, and for each macro collection its derived collections. The users selected their preferred collection and then they entered in an appropriate portal that give access to the collection specific services. The users thus perceived an organization of the information space and services that was related to the publishers and not necessarily dependent on the underlying physical organization.

T. Koch and I.T. Sølvberg (Eds.): ECDL 2003, LNCS 2769, pp. 362–373, 2003.

The notion of collection was thus acting as a pivot for the provision of different views of the underlying DL. In ETRDL these were views "by publisher". This criterion was embedded in the software code and could not be modified. The possible virtual views were thus established and dependent from the number of publishing organizations and their needs.

As our experience in building DLs grew, we understood that the independency between the physical DL and the views of them given to the users through the collection paradigm was the key for satisfying the requirement of specificity raised by the users of large DLs.

Today's DLs store heterogeneous content, often collected from multiple information sources, such as archives, museums, libraries, e-prints archives, databases, etc., that have been created by specific communities of interest to serve their own needs. The aggregation of these documents under the same DL enlarges the clientele that can benefit from the digitized content. This content can be exploited not only by the original users of the component information sources, but also by all the multidisciplinary communities whose interests span across multiple information sources. Serving these new communities implies providing them with their own information space, i.e. the subset of documents that are pertinent to their activity, and offering customized, effective and fast services on these documents. For example, in a scientific DL, historical archivists could be interested in documents about the history of science and might want to retrieve these resources using specific finding aids. Instead astronomers that access the same DL could be interested in astrophysical articles and require services that validate the quality of the data published. Users of these large DLs thus want customized views of the DL centered around a particular collection of documents that satisfies their information needs.

Differently from ETRDL, however, as the requirements of the users are disparate, the collections cannot be pre-defined or dependent from any pre-established criterion. Moreover, in the new DLs the information sources are composed by multi-version, and structured documents in multiple languages that are described by different metadata formats; the users, the usages, the information sources and the services change over the DL lifetime. The collections must then be created dynamically from heterogeneous sources and they must evolve following the evolution of both the underlying physical environment and user needs. Finally, specific services, which exploit the characteristics of the documents in the collections, their access rights and the semantic requirements of the users, must be associated with the collections.

The simple solution adopted in ETRDL could not be used in these complex new DL environments. The CS presented in this paper implements a new approach for supporting dynamic and virtual collections, it supports the dynamic creation of new collections by specifying a set of definition criteria and make it possible to automatically assign to each collection the specialized services that operate on it.

The Collection Service described here has been experimented so far in two DL systems funded by the V Framework Programme, CYCLADES (IST-2000-25456) and SCHOLNET (IST-1999-20664), but it is quite general and can be applied to many other component-based DL architectural frameworks.

The rest of this paper is organized as follows. Section 2 describes our assumptions on the underlying DL architectural framework. Section 3 presents the functionality of the CS and provides a logical description of its internal architecture. Section 4 illustrates how this logical architecture has been implemented in the CYCLADES and SCHOLNET DL systems and the advantages that the introduction of this service has brought to the their functionality. Finally, Section 5 describes our future plans.

## 2   The Reference Architecture

One of the main aims in introducing the CS was to propose a solution that could be widely applied. Therefore, we decided to assume a simple reference architecture based on a set of distinct services that communicate through a given protocol. These services can be distributed and replicated over the Internet.

In this architecture services named *Information Sources* (ISs) perform the storage, access and indexing functionality. Each IS maintains both the documents and the index for these documents. In particular, we assume that in every IS documents are represented using one or more metadata sets (e. g. Dublin Core, MARC), that describe document content in a compact way. The remaining functionality required for the document discovery, i. e. query planning, query optimization, query filtering and so on, is covered by the *Query Mediator* (QM) service. The QM develops plans for the execution of user queries. In particular, it translates and decomposes a query in a way that can be understood by any IS, merges the results of these sub-queries, and sends them back to the *User Interface* (UI) which provides a human front-end for displaying them to the user. The status of the architecture, i. e. which are the type of the existing services, which are their instances, how they have been configured, etc., is maintained by the *Manager*. New service types and new service instances can be added by simply defining them in the Manager. In particular, other ISs can be added at any time without redesigning the infrastructure or any of its components. All the existing architectural components know about the existence of new components by sending requests to the Manager. Finally, the *Registry* maintains information about the registered users and their rights.

As a final hypothesis on this reference architecture we assume that each service is able to describe itself. In particular, this description specifies the preconditions about the documents that can be managed by this service, e. g. the documents and metadata formats, their structure, language, etc.

## 3   The Collection Service

The Collection Service is a DL architectural service, i. e. a service that supports the activity of the other DL services. In order to support the dynamic growth of the content space, the addition of new services and the variability of the

DL user needs it does not gather and store the documents of a collection in an internal repository, as other solutions do [3,4], but instead maintains them "virtually", i. e. characterizes them in such a way that their elements can always be retrieved when they are required. The CS accepts requests for the creation of new collections and stores metadata information about them. Any authorized user can create a new virtual collection by sending a request to the CS specifying a membership condition, e. g. "the document type is **technical report** and the document subject is **digital libraries**", or by refining the definition of an existing collection. The collection represents the set of all the documents of the underlying real DL information space that satisfy this condition. This means that when a new IS joins the DL, or when an existing one is updated, this change is automatically propagated to all the collections.

By exploiting the information given by the creator of the collection and the information about the underlying architectural configuration, which is provided or automatically calculated, the CS dynamically generates collection descriptive metadata and disseminates them upon request. This metadata comprises not only information on how identify the documents of the collection but also the list of functions that can be activated on them. By using this information, for example, a UI can propose a list of collections to the users, invite them to select one, and then visualize only the specialized functions available on this collection. These metadata are periodically refreshed in order to take into account the evolution of the underlying DL infrastructure, ISs set and services particularly.

Access to collections has to be driven by policies. Policies can be posted to regulate access to and selection of ISs, and the access, interpretation, and evaluation of each single document. The CS therefore has to take into account the access right rules specified by each IS, the variety of media technologies and their access licences.

Figure 1 shows a logical representation of the internal architecture of the CS and the main interactions between modules, illustrating how the initial collection description made by a user is manipulated to produce the collection metadata. These are stored in and disseminated on request by the Metadata Repository (MD) via the Collection Service API.

We start our description by listing the collection metadata (CM) fields that are most significant for the purpose of this paper[1]:

- *Identifier* - the formal unique identifier;
- *Name* - the name of the collection;
- *Description* - the textual description associated with the collection;
- *Membership Condition* (MC) - it represents a formal specification of the collection;
- *Parent* - the identifier of the parent collection. It is used to maintain the hierarchical organization among the set of collections;

---

[1] A more detailed set of collection metadata and how to easily generate them about virtual collection is reported in [5] were a set of benefits for DLs that contains collections are presented too.

- *Retrieval Condition* (RC) - the condition that specifies how to retrieve the documents belonging to the collection;
- *Services* - the list of functions implemented by the DL services that are associated with the collection;
- *Policies* - the policies that regulate the access to the collection.

The interaction between the authorized user and the CS is driven by a GUI that makes it possible to formulate, create, edit and remove collection requests. It allows users to easily create the formal description of their needs. This description is then exploited by the main CS functionality, RC Generation, Services Selection, and Policies Specification, as report below.

**RC Generation.** The *RC Generation* module generates the RC which allows the retrieval of the DL information space documents that belong to the collection. It consists of a set of pairs $(IS_i, filtering\_condition_i)$, where $filtering\_condition_i$ is a set of conditions on the fields of a particular metadata format that specify the subset of documents disseminated by the IS $IS_i$. The collection is given by union of all the documents specified by each single pair. As a consequence of this definition, the set of documents in a collection varies according to the state of the ISs. Moreover, the same document can belong to many different collections.

The ISs listed in the RCs are either extracted by the MC, when they are specified, or they can be automatically derived by matching the MC against a description of the instantiated ISs. This automatic derivation is carried out by the *Source Selection* module. This module implements this selection using the IS' *language model*[2]. This language model is either acquired by the *Harvester* module, which sends a request to a specific service, e. g. the Manager or the IS itself, or it is derived automatically, using the *Query Sampling* module. This module automatically acquires the IS language model by running randomly generated queries and processing the documents returned. The automatic generation processes are periodically repeated to update the RC according to the changes in the underlying physical information space.

The RC can be used by any service that needs to identify the documents belonging to the collection. In particular, it can be exploited by the Query Mediator Service that can reduce the search space to only those ISs that are indicated in the RC.

**Services Selection.** The functions associated with a collection must be functions implemented by existing services, or refinements of them, that can work on the documents of the collection. The objective of the *Service Generation* module is to derive which are the admissible functions for each collection. This module operates on the service descriptions stored in the *Service Description Repository*. These descriptions are periodically retrieved from the *Service Description*

---

[2] We consider the language model as the list of (term, weight) of terms that occur in the IS documents.

*Harvester* which contact the Manager in order to acquire the list of existing services and then gather a list of function descriptions from each of them. The Service Generation module compares each function description against the description of the content of the ISs specified in the RC, returning only those that are compliant with the documents belonging to the collection.

**Policies Specification.** ISs can impose some special access rights rules that grant access to their documents only to well identified communities of users, or can impose the use of their own services. Moreover, some specific services can require a fee to be paid, or can specify particular conditions of use. The *Policies Manager* module completes the CM by adding the information about policies derived by the ISs and the services related to the collection. In order to do this, it uses the *Rights Checker* module that acts as mediator between the CS and the DL Registry.

Even though some of the logical modules must interact directly with the DL infrastructure and, therefore, part of their design is strictly dependent on that environment, the CS can be considered infrastructure independent because only a minimal API set has to be realized (see Figure 1).

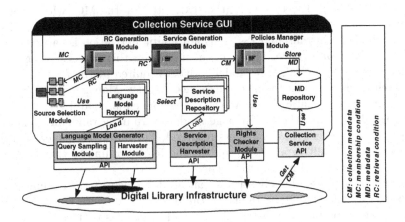

**Fig. 1.** Collection Service Architecture.

## 4   Two Applications

In the previous section we have introduced the general functionality of the CS and its logical architecture. In this section we exemplify what we have described so far by presenting two concrete applications in the CYCLADES and SCHOLNET systems. The requirements of both these systems highlighted the need for a virtual organization of the information space. However, as the requirements and the application contexts were quite different, the implementations are different.

## 4.1   Collection Service in the CYCLADES Project

CYCLADES[3] is an OAI [6] service provider that implements an open collaborative virtual archive service environment supporting both single scholars as well as scholarly communities in carrying out their work. CYCLADES can be configured to gather metadata records from an arbitrary number of OAI compliant archives. The set of these archives is not pre-defined, but new archives can be added over the lifetime of the system. The CYCLADES information space is thus potentially very large and heterogeneous. Each single user, and each community of users, can dynamically activate its own/shared working space. This working space contains information that is relevant for the user/community of users. It can contains documents authored by the owner(s) of the working space, recommendations, results of previous queries, etc. In particular, it contains the subset of the DL information space that is relevant to the user/community. All the services that access and manipulate DL documents operate on this restricted space. Given the dynamic nature of the underlying information space, the potentially large number of users and their variability, we decided to implement these user DL spaces as virtual collections.

In CYCLADES the DL information space is maintained by the *Access Service* which gathers metadata records from the OAI compliant archives. This service organizes the information space internally in order to index the information gathered by different OAI data providers separately. From the logical point of view, the Access Service is thus a common access point for many ISs as there are many OAI data providers. The functionality of the Manager Service is spread over different services. In particular, the list of ISs and generic information about them, such as their name, a brief textual description of their content, etc., are provided by the Access Service itself.

The CYCLADES system users do not know anything about the provenance of the underlying content. They create their own collections by simply giving a MC that characterizes their information needs and do not provide any indication about which are the ISs that store these documents. They must then be calculated automatically. The Source Selection module and the Language Model Generator module implement particular algorithms for carrying out this automatic computation. The former module implements a ranking algorithm that has been obtained by adapting the CORI algorithm [7] to work on structured documents. The latter uses a *query-based sampling* technique [8] to automatically acquire the language model of an IS. This technique does not require the cooperation of IS providers, nor does it require that IS use a particular search engine or presentation technique. Language models are created by running randomly

---

[3] http://www.ercim.org/cyclades/

generated queries and examining the documents returned. Both algorithms are fully described in [9].

Note that the accuracy of the automatic source selection obtained by combining the two algorithms is high, i. e. the RC that is generated approximates very well the MC. This is demonstrated by a set of experiments the we carried out on a CYCLADES configuration that was working on 62 OAI compliant archives. In particular, in these experiments we generated randomly 200 collections using Dublin Core fields. The collections generated are of two kinds: 100 collections (T1) are generated using a combination of conditions on `description` and `title` fields, 100 collections (T2) are generated using a combination of conditions on all fields of the DC schema.

Figure 2 shows tests on the quality of the source selection. *Precision* is defined as $gcd/(gcd+bcd)$ and *recall* is defined as $gcd/(gcd+gncd)$ were $gcd$ is the number of documents belonging to the collection that are found, $bcd$ is the number of documents that do not belong to the collection that are found (also called false positives) and $gncd$ is the number of documents belonging to the collection that are not found (also called false negatives).

The current release of the CYCLADES system does not fully exploit the potentiality of the CS since it uses the CS only as a means to construct virtual information spaces that are semantically meaningful from some community's perspective. Services such as search and browse are activated on the restricted information space described by the collection, but this is the only customization option. The CS does not support collection specific services, i. e. all the users perceive the same services in their working space.

Despite this partial exploitation of the potential of the CS in providing virtual views of the DL, its introduction has brought a number of other important advantages to the CYCLADES users. By reducing the information space to a meaningful subset, the collections play the role of a *partitioning query* as described in [10], i. e. they define a "searchable" subset of the documents which is likely to contain the desired ones. This has the effect of reducing both *false positives*, i. e. useless documents that fail to fulfill the user's needs, and *false negatives*, i. e. useful documents that the system fails to deliver, from the retrieved set.

Moreover, the list of ISs specified in the RC can be exploited by the CYCLADES search and browse services to improve their performance. Figure 3 shows a measure of this improvement. In particular, it compares the query response times obtained by retrieving the set of documents matching the MC with those obtained using the RC (asking for the top 100, 500 and 1000 records for each kind of query). This picture shows that there is an high improvement in response time with little loss in the set of records retrieved (see Figure 2).

Furthermore, resources aggregated in a collection can be found more easily than if they were disjoint. CYCLADES includes a recommender system that is able to recommend a collection to a user on the basis of his own profile and the collection content, so all resources belonging to a collection are discovered together.

Finally a simple list of the collections stored in CYCLADES can provide a good introduction and overview of the large and heterogeneous DL information space.

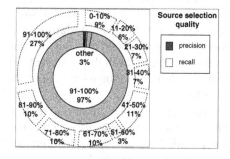

**Fig. 2.** Source selection: precision and recall.

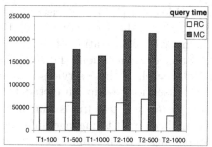

**Fig. 3.** Source selection: response time.

## 4.2    Collection Service in the SCHOLNET Project

SCHOLNET[4] is a digital library service system, i.e. a system that can be instantiated to create DLs. In order to be able to adapt itself to different application contexts it is extremely flexible and extensible.

It provides mechanisms for supporting new forms of communication among scholars communities. These can be communities of students, researchers, professors and scientists that need to access, manage and disseminate documents and other reference material. The SCHOLNET documents belong to publishing organizations. These are research institutions, universities, companies that decided to collaborate in the setting up of a scientific DL.

SCHOLNET supports multimedia, structured and annotated documents in multiple languages that can be described by multiple metadata in different formats. These documents can be disseminated by scholars in draft or preliminary form, or they can be reviewed before becoming publicly available. Particular policies regulates the access to these documents.

From the technical point of view, the SCHOLNET infrastructure is built as a networked federation of different services that can be distributed or replicated. This federation is "open", i.e. it supports an incremental service extensibility to meet the specific needs of existing or new different scholarly communities. It also allows the addition of new service instances located on different servers, for example, to accommodate new publishing institutions that join the DL or to redistribute the workload.

In this infrastructure, the IS functionality is carried out jointly by the *Repository Service*, which provides access to the documents physically distributed on

---

[4] http://www.ercim.org/scholnet/

multiple servers, and the *Index Service*, which serves queries on different languages and metadata formats. Each of these services handles the documents of one or more publishing institutions. A *Query Mediator* dispatches queries to appropriate Index servers; a *Registry Service* maintains information about users, communities and publishing institutions; a *Meta Service* implements the functionality of the Manager service, i. e. it maintains a continuously update status of the networked federation of services, checks its consistency and controls the flow of the communications. These services communicate through a protocol. In particular, each of these services disseminates a description of its functions in an agreed service description metadata format.

The SCHOLNET scenario is thus flexible, heterogeneous and dynamic. It has explicitly been built to manage different kinds of users, dynamically organizable in communities. Each community has its own needs both in terms of content an services. The underlying architectural environment is strongly heterogeneous. The Repository and Index services differ for languages, metadata formats, access rights and management rules. Moreover, the environment is also highly expandable. The set of servers able to host specific services can grow and the plug-ins of new and unpredictable service types is supported.

The CS was introduced in SCHOLNET to implement a level of independency from the underlying infrastructure and the customized views of the DL content and services required to satisfy the needs of the heterogeneous communities.

In SCHOLNET the collections can be created by authorized users by specifying a Membership Condition that explicitly indicate which are the publishing organizations that disseminate the collection documents. The ISs in the Retrieval Condition are derived by list of these publishing organizations.

The CS Service Selection module uses the common and well defined description of each service and ISs, which can automatically be gathered through protocol calls, in order to identify the appropriate set of service functions that can be activated on the collection space. This selection is done by matching the characteristics of documents and their calculated policies against the functions specifications. Note that the gathering of the service descriptions and the generation of the service functions is periodically repeated in order to accommodate the possible changes in the underlying DL infrastructure.

The SCHOLNET CS provides, in addition to the advantages that have been discussed for CYCLADES a number of other specific advantages that derive from the combination of the collection notion with the specific SCHOLNET functionality. In particular, it has been possible to:

- simply organize the different user communities, allowing for the different access rights. It has been possible to create collections of candidate documents that are accessible only by given teams that, in this way, can share draft and preliminary documents in a shared workspace; collections that present the content extracted from the different ISs taking into account the potential audience, e. g. blinding detailed information to students, partially granting access to teachers, and showing all documents content to scientist;

- grant access to the information space through virtual views organizing it by document content, form, or type;
- improve the performance of the services. The SCHOLNET infrastructure is dynamic and expandable with respect to the number of servers and service types: in the experimentation phase, for example, more than half a million documents have been indexed using different Index servers located in many countries (different in metadata types, languages, controlled vocabulary, stemming rules, and stop-words list). The Query Mediator using the services metadata section contained in each collection is able to route the query only to the most appropriate Index servers, improving the response time and in the same time, reducing the workload of each server.

The collections metadata are then used by the SCHOLNET UI to present a personalized virtual environment in which users can select, using the appropriate services, only the appropriate documents.

## 5   Conclusions

This paper has introduced a new DL infrastructure service for supporting dynamic virtual collections. This service can be exploited by other services to provide virtual views of the DL customized according to the needs of the different communities of users.

The notion of collection that we have used here was initially proposed by Lagoze and Fielding [11]. Others [3] have proposed an approach collection-centric, where each collection has a user interface that allows users to search and browse over the collection content. This kind of collection is similar to an IS, as the collection creator has to supply the documents belonging to it. Moreover, the set of services available on a collection can be configured by the collection creator but has to be decided during the creation phase. This approach is quite static, however less dynamic than the approach we have proposed.

The paper has also shown how this service has been used to satisfy specific application requirements in the CYCLADES and SCHOLNET systems. The CYCLADES system is now available[5] and the SCHOLNET access address will be published soon on the OpenDLib web site[6].

We consider the CS we described in this paper as a first prototype of a more general "mediator infrastructure service" that can be used by the other DL services to efficiently and effectively implement a dynamic set of virtual libraries that match the user expectations upon the concrete heterogeneous information sources and services. In particular, we are now working on the generalization of the CS to include other aspects of the information space in the virtual view, like the structure of the documents, their descriptive metadata formats, and the used controlled vocabularies, i.e. terms used in describing a document.

---

[5] http://calliope.ics.forth.gr:7007/Cyclades/LoginForm.html
[6] http://www.opendlib.com

**Acknowledgements.** This work was partially founded by the CYCLADES and SCHOLNET EU projects. Thanks are due to the DLib Group at CNR-ISTI for the considerable support received.

# References

1. Andreoni, A., Baldacci, M.B., Biagioni, S., Carlesi, C., Castelli, D., Pagano, P., Peters, C.: Developing a European Technical Reference Digital Library. In: Proceedings of the third European Conference on Digital Libraries (ECDL'99), Springer-Verlag Berlin Heidelberg New York (1999) 343–362
2. Davis, J., Lagoze, C.: The Networked Computer Science Technical Report Library. Technical Report TR94-1595, Department of Computer Science, Cornell University (1996)
3. Witten, I.H., Bainbridge, D., Boddie, S.J.: Power to the People: End-user Building of Digital Library Collections. In: Proceedings of the first ACM/IEEE-CS joint conference on Digital libraries, ACM Press (2001) 94–103
4. Bergmark, D.: Collection Synthesis. In: Proceeding of the second ACM/IEEE-CS Joint Conference on Digital Libraries, ACM Press (2002) 253–262
5. Geisler, G., Giersch, S., McArthur, D., McClelland, M.: Creating Virtual Collections in Digital Libraries: Benefits and Implementation Issues. In: Proceedings of the second ACM/IEEE-CS Joint Conference on Digital Libraries, ACM Press (2002) 210–218
6. Lagoze, C., Van de Sompel, H.: The open archives initiative: building a low-barrier interoperability framework. In: Proceedings of the first ACM/IEEE-CS Joint Conference on Digital Libraries, ACM Press (2001) 54–62
7. French, J.C., Powell, A.L., Callan, J., Viles, C.L., Emmitt, T., Prey, K.J., Mou, Y.: Comparing the performance of database selection algorithms. In: Proceedings of the 22nd annual international ACM SIGIR conference on Research and development in information retrieval, ACM Press (1999) 238–245
8. Callan, J., Connell, M.: Query-based sampling of text databases. ACM Transactions on Information Systems (TOIS) 19 (2001) 97–130
9. Candela, L., Castelli, D.: The Cyclades Collection Service. Technical report, Istituto di Scienza e Tecnologie dell'Informazione "Alessandro Faedo", CNR (2003)
10. Blair, D.C.: The challenge of commercial document retrieval, Part II: a strategy for document searching based on identifiable document partitions. Information Processing and Management 38 (2002) 293–304
11. Lagoze, C., Fielding, D.: Defining Collections in Distributed Digital Libraries. D-Lib Magazine (1998) http://www.dlib.org.

# A Framework for Unified Authority Files: A Case Study of Corporate Body Names in the FAO Catalogue

James Weinheimer and Kafkas Caprazli

FAO of the UN, Library and Documentation Systems Division, 00100 Rome, Italy
{Jim.Weinheimer,Kafkas.Caprazli}@fao.org

**Abstract.** We present a Unified Authority File for Names for use with the FAO Catalogue. This authority file will include all authorized forms of names, and can be used for highly precise resource discovery, as well as for record sharing. Other approaches of creating unified authority files are discussed. A major advantage of our proposal lies in the ease and sustainability of sharing records across authority files. The public would benefit from the Unified Authority File with its possibilities for cross-collection searching, and metadata creators would also have a greater possibility to utilize bibliographic records from other collections. A case study describes the treatment and use of corporate body names used in the catalogue of The Food and Agriculture Organization of the United Nations.

## 1 Introduction

It is no secret that a heading in a metadata record can be highly difficult to find. For example, what is the heading for The United Nations? It depends on which catalogue you are using. It can be United Nations, UN, U.N., O.N.U., OON, Forente nasjoner, or many other forms. No one can be expected to know the form that happens to be in use in a particular catalogue, so there is authority control. The idea of authority control is simply to choose a single form of name as an organizational point. This form will then serve to bring together all metadata records of items originating from that corporate body. Authority control then provides cross-references from any other forms. Therefore, a Russian catalogue might use the form Организация Объединенных Нации, with references from other forms, as shown in Figure 1.

What is important is that a single heading is used consistently within a collection, i.e. the authorized form. For example in the following catalogue, items authored by the United Nations, UN, U.N., O.N.U., OON, Forente nasjoner, and so on will use the single form Организация Объединенных Нации.

The authority record will work in the following way. Someone will search for United Nations and find the cross-reference *Use: Организация Объединенных Нации* – and the user will be able to make the correct search, so long as a single form of the name is used in the catalogue.

T. Koch and I.T. Sølvberg (Eds.): ECDL 2003, LNCS 2769, pp. 374–386, 2003.

**Fig. 1.**

## 2  Multiple Catalogues, or, Union Catalogues

The method described above works fine so long as the catalogue remains isolated. When catalogues start to interact, things become much more complicated.

For the illustration shown in Figure 2, we will assume that each metadata collection uses a consistent form of the name, but a different one chosen by the Russian catalogue. Therefore, in the French catalogue, all resources authored by the United Nations have the corporate name *O.N.U.*, but in the Norwegian catalogue, it is *Forente nasjoner*.

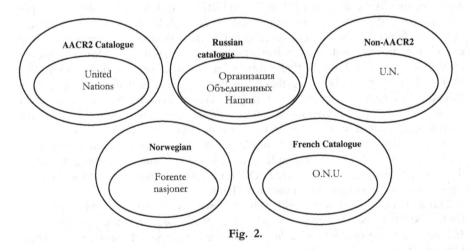

**Fig. 2.**

So, each metadata collection can be fully consistent when considered individually, but when these collections are brought together, their incompatibility becomes obvious. Therefore, when collections are brought together, there is tremendous pressure on the managers of each collection to accept a single form of name, since if they do not, the integrated collection will be inconsistent. This no longer needs to be the case.

## 3  Current Efforts at International Authority Control

Currently, several projects deal with international authority control. These projects rely on maintaining separate records and linking them in some way. In the proposal of the International Federation of Library Associations (IFLA), this link is made with an *International Standard Authority Data Number* (ISADN). All authority records dealing with this corporate body would get the same ISADN.

```
Authorised heading: British Columbia Youth Soccer Association
Information note: Name changed in 1977 from British Columbia
    Juvenile Soccer        Association.
See reference tracing: < B.C. Youth Soccer Association
See also reference tracing: << British Columbia Juvenile
    Soccer Association
Source area: National Library of Canada/Bibliothèque
    nationale du Canada  AACR2, 1981-08-01
ISADN area: NCL/BNC 0011-A-0719
```

There is also the recommended Machine-Readable Bibliographic Information Committee (MARBI) proposal from the American Library Association also recommends maintaining separate records, but instead of using ISADNs, they use the actual headings with local record numbers. This envisions a system interlinked through local record numbers as shown in Figure 3.

*English record*

```
001              ea55555
008/10 (Cataloging rules): c (AACR2)
008/11 (Subject system/thesaurus rules): a (LCSH)
040      $b (Language of cataloging): eng (English)
100 0# $a Cleopatra, $c Queen of Egypt, $d d. 30 B.C.
400 0# $a Cleopatra, $c Queen of Egypt, $d d. 30 B.C.
700 04 $a Cleopatre $b VII $c (reine d'Egypte ; $d 0069-0030
           av. J.-C.) $0 fa44444
700 04 $a Kleopatra, $c Agypten, Konigin, $b VII $d av69-v30 $0
           ga33333
700 04 $a <Heading for Cleopatra in Arabic, formulated
           according to appropriate convention> $0 aa66666
700 06 $a Cleopatre $b VII $c reine d'Egypte, $d 30 av. J.-C.
           $0 cfa77777
```

*French Record*

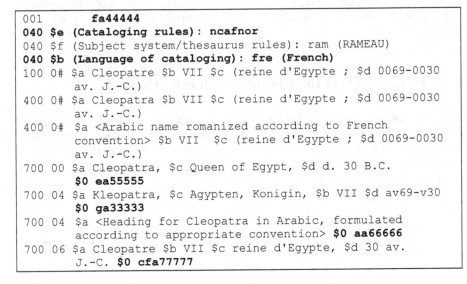

```
001       fa44444
040 $e (Cataloging rules): ncafnor
040 $f (Subject system/thesaurus rules): ram (RAMEAU)
040 $b (Language of cataloging): fre (French)
100 0# $a Cleopatre $b VII $c (reine d'Egypte ; $d 0069-0030
       av. J.-C.)
400 0# $a Cleopatra $b VII $c (reine d'Egypte ; $d 0069-0030
       av. J.-C.)
400 0# $a <Arabic name romanized according to French
       convention> $b VII  $c (reine d'Egypte ; $d 0069-0030
       av. J.-C.)
700 00 $a Cleopatra, $c Queen of Egypt, $d d. 30 B.C.
       $0 ea55555
700 04 $a Kleopatra, $c Agypten, Konigin, $b VII $d av69-v30
       $0 ga33333
700 04 $a <Heading for Cleopatra in Arabic, formulated
       according to appropriate convention> $0 aa66666
700 06 $a Cleopatre $b VII $c reine d'Egypte, $d 30 av.
       J.-C. $0 cfa77777
```

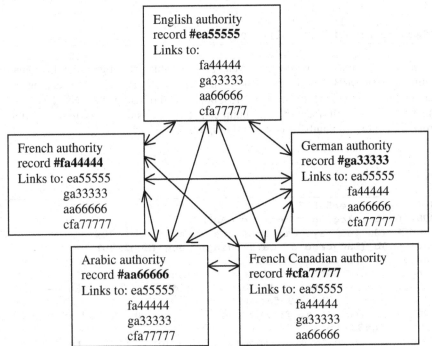

**Fig. 3.**

There would be separate records for the authorized German and Arabic forms, as well as any additional authorized forms that will be included. As we see from Figure 3, this would entail a significant amount of extra work since each record could become quite complex, with the task to keep all of the records, record numbers, and headings correct.

Adding a new authority record into this system creates a great deal of additional work for each database. Adding a new system of authorized forms (e.g. Chinese) would be a tremendous undertaking for the entire structure. Even then, once this system is fully completed, the next steps of creating a practical system from it remain unclear.

We feel these proposals, although very ambitious and laudable, are still thinking in a paper environment, while new possibilities are now available with computers. Our proposal attempts to answer the problems raised by the earlier proposals and to build a mechanism that can be utilized immediately. This will be explained after a short discussion about corporate bodies as used at FAO.

## 4 A Case Study: The Current Situation with FAO Corporate Bodies

The catalogue of the Food and Agriculture Organization of the United Nations follows the rules according to the AGRIS, the international information system for the agricultural sciences and technology. Currently there is nothing in the FAO catalogue that provides cross-references to variant forms of names of corporate bodies. To find items authored by the Food and Agriculture Organization, the user must know to search under FAO, Rome (Italy).

We would like to use the extremely rich cross-reference structure in the LC authority file. Using the cross-reference structure does not mean that we want to use their authorized forms in our collection, since, as an international organization, FAO is a normative organization and cannot favour any language.

## 5 Greater Efficiency for Users and Cataloguers

Obviously, it would be valuable for users and FAO cataloguers to be able to use these references. Users could immediately gain from not having to know the precise form of a corporate name and they could search for it in multiple languages and other forms. In a similar way cataloguers would also gain, since there would be no need for them to memorize all the variant forms of names and they could find them under other language forms.

# 6 Proposal

As a preliminary step in the creation of the Unified Authority File, we will take the records from the LC NAF that are associated with the divisions in FAO, and put them into a local authorities database. We shall also display the LC NAF form so that users will know how they can find items for this corporate body under this name in an AACR2 catalogue.

```
010  ^a n 80004214
035  ^a (OCoLC)oca00386864
040  ^a DLC ^c DLC ^d DLC ^d DLC-R ^d              110: Authorized form
110  ^a Food and Agriculture Organization of the
     United Nations
410  ^a FAO
410  ^a United Nations Food and Agriculture Organization
410  ^a Organización de las Naciones Unidas para la Agricultura y
     la Alimentación
410  ^a Organisation des Nations Unies pour        410: Non-Authorized
     l'alimentation et                                    forms
     l'agriculture
410  ^a Prodovol'stvennaia i sel'skokhoziaistvennaia organizatsiia
     Organizatsii Ob''edinennykh Natsii
410  ^a Delkhiin Khuns Khodoo Azh Akhuin Baiguullaga
410  ^a United Nations. ^b Prodovol'stvennaia i
     sel'skokhoziaistvennaia organizatsiia
410  ^a United Nations. ^b Food and Agriculture Organization
410  ^a Munazzamat al-Aghdhiyah wa-al-Zir⁻a`ah al-t⁻abi`ah lil-Umam
     al-Muttahidah
410  ^a Organizacija Ujedinjenih Nacija za ishranu i poljoprivredu
410  ^a United Nations. ^b Munazzamat al-Aghdhiyah wa-al-Zir⁻a`ah
     al-t⁻abi`ah lil-Umam al-Muttahidah
410  ^a Forenede nationers organisation for ernæring og landbrug
410  ^a Organisatie voor Voedsel en Landbouw
410  ^a Organizatsiia Ob''edinennykh Natsii po voprosam
     prodovol'stviia i sel'skogo khoziaistva
410  ^a United Nations. ^b Organizatsiia po voprosam
     prodovol'stviia i sel'skogo khoziaistva
410  ^a Potravinová a zemedelská organisace Spojených národ°u
410  ^a United Nations. ^b Potravinová a zemedelská organisace
410  ^a Yuen Singnyang Nongop Kigu
410  ^a Kukche Yonhap Singnyang Nongop Kigu
410  ^a F.A.O.
410  ^a Kokuren Shokury⁻o N⁻ogy⁻o Kik⁻o
410  ^a Organizzazione delle Nazioni Unite per l'alimentazione e
     l'agricoltura
410  ^a Food and Agriculture Organization (United Nations)
410  ^a Lien ho kuo liang shih chi nung yeh tsu chih
410  ^a Food and Agriculture Organisation of the United Nations
410  ^a United Nations Food and Agriculture Organisation
410  ^a Samyukta R⁻ashtra Sangha k⁻a Kh⁻adya va K°rshi Sangathana
410  ^a Office and Agriculture Organisation of the United Nations
410  ^a Food and Agricultural Organization of the United Nations
410  ^a Food and Agricultural Organization
410  ^a Tô ch'u'c lu'o'ng nông Liên Hiêp Qu'ôc
410  ^a Food and Agricultural Organisation of the United Nations
410  ^a Tô ch'u'c lu'o'ng thu'c nông nghiêp cua Liên Hiêp Qu'ôc
410  ^a Kokusai Reng⁻o Shokury⁻o N⁻ogy⁻o Kikan
410  ^a Tô ch'u'c nông nghiêp và lu'o'ng thu'c cua Liên Ho'p Qu'ôc
```

Therefore, we propose taking the LC authority record and changing it in the following way: All fields will be changed to include additional information concerning the *authority file it comes from*, and the *language of the heading.*

**^σ source authority file**
**^λ language (ISO 639-2 code), or "all"**
*(the subfield delimiters are subject to change. These have been chosen only for demonstration purposes)*
This differs from current proposals in that we have a *single record* for all existing authority records. Here is an example of a record, including the FAO heading.

```
110 2_ ^σ FAONAF ^λ all ^a FAO, Rome (Italy)
110 2_ ^σ LCNAF ^λ all ^a Food and Agriculture Organization of the
       United Nations
410 2_ ^σ LCNAF ^λ all ^a FAO
410 2_ ^σ LCNAF ^λ all ^a United Nations Food and Agriculture
       Organization
410 2_ ^σ LCNAF ^λ all ^a Organización de las Naciones Unidas para
       la Agricultura        y la    Alimentación
410 2_ ^σ LCNAF ^λ all ^a Organisation des Nations Unies pour
       l'alimentation et l'agriculture
410 2_ ^σ LCNAF ^λ all ^a Prodovol´stvennaia i
       sel´skokhoziaistvennaia organizatsiia Organizatsii
       Ob´´edinennykh Natsii
410 2_ ^σ LCNAF ^λ all ^a Delkhiin Khuns Khodoo Azh Akhuin
       Baiguullaga
410 2_ ^σ LCNAF ^λ all ^a United Nations. ^b Prodovol´stvennaia i
       sel´skokhoziaistvennaia        organizatsiia
410 2_ ^σ LCNAF ^λ all ^a United Nations. ^b Food and Agriculture
       Organization
410 2_ ^σ LCNAF ^λ all ^a Munazzamat al-Aghdhiyah wa-al-Zirⁱa`ah
       al-tⁱabi`ah lil-Umam al-Muttahidah
410 2_ ^σ LCNAF ^λ all ^a Organizacija Ujedinjenih Nacija za
       ishranu i poljoprivredu
410 2_ ^σ LCNAF ^λ all ^a United Nations. ^b Munazzamat al-
       Aghdhiyah wa-al- Zirⁱa`ah al- tⁱabi`ah lil-Umam al-Muttahidah
...
```

This record shows the authorized form used at FAO and the AACR2 form used in the LC Name Authority File, necessary for searching in English language libraries. The authorized form of the corporate body (110) can now *repeat*, since the 110 must include languages and sources.

The subfield λ is used for those catalogues that base the form of a corporate name on the language of the item. For example, there is a United Nations mandate that states that no language can be given precedence over any others. Therefore, a document can have many valid forms of a heading. The user must search under several language forms to make a complete search for the name of many corporate bodies. The example below shows the NAF record with the FAO forms added to it. As we can see, the record now contains additional, and valuable, information not contained in the original NAF record.

```
000           00739cz 2200145n 450
001           4399165
005           19890408080517.8
008           890217n^ acannaab ^n ana
010  __  ^a n 88103322
035  __  ^a (DLC)n 88103322
040  __  ^a DLC ^c DLC
110 2_  ^σ FAONAF ^λ eng ^a FAO, Rome (Italy). Animal Production and
        Health Div.
110 2_  ^σ FAONAF ^λ fre ^a FAO, Rome (Italy). Div. de la Production
        et de la Sante Animales
110 2_  ^σ FAONAF ^λ esp ^a FAO, Rome (Italy). Direccion de
        Produccion y Sanidad Animal
110 2_  ^σ LCNAF ^λ all ^a Food and Agriculture Organization of the
        United Nations. ^b Animal Production and Health Division
```

# 7  Public Displays

The public display could be completely flexible and the authorized fields could also be made to **search the correct catalogues**. For users of the FAO catalogue, they could see something similar to:

> *Search:* Organizacija Ujedinjenih Nacija za ishranu i poljoprivredu
> *Use:*
> **FAONAF (All):** FAO, Rome (Italy) [Search the FAO Catalogue]
>
> *Other preferred forms:*
> **LCNAF (All):** Food and Agriculture Organization of the United Nations [Search associated catalogues]

Clicking on the FAO form of the name would automatically search the FAO Catalogue, while searching the LCNAF form of the name would automatically search any associated catalogues that use the AACR2 form of the name. In this way, the Unified Authority File could be useful from very quickly, and perform international searches effortlessly.

Users of an AACR2 catalogue could see the following display:

> *Search:* Organizacija Ujedinjenih Nacija za ishranu i poljoprivredu
> *Use:*
> **LCNAF (All):** Food and Agriculture Organization of the United Nations [Search associated catalogues]
>
> *Other preferred forms:*
> **FAONAF (All):** FAO, Rome (Italy) [Search the FAO Catalogue]

This format could easily be expanded to include preferred terms from other institutions. For example, the French form *(RAMEAU)* and the German form *(Gemeinsame Körperschaftsdatei-GKD)* could be added easily.

```
110 2_  ^o FAONAF ^λ all ^a FAO, Rome (Italy)
110 2_  ^o LCNAF ^λ all ^a Food and Agriculture Organization of the
        United Nations
110 2_  ^o RAMEAU ^λ all ^a Organisation des Nations unies pour
        l'alimentation et l'agriculture
110 2_  ^o GKD ^λ all ^a Food and Agriculture Organization
410 2_  ^o LCNAF ^λ all ^a FAO
410 2_  ^o LCNAF ^λ all ^a United Nations Food and Agriculture
        Organization
    ...
```

In the FAO Catalogue, the record above could display as:

**Search:** Organizacija Ujedinjenih Nacija za ishranu i poljoprivredu
**Use:**
**FAONAF (English):** FAO, Rome (Italy) [Search the FAO Catalogue]

*Other preferred forms:*
**AACR2:** Food and Agriculture Organization of the United Nations [Search associated catalogues
**RAMEAU:** Organisation des Nations unies pour l'alimentation et l'agriculture [Search associated catalogues]
**GKD:** Food and Agriculture Organization [Search associated catalogues]

Clicking on each form of name would search the correct form in the correct catalogue, no matter where it is in the world.

This new record structure could increase indefinitely, adding as many authorized and unauthorized forms as desired.

# 8  Duplicated Forms

Duplicated authorized forms are allowed to duplicate. For example, if the LCNAF and French forms were the same, it would still be important to indicate this.

```
110 2_  ^o LCNAF ^λ all ^a Microsoft Corporation
110 2_  ^o RAMEAU ^λ all ^a Microsoft Corporation
110 2_  ^o GKD ^λ all ^a Microsoft Corporation <Redmond, Wash.>
110 2_  ^o FAONAF ^λ all ^a Microsoft Corporation, Redmond, WA
        (USA)
410 2_  ^o LCNAF ^λ all ^a Microsoft (Firm)
410 2_  ^o LCNAF ^λ all ^a Microsoft, Inc.
```

Although the LCNAF and RAMEAU headings are identical, they are still the correct forms to search under in the associated catalogues. Unauthorized forms can be duplicated in the same way, since there is a great deal of flexibility in display.

# 9  Work Displays

Displays for cataloguers could be handled as easily as public displays. Since each field will have its own source file, cataloguers could view only the information pertinent to their own catalogues. Cross-references could be duplicated just as headings can be:

```
110 2_  ^σ FAONAF ^λ all ^a FAO, Rome (Italy)
110 2_  ^σ LCNAF ^λ all ^a Food and Agriculture Organization of the
        United Nations
110 2_  ^σ RAMEAU ^λ all ^a Organisation des Nations unies pour
        l'alimentation et l'agriculture
110 2_  ^σ GKD ^λ all ^a Food and Agriculture Organization
410 2_  ^σ LCNAF ^λ all ^a FAO
410 2_  ^σ LCNAF ^λ all ^a United Nations Food and Agriculture
        Organization
410 2_  ^σ FAONAF ^λ all ^a Organización de las Naciones Unidas para
        la Agricultura y la Alimentación
410 2_  ^σ LCNAF ^λ all ^a Organización de las Naciones Unidas para
        la Agricultura y la Alimentación
```

A cataloguer who uses only the FAONAF, can choose to see only the fields marked FAONAF.

```
110  2_  ^σ FAONAF ^λ all ^a FAO, Rome (Italy)
410  2_  ^σ FAONAF ^λ all ^a Organización de las Naciones Unidas para
         la Agricultura y la Alimentación
```

Likewise, a cataloguer using GDK could choose to see only those fields. Additionally, the view could be in any format: USMARC, UNIMARC, or anything else.

It should be clear that in such a structure, all forms of name are equally valid, and no catalogue needs to change their forms in order to participate. The old problem faced by Union catalogues, discussed at the beginning of the paper, no longer need to plague us. All that is needed is sharing of records.

# 10  Benefits for Libraries

The FAO Library is currently searching OCLC WorldCat, which uses AACR2, to find if another library has created catalogue records for their items. If a cataloguer finds a matching record in WorldCat, there still remains a lot of work to transform the record from an AACR2 record to the standards used at FAO.

Every time library staff find a matching record in WorldCat, they must also search the local authority file and determine the form of each corporate body's name. With the Unified Authority File, the decision will still need to be made, but it will be needed *only once* and not every time a record is taken from WorldCat. Below is an example of how this would work:

*AACR2 record (extract)*

```
245 00 ^a Somalia : ^b a country study / ^c Federal Research
        Division, Library of Congress ; edited by Helen Chapin Metz.
250 __ ^a 4th ed.
260 __ ^a Washington, D.C. : ^b The Division : ^b For sale by the
        Supt. of Docs., U.S. G.P.O., ^c 1993.
300 __ ^a xxxvii, 282 p. ; ^b ill., maps ^c 24 cm.
710 2_ ^a Library of Congress. ^b Federal Research Division.
```

*FAO Library record (extract)*

```
English title: Somalia: a country study
Serial:        Area Handbook Series (USA). 1057-5294, no. 550-86
Authors:       Metz, H.C. (ed.)
Corp.authors:  Library of Congress, Washington, DC (USA). Federal
    Research Div.
Publ.place:    Washington, DC (USA)
Publ.date:     1993
Edition:       4. ed.
Collation:     282 p., illus.
```

*Authority Record (extract)*

```
110 2_ ^σ FAONAF ^λ all ^a Library of Congress, Washington,
       DC (USA).   Federal Research Div.
110 2_ ^σ LCNAF ^λ all ^a Library of Congress. ^b Federal
       Research    Division.
```

The FAO cataloguer finds the AACR2 record in WorldCat and downloads it to the local machine. The authority record 110 2_ Library of Congress. ^b Federal Research Division exists in the authority file. The cataloguer must determine the form of name of the corporate body according to FAO rules in any case. This information will then be added to the record in the Unified Authority File. After this, any new records from WorldCat with this corporate body using the AACR2 form of the name can be transformed to FAO standards semi-automatically.

If this cooperative database is adopted and maintained, record sharing could become extensive with an increasing efficiency of library resources. AACR2 libraries could then take records from FAO, since sharing could occur in reverse. If other authorized forms of names were added (German, French, Chinese, etc.) truly international record sharing could be achieved, since a German record or French record could be imported just as easily, and vice versa.

# 11  Perspectives

The Unified Authority File shown in Figure 4 can serve as a platform for cross-catalogue searching. Correctly implemented with new web technologies, a single click could search all catalogues in the world using their authorized forms. The same structure could be used for all types of authorized forms, such as personal and geographic names, and subjects.

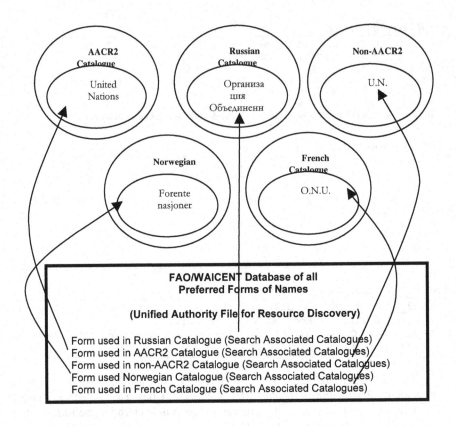

**Fig. 4.**

This paper presents is a MARC-based solution, but of course the choice of system is not so important, as it could be stored in almost any format, including XML if so desired. The system that we propose can have a variety of displays, from MARC21, UNIMARC, or any other. This same mechanism would allow for ease of data exchange.

Generations before us have collected a vast amount of information that is of critical importance for resource discovery. By building on their efforts, our generation now has the task of bringing this information together.

# References

1.   Library of Congress Authority File: http://authorities.loc.gov/
2.   USMARC21 Authorities Format:  http://lcweb.loc.gov/marc/authority/ecadhome.html
3.   Authorites RAMEAU: http://noticesrameau.bnf.fr:8096/
4.   Catalogue of the Deutsche Bibliothek Frankfurt am Main
5.   http://dbf-opac.ddb.de/index_e.htm

6.  German Authority Work and Control / Monika Muennich
7.  http://www.oclc.org/oclc/man/authconf/muennich.htm
8.  Description Conventions (from LC) http://www.loc.gov/marc/relators/reladesc.html
9.  Guidelines for Authority Records and References, 2nd ed. / revised by the IFLA Working Group on GARE Revision http://www.ifla.org/VII/s13/garr/garr.pdf
10. Discussion Paper No. 2001-DP05: Multilingual authority records / MARBI Multilingual Record Task Force. http://lcweb.loc.gov/marc/marbi/2001/2001-dp05.html

# geoXwalk – A Gazetteer Server and Service for UK Academia

James Reid

GeoService Delivery Team, EDINA, University of Edinburgh, George Square, Edinburgh, EH8 9LJ, Scotland.
James.Reid@ed.ac.uk

**Abstract.** This paper will summarise work undertaken on behalf of the UK academic community to evaluate and develop a gazetteer server and service which will underpin geographic searching within the UK distributed academic information network. It will outline the context and problem domain, report on issues investigated and the findings to date. Lastly, it poses some unresolved questions requiring further research and speculates on possible future directions.

## 1 Introduction

The Joint Information Systems Committee (JISC) is a strategic advisory committee working on behalf of the funding bodies for further and higher education (FE and HE) in the United Kingdom. The JISC promotes the innovative application and use of information systems and information technology in FE and HE across the UK by providing vision and leadership and funding the network infrastructure, Information and Communications Technology (ICT) and information services, development projects and high quality materials for education in what is referred to as the JISC 'Information Environment' (JISC IE). The JISC IE provides access to heterogeneous resources for academia, ranging from bibliographic, multimedia and geospatial data and associated materials.

The geoXwalk project was conceived as a development project to build a shared service which would service the JISC IE by providing a mechanism for geographic searching of information resources. This would complement the traditional key term and author type searches that have been supported. 'Geo-enabling' other JISC services would provide a powerful mechanism to support resource discovery and utilisation within the distributed JISC IE.

## 2 Problem Domain

Geographic searching is a powerful information retrieval tool. Most information resources pertain to specific geographic areas and are either explicitly or implicitly

T. Koch and I.T. Sølvberg (Eds.): ECDL 2003, LNCS 2769, pp. 387–392, 2003.

geo-referenced. The UK's National Geospatial Data Framework (NGDF) estimates that as much as eighty per cent of the information collected in the UK today is geo-referenced in some form. Geography is frequently used as a search parameter, and there is an increasing demand from users, data services, archives, libraries, and museums for more powerful geographic searching. However, there are serious obstacles to meeting this demand.

Geographic searching is often restricted because geographic metadata creation is excessively resource intensive. Accordingly, many information resources have no geographic metadata, and where it exists, it usually only extends to geographic names. Search strategies based on geographic name alone are very limited (although they are a critical and often the only access point). An alternative is to geo-reference the resources using a spatial referencing system such as latitude and longitude or, in the UK, the Ordnance Survey National Grids (of Great Britain and Northern Ireland).

The existence of a maze of current and historical geographies has created a situation where there is considerable variation in the spatial units and spatial coding schemes used in geographic metadata. Many geographic names have a number of variant forms, the boundaries in different geographies do not align, and names, units and hierarchies have changed in the past, and will continue to change. In 1990, the UK Data Archive (University of Essex) identified ninety different types of spatial units and spatial coding schemes in use in their collection and more have since been added. By way of illustration, the Resource Discovery Network (RDN) ResourceFinder (http://www.rdn.ac.uk/) does not currently have a specific geographic search function, instead it simply searches using a text based mechanism, thus to find information referring to a particular place the place must be referred to by name in the description field of the resource's accompanying metadata. Using geoXwalk, the place-names in the metadata can be turned into other geographical identifiers enabling searching by e.g. minimum bounding rectangle, postcode, county.

Clearly, no single system of spatial units and coding will suit all purposes as people conceptualise geographic space in different ways and different servers deploy differing geographic naming schemes. Ideally, users should not be forced to have to explicitly convert from one 'world' view to another. However, it is impractical for most service providers to support more than a few geo-referencing schemes, or develop the means to convert from one to another. A comprehensive gazetteer linking a controlled vocabulary of current and historical geographic names to a standard spatial coding scheme (such as latitude and longitude and/or the Ordnance Survey National Grid(s)) would be necessary to perform these translations (or 'cross-walks' – hence the name) and would therefore provide the capacity to be, what might be referred to as 'geographical agnostic' . This is what the geoXwalk project aims to deliver. geoXwalk was funded by the JISC as a multi Phase development project, the principle aim of which was to assess the feasibility of developing and providing an online, fast, scaleable and extensible British and Irish gazetteer service, which would play a crucial role in supporting geographic searching in the JISC IE. The project was a joint one between EDINA, Data Library, University of Edinburgh, and the History Data Service, Data Archive, University of Essex.

The general aim of the project is to investigate the practicability of a gazetteer service, (a network-addressable middle-ware service), implementing open protocols, specifically the Alexandria Digital Library Gazetteer Protocol (ADL 1999, Janée and Hill 2001) and the Open GIS Consortium's (OGC) Filter Specification (OGC 2001), to support other information services within the JISC IE. Firstly, by supporting geographic searching and secondly, by assisting in the geographic indexing of information resources. As the project has progressed it has become clear that there is also a requirement for it to act as a general reference source about places and features in the UK and Ireland. Phase I was conducted as a scoping study to determine the feasibility and the requirements for such a service while Phase II which commenced in June 2002 aims to develop an actual working demonstrator geo-spatial gazetteer service suitable for extension to full service within the JISC IE.

## 3  Technical Implementation

For conceptual purposes the geoXwalk project can be decomposed into a number of interdependent though to some degree independent features:

i)       a gazetteer database supporting spatial searches;
ii)      middleware components comprising APIs supporting open protocols to issue spatial and/or aspatial search queries;
iii)     a semi-automatic document 'scanner' that can parse non-geographically indexed documents for placenames, relate them to the gazetteer and return appropriate geo-references (coordinates) for confirmed matches – a 'geoparser'.

### 3.1  The Gazetteer Database

The gazetteer database itself is of course crucial but what is of particular relevance is that geoXwalk extends the concept of a traditional gazetteer which typically only hold details of a placename/feature along with a single x/y coordinate to represent geographic location . In order to provide answers to the sorts of sample queries that geoXwalk will be expected to resolve (e.g. What parishes fall within the Lake District National Park?; What is at grid ref. NT 258 728?; What postcodes cover the Fife Region? etc. ) each geographical feature held in the database needs to provide, as a minimum: a) a name for the feature, b) a feature type and c) a geometry (spatial footprint).

In the case of the latter, the simplest geometry would be a point location but significantly, geoXwalk accommodates recording of the actual spatial footprint of the feature i.e. polygons as opposed to just simple points. By using a spatially enabled database, geoXwalk can then determine at runtime the implicit spatial relationships between features (this contrasts with the classic 'thesaurus' approach in which predetermined hierarchies of features are employed to capture the spatial relationships between features). Holding such extended geometries in the database therefore permits more flexible and richer querying than could be achieved by only holding reduced geometries. Furthermore, all polygonal features can be optionally queried as point features if desired.

A feature type thesaurus has been implemented based on a national dialect of the ADL Feature Type Thesaurus (FTT) (http://www.alexandria.ucsb.edu/~lhill/FeatureTypes/) and provides a means of controlling the vocabulary used to describe features when undertaking searches. Phase I of the project had identified the ADL FTT as a suitable candidate given its relative parsimony balanced against its richness and adaptability.

The database schema used in geoXwalk is itself based upon the ADL Content Standard (http://www.alexandria.ucsb.edu/gazetteer/gaz_content_standard.html). Examination of the ADL standard showed that it could embody the richness of an expanded gazetteer model. It further allows temporal references to be incorporated into entries and defines how complicated geo-footprints can be handled. Explicit relationships can be defined, which is of particular use when a gazetteer holds significant amounts of historical data for which geometries do not exist (although implicit spatial relationships between features based on their footprints is arguably the more flexible approach to favour).

The standard also recognises that data sources will not hold all the detail permitted by the standard. Furthermore, features can be easily introduced into a gazetteer and be updated with additional information from other sources at a later date. Potentially this could save a significant amount of time when the gazetteer is constructed from a variety of data sources (as in fact geoXwalk is). Also, from a pragmatic point of view, the proposed standard has been implemented in a web based gazetteer service, containing over 10 million entries.

### 3.2    The Middleware Components

Two protocols are currently supported by geoXwalk – the ADL Gazetteer Protocol (Janée and Hill 2001) and the OGC Filter Encoding Implementation Specification (OGC 2001). In order to process incoming queries a suite of servlets has been written that transforms the XML based queries generated by the client and maps these to database specific SQL statements. Additionally, in a sample demonstrator that has been developed, an OGC Web Map Server (WMS) is deployed to produce map based visualisations of the returned geographical features. The demonstrator is purely for illustrative purposes as the primary focus of the geoXwalk server is to service machine to machine (m2m) queries. A related project, Go-Geo! (www.gogeo.ac.uk), which is a geospatial metadata discovery service for UK academia, utilises the geoXwalk server to perform enhanced spatial searching.

## 3.3  The Geoparser

Much of the data and metadata that exists within the JISC IE, while having some sort of georeference (such as placename, address, postcode, county etc.) is not in a format that allows it to be easily spatially searched. One task of the project was to investigate how existing, non-spatially referenced documents could be spatially indexed. Using the gazetteer as reference, a prototype rule based geoparser has been implemented that can semi-automatically identify placenames within a document and extract a suitable spatial footprint .

The approach taken has not relied on a 'brute force' approach as this is too resource intensive and in tests proved too unreliable. The rule based approach takes account of the structure of the document and the context within which the word occurs. As a refinement to the basic geoparser, a web-based interface has also been developed to allow interactive editing/confirmation of the results of the geoparser. Resultant output from this stage can then be used to update the document's metadata to include the georeferences thus making the original document explicitly spatially searchable.

## 4   Outstanding Issues

The development of both the gazetteer and the geoparser have identified a series of questions that require further investigative research. Amongst the more intractable of these are issues associated with feature disambiguation and improvements to the geoparser.

The first of these, referred to elsewhere as 'map conflation' (Yuan 1999) essentially is concerned with the identification and resolution of duplicate entries in the gazetteer. In essence the problem is one of being able to discriminate between existing and new features and to be able to determine when two (or more) potentially 'similar' geographic features are sufficiently 'similar' to be considered as the same feature. As geoXwalk dimensions a geographic feature on the basis of: (i) its name; (ii) its feature type (ADL FTT entry) and (iii) its geometry (spatial footprint),there are thus three distinct 'axes' along which the candidate features must be compared .

The critical question arises of how closely on all three axes must the features correspond and whether one axis should be weighted more highly than another. As geoXwalk relies on answering queries by using the implicit spatial relations between features using their geometries, one rule-of-thumb would be that a features geometry is it's principal axis and takes precedence over name and type. However, as more historical data is added to the gazetteer this problem intensifies – take for example the case of London (contemporary) and Londinium (Roman) – while both may be regarded as the same place, they exhibit radically different spatial footprints (and possibly feature types - town vs. city). The derivation of some metric that would allow confidence limits to be attached to features as they are added to the gazetteer is therefore a pressing research priority.

A lot of refinement work could be conducted on the current basic implementation of the geoparser, specifically optimising it in terms of performance and accuracy in order to facilitate realtime geoparsing as well as minimising the number of false positives identified. Additionally, the capacity to derive a feature type automatically as well as the footprint itself would be extremely useful.

## 5  The Future

The project ends in June 2003 at which point evaluation by JISC may lead to an extension to a fully resourced shared service within the JISC IE. However, significant interest in the project exists outside the academic community that could forseeably lead to a more 'public' service that is of relevance to a wider audience that just the UK academic sector. Indeed, the model employed is sufficiently adaptable to scale to the development of a European geoXwalk comprising a series of regional geoXwalk servers. Such a facility would form a critical component of any European Spatial Data Infrastructure (ESDI).

## References

1.  Joint Information Systems Committee, *Information Environment: Development Strategy 2001–20*, (JISC 2001).
2.  *Alexandria Digital Library Project.* [online] http://www.alexandria.ucsb.edu/ (01 October 1999) and ADL. *Alexandria Digital Library Gazetteer Development Information.* [online] http://www.alexandria.ucsb.edu/gazetteer/ (01 October 1999).
3.  Janée G. and Hill, L., The ADL Gazetteer Protocol, Version 1. Available online: < http://alexandria.sdc.ucsb.edu/~gjanee/gazetteer/specification.html>,(2001).
4.  Open GIS Consortium Inc., Filter Encoding Implementation Specification Version 1.0.0, (19 September 2001). Available online at: <http://www.opengis.org/techno/specs/02-059.pdf>
5.  Yuan S., Development of Conflation Components, *Geoinformatics and Socioinformatics* '99 Conference Ann Arbor,19–21 June (1999),pp. 1–13.

# Utilizing Temporal Information in Topic Detection and Tracking

Juha Makkonen and Helena Ahonen-Myka

Department of Computer Science, University of Helsinki, P.O. Box 26,
00014 University of Helsinki, Finland
{jamakkon,hahonen}@cs.helsinki.fi
http://www.cs.helsinki.fi/group/doremi/

**Abstract.** The harnessing of time-related information from text for the use of information retrieval requires a leap from the surface forms of the expressions to a formalized time-axis. Often the expressions are used to form chronological sequences of events. However, we want to be able to determine the temporal similarity, i.e., the overlap of temporal references of two documents and use this similarity in Topic Detection and Tracking, for example. We present a methodology for extraction of temporal expressions and a scheme of comparing the temporal evidence of the news documents. We also examine the behavior of the temporal expressions and run experiments on English News corpus.

## 1 Introduction

News documents contain a wealth of information coded in the natural language temporal expressions. Automatic processing of news often neglects these expressions for several reasons: temporal expressions are difficult to spot, their surface forms themselves are hardly of any direct use, the meaning of an expression is often somewhat ambiguous or at least very difficult to resolve, and the expressions do not lend themselves easily to any kind of comparison. However, this temporal information would be highly useful for many areas of applications: (context aware) information retrieval, information extraction, question answering, document summarization, and topic detection and tracking, for example [1].

There are three problems one has to deal with before temporal information can be applied automatically in any of these tasks: *recognition, formalization* and *comparison* of the temporal expressions. First, the expressions have to be extracted from the text. Second, the expressions need to be provided with formal meaning. In addition to the expression, one often needs some context information, such as the utterance time and the tense of the relevant verb, in order to map the expression. And finally, there has to be a suitable method of employing the formalized expression.

In this paper, we examine these problems in the context of topic detection and tracking (TDT) [2] where one attempts to detect new, previously unreported *events* from online news-stream and track documents discussing the same event. Clearly, an event as well as the news-stream itself are intrinsically sensitive to

T. Koch and I.T. Sølvberg (Eds.): ECDL 2003, LNCS 2769, pp. 393–404, 2003.

time. In TDT, an event is usually understood as *"some unique thing that happens at some point in time"* [3]. Note that this definition differs from the concept of event in AI and dialog systems.

In recognizing temporal expressions, we employ functional dependency parsing (see, e.g., [4]) and finite-state automata. Once an expression is recognized, the terms it contains are converted to *shift* and *span* operations that move the utterance time to the past or to the future. We define these operations on top of a *calendar* [5] that defines the global time-line and its various granularities of time. In addition, we provide semantics for expressions with considerable degree of indexical variety: *by early May, later this month* etc.

Finally, we outline an approach to comparing the temporal similarity of two documents. Unlike in some of previous approaches (see e.g. [6,7]), we are not attempting to establish a chronological order for various actions occurring in the text of a news document. The result of comparison characterizes the proportion of overlap in the resolved expressions of two documents. We show that this overlap, *coverage*, is higher when two documents discuss the same event than when they are not. Naturally, a TDT system would not make decision based on sheer temporal similarity, but we believe it will provide valuable additional evidence.

This paper is organized as follows: In Section 2 we present some of the previous work. Our approach is discussed in Section 3.1 and Section 5 contains experimental results with English TDT2 corpus. Section 6 is a conclusion.

## 2    Related Work

Mani and Wilson have presented an approach for resolving temporal expressions from news-feed with manually produced and machine-learned rules [6]. They could resolve expressions with explicit ('tomorrow') and positional ('next week') offsets based on the reference time and implicit ('Thursday', 'February') offsets based on reference time and the verb tense. While Mani and Wilson confined their experiments to core expressions and neglected prepositions, Schilder and Habel introduced prepositions in their finite-state automata [7] using Allen's previous work [8]. Both of these approaches make efforts in assigning a temporal tag for events [1] occurring in the news document. Setzer and Gaizauskas have proposed annotation schemes for such events and temporal information [9].

Dialog systems have had similar aspirations to these approaches. For example, Wiebe *et al.* presented a machine learning approach for a scheduling dialog, where two agents, a human and a computer, are trying to agree on meetings via natural language [10].

Temporal information has been used in detecting events from the text. Smith employed spatio-temporal attributes in detecting historical events from a digital library [11]. His method employs place–time collocations. Koen and Bender augmented the news documents with external temporal information and thus

---

[1] Here, an event is understood differently from TDT. An event is defined by a verb (e.g., the spokesman *said*) or by event-denoting nouns (e.g., *elections*).

anchored the temporal expression occurring in the text into events more familiar to the reader [12]. The temporal references have nurtured the domain of topic detection and tracking in various forms [3,13] as well as more recent area of temporal summarization [14].

All of the approaches require a temporal ontology or time-line that provides terms such as *year, Monday* and *week* a semantical interpretation. Often time-line simply relies on system date, but temporal algebras have been proposed in order to formalize the time-line and the units of time it contains [5,15].

## 3  Resolving Temporal Expressions

Some temporal expressions are *explicit* [7], e.g., *on the 24th of August 2003, in October 2001* etc. No additional information is required in resolving them. There are also *implicit* expressions that contain a varying degree of indexical features: *last February, two weeks ago, on Tuesday* etc. In order to formalize these expressions, we need to know the reference time and the verb tense. Yet, the are *vague* expressions such as *after several weeks* and *before June* the formalization of which is difficult.

We map all the expressions as an interval, i.e., a pair of dates, on a global time-line, *calendar*. This is accomplished by moving either the *utterance time* or the *reference time* according to the operators occurring in the expression. The outcome is called *event time*. This distinction has usually been attributed to Reichenbach (see, e.g., [16]) and can be exemplified by following sentences:

> *The winter of 1974 was a cold one. The next winter will be even colder.*
> *The winter of 1974 was a cold one. The next winter was even colder.*

In the first sentence, the expression *next winter* (*event time*) refers to the next winter with respect to the time of utterance. In the latter, due to the past-tense of the verb, *next winter* refers to the following winter, i.e., the winter of 1975.

### 3.1  Recognizing Temporal Expressions

We divide the terms occurring in the temporal expressions into categories presented in Table 1. We consider the baseterms to be more like sub-categories. For example, the baseterm *day* contains terms referring to a day: morning, noon, day, afternoon, evening, night. Similarly, *weekday* consists of weekdays from Monday to Sunday.

We employ a finite-state automata in recognizing temporal expressions. Figure 1 portrays a simplified automata that recognizes temporal expressions with *monthname* as the baseterm. The input comprises a natural language sentence that is examined a word at a time. The automata remains in the initial state unless a *temporal*, a *determiner* or an *ordinal* is encountered. If there is no valid transition from a given state, the automata returns to the initial state. The valid end-states have double circles.

**Table 1.** A list of categories of terms occurring in temporal expressions.

| category | terms |
|---|---|
| baseterm | day, week, weekday, month, monthname, quarter, season, year, decade |
| indexical | yesterday, today, tomorrow |
| internal | beginning, end, early, late, middle |
| determiner | this, last, next, previous, the |
| temporal | in, on, by, during, after, until, since, before, later |
| postmodifier | of, to |
| numeral | one, two, ... |
| ordinal | first, second, ... |
| adverb | ago |
| meta | throughout |
| vague | some, few, several |
| recurrence | every, per |
| source | from |

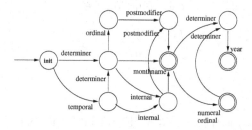

**Fig. 1.** A simplified automata recognizing *monthname* related temporal expressions.

The automata can deal with input such as "The strike started *on the 15th of May 1919*. It lasted *until the end of June*, although there was still turmoil *in late January next year*". Clearly, the automata would accept invalid expressions as well, but we have assumed a non-hostile environment, i.e., we assume the news articles are good English. There is also a filter for recognized invalid expressions. The expressions with a *vague* term, *a few weeks ago*, are recognized, but omitted from further processing at this stage.

We have employed Connexor's Functional Dependency Grammar parser [2]. It is fairly easy to determine the tense of the relevant verb, since the parser typically finds a link between the verb and the first term of the temporal expression [4].

## 3.2   Calendar-Based Time-Line

In order to formalize the structure of the time-line, we adopt the calendar model from Goralwalla *et al.* [5] to construct an algebra for temporal expressions. In the core of it all, we have the time-line.

**Definition 1** *A global time-line $\mathcal{T}$ is a point structure with precedence relation $<_{\mathcal{T}}$. An interval $[t_i, t_k] \subset \mathcal{T}, t_i < t_k$ is a set of instants $\{[t_j, t_j] \mid i \leq j \leq k\}$.*

[2] http://www.connexor.com

A *calendar* provides a space, where elements can be compared, ordered and moved, i.e., where elements are in relation with other elements. Without a calendar, expressions like *last April* and *two weeks ago* would hardly make sense.

**Definition 2** *A calendar $C$ is a triplet $\langle \mathcal{T}, \mathcal{G}, \mathcal{F} \rangle$, where $\mathcal{T}$ is the global timeline of $C$, $\mathcal{G}$ is the set of granularities $\mathcal{G} = \{G_1, G_2, \ldots G_n\}$. $\mathcal{F}$ is the set of conversion functions between the granularities.*

Granularities are the basic units of time. For example, a Gregorian calendar has a granularities

$$\mathcal{G} = \{G_{year}, G_{month}, G_{week}, G_{day}, \ldots\}.$$

A stock exchange related calendar could augment this set with $G_{quarter}$, and another related to sports could have $G_{season}$ which would differ from the 'four seasons'. for example. One can conduct a conversion from a granularity to another by the virtue of a conversion function $f \in \mathcal{F}$,

$$f_C^{G_1 \to G_2}(i_1) \to N_{G_2},$$
$$f_C^{G_2 \to G_3}(i_1, i_2) \to N_{G_3},$$
$$\vdots$$
$$f_C^{G_n \to G_{\mathcal{T}}}(i_1, i_2, \ldots i_n) \to R_{G_{\mathcal{T}}},$$

where $i_j (1 \leq j \leq n)$ is the ordinal of the calendric element of the $j^{th}$ calendric granularity in calendar $C$. The result $N_{G_{j-1}}$ is the number of units of $G_{j-1}$ contained by $i_1, \ldots, i_j$. The final outcome, $R_{G_{\mathcal{T}}}$ is the (real) number of the units of *bottom granularity* of $\mathcal{T}$. The bottom granularity is the basis for other granularities. It could be a day, a second, a nanosecond etc. Naturally, the values $N_{G_{j-1}}$ have a lower and upper bound depending on the values of $i_1, \ldots, i_n$. For example, $f_C^{G_{month} \to G_{day}} \in \{28, 29, 30, 31\}$:

$$f_C^{G_{month} \to G_{day}}(2002, 12) = 31, \quad f_C^{G_{month} \to G_{day}}(2001, 11) = 30,$$
$$f_C^{G_{month} \to G_{day}}(2000, 2) = 29, \quad f_C^{G_{month} \to G_{day}}(1999, 2) = 28.$$

The granularity $G_{monday}$ contains every seventh element of $G_{day}$, and $G_{December}$ every twelfth element of $G_{month}$. Analogously, $G_{weekend}$ comprises all the Saturday-Sunday pairs.

### 3.3    Canonization

We want to transform the natural language expression into operators that shift the back or forth, i.e., left or right on the time-line. We call this process *canonization*, since it determines the formal meaning of a temporal expression.

**Definition 3** *A canonized form is a pair $\langle t_i, t_j \rangle$, $t_i, t_j \in \mathcal{T}$ of points on the timeline that denotes an interval $[t_i, t_j] \subset \mathcal{T}$ if $t_i < t_j$, or an instant $[t_i, t_i] \subset \mathcal{T}$ if $t_i = t_j$.*

In the following, we content ourselves with day-level, i.e., $G_{\mathcal{T}} = G_{day}$. Thus all the references to mornings, evenings etc. are interpreted as the baseterm *day*. In the following, we assume the reference time of $t_r = 20020626$, that is, Wednesday, June 26th 2002.

**Definition 4** *A function* $\pi : \mathcal{G} \times \mathcal{T} \to \mathcal{T}$, $\pi(G, t_r) = t_i$ *returns the previous start point of an element of the granularity G. Similarly, a function* $\rho : \mathcal{G} \times \mathcal{T} \to \mathcal{T}$, $\rho(G, t_r) = t_i$ *returns the start point of the next element of the granularity G.*

For example, $\pi(G_{week}, t_r) = 20020624$, $\pi(G_{july}, t_r) = 20010701$, $\rho(G_{year}, t_r) = 20030101$ and $\rho(G_{tuesday}, t_r) = 20020702$.

**Definition 5** *A function* $\delta_L : \mathcal{G} \times \mathbb{N} \times \mathcal{T} \to \mathcal{T}$, $\delta(G, n, t_r) = t_i$ *shifts the point* $t_r$ *n elements of granularity G to the left on the time-line. A function* $\delta_R : \mathcal{G} \times \mathbb{N} \times \mathcal{T} \to \mathcal{T}$ *performs a shift similarly to the right on the time-line.*

The size of the shift is converted into days, because the length of the granularity $G_{month}$, for example, varies considerably. For instance, *three months ago* would result in left shift

$$\delta_L(G_{months}, 3, t_r) = \delta_L(G_{day}, \sum_{k=1}^{n} f_C^{G_{month} \to G_{day}}(y(t_r), m(t_r) - k), t_r)$$
$$= \delta_L(G_{day}, (31 + 30 + 31), t_r)$$
$$= 20020326,$$

where functions $y : \mathcal{T} \to \mathbb{N}$ and $m : \mathcal{T} \to \mathbb{N}$ return the year and the month of a given point on the time-line $\mathcal{T}$. The end point of a canonized temporal expression is obtained by a shifting the start point to the right for the length of the baseterm (minus one day) as shown in Table 2.

**Table 2.** A list of canonized baseterms (here start point is in the past). Once the right shift is converted to days, the number of days should be decreased by one.

| baseterm | start | end |
|---|---|---|
| year | $\pi(G_{year}, t_r)$ | $\delta_R(G_{year}, 1, \pi(G_{year}, t_r))$ |
| season | $\pi(G_{season_x}, t_r)$ | $\delta_R(G_{season_x}, 1, \pi(G_{season_x}, t_r))$ |
| quarter | $\pi(G_{Q_n}, t_r)$ | $\delta_R(G_{Q_n}, 1, \pi(G_{Q_n}, t_r))$ |
| month | $\pi(G_{month}, t_r)$ | $\delta_R(G_{month}, 1, \pi(G_{month}, t_r))$ |
| week | $\pi(G_{week}, t_r)$ | $\delta_R(G_{week}, 1, \pi(G_{week}, t_r))$ |
| day | $t_r$ | $t_r$ |

Sometimes the expressions contain prepositions such as *by*, *before*, *until* and *since* that would have to be interpreted. We call these *span* operators, and they manipulate the start and end points once the points have been resolved. For example, *before* can be understood to the leave start point open when it refers to the past. In case it refers to the future, the start point can be understood as the utterance time. Table 3 lists interpretations for some of the most common non-baseterms.

**Table 3.** The interpretation of non-baseterms.

| term | span |
|------|------|
| after, from, since | $[t_i, varies]$ |
| before, by, until | $[varies, t_i]$ |
| during, in, throughout | $[t_i, \delta_R(G, 1, t_i)]$ |
| on | $[t_i, t_i]$ |
| beginning, early | $[t_i, \delta_R(G, \frac{1}{3}, t_i)]$ |
| mid-, middle | $[\delta_R(G, \frac{1}{3}, t_i), \delta_R(G, \frac{2}{3}, t_i]$ |
| late, end | $[\delta_R(G, \frac{2}{3}, t_i), \delta_R(G, 1, t_i]$ |

Since we are aiming for statistical similarity or overlap, we consider *internal-*
terms to represent one third of the baseterm. The expression *the end of August*
would thus cover the time-line from the 20th to 31st of August.

The process of canonization can be outlined as follows. First, we extract the
baseterm of the expression. Second, we evaluate the start point of the interval
denoted by the baseterm by examining the tense and the reference time. Third,
we shift this start point to the left or to the right if need be. Finally, the span
operators modify the start and end points.

Table 4 shows a tripartite division of temporal expressions. The prefix typically modifies the duration of the baseterm (*late*) or shifts the baseterm with
respect to some coarser baseterm (*15th, second*). The postfix then shifts the
baseterm to the left or to the right. Naturally, all expressions do not fall into
this division (e.g., *October 11*). In practice, we employ finite-state automata
with a window (previous-current-next) to be able to cope with the variety of
expressions and to be able to disambiguate terms.

**Table 4.** Examples of expressions canonized with respect to June 26, 2002.

| prefix | baseterm | postfix | start | end |
|--------|----------|---------|-------|-----|
| on the 21st | (day) | of September last year | 20010921 | 20010921 |
| in late | May | | 20020520 | 20020531 |
| during the second | week | of June 2001 | 20010611 | 20010617 |
| before the end of | October | this year | 20020626 | 20021031 |
| after | Friday | | 20020628 | – |
| six | years | ago | 19960626 | 19960626 |

## 4   Comparing Formalized Temporal Expressions

We are interested in how similar two documents are as to temporal references,
that is, how much the references overlap? The documents, or rather their canonized temporal expressions are compared pair-wise. Each start-end pair of one
document is compared to each of the start-end pairs of the other. The relations

between these intervals fall into following seven categories [17]. Note that the first six have also the converse relation. In the following, we are not concerned, whether $A$ is **before** $B$ or vice versa.

$[t_i, t_j]$ is **before** $[t_k, t_l]$ if $t_j < t_k$,

$[t_i, t_j]$ **meets** $[t_k, t_l]$ if $t_j = t_k$,

$[t_i, t_j]$ **overlaps** $[t_k, t_l]$ if $t_i < t_k < t_j < t_l$,

$[t_i, t_j]$ **begins** $[t_k, t_l]$ if $t_i = t_k \wedge t_j < t_l$,

$[t_i, t_j]$ **falls within** $[t_k, t_l]$ if $t_i < t_k \wedge t_j < t_l$,

$[t_i, t_j]$ **finishes** $[t_k, t_l]$ if $t_i < t_k \wedge t_j = t_l$,

$[t_i, t_j]$ **equals** $[t_k, t_l]$ if $t_i = t_k \wedge t_j = t_l$,

Motivated by the reliability investigations of Krippendorff [18] in comparing sets of intervals, we place the two sets on a cross-tabulation as illustrated in Figure 2. The diagonal represents the synchronous points of the two time-axes, and the shaded areas correspond to the intersections between two intervals $A = \{A_1, A_2, A_3\}$ and $B = \{B_1, B_2, B_3, B_4\}$.

Should the two sets be identical, the shaded areas would be of size $A_i \times B_i$ for each $i$. In such case, all of the intervals of $A$ would be covered with and an interval of $B$. We do not wish to attribute each kind of relation a uniform emphasis as to similarity, since we would value more knowing a day falls within a weekend or a week than falling within a year's interval. Therefore, we propose a simple weight function $\mu : \mathcal{T} \times \mathcal{T} \to \mathbb{R}$ such that

$$\mu([t_i, t_j], [t_k, t_l]) = \frac{2\,\Delta([t_i, t_j] \cap [t_k, t_l])}{\Delta(t_i, t_j) + \Delta(t_k, t_l)},$$

where $\Delta : \mathcal{T} \times \mathcal{T} \to \mathbb{R}, \Delta(t_i, t_i) = 1$ is the duration (in days) of the given interval. The weight function results in 1 if the expressions are an exact match and 0 if the expressions are distinct. All of the relations presented above can be expressed with the duration of the intersection, because we do not make the distinction between **begins, falls within** and **finishes**. Rather, they are just cases of having a non-empty intersection.

As to the example of Figure 2, the intersections $A_3 \cap B_4$ and $A_2 \cap B_3$ would result in higher $\mu$-value than the any of the intersections $A_1 \cap B_1$, $A_1 \cap B_3$, and $A_1 \cap B_2$, because the sizes of the intersections $A_3 \cap B_4$ and $A_2 \cap B_3$ are closer to the sums $|A_3| + |B_4|$ and $|A_2| + |B_3|$.

In practice, the pair-wise $\mu$-weights are calculated in what we call a *cover matrix* illustrated in Figure 4. The coverage of an interval $T_{i,j}$ is calculated by choosing the maximum $v_{i,j}$ of the of the weights for that term. If an interval $T_{1,i}$ is covered with an interval $T_{2,j}$ of equal weight, the maximum value is $v_{1,i} = 1$. On the contrary, if it is not covered all, the maximum value yields $v_{1,j} = 0$. In cases of inclusion the cover varies in $(0, 1)$ depending on the sizes of the intervals.

The total coverage of the two sets of intervals is the sum of all the maximum values divided by the number of interval, i.e.,

$$coverage(T_1, T_2) = \frac{\sum_{i=1}^{n} v_{1,i} + \sum_{j=1}^{m} v_{2,j}}{m + n}$$

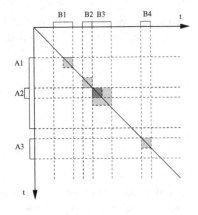

**Fig. 2.** A cross-tabulation of two sets of intervals $A$ and $B$.

| | $T_{2,1}$ | $\ldots$ | $T_{2,m}$ | max |
|---|---|---|---|---|
| $T_{1,1}$ | $\mu(T_{1,1}, T_{2,1})$ | $\ldots$ | $\mu(T_{1,1}, T_{2,m})$ | $v_{1,1}$ |
| $\vdots$ | $\vdots$ | | $\vdots$ | $\vdots$ |
| $T_{1,n}$ | $\mu(T_{1,n}, T_{2,1})$ | $\ldots$ | $\mu(T_{1,n}, T_{2,m})$ | $v_{1,n}$ |
| max | $v_{2,1}$ | | $v_{2,m}$ | |

**Fig. 3.** A cover matrix.

## 5   Experiments

Our test set consisted of 8595 English news documents of TDT2 corpus [19] dating from the 1st of January 1998 to the 31st of January 1998. It contains documents from online newspapers, and radio and television broadcast transcriptions. 2382 documents have been assigned to one of 35 events ranging from cable car crash in the Italian Alps to 1998 Winter Olympics in Nagano, for example.

### 5.1   Extraction Results

We evaluated the extraction performance with 1417 sentences of 65 documents from TDT2 corpus. The set contained as many as 535 temporal expressions, 326 of which were simple and 209 were composite. We evaluated the output of the system manually, and the accuracy, the number of correct assignments over the total number of temporal references in the text, of the recognition and the canonization were as follows.

| type | recognition | canonization |
|---|---|---|
| simple | 0.98 | 0.93 |
| composite | 0.85 | 0.66 |

Naturally, the values for canonization are lower, since in order for an expression to be canonized correctly, it has to be recognized first. In other words, a failure in recognition is also a failure in canonization.

By definition, the simple expressions contain few indexical features or complex syntactic or functional relations, and thus they were easy to spot. They were rather to easy to evaluate as well, though at times the tense of the verb would be misleading, for example. This problem was amplified in the performance of the composite expressions that were still decently recognized. However, the canonization suffered enormously from verbs such as *schedule, plan* and *expect*, for example, that often refer to the future although they may be in past tense. *The meeting was scheduled for Monday* can refer to previous or next Monday.

On the average, we found a little less than 5 temporal expressions from each of the 8595 documents.

## 5.2   Comparison Results

We calculated the average distribution of the temporal relations of the intervals, i.e., what kind of temporal relations to expect when comparing two documents. In the experiments we made the following assumption: if both of the documents are unlabeled, we do not compare them as we do not know whether they discuss the same event or not. Thus, we included only comparisons where at least one of the documents has been associated with a prelabeled event.

The results in Table 5 support the use of temporal evidence in identifying events. The various kinds of inclusion is uniformly higher when two documents discuss the same event. The granularities of Gregorian calendar we used do not meet or overlap each other very often, while the various sorts of inclusion are more frequent. Usually, the overlapping intervals are a week and a month, and they overlap only when the first or the last day of the month is in the middle of the week. Otherwise, the comparison would qualify as relation 'begins', 'finishes' or 'falls within'.

**Table 5.** The average distribution of temporal relations between documents of the same and different event.

| relation | same event | |
|---|---|---|
| | *yes* | *no* |
| before | 0.7824 | 0.8368 |
| meets | 0.0025 | 0.0016 |
| overlaps | 0.0366 | 0.0201 |
| begins | 0.0088 | 0.0054 |
| falls within | 0.1488 | 0.1220 |
| finishes | 0.0089 | 0.0064 |
| exact | 0.0120 | 0.0078 |

The frequency of 'falls within' is quite high compared to the rest. This is a result of comparing days with intervals like a week, a month and a year: it is more likely that a days is in the middle of such interval than that it starts or finishes it. There are almost an equal amount of occurrences of 'begins' and 'finishes'; the latter is just slightly more frequent. This is due to the test corpus dating from January 1998: there are more references to 'year 1997' and to 'December 1997' than to 'year 1998' and to the whole month of 'January 1998', respectively.

We also performed temporal comparisons using the coverage-function and the average of $\mu$-values represented in Table 6. The results show higher scores when two documents discuss the same event, but there really is no difference in the two approaches; the ratio between 'yes' and 'no' categories is around 1.47 with both functions. Hence, it would seem that finding the maximum similarity for each expression does not return any advantage over a simple average of the similarities.

**Table 6.** The averages of the sum of $\mu$-values and the coverage.

|  | same event | |
|---|---|---|
|  | yes | no |
| avg $\mu$ | 0.0034 | 0.0023 |
| coverage | 0.0059 | 0.0040 |

Although the detection and tracking would not rely on mere time-based evidence, the temporal expressions seem to be of use in topic-based information organization. These results would likely improve from more accurate canonization. In addition, it could be beneficial – especially for detecting the first story of previously unreported event – to examine the distance and direction of the referenced intervals with respect to the time of utterance.

## 6 Conclusion

We have presented an approach to recognize, formalize and compare temporal expressions. Our application are has been topic detection and tracking which is intrinsically sensitive to time. We employed automata based on dependency functions in recognition phase and augmented a calendar with shift and span functions. Our main contribution was an approach to compare two sets of intervals in terms of coverage.

An obvious improvement is to make the canonization more efficient. In addition, in order to expand the domain of canonizable expressions, one could introduce a vagueness function that would reflect the inaccuracy of the temporal expression. For example, *a couple of weeks ago* covers an interval of certain amount of points on the time-line, some more vaguely than others.

## References

1. Setzer, A.: Temporal Information in Newswire Articles: An Annotation Scheme and Corpus Study. PhD thesis, University of Sheffield, UK (2001)
2. Allan, J., ed.: Topic Detection and Tracking – Event-based Information Organization. Kluwer Academic Publishers (2002)

3. Allan, J., Carbonell, J., Doddington, G., Yamron, J., Yang, Y.: Topic detection and tracking pilot study: Final report. In: Proc. DARPA Broadcast News Transcription and Understanding Workshop. (1998)

4. Tapanainen, P., Järvinen, T.: A non-projective dependency parser. In: Proc. 5th Conference on Applied Natural Language Processing. (1997)

5. Goralwalla, I.A., Leontiev, Y., Özsu, M.T., Szafron, D., Combi, C.: Temporal granularity: Completing the puzzle. Journal of Intelligent Information Systems 16 (2001) 41–63

6. Mani, I., Wilson, G.: Robust temporal processing of news. In: Proc. Association for Computational Linguistics (ACL-2000). (2000) 69–76

7. Schilder, F., Habel, C.: From temporal expressions to temporal information: Semantic tagging of news messages. In: Proc. ACL-2001 Workshop on Temporal and Spatial Information Processing. (2001) 65–72

8. Allen, J.F.: Maintaining knowledge about temporal intervals. Communications of ACM 26 (1983) 832–843

9. Setzer, A., Gaizauskas, R.: Building a temporally annotated corpus for information extraction. In: Proc. 2nd Intl. Conference on Language Resources and Evaluation (LREC) workshop: Information Extraction Meets Corpus Linguistics. (2000)

10. Wiebe, J., O'Hara, T., McKeever, K., Öhrström-Sandgren, T.: An empirical approach to temporal reference resolution. Journal of Artificial Intelligence Research 9 (1998) 247–293

11. Smith, D.A.: Detecting events with date and place information in unstructured text. In: Proc. 2nd Joint Conference on Digital Libraries (JDCL'02). (2002) 191–196

12. Koen, D.B., Bender, W.: Time frames: Temporal augmentation of the news. IBM systems journal 39 (2000) 597–616

13. Makkonen, J., Ahonen-Myka, H., Salmenkivi, M.: Applying semantic classes in event detection and tracking. In: Proc. International Conference on Natural Language Processing (ICON'02), Mumbai, India (2002)

14. Allan, J., Gupta, R., Khandelal, V.: Temporal summaries of news topics. In: Proc. ACM SIGIR. (2001) 10–18

15. Ning, P., Wang, X.S., Jajodia, S.: An algebraic representation of calendars. Annals of Mathematics and Artificial Intelligence 36 (2002) 5–38

16. Allen, J.: Natural Language Understanding. 2nd edn. The Benjamin/Cummings Publishing Company (1995)

17. Galton, A.: Time and change for AI. In Gabbay, M., Hogger, C.J., Robinson, J.A., eds.: Handbook of Logic in Artificial Intelligence and Logic Programming, Volume 4, Epistemic and Temporal Reasoning. Oxford University Press (1995) 175–240

18. Krippendorff, K.: On the reliability of unitizing continuous data. In Marsden, P.V., ed.: Sociological Methodology. Blackwell (1995) 47–76

19. Cieri, C., Strassel, S., Graff, D., Martey, N., Rennert, K., Liberman, M.: Corpora for topic detection and tracking. In Allan, J., ed.: Topic Detection and Tracking – Event-based Information Organization. Kluwer Academic Publisher (2002) 33–66

# Automatic Conversion from MARC to FRBR

Christian Mönch[1] and Trond Aalberg[2]

[1] Hungarian Academy of Sciences,
Computer and Automation Research Institute,
Budapest, Hungary
moench@dsd.sztaki.hu
[2] Norwegian University for Science and Technology,
Department of Computer and Information Science,
Trondheim, Norway
trondaal@idi.ntnu.no

## 1 Introduction

Catalogs have for centuries been the main tool that enabled users to search for items in a library by author, title, or subject. A catalog can be interpreted as a set of bibliographic records, where each record acts as a surrogate for a publication. Every record describes a specific publication and contains the data that is used to create the indexes of search systems and the information that is presented to the user. Bibliographic records are often captured and exchanged by the use of the MARC format. Although there are numerous "dialects" of the MARC format in use, they are usually crafted on the same basis and are interoperable with each other —to a certain extent. The data model of a MARC-based catalog, however, is "[...] extremely non-normalized with excessive replication of data" [1]. For instance, a literary work that exists in numerous editions and translations is likely to yield a large result set because each edition or translation is represented by an individual record, that is unrelated to other records that describe the same work.

Different conceptual models have been defined for bibliographic entities and the relations between them in order to address the lack of bibliographic structure in catalogs, for instance [2]. The most influential model is provided by the *Study group on the Functional Requirements for Bibliographic Records* of the *International Federation of Library Associations and Institutions* (IFLA) This model is commonly refered to as the *FRBR model* [3]. Because it explicitly models abstract concepts that are only implicitly represented in traditional catalogs, it can greatly improve search and navigation in bibliographic catalogs [4].

However, the creation of an entity of the FRBR model is a time consuming and expensive process, and an automated or at least computer supported transformation of existing records is needed. In this paper we describe an ongoing effort to create a framework for the automatic extraction of FRBR model entities from MARC records.

## 2 The Framework for the Conversion

### 2.1 The BIBSYS Catalog

As a case study for our framework we use *BIBSYS*, the Norwegian bibliographic database for university and college libraries. BIBSYS is based on the MARC format. The various

T. Koch and I.T. Sølvberg (Eds.): ECDL 2003, LNCS 2769, pp. 405–411, 2003.

entries of a MARC record are identified by the use of fields and subfields. Field identifiers are three-numbered values whereas subfields are identified by a single letter. BIBSYS adds a few extensions to MARC, for example field 491 which allows to put BIBSYS records into a *part of* relationship, in order to deal with multipart items.

## 2.2   The FRBR Model

The FRBR model is an entity relationship model that defines three groups of entities, and the attributes and relationships between these entities. It further defines how the attributes and relations are used when performing the four operations: *searching, identifying, selecting,* and *obtaining* on the entities in group 1, respectively on a subset of these entities.[1] The entity group 1 contains entities that describe the products of artistic or intellectual endeavor. The entities of group 2 represent those responsible for the content, and the entities of group 3 represent subjects of works. In this paper we focus on the entities in group 1 and in group 2. The entities in group 1 of the FRBR model are: *work, expression, manifestation,* and *item*. The entities in group 2 are: *person* and *corporate body.* A *work* is realized through one or more *expressions,* an *expression* is embodied in one or more *manifestations,* and a *manifestation* may embody one or more *expressions.* A *manifestation* is exemplified by one or more *items.* Figure 1 shows these entities and some of the relations between them.[2] We have just depicted the basic relations, a range of additional relations are defined, e. g. *is part of* between *works* and *is translator* relation between *persons* and *works.* For a complete description of all entities and relations in the FRBR model refer to [3].

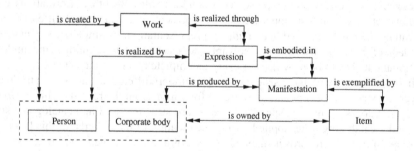

**Fig. 1.** Entities in Group 1 and 2 of the FRBR Model and Relationships between them

It is important to notice, that the primary relationship between *expressions* and *manifestations* is a M-to-N relationship, in contrast to all other primary relationships, which are 1-to-N relationships.

---

[1] The obtain operation is not defined on the abstract entities *work* and *expression.*
[2] We adopted the notion from [3], where double arrows indicate are cardinality greater than or equal to one.

## 2.3   The Conversion Process

The record-based catalog is viewed as a set of records. Each record consists of a sequence of attributes. An attribute is represented by a 2-tuple containing the attribute name and the attribute value. Attribute names may appear more than once in a record. The conversion process has four main steps:

1. Extraction of manifestation and item entities from the records.
2. Identification of aggregated manifestations, i. e. of manifestations that embody more than one expression.
3. Clustering of the record set in order to identify works and expressions.
4. Creation of entities and extraction of entity attributes from the clusters.

These four steps are based on the information stored in the records. Unfortunately the information can not be easily retrieved from the records. The reasons are that records might have different structures and that attribute values may be insufficient or erroneous. We distinguish two classes of errors in record based catalogs:

**Inconsistency.** Identical information might be represented differently in different records. It might be stored in different attributes and/or stored as different values. Other entries in the records might be erroneous, e. g. spelling errors.

**Incompleteness.** Information that is required to identify an entity or a relationship defined in the FRBR model is not present in the records, or in a subset of the records.

Inconsistency errors in names or titles can often be corrected by classifying attribute values according to the classes represented by authority files. But other informations, e. g. relations between manifestations, are usually represented in a number of different ways and can not be easily mapped onto a uniform representation. Incompleteness can result from lack of data, but also from unresolvable inconsistencies. If a catalog is incomplete, additional data has to be provided for every incomplete record in the catalog.

In order to cope with inconsistencies and to support different catalogs we introduced a layer to extract consistent and error-free information from the records. This *attribute layer* is catalog-specific, i. e. specific to the record structure used in a catalog and specific to the cataloging rules applied during the creation of the records. In this layer the information from the records is mapped on a set of uniquely named *selected attributes*, e. g. *title, original title, creator*.

The conversion process is shown in figure 2. The first step consists of the creation of manifestation and item entities. The next step consists of a cluster run to identify the works. Every work set is then clustered in order to identify expressions. The cluster algorithms access the information in the records through the attribute layer. During the cluster process the primary relations and additional relations, e. g. *is translation of*, are identified. The identification of aggregated manifestations is performed in the attribute layer.

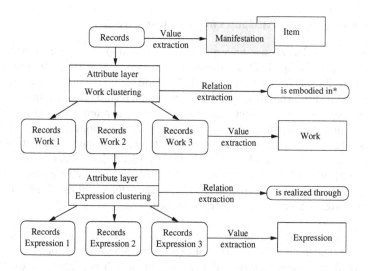

**Fig. 2.** Clustering Works and Expressions and Extracting FRBR Model Entities and Relations

## 3   The Attribute Layer for BIBSYS

### 3.1   Record Classes

For the scope of this paper we only concentrate on records, that describe monographs or series, ignoring, for example, audio recordings. Records in BIBSYS can be classified according to different characteristics. We divide records into two classes that are treated differently in the BIBSYS attribute layer:

**Series records.**   Records of this class describe a periodical publication. They are usually identified by the existence of field 022, which is ISSN-related, but also by the existence of fields 310, 440, and 490. Records describing series' are usually not linked —via the 491$n subfield— to other records. We investigated over 100.000 records and found only one example where a series had a 491$n subfield.

**Monograph records.**   All records that do not belong to the series class fall into the class of monographs. Monographs may be linked to records describing either monographs or series'. Monograph records can have the following characteristics:

**Linked.**   A monograph record may reference another record. This is done by storing the object-id of the referenced record in the subfield 491$n.

**Aggregative.**   A monograph record may describe a manifestation, that contains multiple expressions, and therefore also multiple works. This is usually indicated by the existence of multiple titles and of multiple authors.

Records of different classes are treated differently in order to extract the required attributes. If a monograph record is linked, the record that it refers to usually stores information common to all records that link to it. If a record is aggregative, it stores information relevant to more than one work and hence to more than one expression.

## 3.2    Retrieving Generic Attributes for the Cluster Runs

In order to find works, we use fingerprints (or signatures). The fingerprint of a work consists of data that uniquely identifies a work. In a series record this is the name of the series and the publisher (or the editor). In a monograph record it is the original title and the creator, a person or a corporate body. If the monograph record is aggregative, it contains multiple fingerprints of works. Our system allows for the dereferencing of linked records and it tries to find all fingerprints of the works contained in an aggregative record. The list below describes some of the heuristics we apply the identify the generic attributes. We could partly rely on the methods used in different projects that concentrated on MARC records [5,6,7]. We did not describe all generic attributes here and we concentrated on describing the handling of monograph records, because the handling of series records is straight forward, since they are far more homogeneous.

**Titles** are searched in the following subfields in descending priority: 130$a, 740$a, 240$a (if the subfield 240$l does not exist), and 245$a. If no titles are found and the record references a monograph record, the search is recursively extended to the referenced record. When dereferencing a link, the *part of* relation between the records is preserved. The content of these fields is processed in order to extract single titles from a set of titles, i. e. titles marked off by separators.

**OriginalTitles** are searched in the following subfields in descending priority: 241$a, 240$a (if the subfield 240$l exists), and 500$a if it starts with a function indicator like *originaltitler:*, or *orig.titt.:*. If no original titles are found and the record references a monograph record, the search is recursively extended to the referenced record. Original titles are split in the same way as titles.

**Creator** is searched in the following subfields in descending priority: 100$a (the creator a person), and 110$a (the creator is a corporate body). Again the search is recursively extended to referenced monograph records.

**Translator** is searched in the 700$a subfields in those lines that contain a 700$l, or a 700$e subfield that indicates a translator function, i. e. has a value like *oversetter*, or *overs.*.

**Language** is searched in field 008, and in subfield 240$l. The search is recursively extended to referenced monograph records.

**Edition** is searched in the 250$a, and the 250$b subfield and recursively extended.

## 3.3    Problems in the BIBSYS Attribute Layer and Possible Solutions

The BIBSYS catalog contains records of three different degrees of quality, namely *kat2*, *ukatm*, and *konv*. This leads to varying reliability of the extracted attribute values. The attribute extraction described above is only fully applicable to high quality records. In other records, for example, original titles and translators are hard, if not impossible to identify. It might also be difficult to identify an original work, because in BIBSYS the original language is not recorded in field 041. To resolve some of these problems the knowledge gained when processing reliable records might be used to identify the original language, original titles, and the titles of translations into different languages. This strategy would in general allow to view incompleteness on the level of the catalog instead of the level of single records.

Another error often found in BIBSYS is the repetition of the values from the subject access fields (fields 6xx) in the added entry fields (fields 7xx), presumably because the 7xx fields are indexed by the search machines, while the 6xx fields are not. Therefore the use of information from the 7xx fields leads to very noisy results (cf. [6]). As a countermeasure for this problem, we only used 7xx fields that are not resembling a corresponding 6xx field.

## 4 Conclusion

We applied our prototype system to a set of 4379 BIBSYS records that are related to Henrik Ibsen. These records often describe complex works, containing multiple expressions and/or parts of other works. We chose them because singlecelular works are often easy to convert and studies "[...] suggest that the majority of benefits associated with applying FRBR [...] could be obtained by concentrating on a relatively small number of complex works." [8]. When putting the system into a strict mode that relies on the certain identification of the original title, we identified 48 works by Henrik Ibsen. Of these works 16 were falsely identified because of varying or erroneous spelling, 10 were collections and translations that the system failed to recognize as such. These works could be clustered into 1111 expressions, which are contained in 1072 manifestations, 35 of which contained more than one expression. But due to the strict setting of the rules 3307 records where ignored, because it could not be determined, whether they contain an original title or not. Without this knowledge it is impossible to reliably identify the work cluster. With non-strict settings our system identified 580 works by Ibsen and 3706 expressions in 3567 manifestations, clearly no satisfying result.

The next steps are to apply a more fault tolerant dissimilarity measure to the clustering process, and to use authority files in the attribute layer in oder to cope with spelling variations and errors. In addition, we will try to leverage the reliable information found in high quality records to process incomplete records. It is planned to apply the system to a 100.000 records large subset of the BIBSYS catalog and to evaluate the results.

## References

1. Husby, O.: How can BIBSYS benefit from FRBR? <http://www.lub.lu.se/netlab/conf/husby.ppt> [08-03-2003] (2002) Presentation at the Netlab Conference, Lund, Sweden.
2. Weinstein, P.C.: Ontology-based metadata: Transforming the MARC legacy. In: Third ACM International Conference on Digital Libraries. (1998) 254–263
3. IFLA Study Group on the Functional Requirements for Bibliographic Records: Functional Requirements for Bibliographic Records — Final Report. Volume 19 of UBCIM Publications – New Series. K. G. Saur, München (1998)
4. Aalberg, T.: Navigating in Bibliographic Catalogues. In Agosti, M., Thanos, C., eds.: Research and Advanced Technology for Digital Technology, 6th European Conference, ECDL 2002, Rome, Italy, Springer (2002)
5. Delsey, T.: Functional analysis of the MARC 21 bibliographic and holdings formats. Technical report, Library of Congress (2002)
6. Hegna, K., Murtoma, E.: Data mining MARC to find: FRBR? <http://folk.uio.no/knuthe/dok/frbr/datamining.pdf> [08-03-2003] (2002)

7. Hickey, T.B., O'Neill, E.T., Toves, J.: Experiments with the IFLA Functional Requirements for Bibliographic Records (FRBR). D-Lib Magazine **8** (2002) 9.
8. Bennett, R., Lavoie, B., O'Neill, E.: The concept of a Work in WorldCat: An application of FRBR. Working Draft (2002)

# Musescape: A Tool for Changing Music Collections into Libraries

George Tzanetakis

Computer Science Department, Carnegie Mellon University
5000 Forbes Avenue, Pittsburgh, PA 15213, USA
gtzan@cs.cmu.edu
http://www.cs.cmu.edu/~gtzan

**Abstract.** Increases in hard disk capacity and audio compression technology have enabled the storage of large collections of music on personal computers and portable devices. As an example a portable device with 20 Gigabytes of storage can hold up to 4000 songs in compressed audio format. Currently the only way of structuring these collections is using a file system hierarchy which allows very limited forms of searching and retrieval. These limitations are even more pronounced in the case of portable devices where there is less screen real estate and user attention is limited compared to a personal computer.
*Musescape* is a prototype tool for organizing and interacting with large music collections in audio format with specific emphasis on portable devices. It provides a variety of automatic and manual ways to organize and interact with large music collections using a consistent continuous audio feedback user interface for browsing, searching and annotating. Using this system a user can convert an unstructured or partially structured collection of music with limited retrieval capabilities into a music library with enhanced functionality.

## 1 Introduction

The capacity to store and the ability to distribute large collections of music is increasing every day. A large percentage of current internet traffic consists of music files and it looks likely that complete digital distribution of music might become a reality in the near future. Current portable devices can hold thousands of music files stored in compressed audio formats, such as the MPEG audio compression standard (the well known .mp3 files). A frequent complaint of users of such devices is that although they can store all this music they end up only accessing a small subset of it because such large collections are hard to organize and navigate. Digital libraries provide a variety of concepts and tools that users can use to search and navigate large collections of documents. Although retrieval of music has some similarities with text, image and video retrieval it has unique characteristics that pose new challenges to research in digital libraries. In this paper, we describe *Musescape* a set of tools for converting an unstructured or partially structured collection of music files in audio format to a music library with a variety of ways to search and browse.

T. Koch and I.T. Sølvberg (Eds.): ECDL 2003, LNCS 2769, pp. 412–421, 2003.

Unlike existing music recommendation and metadata systems that rely on experts, the main goal of our system is to enable users to quickly organize their collections by themselves using their own subjective judgments. We believe that especially for the subjective domain of music listening it is important to provide the user with control and flexibility in organizing large music collections without relying on outside sources of information. Although this approach implies significant user involvement it is assisted in two main ways: 1) use of automatic content-analysis techniques such as similarity retrieval and classification and 2) a consistent and common user interface for browsing, searching and annotation utilizing direct manipulation principles and continuous audio feedback. This interface is especially suitable for portable devices as it requires minimal screen real estate and little visual attention from the user.

## 1.1  Overview

The paper is structured as follows: Sect. 2 describes related work. Sect. 3 describes the main underlying representation used behind *Musescape*. There are two main modes of operation: 1) the archive described in Sect. 4 where the user with the assistance of automatic tools provides the necessary metadata and organizational information, and 2) the library described in Sect. 5 that allows the user to search and browse the collection. For consistency and ease of learning the user interface is almost identical for these two modes of operation. It is described in Sect. 6. The implementation of the system is described in Sect. 7 and conclusions and directions for future work are provided in Sect. 8.

## 2  Related Work

The concept of browsing is central to the design of our system. In contrast to directed search where the target is known, in browsing, the user explores a collection of items without a specific goal in mind. Although there is limited work in music browsing, other types of multimedia data such as speech, image and video browsing have received more attention. Representative examples of such systems are: the PhotoFinder system for image organization and retrieval [1], the Informedia system for video retrieval and browsing [2], and the SpeechSkimmer system for speech recordings [3].

A variety of features and systems that analyze audio signals have been proposed. Some representative examples are: beat detection [4,5,6], genre classification [7], and similarity retrieval [8]. The concept of music similarity is discussed in [9] where the importance of providing many different ways of music similarity retrieval is shown.

It is important to emphasize that the emphasis of this work is music stored as audio files rather than symbolic representations such as notated scores or MIDI (Musical Instrument Digital Interface) files. The symbolic and hierarchical nature of these representations allows higher levels of processing and understanding resulting in interesting interactions such as query-by-humming [10]. Unfortunately the automatic conversion of music to symbolic representation is currently an unsolved problem and therefore we do not consider symbolic representations in this work.

A related work to *Musescape* is the Sonic Browser described in [11], which is a graphical user interface based on direct manipulation-sonification for browsing collections of audio signals. Each sound file is represented by a visual shape on a two-dimensional plane and a cursor with an aura around it is used for exploration. The sound files that fall inside the aura are simultaneously played back spatialized based on their distance and location relative to the cursor. The main emphasis of this system is browsing rather than searching and or annotating whereas *Musescape* tries to unify all these three operations under a common continuous audio feedback user interface. Variations to the idea of providing a visual space with objects corresponding to sound files have been proposed in [12] where a heuristic variation of multi-dimensional scaling (FastMap) is used to map sound objects into an Euclidean space preserving their similarities and in [13] where a growing self-organizing map is used to preserve sound similarities calculated using psychoacoustic measures in order to visualize music collections as a set of islands on a map. One drawback of these types of systems especially for portable devices is that they require large screen real estate and significant visual attention from the user.

Many of the ideas behind the design of *Musescape* have been influenced by the concept of direct manipulation. Another inspiration has been the Schneiderman mantra for the design of interactive systems "Overview first, zoom and filter, then details on demand" [14]. The "Sound Slider" component described in Sect. 6 was first proposed in [15] as a alternative method for specifying music queries.

## 3   Representation

Unlike many existing music organization systems that are structured around album titles in *Musescape* the main unit of processing is the song. This reflects our belief that the concept of albums will become gradually obsolete as the recording industry moves from compact disks to digital music distribution. Each song is characterized by a set of attribute-value (AV) pairs. The values can either be strings or numeric and they can either be annotated manually or extracted automatically. In addition some AV pairs allow their values to be edited (mutable) while others are immutable. As an example consider the following song representation: { *title = Lucy in the sky with diamonds, artist = Beatles, album = Sgt. Pepper's Lonely Hearts Club Band, genre = Rock, mood = mellow, collection = Classics, tempo = 90, centroid = 240*} . For example typically *artist* and *album* are immutable whereas *mood* is mutable. Immutable values can be changed but a warning is provided to the user and the options of using synonyms is provided. For each string value an optional list of synonyms can be stored. An example of such a list might be: { *Beatles, The Beatles, beatles*}. All the synonyms are treated as equivalent when searching or browsing.

In addition, for each attribute with string values a distance matrix that holds the distance between each possible value pair is stored. By default this distance matrix has a value of 0 for identical values (using the synonyms) and 1 for different values however any value from 0.0 to 1.0 can be used. As an example, in musical genres, Pop might be closer to Rock than to Jazz. The distance matrix allows such relations to be expressed and used for similarity calculations.

The user can also define new attributes and specify their values. This flexibility is important as it enables the inclusion of subjective information and doesn't force users to comply to a fixed representation. The proposed representation although simple is quite expressive for the domain of music and leads to a consistent user interface that will be described in Sect. 6. Another important concept, is the idea of a collection (or playlist) which is basically a named list of songs and their representations. Examples of collections could be: the songs from the album Revolver by the Beatles, jazz from the 1960, music for waking up in the morning. Collections can be either specified by enumeration of their members or by a query specification which is any subset of AV pairs. For example a collection of all Beatles songs released in 1968 can either be specified by listing all of them or by the following specification: { *artist = Beatles, year = 1968*}.

A distance function is a function that takes as arguments a pair of specifications (subsets of AV-pairs) and some optional parameters and produces a positive number indicating the dissimilarity of the corresponding specifications. The string-valued attributes are converted to numbers using the corresponding distance matrices. Any distance functions can be defined and used depending on the user and/or the application. Currently supported functions are: Manhattan, Euclidean, Cosine, and Mahalanobis. More details about these distances can be found in any textbook on statistical pattern recognition such as [16]. This flexibility in the choice of distance functions, attribute-value pairs is necessary to support the many types of music similarity that are desirable [9].

## 4   Archive

The archive part of *Musescape* provides the automatic tools and user interfaces for annotating and organizing an unstructured or partially structured collection of music into a library. Essentially the main task of the user of the archive is given an unknown song to construct the corresponding representation by specifying all the AV pairs. If done manually this process can be quite time consuming therefore *Musescape* provides a variety of tools to assist in this process.

Initially a large subset of AV-pairs is automatically filled in. Metadata information such as artist name, album, etc, is imported from databases such as freedb (http://www.freedb.org) in the case of compact disks and directly from id3 tags (http://www.id3.org) in the case of individually downloaded mp3 files. In addition, for each song, automatic feature extraction is performed and a set of AV pairs that represent musical content is stored. Currently the feature set described in [7] for the purposes of automatic musical genre classification is used.

This feature set attempts to capture information about timbral, rhythmic and pitch content of music. Both the metadata features and the automatically extracted features are immutable. The remaining AV pairs are specified by the user with the assistance of the user interface described in Sect. 6.

Further assistance is provided by having the possibility to create for each string-valued attribute a predictor which is a statistical pattern recognition classifier trained on the existing data which predicts the value of that attribute. Taking musical genre as an example the classifier based on the existing data creates a statistical model of the feature vectors for each musical genre. Given an unclassified song and the corresponding automatically extracted content features the classifier predicts the genre (the value). Subsequently the user can either confirm the prediction or edit it.

The currently supported classifiers are: Gaussian Mixture Model (GMM) and K-NN (K-Nearest Neighbors) and new classifiers can be added easily. More details about these classifiers can be found at [16]. Another operation that can assist annotation is automatic content-based similarity retrieval where any subset (specification) of the songs representation can be used to retrieve similar files that are already annotated. The user interface allows to use an existing specification to annotate a song or a collection. For example it is easy to mark a whole collection with {*mood = mellow*} in one operation. In addition to the standard methods of input described in Sect. 6 it is possible that certain attributes have specialized methods of input. Currently the only such attribute is tempo which can be specified by tapping along with the music using the mouse key.

## 5   Library

The library part of *Musescape* provides the automatic tools and user interfaces for searching and browsing a structured or partially structured collection of music. Essentially the main operation supported is searching/browsing the library based on a song specification (a subset of AV-pairs). Searching and browsing are essentially unified under this framework as will be described in more detail in the following section. Another important operation that is supported is content-based similarity retrieval. The user can search for the $k$ most similar files based on an arbitrary specification. That way a very rich set of possible interactive explorations is supported. For example the user can start a session by looking for files that are similar to a specific song based on the automatically-extracted features then based on the specification of one of the returned files look for files that have tempo approximately 100BPM and their musical genre is Blues. Although these interactions can be quite complex the consistent user interface, unified representation and continuous audio feedback make them easier to perform. At any point, collections (playlists) that are either constructed manually or using a specification can be saved on the hard disk. It is clear that there are many similarities in how the user interacts with both the archive and library module. This fact will be exploited in the design of a consistent common user interface described in the next section.

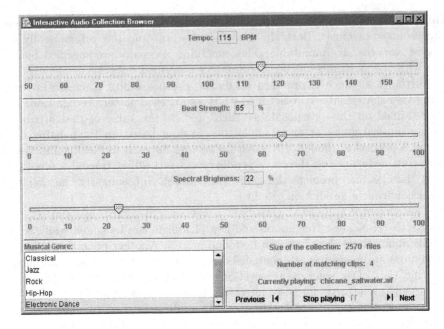

**Fig. 1.** Sound Sliders and Sound List

## 6 User Interface

Interfaces for interacting with large collections of documents typically support three main types of operations: browsing, searching and annotating. In current systems for music collections each of these operations is performed by a separate software system. For example searching is typically done using a file browser or a search engine, browsing is supported through playlists, and annotation is done using a database tool. Another problem with existing interfaces for audio is that the feedback provided to the user is minimal. For example, a typical scenario, is that the user provides a set of attributes such as "pieces of Rock music with tempo 80 BPM" using either a text description or manipulating some components such as sliders or lists. Then the user clicks a " search" button and a play list consisting of the music pieces that satisfy these constraints is returned. The returned files can then be heard and explored by the user. The problem with this approach is that the feedback available during playback is not used at all during the query specification. Therefore, the two problems we would like to address in the design of the user interface is the separation of browsing, searching and retrieving as well as the lack of feedback to the user. The fundamental idea for addressing these issues is to provide components with direct interactive continuous audio feedback to the user and get rid of the "search" button. These components are shared and re-used for searching, browsing and annotation providing a consistent interface to the user.

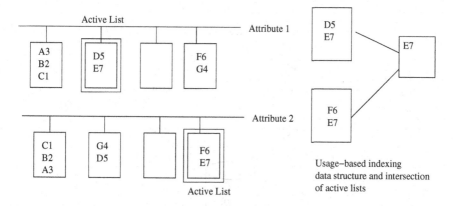

**Fig. 2.** Usage-based indexing

The main idea is simple but powerful and will be illustrated with the example of a volume control slider. If such a slider were to be designed as current music players-organizers, then its value would be adjusted without any actually change in volume, and then a "submit" button would be pressed and the actual volume change would occur. Obviously, the usual way of doing volume change where the sound changes directly based on the user actions is preferable. In developing the user interface our goal has been to provide this type of direct sonification and interaction to all user actions. In the designed interface components continuous audio feedback is provided for each user action and sound never stops playing.

For each attribute, an interface component, which we shall call "filter", is created. The purpose of a "filter" is to allow the user to specify the value of an attribute. Currently two types of filters are supported: a "Sound-Slider" for numerical values and a "Sound-List" for string values. Visually, these "filters" look like the standard slider and list components of user interface toolkits (Figure 1). The only difference is that whenever there is a change of value using a "filter", the sound immediately reflects this change. This simple change in behavior makes a big difference in the effectiveness of the system. For example, if a user sets a "Sound-Slider" corresponding to tempo in Beats-per-minute (BPM) to 80 BPM, a song at that tempo is immediately played back providing direct audio feedback. One obvious question is how to combine all these "filters" in such a way that whenever there is a user action the music that is returned satisfies all the filter settings. The naive solution of searching for all the files that satisfy the attribute settings has the problem that it is too slow even when using indexing methods for the data. Because of the continuous audio feedback it is desired that changes happen as fast as possible else users are confused about the effect of their actions. To address these problems, an indexing-preprocessing step is performed. The idea is to simply pre-sort the songs according to all the possible user settings. Another way to view this process is that rather than indexing to support arbitrary search, indexing only supports the possibilities offered by the user interface. This approach will be referred to as "Usage-based indexing".

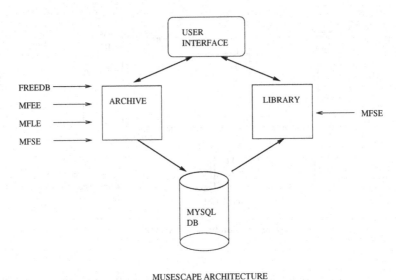

MUSESCAPE ARCHITECTURE

**Fig. 3.** Musescape architecture

Each "filter" is represented as a list of lists of files. The lists are doubly linked. The first level corresponds to the possible settings and the second level (lists of files) corresponds to the files that have a particular value. For string-valued attributes the first level list has an item for each possible value and the second level list contains the files with that particular value. For numerical values, linear quantization bins are used for the first level. As an example, for a tempo slider with quantization size 5 BPM a second level list will consist of the files with tempos from 100-105 BPM. An example of this structure is shown in Figure 2. The list of files corresponding to the current setting of an attribute is called the active list. Therefore, the files that satisfy all "filter" settings can quickly be found by finding the intersection of all the active lists. Because only the active lists are considered rather than the whole dataset this operation is fast. When there is a user action, the active list of the appropriate attribute is changed to the active list of the new value. Using a check box, each "filter" can be enabled/disabled for specification. In addition to providing a consistent and common interface for all three operations of browsing, searching and annotating, the developed interface is especially suited for portable devices as it requires minimal screen real-estate and visual user attention.

## 7   Implementation – Architecture

The main architecture of the system is shown in Figure 3. The user interacts with the system through the user interface module which can either communicate with the archive module or the library module. Both these modules use the same underlying database representation. The following assistive modules can be used to assist browsing, search and annotation: MFEE (Music Feature Extraction Engine) automatically calculates features, MFLE (Music Feature Learning Engine) predicts attribute values using statistical pattern recognition techniques, MFSE (Music Feature Similarity Engine) returns a ranked list of similar files. Essentially the communication between all the modules is done using specifications (arbitrary subsets of attribute-value pairs).

The user interface as well as the archive and library modules are implemented in Java. These modules communicate with a MySQL (www.mysql.org) database that holds the representations of all the songs in the collection. An XML format for song specifications is also supported and used for communication and storage. The various music content modules (MFEE, MFLE and MFSE) are implemented using Marsyas, a free software framework in C++ and JAVA, for audio analysis [17], (www.cs.princeton.edu/~gtzan/marsyas.html). The system has been designed to be extensible and most components can be substituted through the use of standarized interfaces. For example, new classifiers, automatic feature extraction methods, distance metrics can be incorporated to the system without extensive code modifications. We are currently testing the system using a set of various music collections. The largest collection consists of approximately 10000 songs representative of a variety of musical genres and styles. It is our intention, when testing is completed to release *Musescape* as free software.

# 8   Conclusions and Future Work

In this paper, *Musescape*, a system for assisting the organization of personal music collections into libraries was presented. The main goal is to provide the user with complete control and flexibility over the whole process something desired because of the subjective nature of music listening. In order to assist with this process, automatic musical content analysis techniques are used and a consistent continuous audio feedback interface for browsing, searching and annotating is utilized. This interface is especially suitable for portable devices because it required little screen estate and visual attention.

There are many interesting directions for future work. One obvious possibility is the inclusion of more powerful query specification methods which are already supported by the underlying database. However, following this direction one must be careful to retain consistency and simplicity of the user interface. Another interesting direction is the possibility of hands-free interaction something that would be attractive in applications such as music listening while driving. We are currently exploring this direction using the IBM ViaVoice Software Development Toolkit (www.ibm.com/software/speech). MPEG-7 www.mpeg.org is an international standard for the description of multimedia metadata information. We are planning to intergrate our system with MPEG file descriptors. Finally we plan to incorporate relevance feedback for the fine tuning of similarity retrieval to the system.

# References

1. Kang, H., Shneiderman, B.: Visualization Methods for Personal Photo Collections: Browsing and Searching in the PhotoFinder. In: Proc. Int. Con.f on Multimedia and Expo, New York, IEEE (2000)
2. Christel, M.G., Smith, M.A., Taylor, R.C., Winkler, D.B.: Evolving video skims into useful multimedia abstractions. In: Proc. of the SIGCHI Conf. on Human Factors in Computing Systems, Los Angeles, USA (1998) 171–178
3. Arons, B.: SpeechSkimmer: a system for interactively skimming recorded speech. ACM Transactions Computer Human Interaction **4** (1997) 3–38 http://www.media.mit.edu/people/barons/papers/ToCHI97.ps.
4. Scheirer, E.: Tempo and beat analysis of acoustic musical signals. Journal of the .Acoustical Society of America **103** (1998) 588,601
5. Laroche, J.: Estimating Tempo, Swing and Beat Locations in Audio Recordings. In: Proc. Int. Workshop on applications of Signal Processing to Audio and Acoustics WASPAA, Mohonk, NY, IEEE (2001) 135–139
6. Dixon, S.: An Interactive Beat Tracking and Visualization System. In: Proc. Int. Computer Music Conf. (ICMC), Habana, Cuba, ICMA (2002) 215–218
7. Tzanetakis, G., Cook, P.: Musical Genre Classification of Audio Signals. IEEE Transactions on Speech and Audio Processing **10** (2002)
8. Logan, B., Salomon, A.: A Music Similarity Function based on Signal Analysis. In: Int. Conf. on Multimedia and Expo (ICME), IEEE (2001)
9. Aucouturier, J.J., Pachet, F.: Music Similarity Measures : What's the use ? In: Proc. Int. Conf. on Music Information Retrieval (ISMIR), Paris, France (2002) 157–163
10. Ghias, A., Logan, J., Chamberlin, D., Smith, B.: Query by Humming: Musical Information Retrieval in an Audio Database. ACM Multimedia (1995) 213–236
11. Fernstrom, M., Brazil, E.: Sonic Browsing: an auditory tool for multimedia asset management. In: Proc. Int. Conf. on Auditory Display (ICAD), Espoo, Finland (2001)
12. Cano, P., Kaltenbrunner, M., Gouyon, F., Battle, E.: On the use of FastMap for Audio Retrieval and Browsing. In: Proc. Int. Conf. on Music Information Retrieval (ISMIR), Paris, France (2002) 275–276
13. Rauber, A., Pampalk, E., Merkl, D.: Using Psycho-Acoustic Models and Self-Organizing Maps to Create a Hierarchical Structure of Music by Sound Similarity. In: Proc. Int. Conf. Music Information Retrieval (ISMIR), Paris, France (2002) 71–80
14. Shneiderman, B.: Designing the User Interface: Strategies for Effective Human-Computer Interaction. 3rd ed. edn. Addison-Wesley (1998)
15. Tzanetakis, G., Ermolinskyi, A., Cook, P.: Beyond the Query-by-Example Paradigm: New Query Interfaces for Music Information Retrieval. In: Proc. Int. Computer Music Conference (ICMC), Gothenburg, Sweden (2002)
16. Duda, R., Hart, P., Stork, D.: Pattern classification. John Wiley & Sons, New York (2000)
17. Tzanetakis, G., Cook, P.: Marsyas: A framework for audio analysis. Organised Sound **4(3)** (2000)

# A Digital GeoLibrary: Integrating Keywords and Place Names

Mathew Weaver[1], Lois Delcambre[1], Leonard Shapiro[2], Jason Brewster[2], Afrem Gutema[2], and Timothy Tolle[3]

[1]Computer Science and Engineering Department, OGI School of Science and Engineering, Oregon Health & Science University
{mweaver, lmd}@cse.ogi.edu

[2]Department of Computer Science, College of Engineering & Computer Science, Portland State University
{len, jbrew, gutemaa}@cs.pdx.edu

[3]Strategic Planning, Region 6, USDA Forest Service
ttolle@fs.fed.us

**Abstract.** A digital library typically includes a set of keywords (or subject terms) for each document in its collection(s). For some applications, including natural resource management, geographic location (e.g., the place of a study or a project) is very important. The metadata for such documents needs to indicate the location(s) associated with a document – and users need to be able to search for documents by keyword as well as location. We have developed and implemented a digital library that supports – but does not require – georeferenceable documents (i.e., documents with reference to geography through the use of a textual place name). Because of their implicit spatial footprint, place names benefit from spatial reasoning and querying (e.g., to find all documents that describe work performed within a five-mile radius of a certain point) in addition to traditional keyword-based search. This paper presents the architecture for a digital library that combines spatial reasoning and selection with traditional (non-spatial) search. The contributions of this work are: (1) the use of a traditional geographic information system (GIS) for spatial processing rather than a specially tailored GIS system or a separate gazetteer and (2) the seamless integration of GIS with our thesaurus-based Metadata++ system, so users can easily take advantage of the strengths of both systems.

## 1   Introduction

Our work is motivated by the needs of natural resource managers in the USDA Forest Service to develop a distributed digital library to provide easy access to various documents such as Decision Notices, Environmental Impact Statements, and Watershed Assessments [2] produced as a normal part of their work processes and decisions. We seek to provide easy access to these documents for other natural resource managers who might be doing similar work or facing a similar decision. In

T. Koch and I.T. Sølvberg (Eds.): ECDL 2003, LNCS 2769, pp. 422–433, 2003.

our system, called Metadata++ [12], we describe these documents with a rich set of controlled vocabularies for twenty-eight domains of interest such as: air, climate, fire, vegetation, and so forth (as shown in Figure 1).

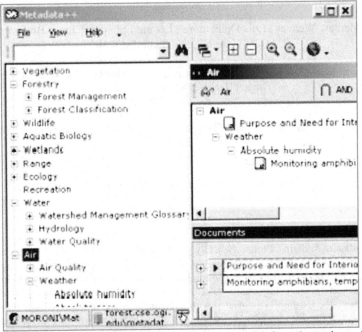

**Fig. 1.** Screenshot of Metadata++ with CVs on the left, and search result (search term "Air") on the right.

In addition to related keywords, the majority of these documents are also associated with one or more geographic areas, e.g., to indicate the area of land where a study was done or where a proposed project will take place. Locations are typically described using standard locations, such as the National Forests/Ranger Districts and Hydrologic Unit Codes as shown in Figure 2. The location schemes can be represented in a controlled vocabulary where spatial containment and equivalence of geographic footprint are represented by narrower/broader term and synonymy. In this application, about a dozen such location schemes are in common use.

The user (quite naturally) often wants to combine search terms from both spatial and non-spatial vocabularies – which presents both challenges and opportunities. We want the benefit of the rich metadata structure and search capability of Metadata++ plus the benefits of spatial reasoning of a standard GIS system. Our approach is to use Metadata++ and a standard GIS system running independently, with communication as shown in Figure 3. GIS datasets containing place names are used to generate controlled vocabularies in Metadata++.

```
-  Locations
   +  Bureau of Land Management
   -  USDA Forest Service
      +  Region 5
      -  Region 6
         +  Umpqua National Forest
         +  Wenatchee National Forest
         -  Willamette National Forest
               Blue River Ranger District
               McKenzie Ranger District
               Oakridge Ranger District
-  Watersheds
   -  Pacific Northwest
      +  Puget Sound
      +  Willamette River Basin
      -  Yakima
         -  Upper Yakima
            +  Cle Elum Creek
            +  Yakima River
                  Big Creek
                  Little Creek
                  Silver Creek
```

**Fig. 2.** Excerpt showing two location CVs: the USDA Forest Service National Forest System, and Watersheds (as named in the Hydrologic Unit Code scheme).

The user may use the standard GIS system to browse and search GIS datasets, e.g., with rainfall or temperature coverages, soil types, and so forth. The user may also, at any time, select a region of interest (in the GIS system) and send the locations to Metadata++ for inclusion in a document search. Additionally, when Metadata++ has a set of documents in a search result, the documents that are associated with locations can be sent to the GIS system for display on a map. Metadata++ may also ask the GIS system to compute broader and narrower terms (i.e., containing and contained places) and synonyms (i.e., significantly overlapping places) for any location term.

Other approaches to this problem include: augmenting a document retrieval system or a GIS in various ways or introducing a gazetteer to sit between the two systems to translate between place names and geographic footprints [6]. More recently, so-called Geographic Information Retrieval (GIR) systems seek to support both types of search directly [4].

The organization of this paper is as follows. Section 2 provides a brief introduction to Metadata++. Our combined architecture is presented in Section 3, with a discussion of the detailed interaction between the two components. Section 4 discusses how our work compares to other approaches in more detail; and the paper concludes in Section 5.

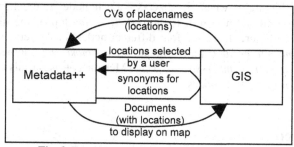

**Fig. 3.** Functions supported by our integration of Metadata++ and a GIS

## 2  Metadata++

Metadata++ is a document retrieval system built on a framework of related terms [13]. *Terms* are words or phrases frequently used in the application domain that may be related using relationships similar to those in a thesaurus [1], including hierarchy, synonymy, and association. Metadata++ assists a user, usually the author or librarian, in selecting terms (as shown on the left side of Figure 1) to associate with a document by suggesting terms found in the full-text index of the document.

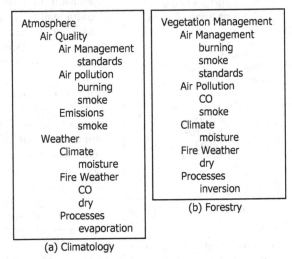

(a) Climatology

(b) Forestry

**Fig. 4.** CVs showing terms that appear multiple times, in different arrangements

One significant difference between Metadata++ and a typical thesaurus is that a term can appear in multiple locations in the broader/narrower term hierarchy. As illustrated in Figure 4, users with different expertise (e.g. climatology and forestry) use some of the same terms but organize them differently within vocabularies. Thus Metadata++ distinguishes between a term, such as *smoke* or *air pollution* and the *node(s)* of the hierarchy where it appears. Each node in the hierarchy is thus identified by its trail where a trail is the path from the top of the hierarchy to the selected term. In Figure 4, we see four different nodes for the term *smoke*. One of the trails is *Atmosphere~Air Quality~Air pollution~smoke* and another is *Vegetation Management~Air Management~smoke*. Thus, Metadata++ uses trails to disambiguate terms that appear in multiple nodes.

## 3  Architecture

This section explains our architecture for integrating Metadata++ and GIS to build a digital geolibrary. The architecture enhances retrieval of geographic information by exploiting functionality of both systems, and communicating information between the two systems (as shown in Figure 5).

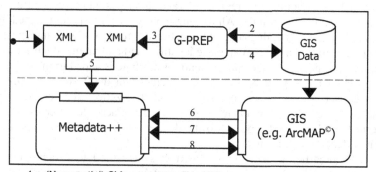

1.  (Non-spatial) CVs are prepared in XML
2.  GIS datasets processed by G-PREP
3.  Location CVs are prepared in XML
4.  Place ID attribute added to GIS datasets
5.  XML CV files are loaded into Metadata++
6.  User-selected locations are passed to Metadata++
7.  Metadata++ asks GIS to compute synonyms
8.  Metadata++ passes documents (with locations) to GIS for display

**Fig. 5.** Architecture

## 3.1   Vocabulary Extraction

The first requirement for integrating Metadata++ with GIS is extracting controlled vocabularies of place names from GIS datasets. Geographical places are often naturally hierarchical based on spatial containment. Larger places, such as states or national forests, contain smaller places, such as counties or ranger districts, respectively. In GIS datasets, this hierarchy is represented implicitly by the fact that some spatial footprints are contained within others. For example, the polygon representing the State of Oregon geometrically contains the polygons that represent the counties within Oregon. A process called G-PREP implements vocabulary extraction by taking GIS datasets and generating hierarchical controlled vocabularies of place names expressed in XML (shown in Figure 5, Steps 2 & 3). The controlled vocabularies are then loaded (along with non-spatial vocabularies from other sources) into Metadata++.

While implementing G-PREP, we encountered a number of problems. GIS datasets are usually separated into layers (also called themes) based on similar feature type. For example, USDA Forest Service ranger districts are contained in one layer and national forests are contained in a separate layer. Because of this separation of layers, G-PREP cannot generate the complete hierarchy within the context of a single layer. Instead, the G-PREP needs to know which layers correspond to which levels in the hierarchy. With the datasets available to us, we could not easily automate this process. We had to process each layer in the proper hierarchical order.

The nature of geographic footprints presents another, more significant, obstacle to vocabulary extraction. A person might imagine a layer consisting of precise, disjoint polygons – such as political county boundaries. However, many geographic places cannot be represented by a simple polygon. For example, a national forest may consist of many non-contiguous regions of varying shapes and sizes – resulting in a complex geographic footprint.   All of these polygons must be mapped to one conceptual place name (i.e. the name of the national forest). G-PREP implements this mapping by generating a conceptual place identifier and adding the identifier as a new attribute for each polygon.  This place identifier attribute is added to the original GIS dataset (as shown in Figure 5, Step 4) and included in the XML hierarchy that is loaded into Metadata++ – serving as an implicit gazetteer that connects spatial footprints with textual place names.  Because the place identifier is a separate attribute in the GIS dataset, updates to the dataset (such as refined footprints) have little or no effect on the indentifiers.

The place identifier generated by G-PREP is also used to disambiguate place names.  For example, the State of Oregon contains twenty six places that are all officially named "Salmon Creek" – three of which are not even creeks! A simple keyword search for "Salmon Creek" would likely yield many irrelevant documents. Using a place identifier in both the GIS and Metadata++ allows the user to precisely select a location of interest – whether from a map or from a controlled vocabulary.

Another significant problem arises because various footprints are generated at different times, using different instruments, for different purposes – and quite often have different precision and accuracy.  Because of complex and imprecise footprints, calculating spatial containment is non-trivial.  For example, the footprint of a ranger district may slightly extend beyond the footprint of the national forest – even though the ranger district is under the administrative jurisdiction of (and contained within) the national forest.   G-PREP uses heuristics to handle these calculations but occasionally requires user interaction.

Representing places as terms in Metadata++ supports the use of unofficial place names – places that are commonly referred to but do not have an official geographic footprint.  Searching for unofficial places names is defined as a necessary feature for digital geolibraries [10].  For example, most people in the State of Washington know about Snoqualmie Pass – many people could take you there without any difficulty. However, Snoqualmie Pass does not have an official geographic footprint – and may not even appear on some maps.  By representing Snoqualmie Pass as a term in Metadata++, the user may still use it for document retrieval – even though it may or may not appear in a GIS dataset.  Furthermore, if an unofficial place does have a footprint, we can easily assign a place identifier – as with official places – and include the place name in a controlled vocabulary within Metadata++.

## 3.2   Place Selection

A primary user task is selecting places within the GIS and communicating those selections to Metadata++ – to associate with a document or specify a search.  Place selection may be as simple as pointing to a region on the map and clicking the mouse to select the polygon.  However, one advantage of using the GIS is the ability to do more advanced spatial analysis.  For example, the user may issue a query to find all counties with geographic area less than two million acres.  The GIS will answer this query by automatically selecting those regions within the active dataset that satisfy the specified query.  In addition to maps, the user may choose to use other types of

GIS data to assist in finding relevant regions – such as a dataset of annual precipitation to find those counties that receive more than one hundred inches of rain per year. The GIS will answer this query by intersecting the qualifying regions of the annual rainfall dataset with the map of counties. This query could be combined with the previous example to find all counties with area less than two million acres that receive over one hundred inches of rain annually.

After using GIS functionality to select the desired place(s), the place names are sent to Metadata++. Selecting a place in GIS is equivalent to selecting the corresponding place name in the Metadata++ hierarchy. The selected place may be used for any Metadata++ function – such as document search or metadata attachment. Users have the flexibility of using either Metadata++ or the GIS – or a combination of both systems – for selecting places. Because all terms are presented to the users in Metadata++, they can easily mix geographic terms (e.g. place names) with any other (non-geographic) terms.

Our implementation adds a new button to ArcMAP© (a popular GIS application produced by ESRI®). The user may use all of the functionality in ArcMAP© to analyze geographic datasets. At any point in that process, the user may select one or more locations (using any of the selection mechanisms in ArcMAP©) and click the button to send the selections to Metadata++. The integrated architecture could easily be extended to work with other GIS applications – transforming any GIS application into a powerful tool for geographic information retrieval.

### 3.3     Synonym Discovery

Metadata++ uses synonyms for query expansion during document retrieval. For non-geographic controlled vocabularies – such as wildlife species or climate terms – synonymous terms are represented explicitly in Metadata++. For geographic controlled vocabularies of place names, Metadata++ uses the GIS to find synonyms. We could explicitly represent synonymous places in Metadata++, but we chose not to do so for two reasons. First, a large number of synonyms exist among places. Every place within every location vocabulary may be considered a synonym with one or more places in many other location vocabularies. For example, the land within Clackamas County is also within the Lower Willamette River basin. All of the land in the State of Oregon belongs to some county and also belongs to some watershed and may also be part of a ranger district – resulting in a large number of possible synonyms.

The second, more significant, reason is the ambiguous semantics of spatial synonymy. If the spatial footprints of two different places exactly coincide, then those places would likely be defined as synonyms. However, that rarely – if ever – occurs in real geography. Clackamas County and the Lower Willamette River Basin are in the same geographic place, but their spatial footprints do not coincide. Some points within Clackamas County are not within the Lower Willamette River basin and vice versa. This type of situation makes it difficult to explicitly represent spatial synonyms as related terms in Metadata++.

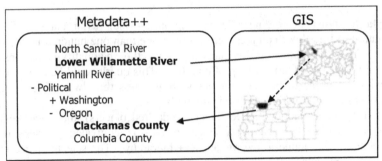

**Fig. 6.** Synonym Discovery

Spatial synonyms are determined in the GIS by computing a percentage of overlap between the polygons based on a user-specified threshold. Because the GIS computes synonyms (instead of representing them explicitly in Metadata++), the user may adjust the threshold to achieve the desired results. In addition to percentage of overlap, the user may also wish to include other GIS computations (such as adjacency or proximity) while discovering synonyms. These computations are performed on a default set of datasets – or on one or more specific datasets chosen by the user.

Figure 6 shows an example of synonym discovery within the GIS. The user selects Lower Willamette River from the Watershed controlled vocabulary. Metadata++ then sends that selection to the GIS. Using the established threshold, the GIS determines which place(s) in other vocabularies (such as political regions) overlap with the selected region. In the example, the GIS determines that the Lower Willamette River basin is a spatial synonym of Clackamas County, and returns that place to Metadata++. In addition to finding synonyms for places selected in Metadata++, synonym discovery may be combined with place selection. If a user selects an area on a map, the GIS can compute the spatial synonyms and send all of the corresponding places (the selected place and its synonyms) to Metadata++ for processing.

### 3.4   Document Display

Because many natural resource documents are attached to one or more place names, it is useful to display the documents on a map. When such a document is part of a query result, Metadata++ can send the appropriate place name(s) to the GIS. The GIS will then display the documents on the appropriate map. For example, consider a document about hazardous tree removal in Clackamas County. Perhaps the user searched for documents about tree removal in the State of Oregon. Metadata++ would show the document in the context of the hierarchy and would notify the GIS that the document was attached to Clackamas County. The GIS would then locate the polygon corresponding to Clackamas County and display an icon representing the document in or near the polygon.

# 4   Related Work

Geographic information retrieval (GIR) focuses on document retrieval based on geographic references within documents. Each document can be uniquely classified as georeferenced, georeferenceable, or non-georeferenceable. Georeferenced documents (such as a digital map) contain explicit reference to geography in the form of a spatial footprint (coordinate, polygon, etc.). Georeferenceable documents (such as an Environmental Impact Statement) do not contain an explicit spatial footprint, but do contain implicit reference to geography in the form of one or more textual place names. Non-georeferenceable documents (such as a scientific report describing the feeding process of spotted owls) are not related – implicitly nor explicitly – to any geographic location. Each type of document must be considered in a GIR system.

Some GIR systems use only spatial queries for document retrieval. Spatial queries execute over geographic footprints – so georeferenced documents are easily retrieved. However, before a georeferenceable document can be considered in a spatial search, the system must somehow associate a footprint with the document [14] – at which point it becomes georeferenced. Automatically associating footprints with georeferenceable documents is non-trivial. Georeferenceable documents contain place names – but place names are often ambiguous. For example, a document about the first president of the United States may be mistakenly associated with the town of George in the State of Washington (which is a real town). Similarly, the city of Portland exists in Oregon and Maine. A related problem is the use of alternate or informal names for places. For example, an older or more informal document may refer to Boston, Massachusetts as "bean town" or Portland, Oregon as "stump town". Metadata++ searches for documents within the context of the term hierarchy – not in context of the spatial footprints of documents. Our architecture uses the GIS to execute spatial queries to extract vocabularies of place names and discover spatial synonyms, but document retrieval occurs in Metadata++ (which does not require that documents be associated with spatial footprints).

The ADEPT [6] Digital Library Architecture provides support for geographic information retrieval using search buckets. A search bucket is an abstract metadata category with defined search semantics. Collections may provide metadata for items (e.g., documents) using various buckets. For example, the "Geographic location" bucket contains coordinates describing a document's spatial footprint and supports three spatial search operators: contains, overlaps, and is-contained-in. The "Assigned term" bucket contains subject-related terms from controlled vocabularies and supports three text-based search operators: contains-all-words, contains-any-words, and contains-phrase. The ADEPT architecture searches multiple heterogeneous collections by specifying queries using the various bucket search operators. By treating place names as terms in controlled vocabularies, Metadata++ uses a single, unified search operation that exploits hierarchical relationships and synonyms. Synonyms discovered by the GIS are handled uniformly with synonyms explicitly represented in Metadata++.

Recent GIR research [3,7,8] relies on ontologies to facilitate information retrieval. SPIRIT [8] attempts to address proximity relationships as well as alternate and informal place names by developing a geographical ontology that "models both the vocabulary and the spatial structure of places". OASIS [3] represents places as explicit objects in an ontology with specific attributes (latitude, longitude, standard name) and relationships (meets, overlap, partOf) to other place objects. These relationships are used to explicitly represent and query spatial relationships between places. Instead of building an explicit ontology, Metadata++ focuses on faithfully representing the controlled vocabularies (both spatial and non-spatial) that are commonly used in the application domain. The hierarchy among place names in Metadata++ is similar to the partOf relationship, but Metadata++ relies on the GIS to discover spatial synonyms instead of representing those relationships (e.g. meets, overlap) explicitly.

Our work is similar in spirit and proposes a similar architecture to that of GeoVSM [4]. The authors argue convincingly that GIR systems must support two kinds of description (keyword as well as spatial) as well as two kinds of search, although they assume that both sides of the system are providing search capability over the same set of documents. They also recommend that the user interface available in a GIR system include two different user interfaces for the two components because they correspond to distinct ways of representing and organizing information. Our architecture follows the same philosophy, with a separate interface for Metadata++ and the (standard) GIS system. Key differences in our work compared to GeoVSM are that: (1) our system explicitly accommodates non-georeferenceable documents; (2) our GIS component is a standard GIS system that is used to browse various kinds of maps and layers and to select locations (but is not explicitly used to search for documents); (3) our document system, Metadata++, does not use a spatial metaphor to display non-spatial keywords, rather we provide a hierarchical display of terms; and (4) because of the explicit use in this domain of controlled vocabularies to describe places, we are able to easily combine place names with any other (non-spatial) terms in our description and search of documents in Metadata++.

G-Portal [9] is a map-based digital library architecture for georeferenced resources. Like Metadata++, G-Portal provides a map-based interface and a classification interface (to support non-georeferenceable documents). The authors emphasize synchronization between the interfaces – documents selected in one interface will be automatically selected in the other interface. Our work differs from G-Portal in the primary purpose of the map-based interface. In Metadata++, the map-based interface (i.e., the GIS) is not used to specify searches for documents. Rather, it is intended to search for geographic places so that the place names can be combined with non-geographic search terms in Metadata++ – as well as displaying georeferenceable documents from search results.

## 5     Conclusions and Future Work

We have implemented a prototype of our architecture (including vocabulary extraction and place selection). Initial user feedback is very positive – and testing will continue with additional users. Future work will include implementation of synonym discovery and document display. We will also consider georeferenced documents that are associated with unnamed places (e.g., a coordinate). Such documents may be handled using spatial synonyms and/or spatial searches within the GIS.

We are continuing our work on Metadata++. This includes implementing templates as a way for users to pre-select certain terms in the hierarchy for search or metadata attachment. For example, a botanist that works in the Wenatchee National Forest may define a template that will automatically select Wenatchee National Forest and Douglas Fir trees. We have also begun a detailed comparison of Metadata++ searches based on trails with vector space searches based on keyword vectors. A detailed comparison will help us better evaluate the overall effectiveness of Metadata++. Our research is currently focused on natural resource management in the Pacific Northwest region of the United States – but the same ideas and technology could be applied to different domains and other geographic areas. Additionally, vocabularies of related terms (e.g. synonyms) may be an interesting approach to building a multilingual digital library.

By combining a rich, vocabulary-based document retrieval system with traditional GIS tools, we enable users in natural resource management to effectively and precisely retrieve geographic (and non-geographic) information. Combining vocabularies of place names with other controlled vocabularies, allows us to provide a simple, unified mechanism for creating and searching metadata. Our architecture lets users easily specify searches involving spatial and non-spatial search terms. The architecture provides a clean separation between the two components: Metadata++ is unaware of spatial footprints and the GIS is unaware of documents. Instead, our architecture simply provides for the GIS to deliver place names to Metadata++, on user request. And such terms in Metadata++ are known to have an external identifier. A term with an external identifier in Metadata++ can have synonyms computed by the designated external system. Also, documents associated with such a term can be passed to the external system for display or other processing. This architecture permits the use of various GIS software tools as well as other external systems, such as an ontology, with Metadata++.

**Acknowledgements.** We acknowledge the helpful collaboration of the USDA Forest Service under the direction of Tim Tolle. We also thank Dale Guenther of the USDA Forest Service for his help in gathering and understanding several GIS datasets. This work is supported, in part, by the National Science Foundation, grant numbers 9817492 and 9983518.

# References

[1] ANSI/NISO Z39.19 – 1993. *Guidelines for the Construction, Format, and Management of Monolingual Thesauri.* NISO Press, 1994.
[2] Delcambre, Lois, and Timothy Tolle. "Harvesting Information To Sustain Forests". *Communications of the ACM*, January 2003 Volume 46, Number 1, pp. 38–39.
[3] Fonseca, F., M. Egenhofer, P. Agouris, and C. Câmara. "Using Ontologies for Integrated Geographic Information Systems". *Transactions In GIS* 6(3), 2002.
[4] Guoray Cai, "GeoVSM: An Integrated Retrieval Model For Geographical Information". Lecture Notes on Computer Science (LNCS) 2478: *Geographic Information Science*, M. Egenhofer and D. Mark, (ed) Springer-Verlag (2002)

[5]   Guoray Cai, :GeoVIBE: A Visual Interface For Geographic Digital Libraries", Lecture Notes on Computer Science (LNCS) 2539: *Visual Interfaces to Digital Libraries*, K. Borner and C. Chen, Eds.: Springer-Verlag (2002)

[6]   Janée, Greg and James Frew. "The ADEPT digital library architecture". JCDL 2002: *Proceeding of the second ACM/IEEE-CS Joint Conference on Digital libraries*, 2002, Portland, Oregon, USA., ACM Press, pp. 342–350.

[7]   Jones, Christopher B., Harith Alani, and Douglas Tudhope. "Geographical information retrieval with ontologies of place". Lecture Notes in Computer Science (LNCS) 2205: *Spatial Information Theory Foundations of Geographic Information Science*, D. Montello (ed), COSIT 2001, Springer-Verlag (2001)

[8]   Jones, Christopher B., R. Purves, A. Ruas, M. Sanderson, M. Sester, M. van Kreveld, R. Weibel. "Spatial Information Retrieval and Geographical Ontologies: An Overview of the SPIRIT project" in 'SIGIR 2002: *Proceedings of the 25th Annual International ACM SIGIR Conference on Research and Development in Information Retrieval*, August 11–15, 2002, Tampere, Finland', ACM Press, pp.387–388.

[9]   Lim, Ee-Peng, Dion Hoe-Lian Goh, Zehua Liu, Wee-Keong Ng, Christopher Soo-Guan Khoo, Susan Ellen Higgins. "G-Portal: a map-based digital library for distributed geospatial and georeferenced resources". JCDL 2002: *Proceeding of the second ACM/IEEE-CS Joint Conference on Digital libraries*, 2002, Portland, Oregon, USA., ACM Press, pp. 351–358.

[10]  National Research Council, "Distributed Geolibraries: Spatial Information Resources, Summary of a Workshop". Panel on Distributed Geolibraries, National Academy Press, 1999.

[11]  Seaber, P.R., F.P Kapinos, G.L. Knapp. "Hydrologic Unit Maps". *U.S. Geological Survey Water-Supply Paper* 2294, 1987, 63 p.

[12]  Weaver, Mathew, Lois Delcambre, David Maier. "A Superimposed Architecture for Enhanced Metadata". *Proceedings of the DELOS Workshop on Interoperability in Digital Libraries*, Darmstadt, Germany, September 2001.

[13]  Weaver, Mathew, Bill Howe, Lois Delcambre, Timothy Tolle, David Maier. "Representing, Exploiting, and Extracting Metadata using Thesaurus++". *National Conference for Digital Government Research* (dg.o 2002), Los Angeles, California, May 2002.

[14]  Woodruff , A. G. & Plaunt, C. "GIPSY: Geo-referenced Information Processing System". *Journal of the American Society for Information Science*, (1994a), 45, 645–655.

# Document-Centered Collaboration for Scholars in the Humanities – The COLLATE System

Ingo Frommholz[1], Holger Brocks[1], Ulrich Thiel[1], Erich Neuhold[1],
Luigi Iannone[2], Giovanni Semeraro[2], Margherita Berardi[2], and
Michelangelo Ceci[2]

[1] Fraunhofer IPSI, Darmstadt, Germany
{frommholz, brocks, thiel, neuhold}@ipsi.fraunhofer.de
[2] Dipartimento di Informatica, University of Bari, Italy
{iannone, semeraro, berardi, ceci}@di.uniba.it

**Abstract.** In contrast to electronic document collections we find in contemporary digital libraries, systems applied in the cultural domain have to satisfy specific requirements with respect to data ingest, management, and access. Such systems should also be able to support the collaborative work of domain experts and furthermore offer mechanisms to exploit the value-added information resulting from a collaborative process like scientific discussions. In this paper, we present the solutions to these requirements developed and realized in the COLLATE system, where advanced methods for document classification, content management, and a new kind of context-based retrieval using scientific discourses are applied.

## 1 Introduction

Much scientific work with historical document collections is characterised by additional requirements compared to those usually found in contemporary digital libraries. For instance, the original source material might be lost and no longer be available, hence research has to rely on references found in secondary documents describing the original artifacts. Since working with cultural content is highly interpretative and incremental, the examination of scientific discussions about the material might grant more insight than the documents themselves. Therefore, a digital library dealing with historical material should offer support for storage, identification and access to the cultural documents, as well as providing the means to assist collaborative knowledge working processes where additional knowledge is gained based on the discussions about the material at hand. In this context, annotations entered by domain experts serve as building blocks for establishing scientific discourses. In addition to metadata generated by traditional formal indexing (e.g., cataloguing, controlled keywords) the value-added information represented in those discourses can be exploited in order to provide advanced content- and context-based access to the underlying digital repository.

The COLLATE system, which will be presented in this paper, employs advanced techniques to provide adequate access to historic film-related documents and their associated metadata, as well as to support collaboration between its

T. Koch and I.T. Sølvberg (Eds.): ECDL 2003, LNCS 2769, pp. 434–445, 2003.

professional users working with the material. Based on the reference model for an OAIS (Open Archival Information System, [8]) we will first outline the motivation behind the COLLATE system architecture, which is a revised version of an older one presented in [6], and then demonstrate the necessity to extend OAIS in order to support collaborative work processes. Then, we will take a closer look at some of the major system components, in particular those responsible for automatic document classification, XML-based content management and advanced, discourse-related retrieval functions.

## 2   The COLLATE System

The COLLATE[1] system focuses on historic film documentation, dealing with digitized versions of documents about European films of the 20ties and 30ties of the last century. Such documents can be censorship documents, newspaper articles, posters, advertisement material, registration cards, and photos. The system has to support several tasks required for managing its cultural content like, e.g., metadata creation, in-depth analysis and interpretation, and collaborative discussions about the documents and their related metadata. Advanced embedded search and retrieval functionality, both concept- and context-based, represents a fundamental requirement to maintain a continuous flow of information between the various actors involved.

### 2.1   Adding Collaboration to an Open Archival Information System

In [6], we presented an overall architecture of the COLLATE system which is based on a task-oriented layer concept. However, it turned out that the work of film scientists is not dividable into static tasks, but into phases manifesting themselves as discourses about specific topics. In contrast to tasks, such phases may be resumed if new contributions are added. In this case, a user can refer to an earlier point in the discourse. Our analysis of user behavior resulted in a revised COLLATE system architecture, as shown in Figure 1, which reflects our shift from a task-oriented towards a discourse-oriented view. The architecture is based on the reference model for an Open Archival Information System (OAIS). According to the definition in [8], "an OAIS is an archive, consisting of an organization of people and systems, that has accepted the responsibility to preserve information and make it available to a designated community". As the OAIS approach explicitly addresses organizational needs, it is more focused on our application domain than the framework defined by the Open Archives Initiative[2], which was founded in the area of e-print archives for enhancing communication among scholars. An OAIS consists of several modules, which are Ingest, Data Management, Archival Storage, Access, and Administration. We slightly modified this model by introducing an additional collaboration layer and neglecting the preservation planning layer described in [8]. An OAIS is surrounded

---

[1] Collaboratory for annotation, indexing and retrieval of digitized historical archive material IST-1999-20882, http://www.collate.de/.

[2] http://www.openarchives.org/

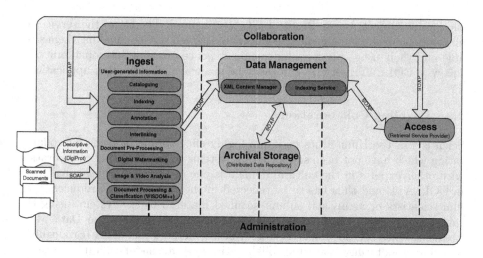

**Fig. 1.** The COLLATE system architecture

by a *producer-management-consumer* environment; *producers* are those actors providing the content or the information to be preserved; *managers* define the overall policy of an OAIS (and thus do not perform day-to-day archive operations); *consumers* use the services provided by an OAIS in order to find the information they are interested in.

The *Ingest* component provides functionality for the submission of information or objects to be stored in the system. Producers can insert scanned documents (together with some descriptive information) and user-generated information. The pre-processing contains the creation of digital watermarks, an image & video analysis, and certain document processing and classification techniques for the automatic generation of metadata. User-generated information is created by producers in a collaborative process. Documents and information prepared by Ingest services are sent to the *Data Management* component. In COLLATE, Data Management consists of two modules: The *XML Content Manager* realizes the storage of and access to digitized documents and user-generated information, which is serialized in XML. The *Indexing Service* updates the retrieval index on the arrival of new data objects. All Data Management modules are closely connected to the *Archival Storage* component, which is responsible for the maintenance of the distributed data repository by providing some low-level database access. Consumers access the system by invoking services of the *Access* component. Advanced retrieval functionality, e.g., based on scientific discourses, is provided here, which calls Data Management services. The *Administration* component is used, e.g., to monitor and improve archive operations, as well as to manage the configuration of the system. COLLATE also introduces an additional *Collaboration* component, which is responsible for the collaborative process described in Section 2.2. For the communication between all system components, the Simple Object Access Protocol (SOAP)[3] is used. Therefore, the services of all components are implemented as SOAP-based web services, making them scalable and their usage platform-independent, hence enabling interoperability. In this way, COLLATE services can easily be made available to other applications.

## 2.2 Enabling Collaboration

Scientists in the Humanities maintain highly effective mechanisms for collaboration which have not been supported by systems so far. Ensuring collaboration with other experts in the cultural domain is one of the most crucial challenges in COLLATE and thus has to be reflected in the architecture. Producers (i.e., film scientists or archivists) submit scanned material to the system, using the Ingest component, which is being pre-processed and sent to the Data Management. Once the document is stored, user-generated metadata (cataloguing, indexing, annotating) is created collaboratively. If, for instance, a user retrieves a specific document and the metadata already associated with it, she might be willing to contribute additional knowledge, e.g., comment upon an annotation by another user or complete missing cataloguing information. This kind of rather passive collaboration alone would be insufficient to justify complex collaboration services. In COLLATE we focus on active, system-internal support for collaboration, in particular proactive notifications about, e.g., newly submitted documents, and requests for comments broadcast to relevant domain experts. It should also be possible to bring together experts working in similar contexts, but who did not know of each other until now. In COLLATE's *collaboration* component, we therefore apply an agent-based approach, the MACIS (Multiple Agents for Collaborative Information Systems) framework, which has been developed to implement collaborative, distributed information environments (see also[5]).

## 3   System Components

### 3.1   Ingest

The Ingest component is responsible for document and metadata submission. In COLLATE, we distinguish between two kind of metadata: user-generated information and metadata which are automatically generated during document pre-processing.

The cultural material in COLLATE, which consists of scanned versions of the original resource, cannot be used for access and retrieval as it is. Therefore, methods have to be applied to extract as much information from both textual and pictorial material and make them as machine-accessible as possible. This requires us to go beyond mere OCR techniques for textual documents, and to apply methods for image analysis in order to automatically index pictorial documents. *WISDOM++*[4] is a document analysis system that can transform textual

---

[3] http://www.w3.org/TR/2002/CR-soap12-part1-20021219/

[4] http://www.di.uniba.it/~malerba/wisdom++/

paper documents into XML format [2]. This is a complex process involving several steps performed by WISDOM++. First, the image is *segmented* into basic layout components (non-overlapping rectangular blocks enclosing content portions). These layout components are *classified* according to the type of their content which can be, e.g., text, graphics, etc. Second, a perceptual organization phase called *layout analysis* is performed to detect structures among blocks. The result is a tree-like structure which is a more abstract representation of the document layout. This representation associates the content of a document with a hierarchy of layout components, such as blocks, lines, and paragraphs. Third, the *document image classification* step aims to identify the membership class (or type) of a document (e.g. censorship decision, newspaper article, etc.), and it is performed using some first-order rules which can be automatically learned from a set of training examples [13]. *Document image understanding* (or *interpretation*) [18] creates a mapping of the layout structure into the *logical structure*, which associates the content with a hierarchy of logical components, such as title/authors of a scientific article, or the name of the censor in a censorship document, and so on. In many documents the logical and the layout structures are closely related. For instance, the title of an article is usually located at the top of the first page of a document and it is written with the largest character set used in the document. Once logical and layout structure have been mapped, OCR can be applied only to those textual components of interest for the application domain, and its content can be stored for future retrieval purposes. Document image understanding also uses first-order rules [13]. The result of the document analysis is an XML document that makes the document image retrievable. In this way, the system can automatically determine not only the type of document, but is also able to identify interesting parts of a document and extract the information given in this part plus its meaning. As an example, we can automatically identify a document as being a censorship document coming from a specific authority and can additionally identify, e.g., the name of the censor (which is usually in a certain part of censorship documents by this institute).

For pictorial material, we can automatically extract metadata by performing an image & video analysis. The result of such an analysis is the extraction of basic image features like, e.g., edge analysis values, grayscale, and entropy, which support the classification of the pictorial material and the extraction of index terms describing the picture. See [11] for further details. Documents can optionally be supplied with digital watermarks. Watermarking is beyond the focus of this paper; refer to [7] for a description.

User-generated metadata ranges from formal indexing to content-based information gathered in collaborative processes (such as, e.g., in discussions about certain interpretations of documents or annotations). Well established in library science, formal indexing in COLLATE corresponds to collecting bibliographic metadata and the assignment of keywords to a document or certain passages of it. While formal indexing represents a fundamental prerequisite for enabling access to the documents, our focus is set on collaborative, content-based indexing and the resulting discourses established in scientific discussions about certain topics. Source analysis in the Humanities is an interpretative process, which reflects the current subjective point of view of the scientist. If in a col-

**Fig. 2.** Annotation thread, keywords, cataloguing

laborative digital library like COLLATE this point of view can be expressed and manifested (in an annotation), the expert tacit knowledge becomes explicit and can be accessed by other users. This in turn means that certain subjects in the experts' statements themselves become the focus of interest and are controversially discussed, i.e. they are commented upon. Since we interpret discussion threads associated to a document as coherent linguistic entities, we have empirically devised a set of admissible discourse structure relations which classify the interrelations between the annotations. Ranging from factual (e.g., providing additional information) to more interpersonal levels (i.e. focusing on certain expertise of the participants of a discussion), we use these relations to structure the resulting discourses (see [4] for a detailed definition of discourse structure relations). Using the Resource Description Framework[5] (RDF) to represent the interrelations[6], we obtain a directed acyclic graph with the digitized document as the root node. The set of nodes in the graph is the set of the document and the annotations occurring in the discussion; the typed links between the annotations, or the document and its direct annotations, respectively, form the vertices of the graph. We call this graph the *annotation thread*. An annotation thread forms a *collaborative discourse* about a specific topic (which is, in our case, the digitized document). With the typed links and the interpretation of annotations as node, an annotation thread can be seen as a hypertext (according to the definition of hypertexts in [1]). Figure 2 shows an example of an annotation thread (on the left side) with the digitized document as root node, and additional cataloguing and indexing information (on the right side). We can see an interpretation of the document, which is attacked by another scientist, using an annotation together with a "counterargument" relation type.

---

[5] http://www.w3c.org/RDF/

[6] The corresponding RDF Schema can be found at http://www.collate.de/RDF/collate.rdfs.

## 3.2   Data Management and Archival Storage

Data submitted to and set up by the Ingest component is forwarded to the Data
Management component, which is coupled to the Archival Storage. Archival Storage provides functionality for the distributed data repository, which consists of
relational database management systems. Archival storage offers low level access and storage capabilities, mainly based on SQL. Data Management modules
make use of these capabilities. Data Management consists of two components,
which are the XML Content Manager and the Indexing Service.

**XML Content Manager.** The COLLATE system has been devised as a distributed architecture. In fact, the idea of a collaboratory entails the new concept
of entities - software components and users - that need to work together, but
both in different locations (distribution along space) and asynchronously (distribution in time). This vision justifies our approach to developing a platform
that is capable of tackling the distribution issue along these two dimensions
while providing complete transparency w.r.t. Data Management and Archival
Storage to end users. Hence the task of content management is delegated to
a dedicated component named *XML Content Manager* (XMLCM)[7]. Content
management components have to deal with all kinds of processes, e.g., the insertion of a scanned document in the repository, and the insertion/access of some
metadata on a specific resource. XMLCM comprises three layers: the integration layer, core components, and the persistence layer. The *integration layer* is
the handle which external applications can rely on to use XMLCM services. It
has been developed within the Web Services paradigm, using SOAP technology. Thus, the integration layer allows the communication with services of other
COLLATE components, like those from Ingest and Access. *Core components*
are those components that have to manage COLLATE resources represented
as XML documents inside XMLCM. As sketched in Figure 3 they provide: access to XML documents at different levels of granularity (DocumentManager,
ElementManager), the possibility of managing XML Schemas or DTDs for the
documents in the Repository (MetadataManager), full support for accessing the
repository (QueryManager), the possibility of managing the underlying RDBM-
Ses, thanks to the BridgeXMLSQL component (in this way allowing the stor-
age/retrieval of non XML resources such as scanned documents), and a complete
layer for managing RDF Descriptions (models as well as single RDF statements)
used for connecting COLLATE resources. *XML Persistence layer* is the set of
components that cope with the problems of effective storage/retrieval of XML
resources, using the low-level access and storage functionality provided by the
Archival Storage.

**Indexing Service.** The *Indexing Service* is responsible for the maintenance
of the index used for retrieval. Every time new data arrive from the Ingest,
XMLCM stores the data in the repository and contacts the indexing service,

---

[7] XMLCM has been developed by one of our project partners, SWORD ICT
(http://www.sword.it/english/index.htm).

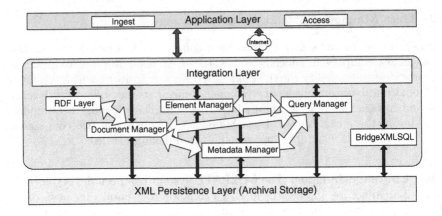

**Fig. 3.** XML Content Manager Architecture

which has to update the index accordingly. For annotations, full-text indexing is performed by calculating term weights based on the well-known $tf \times idf$ (term frequency, inverse document frequency) measure.

## 3.3 Access

To provide access to the cultural material, we have devised a set of advanced customizable retrieval functions for COLLATE [6]. Given a query $q$, we calculate for each document $d$ the *retrieval status value* of $d$ w.r.t. $q$, denoted by $r(d, q) \in [0, 1]$. Having such retrieval weights for all documents, we rank the documents based on descending retrieval status values. Using standard IR techniques, COLLATE provides functions for calculating $r_{meta}(d, q)$, which is the retrieval weight based on cataloguing and keyword metadata or data automatically derived from document pre-processing. Hence $r_{meta}(d, q)$ is computed on the information we can gain from the document itself. In contrast to that, we focus on a more advanced retrieval method called *context-based retrieval* which regards the annotation thread as extension of the document it belongs to, conveying additional information which could not be derived from the document itself and has an interpretative, thus subjective nature.

**Context-based Retrieval.** The context we are talking about in context-based retrieval is the *discourse context*; not only a statement in the discourse is considered, but also its position in the discourse and is type, given by a discourse structure relation. Thus, we do not only consider *what* is said (in an annotation), but also *where, when* and to *what purpose* it was said (the position of the annotation in the annotation thread plus the link type connecting it with its source). Furthermore, a document is judged in the light of the discussion about it. To demonstrate the value of context-based retrieval, we provide a simple example. Suppose a user is looking for censorship decisions mainly taken for political reasons. Returning to the document $d$ and metadata depicted in Figure 2, we do not find any evidence on political reasons in the cataloguing information or keywords. Based on this only, $r(d, q)$ is very low for this document, say 0.01. Nevertheless, another film scientist has put her interpretative analysis of the document into an annotation, stating that she thinks the censorship decision has a political background, even though it is not mentioned explicitly in the censorship document. Therefore, the document (together with this annotation) can be interesting for a user seeking political censorship. The retrieval engine would take this fact into account by raising the retrieval weight for the document $d$ to the value of, say, 0.4. Going further, a second film scientist has attacked the statement of the first one by annotating the first annotation and using the "counterargument" relation type [4]. This means the statement of the first scientist is controversial and far away from being safely regarded as a fact. To reflect this situation, the retrieval engine now lowers the previously raised retrieval weight for document $d$ to, e.g., 0.25. If the discussion were to go on, all contributions would have an impact on the overall weight of document $d$, depending on their position in the discourse, their content and the type of the incoming link. The kind of retrieval weight for $d$ which is based on the discourse on $d$ is referred to as $r_{dis}(d, q)$, which is computed in a recursive way. For each annotation $A$ in the annotation thread, we need to calculate $r_{dis}(A, q)$, the retrieval status value of this annotation w.r.t. the query, taking the annotation subthread with $A$ as the root element into account. The direct relation between a source annotation $A$ and the destination $A'$ with a link of type $X$ (with $X$ being a discourse structure relation) is defined as the triple $rel(X, A, A')$. Then, $r_{rel}(A, A', rel(X, A, A'), q)$ is the retrieval weight of $A$ w.r.t. $q$, having a directly connected annotation $A'$ linked with type $X$. To compute $r_{dis}(A, q)$, we look at each direct successor of $A$ (the set $succ(A)$) in the annotation thread, with

$$r_{dis}(A, q) = \frac{1}{|succ(A)|} \sum_{A' \in succ(A)} r_{rel}(A, A', rel(X, A, A'), q) \qquad (1)$$

It is $r_{rel}(A, A', rel(X, A, A'), q) = f(r_{ann}(A, q), r_{dis}(A', q), X) \in [0, 1]$ with $r_{ann}(A, q)$ as the retrieval status value of annotation $A$ without taking any context into account (calculated, e.g., by applying full-text retrieval methods), so (1) is a recursive function. Furthermore, it is $r_{dis}(A, q) = r_{ann}(A, q)$, if $A$ is a leaf in the annotation thread, so the recursion terminates. We are currently evaluating several strategies for the calculation of $r_{rel}(A, A', rel(X, A, A'), q)$. For $X$ being a counterargument, it should be $r_{rel}(A, A', rel(X, A, A'), q) < r_{ann}(A, q)$ ($A'$ being direct successor of $A$ in the annotation thread), since counterarguments weaken the argument made in $A$. On the other hand, if $X$ is a supportive argument, then $r_{rel}(A, A', rel(X, A, A'), q) > r_{ann}(A, q)$. Supportive arguments therefore strengthen a statement made in $A$. Finally, for a document $d$, let

$$r_{dis}(d, q) = \max_{A \in succ(d)} r_{dis}(A, q) \qquad (2)$$

(2) is justified by our view of direct annotations to a document being interpretations; we take the weight of the best-matching interpretation since we need a

measure which is independent of the number of interpretations. To achieve one single ranking, it should be possible to use both $r_{meta}(d, q)$ and $r_{dis}(d, q)$ in a balanced way. This leads to $r(d, q) = \alpha \cdot r_{dis}(d, q) + (1 - \alpha) \cdot r_{meta}(d, q)$. Depending on the user's preferences, $\alpha \in [0, 1]$ can be high (emphasizing the scientific discourse) or low (emphasizing the "hard facts" only).

**Retrieval Engine and Result-Set Enrichment.** We apply *HySpirit*[8][10], which is an implementation of probabilistic Datalog, providing the required support for retrieval based on metadata, full texts, and even hypertexts. HySpirit can access Datalog clauses stored in an RDBMS. After submitting a query, the retrieval engine calculates, depending on the kind of retrieval to be performed, a document ranking. This ranking is enriched with appropriate metadata obtained from the Data Management, and then set up in order to present it to the user.

# 4   Related Work

Some efforts have been made before to create collaborative information spaces. *BSCW* [3] provides web-based access on shared objects for collaborative environments. A commercial groupware product providing means for information sharing, but with limited collaboration support is *Lotus Notes*[9]. Collaboratories (e.g., [12]) more thoroughly support studies of the source material, which is stored as a distributed set of digitized source documents. *DEBORA* [14] enables digital access to books of the Renaissance, also offering annotation functionality, but without an explicit discourse model. *Annotea*[10] is a web-based annotation system using RDF. Similar to COLLATE, annotations are seen as statements about web pages, but do not establish a scientific discourse. Hypertext Information Retrieval (HIR) has been a research topic for many years. Besides direct search, hypertext information systems also offer the means to navigate and browse through the information space, resulting in the definition of combined models covering text retrieval and benefits gained from hypertext structures [1]. *Google* regards the whole World Wide Web as a hypertext and makes use of its link structure by applying the PageRank algorithm [15], but, as a Web search engine, does not take any link types into account. Frei and Stieger present an algorithm using typed links based on spreading activation [9], which is similar to the one presented in this paper, but cannot be applied to special hypertexts modeling a discourse like we have in COLLATE. Besides these few examples, there exist a number of other HIR systems. Link types similar to those defined in the COLLATE project, but not focused on scientific discourses, were introduced in 1983 by Randall Trigg [17] as well as, to state another example, in the authoring environment *SEPIA* [16].

---

[8] http://www.hyspirit.com/
[9] http://www.lotus.com/home.nsf/welcome/notes
[10] http://www.w3.org/2001/Annotea/

## 5   Conclusions

In this paper, we presented the COLLATE system and its advanced ingest, data management, access and collaboration methods which make it a system capable of dealing with the requirements arising from maintaining and working with historical cultural material. WISDOM++, a tool for advanced automatic document processing and classification, is applied. XMLCM is used to manage the digitized and user-generated content stored in the distributed data repository. In order to make use of the results coming from collaborative discussions, we have modeled scientific discourses as hypertext and, with discourse structure relations, introduced appropriate link types. Context-based retrieval directly uses the value-added information contained in scientific discourses, taking its subjective nature into account.

**Lessons learned.** The solutions described in this paper are rooted in user requirements we identified in [6]. Taking these as a starting point, we had many discussions with our targeted users, namely three European film archives which are part of the COLLATE consortium. Considering the valuable empirical input we got from them, many of the methods described in [6] have been implemented and are in use; other concepts had to be modified (as can be seen in particular by our shift from a task-oriented to a discourse-oriented view as described in Section 2.1). We provided our users with an external web-based discussion tool; evaluating their discussions formed the basis for our model of scientific discourses using discourse structure relations, and for the context-based retrieval. The need to offer a proactive collaboration component was derived from empirical data as well. A COLLATE prototype has been implemented and is used at the three film archives' sites. Discourse structure relations and context-based retrieval have recently been introduced to our users. We will collect feedback from the users in order to evaluate the acceptance of our approaches as well as to measure the efficiency and effectiveness of our context-based retrieval approach.

## References

1. Maristella Agosti. An overview of hypertext. In Maristella Agosti and Alan F. Smeaton, editors, *Information Retrieval and Hypertext*, chapter 2. Kluwer Academic Publishers, Boston et al., 1996.
2. O. Altamura, F. Esposito, and D. Malerba. Transforming paper documents into XML format with WISDOM++. *International Journal for Document Analysis and Recognition*, 4:2–17, 2001.
3. R. Bentley, T. Horstmann, K. Sikkel, and J Trevor. Supporting collaborative information sharing with the World-Wide Web: The BSCW shared workspace system. In *4th International WWW Conference*, Boston, 1995.
4. H. Brocks, A. Stein, U. Thiel, I. Frommholz, and A Dirsch-Weigand. How to incorporate collaborative discourse in cultural digital libraries. In *Proceedings of the ECAI 2002 Workshop on Semantic Authoring, Annotation & Knowledge Markup (SAAKM02)*, Lyon, France, July 2002.

5. H. Brocks, U. Thiel, and A. Stein. Agent-based user interface customization in a system-mediated collaboration environment. In *Proceedings of the 10th International Conference on Human-Computer Interaction*, 2003.

6. H. Brocks, U. Thiel, A. Stein, and A. Dirsch-Weigand. Customizable retrieval functions based on user tasks in the cultural heritage domain. In Panos Constantopoulos and Ingeborg Sølvberg, editors, *Proceedings of the ECDL 2001, Darmstadt, Germany, Sept. 2001*, Lecture Notes in Computer Science, pages 37–48, Berlin et al., 2001. Springer.

7. J. Dittmann. Content-fragile watermarking for image authentication. In *Proceedings of SPIE: Security and Watermarking of Multimedia Contents III*, volume 4314, San Jose, California, USA, 2001.

8. Consultive Committee for Space Data Systems. Reference Model for an Open Archival Information System (OAIS), January 2002. http://wwwclassic.ccsds.org/documents/pdf/CCSDS-650.0-B-1.pdf.

9. H. P. Frei and D. Stieger. The use of semantic links in hypertext information retrieval. *Information Processing and Management: an International Journal*, 31(1):1–13, 1995.

10. N. Fuhr and T. Rölleke. Hyspirit — a Probabilistic Inference Engine for Hypermedia Retrieval in Large Databases. In H.-J. Schek, F. Saltor, I. Ramos, and G. Alonso, editors, *Proceedings of the 6th International Conference on Extending Database Technology (EDBT), Valencia, Spain*, Lecture Notes in Computer Science, pages 24–38, Berlin et al., 1998. Springer.

11. Silvia Hollfelder, Andre Everts, and Ulrich Thiel. Designing for semantic access: A video browsing system. *Multimedia Tools and Applications*, 11(3):281–293, August 2000.

12. R.T. Kouzes, J.D. Myers, and W.A. Wulf. Doing science on the internet. *IEEE Computer*, 29(8), 1996.

13. D. Malerba, F. Esposito, and F.A. Lisi. Learning recursive theories with ATRE. In *Proc. of the 13th European Conf. on Artificial Intelligence*, pages 435–439. John Wiley & Sons, 1998.

14. D.M. Nichols, D. Pemberton, S. Dalhoumi, O. Larouk, C. Belisle, and Twindale M.B. DEBORA: Developing an Interface to Support Collaboration in a Digital Library. In J.L. Borbinha and T. Baker, editors, *Proceedings of the 4th European Conference on Research and Advanced Technology for Digital Libraries (ECDL 2000)*, Lecture Notes in Computer Science, pages 239–248, Berlin et al., 2000. Springer.

15. L. Page, S. Brin, R. Motwani, and T. Winograd. The PageRank citation ranking: Bringing order to the web. Technical report, Stanford Digital Library Technologies Project, 1998.

16. M. Thüring, J.M. Haake, and J. Hannemann. What's ELIZA doing in the Chinese Room? Incoherent hyperdocuments - and how to avoid them. In *Hypertext '91 Proceedings*, pages 161–177, New York, 1991. ACM Press.

17. Randall Trigg. *A Network-Based Approach to Text Handling for the Online Scientific Community*. PhD Thesis, Department of Computer Science, University of Maryland, November 1983.

18. S. Tsujimoto and H. Asada. Understanding multi-articled documents. In *Proceedings of the 10th International Conference on Pattern Recognition*, pages 551–556, 1990.

# DSpace as an Open Archival Information System: Current Status and Future Directions

Robert Tansley[1], Mick Bass[1], and MacKenzie Smith[2]

[1]Hewlett-Packard Laboratories, 1 Cambridge Center suite 12, Cambridge, MA 02142, USA
{robert.tansley, mick.bass}@hp.com
[2]Massachusetts Institute of Technology Libraries, Cambridge, MA 02139, USA
kenzie@mit.edu

**Abstract.** As more and more output from research institutions is born digital, a means for capturing and preserving the results of this investment is required. To begin to understand and address the problems surrounding this task, Hewlett-Packard Laboratories collaborated with MIT Libraries over two years to develop DSpace, an open source institutional repository software system. This paper describes DSpace in the context of the Open Archival Information System (OAIS) reference model. Particular attention is given to the preservation aspects of DSpace, and the current status of the DSpace system with respect to addressing these aspects. The reasons for various design decisions and trade-offs that were necessary to develop the system in a timely manner are given, and directions for future development are explored. While DSpace is not yet a complete solution to the problem of preserving digital research output, it is a production-capable system, represents a significant step forward, and is an excellent platform for future research and development.

## 1 Introduction

Increasingly, research and educational institutions produce born-digital output. As well as traditional document-based material, researchers and teachers produce data in more complex outputs, such as audio, video, legacy application data, statistical databases, software, and others. Presently, constituents of these institutions do not have a suitable place to put these digital objects such that they will be preserved for the long-term. Organisational changes and the now well-understood problems of digital preservation mean that much of this valuable output, and hence initial investment, is lost.

To begin addressing this need, Hewlett-Packard Laboratories and MIT Libraries collaborated on a two-year project to develop DSpace, an open source repository system for the capture and preservation of digital materials. DSpace was designed as a production quality system offering the breadth of functionality required for a long-term institutional repository in a relatively simple fashion. After several months of working with early adopter communities at MIT, DSpace went into production at MIT Libraries in November 2002, and has been available as open source software since that time.

T. Koch and I.T. Sølvberg (Eds.): ECDL 2003, LNCS 2769, pp. 446–460, 2003.

Of course, we cannot claim to have solved the problem. Of those issues that are technical, many are at present research problems. DSpace is serving as the starting point for a number of development and research efforts looking into these issues.

The focus of this paper is to document the present functionality of DSpace, using the Consultative Committee for Space Data Systems' Reference Model for an Open Archival Information System (OAIS) [5] as a basis to demonstrate how far DSpace is towards becoming a comprehensive long-term institutional repository system. Decisions and necessary tradeoffs made during the development to meet production deadlines are explained. Also described are some thoughts on possible future research and development on the DSpace platform.

## 2  Related Work

DSpace draws on previous work and experiences from the field of digital libraries and repositories. The DSpace architecture has roots in Kahn and Wilensky's Framework for Distributed Digital Object Services [4], as well as Arms et al.'s work on digital library architecture [1], [2].

Comparable systems to DSpace are surprisingly few. The EPrints system developed at the University of Southampton [12] has many similar features to DSpace, but is targeted at author self-archiving of document-style material rather than long-term preservation of digital material. Interoperability with EPrints is of course desirable, and can currently be achieved through use of the OAI metadata harvesting protocol [11]. The Greenstone software from New Zealand Digital Library Project at the University of Waikato [13] is another open source digital library tool with a focus on publishing digital collections.

## 3  The Open Archival Information System Reference Model

One very relevant piece of prior work is CCSDS' Open Archival Information System (OAIS) reference model [5]. This describes the functional components of a system intended to preserve information for the benefit of a 'designated community'. It is a useful guide to the various aspects of archival systems, and the terminology is useful for describing existing systems, even if they do not exactly map onto the model.

The remainder of this paper describes DSpace's current capabilities in terms of these functional components. Note that DSpace's architecture does not directly correspond to the OAIS model. For example, archival information and data management information are both stored in the database. However, describing the functionality in terms of OAIS is a good way of expressing the functionality of the system to those familiar with the model. Additionally, since the OAIS represents mature thinking about what is really required to archive digital information, mapping DSpace functionality onto OAIS is a very effective way of finding out DSpace's strengths and where future work should be most urgently directed.

## 4  Archival Storage

Currently in DSpace, archival information is stored in a typical relational database, and the content itself is stored in the file system on the server. Thus, in DSpace, an OAIS Archival Information Package (AIP) is currently a logical object that is located in variety of database tables and files. This means that accessing archival information in DSpace is easy and efficient, but this is not optimal for preservation, since the representation information for much of the data is implicit in the DSpace code, and extracting an AIP requires the use of the DSpace code.  Since we are using contemporary, actively maintained software and hardware, we feel this is an acceptable risk for the short term. To address this for the long term we are designing a means of storing DSpace AIPs in open, standard formats, for example based on METS [7] or RDF [8]. These will allow the reconstruction of the data in a DSpace given the AIPs, even if the DSpace code and runtime environment is not available. These would become the real archival storage in the system, and the information in the relational database would become access information. Since the logical contents are the same, the discussion that follows equally applies to both the relational database storage in place now and the future AIPs.

OAIS describes a specialisation of AIP called an Archival Information Unit (AIU) that represents the 'atoms' of information the archive is storing. In DSpace, the basic unit of archival storage, constituting an AIU in the OAIS model, is the **Item**. An Item is a logical work and can consist of many **Bitstreams**, the digital files that make up the content of the work. The structure of Items is depicted in figure 1.

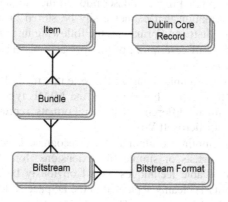

**Fig. 1.** DSpace Item Structure

Items all have one Dublin Core descriptive metadata record.  This allows basic metadata interoperability across all of the items in DSpace. DSpace as shipped uses a derivation of the Library Application Profile, though the registry may be edited via means of an administrative user interface to suit an institution's particular need. This Dublin Core record also contains free text provenance information about who submitted the Item, and with which tool(s).

While Dublin Core is not nearly as descriptive as many of the metadata schemas and standards used by various communities, it is nearly always trivial to crosswalk from the richer description to Dublin Core. Serialisations of the richer metadata may be stored as Bitstreams within the item. Various efforts are under way to enable DSpace to make use of the richer metadata, such as the SIMILE project [9], which is investigating applying some or all of the Semantic Web tool stack and RDF.

Content within Items is divided into **Bundles**, each of which contains one or more Bitstreams. A Bundle may contain Bitstreams that are somehow closely tied, for example an HTML document containing images; the HTML source file and associated JPEG image files would be stored as separate Bitstreams within a single Bundle.

Presently, we do not have a way to express the exact relationship between such Bitstreams, for example expressing that a sequence of TIFF images are ordered pages of a book. Expressing and storing this part of the representation information for an item is a non-trivial problem, though efforts such as METS are well on the way to addressing it. We decided delaying the deployment and distribution of DSpace until a solution is implemented was unnecessary. We felt this was a reasonable, managed risk, since most of the initial content targeted for DSpace was in single document files or well-understood multi-file formats like HTML.

Bitstreams are individual digital content files, such as a JPEG image, HTML source document, PDF file, MP3 audio file, or MPEG movie file. Each Bitstream is associated with exactly one **Bitstream Format** from the system's Bitstream Format Registry. For each Bitstream some technical metadata is also stored: The Bitstream's size and MD5 checksum for integrity checking ('fixity information' using OAIS terminology), and an optional free text description of the file (always a useful fallback for catching any information that cannot easily be stored in a machine-processible way.) Currently, each Bitstream Format has the following information:

- A short name and a full description of the format, e.g. 'HTML 4' and 'Hypertext Markup Language version 4.'
- The MIME type, for example 'image/gif'. Note that many Bitstream Formats may have the same MIME type. For example, the MIME type 'application/msword' may be used by many different Bitstream Formats representing the output of different versions of Microsoft Word.
- Information for attempting to automatically recognise Bitstreams in this format. Currently this is consists of simple file extensions, for example '.jpg'. More sophisticated and reliable techniques would obviously be advantageous, so this piece of functionality is cleanly separated in the DSpace code.
- The 'support level' for the format. This is decided by the institution and indicates how well the hosting institution is likely to be able to preserve content in the format in the future, through migration or emulation. Factors influencing the support level for a particular format may be availability of detailed representation information (format specifications), availability of tools and source code for manipulating the format, available resources and demand from the institution's communities.

There are three possible support levels that Bitstream formats may be assigned by the hosting institution. The host institution should determine the exact meaning of each support level, after careful consideration of costs and requirements. MIT Libraries' interpretation is shown in Table 1.

Note that the Bitstream Format registry does not contain representation information; however, to ensure preservation (a 'supported' format), the hosting institution should have extensive representation information for a format available and securely archived.

## 4.1  Archival Information Collections

The OAIS describes the concept of the Archival Information Collection (AIC), which is a kind of AIP that represents a collection of other AIPs. In DSpace, there are currently two kinds of AIC: **Community** and **Collection**.

**Table 1.** Bitstream Format Support Levels

| Supported | The format is recognised, and the hosting institution is confident it can make Bitstreams of this format useable in the future, using whatever combination of techniques (such as migration, emulation, etc.) is appropriate given the context of need. In other words, the hosting institution has full representation information for this format and the resources to use it. |
|---|---|
| Known | The format is recognised, and the hosting institution will promise to preserve the Bitstream as-is, and allow it to be retrieved. The hosting institution will attempt to obtain enough information to enable the format to be upgraded to the 'supported' level. |
| Unsupported | The format is unrecognised, but the hosting institution will undertake to preserve the Bitstream as-is and allow it to be retrieved. |

A DSpace Collection consists of DSpace Items that are somehow related. A Collection might be a technical report series, or a series of statistical data sets produced during a research project.

DSpace Collections are organised into Communities. These typically correspond to a laboratory, research centre or department. This structure is depicted in figure 2. Note that Collections may appear in more than one Community, and Items may appear in more than one Collection.

**Fig. 2.** DSpace Communities, Collections and Items

In DSpace, the each Community and Collection has some metadata corresponding to the OAIS Collection Description and Preservation Description Information. This includes the name of the Community or Collection, a free-text description of the content and/or purpose of the collection, and a free-text provenance description.

## 4.2  Identifiers

One important aspect of preservation is naming; archiving something isn't particularly useful unless it can be referred to and accessed. The OAIS describes two sorts of names: AIP Identifiers and Content Information Identifiers.  Presently, DSpace uses CNRI's Handle system [10] to identify Items, Collections and Communities.  Since these objects are stored in the relational database and are both archival and access-optimised, these Handles in are effect both AIP Identifiers and Content Information Identifiers.  When AIPs are stored in an open, standard format outside of the relational database, the Handles are likely to become the Content Information Identifiers, and the AIP Identifiers may become something different.  It may be that for each Item there exists a number of AIPs, corresponding to different storage formats and versions of that Item; the exact details have not yet been nailed down.

The advantages of using Handles are guaranteed global uniqueness, and a global resolution mechanism.  Even if for some reason the global resolution mechanism becomes unavailable, the fact that the Handles are globally unique is still valuable, and they may still be used within DSpace to locate items.

DSpace does not assign Handles to subparts of Items, such as Bitstreams.  While direct, programmatic access to subparts is often desirable, providing access in a preservable way is very difficult, since exactly what the intended subpart is may be unclear.  Is it the particular bit-encoding or a higher-level concept such as 'the image on page 3,' in which case a bit-encoding in an appropriate contemporary format is required?  Thus we decided it was inappropriate to give Handles to entities while we have no way of expressing exactly what it is that is being identified by the Handle.

Bitstreams within an Item do have a numerical ID (a database primary key) that is unique to a DSpace instance.  Thus, as a compromise, individual Bitstreams may still be accessed directly using the numerical ID if necessary for a particular purpose. Modifying the code to allow Handles to be assigned to Bitstreams would be a trivial change, if such a path was deemed appropriate in the future.

## 4.3  History Information

While the provenance information in the form of prose in the DC record is very useful, it is not easily programmatically manipulated.  DSpace includes a History system that captures a time-based record of significant changes in DSpace, in a manner suitable for later repurposing, for example to create audit trails and track where some change to information in the archive might have been changed.

Currently, the History subsystem is explicitly invoked when significant events occur (e.g., DSpace accepts an item into the archive). The History subsystem then creates RDF data describing the current state of the object. The RDF data is modelled using the ABC Model [4], an ontology for describing temporal-based data.

## 4.4  A Sample DSpace AIP

Figure 3 shows an example DSpace Item as an AIP.  Preservation Description Information is shown in italics. Representation Information for the Bitstreams is not held within the system, but is linked by reference to the Bitstream Formats.

Representation Information for the AIP as a whole is not stored explicitly, as has been previously discussed. When AIPs are generated and stored using the METS, this will be addressed.

## 4.5   Migration and Disaster Recovery

Important aspects of the archival storage part of an OAIS system are backup and disaster recovery. These are not directly addressed by the DSpace code; the wealth of existing backup and recovery tools available for different operating systems may be employed with DSpace without difficulty. At MIT Libraries, the server's file systems are backed up to magnetic tapes which are then shipped off-site. A drawback with this approach is that disaster recovery would rely on the availability of the appropriate hardware and software, since the data would be recovered in the PostgreSQL database storage formats. This is an acceptable risk while we are using actively maintained hardware and software, however backing up DSpace AIPs in an open, standard format such as METS as discussed above is necessary for reliable long-term recovery.

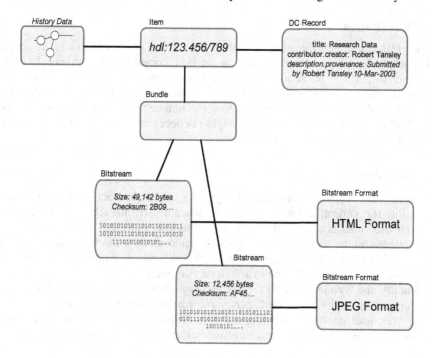

**Fig. 3.** A Sample DSpace Archival Information Package

Storing DSpace AIPs in the standard format would also make migration between physical storage media simpler, since it would not be necessary to use exactly the same database application with the new storage media.

# 5  Data Management

DSpace has a number of functions that fall within the data management part of the OAIS functional model. These include records of users of the system, authorisation control, and metadata indices.

## 5.1  E-people

DSpace holds information about users of the system for authorisation and authentication, for keeping records of who did what, and for subscriptions (described in section 8.2.) In OAIS these are termed 'Customer Profiles'. DSpace calls them **E-people**. These E-person records are not 'authority records' for authors and contributors to archived content. The term 'E-person' is used as opposed to 'user' since many parties accessing DSpace may be machines rather than real users.

E-people may also be organised into **E-person Groups**, so that authorisation policies and so on can be easily administered.

## 5.2  Authorisation

DSpace features a fine-grained authorisation system that enables individual E-people and E-people Groups to be permissions on individual objects in the system. In order for a user to perform an action on an object, they must have permission; DSpace operates a 'default deny' policy. Different permissions can apply to individual Bitstreams within an Item. Permissions do not 'commute'; for example, if an E-person has READ permission on an Item, they might not necessarily have READ permission on the Bundles and Bitstreams in that item.

## 5.3  Authentication

In general, the access mechanisms that people use to interact with DSpace are responsible for authentication. For example, when a user interacts with DSpace via the Web user interface, it is the Web user interface code that is responsible for determining who the user is. This is because authentication mechanisms tend to be specific to interfaces. MIT Libraries use X509 certificates to authenticate users; this mechanism may not be applicable to a Web services interface.

Naturally, the Web user interface code, and any other code that must authenticate a user, can and will make use of the E-person records held within the database.

The Web user interface code shipped with DSpace has been designed to make interoperating DSpace with any local authentication schemes as simple as possible.

## 5.4  Indexing

DSpace stores storing objects and metadata in normalised relational database tables, allowing efficient programmatic access and retrieval. In addition, DSpace maintains two kinds of index for access services.

The first kind is an ordered index of Items (by title or date) or authors of Items in the archive. This allows access mechanisms such as the Web user interface to retrieve and present to the user ordered lists of objects to browse through. These indices are maintained in the database.

The second kind of index is a quick look-up index for responding to user's keyword search queries. DSpace uses the open source Jakarta Lucene search engine to manage and query this index. Presently, a subset of the Dublin Core fields is indexed. Lucene supports full-text indexing but DSpace does not use that feature yet.

# 6   Administration

Presently, DSpace administration is performed centrally by staff knowledgeable of the system and how it works. Future development will allow some of the administrative functions of the archive to be performed by individual communities if desired. This allows communities to retain a sense of control over their content in the archive, and to relieve central administrative burden.

Examples of the sort of administration that communities will be able to perform are authorising submitters, creating Collections, assigning roles in the submission workflow such as reviewers, and changing cosmetic aspects of the Web user interface specific to their Collections.

It was decided to have all administration performed centrally for now since the number of communities at MIT using DSpace is currently quite small, and it would have taken too long to develop a user interface sufficiently user-friendly and robust. Such an interface would have to ensure that mistakes made by community administrators do not cause damage.

There are two main means of administering the DSpace archive. Most administration can be performed via an administration Web UI. Some low-level tasks are performed by running shell scripts and commands on the server machine.

The administration Web UI contains tools for:

- Creating and editing metadata for Communities and Collections
- Creating and maintaining E-person records
- Controlling authorisation Groups and access control lists
- An interface for modifying Items in the archive. Although this allows any edits to be made to the item, in general it is just used to correct spelling mistakes and the like
- Withdrawing Items from the archive.
- Viewing and editing the registry of Dublin Core elements and qualifiers. Presently, this must be done with care, since various parts of the system such as the submission UI expect particular elements and qualifiers to be present
- View and edit the Bitstream Format registry
- View and abort active submission workflows

Tasks that must be performed via shell scripts and commands include:

- Importing many SIPs at once (batch importing)
- Administering backups
- Search and browse index maintenance

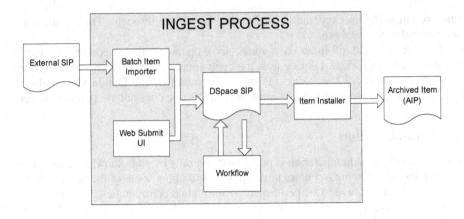

**Fig. 4.** The DSpace Ingest Process

## 7  Ingest

The basic task of the ingest part of an OAIS is to receive a Submission Information Package (SIP) and transform it into an AIP suitable for inclusion in archival storage. The DSpace ingest process is depicted in figure 4. At present, DSpace supports two methods of ingest.

Firstly there is a batch item importer. For this importer we have defined a simple external SIP format, in which the metadata (Dublin Core) is stored in an XML file, in a directory with the associated content files. The batch importer takes these external SIPs, and converts them into DSpace SIPs stored in the DSpace database and Bitstream store. Currently, content to be imported must be copied to a temporary directory on the server running DSpace, and the batch importer tool run via a remote shell.

Secondly, DSpace features a Web-based submission user interface. Using this, a submitter (producer using OAIS terminology) fills out appropriate metadata fields, and uploads the content files to DSpace. This information is used by the submission UI to construct a DSpace SIP in the database and Bitstream store.

Once the SIP has been constructed in DSpace, the workflow associated with the target collection is started. This corresponds to the 'quality assurance' function in the OAIS model. Presently, the workflow system in DSpace is quite simple. There are three possible workflow roles:

1. *Reviewers* can accept the submission, or reject it
2. *Approvers* can accept or reject the submission, and can edit the metadata of the item
3. *Editors* can edit the metadata of the submission, but may not reject the submission; when they have performed any necessary edits, they commit it to the archive.

456   R. Tansley, M. Bass, and M. Smith

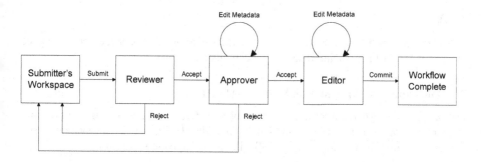

**Fig. 5.** DSpace Workflow Process

An incoming submission passes through these three steps in order, as depicted in figure 5. Zero or more E-people can be assigned to each role for a collection. If more than one E-person is assigned to a role, only one E-person actually has to perform it. In this case, the E-person performing the role 'locks' the submission so that the other E-people in that role know it is being worked on. If no E-people are assigned to a role for a collection, the submission passes straight through that step.

This relatively simple workflow will not cover every conceivable submission workflow, but does cover the needs of most communities. The exact semantics of each role may be determined individually for each Collection. For example, the Reviewer of one Collection might simply check that the uploaded files have been received correctly. The Reviewer of another might look at and make recommendations about the content of the submission.

Once the workflow process is successfully complete, the Item Installer is responsible for transforming the DSpace SIP into a DSpace AIP. This performs the 'Generate AIP,' 'Generate Descriptive Info,' and 'Coordinate Updates' functions in the OAIS model. Specifically, the operations it performs are:

- Assigns an accession date
- Adds a "date.available" value to the Dublin Core metadata record of the Item
- Adds an issue date if none already present
- Adds a provenance message (including bitstream checksums)
- Assigns a Handle persistent identifier
- Adds the Item to the target Collection, and adds appropriate authorisation policies
- Adds the new item to the search and browse indices

DSpace contains Java APIs for constructing a DSpace SIP, and invoking the workflow system and Item Installer. Thus, an institution may implement their own submission mechanism by building on those APIs. For example, a department within an institution might have an existing application for submitting content to a departmental Web site. A bridging application might automatically take new content from the departmental Web site and use the DSpace APIs to add the content to DSpace.

Another possibility is to convert metadata and content exported from another system into the simple DSpace XML SIP format for the batch import tool.

# 8  Access

There is little point in archiving things if they cannot later be accessed! DSpace offers a variety of access and discovery mechanisms.

## 8.1  Dissemination Information Packages (DIPs)

DSpace presently can disseminate three sorts of DIP: Community, Collection and Item record Web pages, individual Bitstreams via HTTP, and a file system based format including the metadata in an XML file and composite Bitstreams.

### 8.1.1  Community, Collection, and Item Record Web Pages

Each Community and Collection in DSpace has a 'home page' in the Web UI. This displays information such as the name and description, most recent new Items, and access to common functions such as submission and subscriptions.

For each Item in DSpace, the Web UI can present an Item record display page. This displays a subset of the Dublin Core metadata associated with the Item, a link to a version of the page displaying all of the Dublin Core metadata, and a list of Bitstreams within the Item which can be individually downloaded and viewed. Essentially, this Item record display page is the default DIP of each Item in DSpace.

If an Item has been withdrawn for some reason, the default DIP is a 'tombstone' page, which explains that the Item has been withdrawn and is no longer accessible.

### 8.1.2  Bitstreams

Besides the Item record display page, DIPs available to users take the form of simple, individual Bitstream downloads via HTTP or HTTPS. The MIME type of each format being downloaded is sent in the HTTP header, allowing the browser to select the most appropriate view or application for displaying the Bitstream to the end user.

DSpace currently has no more sophisticated DIP mechanisms than this. There is no tool that negotiates an appropriate Bitstream Format to send to the user or that can transform between Bitstream Formats. For now the communities using DSpace tend to use the same contemporary formats, so this is only a barrier to a small minority of users. The need for transformations is likely to increase over time as DSpace is used to archive more complex rich media material, so this is obviously an important development area for DSpace. A possible solution is a mechanism whereby available transformations are determined by the system, the user selects one (or one is somehow negotiated automatically), and the system then either performs the transformation and disseminates the results or sends a cached copy.

An additional possibility is that Bitstream(s) are embedded in some sort of emulation environment that is disseminated to the end user. For example, a software executable might be sent embedded in a Java Applet that emulates the software and hardware environment that executable runs in.

### 8.1.3  Batch Item Exporter

DSpace also features a batch export tool which can write DIPs for desired Items in the same XML format and directory structure that the batch import tool recognises. This allows 'round trips' Items between DSpace instances. The exporter must be run using a shell on the server computer, and thus is not in general available to end users.

While DSpace does not have a standard, open AIP storage format, this is also a way of backing up data in the archive so that the DSpace software and hardware does not have to be available to reconstruct the archive in the event of some disaster. The forthcoming open, standard AIP format mentioned in section 4 above may be used as a DIP, probably replacing the current, simple format.

### 8.2 Discovery Mechanisms

DSpace already provides a variety of discovery mechanisms:

*Handle Resolution.* The CNRI Handles assigned to new DSpace Items may be resolved using the global Handle resolution mechanism. A Handle resolution request will result in the URL of the relevant Item record display page. In the future, Handle resolution requests may result in a variety of URIs or other means of accessing different available disseminations of a particular Item, Collection or Community.

*Open Archives Initiative Protocol for Metadata Harvesting (OAI-PMH).* As more institutions bring up DSpace and similar institutional repositories, the resultant availability of on-line material presents a great opportunity for cross-institution access and discovery. One important effort in realising this is the Open Archives Initiative (OAI) [11]. DSpace functions as an OAI data provider; it will respond to OAI-PMH requests with appropriate descriptive metadata (Dublin Core.)

*Search and Browse.* The DSpace Web UI provides an interface to the search index. End users can enter search terms and view matching Items. These searches can be scoped to particular Communities and Collections. The Web UI also allows users to browse through the lists of Items ordered by author, title and date.

*Subscriptions.* Any E-person registered with DSpace can elect to 'subscribe' to one or more collections. When new Items appear in any of their subscribed Collections, the E-person is sent an e-mail summarising these new Items.

*OpenURLs.* DSpace supports the OpenURL protocol in a rather simple fashion. DSpace can display an OpenURL link on every Item record page, automatically using the Dublin Core metadata. Additionally, DSpace can respond to incoming OpenURLs. Presently it simply passes the information in the OpenURL to the search subsystem. The relevant item (if it is in DSpace) is usually at the top of the list of results.

## 9  Transformation

A final aspect of digital preservation that is not specific to any particular part of the OAIS functional model is the necessary migration of content in one format to another, as the hardware and software used to access digital material changes over time. In OAIS terminology this is referred to as Transformation.

At present, DSpace as shipped does not have any facility for automated Transformations. Although this seems like a serious omission, it is not a barrier to operating a DSpace; a suitable update will be available before any hardware, software and Bitstream Format specifications become truly obsolete and unknown.

The future Transformation functionality is likely to take the form of some administrative tool which is given some heuristic to decide what needs to be transformed. This may be as simple as a particular Bitstream Format, or a pattern of Bitstream Formats within a Bundle. The tool to perform the actual transformation would also be specified.

The Transformation tool would then apply the transformation to each Bitstream or set of Bitstreams in the appropriate archive, Community or Collection. These new Bitstreams would be stored in new Bundles within the Item, and hence available through the same Handle as the original(s).

Transformations are often 'irreversible' and may result in the loss of some information. It is not always possible to represent every piece of information that can be held in one format in another. Hence, the following precautions would be taken:

- Bitstreams that are superseded by the Transformation would not be removed, so that any future, improved version of the Transformation can be applied. The superseded Bitstreams might be moved to cheap 'off-line' media, however.
- The provenance information (currently stored in the Dublin Core record) of the Item would be updated to include information about the Transformation.
- The History system would store information about the Transformation event, including when it occurred, the tool used, the person who initiated it, and the state of the Item and its contents before and after the Transformation.

Should the Transformation later prove to have been problematic, for example if it resulted in loss or garbling of important information, the data stored by the History system could be used to automatically 'back-track' the Transformation, and re-apply an improved Transformation tool. Since the History system stores the state of the Item before and after Transformation, it is also possible to verify that Transformations have been successfully undone.

## 10  Conclusion

With DSpace, we feel we have made significant progress towards providing a tool to address an institution's long-term digital repository needs. It is not yet a complete solution, and by considering DSpace in the context of the OAIS model, we have been able to highlight the areas in which DSpace needs work:

- Describing complex relationships between Bitstreams (Bundle descriptions)
- It would be relatively easy to write a tool that migrated Bitstreams from one format to the other using the DSpace Java API. Preferable would be a standardised way in which this can be achieved so that migrations and transformations can be shared between DSpaces, and so the effort required to perform future migrations is small.
- We need a way to use these complex relationships between Bitstreams and transformation tools to provide more useful disseminations, especially as the complexity of data and media in the system increases. The FEDORA work [6] in particular provides a useful framework for addressing this issue.

By working with a host institution we have been able to focus on the providing the functionality required to run as a live service now and to immediately start capturing digital information that would otherwise be lost. In building DSpace as a simple, modular system, we have given future research and development in the above areas a head start, since it is clear where in the system each piece of functionality should reside. Additionally, since DSpace is open source, it can potentially provide value to a great many institutions, and stands to benefit from a large community of developers and information science professionals.

We are confident that DSpace represents a great step forward in the fight by institutions to capture the digital output of research investment, and is in an excellent position to provide a comprehensive solution to this problem in the future.

# References

1.  William Y. Arms: Key Concepts in the Architecture of the Digital Library, *D-Lib Magazine*, July 1995 <http://www.dlib.org/dlib/July95/07arms.html>.
2.  William Y. Arms, Christophe Blanchi, and Edward A. Overly: An Architecture for Information in Digital Libraries, *D-Lib Magazine*, February 1997 <http://www.dlib.org/dlib/february97/cnri/02arms1.html>.
3.  The GNU EPrints Software <http://software.eprints.org/>
4.  Robert Kahn and Robert Wilensky, *A Framework for Distributed Digital Object Services*, May 1995 <http://www.cnri.reston.va.us/home/cstr/arch/k-w.html>.
5.  Consultative Committee for Space Data Systems, *Reference Model for an Open Archival Information System (OAIS)*, CCSDS 650.0-R-2, Red Book, Issue 2, July 2001 <http://ccsds.org/documents/pdf/CCSDS-650.0-R-2.pdf>.
6.  Sandra Payette and Carl Lagoze, "Flexible and Extensible Digital Object and Repository Architecture," in *Research and Advanced Technologies for Digital Libraries: Proceedings of the Second European Conference, ECDL '98*, Crete, Greece, 1998., G. Goos, J. Hartmanis, and J. van Leeuwen, eds., *Lecture Notes in Computer Science*, 1513 (Berlin: Springer, 1998) <http://www.cs.cornell.edu/payette/papers/ECDL98/FEDORA.html>.
7.  Metadata Encoding and Transmission Standard (METS) <http://www.loc.gov/standards/mets/>
8.  W3C Resource Description Framework (RDF) <http://www.w3.org/RDF/>
9.  SIMILE: Semantic Interoperability of Metadata and Information in unLike Environments <http://web.mit.edu/simile>
10. Handle System Overview. <http://www.ietf.org/internet drafts/draft-sun-handle-system-10.txt>
11. The Open Archives Initiative <http://www.openarchives.org/>
12. The Greenstone Digital Library Software <http://www.greenstone.org/>

# Preserving the Fabric of Our Lives: A Survey of Web Preservation Initiatives

Michael Day

UKOLN, University of Bath, Bath BA2 7AY, United Kingdom
m.day@ukoln.ac.uk

**Abstract.** This paper argues that the growing importance of the World Wide Web means that Web sites are key candidates for digital preservation. After an brief outline of some of the main reasons why the preservation of Web sites can be problematic, a review of selected Web archiving initiatives shows that most current initiatives are based on combinations of three main approaches: automatic harvesting, selection and deposit. The paper ends with a discussion of issues relating to collection and access policies, software, costs and preservation.

## 1   Introduction

In a relatively short period of time, the Internet has become a pervasive communication medium. For example, Castells opens his book on *The Internet Galaxy* by saying, "the Internet is the fabric of our lives" [1]. Of the many tools that make-up the Internet, perhaps the most widely used is the World Wide Web.

The Web now plays a major role in research, e.g., being used as a medium for the dissemination of information about institutions and research projects, and as a means of distributing data, publications, learning resources, etc. The Web is also used to provide user-friendly interfaces to a wide range of important databases, e.g. of bibliographic or sequence data, many of which predate the Web itself. Hendler has accurately written that scientists have become "increasingly reliant" on the Web for supporting their research. For example, he notes that the "Web is used for finding preprints and papers in online repositories, for participating in online discussions at sites such as Science Online, for accessing databases through specialized Web interfaces, and even for ordering scientific supplies" [2].

The Web is also now widely used in non-research contexts. It has developed very rapidly as a major facilitator of personal communication, electronic commerce, publishing, marketing, and much else. Since its inception, the Web has seen the development of new types of online commerce (e.g., companies like eBay or Amazon.com) as well as a major move by existing organisations (e.g., the news media, television companies, retailers, etc.) to develop a significant presence on the Web. On a smaller scale, many individuals have begun to use services like GeoCities (http://geocities.yahoo.com/) to create Web pages that focus on their personal interests and hobbies, e.g. for genealogy. In summary, the Web's importance can be

T. Koch and I.T. Sølvberg (Eds.): ECDL 2003, LNCS 2769, pp. 461–472, 2003.

gauged by Lyman's recent comment that it has become "the information source of first resort for millions of readers" [3]. For this reason, the preservation of Web sites has begun to be addressed by a variety of different initiatives.

UKOLN undertook a survey of existing Web archiving initiatives as part of a feasibility study carried out for the Joint Information Systems Committee (JISC) of the UK further and higher education funding councils and the Library of the Wellcome Trust [4]. After a brief description of some of the main problems with collecting and preserving the Web, this paper outlines the key findings of this survey.

# 2    Problems with Web Archiving

There are a number of reasons why the Web or Web sites can be difficult to collect and preserve. Some of these are technical, e.g. related to the size and nature of the Web itself, while others are related to legal or organisational issues.

## 2.1    Technical Challenges

One general problem is that the Web is huge and still growing. This means that no single organisation can realistically hope to collect the entire Web for preservation. Until now, the Internet Archive has attempted to do this, but in the longer term Web preservation will be best seen as a collaborative activity. Estimates of Web size and growth rates vary, but all agree that the Web has until now demonstrated a consistent year on year growth. Rapid growth rates are attested by studies undertaken in the late 1990s at the NEC Research Institute [5, 6], by a survey undertaken in 2000 by Cyveillance [7] and by the annual statistics on Web server numbers collected by the Web Characterization Project of OCLC Research (http://wcp.oclc.org/). In 2000, Lyman and Varian collated these (and other) figures and concluded that the total amount of information on the 'surface Web' was somewhere between 25 and 50 terabytes [8]. It is likely to be far larger by now.

It is worth pointing out that these figures hide a large proportion of the Web. In 2001, Bar-Ilan pointed out that size estimates of the Web only tended to count "static pages, freely accessible to search engines and Web users" [9]. A large number of other pages were not so accessible; chiefly those created dynamically from databases, or with other accessibility barriers (e.g., with password protection) or format problems. A much-cited paper produced by the search company BrightPlanet estimated that this subset of the Web - sometimes known as the 'invisible,' 'hidden' or 'deep Web' - could be up to 400 to 500 times bigger than the surface Web [10].

Another potential problem is the Web's dynamic nature, meaning that many pages, sites and domains are continually changing or disappearing. In 2001, Lawrence, et al. cited an Alexa Internet (http://www.alexa.com/) estimate that Web pages disappear on average after 75 days [11]. This rate of decay means that, without some form of collection and preservation, there is a danger that invaluable scholarly, cultural and scientific resources will be unavailable to future generations. The process of change often leaves no trace. Casey has commented that she got the impression that "a significant percentage of Web sites have the life span of a housefly and about as much chance as meeting an untimely end" [12]. A major concern has been the Web sites of major events, e.g. political elections or sporting events. Colin Webb of the National Library of Australia (NLA) noted that much of the Web presence associated with the Sydney Olympic Games in 2000 disappeared almost faster than the athletes themselves [13].

A further set of problems relates to the ongoing evolution of Web-based technologies. While some basic Web standards and protocols have remained relatively stable since the 1990s, there have been major changes in the way some Web sites are managed. For example, Web content is increasingly beginning to be delivered from dynamic databases. Some of these may be extremely difficult to replicate in repositories without detailed documentation about database structures and the software used. Other sites may use specific software that may not be widely available, or may adopt non-standard features that may not work in all browsers. All of this provides technical challenges for those wishing to collect and preserve Web sites.

It is perhaps also worth emphasising that the Web is also a 'moving-target' for preservation purposes. In the near future, there are likely to be changes as the Web evolves to take account of the W3C's vision of a 'Semantic Web,' whereby information is given well-defined meanings, so that machines can begin to understand it, and process it accordingly (http://www.w3c.org/2001/sw/). Other drivers of change will be the development of Web services technology for business to business activity and the continued adoption of computational grid technologies by scientists.

## 2.2   Legal Challenges

Some of the most significant challenges to Web archiving initiatives are legal ones, chiefly related to copyright or liability for content made available through archives. As part of the JISC/Wellcome Trust feasibility study, Charlesworth undertook a detailed survey of the legal issues related to the collection and preservation of Internet resources [14]. This noted that the legal environment in many countries is unappreciative of - or sometimes inhospitable to - the potential role of Web archives. While the most obvious legal problem relates to copyright law, there are also potential problems with defamation, content liability and data protection. The 'safest' way of overcoming these challenges would be to select resources carefully - thus excluding at source those resources that may have liability problems - and to develop effective rights management policies, combined with effective processes for the removal of (or the limiting of access to) certain types of material.

## 2.3   Organisational Challenges

The Web developed in a decentralised way. There is, therefore, no single organisation (or set of organisations) that can be held responsible for the Web. It has no governing body that can mandate the adoption of standards or Web site preservation policies.

Instead, most decisions about Web content and delivery are devolved down to Web site owners themselves. Bollacker, Lawrence and Giles point out that "the Web database draws from many sources, each with its own organization" [15].

With the exception of the Internet Archive, Web preservation initiatives tend to focus on defined subsets of the Web, e.g. by national domain, subject or organisation type. Those cultural heritage organisations interested in the preservation of the Web tend to approach it from their own professional perspective. Archives will be interested in the recordkeeping aspects of Web sites, art galleries in conserving artworks that use Web technologies, historical data archives in those sites considered to have long-term social or political importance, etc. Some national libraries have provided a slightly wider perspective, for example, viewing a whole national Web domain (however defined) as suitable for collection and preservation. In practice, this decentralised approach to Web archiving may prove useful, although it will need significant co-operation to avoid duplication and to help facilitate user access to what could become a confusing mess of different initiatives and repositories.

Another general issue is quality. While the Web contains much that would definitely be considered to have continuing value, (e.g., the outputs of scholarly and scientific research, the Web sites of political parties, etc.), there is much other content that is of low-quality (or even worse). Chakrabarti, et al. note that each Web page might "range from a few characters to a few hundred thousand, containing truth, falsehood, wisdom, propaganda or sheer nonsense" [16]. A survey of academic opinion in 2001 showed that while there was a general satisfaction with the Web as a research tool, many had significant concerns about accuracy, reliability and value of the information available [17].

## 3  Web Archiving Initiatives

At the present time, there are a variety of different organisation types pursuing Web archiving initiatives. These have been initiated by archives, national libraries, historical data archives and even some Web site owners themselves (e.g., the British Broadcasting Corporation). Perhaps the most ambitious and well-known Web archiving initiative at the moment is that run by the US-based Internet Archive [18]. This privately funded organisation has been collecting Web pages since 1996 and has generated a huge database of Web pages that can be accessed via the 'Wayback Machine' as well as co-operating with the Library of Congress and the Smithsonian Institution on the creation of special collections.

National Libraries are responsible for some of the more visible and successful Web archiving initiatives. Following the early examples of the Swedish and Australian national libraries, pilot Web archiving initiatives have now been launched in many other countries, including Austria, Denmark, Finland, France, Germany, Iceland, New Zealand, the United States and the United Kingdom. A survey by Hallgrímsson of European national libraries in late 2002 and early 2003 showed that 15 out of the 25 libraries that responded had some kind of Web-archiving initiative underway [19]. In some countries (e.g., France) some of the intellectual property rights issues have been dealt with by including Web archiving amongst the national library's legal deposit responsibilities. Other national library initiatives, following the example of the National Library of Australia in the PANDORA archive, seek permission from Web site owners before adding them to the library's collections.

National archives have also begun to get involved in the collection and preservation of Web sites, especially where Web sites are understood to have evidential value. Sometimes this interest manifests itself in the form of guidance for Web managers. For example, the National Archives of Australia [20, 21] and the Public Record Office (now the National Archives) in the UK [22] have each issued detailed electronic records management (ERM) guidelines for Web site managers. Some other archives have already begun to capture and accession Web sites. For example, the US National Archives and Records Administration (NARA) arranged for all federal agencies to take a 'snapshot' of their public Web sites at the end of the Clinton Administration for deposit with their Electronic and Special Media Records Services Division [23]. In the UK, the Public Record Office (PRO) accessioned a snapshot of the No. 10 Downing Street Web site (http://www.number-10.gov.uk/) just before the General Election of June 2001. Ryan has described some of the technical problems that the PRO had with migrating the Web site so that it could work in a different technical environment [24].

Some universities and scholarly societies have supported smaller Web archiving initiatives. These include the Archipol project (http://www.archipol.nl/), dedicated to the collection of Dutch political Web sites, and the Occasio archive of Internet newsgroups gathered by the Dutch International Institute of Social History (http://www.iisg.nl/occasio/).

## 3.1   Approaches to the Collection of Web Sites

Currently, there are three main approaches to the collection of Web sites. The first of these is based on the deployment of *automatic harvesting* or gathering tools, generally utilising Web crawler technologies. The second is based on the *selection and capture* of individual Web sites. The third approach is based on a more traditional *deposit* model.

### Automatic harvesting approaches

The Internet Archive (http://www.archive.org/) and the Swedish Royal Library's Kulturarw[3] project (http://www.kb.se/kw3/) were amongst the first to adopt the automatic harvesting approach. In this, Web crawler programs - similar to those used by Web search services - are used to follow links and download content according to particular collection rules. The Kulturarw[3] crawler, for example, is set-up to only collect Web sites in the .se domain, those sites physically located in Sweden, and sites in other domains selected for their relevance to Sweden [25]. The Internet Archive collects the Web on a much broader scale, but their crawlers will not harvest sites (or parts of them) protected by the robot exclusion protocol. A number of other national-based initiatives have followed the automatic approach, most notably the

Helsinki University Library in its experiments with the NEDLIB harvester [26] and the Austrian On-Line Archive (AOLA) [27].

## Selective capture approaches

Some initiatives have taken a much more selective strategy based on the selection of individual Web sites for inclusion in an archive. This was the general approach pioneered by the National Library of Australia (NLA) with the development of its PANDORA archive (http://pandora.nla.gov.au/). This was initiated in 1997 with the development of a 'proof-of-concept' archive and a conceptual framework for a sustainable service. Sites are first selected according to the NLA's selection guidelines and the appropriate rights negotiated with their owners. Once this has been agreed, the sites are collected using gathering or mirroring tools. If this is not possible, the national library makes arrangements with the site owner to receive the files on physical media or via ftp or e-mail. The general selection criteria for PANDORA include the resource's relevance to Australia (regardless of physical location), its 'authority' and perceived long-term research value. There are more 'inclusive' selection guidelines for particular social and topical issues and specific ones for particular types of material (http://pandora.nla.gov.au/selectionguidelines.html). The NLA has also developed a suite of software tools known as the PANDORA Digital Archiving System (PANDAS) that can initiate the gathering process, create and manage metadata, undertake quality control and manage access to gathered resources. The selective approach has also been experimented with by the Library of Congress in its Minerva project [28] and the British Library for the 'Britain on the Web' pilot.

## Deposit approaches

Deposit approaches are based on site owners or administrators depositing a copy or snapshot of their site in a repository. This is a strategy used, for example, by NARA for its collection of US federal agency Web sites in 2001 and by Die Deutsche Bibliothek (DDB) for the collection of dissertations and some online publications (http://deposit.ddb.de/).

## Combined approaches

There has been some discussion as to which one of the three approaches is best. In practice, however, they all have advantages and disadvantages.

The deposit approach, for example, may work in particular situations where there is agreement with depositors and where the incremental cost of deposit (to the depositors) is not too expensive. Supporters of the automatic crawler-based approach argue that it is by far the cheapest way to collect Web content. Thus Mannerheim notes that, "it is a fact that the selective projects use more staff than the comprehensive ones" [29]. However, the current generation of Web crawler technologies cannot cope with some database-driven sites and can sometimes run into difficulty with items that need browser plug-ins or use scripting techniques. The selective approach allows more time to address and rectify these problems but limits the range of resources that can be collected. For some of these reasons, some initiatives are increasingly emphasising the need to use a combination of approaches. The pioneer of this approach has been the Bibliothèque nationale de France (BnF), which has investigated the preservation of the 'French Web' as part of its responsibilities for the legal deposit of French publications.

The French initiative has, for example, experimented with refining the automatic harvesting approach by taking account of a Web page's change frequency and by attempting to measure site importance automatically:

- Change frequency - the French Web crawling experiments collected information about when each page was retrieved and whether there had been any updating. This information was then stored in an XML-based 'site-delta' that could be used to judge the required frequency of crawl [30].
- Page importance - this can be calculated in a similar way to that used by search services like Google [31]. The BnF regards the automatic calculation of page importance based on link structures as a way of focusing attention on the part of the Web that is most well-used. An initial evaluation, comparing a sample of automated rankings with evaluations of site relevance by library staff, showed a good degree of correlation [32].

The BnF have also proposed a selective strategy for the collection of the 'deep Web' - known as the 'deposit track.' This follows a similar approach to PANDORA, and is based on the evaluation of sites by library staff followed by liaison with site owners over their deposit into the library. The BnF undertook a pilot project to test this approach in 2002. The BnF notes that Web harvesting technologies may have some uses in helping to support the deposit track. For example, robots can be used to analyse the technical features of crawled material, helping to detect deep-Web sites for which selective attention may be required.

# 4   Discussion

The survey of Web archiving initiatives looked in particular at a number of issues of relevance to the feasibility study. These included collection and access policies, software, relative costs and sustainability.

## 4.1   Collection Policies and Coverage

Both automatic harvesting-based and selective approaches to Web archiving are dependent to some extent upon the development of collection policies. The automatic approaches will usually define this by national domain and server location, supplemented by a list of other sites that have been individually judged to be of interest. In some cases, sites can be automatically excluded from the collection process, e.g. by taking account of standards for robot exclusion. Selective approaches will normally develop more detailed collection guidelines, often based on a resource's relevance to the collecting institution's designated communities, their provenance or their suitability for long-term research. Sites that change frequently may have to be collected on a regular basis. In addition, many of the Web sites that meet selection guidelines on other criteria may include errors, be incomplete or have broken links. The collecting institution will need to decide whether these 'features' are an essential part of the resource being collected and act accordingly. Once a site loses its active hyperlinks with the rest of the Web, it will be very difficult to evaluate whether these links were working at the time of collection. Whether this is a problem will depend on whether the Web site is being preserved for its informational or evidential value.

Table 4.1 is an attempt to show the relative size (in Gigabytes) of selected Web-archives as of late 2002 and early 2003. Although the figures are approximate and do not take into account things like compression or crawl frequency, it shows that those initiatives based on automatic harvesting have normally resulted in collections that are considerably larger than those using the selective approach. As may be expected, the initiative with the largest collection is the Internet Archive with over 150 tera-bytes of data (and growing). While the largest of the selective archives (PANDORA) has a size not dissimilar to two of the smaller harvesting-based archives (Austria and Finland), by comparison, the British Library and Library of Congress pilot archives are extremely small.

**Table 1.** Approximate size of selected Web-archiving initiatives, 2002

| Country | Initiative/Organisation | Approach | Size (Gb.) | No. sites |
|---|---|---|---|---|
| International | Internet Archive | harvesting | > 150,000.00 | |
| Sweden | Kulturarw3 | harvesting | 4,500.00 | |
| France | Bibliothèque nationale de France | combined | < 1,000.00 | |
| Austria | AOLA | harvesting | 448.00 | |
| Australia | PANDORA | selective | 405.00 | 3,300 |
| Finland | Helsinki University Library | harvesting | 401.00 | |
| UK | Britain on the Web | selective | 0.03 | 100 |
| USA | MINERVA | selective | | 35 |

Source: Day, 2003 [4]

## 4.2   Access Policies

More thought needs to be given to how access is provided to the large databases that can be generated by the automatic harvesting approach. The Internet Archive's Way-back Machine is a useful and interesting 'window' on the old Web, but currently users need to know the exact URLs that they are looking for before they can really begin to use it. Alternative approaches to access might involve the generation or reuse of metadata or the development of specialised Web indexes designed to search extremely large databases of Web material, possibly including multiple versions of pages harvested at different times. From 2000 to 2002, the Nordic Web Archive Access project (NWA) investigated the issue of access to collections of Web documents [33]. The result was an open-source NWA Toolset (http://nwa.nb.no/) that searches and navigates Web document collections. The current version of the NWA Toolset supports a commercial search engine provided by the Norwegian company FAST (http://www.fastsearch.com/).

## 4.3  Software

Specific software tools have been developed or adapted to support both collecting approaches. The Swedish Royal Library's Kulturarw³ initiative adapted the Combine crawler [34], while other countries have used or evaluated the NEDLIB harvester developed by the Finnish CSC [26]. The experiments at the BnF tested the Xyleme crawler for Web collection. The Internet Archive uses the Alexa crawler, and this software is completely rewritten every other year.

The selective approach has seen the use of a variety of site mirroring and harvesting tools. PANDORA started using Harvest, but currently has adopted a twin approach, using HTTrack and Teleport Pro/Exec. The British Library, the Library of Congress and the BnF have also used HTTrack in their pilot projects. The NLA have themselves developed an archive management system called PANDAS to help facilitate the collection process, to deal with metadata and quality control, and to manage access. This has had a significant impact by increasing automation and tools for these processes and consequently reducing staff time and costs incurred.

## 4.4  Costs

Costs between the initiatives vary widely. Arms, *et al.*, have estimated that the selective approach - as carried out in the Library of Congress's Minerva pilot - is "at least 100 times as expensive as bulk collection" on the Internet Archive model [28]. In addition it should be recognised that a significant element of the additional cost of the selective approach can be incurred in undertaking rights clearances. However, although this approach has additional costs, it does allow many materials gathered in this way (for example in PANDORA), to be made publicly accessible from the archive via the Web. This generates substantially higher use and gives wider accessibility than other methods.

## 4.5  Long-Term Preservation

Many current Web archiving initiatives have been, until now, focused on the collection of resources rather than on their long-term preservation. In the short to medium-term, there is nothing wrong with this, but there remains a need to consider how those Web sites being collected at the moment can be preserved over time, and what this may mean. This may include assessments of various proposed preservation strategies (migration, emulation, etc.) and the implementation of repositories based, for example, on the standard *Reference Model for an Open Archival Information System (OAIS)* [35]. One key issue for repositories will be how to ensure the authenticity of digital objects, i.e. to verify that they are exactly what they (or their metadata) claim to be [36]. This may be dependent on cryptographic techniques applied by the repository or by the encapsulation of objects in descriptive metadata. What is clear, however, is that in many cases the nature of the repository itself will serve as a surrogate for an object's authenticity. So, for example, Hirtle has said, "the fact that digital information is found within a trusted repository may become the base upon which all further assessment of action builds" [37].

Ways of defining trusted repositories have recently been investigated by a working group established by the Research Libraries Group (RLG) and OCLC. In 2002, this group published a report outlining a framework of attributes and responsibilities of trusted digital repositories. Trusted repositories are defined as "one whose mission is to provide reliable, long-term access to managed digital resources to its designated community, now and in the future" [38]. The report defines the key attributes of such repositories (e.g. organisational viability and financial sustainability) and outlines their main responsibilities. The working group further recommended that a framework should be developed in order to support the certification of digital repositories. The RLG together with NARA is currently setting up a task force to undertake this (http://www.rlg.org/longterm/certification.html).

Web archiving initiatives need to be aware of the requirements for becoming trusted digital repositories. Those that are now essentially project-type activities will need to be become firmly embedded into the core activities of their host institutions and have sustainable business models. In this regard, it is encouraging to note how many of the current initiatives have been funded from the host organisations' own budgets.

## 5   Conclusions

It is hoped that this short review of existing Web archiving initiatives has demonstrated that collecting and preserving Web sites is an interesting area of research and development that has now begun to move into a more practical implementation phase. To date, there have been three main approaches to collection, characterised in this report as 'automatic harvesting,' 'selection' and 'deposit.' Which one of these has been implemented has normally depended upon the exact purpose of the archive and the resources available. Naturally, there are some overlaps between these approaches but the current consensus is that a combination of them will enable their relative strengths to be utilised. The longer-term preservation issues of Web archiving have been explored in less detail.

**Acknowledgements.** This paper is based on work undertaken for a feasibility study into Web-archiving undertaken for the Joint Information Systems Committee and the Library of the Wellcome Trust. UKOLN is funded by the JISC and Resource: The Council for Museums, Archives & Libraries, as well as by project funding from the JISC and the European Union. UKOLN also receives support from the University of Bath, where it is based.

## References

1.   Castells, M.: The Internet galaxy: reflections on the Internet, business, and society. Oxford University Press, Oxford (2001)
2.   Hendler, J.: Science and the Semantic Web. Science **299** (2003) 520–521

3. Lyman, P.: Archiving the World Wide Web. In: Building a national strategy for digital preservation. Council on Library and Information Resources and Library of Congress, Washington, D.C. (2002) 38–51 http://www.clir.org/pubs/abstract/pub106abst.html

4. Day, M.: Collecting and preserving the World Wide Web: a feasibility study undertaken for the JISC and Wellcome Trust (February 2003) http://library.wellcome.ac.uk/projects/archiving_feasibility.pdf

5. Lawrence, S., Giles, C.L.: Searching the World Wide Web. Science **280** (1998) 98–100

6. Lawrence, S., Giles, C.L.: Accessibility of information on the Web. Nature **400** (1999) 107–109

7. Murray, B., Moore, A.: Sizing the Internet. Cyveillance White Paper. Cyveillance, Inc. (10 July 2000) http://www.cyveillance.com/web/downloads/Sizing_the_Internet.pdf

8. Lyman, P., Varian, H.R.: How much information? University of California at Berkeley, School of Information Management and Systems, Berkeley, Calif. (2000) http://www.sims.berkeley.edu/research/projects/how-much-info/internet.html

9. Bar-Ilan, J.: Data collection methods on the Web for informetric purposes: a review and analysis. Scientometrics **50** (2001) 7–32

10. Bergman, M.K.: The deep Web: surfacing hidden value. Journal of Electronic Publishing **7** (August 2001). Available at: http://www.press.umich.edu/jep/07-01/bergman.html

11. Lawrence, S., Pennock, D.M., Flake, G.W., Krovetz, R., Coetzee, F.M., Glover, E., Nielsen, F.Å, Kruger, A., Giles, C.L.: Persistence of Web references in scientific research. Computer **34** (February 2001) 26–31

12. Casey, C.: The cyberarchive: a look at the storage and preservation of Web sites. College & Research Libraries **59** (1998) 304–310

13. Webb, C.: Who will save the Olympics? OCLC/Preservation Resources Symposium, Digital Past, Digital Future: an Introduction to Digital Preservation, OCLC, Dublin, Ohio (15 June 2001) http://www.oclc.org/events/presentations/symposium/preisswebb.shtm

14. Charlesworth, A.: A study of legal issues related to the preservation of Internet resources in the UK, EU, USA and Australia (February 2003) http://library.wellcome.ac.uk/projects/archiving_legal.pdf

15. Bollacker, K.D., Lawrence, S., Giles, C.L.: Discovering relevant scientific literature on the Web. IEEE Intelligent Systems **15** (2000) 42–47

16. Chakrabarti, S., Dom, B.E., Kumar, S.R., Raghavan, P., Rajagopalan, S., Tomkins, A., Kleinberg, J., Gibson, D.: Hypersearching the Web. Scientific American **280** (June 1999) 44–52

17. Herring, S.D.: Using the World Wide Web for research: are faculty satisfied? Journal of Academic Librarianship **27** (2001) 213–219

18. Kahle, B.: Way back when ... New Scientist **176** (23 November 2002) 46–49

19. Hallgrímsson, T.: Survey of Web archiving in Europe. E-mail sent to list web-archive@cru.fr (3 February 2003)

20. National Archives of Australia: Archiving Web resources: a policy for keeping records of Web-based activity in the Commonwealth Government (January 2001) http://www.naa.gov.au/recordkeeping/er/web_records/archweb _policy.pdf

21. National Archives of Australia: Archiving Web resources: guidelines for keeping records of Web-based activity in the Commonwealth Government (March 2001) http://www.naa.gov.au/recordkeeping/er/web_records/archweb _guide.pdf

22. Public Record Office: Managing Web resources: management of electronic records on Websites and Intranets: an ERM toolkit, v. 1.0 (December 2001)

23. Bellardo, L.J.: Memorandum to Chief Information Officers: snapshot of public Web sites. National Archives & Records Administration, Washington, D.C. (12 January 2001) http://www.archives.gov/records_management/cio_link/memo_to_cios.html

24. Ryan, D.: Preserving the No 10 Web site: the story so far. Web-archiving: managing and archiving online documents, DPC Forum, London (25 March 2002) http://www.jisc.ac. uk/dner/preservation/presentations/pdf/Ryan.pdf

25. Arvidson, A., Persson, K., Mannerheim, J.: The Royal Swedish Web Archive: a "complete" collection of Web pages. International Preservation News **26** (December 2001) 10–12 http://www.ifla.org/VI/4/news/ipnn26.pdf

26. Hakala, J.: The NEDLIB Harvester. Zeitschrift für Bibliothekswesen und Bibliographie **48** (2001) 211–216

27. Rauber, A., Aschenbrenner, A., Witvoet, O.: Austrian Online Archive processing: analyzing archives of the World Wide Web. In: Agosti, M., Thanos, C. (eds.): Research and advanced technology for digital libraries: 6th European conference, ECDL 2002, Rome, Italy, September 16–18, 2002. Lecture Notes in Computer Science, Vol. 2458. Springer-Verlag, Berlin (2002) 16–31

28. Arms, W.Y., Adkins, R., Ammen, C., Hayes, A.: Collecting and preserving the Web: the Minerva prototype. RLG DigiNews, **5** (April 2001) http://www.rlg.org/preserv/diginews/ diginews5-2.html#feature1

29. Mannerheim, J.: The new preservation tasks of the library community. International Preservation News **26** (December 2001) 5–9 http://www.ifla.org/VI/4/news/ipnn26.pdf

30. Abiteboul, S., Cobéna, G., Masanès, J., Sedrati, G.: A first experience in archiving the French Web. In: Agosti, M., Thanos, C. (eds.): Research and advanced technology for digital libraries: 6th European conference, ECDL 2002, Rome, Italy, September 16–18, 2002. Lecture Notes in Computer Science, Vol. 2458. Springer-Verlag, Berlin (2002) 1–15

31. Brin, S., Page, L.: The anatomy of a large-scale hypertextual Web search engine. Computer Networks and ISDN Systems **30** (1998) 107–117

32. Masanès, J.: Towards continuous Web archiving: first results and an agenda for the future. D-Lib Magazine **8** (December 2002) http://www.dlib.org/dlib/december02/masanes/ 12masanes.html

33. Brygfjeld, S.A.: Access to Web archives: the Nordic Web Archive Access Project. Zeitschrift für Bibliothekswesen und Bibliographie **49** (2002) 227–231

34. Ardö, A., Lundberg, S.: A regional distributed WWW search and indexing service - the DESIRE way. Computer Networks and ISDN Systems **30** (1998) 173–183

35. CCSDS 650.0-B-1: Reference Model for an Open Archival Information System (OAIS). Consultative Committee on Space Data Systems (2002) http://wwwclassic.ccsds.org/ documents/pdf/CCSDS-650.0-B-1.pdf

36. Lynch, C.: Authenticity and integrity in the digital environment: an exploratory analysis of the central role of trust. In: Authenticity in a digital environment. Council on Library and Information Resources, Washington, D.C. (2000) 32–50 http://www.clir.org/pubs/abstract/ pub92abst.html

37. Hirtle, P.B: Archival authenticity in a digital age. In: Authenticity in a digital environment. Council on Library and Information Resources, Washington, D.C., (2000) 8–23 http://www.clir.org/pubs/abstract/ pub92abst.html

38. RLG/OCLC Working Group on Digital Archive Attributes: Trusted digital repositories: attributes and responsibilities (2002) http://www.rlg.org/longterm/repositories.pdf

# Implementing Preservation Strategies for Complex Multimedia Objects

Jane Hunter[1] and Sharmin Choudhury[2]

[1]DSTC, Brisbane Australia
jane@dstc.edu.au
[2]ITEE Dept. University of Queensland, Brisbane Australia
sharminc@dstc.edu.au

**Abstract.** Addressing the preservation and long-term access issues for digital resources is one of the key challenges facing informational organisations such as libraries, archives, cultural institutions and government agencies today. A number of major initiatives and projects have been established to investigate or develop strategies for preserving the burgeoning amounts of digital content being produced. To date, the alternative preservation approaches have been based on emulation, migration and metadata - or some combination of these. Most of the work has focussed on digital objects of a singular media type: text, HTML, images, video or audio and to date few usable tools have been developed to support or implement such strategies or policies. In this paper we consider the preservation of composite, mixed-media, objects, a rapidly growing class of resources. Using three exemplars of new media artwork as case studies, we describe the optimum preservation strategies that we have determined for each exemplar and the software tools that we have developed to support and implement those strategies.

## 1 Introduction and Objectives

A number of major initiatives have been established to tackle the problem of preservation of digital content. The US Congress recently appropriated $100 million to the Library of Congress to establish a National Digital Information Infrastructure and Preservation Program (NDIIPP) [1]. The program has begun by reviewing the current state of digital preservation. In 2002, it commissioned a series of essays by recognized experts on the preservation of: Web sites, electronic journals, electronic books, digitally recorded sound, digital moving images and digital television. [2]. Other initiatives such as the CEDARS project [3], CAMiLEON [4], the National Library of Australia's PANDORA project [5,6], Networked European Deposits Library (NEDLIB) [7] and the OCLC/RLG Working Group on Preservation Metadata [8] have all been investigating strategies for the preservation of digital content. These initiatives have been focusing on three main strategies: emulation, migration and metadata - or some amalgam of these which relies on the encapsulation of the digital object with detailed preservation metadata. In addition, these initiatives have all been focussing on digital objects of one particular media type e.g., web sites (HTML), electronic journals, electronic books, digitally recorded sound and digital moving images. The work we describe here focuses on the problem of preserving composite digital objects consisting of multiple media types.

Only recently have a couple of mixed-media preservation initiatives emerged from arts organizations and museums, wanting to preserve multimedia, new media or

T. Koch and I.T. Sølvberg (Eds.): ECDL 2003, LNCS 2769, pp. 473–486, 2003.

variable media artworks in their collections. For example, *Archiving the Avant Garde* [9] is a collaborative preservation project between the Berkeley Art Museum and Pacific Film Archive (BAM/PFA), the Solomon R. Guggenheim Museum, the Walker Art Center, Rhizome.org, the Franklin Furnace Archive, and the Cleveland Performance Art Festival and Archive. The Guggenheim Museum has also established the Variable Media Initiative [10] which is inviting media artists, curators, and museum specialists to a series of meetings to brainstorm strategies for preserving specific case study works in the Guggenheim collection.

The main outcome (to date) of the *Archiving the Avant Garde* project has been a Variable Media Questionnaire [11], a set of descriptive elements to be completed by the artist and collector, outlining the parameters for recreating the work in a new medium once the original medium is obsolete, including whether such an option is allowed or prohibited by the artist. In addition, they are investigating the development of hardware and software emulators to enable the preservation of digital artworks, originally developed on hardware and software which has become obsolete.

Rothenberg [12] argues that emulating hardware is cost effective because, once a platform has been emulated, that emulator can be used to run any software written for that platform. However he also admits there are problems with emulation: future users will need to know how to run obsolete software, so we may need use-copies for non-scholarly access to documents; we may have to emulate more than hardware; and emulation requires an emulator specification and environment per platform, which is an ambitious goal. A number of other authors have also outlined the problems associated with using emulation as a preservation strategy [13]. Problems include cost, which may be prohibitive because of issues associated with intellectual property rights. David Bearman [14] also has problems with emulation, suggesting that it would not preserve electronic records as evidence even if it could be made to work and is serious overkill for most electronic documents. He argues that Rothenberg, a major proponent of emulation, is concentrating too much on the functionality of computer systems, and not enough on the actual content of records.

Although we believe that emulation may be the optimum approach for certain multimedia/new media objects - particularly those objects dynamically generated by software programs - we also believe that there exists a large class of multimedia objects for which emulation is not the best strategy. In particular, for those multimedia objects composed of multiple audio and video channels, images, text and even physical objects combined in some spatio-temporal structure, we propose an approach based on a combination of metadata and migration to high quality, platform-independent, standardized formats. More specifically we propose the following preservation steps:

1. Store the multimedia object's components in formats which are as high quality, standardized and platform-independent as possible (e.g., MPEG-2, MP3, TIFF) and the complete object in a simple structural markup such as SMIL [15] or HTML+TIME [16] rather than Shockwave, Flash etc.;
2. Record sufficient descriptive, structural, administrative and technical metadata to interpret and display the canonicalized object;
3. Use METS [17] (the Library of Congress's Metadata Encoding and Transmission Standard) to encapsulate the platform-independent digital object with its

descriptive, administrative, technical and structural metadata, into a complete preservation package;

4. Update the links to the required software/technical requirements as required;
5. Only reformat on request – not automatically and only migrate those objects deemed to be of significant value and hence requiring preservation.

In the remainder of this paper we investigate the optimum preservation strategies for a number of case studies and present the results of our investigations. The remainder of the paper is structured as follows. The next section describes related initiatives and projects and outlines how the work described here differs from and builds upon these approaches. Section 3 describes three case studies. Section 4 provides details of the actual software tools which we developed to support the identified preservation strategies and Section 5 concludes with a discussion of problem issues and future work.

## 2  Background

Most of the literature regarding digital preservation refers to three main strategies:
1. Technical Preservation - maintaining the original software, and sometimes hardware, of the original operating environment.
2. Emulation - re-creating the original operating environment by programming future platforms and operating systems to emulate the original environment.
3. Migration - transferring digital information to new platforms before the earlier one becomes obsolete.

The first strategy is not considered to to be a realistic or viable solution. The two main contenders have been emulation and migration. However recent research [3,4] recommends an amalgam of these strategies which relies on the preservation of both the original bytestream as well as detailed metadata which will enable it to be interpreted in the future. In the next subsections we analyse each of these approaches.

### 2.1  Emulation

Jeff Rothenberg [18,19], is the principle proponent of the emulation method - in which one saves not just the data but also the program that was used to create/manipulate the information in the first place. Rothenberg suggests that the only way to decode the bit stream would be to run the old program, which would require the use of an emulator. Several different methods for defining how an emulator can be specified have been suggested, but the feasibility of these methods has not yet been fully demonstrated.

The emulation approach suffers from two major drawbacks:

1. Saving the original program is justifiable for re-enacting the behaviour of a program, but it is overkill for data archiving. In order to archive a collection of pictures, it is hardly necessary to save the full system that enabled the original user to create, modify, and enhance pictures when only the final result is of interest for posterity.
2. The original program generally shows the data (and more often, results derived from the data) in one particular output form. The program does not make the data

accessible; it is therefore impossible to export the original data from the old system to a new one.

Lorie [20,21] suggests an approach which relies only partially on emulation by differentiating between data archiving, which does not require full emulation, and program archiving, which does. Lorie's approach relies on a Universal Virtual Computer (UVC). For data archiving the UVC can extract the data from the bit stream and return it to the caller in an understandable way, so that it may be exported to a new system. To archive a program's behaviour, emulation cannot be avoided and the UVC will emulate the current computer when interpreted on a future one.

## 2.2   Migration

*Migration* is the most commonly applied approach for digital preservation. It involves converting a document from its original format into successive subsequent formats as each previous format becomes obsolete. The disadvantages of migration are that it is highly labour-intensive and that in some situations, it may either corrupt or alter the appearance, structure, meaning or behaviour of a digital resource. The advantage is that in the majority of cases it extends the longevity of a digital resource, at least until the new format becomes obsolete.

The CAMILEON project has developed an alternative approach, called *Migration on Request* [22]. The investigators claim that by maintaining the original bytestream along with a tool to migrate the object at the point of use, the preservation strategy can be more accurate and cost effective. However the task of actually writing the migration tool may be extremely difficult, time consuming and expensive and many different tools may need to be developed.

## 2.3   Preservation Metadata

Most metadata initiatives (Dublin Core, MPEG-7, IMS) have focussed on facilitating resource discovery through standardized resource descriptions. Although such metadata standards are important to avoid a completely chaotic repository of information on the Web, they do not guarantee continual long-term access to digital resources. Hence a number of initiatives have been focussing on the use of metadata to support the digital preservation process. Such initiatives include: Reference Model for an Open Archival Information System (OAIS) [23], the CURL Exemplars in Digital Archives project (CEDARS) [3], the National Library of Australia's (NLA) PANDORA project [5], the Networked European Deposit Library (NEDLIB) [7] and the Online Computer Library Centre/Research Libraries Group (OCLC/RLG) Working Group on Preservation Metadata [8]. These initiatives rely on the preservation of both the original bytestream or digital object, as well as detailed metadata which will enable it to be interpreted in the future.

The preservation metadata provides sufficient technical information about the resources to support either migration or emulation. Metadata can facilitate the long-term access of the digital resources by providing a complete description of the technical environment needed to view the work, the applications and version numbers needed, decompression schemes, other files that need to be linked to it etc.

However associating appropriate metadata with digital objects will require new workflows and metadata input tools at the points of creation, acquisition, reuse, migration etc.. This will demand effort the first time a particular class of digital resource is received into a collection. However assuming many of the same class of resource are received, economies of scale can be achieved by re-using the same metadata model and input tools.

The Library of Congress's Metadata Encoding and Transmission Standard (METS) [17] schema - provides a flexible mechanism for encoding descriptive, administrative, and structural metadata for a digital library object, and for expressing the complex links between these various forms of metadata. We believe that it may provide a good approach for encapsulating the complex preservation metadata required by multimedia digital objects, such as new media artworks, but that certain extensions to the METS schema may be required. We investigate this hypothesis and possible extensions to METS in sections 3 and 4.

### 2.4   Our Approach

We believe that no single approach is the right one. Each object or class of objects will need to be evaluated on a case-by-case basis and in many cases, the optimum approach will be some combination of emulation or migration together with preservation metadata and will involve the use of METS to wrap the canonicalized digital object and its metadata within a preservation package. However we do believe that optimum storage formats and metadata schemas can be determined for specific classes of objects and that the development of metadata input tools (based on these schemas) and their integration into workflows will facilitate the long term preservation and archival of complex multimedia objects. In the next section we test this hypothesis by considering the optimum preservation strategies for three different exemplars of new media artworks and the software tools which could support the determined strategies.

## 3   Case Studies

We decided to use new media artworks as the case studies for analysing multimedia preservation. This genre represents a significant preservation problem for the following reasons:

- They often comprise a highly heterogeneous mix of many media types: images, video, audio, text, hyperlinks, programs and physical objects;
- They are often highly proprietary - developed on all sorts of hardware platforms using old or eclectic combinations of software;
- They are often fragile and have a very high obsolescence rate;
- Standards are not employed and best practice guides for artists, curators or collectors rarely exist or not used if they do;
- They are often part of a travelling exhibition, requiring frequent deconstruction and reconstruction;
- They often include an element of randomness, chaos or dynamism due to uncontrollable real-time environmental input e.g., Ouija 2000 in which the planchette on a Ouija board is controlled by internet users;

- Art galleries and Museums of Contemporary Art are collecting them in greater numbers and they are often expensive or of significant cultural value.

In the next three sub-sections we consider the preservation of three different types of newmedia art:

1. *Verbum Interactive* - an interactive digital art magazine on CD-ROM;
2. *Eurovision* - a video artwork on VHS; and
3. *The elements* - a new media artwork by Nam June Paik comprising physical objects combined with video monitors and audio speakers in a particular layout.

## 3.1     Verbum Interactive

### 3.1.1     About Verbum

Verbum Interactive is described as a digital art and design CD ROM Magazine. In fact it is claimed to be the world's first fully integrated multimedia magazine. Verbum Interactive combines text, sound, graphics, animations, talking agents, video and music, accessible via a point and click interface. Two CDs make up the magazine: the first CD features stories with on-screen and printable text, sound, video clips and sample multimedia files. The second CD is an interactive panel discussion between six industry leaders on the state of the multimedia industry.

### 3.1.2     The Problem

Verbum Interactive was published in 1991. This edition was developed on a Macintosh Classic and required very specific system configuration to function. When the Macintosh Classic became obsolete so did this edition of Verbum Interactive. The contents of the two CDs became inaccessible and this historically important inaugural interactive multimedia magazine became lost despite the fact that the physical storage medium, the CDs, have not deteriorated.

As no step-wise migration had taken place before the contents of the CD became inaccessible, migration could not be performed. Reinterpretation was also not an option since there was no information regarding the structure of the work or links to the various components of the work to enable reconstruction. This highlights the role that metadata can play in preservation. If preservation information had been recorded, including the location of the various components of text, images and other multimedia files and more importantly the information regarding the structure of the work, then it may have been possible to re-create the work on the latest platform with the original content. However the lack of metadata meant that the only strategy available to us was to attempt to play the CDs on an emulated Macintosh.

### 3.1.3     The Preservation Strategy

The emulator which we used was the Basilisk II, an Open Source 68k Macintosh emulator which enables you to run 68k MacOS software on any computer. However, a copy of MacOS and a Macintosh ROM image was required in order to use Basilisk II [24]. We were able to access approx. two thirds of the original content of Verbum using Basilisk II. Most of the problems that arose were in relation to the first CD. The second CD appeared to be fully accessible. The problems we encountered included:

- When the emulator was set to emulate a MAC OS with optimal setting for the two CD then the animated graphics interfered with the emulation software and the

emulator froze. With less than optimal setting many of the graphics in the CD would not work.
- Certain parts of the first CD could not be accessed because the emulator is not a perfect or complete emulation of the MAC OS system.

An interesting point to note is that Verbum Interactive does contain some information that can be used to reconstruct the CDs, but because the data is stored on the CDs the information is also rendered inaccessible because the CD is inaccessible. Thus it makes sense to store the preservation metadata separate to the actual content and to link or point from the metadata to the content.

## 3.2    Eurovision

### 3.2.1    About Eurovision

Eurovision [25] is a video artwork by Linda Wallace, completed in March 2001, recorded as a PAL format video of length 19.2 minutes. Using video compositing software, Linda Wallace has combined four sequences from the Eurovision song contest with footage from Bergman and Godard films, a Russian documentary about the space race from the 50s/60s, images from the Louvre and icons of the Madonna, with a background music track and overlaid text - in a multi-framed video stream.

### 3.2.2    The Problem

Currently there is no problem accessing this work via any VCR which supports PAL. Ancillary contextual information (metadata) is also available via the associated web site [25]. However with video cassettes fast becoming superseded by DVD players and the indifferent durability of magnetic tapes in the long run, there is a good chance that Eurovision will not be viewable in years to come unless refreshing (transfer to a better physical storage) and migration (reformatting to a high quality, standardized format e.g., Motion-JPEG or MPEG-2 (HDTV)) steps are taken.

### 3.2.3    The Preservation Strategy

Besser [26] and Wactlar et.al. [27] have both proposed similar approaches to the preservation of moving image materials. Both groups propose the digitisation of the film/video in a high quality standardized format (e.g., Motion JPEG or HDTV-quality MPEG-2) and storage on RAID storage systems, which are periodically refreshed. In addition, both assert that the recording of associated metadata is essential for ensuring long-term accessibility to moving image content.

MPEG-7, [28], the Multimedia Content Description Interface, is a standard developed by the Moving Pictures Expert Group (MPEG), a working group of ISO/IEC. Its goal is to provide a rich set of standardized tools to enable both humans and machines to generate and understand audiovisual descriptions which can be used to enable fast efficient retrieval from digital archives (pull applications) as well as filtering of streamed audiovisual broadcasts on the Internet (push applications).

Although MPEG-7 provides a very comprehensive set of description tools, to enable the creation of (XML) descriptions of multimedia content, it does not support the preservation needs of moving image content, which requires metadata such as:

• Contextual information provided by the artist e.g., the meaning behind the work, how it was created, how they would like it displayed etc.

- Types of reformatting, refreshing, preservation actions permitted by the artist/owner;
- Details of refreshing and migration events.

Some of this metadata may be provided in the future by MPEG-21, the Multimedia Delivery Framework [29] which aims to provide a framework to enable transparent and augmented use of multimedia resources across a wide range of networks and devices to meet the needs of all users. However until the MPEG-21 standard is final and complete, the extent to which it will satisfy the preservation metadata requirements of moving image content, will remain fuzzy. The Library of Congress Audio-Visual Prototyping Project has also developed a draft set of extension schemas to use within METS for encoding preservation metadata specific to audiovisual content [30]. The additional metadata is primarily technical metadata (specific to audio, images, video and text e.g., sampling rate, compression codec etc.) for both the current object and its source plus details of reformatting and migration events.

Until MPEG-21 is available, the optimum approach to capturing the preservation metadata for Eurovision would be to use the LoC's Audio-Visual Prototyping Project schemas for video [30] but further extended with some additional metadata specific to artworks, such as the artist's intention and perspective, technique, tools used and their views on how the artwork should be installed and screened and which preservation strategies are permissible. The Variable Media Questionnaire [11] could be used to provide this additional set of artwork-specific metadata elements. The complete set of metadata elements and links to the various digital components would be stored within a METS container.

## 3.3    The Elements

### 3.3.1    About *the Elements*

*The elements* by Nam June Paik, is a typical example of a large class of new media artworks. DVD players stream multiple synchronized audio and video streams to a number of television monitors and speakers arranged in some artistic juxtaposition with physical artefacts in a real gallery space. In *The elements*, Nam June Paik has set six television monitors into an oriental red lacquer cabinet and plays video footage featuring early Hollywood film stars alongside avant-garde artists and rapid sequences of images of the natural world.

**Fig. 1.** *The elements*, Nam June Paik, 1989 Courtesy of Qld Art Gallery

### 3.3.2    The Problem

New media artworks such as *The elements* are notoriously difficult to install or move. They rely on a large set of fragile physical and digital components with complex interdependencies and physical, spatial and temporal relationships which need to be satisfied in order to maintain the integrity of the artwork according to the artist's wishes. The problem is one of ensuring that all of the metadata which is required to recreate the artwork has been precisely recorded and that the various components do not degrade or alter with time or during refreshing or migration steps.

### 3.3.3    The Preservation Strategy

For complex mixed-media artworks such as *The elements* which are composed of multiple audio and video channels, images, text and even physical objects combined in some spatio-temporal structure, we propose an approach based on a combination of metadata and migration to high quality, platform-independent, standardized formats. More specifically we propose an approach based on the five preservation steps described at the end of Section 1. In order to ensure that all of the relevant metadata is recorded, an analysis of the workflow from content creation to acquisition to exhibition to archival to re-use and preservation was carried out. *Figure 2* illustrates the typical life cycle of a new media artwork and the kinds of metadata which are acquired/modified at each stage. Based on this analysis of the content and metadata workflows and the proposed preservation approach, we were able to determine an optimum metadata schema to support the preservation needs of new media artworks such as the Elements. This is available at: http://metadata.net/newmedia/schma.xsd.
A summary of the key extensions to METS are listed below:

- Descriptive Metadata
  - o Dublin Core Metadata Initiative
  - o Guggenheim Variable Media Questionnaire
- Administrative Metadata
  - o Technical schemas proposed for use in the Library of Congress Audio-Visual Prototyping Project
- Structural Metadata
  - o SMIL 2.0

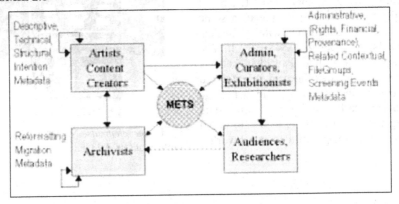

**Fig. 2.** Typical Metadata Workflow associated with Multimedia Artworks

Once the schema had been designed, the next step was to develop actual metadata input tools to facilitate the recording of preservation metadata, at the points of creation, acquisition, reuse, migration etc. The next section describes the metadata input tools which we've developed specifically to support the preservation of new media artworks but which can be applied more broadly to complex mixed-media objects from any domain.

# 4    Software Tools for Inputting Preservation Metadata

Both a stand-alone Java application and a JSP (Java Server Pages) version of the metadata input tools were developed. The application consists of a set of metadata input forms, constrained by the underlying XML Schema, which can be partitioned into four categories:

1. Descriptive and presentation metadata;
2. Purpose and intent metadata;
3. Preservation metadata; and
4. Digital Object Definition and Structural metadata.

## 4.1    Descriptive and Presentation Metadata

Descriptive metadata consists of the DCMES e.g., Title, Creator, Subject, Description etc. For the "Type" of a newmedia artwork, we have used the classifications developed by the Guggenheim Museum:

1. *Installation*: this form of artwork has physical objects, such as a rocks or flowers, as part of a piece;
2. *Interactive*: artwork that requires audience interaction.
3. *Reproduced*: artwork that can be reproduced from a master.
4. *Encoded*: born-digital works of art.
5. *Networked*: digital artwork that is dynamically created using a network.

The chosen *Type* then determines the presentation and installation metadata. The descriptive metadata will be used for search and retrieval and the presentation/installation metadata will be used to set up the artwork for exhibitions. *Figure 3* illustrates the description metadata input tool.

## 4.2    Purpose and Intent Metadata

This type of metadata is concerned with capturing the intention of the artist when he/she created the artwork. It is important to capture this information to ensure that the key message is not lost or corrupted during the preservation process. We extended the METS schema to include specific tags to support this. *Figure 4* illustrates the metadata input form that collects this information.

## 4.3    Preservation Metadata

The preservation metadata is designed to gauge the willingness of the artist to have their work preserved, the kinds of preservation methods permitted and the extent to which the artwork may be modified. *Figure 5* illustrates the metadata input form for *Preservation* metadata.

**General Questions**

What is the title of the work?

Who is the creator of the work?

What date was the work created?

If applicable who is the publisher of the work?

What classification(s) does the work fall under?

☐ Installation ☐ Interactive ☐ Reproduced ☐ Encoded ☐ Networked

**Fig. 3.** Dublin Core Metadata Input Form

**Intention Questions**

What was the message behind the work?

[                    ] **Browse**

Describe the work in your own words

[                    ] **Browse**

**Fig. 4.** Intent Metadata Input Form

**Preservation Questions**

| Attitude to preservation | Installation | Interactive | Reproduced | Encoded | Networked |
| --- | --- | --- | --- | --- | --- |

Q1. Is the work to be preserved after it is no longer variable in its current form? **Yes** ▼

Q2. Can new preservation strategies be applied to this piece? **Yes** ▼

Q3. What new strategies can be applied to this piece? **Not applicable** ▼

Q4. Who has the authority to change preservation strategies and fate of work?

**Fig. 5.** Preservation Metadata Input Form

## 4.4    Specifying the Digital Objects Definitions and Structure

There are two components to the structural metadata: multimedia object definition metadata and overall structural metadata. The multimedia object definition metadata is required for each component of the artwork. This includes the format of the digital object, the compression characteristics and details of the software that was used to create the media object. This data will be used to migrate the multimedia objects to the current standard. The extensions to METS for encoding preservation metadata specific to audiovisual content [30] were used. *Figure 6* illustrates the input form.

We believe that SMIL 2.0 [15] is capable of providing a simple platform-independent XML-approach to specifying the structure of the artwork as a whole. Because of its simplicity, human-readability and platform-independence, it is preferable to application-dependent formats such as *Director, Acrobat, Shockwave* or *Flash*. Rather than build our own SMIL editing tool to specify the object's structure, we have chosen to invoke an existing SMIL authoring tool, *Fluition*, by *Confluent Technologies*, [31] from within our Java application.

Users specify the location of the digital objects and their temporal and spatial layout relative to each other by defining regions and attaching the digital objects to them. When the specification is complete, users have a choice of either saving both the structural metadata and a digital version of the object to SMIL or HTML+TIME. *Figure 7* illustrates the structural specification of *The elements*.

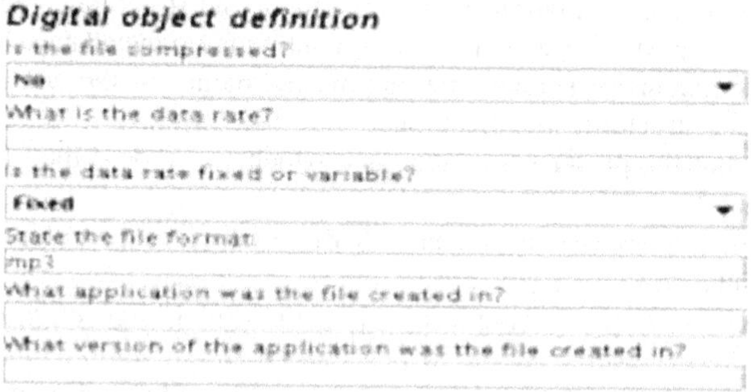

Digital object definition
Is the file compressed?
No
What is the data rate?
Is the data rate fixed or variable?
Fixed
State the file format
mp3
What application was the file created in?
What version of the application was the file created in?

**Fig. 6.** Digital Object Definition metadata form for an audio object.

Region ID
X
Y
W
H
Layer
Color
Fit
Group
Apply
Delete
Color
Width
Height
Preview
Publish
Add
Copy
Modify
Browse...

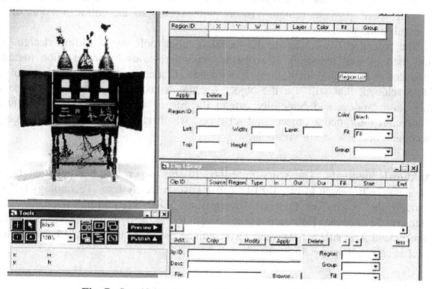

**Fig. 7.** Specifying Structural Metadata using *Fluition*

## 5 Conclusions and Future Work

In this paper we have proposed a new approach to the preservation of mixed-media objects, based on a combination of reformatting, metadata, encapsulation and migration. We then investigated the feasibility of this approach by investigating the preservation options for three case studies - exemplars of new media artworks. From the analysis of the case studies, we concluded that although our proposed approach is not the optimum for all mixed-media objects, it is the best strategy for a large subset - those objects consisting of images, video, audio, text and physical objects combined in some spatio-temporal structure or format.

We then determined the optimum metadata schema and tools which could be developed to support and implement this preservation strategy and set about building them. The tools are a combination of metadata input and structural specification tools - the outcome is an XML file which is conformant with the metadata schema based on METS, with extensions to support the audiovisual nature of the content and which uses SMIL for the structural specifications.

We believe that the preservation approach which we've described here offers the following advantages:

- Storage of the preservation metadata in XML ameliorates the potential problem of database redundancy;
- The approach is relatively simple and it works for a large class of multimedia objects;
- The metadata input tools need only be developed once but will apply to large sets of objects;
- It not only preserves the artworks but also provides an accurate digital reproduction which will provide remote visitors with access to an online version of the exhibition.

The next step is to integrate the metadata input tools into workflow design tools and then to link registries of software version releases to preservation metadata repositories in cultural institutions. It is intended that an automatic migration tool will be developed, that will use the object specific metadata to greatly streamline the migration process and hopefully extend the life of many valuable and culturally significant multimedia objects and artworks, which are currently in real danger of becoming obsolete or not viewable.

**Acknowledgements.** The work described in this paper has been funded by the Cooperative Research Centre for Enterprise Distributed Systems Technology (DSTC) through the Australian Federal Government's CRC Programme (Department of Industry, Science and Resources). Thanks also to Paul Brown, Linda Wallace and the Queensland Art Gallery for providing us with access to the three artworks which were used as case studies for this research.

# References

[1]  National Digital Information Infrastructure and Preservation Program, http://www.digitalpreservation.gov/ndiipp/

[2]  Building a National Strategy for Preservation: Issues in Digital Media Archiving, commissioned for and sponsored by the National Digital Information Infrastructure and Preservation Program, Library of Congress, April 2002, copublished by the Council on Library and Information Resources (CLIR), ISBN 1-887334-91-2 http://www.clir.org/pubs/reports/pub106/contents.html

[3]  CEDARS, CURL Exemplars in Digital Archives http://www.leeds.ac.uk/cedars/

[4]  CAMiLEON http://www.si.umich.edu/CAMILEON/

[5]  PANDORA http://pandora.nla.gov.au/

[6]  National Library of Australia, Digital Archiving and Preservation at the National Library http://www.nla.gov.au/initiatives/digarch.html

[7]   Networked European Deposits Library (NEDLIB) http://www.kb.nl/coop/nedlib/
[8]   OCLC/RLG Working Group on Preservation Metadata
      http://www.oclc.org/research/pmwg/
[9]   Archiving the Avant Garde http://www.bampfa.berkeley.edu/ciao/avant_garde.html
[10]  Guggenheim Museum, Variable Media Initiative
      http://www.guggenheim.org/variablemedia
[11]  Guggenheim Museum, Variable Media Questionnaire
      http://three.org/ippolito/variablemedia/var_questionnaire_beta.html
[12]  Jeff Rothenberg, Avoiding Technological Quicksand: Finding a Viable Technical
      Foundation for Digital Preservation, Washington, D.C.: Council on Library and
      Information Resources. 1999
      http://www.clir.org/pubs/abstract/pub77.html
[13]  Stewart Granger, "Emulation as a Digital Preservation Strategy", D-Lib Magazine, Vol 6
      No. 10, October 2000 http://www.dlib.org/dlib/october00/granger/10granger.html
[14]  David Bearman, "Reality and Chimeras in the Preservation of Electronic Records", D-Lib
      Magazine, Vol 5, No. 4, April 1999
      http://www.dlib.org/dlib/april99/bearman/04bearman.html
[15]  Synchronized Multimedia Integration Language SMIL 2.0, W3C Recommendation 7
      August 2001 http://www.w3.org/TR/smil20/
[16]  Timed Interactive Multimedia Extensions for HTML (HTML+TIME) Extending SMIL
      into the Web Browser http://www.w3.org/TR/NOTE-HTMLplusTIME
[17]  METS Metadata Encoding and Transmission Standard
      http://www.loc.gov/standards/mets/
[18]  Jeff Rothenberg: Ensuring the Longevity of Digital Documents. Scientific American,
      272(1), January 1995.
[19]  Jeff Rothenberg, An Experiment in Using Emulation to Preserve Digital Publications,
      RAND-Europe April 2000, published by The Koninklijke Bibliotheek, Den Haag
      http://www.kb.nl/coop/nedlib/results/emulationpreservationreport.pdf
[20]  Raymond Lorie, A Project on Preservation of Digital Data,
      http://www.rlg.org/preserv/diginews/diginews5-3.html#feature2
[21]  Raymond Lorie, The UVC: A Method for Preserving Digital Documents - proof of
      concept (2002) http://www.kb.nl/kb/ict/dea/ltp/reports/4-uvc.pdf
[22]  Mellor, P, Wheatley, P, Sergeant, D., "Migration on Request : A practical technique for
      digital preservation" ECDL 2002.
      http://www.si.umich.edu/CAMILEON/reports/migreq.pdf
[23]  OAIS Resources http://www.rlg.org/longterm/oais.html
[24]  Basilisk. Basilisk II Official site. http://www.uni-mainz.de/~bauec002/B2Main.html
[25]  Eurovision http://www.machinehunger.com.au/eurovision
[26]  Howard Besser, "Digital Preservation of Moving Image Material", accepted for
      publication in: The Moving Image, Fall 2001, written March 2001
      http://www.gseis.ucla.edu/~howard/Papers/amia-longevity.html
[27]  Howard D. Wactlar and Michael G. Christel, "Digital Video Archives: Managing through
      Metadata", http://www.digitalpreservation.gov/ndiipp/repor/repor_back_archi.html
[28]  MPEG-7 Overview, http://mpeg.telecomitalialab.com/standards/mpeg-7/mpeg-7.htm
[29]  ISO/IEC TR 21000-1:2001(E) (MPEG-21) Part 1: Vision, Technologies and Strategy,
      MPEG, Document: ISO/IEC JTC1/SC29/WG11 N3939
      http://www.cselt.it/mpeg/public/mpeg-21_pdtr.zip
[30]  AV Prototype Project Working Documents, Extension Schemas for the Metadata
      Encoding and Transmission Standard, Revised February 2003.
      http://lcweb.loc.gov/rr/mopic/avprot/metsmenu2.html
[31]  Fluition, Confluent Technologies http://www.confluenttechnologies.com/fluition.html

# Distributed IR for Digital Libraries

Ray R. Larson

School of Information Management and Systems
University of California, Berkeley
Berkeley, California, USA, 94720-4600
ray@sherlock.berkeley.edu

**Abstract.** This paper examines technology developed to support large-scale distributed digital libraries. We describe the method used for harvesting collection information using standard information retrieval protocols and how this information is used in collection ranking and retrieval. The system that we have developed takes a probabilistic approach to distributed information retrieval using a Logistic regression algorithm for estimation of distributed collection relevance and fusion techniques to combine multiple sources of evidence. We discuss the harvesting method used and how it can be employed in building collection representatives using features of the Z39.50 protocol. The extracted collection representatives are ranked using a fusion of probabilistic retrieval methods. The effectiveness of our algorithm is compared to other distributed search methods using test collections developed for distributed search evaluation. We also describe how this system in currently being applied to operational systems in the U.K.

## 1  Introduction

Users of the World Wide Web (WWW) have become familiar with and, in most cases, dependent on the ability to conduct simple searches that rely on information in databases built from billions of web pages harvested from millions of HTTP servers around the world. But this "visible" web harvested by services such as Google and Inktomi is, for many of these servers, only a small fraction of the total information on a particular web site. Behind the myriad "search pages" on many web sites are the underlying databases that support queries on those pages and the software that constructs pages on demand from their content.

This huge set of databases make up the content of today's digital libraries and has been called collectively the "Deep Web". Estimates of the size of the Deep Web place it at over 7500 Terabytes of information [12]. As increasing numbers of digital libraries around the world make their databases available through protocols such as OAI or Z39.50 the problem arises of determining, for any given query, which of these databases are likely to contain information of interest to a world-wide population of potential users. Certainly one goal must be to aid information seekers in identifying the digital libraries that are pertinent to their needs regardless of whether the desired resources are part of the visible web or the deep web.

T. Koch and I.T. Sølvberg (Eds.): ECDL 2003, LNCS 2769, pp. 487–498, 2003.

However, currently information seekers must rely on the search engines of the visible web to bring them to the search portals of these "Deep Web' databases, where they then must submit a new search that will (it is hoped) obtain results containing information that will satisfy their original need or desire. Today's searcher, therefore, must learn how to search and navigate not only the visible web search engines, but also the differing and often contradictory search mechanisms of the underlying Deep Web databases once those have been identified. The first challenge in exploiting the Deep Web is to decide which of these myriad databases is likely to contain the information that will meet the searcher's needs. Only then can come the challenge of how to mix, match, and combine one or more search engines for diverse digital libraries for any given inquiry, and also how to navigate through the complexities of largely incompatible protocols, metadata, and content structure and representation.

Buckland and Plaunt[1] have pointed out, searching for recorded knowledge in a distributed digital library environment involves three types of selection:

1. Selecting which library (repository) to look in;
2. Selecting which document(s) within a library to look at; and
3. Selecting fragments of data (text, numeric data, images) from within a document.

The research reported in this paper focuses on two aspects of the first type of selection, that is, creating a representative of the distributed databases and then, at search time, using these representatives to discover which of distributed databases are likely to contain information that the searcher desires. This problem, distributed information retrieval, has been an area of active research interest for many years. Distributed IR presents three central research problems that echo the selection problems noted by Buckland and Plaunt. These are:

1. How to select appropriate databases or collections for search from a large number of distributed databases;
2. How to perform parallel or sequential distributed search over the selected databases, possibly using different query structures or search formulations, in a networked environment where not all resources are always available; and
3. How to merge results from the different search engines and collections, with differing record contents and structures (sometimes referred to as the collection fusion problem).

Each of these research problems presents a number of challenges that must be addressed to provide effective and efficient solutions to the overall problem of distributed information retrieval. However, as noted above, the first challenge in exploiting the digital library databases of Deep Web is to identify, for any given query, those databases that are likely to contain information of interest to the user. This has been the central problem of distributed Information Retrieval (IR) and has been a focus of active research interest.

Some of the best known work in this area has been that of Gravano, et al. [6] on GlOSS and Callan's [2] application of inference networks to distributed IR (CORI). French and Powell, along with a number of collaborators [5,4,11], have enabled comparative evaluation of distributed IR by defining test collections derived from TREC data, where the TREC databases are divided into sub-collections representing virtual distributed collections. In addition they defined a number of measures for evaluation of the performance of distributed IR[5]. We use one of these test collections and these metrics in this paper to compare previously published results on collection selection with our probabilistic model based on logistic regression.

In the remainder of paper we first describe the methods that we have been developing to harvest content descriptions, or "collection representatives" from distributed collections and examine its efficiency using the TREC-derived testbed databases. Then we examine the probabilistic algorithm used for searching and ranking these collection representatives and compare its performance with earlier approaches to distributed information retrieval. Finally we describe some actual applications of our approach.

## 2    Building a Distributed Collection Database

Research in distributed IR has focussed on the three major aspects of collection selection, distributed search, and merging results. Far more rarely have researchers discussed how the databases to be used in collection selection are to be built. In most of the experimental work in distributed IR the researchers have assumed that the collections would be accessible and that statistics normally derived during indexing of a single database would be available. Obviously this will not be the case in true distributed environment. Some have suggested sampling methods are sufficient for extracting adequate information for representation of distributed collection contents (see, for example [7,10]. This section is based on a short description of this method that appeared in [8] and discusses how the collection representatives were derived.

Our approach to "harvesting" the collection representatives used for the subsequent retrieval and ranking of those collections exploits some features of the Z39.50 Information Retrieval protocol. However, other harvesting method are possible to create similar collection representations, including the sampling methods cited above.

We use only two functional aspects of the Z39.50 protocol in our harvesting method, the Explain Facility and the Browse Facility. In Z39.50 a "facility" is a logical group of services (or a single service) to perform various functions in the interaction between a client (origin) and a server (target).

### 2.1    The Explain Facility

The Z39.50 Explain facility was designed to enable clients to obtain information about servers. Servers can provide a large amount of information on themselves including names and descriptions of the databases that they support, the "attribute sets" and elements used (an attribute set specifies the allowable search fields and semantics for a database), diagnostic or error information, record syntaxes and information on defined subsets of record elements that may be requested from the server (or "elementsets" in Z39.50 parlance). This explain database appears to the client as any other database on the server, and the client uses the Z39.50 Search and Retrieval facilities (with explain-specific attribute sets and record syntaxes) to query and retrieve information from it. These attribute sets, explain search keywords, and record syntaxes terms defined in the standard for the Explain database facilitate interoperability of explain among different server implementations.

## 2.2 Z39.50 Browse Facility

As the name of this facility implies, it was originally intended to support browsing of the server contents, specifically the items extracted for indexing the databases. The Browse facility consists of a single service called the Scan service. It can be used to scan an ordered list of terms (subject headings, titles, keyword, text terms, or other attribute set elements) drawn from the database. Typical implementations of the Scan service directly access the contents of the indexes on the server and return requested portions of those indexes as an ordered list of terms along with the document frequency for each term. This is exactly the kind of information required for information retrieval purposes, or at least for the type of information needed by most distributed search algorithms.

## 2.3 Implementation

Our harvesting method uses these two Z39.50 Facilities to derive information from Z39.50 servers (which including library catalogs, full-text search systems, and digital library systems) in order to build representatives of the distributed resources. The sequence of operations followed to build these representatives is:

1. Use the Z39.50 protocol to connect to the target server.
2. Search the Explain Database to obtain the list of (one or more) databases that are available on that server. Explain also will provide information about some of the collection level statistics useful in retrieval (such as the total number of records in each database).
3. We can then determine, for each database, which search attributes are supported using the Explain "AttributeDetails" query.
4. For each of the searchable attributes discovered, we send a sequence of Scan requests to the server and collect the resulting lists of index terms. As the lists are collected they are verified for uniqueness (since a server may allow multiple search attributes to be processed by the same index) so that duplication is avoided.
5. For each database an XML collection document is constructed to act as a surrogate for the database using the information obtained from the server Explain database and the Scans of the various indexes.
6. A database of collection documents is created and indexed using all of the terms and frequency information derived above.

The result of this process is a database of collection representatives that may be searched by any of the index terms that would be searchable via the various search attributes of the Z39.50 protocol, each grouped within the XML collection representatives. This permits, for example, terms that occur in titles of a particular collection to be searched separately. In the evaluation study described below the average time required to apply the above steps and create a collection representative from a remote database over the network was about 24 seconds. This time is quite reasonable considering that the underlying 236 collections used in this evaluation contained the full contents of TREC disks 1, 2, and 3, with individual collection sizes ranging from less than ten to over 8000 full-text documents.

Although the Z39.50 protocol has been used previously to construct collection representative databases[10], in that work random samples of the records in the collection were used to build the indexes. An advantage of the method described here is its ability to exploit the server's work in processing its records while extracting the terms to be matched in the collection representative index.

In the collection representative each harvested index of the source databases can become a separately searchable element in the collection database. This permits us to apply the same index restrictions to distributed searching as are applied in searching the individual databases. For example, if the harvested databases maintain an author index, this can be used to limit the possible matching collections to that do support an author search.

## 3    Probabilistic Distributed IR

Once the collection representatives have been constructed they must retrieved and ranked to attempt to predict which of the distributed collections are likely to contain the documents that would match the searcher's query. For this retrieval, we use a probabilistic collection ranking algorithm.

The probabilistic retrieval algorithms derived for this work are based on the *logistical regression* algorithms developed by researchers at U.C. Berkeley and tested in TREC evaluations [3]. Since the "collection documents" used for this evaluation represent collections of documents and not individual documents, a number of differences from the usual logistic regression measures were used. In addition, analysis showed that different forms of the TREC queries (short queries using topic titles only, longer queries including the title and concepts fields and the "very long" queries including the title, concepts, description and narrative) behaved quite differently in searching the distributed collection, so three different regression equations were derived and applied automatically based on the length of the query. In a following section we will examine the effectiveness of the algorithms when compared to the CORI collection ranking algorithm for the same queries.

In the logistic regression model of IR, the estimated probability of relevance for a particular query and a particular collection (or collection document) $P(R \mid Q, C)$, is calculated and collections are ranked in order of decreasing values of that probability. In the current system $P(R \mid Q, C)$ is calculated as the "log odds" of relevance $\log O(R \mid Q, C)$, Logistic regression provides estimates for a set of coefficients, $c_i$, associated with a set of $S$ statistics, $X_i$, derived from the query and database of collection documents, such that:

$$\log O(R \mid Q, C) \approx c_0 \sum_{i=1}^{S} c_i X_i \qquad (1)$$

where $c_0$ is the intercept term of the regression. For the set of $M$ terms that occur in both a particular query and a given collection document. The statistics used in this study were:

$X_1 = \frac{1}{M} \sum_{j=1}^{M} \log QAF_{t_j}$ . This is the log of the absolute frequency of occurrence for term $t_j$ in the query averaged over the $M$ terms in common between the query and the collection document.

$X_2 = \sqrt{QL}$ . This is square root of the query length (i.e., the number of terms in the query disregarding stopwords).

$X_3 = \frac{1}{M} \sum_{j=1}^{M} \log CAF_{t_j}$ . This is is the log of the absolute frequency of occurrence for term $t_j$ in the collection averaged over the $M$ common terms.

$X_4 = \sqrt{\frac{CL}{10}}$ . This is square root of the collection size. (We use an estimate oc collection size based on the size of the harvested collection representative).

$X_5 = \frac{1}{M} \sum_{j=1}^{M} \log ICF_{t_j}$ . This is is the log of the *inverse collection frequency*(ICF) averaged over the $M$ common terms. ICF is calculated as the total number of collections divided by the number that contain term $t_j$

$X_6 = \log M$ . The log of the number of terms in common between the collection document and the query.

For short (title only) queries the equation used in ranking was:

$$\log O(R \mid Q, C) = -3.70 + (1.269 * X_1) + (-0.310 * X_2)$$
$$+(0.679 * X_3) + K$$
$$+(0.223 * X_5) + (4.01 * X_6);$$

($K$ is a constant because query term frequency is always 1 in short queries) For long (title and concepts) the equation used was:

$$\log O(R \mid Q, C) = -7.0103 + (2.3188 * X_1) + (-1.1257 * X_2)$$
$$+(1.0695 * X_3) + (-0.00294 * X_4)$$
$$+(5.9174 * X_5) + (2.3612 * X_6);$$

And for very long queries the equation used was:

$$\log O(R \mid Q, C) = -20.9850 + (9.6801 * X_1) + (-1.8669 * X_2)$$
$$+(1.1921 * X_3) + (-0.00537 * X_4)$$
$$+(6.2501 * X_5) + (7.5491 * X_6);$$

For the evaluation discussed below we used the "Fusion Search" facility in the Cheshire II system to merge the result sets from multiple probabilistic searches. For all of the results reported here separate probabilistic searches were performed

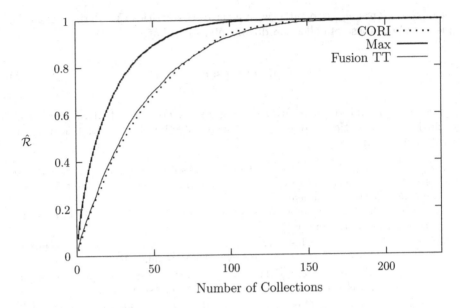

**Fig. 1.** Distributed Search Evaluation - Title Queries

on two different elements of the collection representatives (information derived from the titles of the documents in the harvested collections, and terms derived from anywhere in the documents. The ranked results (obtained using the algorithm above) for each search were then merged into a single integrated result set for a given query. The "Fusion Search" facility was developed originally to support combination of results from different searches. We have used this approach in both single document collections, and for distributed collection representative databases with good results. For example, we have exploited this facility in our retrieval processing for the INEX information retrieval of XML evaluation[9].

The "Fusion Search" facility functions by combining the ranking weights of separated searches. When the same documents, or document components, have been retrieved in differing searches, their final ranking value is based on combining the weights from each of the source sets. It should be noted, however, that in the current implementation this final ranking value is not a an estimated probability but a simple summation of probabilistic collection representative weights. The facility also permits combinations of weighted and Boolean values, although only the estimated probabilities for harvested title terms and full-text terms were combined in the following evaluation.

## 4   Evaluation

For this study we used collections formed by dividing the documents on TIP-STER disks 1, 2, and 3 into 236 sets based on source and month[5]. Collection relevance information was based on based on whether one or more individual documents in the collection were relevant according to the relevance judgements for TREC queries 51-150. The relevance information was used both for estimating the logistic regression coefficients (using a sample of the data) and for the evaluation (with full data).

In French, et al.[4], the authors describe three effectivenes measures for evaluation of distributed information retrieval. The effectiveness measures assume that each database of the distributed collection has (potentially) some *merit* for a given query $q$. As "ground truth" we assume the that optimal ranking is one in which each database containing any relevant documents is ranked before all databases that do not, and for all of the databases that do have one or more relevant documents, the ranking is in descending order of the number of relevant documents in the database. This forms the upper limit on the performance possible for the ranking algorithm. So, for this optimal ranking $B$ and an estimated or test ranking $E$, let $db_{bi}$ and $db_{ei}$ denote the database in the $i$-th ranked position of rankings $B$ and $E$. Also, let $B_i = merit(q, db_{bi})$ and $E_i = merit(q, db_{ei})$, where $merit(q, db)$ is simply the number of relevant documents in $db$. Using these, French, et al., define two "Recall Analogs" and a "Precision Analog". The first Recall analog (suggested by Gravano, et al.[6])

$$\mathcal{R}_n = \frac{\sum_{i=1}^{n} E_i}{\sum_{i=1}^{n} B_i} \tag{2}$$

However, as French, et al. point out this measure operates over all databases whether or not they have any relevant documents. They suggest a more appropriate measure might be one where the denominator only takes into account the databases with at least one relevant document:

$$\hat{\mathcal{R}}_n = \frac{\sum_{i=1}^{n} E_i}{\sum_{i=1}^{n^*} B_i} \tag{3}$$

Where $n^* = \max k$, such that $B_k \neq 0$.

The Precision analog is simply the fraction of top $n$ databases in the estimated ranking that have non-zero merit:

$$\mathcal{P}_n = \frac{|db \in \text{Top}_n(E)|merit(q, db) > 0|}{|\text{Top}_n(E)|} \tag{4}$$

Figures 1, 2 and 3 summarize the results of the evaluation. The X axis of the graphs is the number of collections in the ranking and the Y axis, $\hat{\mathcal{R}}$, is the suggested Recall analog measuring the proportion of the total possible relevant documents that have been accumulated in the top $N$ databases, averaged across all of the queries. The Max line in the figures shows the optimal (baseline) results based where the collections are ranked in order of the number of relevance documents they contain. The figures contain the results of Callan's Inference net approach[2], indicated by CORI (described in [11]). The "Fusion TT" line is the fusion and logistic regression method described above using the title and fulltext elements of the harvested database representatives. The CORI results are the best (to date) results reported for distributed search using the collection used in this evaluation.

For title queries (i.e. those that use only the title portion of the TREC queries), shownFigure 1) the described method achieves higher recall than the CORI algorithm for up to about 100 collections, where CORI exceeds it. Similar performance is shown for long queries where the the fused logistic regression method and CORI perform virtually identically. However, for very long queries shown in Figure 3, the CORI results exceed those of our fusion approach. We would suggest based on these results that CORI would be a better approach for very large queries (such as using an entire document as a query) where the user (or system) is willing to search across many databases. However, for the short queries typical of most user interaction with digital libraries and search systems, the fusion approach with the logistic regression coefficients described above appears to be a better choice.

We are still examining different combinations of elements for the fusion approach, and also examining fusing different probabilistic models. We have tested a version of the well-known Okapi BM-25 (altered for application to collection representatives instead of documents) both alone and fused with the "Fusion TT" results above. The fused results were virtually indistinguishable from the "Fusion TT" results, while the Okapi BM-25 used along performed very poorly.

Preliminary analyses suggest that, since it is impossible to know or estimate from the summary frequency information available in the collection representatives how *many* relevant documents may occur in a given database, there may not be enough information to significantly improve over the results reported here.

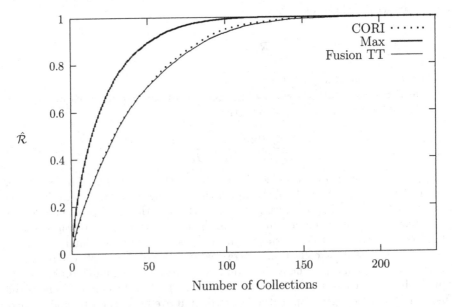

**Fig. 2.** Distributed Search Evaluation - Long Queries

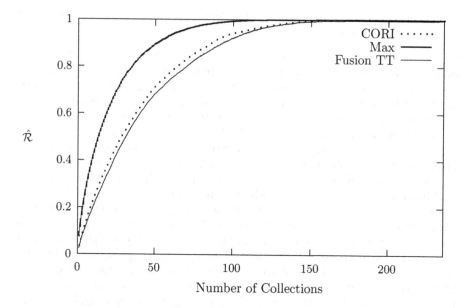

**Fig. 3.** Distributed Search Evaluation - Very Long Queries

# 5   Applications

Over the past several years we have started to use the Cheshire II system to implement production-level services providing access to full-text SGML and XML document for a number of digital library systems in the United States and the United Kingdom, including the UC Berkeley Digital Library Initiative project sponsored by NSF, NASA and ARPA, The Archives Hub sponsored by JISC in the UK, The History Data Service of AHDS in the UK and the Resource Discovery Network in the UK. The Cheshire system is also beginning to be used to provide scalable distributed retrieval for consortia of institutions providing access to online catalogs and archival collections. At present there are two major distributed systems using the techniques and algorithms described above: the Merseylibraries.org system and the Distributed Archives Hub.

MerseyLibraries.org is sponsored by an organization known as "Libraries Together: Liverpool Learning Partnership" with support from The British Library's Co-operation and Partnership Programme (CPP) and the Library and Information Cooperation Council in the UK. Its aims are:

- To provide a web-searchable interface for all the libraries in the Merseyside region.
- To publicize and promote the collections of Merseyside.
- To highlight the benefits of cooperative activity for regional libraries.
- To bring together information about library, archives, and information services.

– To provide a platform for the implementation of cutting edge technologies in libraries and archive repositories.

Currently, the service provides access to the catalogues from of the region's major libraries including: Liverpool City Libraries, Wirral Libraries, Halton Libraries, Sefton Libraries, Warrington Libraries, University of Liverpool Library, Liverpool Hope University College, Liverpool John Moores University, Liverpool Community College, Liverpool Institute for Performing Arts, University of Liverpool Library (archives), and the Liverpool and Merseyside Record Offices. The "virtual union catalog" provided by this service can be searched at http://www.merseylibraries.org. This represents millions of catalog records.

The Distributed Archives Hub is the developing distributed version of the Archives Hub (http://www.archiveshub.ac.uk – which is a centralized Cheshire II based system). The Archives Hub provides a single point of access to descriptions of archives held in repositories throughout the UK. The repositories (libraries, archives, or special collections departments) with archival descriptions available on the Hub currently include over sixty UK institutions, primarily Universities and Colleges, and thousands of archival descriptions. In the distributed version of the Archives Hub each repository (or consortia of repositories) will maintain their own individual servers, which will then amalgamated and made accessible using the techniques discussed in this paper.

## 6    Conclusion

In this paper we have described a standards-based method for building a resource discovery database from distributed Z39.50 servers and examined the algorithms that can be used to select collection representatives likely to contain information relevant to a given query. In addition we have described algorithms that can be used to search these collection representatives and to rank the databases for more effective searching.

We have shown how the presented algorithms and fusion methods appear to perform quite well for the kinds of short queries typically submitted by searchers to digital libraries and search systems.

We have also briefly described the application of the techniques described in two large-scale distributed systems in the UK. We believe that these distributed search techniques can be applied in a wide variety of Digital Library context and can provide an effective and scalable way to provide distributed searching across diverse Digital Libraries.

**Acknowledgments.** The author would like to thank James French and Allison Powell for kindly suppling the CORI results used in this paper. In addition thanks go to Paul Watry and Robert Sanderson of the University of Liverpool for their work in setting up and managing the implementation of distributed systems described above.

This work was supported by the National Science Foundation and Joint Information Systems Committee(U.K) under the *International Digital Libraries Program* award #IIS-9975164.

# References

1. M. K. Buckland and C. Plaunt. Selecting libraries, selecting documents, selecting data. In *Proceedings of the International Symposium on Research, Development & Practice in Digital Libraries 1997, ISDL 97, Nov. 18-21, 1997, Tsukuba, Japan*, pages 85–91, Japan, 1997. University of Library and Information Science.
2. J. Callan. Distributed information retrieval. In W. B. Croft, editor, *Advances in Information Retrieval: Recent research from the Center for Intelligent Information Retrieval*, chapter 5, pages 127–150. Kluwer, Boston, 2000.
3. W. S. Cooper, F. C. Gey, and A. Chen. Full text retrieval based on a probabilistic equation with coefficients fitted by logistic regression. In D. K. Harman, editor, *The Second Text Retrieval Conference (TREC-2)*, pages 57–66, Gaithersburg, MD, 1994. NIST.
4. J. C. French, A. L. Powell, J. P. Callan, C. L. Viles, T. Emmitt, K. J. Prey, and Y. Mou. Comparing the performance of database selection algorithms. In *SIGIR '99*, pages 238–245, 1999.
5. J. C. French, A. L. Powell, C. L. Viles, T. Emmitt, and K. J. Prey. Evaluating database selection techniques: A testbed and experiment. In *SIGIR '98*, pages 121–129, 1998.
6. L. Gravano, H. García-Molina, and A. Tomasic. GlOSS: text-source discovery over the Internet. *ACM Transactions on Database Systems*, 24(2):229–264, 1999.
7. Jamie Callan and M. Connell. Query-based sampling of text databases. Technical report, Center for Intelligent Information Retrieval, Dept. of Computer Science, University of Massachusetts, 1999. Technical Report IR-180.
8. R. R. Larson. Distributed resource discovery: Using Z39.50 to build cross-domain information servers. In *JCDL '01*, pages 52–53. ACM, 2001.
9. R. R. Larson. Cheshire II at INEX: Using a hybrid logistic regression and boolean model for XML retrieval. In *Proceedings of the First Annual Workshop of the Initiative for the Evaluation of XML retrieval (INEX)*, page IN PRESS. DELOS workshop series, 2003.
10. Y. Lin, J. Xu, E.-P. Lim, and W.-K. Ng. Zbroker : A query routing broker for z39.50 databases, 1999.
11. A. L. Powell. *Database Selection in Distributed Information Retrieval: A Study of Multi-Collection Information Retrieval*. PhD thesis, University of Virginia, Virginia, 2001.
12. H. Varian and P. Lyman. How much information? Available as *http://sims.berkeley.edu/research/projects/how-much-info/.*, 2002.

# Reference Directed Indexing: Redeeming Relevance for Subject Search in Citation Indexes

Shannon Bradshaw

Department of Management Sciences
The University of Iowa
Iowa City, IA 52242
shannon-bradshaw@uiowa.edu

**Abstract.** Citation indexes are valuable tools for research, in part because they provide a means with which to measure the relative impact of articles in a collection of scientific literature. Recent efforts demonstrate some value in retrieval systems for citation indexes based on measures of impact. However, such approaches use weak measures of relevance, ranking together a few useful documents with many that are frequently cited but irrelevant. We propose an indexing technique that joins measures of relevance and impact in a single retrieval metric. This approach, called Reference Directed Indexing (RDI) is based on a comparison of the terms authors use in reference to documents. Initial retrieval experiments with RDI indicate that it retrieves documents of a quality on par with current ranking metrics, but with significantly improved relevance.

## 1   Introduction

In order to contribute to a field of study a researcher must be aware of prior work related to her own and appropriately position new work within that space. For such tasks researchers have long noted the utility in determining the relative impact of a set of related papers [8,25,11]. Citation indexes have proven useful in that they permit a searcher to traverse a network of documents linked together by citations and thereby locate important contributions in an area of research. In addition, recent work has demonstrated that retrieval metrics based on the number of citations papers receive can be an effective means of pointing searchers to useful information [13,9]. While for every user it is not necessarily true that a document that is frequently cited will be more useful than one that is not, it is difficult to argue in an academic setting that a ranking metric based on citation frequency does not provide an effective means of prioritizing one's reading. However, work to date has largely left open the question of how relevance is to be determined when ranking search results based primarily on measures of impact. Previous efforts have employed Boolean retrieval methods; therefore, any document using the query terms even a single time is a likely candidate for retrieval. In any large citation index many irrelevant documents may rank highly in the set of search results for a query simply because they are frequently cited. In Web search engines such as Google, which use similar

T. Koch and I.T. Sølvberg (Eds.): ECDL 2003, LNCS 2769, pp. 499–510, 2003.

techniques based on popularity this approach is quite effective given that the average information need can be satisfied by a single popular web page. Users of citation indexes, however, often require an extensive treatment of a topic – information that can only be found by reviewing many documents. Therefore, users of citation indexes often resort to the tedious process of shuffling through long lists of search results sorting the good from the bad or the equally difficult task of traversing many citation paths beginning at a few known relevant documents. This problem can be made much less severe if stronger measures of relevance are employed to provide users with a higher percentage of documents that are significant for what they have to say about the topic of interest. To this end, we present an indexing technique that pulls together measures of relevance and impact in a single metric. This approach, which we call Reference Directed Indexing (RDI), is based on a comparison of the terms authors use in reference to documents. Initial experiments with this approach indicate that it performs quite favorably when compared to a traditional vector-space approach [18] using TFIDF [19] as a term weighting metric. In addition, these experiments demonstrate that RDI selects papers that are not only relevant to a query, but those that are also among the most frequently cited for their contributions to the research area of interest.

## 2    Reference Directed Indexing

The intuition driving RDI is that in the context of citing a document an author uses words that make good index terms for the cited document because they identify what it is about and the terms people typically use to identify the information it contains. For example, Figure 1 depicts a reference to a paper by Ronald Azuma and Gary Bishop entitled "Improving Static and Dynamic Registration in an Optical See-through HMD". This is an early paper on track-

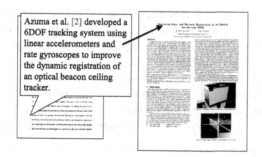

**Fig. 1.** The words of one referrer when citing Azuma and Bishop.

ing the head of a user in augmented reality environments in order to present her with the appropriate perspective view for each frame of an immersive experience.

The citing author in Figure 1 describes this paper as addressing a six degrees of freedom optical tracking system in addition to listing details concerning its implementation. In this paper, we will refer this type of statement as "referential text", or simply a "reference". While this particular reference contains words that serve as excellent index terms, it would be difficult to build a system that automatically extracts just the right index terms on the basis of a single reference. Therefore, RDI leverages the fact that sufficiently useful documents are cited by multiple authors. Repeated reference to a document provides a means of comparing the words of many referrers. Our theory is that if several authors use the same words in reference to a document then those words make good index terms for that document. Figure 2 depicts three additional references to the same paper.[1] In this example, each piece of text written in reference to Azuma

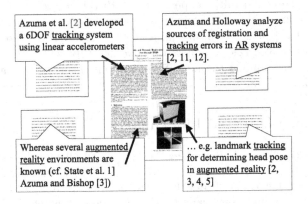

**Fig. 2.** Several references to Azuma and Bishop.

and Bishop contains many words that accurately label one or more of the key ideas in this paper, and each reference contains words also found in the words of one or more of the other authors citing this document. Note the repeated use of the underlined terms "augmented reality" and "tracking" in Figure 2.

RDI treats each citing author as a voter given the opportunity to cast one vote for any index term for a cited document. A vote of "yes" is determined by the presence of that term in the text the citing author writes in reference to the document, a "no" vote by the absence of the term. Provided a term is

---

[1] Clockwise beginning with upper left from: S. You and U. Neumann. Fusion of vision and gyro tracking for robust augmented reality registration. In Proc. of IEEE Virtual Reality, pages 71-78, 2001; E. S. McGarrity. Evaluation of calibration for optical see-through augmented reality systems. Master's thesis, Michigan State University, 2001; T. Auer, A. Pinz, and M. Gervautz. Tracking in a Multi-User Augmented Reality System. In Proc. of the IASTED Int. Conf. on Computer Graphics and Imaging, 249-253, 1998; C.P. Lu and G. Hager. Fast and globally convergent pose estimation from video images. PAMI, 22(2), 2000.

not widely used in reference to many documents (i.e. articles, prepositions, and other terms that rarely identify content), the more votes that term receives the greater its weight will be as an index term for the document. At retrieval time, the highest ranking documents are those that have been most often referenced using the words in a query. The experimental evidence presented in Section 4 suggests that a retrieval system based on this technique provides search results that are both highly relevant and significant in their contribution to the topic of interest.

## 3  Rosetta

We implemented RDI in a search engine for scientific literature called Rosetta. For the experiments reported in this paper we indexed data provided by CiteSeer/ResearchIndex [13] with their permission. As referential text to index the documents in Rosetta, we used the "context of citations" provided by CiteSeer by following the "Context" link from the "Document Details" page representing each document. Each piece of referential text is approximately 100 words long, with 50 words on either side of the point of citation. Rosetta's term weighting metric is defined by:

$$w_{id} = \frac{n_{id}}{1 + logN_i}$$

where $w_{id}$ is the importance of a word $i$ as an index term for document $d$, $n_{id}$ is the number of times word $i$ was used in reference to $d$, and $N_i$ is the total number of documents to which authors have referred using word $i$. In response to queries, the current implementation gathers all documents indexed by the query terms and sorts them based on the number of query terms they match and the weight of those words as index terms. The metric used to rank documents during retrieval is designed to favor documents that have been described most often using language that closely matches the query. Specifically, the score of a document is calculated as

$$s_d = n_d + \sum_{i=1}^{q} w_{id}$$

where $n_d$ is the number of query words matching some index term for document $d$, $q$ is the set of words in the query, and $w_{id}$ is the weight of query word $i$ as an index for document $d$. This metric causes documents to be sorted first by the number of query words their index terms match and then by the sum of the weights of the query words as index terms for the document. The theory here is that when citing a document, authors describe it using terms similar to those a searcher is likely to use in queries for the information the document contains. Therefore, in response to a query, the retrieval metric associates the most importance with documents that have been described using all of the terms contained in a query and then ranks search results according to the frequency with which the matching query terms have been used in reference to each document. This metric may seem a contradiction given that we are interested overcoming weak measures of relevance provided by Boolean-based retrieval. While we acknowledge that this metric can be improved by eliminating its Boolean component, overall, as we demonstrate in Section 4 this approach seems less prone to retrieval errors than even relevance-based retrieval techniques. We discuss this in more detail in the next section.

## 4   Retrieval Performance

We evaluated the retrieval performance of Rosetta on a small sample of 32 queries with appropriate T-tests. For our experiment we randomly selected 24 documents from our collection that contained a keywords section. By this we do not mean conference-specific categories and subject descriptors such as one often finds in ACM publications. Rather we mean a section containing a list of terms describing a paper written in the authors own words. As queries we randomly selected words as phrases listed as keywords in these documents (See Table 1). The average query length was 2 words, which is in keeping with the average length of queries submitted by users of both Web search engines [23] and digital libraries [10]. We chose to test Rosetta using queries collected in this way, when

**Table 1.** Queries used in experiments testing RDI's retrieval performance.

| | | |
|---|---|---|
| adaptive estimation | sonic feedback | groupware |
| supervised learning | haptic | topology changes |
| hardware performance counter | transient interactions | inductive transfer |
| reliable data distribution | information sharing | erasure codes |
| reinforcement learning | virtual finger | user interfaces |
| visual reconstruction | reliable multicast | wait free |
| semistructured data | wavelets | shared variables |
| simulation acceleration | wireless routing | wrapper induction |
| software architecture diagrams | code reuse | digital audio |
| architecture cost model | virtual environments | force shading |
| graphical editors | laser rangefinding | |

people use a retrieval system to locate needed information they are motivated by a specific task or context. The context in which a user submits a query determines which documents will be useful to her in the space of all information on which her query might touch. Having selected queries from the terms authors used to describe their work, we used as context for each query the paper from which the query was drawn. We determined the relevance of each retrieved document based on whether or not it addressed the same topic identified by the query in the paper from which it was drawn. For example, one term, "reliable data distribution", was used by authors to describe research on multicast technology for distributing bulk data such as video feeds to many clients simultaneously with error detection and congestion control.[2] For this query we marked as relevant documents that discuss multicast technology that ensures reliable distribution. We compared the performance of RDI as implemented in Rosetta to a vector-space approach [18] using a cosine retrieval metric [20] and TFIDF [19,21] for term weighting. Boolean retrieval is well-known to be a poor identifier of relevant information; therefore, we felt that a more convincing argument could be made by comparison to a relevance-based retrieval technique. We compared RDI to Cosine/TFIDF, because this approach or some variant is widely used and has proven to be among the best relevance-based retrieval technologies developed by the IR community [19]. We implemented the TFIDF/Cosine system using the following term-weighting metric:

$$w_{id} = TF_{id} \cdot (log_2 N - log_2 DF_i)$$

where $TF_{id}$ is the term frequency of term $i$ in document $d$, that is the number of times term $i$ occurs in document $d$. $N$ is the total number of documents in the collection and $DF_i$ is the document frequency of term $i$ or the number of documents in the entire collection that contain term $i$ [18]. As the cosine retrieval metric we used:

$$cos(d, q) = \frac{\sum_{i=1}^{T}(w_{id} \cdot w_{iq})}{\sqrt{\sum_{i=1}^{T} w_{id}^2 \cdot \sum_{i=1}^{T} w_{iq}^2}}$$

as described in [20] where $T$ is the number of unique terms used in a collection of documents. The magnitude of a document vector in any dimension is the weight of that term as an index for the document ($w_{id}$). For a term not contained in a document the weight is assumed to be zero. The weight of a query term is $w_{iq}$ and is in this system always equal to 1.

As data for our experiment we selected 10,000 documents from the collection maintained by CiteSeer. Each document was required to be the target of at least one citation, but otherwise the documents were selected at random. Since RDI is entirely based on references to documents this requirement guaranteed that both Rosetta and the TFIDF/Cosine system indexed exactly the same collection of documents. For each of the 32 test queries we evaluated 20 search results, the top 10 from both Rosetta and the TFIDF/Cosine system. We constructed a meta-search interface that searched both systems and combined the results on a single page. The meta-search interface presented the documents retrieved in random order, with no indication of the system from which each was drawn. If a document was retrieved by both systems it was displayed only once so as not to give away its origin.

## 4.1   Precision at Top 10

Having evaluated the search results for each query we found that RDI compares favorably to TFIDF/Cosine. RDI identified documents relevant to queries with

---

[2] J. W. Byers, M. Luby, M. Mitzenmacher, and A. Rege. A Digital Fountain Approach to Reliable Distribution of Bulk Data. In Proc. of SIGCOMM '98.

better precision, making fewer of the kind of retrieval errors common to the vector-space technique. The two approaches exhibited largely the same pattern of retrieval, reflecting variables such as query ambiguity and coverage of each topic within the collection. However, on average Rosetta placed 1.66 more relevant documents in the top ten than the TFIDF/Cosine system. Rosetta's mean precision at top ten was .484 compared to .318 for the TFIDF/Cosine system. In a T-test for the significance of this result, the value of the test statistic is 3.227, indicating that the difference in performance is significant at a confidence level of 99.5%. Rosetta performed better than the TFIDF/Cosine system for 60% of the queries and as good or better for 78% of the queries. Rosetta retrieved at least 2 more relevant documents than TFIDF/Cosine in the top ten for one-half of the queries and 3 more relevant documents or more for one-third of the queries. In contrast, the TFIDF system found 2 more relevant documents than Rosetta for only 2 queries and 3 more for only 1 query. Figure 3 depicts a side-by-side comparison over the 32 queries that comprise this experiment. Please note that the queries have been sorted in descending order by the percentage of relevant documents retrieved by Rosetta. A closer examination of the types

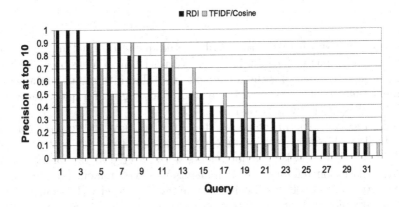

**Fig. 3.** Precision at top 10 for 32 queries: RDI vs. TFIDF/Cosine.

of retrieval errors made by each system in this study indicates that overall RDI is less prone to many common retrieval errors than a TFIDF/Cosine approach and perhaps other content-based approaches. For example, one paper retrieved by the TFIDF/Cosine system in response to the query, "inductive transfer", had nothing to do with Machine Learning or any topics related to the query. However, this paper was retrieved with a cosine score less than 0.02 different from a very relevant document. It was retrieved because the paper contains a very lengthy banking example in which the word "transfer" is used repeatedly. Another paper, "Test Data Sets for Evaluating Data Visualization Techniques" by Bergeron et al.[3] was retrieved erroneously by the TFIDF/Cosine system in response to the query "reliable data distribution". This paper is about creating test data sets for scientific visualization applications. Because the authors discuss the appropriate distribution of values within the test data sets they create, the TFIDF/Cosine system ranked it number one in the list of search results for this query. Finally, one query used in the study was "software architecture diagrams" extracted from a software engineering paper on a formal specification for constructing software architecture diagrams. The TFIDF/Cosine system did not retrieve a single document directly related to this topic. Many of the papers it retrieved for this query concern software engineering topics and thus use the query words repeatedly; however, none deals directly with the topic of "software architecture diagrams". In contrast, Rosetta accurately identified four papers discussing models and tools for constructing software architecture diagrams, placing three of the four it retrieved in the top five search results. Overall, the RDI approach seems less prone to such errors. We believe this is because multiple referrers to a document seldom use many of the same words to describe it unless those words directly identify what that document is about. In contrast, the author of a document inevitably uses many words in telling the story of her research that may cause that document to be retrieved erroneously for a number of queries.

We also discovered two problems with RDI as implemented in Rosetta. We believe these two problems are to blame for the poor performance of Rosetta on queries 11, 14, and 19 depicted in Figure 3. First, although the ranking metric we have implemented performs well overall, the fact that it rewards as little as a single use of all query terms is a problem for some queries. For queries 11, 14, and 19 a few irrelevant documents were retrieved because a single reference to those documents used all the query terms even though one or more of those terms did not directly identify what the cited document was about. We are currently experimenting with retrieval metrics that reward documents frequently referenced using each of the query terms. The second problem we discovered stems from the fact that many authors reuse portions of text in several papers. As a result, the same or very similar text will often appear in many pieces of referential text Rosetta uses to index a document. Because term weighting in Rosetta is based on the number of referrers that use a term, if this text contains any poor index terms, these can be a source of a false positives at retrieval time. We are currently developing a parser to detect such situations and only count the terms used in such texts a single time.

## 4.2    Measuring the Impact of Retrieved Documents

We looked next to the average number of citations per year made to documents retrieved by Rosetta as a measure of the overall significance of search results

---

[3] D. Bergeron, D. A. Keim, and R. Pickett. Test Data Sets for Evaluating Data Visualization Techniques. In Perceptual Issues in Visualization, Springer-Verlag, Berlin, 1994.

provided by RDI. As a baseline for comparison we contrast the citation frequency of documents retrieved by Rosetta with those retrieved by the TFIDF/Cosine system. However, there is no reason to expect that the TFIDF/Cosine approach should prefer frequently cited documents, so we are not comparing one approach to the other here. Rather, we do this merely to illustrate the difference between the frequency with which the documents selected by RDI are cited and the frequency with which an average document on a given topic in our collection is cited. Figure 4 depicts this comparison, graphing the median number of citations per year for the set of documents retrieved by each system in response to each query. Please note that the order in which the queries are displayed in Figure 4 differs from that of Figure 3.

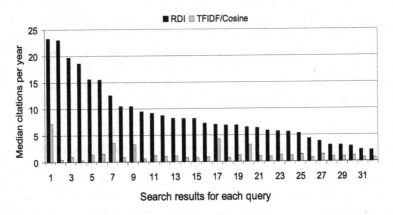

**Fig. 4.** Median number of cites per year to search results in our experiment.

We calculated the average number of citations per year to each document since its year of publication by dividing the number of years since publication by the total number of citations. The median used here then, is the median of the average number of citations per year for the set of documents retrieved for a given query. We use the median instead of mean, because it is less sensitive to a single document receiving many citations, and therefore, more reflective of the overall impact of each set of search results. We used the average number of citations per year rather than simply the total number of citations, so that the age of a document was a less significant factor in the measure of the frequency with which it is cited. As a further step we measured the distribution of publication year for documents retrieved by both systems and found no significant difference. The mean year of publication for documents retrieved by Rosetta is 1994, while the mean year of publication for documents retrieved by the TFIDF/Cosine system is 1995, with publication years ranging from 1984 to 2000. The frequency with which Rosetta's search results are cited far exceeds the baseline. For the average query, the median number of citations/year to search results retrieved by Rosetta was 8.9, while the baseline was only 1.5. Overall, this result combined with the study of retrieval precision supports our claim that RDI provides search results that are both highly relevant and extremely important to the research communities to which they contribute. Though further study is required, this indicates that RDI may provide subject search performance in citation indexes, superior to other methods previously presented.

## 5   Related Work

We are not the first to make use of referential text for indexing and retrieval of information; however, to our knowledge the effectiveness of the type of voting technique we propose has never been demonstrated for subject search. Furthermore, we know only of work exploiting referential in relation to hypertext documents and none directed toward scientific literature. McBryan with the World Wide Web Worm (WWWW) [14] was the first to build a search engine that incorporated anchor text. However, the WWWW provided a structured type of interface allowing users to search in anchor text as one of several choices. In addition, the WWWW provided no ranking, but simply used egrep as the underlying technology to list documents linked to using the words in the query. In other work, Spertus as a demonstration of her work in implementing structured relational database-like search of the Web built a "Parasite" tool in her SQUEAL language that successfully identified home pages using only anchor text as the basis for matches to queries [22]. Craswell et al. [4] use anchor text, which is another form of referential text, as the basis for finding homepages of companies, people, and other entities. Aside from the fact that their work is with web pages and ours with scientific literature, the primary difference between this work and ours is that while they focus on finding a specific class of documents within their domain, our approach is more generally applicable to subject searching within our domain as a whole. Other researchers have explored the idea of a reference-based approach to general-purpose indexing and retrieval to a limited extent. Bharat and Mihaila [1] use Web pages containing many links to like items as "expert pages". At retrieval time, their system identifies the expert pages most relevant to the query and retrieves the links found on those pages to which the majority of expert pages point. Of course the Google Web search engine also employs anchor text in the indexing and retrieval of web pages; however, their approach is different in that anchor serves largely just to identify candidate retrieval results, while the ranking for pages is determined primarily by PageRank [2], which is entirely subject independent. As a result, Google at times suffers from some of the same problems as citation indexes which rank documents based on their impact.

Others have employed referential text in classification and categorization rather than subject search. Chakrabarti et al. [3] extend HITS [12] in order to categorize Web pages into broad Yahoo-like categories, using anchor text to enhance the topic specificity of the algorithm. Furnkranz [7] uses anchor text an other elements of web pages in a Machine Learning approach to classify University web pages into one of seven categories including "Student", "Department", and "Research Project" among others.

Another body of work employs anchor text to select from among several choices of links to follow. The majority of this work deals with focused crawling of Web pages. Several researchers use anchor text as at least in part to select the next page to call from a pool of candidate links, recognizing that anchor text can be a good indicator of the content of a document [24,16,15]. In related work, Davison [5] demonstrated that anchor text and that which surrounds the anchor text contains many terms that overlap with terms in the content of documents. In later work, [6] he used this finding as a basis for technology to guess and prefetch pages that users of Web browsers are likely to request following the page they are currently viewing.

Little work has focused on techniques that merge measures of relevance and utility or significance. One notable exception is that of Richardson and Domingos [17] in which the authors present a topic-sensitive version of PageRank.

## 6  Conclusions and Future Work

In this paper we describe preliminary work on an indexing and retrieval technique called RDI that promises to enhance the effectiveness of subject search in citation indexes. Though the results are preliminary, they do suggest that RDI not only outperforms weak methods of relevance such as those currently employed by citations indexes, but that it performs favorably when compared to one of the most widely used and well-established techniques for relevance ranking in retrieval systems. In future work we plan to further demonstrate the effectiveness of this technique and explore other ways in which we might leverage the precision of referential text.

## References

1. Krishna Bharat and George A. Mihaila. When experts agree: Using non-affiliated experts to rank popular topics. In *Proc. of the 10th World Wide Web Conf.*, 2001.
2. S. Brin and L. Page. The anatomy of a large-scale hypertextual Web search engine. *Computer Networks*, 30(1–7):107–117, 1998.
3. S. Chakrabarti, B. Dom, P. Raghavan, S. Rajagopalan, D. Gibson, and J. Kleinberg. Automatic resource compilation by analyzing hyperlink structure and associated text. *Computer Networks*, 30(1–7):65–74, 1998.
4. N. Craswell, D. Hawking, and S. Robertson. Effective site finding using link anchor information. In *Proc. of the ACM SIGIR Conf. on Research and Development in Information Retrieval*, 2001.
5. Brian D. Davison. Topical locality in the Web. In *Proc. of the ACM SIGIR Conf. on Research and Development in Information Retrieval*, pages 272–279, 2000.
6. Brian D. Davison. Predicting web actions from html content. In *Proc. the ACM Conf. on Hypertext and Hypermedia*, pages 159–168, College Park, MD, June 2002.
7. Johannes Furnkranz. Exploiting structural information for text classification on the WWW. In *Intelligent Data Analysis*, pages 487–498, 1999.

510    S. Bradshaw

8. E. Garfield. *Citation Indexing: Its Theory and Application in Science, Technology and Humanities.* The ISI Press, Philadelphia, PA, 1983.
9. Steve Hitchcock, Donna Bergmark, Tim Brody, Christopher Gutteridge, Les Carr, Wendy Hall, Carl Lagoze, and Stevan Harnad. Open citation linking. *D-Lib Magazine*, 8(10), 2002.
10. Steve Jones, Sally Jo Cunningham, Rodger J. McNab, and Stefan J. Boddie. A transaction log analysis of a digital library. *Int. Journal on Digital Libraries*, 3(2):152–169, 2000.
11. M. M. Kessler. Technical information flow patterns. In *Proc. of the Western Joint Computing Conf.*, pages 247–257, Los Angeles, CA, 1961.
12. Jon Kleinberg. Authoritative sources in a hyperlinked environment. *Journal of the ACM*, 46(5):604–632, 1999.
13. Steve Lawrence, Kurt Bollacker, and C. Lee Giles. Indexing and retrieval of scientific literature. In *Proc. of the 8th Int. Conf. on Information and Knowledge Management*, pages 139–146, Kansas City, MO, November 2–6 1999.
14. Oliver A. McBryan. GENVL and WWWW: Tools for taming the web. In *Proc. of the First Int. World Wide Web Conf.*, Geneva, Switzerland, May 1994.
15. Filippo Menczer and Richard K. Belew. Adaptive retrieval agents: Internalizing local context and scaling up to the Web. *Machine Learning*, 39(2–3):203–242, 2000.
16. J. Rennie and A. K. McCallum. Using reinforcement learning to spider the Web efficiently. In *Proc. of the 16th Int. Conf. on Machine Learning*, pages 335–343. Morgan Kaufmann, San Francisco, CA, 1999.
17. Mathew Richardson and Pedro Domingos. The intelligent surfer: Probabilistic combination of link and content information in pagerank. In *Advances in Neural Information Processing Systems 14*. MIT Press, 2002.
18. G. Salton, A. Wong, and C. S. Yang. A vector space model for automatic indexing. *Communications of the ACM*, 18(11):613–620, 1975.
19. Gerard Salton and Christopher Buckley. Term weighting approaches in automatic text retrieval. *Information Processing and Management*, 24(5):513–523, 1988.
20. Gerard Salton and M. J. McGill. *Introduction to Modern Information Retrieval*, chapter The SMART and SIRE Experimental Retrieval Systems, pages 118–155. McGraw-Hill, New York, 1983.
21. Karen Sparck-Jones. A statistical interpretation of term specificity and its application to retrieval. *Journal of Documentation*, 28(1):11–20, March 1972.
22. Ellen Spertus. *ParaSite: Mining the Structural Information on the World-Wide Web.* PhD thesis, MIT, February 1998.
23. A. Spink, D. Wolfram, B. Jansen, and T. Saracevic. The public and their queries. *Journal of the American Society for Information Science and Technology*, 52(3):226–234, 2001.
24. Michiaki Iwazume Hideaki Takeda and Toyoaki Nishida. Ontology-based information gathering and text categorization from the internet. In *Proc. of the 9th Int. Conf. in Industrial and Engineering Applications of Artificial Intelligence and Expert Systems*, pages 305–314, 1996.
25. J. H. Westbrook. Identifying significant research. *Science*, 132, October 1960.

# Space-Efficient Support for Temporal Text Indexing in a Document Archive Context

Kjetil Nørvåg

Department of Computer and Information Science
Norwegian University of Science and Technology
7491 Trondheim, Norway
Kjetil.Norvag@idi.ntnu.no

**Abstract.** Support for temporal text-containment queries (query for all versions of documents that contained one or more particular words at a particular time $t$) is of interest in a number of contexts, including web archives, in a smaller scale temporal XML/web warehouses, and temporal document database systems in general. In the V2 temporal document database system we employed a combination of full-text indexes and variants of time indexes to perform efficient text-containment queries. That approach was optimized for moderately large temporal document databases. However, for "extremely large databases" the index space usage of the approach could be too large. In this paper, we present a more space-efficient solution to the problem: the interval-based temporal text index (ITTX). We also present appropriate algorithms for update and retrieval, and we discuss advantages and disadvantages of the V2 and ITTX approaches.

## 1 Introduction

The amount of information made available on the web is increasing very fast, and an increasing amount of this information is made available *only* on the web. While this makes the information readily available to the community, it also results in a low persistence of the information, compared to when it is stored in traditional paper-based media. This is clearly a serious problem, and during the last years many projects have been initiated with the purpose of archiving this information for the future. This essentially means crawling the web and storing snapshots of the pages, or making it possible for users to "deposit" their pages. In contrasts to most search engines that only store the most recent version of the retrieved pages, in these archiving projects all (or at least many) versions are kept, so that it should also be possible to retrieve the contents of certain pages as they were at a certain time in the past. The Internet Archive Wayback Machine [4] is arguably the most famous project in this context, and aims at providing snapshots of pages from the whole Web. Similar projects at the national level also exist in many countries, often initiated through the national libraries.

Most current web archives still only support retrieval of a web site as they were at a particular time $t$ (i.e., returning a snapshot), and several (including the Internet Archive Wayback Machine [4]) also do not support text-containment queries yet (a text-containment query is a query for all versions containing a particular set of words, similar to the service offered by a search engine). The restrictions are understandable based on

T. Koch and I.T. Sølvberg (Eds.): ECDL 2003, LNCS 2769, pp. 511–522, 2003.
© Springer-Verlag Berlin Heidelberg 2003

the large amount of text stored in these archives. However, in order to increase the usefulness of these archives as research tools, *temporal text-containment queries* (query for all versions of pages that contained one or more particular words at a particular time $t$) should also be supported. Support for temporal text-containment queries is also useful in a more general context, in document databases as well as in *temporal XML/web warehouses*, which are archives similar to the one discussed above, but in a smaller scale. We denote a generic system supporting these features a *temporal document database system*.[1] In our project we have studied this issue in the V2 temporal document database system [9]. In the V2 prototype we employed a combination of full-text indexes and variants of time indexes for performing efficient text-containment queries [8]. That approach was optimized for moderately large temporal document databases. However, for "extremely large databases" as in the contexts discussed above, the index space usage of the approach used in V2 could be too large. In this paper we present a more space-efficient solution to the problem, which we call the interval-based temporal text index (ITTX), we present appropriate algorithms for update and retrieval, and we discuss advantages and disadvantages of the V2 and ITTX approaches to temporal text-containment querying.

The organization of the rest of this paper is as follows. In Section 2 we give an overview of related work. In Section 3 we give an overview of the V2 temporal document database system. In Section 4 we describe the ITTX approach. Finally, in Section 5, we conclude the paper.

## 2    Related Work

We have previously described the use of variants of time indexes to support temporal text-containment queries [8] (one of these variants will be presented in Section 3.4).

Another approach to solve some of the problems discussed in this paper, is the proposal from Anick and Flynn [1] on how to support versioning in a full-text information retrieval system. In their proposal, the current version of documents are stored as complete versions, and backward deltas are used for historical versions. This gives efficient access to the current (and recent) versions, but costly access to older versions. They also use the timestamp as version identifier. This is not applicable for transaction-based document processing where all versions created by one transaction should have same timestamp. In order to support temporal text-containment queries, they based the full-text index on bitmaps for words in current versions, and delta change records to track incremental changes to the index backwards over time. This approach has the same advantage and problem as the delta-based version storage: efficient access to current version, but costly recreation of previous states is needed. It is also difficult to make temporal zig-zag joins (needed for multi-word temporal text-containment queries) efficient.

---

[1] Note that such a system is different from traditional systems where versions of documents are stored and retrieved using the document name and a version/revision number. In our system we can take advantage of the temporal aspect, and make it possible to retrieve documents based on predicates involving both *document contents* and *validity time*, and in this way satisfy temporal queries.

Xyleme [12] supported monitoring of changes between a new retrieved version of a page, and the previous version of the page, but did not actually support maintaining and querying temporal documents (only the last version of a document was actually stored).

Storage of versioned documents is studied by Marian et al. [6] and Chien et al. [3]. Algorithms for temporal XML query processing operators are proposed in [7], where queries can also be on structure as well as text content.

Another approach to temporal document databases is the work by Aramburu et al. [2]. Based on their data model TOODOR, they focus on static document with associated time information, but with no versioning of documents. Queries can also be applied to metadata, which is represented by temporal schemas.

# 3   An Overview of the V2 Temporal Document Database System

In order to make this paper self-containing, and provide the context for the rest of this paper, we will in this section give a short overview of V2. We omit many optimizations in this overview, and for a more detailed description, and a discussion of design choices, we refer to [9,8].

## 3.1   Document Version Identifiers and Time Model

A document version stored in V2 is uniquely identified by a *version identifier* (VID). The VID of a version is persistent and never reused, similar to the object identifier in an object database.

The aspect of time in V2 is *transaction time*, i.e., a document is stored in the database at some point in time, and after it is stored, it is *current* until logically deleted or updated. We call the non-current versions *historical versions*. When a document is deleted, a tombstone version is written to denote the logical delete operation.

## 3.2   Functionality

V2 provides support for storing, retrieving, and querying temporal documents. For example, it is possible to retrieve a document stored at a particular time $t$, retrieve the document versions that were valid at a particular time $t$ and that contained one or more particular words. A number of operators is supported, including operators for returning the VIDs of all document versions containing one or more particular words, support for temporal text-containment queries, as well as the Allen operators, i.e., *before, after, meets,* etc.

V2 supports automatic and transparent compression of documents if desired (this typically reduces the size of the document database to only 25% of the original size).

## 3.3   Design and Storage Structures

The current prototype is essentially a library, where accesses to a database are performed through a V2 object, using an API supporting the operations and operators described previously. The bottom layers are built upon the Berkeley DB database toolkit [11], which is used to provide persistent storage using B-trees.

The main modules of V2 are the version database, document name index, document version management, text index, API layer, operator layer, and optionally extra structures for improving temporal queries. We will now give an overview of the storage-related modules.

**Version database.** The document versions are stored in the version database. In order to support retrieval of parts of documents, the documents are stored as a number of chunks (this is done transparently to the user/application) in a tree structure, where the concatenated VID and chunk number is used as the search key. The VID is essentially a counter, and given the fact that each new version to be inserted is given a higher VID than the previous versions, the document version tree index is append-only.

**Document name index.** A document is identified by a *document name*, which can be a filename in the local case, or an URL in the more general case. Conceptually, the document name index has for each document name some metadata related to all versions of the document, followed by specific information for each particular version.

**Text indexing.** A text-index module based on variants of inverted lists is used in order to efficiently support text-containment queries, i.e., queries for document versions that contain a particular word (or set of words). In our context, we consider it necessary to support dynamic updates of the full-text index, so that all updates from a transaction are persistent as well as immediately available. This contrasts to many other systems that base the text indexing on bulk updates at regular intervals, in order to keep the average update cost lower. In cases where the additional cost incurred by the dynamic updates is not acceptable, it is possible to disable text indexing and re-enable it at a later time. When re-enabled, all documents stored or updated since text indexing was disabled will be text indexed. The total cost of the bulk updating of the text index will in general be cheaper than sum of the cost of the individual updates.

### 3.4 Temporal Text-Containment Queries in the V2 Prototype

Several approaches for text-containment queries are supported by V2 [8]. We will now describe the most general of these, the VP-index-based approach, where the validity period of every document version is stored in a separate index. This index maps from VID to validity period, i.e., each tuple in the VP index contains a VID, a start timestamp, and an end timestamp. In the V2 prototype the VP index is implemented as a number of chunks, where every chunk is an array where we only store the start VID which the period tuples are relative to. In this way we reduce the space while still making delete operations possible.

Even for a large number of versions the VP index is relatively small, but it has a certain maintenance cost: 1) at transaction commit time the VID and timestamp has to be stored in the index, and 2) every document update involves updating the end timestamp in the previous version, from UC (until changed) to a new value which is the start (commit) timestamp of the new version. The first part is an efficient append operation, but the second is a more costly insert. However, considering the initial text indexing cost for every version, the VP-index maintenance cost is not significant in practice.

Temporal text-containment queries using the VP-index-based approach can be performed by 1) a text-index query using the text index that indexes all versions in the database, followed by 2) a time-select operation that selects the actual versions (from stage 1) that were valid at the particular time or time period.

## 4   Space-Efficient Support for Temporal Text-Containment Queries

Many of the design decisions in V2 are based on the assumption that it shall support typical database features as transaction-based consistency, arbitrarily large transactions, and (relatively) fast commit. However, in a document warehouse context, these can be relaxed. For example, it is possible to assume only one write/update process.

Before we continue the discussion of the text index, we emphasize that as a minimum, the text index should:

- Support the mapping operation from a word $W$ to the identifiers of all the document versions that contain the word.
- Ensure that *if* a identifier is returned by a lookup, it should be *guaranteed* that the document version with this identifier actually exists and contains the word $W$.

### 4.1   A New Storage Architecture

One problem with the original text index in V2 is that each occurrence of a word in a version require a separate posting in the text index. This makes the size of the text index proportional with the size of the document database. For a traditional document databases where only current versions are stored it is difficult to improve on this property (although compression of index entries normally is used to reduce the total index size). However, in a document database with several versions of each document, the size of the text index can be reduced by noting the fact that the difference between consecutive versions of a document is usually small: frequently, a word in one document version will in also occur in the next (as well as the previous) version. Thus, we can reduce the size of the text index by storing word/version-range mappings, instead of storing information about individual versions.

In V2 every document version is assigned a VID=$v$, where the new VID is one higher than the previous assigned VID, i.e., VID=$v+1$. There is no correlation between VID and document, i.e., VID=$v$ and VID=$v+1$ would in general identify versions of different documents. The advantage of this strategy of assigning VIDs is that it gives the version database an efficient append-only property when the VIDs are used as the keys of the versions. In a range-based index a number of versions with VID=$\{5,6,7,8\}$ containing the word $W$ could be encoded as $(W, 5, 8)$. However, there is not necessarily much similarity between document versions VID=$v$ and VID=$v+1$ when the versions are versions of different documents. Except for the most frequently occurring words, there

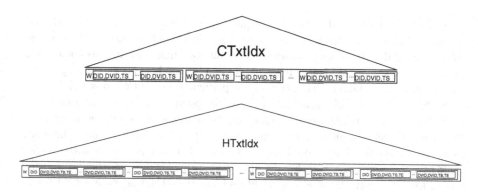

**Fig. 1.** The ITTX temporal text-index architecture.

will not be many chances to cover large intervals using this approach. In order to benefit from the use of intervals, we instead use *document version identifiers* (DVIDs). Given a version of a document with DVID=$v$, then the next version of the same document has DVID=$v+1$. In contrast to the VIDs that uniquely identify a document version stored in the system, different versions of different documents can have the same DVID, i.e., the DVIDs are not unique between different versions of different documents. In order to uniquely identify (and to retrieve) a particular document version, a *document identifier* (DID) is needed together with the DVID, i.e., a particular document version in the system is identified by (DID||DVID). In this way, consecutive versions of the same document that contain the same word can form a range with no holes.

Conceptually, the text index that use ranges can be viewed as a collection of $(W,DID,DVID_i,DVID_j)$-tuples, i.e., a word, a document identifier, and a DVID range. Note that for each document, there can be several tuples for each word $W$, because words can appear in one version, disappear in a later version, and then again reappear later. A good example is a page containing news headlines, where some topics are reoccurring.

When a new document version with DVID=$DVID_i$ is inserted, and it contains a word that did not occur in the previous version, a $(W,DID,DVID_i,DVID_j)$ tuple is inserted into the index. $DVID_i$ is the DVID of the inserted version, but $DVID_j$ is set to a special value UC (until changed). In this way, if this word is also included in the next version of this document, the tuple does not have to be modified. This is an important feature (a similar technique for avoiding text index updates is also described in [1]). Only when a new version of the document that does not contain the word is inserted, the tuple has to be updated. It is important to note that using this organization, it is impossible to determine the DVIDs of the most recent versions from the index. For the [$DVID_i$,UC] intervals only the start DVID is available, and we do not know the end DVID. As will be described later, this makes query processing more complicated.

Under the assumption that queries for current documents will be frequent enough to compensate for the additional cost of having separate indexes for currently valid entries, a separate index is used for the entries that are still valid (an assumption and solution also used in some traditional temporal database systems), i.e., where the end of the interval is UC. In this index the end value UC is implicit, so that only the start DVID needs to be stored. We denote the index for historical entries *HTxtIdx* and the index for valid entries *CTxtIdx*. Note that the space possibly saved by this two-index approach is not an issue, the point is the smaller amount of index entries that have to be processed during a query for current versions (and prefix queries can in particular benefit from this architecture).

So far, we have not discussed how to make temporal text-containment queries efficient. The first issue is whether timestamps can be used *instead* of DVIDs in the index. This would be very useful in order to have document version validity time in the index. However, this is difficult for several reasons. First of all, more than one document version could have the same timestamp, because they were created at the same time/by the same transaction. However, the most important problem is that the intervals would not be "dense": in general, given a document version with timestamp $T = t_i$, the next version of the document will not have timestamp $T = t_i+1$. The result is that it is impossible to determine the actual timestamps or document identifiers of the document versions from the index.

In V2, the VP index is used to make temporal text-containment queries more efficient (see Section 3.4) by providing a map from VID to version validity period (i.e., conceptually each tuple in the VP index contains a VID, a start timestamp, and an end timestamp). With sequentially allocated VIDs as in V2, the VP index is append-only. The result is a low update cost, and it is also space efficient because the VIDs do not have to be explicitly stored.

One of the main reasons why the VP index is very attractive in the context of V2, is that storing the time information in the VP index is much more space efficient than storing the timestamps replicated many places in the text index (once for each word). However, when intervals are used, one timestamp for each start- and end-point of the intervals is sufficient, and the increase in total space usage, compared with using a VP index, is less than what is the case in V2. It is also more scalable, because the V2 approach is most efficient when the VP index can always be resident in main memory. To summarize, our final solution for the ITTX is to store $(W,\text{DID},\text{DVID}_i,\text{DVID}_j,T_S,T_E)$ in the HTxtIdx (where $T_S$ and $T_E$ are the start- and end-timestamps of the interval $[\text{DVID}_i,\text{DVID}_j>$, and to store $(W,\text{DID},\text{DVID},T_S)$ in the CTxtIdx.

## 4.2  Physical Organization

The physical organization of the ITTX is illustrated in Figure 1. In the HTxtIdx there are for each word a number of document identifiers (DIDs), and for each DID there is a number of $[\text{DVID}_i,\text{DVID}_j>/[T_S,T_E>$ ranges. The CTxtIdx is similar, except that the end DVIDs and end timestamps implicitly have the value UC and are therefore omitted. In an actual implementation based on B-trees, this data is stored in chunks in the leaf. The key of a chunk is $(W,\text{DID},\text{DVID})$, where DID is the smallest DID in the chunk, and the DVID is the start of the first interval for this DID. As will be explained below, this information is needed in order to efficiently implement multi-word queries where we only need to retrieve postings for a subset of the DIDs. Note that the size of a chunk must be smaller than a page, and as a result there will in general be more than one chunk for each word, and there can also be more than one chunk for each DID.

The *document name index* is basically the same as the one used in V2, except that for each document name there is also a document identifier. We emphasize that the document name index is a map from document name to DID *and* the DVID/timestamp of all the document versions.

The *document version database* is also identical to the one used in V2, except that (DID‖DVID) is used as the key, instead of only a VID. The append-only property it had in V2 when using VID as the key is lost, but the cost of updating the version database is much smaller than the text indexing cost, so this cost is compensated by a more efficient text indexing. By including some time information in the ITTX we also avoid having a separate VP index.

### 4.3   Operations

Given the description of the ITTX, the algorithms for the most important operations are as follows.

**Insert document:**  When inserting a new document (i.e., a document with a document name not already stored in the database) at time $t$:

1. A new DID is allocated, and the document is inserted into the version database.
2. For all distinct words $W$ in the document, a $(W,\text{DID},\text{DVID}=0, T_S=t)$ tuple is inserted into the CTxtIdx.

**Update document:**  If the document to be inserted at time $t$ is a new version of a document that is already stored in the database:

1. The previous version of the document with DVID=$j$ has to be read in order to determine the difference (or delta) between the two versions. The difference is needed for several purposes: 1) often we do not want to store identical versions, 2) we might want to reduce the storage costs by storing delta versions instead of complete versions, and 3) we need to determine which *new words* appear in the new version, and which words that existed in the previous version *do not* occur in the new version.
2. A new DVID=$j+1$ is allocated and the document is inserted into the version database. In addition, if we want to store delta versions, the previous document version is replaced with the delta version.
3. For all *new* distinct words $W$ in the document, a $(W,\text{DID},\text{DVID}=j+1,T_S=t)$ tuple is inserted into the CTxtIdx.
4. For all words that disappeared between the versions, $(W,\text{DID},\text{DVID}=i,T_S)$ is removed from the CTxtIdx and $(W,\text{DID},\text{DVID}=i,\text{DVID}=j,T_S,T_E=t)$ is inserted into the HTxtIdx.

**Delete document:**  A document delete in a temporal database is a *logical* operation, in contrast to non-temporal databases where it is a *physical* operation. The delete operation in a temporal database can be realized as an update that creates a (logical) *tombstone* *version*. This tombstone can be considered as an empty document, and using the procedure for documents as described above, all the words of the previous version is moved to the HTxtIdx, but none are inserted into the CTxtIdx.

**Retrieve document version:** A document version can be retrieved from the version database using (DID,DVID) as the key. If a document with a particular name *DocName* is to be retrieved, a lookup in the document name index is performed first. The (DID,DVID) for all versions are stored here, sorted on DVID/time so that if a document version valid at a particular time $t$ is to be retrieved, the actual (DID,DVID) can be found by a simple lookup in the document name index. The current version of a particular document DID is simply the version with the largest DVID.

**Non-temporal single-word text-containment query:** All *documents* currently containing a particular word $W_S$ can be found by a lookup in the CTxtIdx for all $(W, \text{DID}, \text{DVID}_i, T_S)$ where $W=W_S$. However, it is impossible from the CTxtIdx alone to know the most recent DVID for the actual DIDs. This can be found from the version database, where the most recent DVID for a document is found by searching for the largest DVID for the actual DID. Note that this is a simple lookup operation, the actual document(s) do not have to be retrieved.

**Non-temporal multi-word text-containment query:** A multiword query, i.e., a query for all documents that contain a particular set of words $W_1, ..., W_n$, can be executed by:

1. A lookup for word $W_1$ in the CTxtIdx, resulting in a set of DIDs which initializes the set $R_1$.
2. For each of the words $W_2, ..., W_n$, lookup the word $W_i$ in the CTxtIdx, let the set $S_i$ be the resulting DIDs, and let $R_i = R_{i-1} \cap S_i$. When finished, $R_n$ will contain the DIDs of the documents that contain the words. In practice an optimized version of this algorithm will be used. For example, if the number of entries for each word is known in advance, it is possible to start the query with retrieving the entries for the most infrequently occurring word(s), and only do lookups where a possible match can occur, e.g., given $R_1$, only do lookups for all $(W_2, \text{DID}_x)$ where $\text{DID}_x$ is a member of $R_1$. In order to be able to do this, statistics for word occurrences is needed. In static document databases this information is often stored in the index. However, maintaining this statistics considerably increases the update cost, so in a dynamic document database we rather advocate maintaining a *word-frequency cache* for the most frequently occurring query words. This approximation should be enough to reduce the query cost. Even without the help of a word-frequency cache or statistics, the size of $R_i$, where $i \geq 2$, will in general be small enough to make it possible to reduce the cost by doing selective lookups.

**Temporal single-word text-containment query (snapshot):** When querying for all document versions that contained a particular word $W_S$ at a particular time $t$, both the CTxtIdx and the HTxtIdx have to be searched:

- Search HTxtIdx: All $(W,\text{DID},\text{DVID}_i,\text{DVID}_j,T_S,T_E)$ where $W=W_S$ and $T_S \leq t \leq T_E$ are retrieved.
- Search CTxtIdx: All $(W,\text{DID},\text{DVID}_i, T_S)$ where $W=W_S$ and $t \geq T_S$ are retrieved.
- At most one version of each document can be valid at a particular time, so the interesting part of the result is essentially a set of $(\text{DID}, \text{DVID}_i,\text{DVID}_j)$ tuples. In general we do not know the actual DVIDs of the matching versions (assuming a fine-granularity timestamp, a match on $t=T_S$ or $t=T_E$ has a low probability). Given a $(\text{DID}, \text{DVID}_i,\text{DVID}_j)$ tuple and a time $t$, the actual DVID can in most cases efficiently be determined by first doing a lookup in the document version database in order to find the name of the document with the actual DID, followed by a lookup in the document name index to find the DVID of the version of the document that were valid at time $t$.

**Temporal multi-word text-containment query (snapshot):** The single-word temporal text-containment query can be extended to multi-word similar to the case of a non-temporal query. However, determining the actual DVIDs should be postponed until the final step.

**Temporal text-containment query (time range):** Querying for all document versions that contained a particular word at some point during a specified time *interval* is performed similar to the temporal snapshot query as described above, the only difference is that there can be more than one matching version of each document, resulting in more than one $(\text{DID}, \text{DVID}_i,\text{DVID}_j)$ tuple for each DID.

### 4.4  Comparison

The most important advantages of the ITTX, compared to the original V2 indexing approach, are:

- Smaller index size.
- More efficient non-temporal (current) text-containment query (i.e., on the documents that are currently valid). In the V2 approach, it was impossible to tell from the text index whether a version with a certain VID was a current version or not. In addition, it was impossible to determine whether two VIDs in the text index were VIDs of the same document or not, resulting in a larger number of VIDs to inspect than desired.
- The time intervals in the index drastically reduce the number of DVIDs that have to be checked. For example, for a snapshot query only one lookup is needed for each matching document in order to determine the DVID.
- The average cost of updating a document is much lower. Assuming most words in version DVID=$i$ also occur in version DVID=$i+1$, only a few postings need to be updated.

However, as with most indexing problems, there is not a single index structure that is best in all situations: the context decides which indexing method is most beneficial. This is also the case in our case, and in some contexts the V2 indexing approach can be better than the ITTX:

- Although the insert of new documents will have the same *indexing cost* (for new documents, all words have to be indexed), the actual insert into the version database will be slightly more expensive because it is not an append operation as before. Another result of insert instead of append is that the storage utilization in the version database is likely to be lower.
- In the V2 system, two important operations that can be used to reduce the amount of data that is stored in the system (or identify candidates for tertiary-storage migration) are *vacuuming* and *granularity reduction* [10]. Vacuuming is the traditional temporal database method for data reduction, and removes the oldest versions. However, in a document database context, granularity reduction is often more appropriate. Two simple granularity reduction approaches that illustrate the concept, are deleting versions of an document that are closer in time than $t_t$, or simply removing every second version of a document. This can be useful when we have a large number of document versions created during a relatively short time period, and after a while we do not really need all these versions. Although a (logical) delete in a temporal database does not result in removal of any historical versions, physical deletion can be performed as a result of vacuuming and granularity reduction operations [10]. When versions are physically removed from the database, fragmentation of time ranges can occur. For example, the use of a granularity reduction strategy that removes every second version will have as a result that all intervals only cover one DVID. Vacuuming on the other hand removes all versions older than a certain age, and does not affect the efficiency of the interval representation of DVIDs. Thus, the ITTX approach is most suitable for application areas where vacuuming, and not granularity reduction, is employed. In the context of this paper, we can assume that all versions will be kept (and that eventual granularity reduction has already been applied to the data), and there is less need for granularity reduction.
- Bulk-updating can be performed relatively efficiently using the original V2 approach. VIDs are assigned sequentially, so that new VIDs are appended to the posting lists. Even of a large number of VIDs are inserted for a particular word, they are stored clustered in the leaf nodes of the index, so that only a much smaller number of writes are actually needed. In the ITTX, the DVIDs are clustered on DIDs, so that in worst case one write is needed for each word in a document (however, we emphasize that when updating documents only a few entries actually have to be updated in the index).

## 5   Conclusions and Further Work

In our V2 temporal document database system we employed a combination of full-text indexes and variants of time indexes for performing efficient text-containment queries. That approach was optimized for moderately large temporal document databases. However, for "extremely large databases" the index space usage of the V2 approach could be too large. In this paper we have presented a more space-efficient solution to the problem, the interval-based temporal text index (ITTX). We have presented appropriate algorithms for update and retrieval, and we discussed advantages and disadvantages of these two approaches.

Future work includes integrating the ITTX into V2 and use our temporal document database benchmarks to compare the performance of ITTX with the VP index approach currently used in V2. We also plan to investigate approaches that can achieve better clustering in the temporal dimension, for example by using an extension of indexing structures like the TSB-tree [5].

**Acknowledgments.** This work was done when the author visited Athens University of Economics and Business in 2002, and Aalborg University in 2003, supported by grant #145196/432 from the Norwegian Research Council.

# References

1. P. G. Anick and R. A. Flynn. Versioning a full-text information retrieval system. In *Proceedings of the 15th Annual International ACM SIGIR Conference on Research and Development in Information Retrieval*, 1992.
2. M. J. Aramburu-Cabo and R. B. Llavori. A temporal object-oriented model for digital libraries of documents. *Concurrency and Computation: Practice and Experience*, 13(11), 2001.
3. S.-Y. Chien, V. Tsotras, and C. Zaniolo. Efficient schemes for managing multiversion XML documents. *VLDB Journal*, 11(4), 2002.
4. Internet archive. http://archive.org/.
5. D. Lomet and B. Salzberg. Access methods for multiversion data. In *Proceedings of the 1989 ACM SIGMOD*, 1989.
6. A. Marian, S. Abiteboul, G. Cobena, and L. Mignet. Change-centric management of versions in an XML warehouse. In *Proceedings of VLDB 2001*, 2001.
7. K. Nørvåg. Algorithms for temporal query operators in XML databases. In *Proceedings of Workshop on XML-Based Data Management (XMLDM) (in conjunction with EDBT'2002)*, 2002.
8. K. Nørvåg. Supporting temporal text-containment queries. Technical Report IDI 11/2002, Norwegian University of Science and Technology, 2002. Available from http://www.idi.ntnu.no/grupper/DB-grp/.
9. K. Nørvåg. V2: A database approach to temporal document management. In *Proceedings of the 7th International Database Engineering and Applications Symposium (IDEAS)*, 2003.
10. K. Nørvåg. Algorithms for granularity reduction in temporal document databases. Technical Report IDI 1/2003, Norwegian University of Science and Technology, 2003. Available from http://www.idi.ntnu.no/grupper/DB-grp/.
11. M. A. Olson, K. Bostic, and M. Seltzer. Berkeley DB. In *Proceedings of the FREENIX Track: 1999 USENIX Annual Technical Conference*, 1999.
12. L. Xyleme. A dynamic warehouse for XML data of the web. *IEEE Data Engineering Bulletin*, 24(2), 2001.

# Clustering Top-Ranking Sentences for Information Access

Anastasios Tombros[1], Joemon M. Jose[1], and Ian Ruthven[2]

[1] Department of Computing Science, University of Glasgow, Glasgow G12 8QQ, U.K.
{tombrosa, jj}@dcs.gla.ac.uk
[2] Department of Computer and Information Sciences, University of Strathclyde,
Glasgow G1 1XH, U.K.
Ian.Ruthven@cis.strath.ac.uk

**Abstract.** In this paper we propose the clustering of top-ranking sentences (TRS) for effective information access. Top-ranking sentences are selected by a query-biased sentence extraction model. By clustering such sentences, we aim to generate and present to users a personalised information space. We outline our approach in detail and we describe how we plan to utilise user interaction with this space for effective information access. We present an initial evaluation of TRS clustering by comparing its effectiveness at providing access to useful information to that of document clustering.

## 1 Introduction

One of the challenging research issues in Digital Libraries is the facilitation of efficient and effective access to large amounts of available information. Document clustering [1] and automatic text summarisation [2] are two methods which have been used in the context of information access in digital libraries.

Document clustering generates groupings of potentially related documents by taking into account interdocument relationships. By taking into account interdocument relationships, users have the possibility to discover documents that might have otherwise been left unseen [3]. Document clusters, effectively, reveal the structure of the document space. This space however, may not help users understand how their search terms relate to the retrieved documents, which can be long and contain many topics. Therefore, the information space offered by document clusters to users is essentially not representative of their queries.

Text summarisation, in the context of information access, offers short previews of the contents of documents, so that users can make a more informed assessment of the usefulness of the information without having to refer to the full text of documents [2,4]. A particular class of summarisation approaches, query-oriented or query-biased approaches, have proven effective in providing users with relevance clues [4]. Query-biased summaries present to users textual parts of documents (usually sentences) which highly match the user's search terms. The effectiveness of such summaries in the context of interactive retrieval on the World Wide Web has been verified by [4].

T. Koch and I.T. Sølvberg (Eds.): ECDL 2003, LNCS 2769, pp. 523–528, 2003.
© Springer-Verlag Berlin Heidelberg 2003

The aim of this work is to reveal a personalised information space to users by restructuring the initial document space. To this end, we combine clustering and summarisation in a novel way. We cluster sentences which have been selected by a query-biased sentence extraction model (*top-ranking sentences, TRS*) [4]. The sentences form part of single document summaries which represent top-ranked documents retrieved in response to a query. The resulting sentence clusters offer a view of the initial information space which is highly characterised by the presence of query terms. The overall objective of this approach is to facilitate a more effective user interaction with the personalised information space, and to utilise this interaction for improving the quality of the information presented to users.

In this paper, we mainly focus on two issues. First, we present our approach and its aims in detail in section 2. Then, we present an initial evaluation of TRS clustering by comparing its effectiveness at providing access to useful information to that of document clustering in section 3. We conclude in section 4, where we also outline how we propose to take this work further.

## 2   Clustering Top-Ranking Sentences

The essence of our approach consists of generating a list of top-ranking sentences for each document retrieved in the top-ranks in response to a user query, and of clustering these sentences. The set of top-ranking sentences constitutes a summary for each of the documents. These sentences are selected through a query-biased sentence extraction model, presented in detail in [4]. Sentences are scored according to factors such as their position within a document, the words they contain, and the proportion of query terms they contain. A number of the highest scoring sentences can then be selected as the summary. Clusters of TRS can be generated by any clustering method, such as hierarchic methods which are commonly used in information retrieval systems [3], or methods which are specifically designed to cluster short textual units (e.g. [5]).

The main function of TRS clusters is to provide effective access to retrieved documents by acting as an abstraction of the information space. Essentially, TRS clusters form a second level of abstraction, where the first level corresponds to summaries (i.e. sets of TRS) of each of the retrieved documents. Instead of interacting with the retrieved document set, users can access documents by browsing through clusters of TRS. Individual TRS are linked to the original documents (or to representations of the original documents, such as titles, summaries, etc.) in which they occur so that users can access the original information.

Sentences within a single TRS cluster will discuss query terms in the context of the same (or similar) topics. This can assist users in better understanding the structure and the contents of the information space which corresponds to the top-retrieved documents. This may be especially useful in cases where users have a vague, not well-defined information need.

It should be noted that the information space which corresponds to clusters of TRS is different to the one which corresponds to the top-retrieved documents. TRS contain a high proportion of query terms, and therefore each sentence can be seen as providing a local context in which these query terms occur. Consequently, the information space which corresponds to TRS clusters will be restricted to these local contexts, offering a personalised view to users. We believe that users can benefit through interaction with personalised information spaces, since they may gain a better understanding of the different topics under which the query terms are discussed (this of course assumes that the selected TRS are representative of the way query terms are used in documents).

The overall objective of our approach is to utilise information resulting from the interaction of users with this personalized information space in the form of implicit feedback [6]. As mentioned previously, users can access documents, or other shorter representations of documents such as titles and query-biased summaries, by selecting individual sentences in TRS clusters. User interaction with TRS clusters, individual documents and other document representations can be monitored, and the information collected can be used to recommend new documents to users, and to select candidate terms to be added to the query from the documents and clusters viewed. This type of implicit feedback has been used by [6] in order to utilise information from the interaction of users with query-biased document summaries, and has shown to be effective in enabling users to access useful information. The system which combines TRS clustering and implicit feedback is currently under development.

From the previous discussion, some similarities between document and TRS clustering become apparent. Both approaches present an abstracted version of the information space in a structured view which facilitates browsing and interaction. Moreover, both approaches aim to provide users with effective access to useful retrieved information through interaction with the grouped documents or sentences. There are, however, some significant differences between the two approaches. TRS clustering uses finer textual units (sentences instead of full documents), and more importantly, it alters the information space by using textual units which are highly characterised by the presence of query terms. The structuring of the information space by document clustering is not tailored to the query since it offers a grouping of documents which may be long and contain many topics. By using query-biased sentences as the items to be clustered, we offer users a view of the information space which is focused on their query terms.

In the next section, we perform an initial evaluation of the effectiveness of TRS clustering at providing access to useful information. To establish whether pursuing TRS clustering is worthwhile, we compare its effectiveness to that of document clustering. In this way, we can get an indication of whether TRS clustering has the potential to act as a medium for effective information access by improving the quality of the provided information when compared to document clustering. It should be noted that in this initial evaluation we do not use information from the users' interaction with clusters. We plan to evaluate aspects of interaction when the system which combines TRS clustering and implicit feedback is completed.

# 3   Comparing TRS and Document Clustering

For this study we used 16 queries which represented actual information needs. The queries were generated by 4 users. The average length of the queries was 3.7 terms. Each of the queries was input to a web-based IR system [4] which retrieved and presented to the searcher the top-30 retrieved documents. The full text of each of the web pages was downloaded. Each searcher was asked to examine each of the documents retrieved, and to assign a numerical value to it representing his assessment of how useful he found the document in relation to his query. The assessments were on a scale from 1 (not at all useful) to 10 (very useful). We did not require for the documents to be visited in any particular order, and we allowed users to adjust their assessments as they wished. There was no time limit imposed on users.

For each query $Q_i$, the top-30 retrieved documents were clustered, generating a document clustering $DC_i$. The top-ranking sentences for each of these documents (maximum four sentences per document, depending on document length) were also extracted, in a procedure reported in [4]. This generated a respective sentence clustering $SC_i$. Both document and TRS clustering was performed using the group average link method [3]. It is worth noting that for some queries it was not possible to download all 30 top-ranked documents (for example some documents may not be available). On average, 23 documents were downloaded per query, and 3.2 sentences per document were extracted.

The user assessments were used to assign scores to each of the two clusterings. More specifically, for a document cluster $DC_i$, the score assigned is a sum of the assessment scores of its comprising documents, normalised by the number of documents in the cluster. For a sentence cluster $SC_i$, the score assigned is a sum of the assessment scores of the documents in which each of the cluster's TRS belongs to, normalised by the number of sentences in the cluster. The type of clustering which produces the highest score is the one which has the potential to provide users with the more useful information.

## 3.1   Results

In Table 1 we present a summary of the results for document clustering (DC) and TRS clustering (SC). In columns 2 and 3 we present the average score for the best cluster for each query and for all clusters, respectively. In both cases TRS clustering produces a significantly higher score than document clustering (Wilcoxon signed-ranks test, $p<0.05$). Only in 2 out of the 16 queries document clusters produced a higher score. The average size of the best DC and SC was comparable (6.5 and 7.75 items per cluster respectively). TRS clusters also display a lower standard deviation across all scores (column 4).

In columns 5 and 6 we give the average highest precision and highest recall for SC and DC across all queries for the best clusters. In order to calculate these values, we considered, for each query, the set of documents for which users assigned a score in the range of 7-10 as the set of relevant documents. On average, there were 4.2 such documents per query. We view such documents as being the most useful for users. The values in Table 1 demonstrate that SC show a significantly higher average precision ($p<0.05$), and a higher average recall. The relatively low precision for both types of clustering can be explained on the basis of the relatively few "relevant" documents per query.

**Table 1.** Summary of results

|    | Avg. best score | Avg. overall score | Std. deviation of overall scores | Avg. P | Avg. R |
|----|-----------------|--------------------|----------------------------------|--------|--------|
| DC | 4.78            | 3.18               | 1.38                             | 0.38   | 0.73   |
| SC | 5.82            | 3.73               | 1.12                             | 0.49   | 0.77   |

An analysis into the composition of TRS clusters shows that the average size is 5.3 sentences per cluster (compared to 5 documents per cluster for DC). It should be noted that all results presented here for SC have been calculated by considering only one occurrence of TRS from the same document in each cluster. On average, across all queries, 36% of sentences in TRS clusters corresponded to multiple occurrences of TRS from the same original document, a result which is a consequence of the high similarity of TRS from the same documents.

In general, our results suggest that TRS clusters provide access to more useful information than document clusters, and that they also manage to structure the document space in a more effective way than document clusters. Moreover, TRS clusters provided more effective access to the highly useful documents (as these were indicated by the users themselves) than documents clusters.

## 4    Conclusions

The results we presented in the previous section demonstrate that there is scope for the application of TRS clustering. Although the study was of a small scale, its results are positive and they suggest that TRS clusters have the potential to lead users to parts of the information space which contain useful information.

To the best of our knowledge, combining document clustering and text summarisation to create a personalised information space with the aim of utilising the users' implicit feedback is a novel approach. Document clustering and summarisation are typically combined for the purposes of multiple-document summarisation (e.g. [7,8]), where sets of related documents, or of their summaries, are clustered in order to select sentences to be included in a summary.

We plan to examine in more detail the characteristics of generated TRS clusters, and to consider the effect of different clustering methods. The effect of the query-biased model, which generates the TRS, on the generated clusters also needs to be considered. In section 3 we presented results for the best SC and DC. Whether users in an interactive environment will be able to recognise

528     A. Tombros, J.M. Jose, and I. Ruthven

the best cluster depends on how cluster contents are summarised and displayed on the interface level. This is a challenging research issue [9] which does not fall within the aims of this paper.

The overall objective of our approach is to integrate TRS clustering in an interactive environment, and to utilise information from the users' interaction with TRS clusters. We believe that users will benefit from interaction with the personalised information space which is generated by TRS clusters. Although devoid of the interaction aspect, the results we reported in this section paper that TRS clusters have the potential to lead users to useful information. We view these results as suggesting that TRS clustering can provide effective access to information, and we plan to build on this research in order to incorporate aspects of interaction in the TRS clustering system.

**Acknowledgements.** The authors wish to thank Ryen W. White for his help with the top-ranking sentences system. This research is funded by the EPSRC (U.K.) research grant GR/R74642/01.

# References

1. Leuski, A., Allan J.: Evaluating a visual navigation system for a digital library. In: Proceedings of the 2nd ECDL Conference, Heraklion, Greece (1998) 535–554
2. Lopez, M.J.M., Rodriguez, M.B., Hidalgo, J.M.G.: Using and evaluating user directed summaries to improve information access. In: Proceedings of the 3rd ECDL Conference, Paris, France (1999) 198–214
3. Willett, P.: Recent trends in hierarchic document clustering: a critical review. Information Procsessing & Management **24** (1988) 577–597
4. White, R.W., Ruthven, I., Jose, J.M.: A task-oriented study on the influencing effects of query-biased summarisation in web searching. Information Procsessing & Management in press (2003)
5. Zamir, O., Etzioni, O.: Web document clustering: A feasibility demonstration. In: Proceedings of the 21st Annual ACM SIGIR Conference, Melbourne, Australia (1998) 46–54
6. White, R.W., Ruthven, I., Jose, J.M.: Finding relevant documents using top ranking sentences: an evaluation of two alternative schemes. In: Proceedings of the 24th Annual ACM SIGIR Conference, Tampere, Finland (2002) 57–64
7. Radev, D.R., Jing, H., Budzikowska, M.: Centroid-based summarization of multiple documents: sentence extraction, utility-based evaluation, and user studies. In: Proceedings of the ANLP/NAACL Workshop on Summarization, Seattle, U.S.A. (2000)
8. Zha, H.: Generic summarization and keyphrase extraction using mutual reinforcement principle and sentence clustering. In: Proceedings of the 25th Annual ACM SIGIR Conference, Tampere, Finland (2002) 113–120
9. Kural, Y., Robertson, S.E., Jones, S.: Deciphering cluster representations. Information Procsessing & Management **37** (2001) 593–601

# Demonstrations

**2MN – Modules for Multimedia Netbased Teaching Evaluation of Transcurricular Application of eLearning-Modules**
*Achim Oßwald and Dirk Weisbrod*

**DiVA – Electronic Publishing System**
*Eva Müller, Uwe Klosa, and Peter Hansson*

**FACET – Faceted Knowledge Organisation for Semantic Retrieval**
*Douglas Tudhope*

**Greenstone Digital Library Software**
*David M. Nichols, David Bainbridge, and Ian H. Witten*

**Human Rights Issues in the Publication of Digital Images on the Web**
*John Mahoney and Jill Evans*

**Interfaces for Digital Libraries at CNAM (1993-2003)**
*Jérôme Dupire*

**Interoperability Resource Discovery for the Performing Arts**
*Catherine Owen and Iain Wallace*

**Library Catalogues as Authorities in new Scientific Financing Schemes**
*Jens Vindvad, Erlend Øverby, and Jan Erik Kofoed*

**Live Analytics: Real-Time Analysis and Organization of Search Results**
*Aleksander Øhrn and Camilla G. Moen*

**Managing Geospatial and Georeferenced Web Resources Using G-Portal**
*Ming Yin, Ee-Peng Lim, and Zehua Liu*

**Model, Design and Construction of a Service-Oriented Web-Warehouse**
*Benjamin Nguyen and Gregory Cobena*

**Smart Search in Newspaper Archives Using Topic Maps**
*Bert Paepen and Sven Van Hemel*

**The Alexandria Digital Earth Prototype (ADEPT), and the Alexandria Digital Library (ADL)**
*Michael Freeston, Terry Smith, and Greg Janee*

# Posters

A Multimedia Digital Library System Based on MPEG-7 and XQuery
*Ji-Hoon Kang, Mann-Ho Lee, and Sung Hyon Myaeng*

A Pilot Study on the Effect of Anaphora Resolution on Information
Retrieval
*Hyuk-Jin Lee and Giyeong Kim*

A Plethora of Plug-Ins, An Abundance of Applets:
Specialized Web-Based Viewers for Art Images, Maps, and Aerial
Photography in Digital Libraries
*Glee Willis*

A Theoretical Framework for the Holistic Evaluation of Digital
Libraries
*Scott Nicholson*

CITIDEL: Computing and Information Technology Interactive Digital
Educational Library
*Edward Fox*

Clickstream Analysis Using the New XML Logging Format
*Lillian Cassel and Filip Jagodzinski*

Collection Management and the Mature Subject Gateway:
A Spring-Clean Solution?
*Lesly Huxley*

Community Deliverables from the Open Archives Forum
*Philip Hunter and Donatella Castelli*

Concept Maps as Visual Interfaces to Digital Libraries
*Edward A. Fox, Ryan Richardson, and Rao Shen*

DAEDALUS: Digital Repositories at the University of Glasgow
*Morag Mackie*

dLibra – Integrated Framework for Publishers and Libraries
*Cezary Mazurek, Maciej Stroinski, and Andrzej Swedrzynski*

DLIST – Digital Library of Information Science and Technology
*Subramaniam Karthik and Anita Coleman*

Educational Library in the Domain of Electrical Engineering:
Accessing Domain-Specific Formats Intuitively
*Mark Painter*

# Author Index